THE CIVILIZATION OF THE AMERICAN INDIAN SERIES

The
Maya Chontal Indians
of
Acalan-Tixchel

The
Maya Chontal Indians
of
Acalan-Tixchel

*A Contribution to the History and Ethnography
of the Yucatan Peninsula*

FRANCE V. SCHOLES

AND

RALPH L. ROYS

with the assistance of

ELEANOR B. ADAMS AND ROBERT S. CHAMBERLAIN

UNIVERSITY OF OKLAHOMA PRESS
NORMAN

Library of Congress Catalog Card Number: 68-15677

Second edition 1968 by the University of Oklahoma Press, Publishing
Division of the University. Reproduced from the first edition published
by the Carnegie Institution of Washington in 1948. Manufactured in the
U.S.A. All rights reserved.

Preface

THE PREPARATION of this volume was prompted by the discovery in the Archivo General de Indias, Sevilla, of a unique text in the Chontal language spoken at the time of the Spanish conquest by Indians of Tabasco and the nearby province of Acalan. This document was found in the summer of 1933 by Dr. Scholes during a routine search of a series of papers relating to the services of conquerors and colonists of New Spain. The Text and accompanying documents, together with other materials from the same archive, describe the history of the Acalan people from preconquest times to the seventeenth century.

A photograph of the Text was sent to Mr. Roys, who immediately recognized its unusual importance, since it is the only narrative in the Chontal language that has come down to us from colonial times. After Dr. Scholes returned to this country in 1934 tentative plans were made to publish the document, a contemporary Spanish version, and an English translation, with a short introduction and explanatory notes. But since so little is known concerning the history of the Acalan area, first visited by Cortés in 1525, and the Tixchel district, to which the Acalan people were moved in 1557, the original plan was enlarged to comprise a detailed history of these regions.

Dr. Robert S. Chamberlain, of Miami University, collaborated in the early phases of the investigation. He participated in the preliminary discussions concerning the knotty problem of the location of Acalan, and in 1937 he made a trip to Tixchel and the Candelaria area to obtain firsthand information concerning local geography. He also wrote out a series of notes on various points, of which we have made some use in the preparation of Appendix B, and he made a preliminary draft of materials on the Spanish occupation of Acalan, which has been useful in the writing of Chapter 5. Because of Dr. Chamberlain's absence in Guatemala, where he served as Cultural Relations Officer of the United States Embassy from 1941 to 1945, he was unable to participate in the final preparation of the volume as planned.

Miss Eleanor B. Adams has rendered great service. She made extracts of two long series of documents which constitute the most important sources for this study. She also transcribed the Spanish translation of the Chontal Text and prepared the modernized version which appears in Appendix A. Her English translation of this Spanish version was used in working out the final translation as it now stands in Appendix A. In many other ways Miss Adams has given effective assistance.

Although Mr. Roys assumed general responsibility for the ethnological and linguistic portions of the manuscript, including notes, and Dr. Scholes for the historical sections, the preparation of the present volume has been a cooperative project from beginning to end. In personal conferences and in extensive correspondence we have threshed out numerous problems of common interest or relating to the sections for which we agreed to assume individual responsibility. In 1939 we made a trip to Tixchel and the Mamantel area to obtain further geographical data. In the actual writing of the manuscript there has been a division of labor, as follows: Chapters 2–4, part of Chapter 5, Chapter 14, and Appendix C were prepared by Mr. Roys; extensive portions of Chapter 5, Chapters 6–13, and Appendices B and D were prepared by Dr. Scholes; Chapter 1, the introduction to Appendix A, the final English translation of the Chontal Text and notes to same, Appendix E, and the Glossary represent our joint authorship. The maps were made under Dr. Scholes' direction, but they include considerable data originally supplied by Mr. Roys. At all times we have exchanged comments, suggestions, and criticisms, and in the writing of our respective sections we have freely made use of information, ideas, and in many cases, sentences and paragraphs sent by one author to the other. We accept joint responsibility for any errors in the volume.

The omission of accents from Indian words and names, save in direct quotations and bibliographical references, follows the practice of the Division of Historical Research in its recent publications.

Acknowledgements are made to the following persons for assistance received at various times: Sr. Arturo Ramos, owner of Hacienda Tichel; Sr. Eduardo R. Dubost, Sr. P. A. González, and Sr. J. Ignacio Rubio Mañé, of Mexico City; Sr. Pedro C. Sánchez, Sr. Manuel Medina, and Sr. Arnulfo de la Llave, of the Instituto Panamericano de Geografía e Historia, Tacubaya, D. F., Mexico; Mr. Raye R. Platt, American Geographical Society, New York; Dr. Robert Wauchope, Tulane University; Miss Wilma Shelton, Mr. Arthur M. McAnally, and Dr. Leslie Spier, of the University of New Mexico; Dr. Walter S. Adams, Mount Wilson Observatory; Dr. S. G. Morley, Dr. Robert Redfield, Dr. Sol Tax, Mr. J. E. S. Thompson, and Mrs. W. H. Harrison, of the Carnegie Institution of Washington. Mr. Leslie Moore and Sr. David Selem, both of whom are now deceased, provided important information and assistance during our trip to Carmen and Tixchel in 1939.

We also wish to acknowledge the aid and loyal support of Dr. A. V. Kidder, Chairman of the Carnegie Institution's Division of Historical Research.

FRANCE V. SCHOLES

RALPH L. ROYS

Abbreviations

AGI—Archivo General de Indias, Sevilla.

DHY—Documentos para la historia de Yucatán. 3 vols. Mérida, 1936–38.

DII—Colección de documentos inéditos relativos al descubrimiento, conquista y organización de las posesiones españolas de América y Oceanía. 42 vols. Madrid, 1864–84.

Fiscal *v.* López—El fiscal contra Alonso López, vecino de la villa de Santa María de la Victoria de Tabasco, sobre haberse titulado visitador y exigido a los indios de la provincia de Tabasco diferentes contribuciones, 1541–45, AGI, Justicia, leg. 195.

García *v.* Bravo—[Antón García] contra Feliciano Bravo, escribano, y Juan Vázquez y Juan Monserrate, 1569–71, AGI, Justicia, leg. 250, ff. 1885–2255v.

Montejo *v.* Alvarado—El Adelantado Don Francisco de Montejo, gobernador de las provincias de Yucatán, con Don Pedro de Alvarado, gobernador de Guatemala, sobre el derecho a los términos del Río de Grijalva, que dicho Montejo había conquistado y pacificado a su costa, 1530–33, AGI, Justicia, leg. 1005, núm. 3, ramo 1.

RY—Relaciones de Yucatán. 2 vols. Madrid, 1898–1900.

Contents

The
Maya Chontal Indians
of
Acalan-Tixchel

1
Introduction

I N THE PAST the attention of the specialist in Maya research, and indeed
that of the interested reader as well, has been largely centered on that
phase of Maya civilization known as the Old Empire, in which the highest art,
most of the finest architecture, and probably the greatest scientific achievements of aboriginal America were produced. This is very natural and will no
doubt continue to be the case. But since it is doubtful whether historical
legends have come down to us from that time, and a belief is steadily growing
that the inscriptions on the monuments contain no historical information,
there is every reason to suppose that any positive knowledge about the Old
Empire will always be confined to such inferences as may be made from
the archaeological evidence.

This phase of Maya culture was succeeded in Yucatan by a period characterized by a strong foreign influence, usually described as Mexican. For a
time art and architecture continued to flourish, as we see from the handsome
buildings and sculptures of Chichen Itza, which combine much of the best in
both Mexican and Maya culture. Prior to the Spanish conquest a decline gradually set in, although it was more marked in some regions than in others. In
some localities the conquerors found the sites of magnificent cities entirely
deserted; in others, towns of thatched structures stood in the shadow of imposing vaulted stone buildings which were abandoned and covered with trees
and brush. In spite of this change, strangely enough, agriculture and commerce were still thriving, and military organization was distinguished for its
initiative and vigor.

For this period we have a number of historical legends and narratives. Some
of these were related to the Spaniards by the natives. Others dealing with the
history of Yucatan are found in the so-called Books of Chilam Balam, written
during the colonial period in the Maya language but with European script.
The historical material in these books consists of five chronicles, a few isolated
narratives, and many prophecies with historical allusions. In addition, several
Yucatecan Maya land documents refer to events during the century immediately preceding the Spanish conquest.

More or less legendary historical material written in two of the native languages has also survived in the highlands of Guatemala. The most important of
these narratives are found in the *Popol Vuh* of the Quiche and the *Memorial*

of Tecpan-Atitlan, also called the *Annals of the Cakchiquels*. In the former, thirteen generations of rulers prior to the conquest are recorded. Colonial Spanish writers also describe a Tzeltal manuscript, which still existed in Chiapas at the end of the eighteenth century but has since disappeared.

The native literature of these three regions recounts the arrival of foreign immigrants who evidently became the ruling class in their new homes. A site variously named Tulapan, Tollan, or Tullan, apparently referring to Tula, the old Toltec capital north of the Valley of Mexico, is mentioned as the place of their origin. Such mention, however, is either so vague or so closely associated with mythological episodes that it might be considered purely legendary, if it were not for the remarkable similarity between some of the remains at Tula and those of a Mexican character found at Chichen Itza in Yucatan. These accounts, like the Mexican historical legends related by Torquemada, apparently suggest a migration of the bearers of a Nahua culture from the highlands of Mexico to the Gulf coast and another migration of peoples who carried a more or less modified form of the same culture to the Maya area. An analysis of these various stories lies beyond the scope of this study, but it seems evident at least that there was a cultural connection between Tula and Chichen Itza.

In Yucatan and Guatemala the immigrants were said to have come by way of a land called Nonoual, which can be identified with reasonable certainty as the country near Laguna de Términos and southwestern Campeche. The intruders actually mentioned in these legends could hardly have been very numerous, since at the time of the Spanish conquest their descendants were speaking the languages of the countries in which they had settled. Other Mexican immigrants, however, evidently came in larger groups, for they were able to preserve their language. Besides two groups of Mexican towns in Tabasco, the Spaniards found scattered Nahuatl-speaking colonies in various parts of Central America, and some of their descendants are still speaking Mexican dialects down to the present time. Unfortunately no native literature of these peoples is now available, and the few legends of their past which they related to the Spaniards are confused and contradictory. They too may have had the tradition of a Tula origin, but this is only a surmise. Recent investigations, however, have revealed a similarity between sculptures found in or near the Pipil area on the Pacific slope and those of southern Veracruz and western Tabasco.

Generally speaking, however, the historical legends and the Spanish descriptions of native customs constitute an important supplement to the archaeological evidence. Above all, we learn from both the native and Spanish accounts something about personalities and human motives, which gives to the archaeological data a sense of living reality that is lacking for the period of the Old Empire.

At the time of the conquest the peninsula of Yucatan and the adjoining lands along the coast of the Gulf of Mexico and the Caribbean Sea may well be considered to have formed an economic unit. Although this area contained a large number of small, independent states, the entire region was united by commercial relations, which constituted a common bond of interest. Yucatan had what almost amounted to a monopoly of salt production and also made a speciality of exporting cotton cloth and slaves to her neighbors. In exchange, cacao, obsidian, copper, gold, feathers, and many other articles of luxury were imported from Tabasco and the Caribbean coast to the southeast. Merchants from Xicalango and Potonchan in Tabasco and from Champoton and Campeche in southwestern Yucatan visited the island of Cozumel and had warehouses and factors on the Ulua River in Honduras.

This trade was facilitated by the similarity of most of the languages spoken over this large area. As we shall see farther on, Chontal, Chol, and Chorti, which were spoken from Laguna Tupilco in Tabasco to the Ulua River, might be considered little more than dialects of the same language; and Yucatecan Maya, although it is a different language, is sufficiently similar so that a merchant from any one of these linguistic areas was able to learn the language of another with comparatively little effort. In 1533 Alonso de Avila related that the native interpreter whom he employed during his campaigns in Yucatan served him equally well when he arrived in northern Honduras.[1]

This interesting situation, with its various historical, ethnological, and linguistic implications, is hardly to be understood, however, without a more detailed knowledge than we have hitherto possessed of the various peoples who inhabited this extensive area. Although we are fairly well informed in regard to the political geography and ethnology of a large part of northern Yucatan, comparatively little is known of the south, especially the region east of the Usumacinta River and south and southeast of Laguna de Términos.

The *cacicazgo*, or province, of Acalan, inhabited by people who spoke the Chontal language of Tabasco, occupied a strategic position within this economic unit. At the time of the Spanish conquest the Acalan dominated the drainage of the Candelaria River, which flows into Laguna de Términos, and they played an important part in the trade carried on between the Gulf coast and the Caribbean across the base of the Yucatan Peninsula. The merchants of

---

[1] Testimony of Alonso de Avila, Campeche, June 8, 1533, *in* Archivo General de Indias (hereinafter cited as AGI), Justicia, leg. 1005, núm. 3, ramo 1. Cf. note 3, p. 8, *infra*.

Acalan occupied one entire ward of the town of Nito, an important commercial center near the mouth of the Río Dulce in Guatemala. In the west they maintained extensive trade with Xicalango, Potonchan, and other parts of Tabasco. Within Acalan the merchants constituted the dominant class, and the wealthiest of them, a lord named Paxbolonacha, was the supreme ruler of the entire cacicazgo. Although many of the Acalan towns, said to number seventy-six in all, were probably small settlements, some of them had a fairly numerous population. Cortés described Itzamkanac, the capital, as a rich and flourishing town with many temples, and he evidently regarded it as a more imposing place than the island city of Tayasal, the chief settlement of the Itza in the Peten.

Wedged in between Tabasco, the Peten, and southwestern Yucatan, the Acalan lands obviously must have been subjected to the crosscurrents of political and cultural influences which characterized the history of the Yucatecan Maya in preconquest times. Moreover, postconquest events in the Acalan area and its environs should have considerable importance in relation to the history and ethnography of the southern half of the Yucatan Peninsula. It has long been recognized, however, that less has been known concerning this region than of almost any other part of the Maya cultural area. Indeed, the very location of Acalan has been the subject of considerable speculation and debate. This situation has been due to a notable lack of available source material, archaeological, documentary, and cartographical, concerning the Acalan people and the country in which they lived.

Archaeological explorations have been carried on for many years in the central part of Yucatan and in the Peten, but the archaeology of the Candelaria area, where the Acalan settlements were located, has been, and to a very great extent still is, a closed book. The recently published report of E. W. Andrews describing his reconnaissance in southwestern Campeche in 1939–40 shows that the Candelaria drainage and adjacent regions are dotted with ruins. The remains indicate that much of this area was thickly populated in ancient times, especially in its more habitable portions above the long series of rapids culminating in the cataract at Salto Grande. Sculptures are notably absent and standing architecture is scant, but at San Enrique a large ruined site contains many mounds once topped by vaulted stone structures. Although he made no excavations, Andrews found pottery fragments ranging from polychrome sherds roughly correlatable with the latest architectural activity of the Old Empire cities in the Peten to the crude incensarios characteristic of the period preceding the Spanish conquest in northern and eastern Yucatan. Andrews did not succeed in identifying the sites of any Acalan towns, but his findings demonstrate the archaeological importance of the region and the need for more intensive investigation at selected sites.

The Spaniards first entered Acalan in 1525 during the course of the epic march of Hernán Cortés from Mexico to Honduras. On this occasion the great conqueror established peaceful relations with the ruler of the province, who gave at least nominal obedience to the Spanish crown and provided desperately needed supplies of food for the army. The Fifth Letter of Cortés, written in 1526 after his return to Mexico City and probably based on some sort of diary or log kept en route, is the most reliable narrative of the expedition. Here we find the earliest account of Acalan and its far-flung commerce, brief descriptions of some of the towns, and a record of significant events, including the execution of Cuauhtemoc, last ruler of the Aztec, which occurred during Cortés' stay in the province. This narrative is supplemented by another eyewitness account in the *True History* of Bernal Díaz del Castillo, the soldier chronicler. Although Bernal Díaz' story is valuable for the vivid recollection of his own impressions and because it contains a certain amount of data not given in the Fifth Letter, it was written many years later and is not so trustworthy as Cortés' contemporary report. Secondhand accounts of the expedition are given by historians of the Indies, notably Gómara and Herrera, but they add little to the narratives of Cortés and Bernal Díaz. Ixtlilxochitl, a descendant of one of the lords of Tezcuco who accompanied Cortés, gives an interesting account of the Cuauhtemoc episode, based on family traditions and the songs and half-legendary stories of the Mexican soldiers.

On the basis of information received from Cortés' soldiers, Francisco de Montejo, who had made an unsuccessful attempt in 1527–28 to occupy Yucatan from the east coast, concluded that Acalan might serve as a base of operations for conquest of the peninsula from the southwest. In 1530 Montejo's lieutenant, Alonso de Avila, advanced overland from Chiapas to Acalan, where he founded a Spanish villa and granted *encomiendas* to his followers. Within a short time, however, Avila realized that the region was not suitable for the purpose Montejo had envisaged. He abandoned the settlement and moved on, first to the Cehache area, or Mazatlan, east of Acalan, and thence to Champoton. Here he was joined by Montejo, and a second attempt was made to conquer Yucatan, this time from the west.

In 1541 Alonso de Luján, an associate of Avila, gave a report of the entrada to Oviedo, the royal chronicler of the Indies, who incorporated it in his *Historia general y natural de las Indias*. Although Luján's narrative is fairly reliable, the author apparently did not have so vivid or picturesque a memory as Bernal Díaz. The section dealing specifically with Acalan is short, and except for a statement concerning the size of the capital, Acalan-Itzamkanac, it adds little to our knowledge of the life of the Acalan people.

For the period from 1530 to 1548 the colonial chronicles contain no data concerning events in the Acalan area. In 1548 Fray Lorenzo de Bienvenida, one of the early Franciscan missionaries in Yucatan, gave a brief account of the province in a letter to Prince Philip. Here we learn that encomiendas in Acalan were held by certain colonists in Yucatan, indicating that the region had been effectively reduced to Spanish authority. According to Bienvenida, the population, once numerous and prosperous, had rapidly declined since the coming of the Spaniards, and he recommended that the survivors be moved to a site near Campeche or Champoton. The printed sources contain no record that the friar's suggestion was ever carried out, although we now know that in 1557 most of the Acalan were actually moved to Tixchel, a former Chontal site on Sabancuy estuary. Cogolludo, the Franciscan historian of Yucatan, mentions an expedition to the Acalan area in 1559 in connection with a war against the Lacandon, and with this entry the history of the province, as related by the colonial chronicles, comes to an end.

Although the traditional sources mentioned in the preceding paragraphs record valuable data concerning certain events after the coming of the Spaniards, they provide no information whatever in regard to the origins of the cacicazgo of Acalan and its history in aboriginal times, and they tell us relatively little about the political, social, and religious life of the people at the time of the conquest. Moreover, the chronicles do not indicate the language spoken in Acalan, although it is evident that the province formed part of the Maya linguistic area. Other colonial authors, such as León Pinelo and Villagutierre, confuse the Acalan with the Chol-speaking Acala, neighbors of the Lacandon, and this error has evidently misled certain modern writers. This fact and the lack of precise geographical data in the chronicles have been largely responsible for the lack of agreement concerning the location of Acalan that has characterized writings on the early history of Middle America for the past ninety years. Some students have correctly located it in the basin of the Candelaria; others place it farther inland in the drainage of the Río San Pedro Mártir in southeastern Tabasco and western Peten; and two eminent Americanists, Orozco y Berra and Maler, state that the Acalan towns were situated west of the Usumacinta River.

Writers on this subject have also been handicapped by the lack of adequate maps of the area from the lower Usumacinta and Laguna de Términos east into the heart of the Yucatan Peninsula. Most of the colonial maps are notoriously inaccurate, and they record little data of any kind for this region. Indeed, one of the best maps of the peninsula, dating from the middle of the eighteenth century, which traces Laguna de Términos with reasonable accuracy, does not even show the Candelaria River.[2] In 1843 Prescott called attention to the fact that none of the Acalan town names mentioned in the early narratives could be found on any map he had seen, and he prudently made no attempt to fix their location. Although several eighteenth-century maps give a location for the Cehache, the eastern neighbors of the Acalan, we have found only one which records the name Acalan. This is one of the maps by D'Anville, the celebrated French cartographer, but his location of the province northeast of Lake Peten is obviously incorrect. Geographical information slowly increased during the nineteenth century, although the maps of this period are by no means reliable. In recent times the growth of the chicle industry has brought about extensive exploration along the Candelaria and its tributaries, and during the past few years a standard-gauge railroad has been built from Campeche to Tenosique, crossing the Candelaria above Pacaitun. These developments have added much to our knowledge of the geography of the Acalan country and its environs, but even the latest cartographical data are obviously incomplete in certain respects.

In recent years much new documentary material relating to the history of Acalan has been accumulated through investigations in the Archivo General de Indias in Seville by Dr. Scholes and his colleague, Dr. Robert S. Chamberlain. These papers, which include the correspondence of colonial officials, missionary reports, lawsuits, administrative decrees, and *probanzas* of various kinds, contain a rich store of information concerning the Chontal of Acalan-Tixchel from aboriginal times to the first quarter of the seventeenth century. A complete list is given in the bibliography.

Three *expedientes*, or series of documents, in this accumulation of new sources deserve special comment.

The first comprises five probanzas, dated 1530–33, which were intended to demonstrate the geographical, economic, and linguistic unity of the lowland area from western Tabasco to the Ulua River in Honduras. They were formulated to support the claims of Francisco de Montejo to jurisdiction over this region as part of his government of Yucatan. For the present publication the most important of these probanzas is one entitled, "Sobre las provincias de Acalan y Mazatlan," which was drawn up at Montejo's request in the autumn

---

[2] *Plano de la provincia de Yucatán,* made in 1766 by Juan de Dios González (British Museum, Add. 17654a). Another eighteenth-century map which shows the Candelaria records the name of the river as "Osvbisu" (Calderón Quijano, 1944, lámina 4).

of 1531, a few months after Avila's expedition through these provinces. It contains the testimony of twelve witnesses, all of whom had accompanied Avila, concerning the location of Acalan, its trade with Xicalango, and certain events relating to the entrada. Because of its early date and the firsthand knowledge of the witnesses, the document ranks next to Cortés' Fifth Letter as the most valuable of the early sources.[3]

The second series is the record of a lawsuit between Antón García, *encomendero* of Acalan-Tixchel, and Feliciano Bravo, *escribano mayor de gobernación* in Yucatan, over the encomienda of the pueblo of Zapotitlan, where two groups of the Acalan Chontal continued to live after most of them were moved to Tixchel in 1557. Documents filed during the litigation, which lasted from 1569 to 1571, contain information concerning the encomienda history of Acalan, a list of tributaries in Tixchel in 1569 which provides data concerning Acalan personal names and social organization, and an account of missionary activity in the Zapotitlan area. As we shall see farther on, these documents and others relating to the Zapotitlan episode also record evidence which helps to establish the location of Acalan in the Candelaria basin.[4]

The third and most important expediente contains an extensive file of documents which we shall designate as the Paxbolon-Maldonado Papers. These documents, ranging from 1565 to 1628, record the merits and services of Don Pablo Paxbolon, a descendant of the rulers of Acalan, and of his Spanish son-in-law, Francisco Maldonado. Included in the series is a lengthy text in the Chontal language describing the history of Acalan-Tixchel from preconquest times to 1604.[5]

This Chontal Text is in three parts. The first is a brief history of the rulers of Acalan going back six generations before the conquest. The Yucatecan Maya chronicles cover a number of centuries, but they are so fragmentary and such long intervals of time separate many of the entries that it is difficult to reconstruct the chronology of events which they recount. The Acalan narrative, although it deals with a much shorter period of time, at-

[3] El Adelantado Don Francisco de Montejo, gobernador de las provincias de Yucatán, con Don Pedro de Alvarado, gobernador de Guatemala, sobre el derecho a los términos del Río de Grijalva, que dicho Montejo había conquistado y pacificado a su costa, 1530-33. AGI, Justicia, leg. 1005, núm. 3, ramo 1. As the title indicates, Montejo was involved in a controversy with Alvarado over part of the area described in the probanzas which comprise this group of papers. There are two copies of the probanza on Acalan and Mazatlan. The entire series will be cited hereinafter as Montejo *v.* Alvarado.

[4] [Antón García] contra Feliciano Bravo, escribano, y Juan Vázquez y Juan de Monserrate, 1569-71 (hereinafter cited as García *v.* Bravo). AGI, Justicia, leg. 250, ff. 1885-2255*v*. This case record forms part of the first legajo of the *residencia* of Don Luis Céspedes de Oviedo, governor of Yucatan from 1565 to 1571.

[5] The Paxbolon-Maldonado Papers form part of AGI, México, leg. 138. Copies of parts of these Papers are also found in AGI, Patronato, leg. 231, núm. 4, ramo 16, and México, leg. 359.

tempts at least to tell something regarding the reign of nearly every generation of rulers and presents a series of connecting events which give us some idea of historical cause and effect. It seems possible that the aboriginal history of northern Yucatan could well be reinterpreted in the light of this narrative and that a comparison would suggest more satisfactory reasons and motives for the wars, alliances, and migrations recorded in the Maya chronicles than the inferences which have been drawn from the latter in the past.

The second part of the Chontal Text lists seventy-six towns and settlements which comprised the cacicazgo of Acalan. In the traditional accounts of the Cortés expedition we find a few Acalan place names, almost all of them in Mexican. The list in the Chontal Text gives the Chontal names, many of which are derived, as we might expect, from the names of plants, trees, animals, and other natural objects or phenomena.

The third section describes from the native point of view the arrival of Cortés, the coming of a second Spanish expedition (evidently that of Avila), the conversion of the Acalan to Christianity, their removal to Tixchel, and their various activities to 1604. From Tixchel they made a number of expeditions into the interior to bring out groups of pagan Indians, including apostate fugitives from northern Yucatan, and to settle them in Christian villages near the Gulf coast under Spanish jurisdiction. Here the clash between European and native ideas is admirably portrayed from the point of view of the Indians.

The importance of these Chontal narratives can scarcely be exaggerated. They supply information concerning the aboriginal history of Acalan, political and religious life at the time of the conquest, and various later developments not available in any other place. They are also an extremely valuable addition to the corpus of native colonial literature of the Maya. As we have already noted, northern Yucatan and the Cakchiquel and Quiche areas of the highlands of Guatemala are well represented in this field, but except for a few legal documents, Christian prayers, catechisms, and church records, no other documents written in the native languages have hitherto been discovered for the extensive area intervening between these widely separated regions. Finally, the Chontal Text is a linguistic document of the greatest rarity. For most of the peoples of the Maya stock a reasonable amount of grammatical and lexicographical material was compiled by the Spanish missionaries in colonial times, but for the Chontal language of Tabasco and Acalan we have only the word lists published by Stoll and Sapper and the brief studies made by La Farge and Becerra in recent years. Becerra writes with regard to Chontal that "for this dialect there is no literature of any sort."[6] It is not too much to say, therefore,

---

[6] Becerra, 1910, p. 98.

that for the study of Maya linguistics the Chontal Text is the most important
find that has been made in many years.

On the basis of these new sources it is now possible to reconstruct the
history of Acalan from preconquest times to the seventeenth century. For the
first time we learn something about the origins of the cacicazgo, and the
mystery of what happened to the Acalan people after 1559 is cleared up. Data
recorded in these documents also show beyond any reasonable doubt that the
Acalan lands were located in the drainage of the Candelaria River.

The Acalan narrative tells how the ruling family came from northeastern
Yucatan, where, we infer, they were unwelcome intruders from Tabasco.
Subsequently this mobile and aggressive group of warriors and merchants
occupied at one time or another the Usumacinta valley in the neighborhood
of Tenosique, various parts of the region around Laguna de Términos, and
the Candelaria area where Cortés found them in 1525. During this period they
carried on wars with the people of Tabasco, the Yucatecan Maya of Champoton and Bacalar, and the Cehache in the south-central portion of the
peninsula.

As a result of the Cortés and Avila expeditions the Indians of Acalan were
brought into contact with the Spanish régime established in the New World.
Acalan was not subjected, however, to the rigors of a military conquest, and
the Spaniards never established a permanent settlement in the Acalan lands.
The means by which the Chontal were brought within the orbit of Spanish
administration were the encomienda system and missionary enterprise. The
first encomienda grants, as we have seen, were made by Avila in 1530. Although Avila and his followers withdrew from Acalan after a few weeks, the
tribute obligation of the Chontal was reasserted by Montejo, who established
headquarters in Campeche, and henceforth the Indians continued to give labor
and tribute to designated Spaniards. The conversion and baptism of the Acalan
occurred in 1550, and the Chontal Text gives an interesting and circumstantial
account of this important event. The decline of population, to which Bienvenida called attention in 1548, is confirmed by evidence in the tribute documents. This phenomenon was the result of various causes, of which the
disruption of aboriginal commerce and European diseases were probably the
most important.

The isolation of the region and the swamps and rapids along the Candelaria,
which had protected the Acalan people from their enemies in pre-Spanish
times, now made the country difficult of access for the missionaries, and in
the late 1550's most of the survivors were moved to Tixchel on Sabancuy

estuary, from which their ancestors had been driven in former times. Some of
the Acalan resisted the change, and others fled to their old homeland. These
groups settled at a place later known as Zapotitlan, located not far from the
site of the former Acalan capital. In the course of time, however, these remnants of the Acalan people were sought out and eventually settled at sites
nearer Tixchel. Thus within a few decades after the coming of the Spaniards
the old Acalan lands along the Candelaria were almost entirely depopulated.
This undoubtedly explains the fact, noted by Prescott in 1843, that the later
colonial maps do not give locations for the Acalan towns mentioned in the
early colonial chronicles.

Curiously enough, the key to the location of the cacicazgo has been available for many years on the map of Tabasco made by Melchor Alfaro in 1579
(Map 2) and published in the first volume of the *Relaciones de Yucatán* in
1898. This map shows a "River called Çapotitan" tributary to Laguna de
Términos. The position of this river on the map identifies it as the Candelaria.
The name undoubtedly indicates an association with the pueblo of Zapotitlan
located in the old Acalan area, but it is only now, on the basis of the sources
relating to this settlement found in the Archivo General de Indias, that we
are able to identify this Río de Zapotitlan as the river leading to Acalan mentioned in the traditional sources.

For half a century the pueblo of Tixchel was governed by Don Pablo
Paxbolon, grandson of the ruler of Acalan who received Cortés in 1525. Paxbolon was educated by the Franciscans in the convent of Campeche, where
he received training in Spanish, Christian doctrine, and the manual arts. Assuming the governorship of Tixchel in 1566, he rapidly won the confidence
of the colonial officials and the missionary clergy, and it was largely as a result
of his efforts that the pueblo of Zapotitlan was finally pacified in 1568–69. He
shrewdly identified his own interests with those of the new Spanish régime
and succeeded in becoming a local territorial ruler over an extensive area on
the southwestern frontier of Yucatan. In this region he reduced various
heathen and apostate groups to obedience and helped to advance the missionary program. About 1590 Paxbolon married his elder daughter to Francisco Maldonado, a recent immigrant from Spain who became one of the
leading citizens of Campeche. By this alliance the cacique enhanced his prestige
and obtained additional support for his activities as a local Indian leader. Subsequently Paxbolon and his son-in-law, together with other citizens of Campeche, initiated a project to reduce groups of fugitive Indians in the interior of
the Yucatan Peninsula which resulted in the establishment of new missionary
foundations known as the forest missions, "The Missions of Las Montañas."

At Tixchel the Acalan people retained their Chontal language, and occasionally clergy were sent there for linguistic training before taking up duties as missionaries among the Chontal-speaking population of Tabasco. In 1585 the Franciscan mission was made a *guardianía* with jurisdiction over other small settlements, Chontal and Maya, in the Tixchel area. In their new homes, strategically located on the coast, the Indians participated in the local commerce carried on between Yucatan and Tabasco and also shared in the contraband trade with heathen and fugitive groups in the interior. In 1569 the lieutenant governor of Yucatan described the inhabitants of Tixchel as wealthier than the Yucatecan Maya in northern Yucatan, and Ciudad Real, in his account of the travels of Fray Alonso Ponce, Commissary General of the Franciscans of New Spain, states that they were more refined than the Maya. Incidentally, there is no hint in Ciudad Real's report or in the various references to Tixchel in Cogolludo's *Historia de Yucatán* that the Indians of this settlement were Acalan Chontal. This is another reason why historians have not been able hitherto to trace the later history of the Acalan people.

Sometime between 1639 and 1643 the pueblo of Tixchel was destroyed and abandoned, probably as the result of an attack by foreign corsairs. Most of the Indians apparently moved to nearby Usulaban, founded in 1603–04 as a settlement of Maya fugitives from northern Yucatan. During the succeeding half-century the population of Usulaban and other towns in the Tixchel district rapidly declined, due to an epidemic of yellow fever in 1648, the flight of Indians to escape exactions by the Spaniards, continued piratical attacks by the corsairs, and raids by Maya refugees settled in the interior of the peninsula. At the same time the Chontal were rapidly absorbed by the Maya, who became the dominant element in the population of the region. Census reports of 1688 show that a majority of the inhabitants of Usulaban now had Maya names and that in the entire Tixchel district the Maya comprised about 88 per cent of the total population. The sources used in this study come to an end at this point. It is evident, however, that the merging process continued into the eighteenth and nineteenth centuries, and so far as we know there is no trace of the Acalan Chontal or their language in the southwest portion of the Yucatan Peninsula at the present time.

Such, in brief, are the main outlines of the history of Acalan-Tixchel as revealed by the new documentary material. In the chapters which follow we shall tell the story of the cacicazgo and its people in full detail on the basis of all the sources, old and new. We begin, however, in Chapter 2 with a survey of the Chontal of Tabasco and neighboring Indian groups in order to provide a background, linguistic and ethnographic, for the more elaborate treatment of the Chontal of Acalan. Chapter 3 is devoted to an analysis of conditions, political, religious, economic, and social, in Acalan at the time of the conquest, and in Chapter 4 we give an interpretation of the aboriginal history of Acalan as recorded in the first part of the Chontal Text.

Chapters 5 and 6 describe the coming of the Spaniards, with special reference to the Cortés and Avila expeditions, and the establishment of Spanish suzerainty over Acalan as a by-product of the occupation of Tabasco and Yucatan. In Chapter 7 we deal with the encomienda history of Acalan, the introduction of Christianity, and the reasons for the decline of the province in the first quarter-century after the entrada of Cortés. The removal of the Acalan to Tixchel, the course of events there to 1569, and the pacification of Zapotitlan form the subject matter of Chapters 8 and 9. In Chapters 10–13 we describe the later activities of Don Pablo Paxbolon, the history of the missions of Las Montañas, the pretensions of Francisco Maldonado to royal favor as reward for his services and those of his father-in-law, and the decline of the Tixchel area in the seventeenth century. The final chapter (14) is devoted to a general review and conclusions.

These narrative chapters are supplemented by five appendices. In view of the importance of the Chontal Text, we give a facsimile reproduction of the original manuscript, a printed text of the contemporary Spanish translation, and an English translation in Appendix A. In this way the narrative is made available for use by the linguist, the historian who is not trained in the Maya languages, and the interested reader.

Because of the long debate concerning the location of Acalan, it has seemed advisable to review this question in a thoroughgoing manner. In Appendix B we present the views of other writers on the subject and then review the evidence, old and new, in favor of the Candelaria location. The itineraries of Cortés and Avila from the Usumacinta to Acalan are also discussed in this appendix in considerable detail, since the conclusions of earlier writers are largely based on their study of these early expeditions. A detailed examination of Cortés' route to Acalan in the light of new evidence also seems justified in view of the fact that his journey of 1524–25 was one of the greatest feats of overland travel and exploration in American history. In this separate review of the problem it has been possible to introduce data that would be burdensome to the reader if included in the narrative chapters.

Appendix C is a study of the Tixchel matrícula of 1569, with special reference to the meaning of Acalan personal names and such inferences as can be made concerning Acalan family and household organization. Appendix D tells the story of certain hitherto unknown explorations in the Peten in 1573 and 1580. This material is included partly because of its intrinsic interest and partly because it provides significant evidence in relation to the problem of the location of Acalan. An English translation of an interesting report of 1604 describing Indian settlements in the interior of the Yucatan Peninsula is presented in Appendix E.

On various questions it is impossible to be as definite as we might wish, despite the mass of new source material. Archaeological investigation will undoubtedly aid in clearing up many puzzling points and provide a better basis for interpreting trends and cultural crosscurrents in pre-Spanish times. New documentary sources will probably be found from time to time. But the materials at hand provide sufficient data to reconstruct in considerable detail the history and ethnography of a region concerning which we have had little information in the past and to make a contribution to the growing body of knowledge concerning the Maya and their civilization.

2

The Chontal of Tabasco and their Neighbors

WHEN THE FIRST Spanish explorers sailed along the southern shore of the Gulf of Mexico, they found a hot, moist alluvial plain, inhabited largely by a people of the Maya stock, whom they afterward called the Chontal.[1] This country was well populated and prosperous, for it produced large quantities of cacao, the most important article of trade in Middle America. Not only was the land covered by a network of navigable rivers, but it lay across the main trade routes connecting the Veracruz slope, the Valley of Mexico, and the highlands of Chiapas with Yucatan and the rich coast of northern Honduras. Consequently it is not surprising that Tabasco was famous for its commerce in pre-Spanish times.

The Chontal area lies entirely in the hot country. It is noted for its many swamps and bogs, and the tropical rain forest is interspersed with grassy savannas, especially where the rivers overflow the surrounding country during the rainy season.[2] The heavy annual rainfall, actually recorded as 2554 mm. (100.62 in.) for the year 1892–93 at Villahermosa, is probably typical of the country. Here the precipitation rose from 2 mm. or less for the months of March and April to 300.5 mm. (11.84 in.) in May and reached 618.4 mm. (24.36 in.) in September.[3]

The term Chontal was originally applied to these people by the Mexicans, whose language was almost a lingua franca in many parts of Middle America, so it was natural for the Spaniards to do the same. We do not know what the Chontal called themselves. The name itself is somewhat ambiguous. *Chontalli* is an Aztec term meaning "foreigner," and it was also applied to peoples in southern Oaxaca and Nicaragua, whose languages are quite unrelated to that of the Chontal of Tabasco. The latter is one of the lowland group of the languages of the Maya stock. It is closely related to the Maya of Yucatan on one side and to the Chiapas group on the other, which includes Tzeltal, Tzotzil, Chañabal, and Chuj. Even closer is its resemblance to Chol and Chorti, which were formerly spoken over a broad area extending eastward across the base of the Yucatan Peninsula to Copan and in all probability as far as the Ulua River in northwestern Honduras.

[1] As far as we know at the present time, it was only in Yucatan that the natives called themselves Maya.

[2] Relaciones de Yucatán (hereinafter cited as RY), 1: 319; Sapper, 1897, pp. 183–84 and map 2.   [3] Sapper, 1897, pp. 402–03.

On February 6, 1579, Don Guillén de las Casas, governor of Yucatan, transmitted to the *alcalde mayor* of Tabasco royal instructions calling for the preparation of reports on the geography, resources, and history of the various parts of the Indies. In accordance with these instructions a series of *relaciones* on the Tabasco area was drawn up, of which two have been preserved. One of these was prepared by the municipal authorities of the Villa de Santa María de la Victoria; the other was written by Melchor de Alfaro Santa Cruz, citizen of the villa and an encomendero of the province. Alfaro's report was made by order of the alcalde mayor, dated April 10, 1579, in which Alfaro is characterized as "the person who better than any other can give an account of the land." The alcalde mayor's decree also instructed Alfaro to make a map "as best he could" of the province. This map, dated April 26, 1579, was filed with Alfaro's report, dated May 4, 1579.

A statement in Alfaro's report certifies that the author had traveled through most of the province of Tabasco and that the accompanying map gave a true picture of the land. A similar statement is made in one of the legends on the map. Although the drawing of the map is distorted, due in part to the circular design, it portrays in a remarkably accurate manner the principal features of Tabasco hydrography. Some of the town locations are incorrect, but on the other hand the map records the sixteenth-century locations of certain towns that have since disappeared or have been moved to other sites. For the purposes of the present volume the most important detail is the "River called Çapotitan," which is evidently the Río de Acalan. (Cf. discussion of this point in Appendix B, pp. 419-20.) As an historical source the Alfaro map of 1579 is a document of great value.

The Alfaro report and accompanying map, together with the relación of the Villa de Santa María, are now in the Archivo General de Indias in Sevilla. The map is in color and measures 57 by 60 cm. (Torres Lanzas, 1900, 1: 24-25). The two reports and a full-size color reproduction of the Alfaro map were published in the first volume of the *Relaciones de Yucatán* (Madrid, 1898). A color reproduction of the map, somewhat reduced in size, was also included in the fifth volume of A. P. Maudslay's translation of the *Historia Verdadera* of Bernal Díaz del Castillo (Works issued by the Hakluyt Society, 2d ser., no. 40, London, 1916). Comparison of these reproductions of the Alfaro map indicates that the second one is more reliable, especially in regard to the readings of the descriptive legends. The Maudslay copy also bears a certification by Sr. Carlos Jiménez Placer of the Archivo General de Indias that it is an "exact reproduction of the original."

The present reproduction is a drawing based on the RY and Maudslay copies, with English translations of the descriptive legends. In the spelling of Indian names we have tried to adhere as closely as possible to the original forms, giving preference in most cases to the readings on the Maudslay copy. In cases of doubt we have also referred to the spellings recorded in Alfaro's report published in RY.

In view of the certification that Maudslay's copy is an exact reproduction, we have followed the latter's rendering of the name of the river where the remains of Cortés' bridge were still to be seen as "Rio qs de gueimango." It should be noted, however, that the copy in RY gives the name as "gueiapan." This has the appearance of a good Nahuatl name and could mean "large river." It is difficult to understand how a Spanish copyist could have made an error of this sort. Alfaro's report (RY, 1: 324) mentions this river, here called an "estero," and the remains of the bridge, but no name is given for the stream.

Some explanation also seems necessary in the case of the "great savannas which they call cimatans," etc. These savannas were evidently named "cimatanes" for the *cimatl* plant. Among the Aztec this was a medicinal plant which Emmart tentatively identifies as a species of Phaseolus. Sahagún describes its fruit as "wild beans" (*frijoles silvestres*) and states that the root was edible if cooked a very long time; otherwise it was poisonous (Emmart, 1940, p. 300; Sahagún, 1938, 3: 229, 232).

An unusual feature of the Alfaro map is its highly conventionalized circular outline, although the subject matter does not call for such a form. In this respect it resembles two colonial Yucatecan Indian maps. In these, unlike the Alfaro map, the top is toward the east and the border sites are set between double circles at approximately regular intervals. Since the only circular European maps known to us are those of a hemisphere or the world, where such an outline was required by the subject matter, the junior author of this study has elsewhere expressed the belief that the Yucatecan maps followed a native Maya convention. Although the Tabasco map is ascribed to Alfaro's authorship, its style suggests the possibility either that he had a native map before him when he drew this chart or that an Indian collaborator, familiar with the Maya convention, aided him in his work. (Cf. Roys, 1943, p. 184. We are indebted to Capt. R. B. Haselden, Curator of Manuscripts in the Huntington Library, for his assistance in our search for European circular maps.)

Chontal, Chol, and Chorti are indeed so similar that, as J. E. S. Thompson suggests, they might well be considered little more than dialectal variants of a single language.[4] This opinion finds confirmation in a Spanish document written in 1533.

From the Ulua River to the River of Copilco-zacualco it is all one language, and they all trade with one another and consider themselves to be the same; and all the Indians of those parts say that those are their boundaries. Beyond the River of Copilco-zacualco the language is that of New Spain [Nahuatl], and similarly beyond the said Ulua River it is another language [Jicaque?].[5]

Chontal, Chol, and Chorti are not readily delimitable, and they apparently merged into one another. Chontal and Chol were divided into various dialects, and the same was probably true of Chorti. In recent years two dialects have been noted in Tabasco; one is spoken in the Chontalpa and the other, in the vicinity of Macuspana. The former is generally known as Chontal, but we do not know whether the Indians themselves give it this name. The latter, however, is called Yocotan by the people who speak it.[6] The Acalan narrative published in this volume seems to record a third dialect of the same language, and there were doubtless others. The Chontal on the Usumacinta may have had a dialect of their own, or it may have been very similar to Acalan.

The so-called western Chol spoken around Palenque was formerly known as Putun, Putum, or Puctun, which reminds us of Putunthan, the name which the Yucatecan Maya applied to the language of the Acalan at Tixchel. M. J. Andrade, however, informed us that the local Indians now call it Palencano and are unfamiliar with the words Chol and Chontal. He collected a vocabulary of this dialect, which he found to differ as much from the eastern Chol as it does from the Yocotan dialect of Chontal.[7] To the southeast were the Chol-speaking Lacandon and the Acala (not to be confused with the Acalan), of whose language we know little except that it was a dialect of Chol. Farther east lived the northeastern or Manche Chol, whose dialect has survived in a grammar and vocabulary compiled during the first half of the seventeenth century by Fray Francisco Morán at San Lucas Tzalac on the Sarstoon River. Thompson traces the Chol area through northern Verapaz to Lake Izabal and Santo Tomás on the Bay of Amatique. At the beginning of the seventeenth

[4] Thompson, 1938, p. 590. The language of the eastern Chol was called Cholti, which might be translated as "speech of the Chol, or of the farmers."

[5] The quotation is translated from a petition of Alonso López, agent of Montejo the Adelantado, filed before the Council of the Indies in the autumn of 1533. In Montejo v. Alvarado.

[6] Blom and La Farge, 1926–27, 2: 468.

[7] Seler, 1904, p. 81; Andrade to Scholes, January 9, 1937.

century a pagan nation called the Toquegua still lived on the slopes of the
mountains east of the lower Motagua. The name sounds Mexican, but Fray
Francisco Ximénez, who does not distinguish between Chol and Chorti, calls
them Loquehuas and states that they were "of the same Chol nation which, as
noted, extended from the land of Esquipulas and Chiquimula to the mountains
on the other side of the river of the gulf [Río Dulce]."[8]

Somewhere beyond Lake Izabal began the Chorti country. Domingo Juarros found this language in use at Zacapa at the end of the eighteenth century.
It is still spoken in the Department of Chiquimula in Guatemala and about
Copan in Honduras. Although he gives no authority for his statement, J.
Galindo claims that Chorti was formerly spoken at Omoa, so it may have been
the language of the coast country between the Motagua and Ulua Rivers. In
any case it seems to be well established that the language of this region was
closely related to Chol and Chorti.[9]

Chorti and Chol are very similar, the principal difference being that the
l in the latter becomes an *r* in Chorti. C. Wisdom, who has made a thorough
study of modern Chorti, states that the two are almost mutually intelligible.
In an account of Copan written in 1576, Lic. Diego García de Palacio, *oidor*
of Guatemala, tells us that "it is certain that the Apay language which is
spoken here is current and understood in Yucatan and the aforesaid provinces,"
the latter being "Uyajal," Lacandon, Verapaz, Chiquimula, and Copan.[10] We
know that Chol was spoken by the Lacandon and in northern Verapaz, and
this statement that some form of Chol-Chorti was understood in Yucatan re-
calls Alonso de Avila's testimony in 1533 that the same interpreter served him
equally well in Yucatan and on the Ulua River.[11]

The Maya of Yucatan constituted an important part of a large economic
bloc extending from Laguna Tupilco in Tabasco to the Ulua River. Although
Yucatecan Maya and Chontal-Chol-Chorti are distinct languages, they are
similar enough so that merchants and many other persons living on the coast
of one of these areas seem to have often learned the speech of the other, but
this was hardly true of the ordinary farmer or cacao grower.

On the basis of sound correspondences A. M. Halpern associates Yucatecan Maya with his Quichoid and Mamoid groups largely spoken in the
highlands of Guatemala, and he places Chontal-Chol-Chorti in his Chiapas
group with Tzeltal-Tzotzil, Chañabal, and Chuj. J. A. Mason, on the other

[8] Thompson, 1938, pp. 585–92; Morán, 1935; Remesal, 1932, bk. 11, ch. 20; Ximénez, 1929–31,
bk. 4, chs. 3, 5: bk. 5, ch. 29; Roys, 1943, p. 114.
[9] Galindo, 1920, p. 595.
[10] García de Palacio, 1920, p. 542.
[11] Sobre lo del Río de Ulua, 1533, *in* Montejo v. Alvarado.

hand, puts Maya and Choloid (which includes Chontal, Chol, and Chorti) in one group and the Chiapas languages in another.[12]

A comparison of the Chontal Text with a Yucatecan Maya document, preferably of the colonial period, will show much similarity in sentence structure as well as in vocabulary, once the sound shifts have been taken into account. Fray Antonio de Ciudad Real, who was probably the author of the Maya Motul dictionary and not unfamiliar with the languages of Guatemala and Chiapas, states that although Chontal is a different language, "in many words it agrees with Maya, and so, knowing one, the other is easily understood."[13]

From a historical standpoint it is of interest to note that Cortés' interpreters on his journey to Honduras apparently had no trouble with Chontal, Maya, and Chol, including the various dialects of these languages, which they encountered in crossing Tabasco and the base of the Yucatan Peninsula; but they found it difficult to communicate with the people of Chacujal on the Río Polochic.[14] This town was near the border between Pokonchi and Kekchi, which Halpern and Mason both associate with a Quichoid group or family.

No grammar or dictionary of Tabasco Chontal has come down to us from colonial times.[15] O. Stoll has published a word list based upon a vocabulary compiled by C. H. Berendt in the neighborhood of Villahermosa, and this has been copied by K. Sapper. Like Stoll and Sapper, M. E. Becerra has published a vocabulary and made comparisons with other languages of the Maya stock. Dialectal variations are shown by two word lists presented by O. La Farge. One, called Chontal, was compiled by W. Gates at Tecoluta in the Chontalpa, and the other, known as Yocotan, is from the language as it is spoken around

---

[12] Halpern, 1942, p. 54; Mason, 1940, p. 71. Halpern, like Stoll and Sapper, uses the form Tzental instead of Tzeltal. Some of the older writers, like Ciudad Real (1873, 1: 472, 479), seem to consider Tzotzil and Tzeltal a single language, which they call Quelem, or Quelen.

[13] Ciudad Real, 1932, p. 347.

[14] Cortés, 1866, pp. 448–51, and 1916, pp. 400–02.

[15] This paucity of Chontal linguistic material is probably to be explained by the very considerable proportion of the Chontal population who spoke Mexican as a second language. Many of the early missionaries had been trained in the Valley of Mexico, and in Tabasco it was not so necessary for them to know the local language as in many other areas, where such ignorance made them almost helpless in dealing personally with the natives. Although the friars spread the knowledge of Nahuatl to some extent by circulating religious songs, especially among the women, it gradually became evident that their religious functions were impeded by their inability to communicate directly with many Chontal women and children and those of the men who were not bilingual. As late as 1595 it was reported that during the preceding eighteen years only three of the missionaries in Tabasco could speak Chontal, and two of these did not know it very well. These men were now dead, and three friars had recently been sent from Yucatan to Tixchel to learn the language from the priest at that town, who was the only Chontal linguist in the district. In 1606 the bishop was still complaining of a lack of Chontal-speaking clergy (AGI, México, leg. 369). As time went on, other Maya linguists were no doubt sent from Yucatan to Tabasco. Grammars and dictionaries would have been useful to such men, but the languages were so similar that such aids could be dispensed with.

the villages of San Fernando and San Carlos in the district of Macuspana. La Farge has also made a brief grammatical study of Yocotan. The language of the Acalan, presented in the Text, is called *uiba than*, which might be translated as "the language here," and it is stated that it is named Chontal in the Mexican language.[16]

Although Tabasco has been little explored archaeologically, it seems evident that a large part, if indeed not all, of the Chontal-speaking area was once a part of the so-called Old Empire of the Maya. Buildings of brick and mortar apparently dating from this period have been found on an island in Laguna de Mecoacan, and at Comalcalco, close to the western border of the Maya area, is a large ruined city of this type.[17]

The alluvial plain of Tabasco contains no stone, and the structural use of burned brick in this area is, as far as we know, unique in Middle America. At Comalcalco the large flat bricks appear to have been burned in open fires, since a black stripe inside indicates imperfect baking. The platform mounds are large; one is 35 m. high and 175 m. along one side. These are constructed of earth held by brick retaining walls, but the buildings with their corbeled vaults are built of bricks set in thick layers of lime mortar made of burned oyster shells from the neighboring coast. The walls were covered with stucco, sometimes modeled with relief carvings of ornamental scrolls, glyphs, and human figures, all of which are typical of Old Empire Maya art.

We know nothing of the history of Comalcalco. Although the name of the site is mentioned in a document of 1565,[18] it does not appear in any of the sixteenth-century lists of Tabasco towns. No dated inscriptions have as yet been found in the ruins, so it is difficult to place this city in the chronology of the Old Empire. The remains at Tortuguero and El Retiro are less distant, but Palenque was the nearest great cultural center. The last is, of course, a stone city, but Comalcalco resembles it in the use of rectangular piers, the profile of the roof slope, and the stucco reliefs. Of genuine artistic merit are the relief sculptures of a number of men modeled on the walls of one of the rooms. Here is a sound attempt at composition and spatial distribution. These figures wear rather full loincloths, elaborate headdresses—most of them feathered—wristlets, bead necklaces, and breast pendants. Only one of them has a supernatural aspect. Otherwise realistically portrayed, he has the leaf-nose of a bat, an

[16] Stoll, 1884, pp. 45–70; Sapper, 1897, pp. 407–36; Becerra, 1910; Blom and La Farge, 1926–27, 2: 465–502.

[17] Charnay, 1887, pp. 183–210; Blom and La Farge, 1926–27, 1: 104–30.

[18] Información de servicios de Alonso Gómez de Santoyo, teniente de gobernador y justicia mayor en la provincia de Tabasco, 1565–66, AGI, México, leg. 98.

animal which plays an important part in the art of Copan and other parts of the Old Empire and figures in the mythology of the Quiche as one of the fabulous creatures of the underworld. We are also reminded of the Tzotzil, or "bat people," of Chiapas, whose language is closely related to Chontal.

These reliefs have a freshness of aspect which is striking. The drawing is for the most part excellent, and their realism is amazing. The plain, and yet unexaggerated, prolapsis of the abdomen in the figures of the older men is an example of the naturalism with which they are portrayed. Without ceramic evidence it is difficult to correlate these sculptures with the art of Palenque, which is famous for its wealth of decoration, its highly developed composition, and its sophisticated execution of detail. The simpler reliefs of Comalcalco may be earlier, or the difference may well be due to a peripheral lag in artistic development.

In Tabasco, as elsewhere, no tradition of that phase of Maya civilization known as the Old Empire has been found, and how or why it came to an end still remains largely a matter of conjecture. What we do know, however, is that at the time of the conquest the Spaniards found there a people of the Maya stock, the Chontal, whose manner of living had been affected by an intrusive Mexican culture and among whom were at least eight, and possibly more, Mexican-speaking towns.

The presence of these Mexican towns within the Chontal area offers a problem of considerable historical interest. We know little about how this alien people came to settle in what had once been a part of the Maya Old Empire. From Tabasco itself no historical legends have come down to us, but their entrance into the country appears to have been one stage of a movement which extended to many parts of the Maya area and even much farther south. In Yucatan the natives told the Spaniards vaguely of a "great descent" of peoples from the west and more specifically of Mexican intruders, who had come from Tabasco.[19] Although few of these accounts are explicit, we believe that they all deal with migrations of considerable importance, for Nahuatl-speaking colonies were reported by the Spaniards in various parts of Guatemala, Honduras, El Salvador, and Nicaragua. Not only have a number of them preserved their language down to the present time, but archaeological investigations have confirmed the spread of a Mexican culture to these regions.[20]

---

[19] Roys, 1933, pp. 66, 139, 147; 1943, pp. 58–59; Landa, 1941, pp. 32–36 and Tozzer notes. This "great descent" from the west into Yucatan was apparently so named to distinguish it from a smaller invasion of the peninsula believed to have come from the east. We doubt, however, that any of the migrations into Yucatan were as large as those which resulted in the Nahuatl-speaking settlements found in Tabasco and Guatemala.

[20] Roys, 1943, pp. 117, 120; Thompson, 1941, pp. 32–34 and *passim*.

We find some indication that the Nahuatl-speaking peoples who settled among the Chontal of Tabasco, as well as those who left evidence of a Mexican culture in northern Yucatan, came from the Gulf slope of southern Veracruz or the adjacent part of Tabasco west of the Maya area. Peter Martyr ascribes a highly developed civilization to southern Veracruz and tells of courts of justice surrounded by walls and of market places and paved streets.[21] In this region, according to Fray Bernardino de Sahagún, lived a people called the Olmeca Uixtotin. Olmeca has been translated as "the rubber people" and Uixtotin, as "the salt water people." They grew cacao and were great traders and very rich. They were evidently accomplished potters, for a fine orange ware from southern Veracruz has been found at Chichen Itza and in other parts of Middle America. They were armed with copper axes, and they wore rubber sandals and ornaments of gold and precious stones. Sahagún implies that they were not all of the same stock, and he tells us that "there are many of these who are Nahuas, or Mexicans." Thompson notes that the languages spoken in this area are Nahuatl and Mixe-Zoquean. He also observes that the earlier Olmec art, apparently prior to the introduction of a Nahua culture into the region, influenced that of the Maya Old Empire, but that its later manifestations show a marked infusion of Toltec motifs and style.[22]

Little is known of the archaeology of the Maya Chontal area subsequent to the Old Empire, but in northern Yucatan there is evidence of a cultural connection with the highlands of Mexico. The Tutul Xiu rulers of Mani in Yucatan were generally believed to be of Mexican descent, and in the Book of Chilam Balam of Mani we read that their ancestors had originally come from a place named Tulapan, apparently referring to Tula, the ancient Toltec capital north of Mexico City. This is of outstanding interest in view of the similarity between some of the remains at Tula and those dating from the Mexican period at Chichen Itza. Not only do we find the same ceramic horizon at both sites, but the serpent columns, friezes with jaguars and eagles carved in relief, and atlantean figures recently excavated at Tula bear a startling resemblance to sculptures of a similar character at Chichen Itza. Some of these features have not as yet been discovered in southern Veracruz and western Tabasco, and the manner in which they were carried to northern Yucatan still remains a problem. Thompson, however, has shown a number of traits common to both the southern Veracruz–western Tabasco area and Chichen Itza, which, since they seem foreign to the art of the Maya Old Empire, were

    [21] Thompson, 1941, pp. 34–38; Anghiera, 1912, 2: 19.
    [22] Sahagún, 1938, 3: 133–34; Vaillant, 1935, p. 121; Thompson, 1941, pp. 37, 42; Merwin and Vaillant, 1932, p. 80; Seler, 1902–23, 4: 431 and map, p. 432.

evidently introduced into Yucatan during the period of Mexican occupation.[23]

Whether or not the legends of a Tula origin, or even the architectural and sculptural analogies, actually represent a migration from that site to the Maya area is somewhat uncertain. The Quetzalcoatl cult was prominent among the Olmeca and the alleged descendants of the Mexican intruders in the Yucatan Peninsula, and there was a legend in the highlands of Mexico indicating that Cholula, Puebla, succeeded Tula as the center of this cult, which spread to the Gulf coast and parts of the Maya area.[24] This is confirmed to some extent by the archaeological evidence. A post-Teotihuacan culture known as Mazapan was abundantly represented at Tula, and G. C. Vaillant points out its affiliation with certain pottery found on the pyramid at Cholula ascribed by tradition to the worship of Quetzalcoatl. He also describes the rise of a civilization which he calls Mixteca-Puebla, since it appears to have developed in the lands of the Nahua of Puebla and the Mixteca of northern Oaxaca. This was the culture which was carried to southern Veracruz and western Tabasco and from there, it is generally believed, to various parts of the Maya country.[25]

There was also a spread of the Nahuatl language to those regions, but we know little of the circumstances under which it occurred. It would appear, however, that the transplanting of Mexican speech and culture to the Gulf coast and the founding of Nahuatl-speaking towns in Tabasco and on the Pacific slope of Central America were accomplished by true migrations, including women; whereas the mere establishment of ruling dynasties in Yucatan and the highlands of Guatemala, but without changes in local tongues or in the cultural patterns save along ceremonial lines, might have been the result of Manchulike conquest by small groups of military adventurers, accompanied by few or no women.

The intruders into the Maya area considered themselves Mexicans, but, as Thompson notes, the features at Chichen Itza which remind us so strongly of the art of central Mexico probably came indirectly. It is not suggested that the same people who brought them to the Gulf coast actually reached Chichen Itza, but rather that the invaders of Yucatan were inhabitants of southern Mexico, who had been strongly influenced by this intrusive culture and had in turn carried it on to the peninsula, along with some elements of their own. One evidence of this is the phallic cult, which according to the Book of Chilam Balam of Chumayel was introduced by the Itza, and this is confirmed by the archaeological remains. This feature was characteristic of neither central

[23] Thompson, 1941, fig. 19.
[24] Torquemada, 1723, bk. 3, ch. 7.
[25] Vaillant, 1941, pp. 19, 22, 77, 83.

Mexico nor of the Maya Old Empire, but it was strongly developed in Vera-cruz and apparently carried from there to Yucatan.[26] The implication, there-fore, is that the foreign intruders from without the Maya area, although they were Nahuatl-speaking, were not entirely of Nahua descent and that their Mexican culture was modified in some respects by that of the Gulf coast.

Kidder, on the other hand, informs us that he considers the resemblances between the religious architecture of Tula and of Chichen to be so close as to indicate direct contact. He further feels that the apparently total absence of any manifestation of such architecture in southern Veracruz or western Tabasco militates against the belief that that area played a significant role in the transference of highland Mexican traits to northern Yucatan.

Tabasco as a whole was first described in two reports, written in 1579 by Melchor de Alfaro Santa Cruz and other officials of the Villa of Tabasco, and these are accompanied by a detailed map of the province by Alfaro (see Map 2). Here we learn that the most thickly populated part was a region called the Chontalpa, which certainly included a compact group of twenty-three Chontal-speaking towns lying between the present Río Seco, formerly the Río de Dos Bocas, and the Río Nuevo, or González. Alfaro, however, gives the number of towns in the Chontalpa as thirty-three, so this area prob-ably also comprised five others formerly situated west of the Río de Dos Bocas and five more lying a short distance east of the main group.[27]

At the mouth of the Grijalva River was a large commercial center vari-ously named Potonchan and Tabasco. Near the coast and on the Grijalva and its tributaries to the south were a number of other Chontal towns, but they were few compared to the large area over which they were scattered. These towns might be roughly divided into three groups. The first would comprise those on or near the Grijalva. Another was Astapa, Jahuacapa, and Jalapa on the Río Tacotalpa. Alfaro calls them the three Çaguatanes, but Cortés con-siders them barrios of a single town, to which he gives the name of Çagoatan. As E. Seler points out, the name was really Ciuatan, "the place of the woman." Widely scattered on the Río Chilapa and its tributaries was a third group con-sisting of Chilapa, Tepetitan, Tepecintila, and Macuspana.[28]

According to the Alfaro map, in 1579 there were still five towns on the Usumacinta River above·Jonuta. These were Popane, sometimes called Tamulte Popane or Tamulte de Popane, Iztapa, Usumacinta, Petenecte, and

[26] Thompson, 1941, pp. 50, 54; Roys, 1933, p. 83.
[27] RY, 1: 311–74; Roys, 1943, pp. 99–100.
[28] Seler, 1902–23, 3: 583; Alva Ixtlilxochitl, 1891–92, 2: 408; Roys, 1943, pp. 100–01.

Tenosique, going upstream in the order named. Besides these, Cortés, Bernal Díaz, and the Chontal Text mention Ciuatecpan, and the Text also refers to a place named Balancan. Of all these only Tenosique and Balancan can still be identified. Petenecte is believed to have been situated not far below Tenosique, and Ciuatecpan and Usumacinta were 6 and 22 leagues respectively down the river from Petenecte.[29]

Although Yucatecan Maya has been spoken around Tenosique in recent times and we find a few Maya surnames from Petenecte in 1573 and 1605, there is strong evidence that the language of the region was predominantly Chontal in the sixteenth and early seventeenth centuries. In 1573 Fray Pedro Lorenzo, a Dominican stationed at Palenque, was acting as missionary for the river towns. He was a noted Chol and Chontal linguist, but we find no reason to believe that he spoke Yucatecan Maya.[30] In a report dated 1595 is a plea for Chontal-speaking clergy in the benefices of Jalpa and Nacajuca in the Chontalpa and of Usumacinta on the river of that name. Here, we are told, the language is "foreign to and different from the language of Yucatan, because the Indians who speak the language of Yucatan do not understand the Chontal language."[31] Only ten years later Alonso de Mesa, evidently the man of that name who translated our Chontal Text, was ordered to translate a petition by the town officers of Tenosique written in Chontal. Although the number of Yucatecan Maya names may have increased somewhat between 1573 and 1605, it seems evident that in the latter year the language of the region was still principally Chontal.[32]

For the next sixty-six years we have no direct evidence regarding the language spoken in the river towns, but by 1671 it is plain that the situation had changed. At this time the governor of Yucatan and Fray Cristobal Sánchez, a prominent Franciscan missionary of that province, received letters of complaint signed by the Indian officials of Tenosique, Petenecte, and three settlements which now appear for the first time in the documents from this region. These new villages were Santa Ana, Canitzam, and Tumulte, or Multe.[33] They are still found on modern maps. Among the twenty signatures

[29] Cf. discussion concerning these towns in Appendix B, pp. 438–48, *infra*.

[30] See Appendix D.

[31] Información de servicios de Fray Juan de Izquierdo, obispo de Yucatán, 1595, AGI, México, leg. 369. Although the evidence is not conclusive, it is possible that a part of the population of Iztapa and Usumacinta were Nahuatl-speaking at the time of the conquest. Cf. p. 82, *infra*.

[32] Información de los malos tratamientos que los españoles hacen a los indios de la provincia de Tabasco, 1605, AGI, México, leg. 369.

[33] We believe the Multe of these letters to be the modern village of this name lying between Santa Ana and Canitzam, or Canizan, and not the Tamulte Popane already mentioned. The latter was a considerable distance downstream, certainly below Usumacinta and probably

on one of these letters are eleven familiar Yucatecan names. One, Mamas, may be the same as Mas, or Maz, which is also a Yucatecan patronymic, and another, Kau, is the Maya word for the grackle, although we have not encountered it as a name. Possibly Hau, which is a common Maya name, was intended. Of the remaining seven signatures two, Acat and Patzin,[34] are frequent among the Chontal of Acalan, and the other five are Spanish. The last were in all probability those of Chontal Indians, since at this time very few Yucatecan Maya had abandoned their native patronymics, while from the very first many Tabasco Indians had adopted Spanish surnames. Not only are the majority of these names Maya, but the letters themselves are written in that language.[35]

There can be little doubt that there were still Chontal-speaking Indians in the Usumacinta towns above the junction with the San Pedro Mártir, but it seems evident that conditions had changed and that their influence was no longer as predominant as it had been during the sixteenth century. Of the two governors mentioned among the officials of the five towns, one had a Chontal name, although that of the other was Maya. The fact that the people of all these towns were now called "indios de la montaña," however, strongly suggests that a very considerable proportion of the population were Yucatecan Maya-speaking people who had been brought in from the forests.

How long any large number of Maya-speaking Indians had been living in these river towns is hard to tell. We have a brief notice of a secular priest who is said to have brought out many Maya-speaking Indians from the forests toward the end of the sixteenth century, but the report is vague and unsatisfactory.[36] In one of the 1671 letters Don Rafael Canche, the governor with the Maya name, writes, "It is many years since we settled in these towns where we are"; and he was probably referring to his own people and not merely to the older Chontal population.

Where the so-called forest Indians had come from still remains something of a problem. Discussion of the neighbors of the Chontal of Tabasco and Acalan will be found elsewhere in this study. It is of interest to note that by 1670 a large part of the Chontal-speaking Acalan in the Tixchel region had

---

below Iztapa as shown on the Alfaro map. In all probability Tamulte Popane had been moved up the river to the modern site.

[34] Acat is certainly Nahuatl, and Patzin seems to have the honorific suffix -tzin, which is so common in Mexican names. As we shall see farther on (pp. 61–63, infra), many of the Chontal had Mexican names.

[35] Testimonio de las cartas de los indios de las montañas y administración a los dichos del Rdo. P. Fr. Cristóbal Sánchez, y asimismo administración en el beneficio de Sumacintla, 1671–78, AGI, Escribanía de Cámara, leg. 308A, núm. 1, pza. 16. The maps now show Santa Ana, "Canizan," and Multe as three different villages.

[36] Royal cedulas to the viceroy of New Spain and to the governor of Yucatan, Tordesillas, July 20, 1592, AGI, México, leg. 2999, libro D-3.

been absorbed by the descendants of Yucatecan Maya fugitives who had been brought into the area from central southern Yucatan. The Maya language, which is still spoken extensively, even among the mestizo population in the northern part of the peninsula, has shown a persistence which we have found among neither the Chontal nor the Chol.

Cortés and Bernal Díaz describe Iztapa as a very large place, and the latter refers to the caciques and merchants of the town. There was much good farm land around it, and it lay in a well-populated district. Cortés considered it an excellent site for establishing a Spanish town. Of Ciuatecpan we know little. Evidently its temples were set on substructures of some size, for the "houses of their idols" could be seen from across a large swamp. A large quantity of food was found at the place, and many farms are mentioned just across the river from the town. There can be little doubt that the settlement just below the gorge of the Usumacinta River, which Oviedo calls Tanoche, was Tenosique. Here Avila found 100 houses in 1530, but the town had already been subject to continuous raids, and it may have decreased in size. The town of Usumacinta was evidently farther down the river than the present village of that name, for it was 22 leagues below Petenecte and the latter town was downstream from Tenosique. Usumacinta must have been a settlement of some importance, since it later became the residence of the beneficed priest who had charge of the entire region. In 1599 this benefice was still fairly prosperous. It contained 350 tributaries, and the salary of the priest was 800 pesos.[37]

With very few exceptions, such as Potonchan, Petenecte, and Tenosique, the Chontal-speaking towns of Tabasco are known to us only by their Mexican names. This was no doubt partly due to the presence in the area of an intrusive Nahuatl-speaking people. A number of towns were entirely Mexican, and their influence on the autochthonous population was such that Nahuatl had become almost a second language to the latter. One group of five Mexican towns was situated close to the southeastern border of the Chontalpa, and three others lay in the angle between the Grijalva River and the Río Seco. Of these eight Nahuatl-speaking towns Cimatan, which belonged to the latter group, was the most important at the time of the conquest.[38]

In another powerful and important town the dominant element was almost certainly Mexican. This was Xicalango, a large commercial center. It was probably situated at the site locally known as Cerrillos near Lake Atasta, a short distance west of Laguna de Términos. The archaeological maps continue

[37] Cortés, 1866, p. 408; 1916, p. 360; Díaz del Castillo, 1939, ch. 175; Oviedo y Valdés, 1851–55, bk. 32, ch. 9; López de Cogolludo, 1867–68, bk. 12, ch. 7; Documentos para la historia de Yucatán (hereinafter cited as DHY), 2: 118.
[38] RY, 1: 320, 352; DHY, 2: 64, 65.

to apply the name to a ruin close to Xicalango Lighthouse opposite Carmen, but the accounts by Ximénez and Fray Antonio de Remesal of a journey which several friars made from Carmen to Xicalango indicate clearly that the town lay some distance inland near the estuaries and lagoons west of Laguna de Términos. We know little of the neighboring town of Atasta. Although the evidence is by no means conclusive, Jonuta on the lower Usumacinta may have been partly Mexican. The people of Xicalango were moved to this town some time prior to 1579.[39]

A third language, Zoque, was spoken in six prosperous towns near the base of the sierra on the southern border of the province. Although these might perhaps be considered a part of the large Zoque area, which spreads over the mountains immediately to the south, their economic relations with the Mexican and Chontal towns of Tabasco were such that the colonial Spanish writers seem justified in considering them a part of the same province.[40]

In 1606 Tepetitan, a Chontal town, had a number of Zoque inhabitants, but we do not know whether or not they were there in pre-Spanish times. Some Zoque were living at Jalapa, another Chontal-speaking settlement, and even at Jalpa in the Chontalpa in the nineteenth century, which is an interesting example of the migrations of mountaineers to the hot country. In the sixteenth century many of the Mam descended to the Pacific coast near Ayutla; in the seventeenth, the Santa Eulalia Indians attempted to settle in the valley of the Ixcan but were driven back by the Lacandon. In the nineteenth, many Kekchi are known to have spread north to the Peten and southern British Honduras, and Roys has recently found new settlements of the same people at the mouth of the Río Dulce opposite Livingston. It is difficult to escape the conclusion that all this is simply the continuation of a tendency which existed long before the Spanish conquest.[41] If further linguistic research should continue to confirm the sound correspondences of the language of the Yucatecan Maya with those of the highlands, we might well surmise that the relationship was the result of a migration of this sort at a very early time.

The prosperity of Tabasco was due largely to its commerce and its production of cacao, which ripens throughout the year. M. Gil y Sáenz writes that here the yield is divided into four crops. The first is called *la invernada*, which comes in January, February, and March. Next is the *cosecho principal*, gathered from April to July. The third is *el venturero* lasting from August

[39] RY, 1: 340, 346; Ximénez, 1929–31, bk. 2, ch. 37.
[40] RY, 1: 320; Roys, 1943, p. 106.
[41] Nombramiento del obispo de beneficiados a los partidos de Tichel y Tepetitan, 1606, AGI, México, leg. 2606; Rovirosa, 1888, pp. 5–6; Roys, 1932, p. 122.

through October, and finally comes *el alegrón,* which ends sometime in December. Formerly, he states, 1000 trees produced 10 *cargas,* or loads, but this was no longer the case in his time.[42]

Water transportation was everywhere available within a comparatively short distance. Cacao does not grow in the highlands of Mexico, and only a relatively small amount could be produced in especially favorable locations in northern Yucatan. Besides large quantities of this highly prized luxury, the Tabasco merchants exported not only articles of local manufacture, but also a surplus of imported commodities which they had taken in exchange for their own products. The Aztec merchants, who were obliged to cross hostile territory to reach Tabasco, brought handsome fabrics, ornaments and spindle cups of gold, articles of copper and obsidian, dyed rabbit hair, and slaves to Cimatan and Xicalango.[43] Slave labor would be especially profitable in a country where the principal crop was gathered throughout the year, and an extensive commerce required many carriers or paddlers.

In exchange the Aztec carried home cacao, finely tanned jaguar and cougar skins, carved tortoise shell, and various precious stones. Tabasco itself produces neither metals nor precious stones. In the highlands of Chiapas were mines of yellow topaz, the so-called amber, from which nose beads were made, but the origin of the jade and crystalline green stones, which the Aztec purchased in Tabasco, is unknown. Some of these stones may have come from the upper Usumacinta River. On a beach of this stream near El Cayo, T. Maler found many extremely hard stones colored ochre-yellow, green, and red. Some of them he thought he recognized as pieces of petrified wood, carnelian, ophite, and jadeite. It seems doubtful that they included jade, since the source of this mineral in Middle America is still considered an unsolved problem. Other hard stones resembling jade, however, were also highly prized.[44]

Besides the gold brought in by the Aztec, it is probable that some was imported from Honduras and southern Veracruz. The former was known as the land of feathers, gold, and cacao, and in the latter Juan de Grijalva's expedition of 1518 found a large quantity of the metal. In addition to manufactured articles, sheets and plates of gold were probably imported, from which native metalworkers made ornaments to suit the local taste. Ceremonial wooden masks were sometimes covered with turquoises and gold leaf, and at Tabasco, or Potonchan, Grijalva and Cortés obtained gold headbands, necklaces, earplugs, and figures of dogs, ducks, and lizards.[45] It is of interest to note that the

[42] Gil y Sáenz, 1872, pp. 36–37.
[43] Sahagún, 1938, 2: 355.
[44] *Ibid.,* 2: 356; Herrera y Tordesillas, 1726–30, dec. 4, bk. 10, ch. 12; Maler, 1901–03, 2: 84.
[45] Oviedo y Valdés, 1851–55, bk. 17, ch. 3; Blom and La Farge, 1926–27, 1: 98.

last all represented edible fauna. In 1541 Montejo's brother-in-law, Alonso
López, obtained by means of threats a number of gold articles from various
Chontal and Mexican towns in Tabasco. The following list gives some idea of
their character. Most of them were evidently worn on important occasions.

1 piece of gold, thin as paper and the size of a paten.
2 large gold jewels fashioned like marine snails (*cobos*).
2 gold jewels fashioned like butterflies and with pendants.
1 gold "carmel," possibly a floral ornament.
1 gold carmel with some pendants.
1 large medal with some gold pendants.
2 gold jewels, one with a butterfly and the other like a small disk (*en tejuelo*).
1 "gold article which they are accustomed to put on the fleshy part of their
    arms at their festivals, which they call *changolo.*"
1 gold mask three fingers wide.
2 ear coverings (*orejeras*), probably the plates of earplugs.
Some ear drops (*zarcillos*), probably earplugs.
14 strings or necklaces of gold beads.
2 strings of gold grasshoppers (*cigarrones*).
1 necklace of small turtles (*hicoteas*) with several beads between each turtle
    and the next.
1 necklace of gold turtles with its small pendants. There were twenty turtles
    and between them some gold beads.[46]

Salt, cotton cloth, slaves, and probably flint weapons and tools were
brought from Yucatan, and there was an extensive trade across the base of the
Yucatan Peninsula with the northern coast of what are now Guatemala and
Honduras. Much of this passed by way of Acalan, and in 1524–25 Cortés re-
received maps from the merchants of Tabasco, Xicalango, and Acalan showing
this route.[47] Another obvious route would appear to have been up the Usumacinta and Río de la Pasión by canoe and overland across the divide to the
Sarstoon River, which flows into the Bay of Amatique, but little is known
about the Usumacinta above Tenosique during the sixteenth century.

The most suitable land for cacao was in the hands of the Chontal, and they
also raised corn, squash, and beans. Fish, turtles, and manatees were taken
from the Gulf, rivers, bayous, and lakes. Much game was hunted in the forests,
including deer, peccaries, rabbits, armadillos, coatis, iguanas, wild turkeys, and
curassows. In early colonial times the Zoque, whose country was too cold for

[46] El fiscal contra Alonso López, vecino de la villa de Santa María de la Victoria de Tabasco,
sobre haberse titulado visitador y exigido a los indios de la provincia de Tabasco diferentes contribuciones, 1541–45, AGI, Justicia, leg. 195 (cited hereinafter as Fiscal *v.* López).

[47] Cortés, 1866, pp. 397, 419; Herrera y Tordesillas, 1726–30, dec. 3, bk. 6, ch. 12; Díaz del
Castillo, 1939, ch. 177.

cacao, brought large quantities of maize, chile, beans, and fowl, which they exchanged for cacao in the Chontalpa and for salt on the lower Grijalva, and it seems likely that this commerce already existed in pre-Spanish times. Montejo the Younger obtained from the Zoque towns a large number of canoes for the final expedition to western Yucatan.[48]

There were three important commercial centers in Tabasco proper. Of these Cimatan and Xicalango were either wholly or partly Nahuatl-speaking, as we have already noted, and Potonchan was Chontal-speaking.

Cimatan was closely associated with two neighboring towns named Conduacan and Cuaquilteupa. This group, which was known as the three Cimatans, was located on the Grijalva a short distance below the point where the Río de Dos Bocas branched off from it and flowed directly north to the Gulf of Mexico. During the sixteenth century the Dos Bocas was a mighty river, but the channel where it left the Grijalva filled with silt, and Dampier, who observed it in 1676, already described it as the insignificant stream which it is today. Later all three towns were moved to the site of the modern Conduacan, two suburbs of which are named Cimatan and Cuculteupa.[49]

The three Cimatans occupied an important strategic position commercially, for they were the first Tabasco towns encountered by the merchants from the Valley of Mexico. Sahagún tells us that before they arrived they sent word ahead and were met in the hostile territory through which they were passing by the friendly "lords" of Anahuac Xicalanco, as the Aztec called the country between Coatzacoalcos and Laguna de Términos, and conducted to their towns. Since travel in Tabasco was mostly by water, it may well be inferred that these merchants were met by canoes, which carried them to their various destinations. Many of them went to Cimatan and Xicalango, but others traded with the Chontalpa, where they had their factories and warehouses at Mecoacan, Chilateupa, and Teutitlan Copilco, the modern Copilco. Here they sold their goods to local traders who took over the distribution. In 1541 the latter were also from Mexico and resided permanently in Tabasco, but it is hard to tell whether this was the case before the Spaniards came.[50]

At the request of the five Nahuatl-speaking towns lying immediately southeast of the Chontalpa the Spaniards established a market at Huimango in 1541. This suggests that there had been no commercial center in that district, and we infer that these towns had received Mexican commodities through

[48] RY, 1: 371–72; Fiscal v. López.
[49] RY, 1: 338–39 and map; DHY, 2: 64; Dampier, 1906, 2: 213.
[50] Sahagún, 1938, 2: 354–55; Fiscal v. López.

Cimatan in pre-Spanish times, although we have found no evidence of any political connection.[51]

At least four Zoque towns near the border of Tabasco and Chiapas are known to have been subject to Cimatan. Two of these, Teapa and Ixtapanga-joya, are on one of the principal passes leading to the highlands of Chiapas; a third, Nicapa, is at the head of the valley of the Río Platanar, which flows into the upper Grijalva; and the fourth, called Gualtipan, is probably the modern Zoque town of Magdalena Coltipan. It seems evident that Cimatan controlled the most important trade routes from the highlands of Chiapas as well as that from the Valley of Mexico.[52]

We know little about the appearance of Cimatan. Building stone and the materials for making the strong lime-and-sand mortar found near the coast were obviously lacking here. Also burned brick structures have as yet only been found associated with lime mortar. There can be little doubt that the temples of a town of such importance were set on pyramids, and the more important buildings, on raised platforms, presumably of earth in this locality. The dwellings at Cimatan were probably the "good large houses" described by Dampier, with walls of "mud or wattling, plastered on the inside and thatched with palm or palmetto leaves." Bernal Díaz, who knew the town, tells us it was defended by palisades equipped with platforms and loopholes for the archers, who were noted for the strength of their long bows and the accuracy of their aim. When the place was permanently subdued, forty years after the first Spanish expedition against it, the report of the expedition states that they pacified the "pueblos" of Tecpan Cimatan, Acatan, Naguatan, and Senuchuacan, and that they burned the houses of the idols, which were numerous in Tecpan Cimatan. The name Cimatan is derived from *cimatl*, a medicinal plant believed to be a species of Phaseolus, and *tecpan* means government house. Since the neighboring towns of Conduacan and Cuaquilteupa were at peace with the Spaniards, and even took part in the expedition, we conclude that these four so-called pueblos were really the four quarters of the town of Cimatan. Such divisions existed at Tenochtitlan and in other parts of the highlands of Mexico as well as at Itzamkanac in Acalan. Although Cimatan was surrounded by large savannas and many swamps and bogs, the region was thickly populated in pre-Spanish times, and there were cacao groves near the town.[53]

The people of Cimatan resisted the Spaniards for many years, although

[51] Fiscal *v.* López.
[52] Godoy, 1931, p. 468; Díaz del Castillo, 1939, 3: 304.
[53] Díaz del Castillo, 1939, ch. 166; Dampier, 1906, 2: 210; Información de servicios de Alonso Gómez de Santoyo . . . , 1565–66, AGI, México, leg. 98.

armed forces and missionaries occupied the town from time to time. About the year 1550 Fray Hernando de Arbolancha of the Mercedarian Order peacefully persuaded the inhabitants to submit to Spanish rule. He promised them exemption from tribute for two years and apparently made some progress in their conversion. When opportunity offered, however, the natives burned the church and fled to the swamps, and later, returning to their homes, they continued to make war on the Christianized Indian pueblos and the Spaniards. As late as 1564 they raided the Chontalpa, where they occupied Comalcalco and prowled about the outskirts of Chichicapa, terrorizing its inhabitants and those of Amatitan with threats to attack and burn their towns. Their numbers were probably increased by refugees from other parts of Tabasco, for in 1541 a principal of Amatitan named Coatl persuaded a large part of the population to abandon the town for a time and attempted to lead them to Cimatan. In his confession he later admitted frankly that this was in order to evade service and tribute to the Spaniards. In 1564, however, Cimatan was finally reduced to submission by a few Spaniards and a force of native allies from the neighboring town of Cuaquilteupa. Most of the people were settled in other towns, and in 1579 the able-bodied married men remaining numbered only seventeen. Gil y Sáenz relates that the original town of Conduacan was inundated in 1625 and the survivors migrated to the present town, which lay between Cuculteupa and Cimatan. The last are now wards, or suburbs, of Conduacan, and it might be inferred from this account that their inhabitants had already moved there before the arrival of the people of Conduacan. Of the Cimatans, only Conduacan is mentioned in 1688, and it seems probable that at this time all three were considered to be a single town on the present site of Conduacan.[54]

Just as Cimatan was favorably situated to handle foreign trade from the south and west, Xicalango enjoyed a very similar advantage in regard to Yucatan, Acalan, and the Usumacinta valley. Xicalango, however, evidently shared this commerce with Potonchan, or Tabasco, since Cortés obtained maps of the road leading to the Caribbean coast from both these towns, and he mentions their merchants in connection with various places along his route. Pilgrims from Potonchan and Xicalango in Tabasco and from Champoton and Campeche in southwestern Yucatan visited the shrine of the goddess Ix Chel on Cozumel Island off the northeastern coast of Yucatan. It may well be in-

[54] Royal cedula to Lic. Alonso López de Cerrato, president of the audiencia of Confines, concerning the Indians of the province of Cimatan, Valladolid, July 7, 1550, AGI, México, leg. 2999, libro D-1; Información de servicios de Alonso Gómez de Santoyo . . . , 1565–66, AGI, México, leg. 98; Fiscal v. López; Gil y Sáenz, 1872, p. 121. Cuaderno de testimonios . . . de los oficiales reales de Yucatán . . . de las personas que poseían las encomiendas y su producto, 1688, AGI, Contaduría, leg. 920, exp. 2.

ferred that they were mostly merchants whose business took them to that region. Whether they crossed the base of the peninsula to the Caribbean or followed the western and northern coasts of Yucatan is still uncertain. We are inclined to believe that they came by both these routes.[55]

As we have already seen, the merchants of Xicalango and various parts of Yucatan had warehouses and factors on the Ulua River in Honduras. Of Yucatan we are told that "many merchants of this land had their sons and other factors there for the aforesaid traffic," and no doubt the same was true of Xicalango. We are reminded of the son of the murdered Cocom ruler of Mayapan, who was absent in Ulua on business at the time of his father's death, and of the brother of the Acalan ruler who governed the quarter of Nito occupied by the merchants from that country.[56]

Fray Juan de Torquemada states, "There is at the present time a town named Xicalanco, where there used to be much commerce; for from various parts and distant lands merchants assembled, who went there to trade."[57] In 1532 Juan Méndez de Sotomayor, who had served as *alcalde mayor* of Tabasco, testified that he knew how the Indians of the provinces of Cochistlan and Acalan came to Xicalango to traffic. The name Cochistlan is of especial interest, since it is the only well-authenticated Mexican place name for any part of Yucatan that has come down to us. Sometimes it is applied to Campeche and sometimes apparently to Champoton, for Méndez refers to the "province of Cochistlan, and another farther on, which is called Campeche."[58] The name is difficult to translate. *Cochiztli* means "sleep," but the name might be derived from *cocho*, a variety of parrot.

Although we know from Sahagún's account of the expeditions of the Aztec merchants to Cimatan and Xicalango that these towns were not subject to the Mexican confederacy, the influence of the latter must have been very strong at Xicalango. It seems possible that the factors of the Mexican merchants with their employees and slaves occupied a quarter of the town, just as the Acalan merchants did at Nito. Such a situation could have given rise to the story by the authors of the *Relación de la Villa de Santa María de la Victoria* that Montezuma had a fortress at Xicalango.[59] One of the encomenderos of Yucatan in 1579 wrote a similar and more circumstantial account:

I married the niece of Montezuma, the great lord of Mexico, the daughter of his brother, who was named Doña Isabel. The aforesaid Montezuma had sent him as

[55] Roys, Scholes, and Adams, 1940, p. 5; RY, 2: 54.
[56] Sobre lo del Río de Ulua, 1533, *in* Montejo v. Alvarado; Landa, 1941, p. 39.
[57] Torquemada, 1723, bk. 1, ch. 12.
[58] Probanza . . . sobre el río de Grijalva y provincia de Tabasco, 1532, *in* Montejo v. Alvarado.   [59] RY, 1: 364.

captain general with a large number of troops to conquer this province [Yucatan]. Thus he established his headquarters at a place called Xicalango, which is between this land and Tabasco; and when he was already about to begin the conquest of this land, messengers from Mexico came to him, sent by his brother Montezuma, informing him how the City of Mexico and all New Spain were [occupied?] by the Spaniards. And he sent him some Spanish garments, such as a coat, hat, and other things of value, in order that he might see them and know in truth how he [Montezuma] was now subject to the Spaniards. And the captain was so greatly distressed that he died of vexation, leaving his daughter, my wife, a small child.[60]

The story was probably not without some basis of fact; from the analogies we have cited it might well be surmised that a close relative of Montezuma was in charge of a colony of Mexican merchants at Xicalango and that he was planning to extend their activities to Yucatan when Cortés seized Tenochtitlan.

Of the government of Xicalango we know only that a woman could, and did, succeed to the "lordship," a custom apparently alien to Maya political tradition, but she gave no commands and a male relative governed in her stead. Like the Acalan ruler, even he "could do nothing without the counsel and advice of the principal men, who came every day to his house or assembled on the square to discuss whatever came up."[61]

The question naturally arises whether Xicalango was Chontal- or Nahuatl-speaking. All the historical legends point to the latter. To Torquemada's account of the Olmeca-Xicalanca could be added Fray Diego de Landa's story of how the Cocom ruler brought Mexican auxiliaries from Tabasco and Xicalango to Mayapan in northern Yucatan. Then, too, there is the statement in the Tabasco report that the Mexican language was native to comparatively few people, "because it proceeds from two strongholds which Montezuma had in this province and which were Cimatan and Xicalango." While the story is as apocryphal as that of Fuentes y Guzmán, who tells us that the Pipil invasion of southern Guatemala dated only from Ahuitzotl's time and was instigated by him, it does nevertheless point strongly to an association of the Nahuatl language with Xicalango. By inference this would also seem to be confirmed by Sahagún's association of the town with Cimatan, which was certainly Mexican-speaking. All this, however, is offset by a single item of contemporary evidence, which it is difficult to gainsay. In the Tabasco report of 1579 it is stated that there were eight Nahuatl-speaking towns in the province. This is repeated in another of 1582, in which these towns are named, and Xicalango does not appear among them. It should be noted that although the people of Xicalango had been moved to the site of Jonuta by this time, the

[60] Ibid., 2: 221–22.   [61] Remesal, 1932, bk. 5, ch. 10.

town had not lost its identity. It still remained a political entity for purposes of government and taxation.[62]

It seems possible, nevertheless, to reconcile this conflicting evidence. The existence of a woman cacique at Xicalango is a feature common in Mexico,[63] but we have not found it in Yucatan or Guatemala. This suggests that, in addition to an Aztec trading colony, the ruling class of the town, including the more important local merchants, was Nahuatl-speaking. The mass of the population, however, could well have been Chontal.

Although Xicalango was one of the first Tabasco towns to be occupied by the Spaniards for any length of time, little is known of its appearance or architecture. In an account of a visit by some of Bishop Las Casas' companions in 1544, we are told that a league east of the town they came to a small Christian chapel on a small square, and little farther on they reached a larger plaza, where they were entertained by the local cacique and spent the night in a large portico (*portal*), which had been constructed as a rest house for travelers. Some of them slept on an arrangement of boards, and others were given rush mats, handsomely woven in red and black patterns. At Xicalango they were received by "all the nobles of the town with the governor, who acted as the principal cacique." They found it a pleasant place with its shady plaza and fresh groves of trees, but the mosquitoes were troublesome. The unmarried youths were still sleeping in the municipal men's house, as was customary in Mexico and Yucatan.[64]

The name of the site today, Cerrillos, indicates that the temples and some of the more important public buildings were set upon substructures. The latter were probably of earth, but may well have been faced with a layer of mortar composed of quartz sand and a lime of burned shell, such as has been found near the former site of Potonchan.

In Tabasco proper the third important commercial center was Potonchan near the mouth of the Grijalva River. The Spaniards renamed both the town and the entire province after the cacique of the town, according to several of the early chroniclers. If so, they evidently added the suffix -*co*, which is very common in Mexican place names and means "place of." A Spanish town was founded near by and was named Santa María de la Victoria in memory of Cortés' victory at Centla in 1519, but it was often called the Villa de Tabasco. There is probably little doubt that Potonchan was Chontal-speaking. Gerónimo de Aguilar, who understood and spoke the language of the town according to Cortés and Bernal Díaz, was able to act as interpreter for Cortés' expedition,

[62] RY, 1: 320, 364; DHY, 2: 64, 84; Fuentes y Guzmán, 1932–33, 2: 90.
[63] Roys, 1943, p. 166.
[64] Remesal, 1932, bk. 5, ch. 10; Ximénez, 1929–31, bk. 2, ch. 37.

and we know that Aguilar was ignorant of Nahuatl. This of course is not entirely conclusive evidence, since even if it had been Mexican, many people would no doubt have understood Chontal, but the inference is confirmed by Gómara, who states that the local name for canoe was "tahucup," and *hucup* is still the Chontal word for canoe.[65]

It was evidently a populous town. Bernal Díaz tells of thousands of warriors opposing the Spaniards there, "because at that time that town had much commerce, and subject to it were other large towns; and they were all equipped with every kind of arms of the sort they used."[66] We have no specific information regarding the subject towns. Among them no doubt were Centla, Taxaual, and Chayala, which were close by, and others may well have been situated some distance up the Grijalva River.

Scanty as it is, the description of Potonchan is the only one of a Tabasco town that has come down to us from the time of the conquest. Along the river bank it was defended by a palisade of thick timbers. The town covered a large area, for the houses were separated from one another by gardens. The finer dwellings were set on earth substructures, which may well have been faced with plaster or mortar. The Spaniards reported that such houses were constructed of lime, brick, and stone, but it is obvious that building stone was not available on this alluvial plain. No remains of the actual houses have as yet been discovered in the region, but at a neighboring site, believed to be that of Centla, Berendt excavated some earth platforms, which were faced with a thick layer of mortar and ascended by stairs constructed of burned brick, mortar, and pounded earth. The mortar, which is excellent, is composed of sand and a lime made from burned shell. On one of the mounds Berendt found evidence which convinced him that the ruins at Centla were occupied at the time of the Spanish conquest.[67]

[65] Herrera y Tordesillas, 1726–30, dec. 3, bk. 7, ch. 3; RY, 1: 361; Díaz del Castillo, 1939, ch. 31; López de Gómara, 1943, 1: 82; Blom and La Farge, 1926–27, 2: 471. In the name Tabasco, if we consider -*co* a suffix signifying "place of," we are reminded of the Aztec *tlauatztli*, which means "something dry." Such a description would seem appropriate for a town site in a low wet district. Rovirosa derives Tabasco from *tlalli* ("land") and *paltic* ("something wet") and Aguilera less plausibly from "tlauashco" (*tlauaxco?*), which he interprets as "the place which has a master" (Rovirosa, 1888, p. 30; Aguilera, 1942, p. 5). We have, however, found new evidence to connect the name Tabasco with that of the native ruler of the town. In 1543 he was Don Francisco Çipaque (Cipac), apparently the successor of a Don Hernando "Azbaque," who was cacique in 1541 and said to be 50 years old at that time (Fiscal *v.* López). The letter *b* does not occur in Nahuatl, but Spaniards ignorant of the language sometimes substituted it for *p*. Moreover, Acipac is a variant of the name Cipac among the Chontal Acalan, so it is obvious that Azbaque was intended for Acipac (cf. p. 62, *infra*). If the elements *Ta-* and -*co*, so familiar in the place names of the region, are considered simply a prefix and suffix, it seems extremely likely that the remainder is simply a Spanish corruption of this name.

[66] Díaz del Castillo, 1939, ch. 31.

[67] *Ibid.*, ch. 31; López de Gómara, 1943, 1: 98–99; Anghiera, 1912, 2: 34; Brinton, 1896, p. 265; Seler, 1902–23, 5: 150–51; Roys, 1943, p. 103.

Most of the houses of Potonchan were thatched structures, presumably with pole or wattle walls. Gómara and Peter Martyr give descriptions suggesting that some of the more substantial buildings were covered by flat, beamed roofs topped with mortar. Many of the dwellings were probably large ones, since in Tabasco there is evidence of multiple-family homes like those in Yucatan.[68]

The principal square of the town was like a large courtyard, and there was a great ceiba tree in the center. Around it were various buildings, some of them the pyramidal temples which the Spaniards called *cues*. Others were great halls said to be the quarters of the persons who served the idols, which indeed appear to have been found in all the buildings. We surmise that one of the buildings was probably the *tecpan*, or government house, and that possibly another might have been the unmarried men's quarters. Both such buildings could have contained oratories with idols.[69]

Gil y Sáenz relates that Potonchan had once been subject to Xicalango, but he does not disclose the source of his information. The town was depopulated some time subsequent to the Spanish conquest, and in 1579 a few surviving families were still living at Tabasquillo a short distance to the south on an arm of the Grijalva. Here they were chiefly occupied as fishers and potters and in raising fowl and fruit, which they sold at the Villa of Tabasco.[70]

In the mountains of Chiapas southwest of the Chontal area is a large area inhabited by the Zoque. In language, and probably also in their basic culture, they are closely related to the Mixe of southeastern Veracruz and Oaxaca. The latter have always been described as a rude, uncultivated people, and the former, while more intelligent, have been placed in much the same category. So far as the Zoque are concerned, the seventeenth-century reports do not seem to bear this out, although no doubt their civilization in pre-Spanish times was inferior to that of the Nahua, Zapotec, and most of the peoples of the Maya stock. Thomas Gage tells us that the Zoque area was the richest part of Chiapas and the people were witty and ingenious. In his time they were manufacturing fine silk fabrics, which were exported to Spain. At the time of the conquest Teapa was a very large place and Ixtapangajoya was described as a pleasant town of 500 houses with good plazas and fine buildings. They may well have been influenced by the civilization of the Gulf coast, since both were subject to Cimatan.[71]

[68] López de Gómara, 1943, 1: 98–99; Anghiera, 1912, 2: 34; Roys, 1943, p. 103.
[69] Díaz del Castillo, 1939, ch. 31; Tapia, 1939, p. 51; Ximénez, 1929–31, bk. 2, ch. 37.
[70] Gil y Sáenz, 1872, p. 77; RY, 1: 346.
[71] Bancroft, 1882, 1: 669; Gage, 1928, pp. 167–68; Díaz del Castillo, 1939, ch. 166; Godoy, 1931, p. 468.

The Zoque country was mostly too cool for growing cacao, and it produced maize, chile, cotton, cochineal, and honey. The yellow topaz, which the Spaniards called "stone amber" and which the Aztec and Maya used to make lip and nose beads, was mined at Tapalapa and probably exported mostly to Tabasco. The site lies near the headwaters of the Sayula, Platanar, and Teapa Rivers, all of which were controlled by Cimatan. The Aztec supply of this commodity is reported to have been obtained from Zinacatan in the Tzotzil area farther east. The other Zoque products were also marketable in Tabasco, where a large part of the population devoted most of their energy to growing cacao.[72]

In pre-Spanish times the Zoque appear to have exported fine fabrics to both the Valley of Mexico and the Maya area. One of these was a netlike cloth, apparently a gauze, and the other is described as a brocading of sheer plain weave. Fragments of both are reported to have been recovered from the Sacrificial Cenote at Chichen Itza, and large quantities of decorated cloth are said to have been brought to the Valley of Mexico from the Tabasco-Chiapas regions as tribute. This is probably true, but it seems most unlikely that the Zoque towns of Tabasco and Chiapas were tributary to the Aztec confederacy at the time of the conquest, although it is known that the latter had conquered the Tzotzil town of Zinacantan.[73]

Some of the Zoque towns were subject to the Chiapanec, but many of them apparently consisted of independent groups, each yielding obedience to the largest or strongest town of the group, as was the case with Quechula and Solosuchiapa. We know nothing about their political or social organization, except that there was a hereditary ruling class.[74]

Since the latter half of the sixteenth century a Chol-speaking people are known to have dwelt in the mountainous region of northern Chiapas between the Zoque towns of Tabasco and the Usumacinta valley, and some of their descendants are still living at Palenque, Tumbala, and Tila. We first hear of this area about the seventh decade of the sixteenth century. At this time the Dominican Fray Pedro Lorenzo was in charge of these towns and those on the Usumacinta River with his headquarters at Palenque. We have found no record of any military expedition sent to conquer the district, and it was apparently sparsely inhabited. Pedro Lorenzo, however, who had settled a number of Chol Lacandon at Ocosingo in 1564, is credited with having brought many more of the same people to the Palenque region, and it is believed that

[72] Herrera y Tordesillas, 1726–30, dec. 4, bk. 10, ch. 12; Sahagún, 1938, 2: 356–57; Roys, 1943, p. 110.
[73] Cordry and Cordry, 1941, *passim;* Sahagún, 1938, 2: 356.
[74] Díaz del Castillo, 1939, ch. 166; Godoy, 1931, p. 468.

the present Chol-speaking inhabitants are largely descended from these converts.[75]

In view of the archaeological importance of Palenque it would be of considerable interest to be able to identify the occupants of the area at the time
of the conquest. By the time of Pedro Lorenzo's arrival the Spaniards had
occupied Tabasco for at least a generation, and we hear nothing of any
Chontal or Mexican settlement in the region. The Tzeltal are still living immediately to the south and to the southeast were the Chol Lacandon, but it is
difficult to determine who were the predecessors of Pedro Lorenzo's converts.
It is hard to believe that the district was uninhabited at the time of the Spanish
conquest.

Culturally these western Chol are now to a large degree Hispanicized, but
early in the eighteenth century they revolted, killed their priests, and apostatized until a military force brought them back into the fold. J. L. Stephens'
reference to their "impious adoration to an Indian female" would indicate that
this was a part of the Tzeltal insurrection of 1712, and it suggests that at this
time at least they were influenced more by the Tzeltal than by the Chontal,
although their language might be more closely related to that of the latter.
Only a century ago Stephens found some of them still wearing loincloths
and was much impressed by their wild appearance.[76]

In the large area between the Usumacinta and the highlands of Chiapas,
extending southeast from the Chacamax River near Palenque to the Salinas on
the Guatemala border, lived a Chol-speaking people known as the Lacandon.
The word is a Hispanicized form of Lacantun, which still survives as the name
of one of the larger rivers of the region. It is apparently descriptive of a site,
since in Maya *lacam tun* is defined as "large rock." Here also are a river and a
lake called Lacanha, which by analogy would mean "great water," and, indeed,
Lake Lacanha is one of the two largest lakes in the area. The country is mostly
hilly or mountainous and covered with tropical rain forest, but it is interspersed with occasional savannas. The region is well watered with rivers,
smaller streams, and lakes.[77]

The people lived by agriculture, fishing, and hunting, but were also warlike. In colonial times they raided their Tzeltal and Chañabal neighbors in
the highlands of Chiapas and the Ixil town of Chajul in Guatemala, and it
may well be surmised that these forays were only a continuation of their wars
in pre-Spanish times. There was probably some provocation, for, as we have

[75] Thompson, 1938, p. 587; Ximénez, 1929–31, bk. 4, chs. 47, 48, 66.
[76] Stephens, 1841, 2: 273, 286; Cristóbal Molina, 1934, p. 360.
[77] Thompson, 1938, pp. 586–90; Motul Dictionary, 1929, p. 534; Tozzer, 1907, pp. 14–19.

seen, the highland peoples sometimes tended to move down into the fertile hot country.

In 1559 Lic. Pedro Ramírez de Quiñones led the expedition mentioned in the Chontal Text from Comitan into the Lacandon country. After a march of fifteen days he came to the so-called Laguna del Lacandon, on which they found an island stronghold. Ciudad Real tells us that "the lake is not very large, but it is deep and circular." It was large enough, however, so that the Spaniards constructed a barge (*bergantín*) of considerable size to get to the island. Here, above the water, on a great bare rock was a town of "very good, spacious, and white" houses. No idols were found in the temples, and the inhabitants worshipped only the sun, "differing in this from the Itza and the other nations of those forested regions, who possessed, worshipped, and sacrificed to countless idols." Remesal states that the sun was their "god of battles," and we are reminded of the Temple of the Sun at Palenque. Here was a large relief carving portraying the face of the sun on a shield supported by two crossed spears, so it seems evident that this religious conception had come down from a much earlier period. Like the Manche Chol and other peoples little affected by Mexican influences, they probably also worshipped mountains, river whirlpools, and other natural features. It is true that idols were found at the Lacandon town of Dolores in 1695, but this may have been due to a late intrusive culture, which had spread from the Yucatan Peninsula.[78]

In view of this description of the site and the meaning of the name Lacantun, it is difficult to escape the conclusion that the town on the rock was Lacantun and that the term was later applied to the entire region and its inhabitants.

Some of the people were taken captive and others escaped in canoes down a large, swift river "in the direction of Yucatan." After sacking and burning the town, the Spaniards went on to two other important Lacandon settlements. For these only Mexican names are given. Possibly they had long been visited by Nahuatl-speaking traders from Xicalango, who had given Mexican names to them, as we have seen to be the case in Acalan. The first of these towns beyond the lake was Topiltepec, and farther on was Pochutla ("place of the ceibas"?). The latter was on an island in another lake. We do not know its size, but some of the Indian allies of the Spaniards are said to have fought in the water, swimming more than a league from some places to others.[79]

[78] Ciudad Real, 1873, 1: 473; Villagutierre Soto-Mayor, 1701, bk. 1, ch. 11; Remesal, 1932, bk. 10, ch. 12; Tozzer, 1913, *passim;* Thompson, 1938, p. 594. Our knowledge of the Chol Lacandon is derived largely from a letter written in Dolores in 1695 and from Villagutierre Soto-Mayor. Ethnological studies based on these sources have been made by Thompson and by Tozzer, who published the letter.

[79] Villagutierre Soto-Mayor, 1701, bk. 1, ch. 11; Remesal, 1932, bk. 10, ch. 12. Water com-

It would be of interest to know the location of the famous town on the rock. Ximénez tells us that it was opposite Comitan and that it was foolish for the Barrios expedition in 1695 to enter the region by way of Ocosingo.[80]

The Lacandon continued their depredations, and in 1586 Juan de Morales Villavicencio led a second expedition to the lake of the island stronghold, starting from Comitan. Ciudad Real, who was in the latter town shortly after the return of Morales, states that the Lacandon were still at the town on the rock at this time but escaped again. Morales, desiring to explore the country, descended the outlet of the lake with canoes and proceeded downstream until the river narrowed and the party came to rapids which they dared not pass. They were unable to continue by land, since the rocky banks on either side were inaccessible. Ximénez believes they had reached the Río de Sacapulas, which he says was known locally as the Ixlean. By the Sacapulas he means the Usumacinta, for he considers the Chixoy, Salinas, and Usumacinta to be all the same stream, which indeed they are, and he elsewhere distinguishes between this river and the Lacantun. His mention of a river named "Ixlean," however, suggests the upper Lacantun, which begins at the junction of the Ixcan and Jatate Rivers. Possibly the association of the name Ixlean with the Usumacinta is an error, and the Ixcan River or its continuation below the Jatate is meant. Lake Miramar, which is in the Jatate drainage, seems larger than the lake of the rock, as described by Ciudad Real, and we do not know that it contains a high rocky island. The lake on which Pochutla was situated was evidently of some size, and Miramar and Lacanha are the only large lakes shown on the maps. There are probably other unmapped lakes, but it is doubtful that any as large as these two remain to be discovered.[81]

Some time subsequent to the Morales expedition the inhabitants of the "Pueblo de Lacandon" retired farther to the south or southeast, where Don Jacinto de Barrios Leal, president of the *Audiencia* of Guatemala, found them over a century later at a town which he named Dolores. Ximénez locates this place near the Lacantun, apparently north or northwest of the river, and some distance above its junction with the Usumacinta. One exploring party in 1696 reported that they descended the Lacantun for 32 leagues before reaching the great river, which was evidently the Usumacinta. Maler, in the light of the evidence we have cited, places Dolores not far from the Jatate.[82]

---

munication between the southern Lacandon and Xicalango was rendered difficult by many dangerous rapids between Anaite and Tenosique.

[80] Ximénez, 1929–31, bk. 4, ch. 66.

[81] *Ibid.*, bk. 4, ch. 70; Ciudad Real, 1873, 1: 476. Mrs. Stone (1932, p. 240) suggests that the lake of the rock was probably L. Miramar.

[82] Ximénez, 1929–31, bk. 4, ch. 66, and bk. 5, ch. 74; Maler, 1901–03, 2: 106–107. A previous expedition had gone down the Lacantun from Dolores, some of its members by land and others

Here the Barrios expedition found a settlement of 100 dwellings and three communal buildings, the largest of which was the temple. The houses were thatched. Their walls were of thick poles or timbers on three sides, and they were open in front. Various apartments are mentioned, each containing a hurdle bed large enough for four people. A prisoner, who was captured before reaching the town, told of a group of more than sixty houses, each of which was occupied by more than twenty persons. This was not confirmed in the report of the occupation of Dolores, but it would indicate that multiple-family houses existed, as among the Manche Chol, the Itza, and the Yucatecan Maya. The temple building was also the men's house and was divided into three parts. In two of these the unmarried youths and the husbands of the pregnant women slept. The town does not appear to have been fortified.[83]

We know little of the political or social organization of the Lacandon. Groups are mentioned, which the Spaniards, perhaps from analogies in the highlands, called calpuls, or chirimitals.[84] The principal cacique headed the largest group in the town. He was also high priest and was treated with much ceremony. Under him were two important chiefs, each with considerable following, and six minor caciques with small chirimitals are also mentioned by name.[85]

Juan de Villagutierre Soto-Mayor states that both men and women wore only loincloths, but we doubt that this was true of the women. The prisoner mentioned above wore in addition to his loincloth a sleeveless jacket of coarse or thick cotton cloth (*manta gorda*). This was the garment called a *xicul* and worn only by the upper class in northern Yucatan, but the man seems to have been only an ordinary farmer. As in Yucatan, a smock of bark cloth was also worn on certain ceremonial occasions connected with religion. The men wore long hair and were decorated with earplugs and nose beads. Some of the last were inserted in the septum; others, which were round and about the size of a silver *real*, were "of the paste (*pasta*) commonly called amber, from which rosaries are made." We are reminded of the yellow topaz nose and lip beads which were worn in Mexico and Yucatan.[86]

by boat. Although they were absent for a considerable time, they do not appear to have reached the Usumacinta.

[83] Villagutierre Soto-Mayor, 1701, bk. 4, ch. 14 and bk. 5, ch. 6; Ximénez, 1929–31, bk. 5, ch. 63; Thompson, 1938, p. 599.

[84] We also read of calpuls on the highlands of Guatemala. In Mexico the *calpulli* was a land-holding lineage group, and the term was also applied apparently to the building where the council of this organization convened. Chirimital may be a corruption of *chinamitl*, a Cakchiquel word defined as "people of the town"; but, if so, it evidently had a more specialized meaning as used here. Cf. Villacorta, 1934, p. 366. It is referable to the Aztec *chinamitl*, town or enclosure, and in Pipil *chinamit* means "town" (Stoll, 1884, p. 17).

[85] Villagutierre Soto-Mayor, 1701, bk. 5, ch. 5; Thompson, 1938, p. 602.

[86] Ximénez, 1929–31, bk. 5, ch. 62; Villagutierre Soto-Mayor, 1701, bk. 5, ch. 6.

These people were still practically in the stone age, although they probably had a little copper and gold. Well-shaped axes of a hard green stone were used to clear the fields. The only weapons mentioned were bows and arrows, but they also had blowguns. It seems likely that these were used only for hunting small game, and the missile was a clay pellet as in Yucatan.[87]

Dolores was the principal town at this time. A little more than 12 leagues before reaching the settlement, the expedition had passed a lake of some size containing many small islands. Captain Pedro Alvarez de Miranda, who observed it from a hill, noted in his diary that it appeared to be larger than Lake Atitlan. This was no doubt an exaggeration, but it was evidently a considerable body of water. Ximénez expresses a belief that it was the Laguna del Lacandon and not that of Pochutla. The Dolores Indians later reported that there had been five settlements around this lake and a number of others elsewhere. After the arrival of the Spaniards the inhabitants fled to the banks of the Usumacinta and other rivers to the north. The following year, however, two towns were discovered by the Spaniards four days' journey from Dolores. One, named Peta ("circular water"), had a population of 117 families, and the other, Mop (Mexican wine palm?), had 105.[88]

The principal enemies of the southern Lacandon were the Itza of Lake Peten, with whom they had no intercourse. In spite of the distance, which was said to be a journey of twenty days, the Itza raided the Lacandon towns by night, killing the people and stealing their boats.[89]

From the records of the first expedition by Feliciano Bravo in 1573 to the head of canoe navigation on the San Pedro Mártir we know that this enmity was of long standing. About this time 200 Indians from Pochutla and Lacandon attempted to raid this area, but they were defeated and most of them were killed. Later a Yucatecan Indian, who had been in the region at the time of Bravo's expedition, stated that the latter reached a point only a day's journey from a large town in the province of Taitza, which evidently extended some distance west of Lake Peten at the time. In 1580 a cacique, said to be of Pochutla, and some of his men, who accompanied a subsequent expedition to the same region, pointed out to the Spaniards the sierras around the Itza capital in the distance. From this it would appear that these Lacandon Indians had at some time visited Lake Peten.[90]

[87] Thompson, 1938, p. 598.
[88] Ximénez, 1929–31, bk. 5, ch. 62; Villagutierre Soto-Mayor, 1701, bk. 4, ch. 18, and bk. 6, ch. 6. The present Laguna Petha was probably more than four days' journey from Dolores.
[89] Villagutierre Soto-Mayor, 1701, bk. 4, ch. 18. Lake Peten was a considerable distance from this region, but a journey of twenty days seems excessive for a war party. Perhaps the round trip was meant.
[90] See Appendix D.

The identification of the Lacandon, of whom the colonial Spanish chroniclers write, as a Chol-speaking people has only recently been established by Thompson's investigations, although some of them had been considered to be of this stock. The problem was complicated by the circumstance that in modern times only a sparse population speaking Yucatecan Maya has been found throughout the entire area. They have been known as Caribs or Lacandon, and their presence in the region has given rise to speculations as to what became of the Chol Lacandon as well as how and when a Yucatecan people came into the country.[91]

Stephens tells us that in 1840 the Chacamax River was the boundary between the Christian Indians living around Palenque and the pagan people of the forests to the southeast, who were known as Caribs, but he has nothing to say of the language of the latter. We might well infer that it was Chol, for he adds that fifty years before, some of these Indians living near the Chacamax requested and received Christian instruction from the priest at Palenque. Sapper, writing at the end of the nineteenth century, believed that all the surviving Lacandon spoke Maya at this time, but he was told at Palenque that a few decades before, Chol-speaking Caribs still came to the Chacamax River to trade.[92]

All the indications point to a comparatively late penetration of the Maya into the region southwest of the Usumacinta. Nevertheless some of them had established themselves there prior to the fifth decade of the seventeenth century. About this time authorization to pacify the pagan Indians of Manche and Lacandon was given to a certain Diego de Vera Ordóñez de Villaquirán, who named the region El Próspero. Although he did little to carry out this ambitious scheme, he succeeded in subjecting a settlement of Indians called Nohaa ("great water") on a lake. A Dominican friar from Chiapas made little progress in Christianizing the people, since they spoke only Yucatecan Maya, but subsequently Franciscan missionaries came from Yucatan and lived among them for a time. Nohaa is described as being about 15 or 18 leagues from Tenosique on the other side of the river. Later the Barrios expedition to Dolores came to a deserted site called Próspero 12 leagues east of Ocosingo. We are told that it was so named because formerly Villaquirán had established his headquarters there. Nohaa, however, was evidently farther to the east, since the accounts of the Barrios expedition do not mention a lake, and Cogolludo tells us that the town was more accessible from the Usumacinta valley than from Chiapas.[93]

[91] Thompson, 1938, *passim.*
[92] Stephens, 1841, 2: 286–87; Sapper, 1897, p. 259.
[93] Villagutierre Soto-Mayor, 1701, bk. 4, ch. 15; Ximénez, 1929–31, bk. 5, ch. 60.

The missionaries reported that the people of Nohaa were monogamous. From what little we know of their religious organization, it somewhat resembled that of the Maya. A priest had charge of their idols. He was assisted in his ceremonies by an *ah kulel*, or deputy, and an *ah kayom*, which means singer or chanter. A daughter of one of these men prepared the sacred breadstuffs, and no other woman was present at the sacrifices. Human sacrifice was practiced, accompanied by excision of the heart and ceremonial cannibalism. The victims were only foreigners and not their own people, so we infer that they sometimes made war on their neighbors. In cases of adultery the priest acted as judge and took part in the execution of convicted persons. We know nothing of the functions of the chief.[94]

Fray Diego de Cogolludo rather implies that these people came of various tribes, but this statement is somewhat obscure. He tells nothing of their relations with the Lacandon, although he mentions the latter. One of the men of Nohaa had made several visits to a Chol-speaking people called the Locen, who were neighbors of the Lacandon. The Locen had seven or eight settlements, the largest of which contained 800 houses.[95]

It seems very possible that the people of Nohaa had crossed the Usumacinta only since the Spanish conquest. In any case they were evidently the precursors of the present Maya Lacandon. We are inclined to ascribe the presence of these people in the area primarily to the continued flight of thousands of northern Yucatecans in colonial times to the central southern part of the peninsula. Although some of them probably joined the Cehache, there must have been a constant pressure on the latter, who in turn would either press upon the western Itza near the headwaters of the San Pedro Mártir or pass through their country to the forests beyond the Usumacinta. Here was a fairly secure refuge so long, at least, as they remained scattered in small villages and hamlets. Indeed, this has proved to be the case so far as the Maya Lacandon are concerned. These appear to have been left entirely undisturbed until lumber operations began in the last decade of the nineteenth century.

After the Spanish conquest of northern Peten at the end of the seventeenth century this movement was no doubt greatly accelerated. Spanish activities, which apparently did not continue very long, were confined mostly to the remaining Chol Lacandon living near the Lacantun in the south. While it is largely a matter of conjecture, we infer that in the course of the eighteenth century the Yucatecan intruders, although probably never numerous, gradually outnumbered and probably absorbed the constantly diminishing Chol-speaking population.

[94] López de Cogolludo, 1867–68, bk. 12, chs. 3, 4, 7.   [95] *Ibid.*, bk. 12, ch. 7.

An interesting reference to this movement occurs in a letter written about 1670 by Captain Juan de Villareal y Alosa of Campeche to the governor of Yucatan. Many Christian Indians had recently fled from Sahcabchen and other parts of southeastern Yucatan to the interior to escape the exactions of an unusually oppressive administration, and the organization of an armed force to bring them back was being discussed. The captain reported that if soldiers went against them, they were prepared to retire to El Lacandon and would settle on a "river which they call Nohku," where it would be impossible to reduce them. If any of the Christianized Indians ever fled to Lacandon, however, they must have been very few in number. A. M. Tozzer's ethnological investigations have revealed little, if indeed any, trace of Christian influences in the Lacandon religion, and Indians, once Christianized for any length of time, have usually preserved some features of their new faith, even though they have reverted to paganism.[96]

[96] Sobre las diligencias que se han hecho para la reducción de los indios de Sahcabchen y otros pueblos, 1668–70, AGI, México, leg. 307; Tozzer, 1907, *passim;* Roys, 1933, Appendix G; Scholes and Roys, 1938, *passim.*

3

The Province of Acalan

THE PROVINCE of Acalan was a region apart. Although the inhabitants were Chontal, it was not only an independent state but was so separated from Tabasco by forests and swamps that the Spaniards considered it to be a part of Yucatan.

The location of this province has long been the subject of much discussion. It was known to be on a river flowing into Laguna de Términos and above a series of rapids and falls, which made it difficult of access. Opinions have varied, some writers placing it in the Usumacinta–San Pedro Mártir drainage and others, in that of the Candelaria. The documents on which this study is based, however, plainly identify the Río de Acalan with the "River called Çapotitan" shown on the Alfaro map (see Map 2), and the latter is evidently the Candelaria.[1]

The first modern description of the river is contained in a report written by "H. Pauling," the owner of Hacienda Candelaria, at Carmen in 1859.[2] A certain dramatic interest attaches to the name of the writer, since he can hardly be other than Henry, or "Henriques," Pawling, the young American who shared the adventures of the archaeologist, John L. Stephens, on his famous journey from Guatemala by way of Palenque to Carmen in 1840.[3] The river has also been described by J. H. Acevedo in 1910 and R. S. Chamberlain in 1937, but the only detailed description of the region is that of Andrews, whose account has been used extensively in preparing the present study.[4]

For a distance of some 40 km. above its mouth the Candelaria is a sluggish estuary passing through low swampy country. On its banks the forest is interrupted from time to time with open, level spaces. Above Suspiro the land be-

[1] For a detailed discussion of the evidence concerning the location of Acalan, see Appendix B.

[2] Pawling's report is found in vol. 5 of Estadística del Estado de Campeche, Agricultura e industrias anexas, 1859, MS. in the Howard-Tilton Library, Middle American Research Institute, Tulane University, New Orleans.

[3] Stephens, 1841, 2: 230–31. Pawling, who came from Rhinebeck Landing, N. Y., went with a circus to Guatemala and later became superintendent of a cochineal plantation near Amatitlan. Dissatisfied with revolutionary conditions, he joined Stephens' party and left for southern Mexico. When Stephens went on to Yucatan, Pawling remained at Carmen.

[4] Acevedo, 1910, pp. 14–18; Andrews, 1943, *passim*. Chamberlain's description is given in a letter to F. V. Scholes, written April 20, 1937, after he had returned from a trip up the Candelaria and Arroyo Caribe. Brief accounts of the Candelaria are also given in Galindo y Villa, 1926–27, 1: 277, and in Pacheco Blanco, 1928.

gins to rise, and from here to Salto Grande the Candelaria is a swift stream broken by many rapids. Pawling gives the number of these as twenty-one, but Acevedo states that there were more than forty. The former describes them as small cascades approximately 2 to 3 ft. high and tells us that he had opened gaps or channels through the ledges which caused them, so that boats of 4 or 5 tons' burden were able to pass. Even with these improvements navigation continued to be difficult and dangerous, for Acevedo writes: "Indescribable is the impression produced by the flight of the '*canoas barqueras*' down these torrents, which remain mute witnesses of so many fatal disasters." On either side swamps and savannas alternate with low, forest-covered headlands, which show traces of a considerable population in times past, although the mound groups are not of any size.

At Salto Grande there is a cataract 3 m. high, and above this the river broadens to about 50 m. Chamberlain estimates its width somewhat farther up as between 60 and 90 m. Above Salto Grande it is now a fairly deep and sluggish stream, but in Acevedo's time it was broken by slight drops at Pacaitun and Salto Ahogado, described as "mere obstructions removable by modern explosives." Pawling, however, tells us that the elevations (*altos*) at Pacaitun were formed by hard rocks and had been impassable, but that he had improved them at the cost of much labor and 1,000 pesos, so that boats of 50 tons' burden could pass over them. It seems possible that this and later improvements may have slightly lowered the water in the Candelaria and its tributaries above this point and drained many of the shallow waterways which were navigable for canoes at the time of the conquest.

Above Salto Grande as far as San Enrique low hills confine the river on both sides. At San Enrique a broad swamp begins on the north shore, while on the south bank the land still rises, often in a steep cliff, but frequently leaving a level and sometimes swampy strip along the shore. Beyond, a hilly country is to be seen in the distance. From Salto Grande to the east extends a zone of heavy rain forest. Little standing architecture remains, but Andrews reports large mounds, traces of vaulted buildings, and other evidences of a former large agricultural population. It is of interest to note that up and down the river he found, in addition to later wares, many polychrome sherds, which, he believes, may be roughly correlated with the latest ceramic period of the Maya Old Empire in the Peten.[5]

At a high hill called Cerro de los Muertos the Candelaria, here over 150 m. wide in Acevedo's time, divides into two tributaries about equal in size. One is the Arroyo Caribe, which extends to the northeast. Chamberlain estimates

[5] Andrews, 1943, p. 49.

its width as 60 m. at San Rafael, and it is navigable for large motor launches as far as Laguneta. Above this point it separates into small streams, some of which drain a number of lakes and swamps. One of the latter, now called Isla Pac, is the former Bolonpeten, or "nine islands," and covers a large area. Much of it is permanently under water, but it contains a number of islands, from which it derived its name. One branch of the Caribe, which may have been navigable for canoes in the rainy season, extends east to Concepción. Broad swamps lie along the northwest shore of the Caribe, while on the opposite side is a range of hills extending in the direction of Laguneta.[6]

South of Cerro de los Muertos is the other main tributary of the Candelaria, called the Río San Pedro. Its western shore is hilly, and east of it is a swampy area. The stream is navigable almost to the Guatemala border, where rapids and falls are encountered, but beyond this a canoe can go still farther south. The older maps show a water connection with the Río San Pedro Mártir. Acevedo states that this consists of two small swift streams (*dos correntosos arroyos*) named Tablas and Limón, but no such connection appears on the later maps. It would be of considerable interest if it could be shown that the Acalan were able to reach the Usumacinta drainage with canoes.

An important branch of the San Pedro is the Arroyo de Esperanza, which is navigable to Esperanza by motor launch and much farther east by canoe. It finally divides into smaller streams, one of which, the Río Paixban, reached the Cehache area. Villagutierre, who calls it Ixban, describes it as "an estero, or large arroyo," lying between Chumpich (the modern Cumpich) and Batcab, which were Cehache settlements.[7]

Andrews describes the upper Candelaria drainage as an "alternation of fairly high headland capped with heavy rain forest and large swampy stretches with only scrubby growth. These swamps frequently deepen to form lakes of considerable size. . . . The entire region was heavily populated in ancient times, and mound sites cover the raised headlands. These sites, often large, are completely ruined, and no informant has seen a fragment of standing wall or a piece of sculpture."[8] This suggests that the older civilization of the region, at least in its general cultural aspects, had not been very different from that which Cortés and Bernal Díaz observed during their journey through Acalan and the Cehache country in 1525.

Acalan is a Nahuatl word derived from *acalli* ("canoe"), and the name has been translated as "the place of the canoes." Since all travel and transportation

---

[6] *Ibid.*, pp. 45–46.
[7] Villagutierre Soto-Mayor, 1701, bk. 5, ch. 8.
[8] Andrews, 1943, pp. 46, 50.

were by canoe, most of the settlements were probably near navigable waters. All the reports of the early travelers who came up the Candelaria by boat give considerable prominence to the rapids which they encountered, while the accounts by Cortés, Bernal Díaz, and Avila's companions, who entered and left Acalan by land routes, do not mention any rapids, although some of them, particularly Bernal Díaz, traveled by water within the province. They do, however, have much to say about lagoons, bayous, and sluggish rivers. For this reason it seems safe to put the major Acalan settlements above Salto Grande.

Bernal Díaz tells us that while some of the towns were on terra firma, others were on "something like islands," and that he departed from the capital with eighty soldiers by water and obtained one hundred canoe loads of food supplies from "certain [towns] lying between some rivers."[9] Surely this would seem to indicate that a considerable part of the population lived on the tributaries of the Candelaria above Pacaitun and Salto Ahogado.

Whether or not the Chontal-speaking area at the time of the conquest included the region northeast of Laguna de Términos is a problem of ethnographical importance. Certainly the site of Tixchel was uninhabited when the Acalan were moved there in 1557. Shortly afterward, however, Don Luis Paxua, their chief, fled to the town of Chiuoha. This was a Chontal settlement which was not yet under Spanish domination, so it would appear that there were already some Chontal in the region when the Acalan were brought there by the Spaniards.

As we shall see from the Paxbolon narrative, the Acalan had previously established themselves at Tixchel during the fifteenth century and had remained there sixty or eighty years before they were driven back into the interior. It could well be that they encountered other Chontal already living in this area when they arrived, just as they had found them in the Usumacinta valley around Tenosique, for the region was easily accessible by inlets and streams from Laguna de Términos, but it is also possible that the first Acalan settlement at Tixchel represented a Chontal movement into Yucatecan Maya territory. In either case we may well surmise that some of the Chontal-speaking population continued to remain in the region.

As we have seen, the Chontal of Tabasco are known to us only by a Mexican term, which means "foreigner," and we do not know what name they gave themselves. Acalan, "the land of the boats," is also Nahuatl, but the inhabitants of this region called themselves Amactun or Mactun *uinicob*, meaning the Mactun men or the Mactun people. According to the Text, they called their country Tamactun. We cannot translate the name with certainty, but *ta*

[9] Díaz del Castillo, 1939, chs. 176, 177.

can mean "at," and in Maya *mac* means that which covers an aperture, like the lid of a box or vessel and the stopper of a bottle, or that which chokes or obstructs something. *Tun* means "stone" or "rock" in modern Chontal. In Maya the term indicates a precious green stone, a soft limestone overlying the older rock and shell conglomerate, and in compounds something made of stone.[10] The name Mactun may well have referred to the stone ledges which obstructed the flow of the Candelaria River. These were the most important features of the stream which was the main artery of commerce in the region. Today the name Mactun survives as that of a site just above some rapids on the Río San Pedro Mártir in the Peten,[11] and also of a stream that flows into the Usumacinta near Canizan, but we do not know whether such an obstruction occurs on this tributary.

The Yucatecan Maya called the language of Acalan Putun *than* (Putun "language") and they may also have applied this name to the people. The term Putun, also written Poton, has long been considered to be of Nahuatl derivation and designated certain tribes in El Salvador and Honduras. If it is Mexican, it would be a loan word in the Chol language, where it means "peaceful" (*pacífico*).[12]

The province of Acalan was well populated and had seventy-six towns and villages, which are named in the Chontal Text. It is impossible, however, to identify most of these settlements, inasmuch as the traditional sources record names and other specific data for only a few of the Acalan towns. Moreover, there is still some doubt concerning the actual location of the settlements which we can relate to towns mentioned in the chronicles.

The most important town at the time of the conquest was Itzamkanac, where the Acalan ruler, Paxbolonacha, resided. Cortés describes the settlement, which he calls "Izancanac," as a large place with many temples. Bernal Díaz refers to it as Gueyacala, "great Acalan," to distinguish it from another town known as "small Acalan," which we are unable to identify. Most Spanish writers employ the general Mexican term Acalan to designate both the capital and the province. Although the exact location of Itzamkanac cannot be determined at present, it is our belief that the town was situated south of the Candelaria near the junction of the Arroyo Caribe and San Pedro branches.

---

[10] Tozzer, 1907, p. 17; Sapper, 1897, p. 429.

[11] Communication by S. G. Morley.

[12] Ciudad Real, 1932, p. 347. Brinton (1882, p. 125) cites Gómara's derivation of Poton from the Nahuatl *potonia*, "to smell bad." Cf. Morley, 1937–38, 1: 16; Roys, 1933, p. 115. Even as early as 1527 the name Champoton was defined as "lugar hediondo," but we still doubt that this was the original meaning of Putun (Relación hecha por Luis de Cárdenas . . . , AGI, Patronato, leg. 16, núm. 2, ramo 6).

A broad swamp separated the settlement from the shores of the river.[13]

Of Itzamkanac, Oviedo tells us: "In that city of Acalan are some 900 or 1000 very good houses of stone and plastered white, covered with thatch, most of them of principal men." We are reminded of this writer's glowing accounts of other important commercial towns, and one hesitates to accept them without some reservation. At Chauaca he informs us that most of the houses were of hewn stone, but in the *Relaciones de Yucatán* another account of the same town, although it notes the existence of houses "of stone masonry thatched with straw, where they had their assemblies and markets," also tells of "the inhabitants (*vecinos*) of that town having their large houses of wood, very strong, thatched with palm leaves." No doubt there was a considerable number of thatched stone structures at Itzamkanac; some of them probably had walls of stone rubble smoothed with plaster. We are inclined to believe, however, that many of the "plastered white" houses were not unlike a remarkable modern native structure at Champoton illustrated by R. Wauchope. Here the stockade walls with their exterior horizontal stringers are so heavily plastered that they resemble some of the ancient temple profiles.[14]

In any case Itzamkanac probably presented a different appearance from the Chontal settlements on the alluvial plain of Tabasco. At the latter what little stone they had must have been transported a long distance, although near the coast, as we have seen, structures of burned brick and excellent concrete have been found. In both regions, however, the more common type evidently consisted of dwellings with thatched roofs and pole or wattle walls, and in Acalan, as in Tabasco, many of them were no doubt quite large and plastered on the inside.

Although multiple-family dwellings are not actually reported from Acalan, there is reason to believe that they existed. Our principal grounds for this belief are the indications of this manner of living among the Chontal of Tabasco. It is also of interest to note that in a *matrícula*, or list of tributaries, of Tixchel made in 1569 there are certain apparent groups of brothers-in-law and of fathers-in-law and sons-in-law. Assuming that these represent common residence groups, Dr. S. Tax interprets certain extracts from this list as indicating a strong tendency toward matrilocal residence. On the face of it, he suggests the probability that upon marriage most of the daughters brought their husbands to the house and most sons moved out. This material will be studied in more detail in Appendix C.

[13] Cortés, 1866, p. 419; Díaz del Castillo, 1939, ch. 175. Cf. discussion of the location of Itzamkanac in Appendix B.
[14] Oviedo y Valdés, 1851–55, bk. 32, ch. 5; Wauchope, 1938, p. 67 and pl. 14a.

Contemporary sources tell us that multiple-family houses were common among the Yucatecan Maya, the Chol Lacandon, the Manche Chol, and the Itza on Lake Peten.[15] In 1582 small settlements containing large multiple-family houses were also reported some distance east of Tixchel and north of the Candelaria drainage.[16] At Las Ruinas in the same general region Andrews reports late pre-Spanish remains of two large houses, one rectangular and the other apsidal in plan. Both suggest dwellings of some sort; but the latter, which has three doors in front and one in the rear, reminds us of the residence of a chief as described by Landa in northern Yucatan.[17] The Tixchel matrícula of 1569 records nine married couples in the house of the cacique.[18]

If there were many multiple-family dwellings at Itzamkanac, 900 houses would represent an extremely large population, but it is possible that the number was an exaggeration. In 1548 Fray Lorenzo de Bienvenida wrote a letter to Prince Philip, informing him that the town called Acalan had been a mighty province thirty years before, but that the people had melted away and by this time there were only 200 houses. This would still represent a good many inhabitants, but we infer from the statement that a considerable part of the remaining population of the province had come in from other settlements and were now living at the former capital. In any case, Itzamkanac was unquestionably a large town at the time of the conquest. Cortés' Spanish soldiers with their horses were quartered in a single structure near the home of the ruler, which was probably the *tecpan*, or government building. Itzamkanac evidently impressed Cortés more than did the Itza capital Tayasal, for in describing Chacujal on the Polochic River in northern Guatemala he tells of the large plaza with temples and other buildings around it and states that nothing like it had been seen since leaving Acalan.[19]

Itzamkanac appears to have been divided into four quarters. When Cortés entered the country, the ruler, Paxbolonacha, called together his four principal men from Padzunun, Atapan, Chabte, and Taçacto. The Spanish version of the Chontal Text states that these were towns, but the Text itself refers to them as the "chan tzucul cab," which could be translated as the "four divisions of the town." The Maya word *tzucul* is defined as "small town, or subdivision or part of a town."[20] Since none of the four names appear in the long list of

---

[15] Roys, 1943, pp. 21, 103; Villagutierre Soto-Mayor, 1701, bk. 8, ch. 12; Thompson, 1938, p. 599.
[16] Testimony of Pedro Uc of Tecumche, October 15, 1582, *in* Probanzas of Feliciano Bravo, *escribano mayor de gobernación* in Yucatan, 1562-82, AGI, México, leg. 109.
[17] Andrews, 1943, pp. 36, 72-73; Landa, 1941, pp. 85-86.
[18] The Tixchel matrícula is found in García *v.* Bravo, ff. 2116v-2128v.
[19] Cartas de Indias, 1877, p. 75; Cortés, 1866, pp. 447, 448.
[20] Motul Dictionary, 1929, p. 268.

Acalan towns, we infer that they were the four subdivisions of Itzamkanac, which heads the list.

Information concerning other towns named in the Text is scant. Çacchute, the first Acalan town entered by Cortés in 1525, is apparently the same as Tizatepelt mentioned in Cortés' Fifth Letter. Tuxakha may be identified as Teutiercas, 5 leagues from Tizatepelt in the direction of Itzamkanac. Concerning Teutiercas (or Teutiaca) Cortés states: "It is a very beautiful pueblo . . . and has most beautiful mosques, especially the two in which we took up our quarters after having thrown out the idols." Ixtlilxochitl calls the place Teotilac and states that it was situated on a large river.[21] We tentatively locate these towns on or near the San Pedro branch of the Candelaria. The pueblo of Chakam, where a group of runaway slaves later took refuge, also appears to have been on or near the San Pedro.

The title of the Acalan chief was *ahau*, which means "ruler" and is frequently translated from both Chontal and Yucatecan Maya as "king." One of Paxbolonacha's four principal men, Mututzin Ahau, had the same title, and the Text mentions a number of other ahaus. The head chief's power was by no means absolute, for he could take no action without consulting his principal men, so it is difficult to determine the precise significance of the title.

The Spanish version of the Text refers to the Acalan ruler as the "rey" and to all the other civil authorities generally as "principales," except in one case where the local town executives are called "gobernadores." In the Text, however, the so-called king, the heads of the four quarters of Itzamkanac, and the chiefs of other towns are designated as ahaus. All the lesser dignitaries are called "nucalob" or "nuc uinicob," which mean "principal men." These terms are very similar to the Yucatecan Maya *nucil*, *nucil uinicob*, and *nucbe uinicob*, which have much the same meaning. In Yucatan, however, the territorial ruler was called the *halach uinic*, or "real man"; the local town executive was the *batab*; and the head of a subdivision of a town, who was also a member of the council, was an *ah cuch cab*. The data found in the Acalan narrative, however, are insufficient to reconstruct the details of the Acalan political organization. There can be little doubt that there were town councils, of which at least some of the members were the nucalob or nuc uinicob; also the ruler and the local town heads may well have had a staff of deputies like the ah kulels of Yucatan.[22]

We are reminded not only of the Mexican political organization, where we

[21] Cortés, 1866, pp. 417–18, and 1916, pp. 368–69; Alva Ixtlilxochitl, 1891–92, I: 412.
[22] Roys, 1943, p. 62.

find a "chief of men" like Montezuma and the captains of the four quarters of Tenochtitlan, but also of the Nahuatl-speaking Pipil in southern Guatemala, who also had four captains and a commander in chief. Of the Xiu in Yucatan, who were of Mexican origin, we read in one of the Maya chronicles that when Mayapan fell, "the halach uinic Tutul departed with the chiefs and the four divisions of the town." It is of course quite possible that such an organization was as much a political tradition among the Maya as it was Mexican, but as yet we know of it only among the Nahua peoples or those of the Maya stock who had been subject to Mexican influences. As we shall see from the number of Mexican personal names among the Acalan, there are strong indications that they belonged to the latter class.[23]

The Chontal Text tells us little of Acalan social organization, except that slaves of the ruler and principals are mentioned. They are called "meya uinicob" or "working people," in Chontal and "esclavos" in Spanish. The Yucatecan Maya manuscripts, with the exception of the Crónica de Calkini, avoid mention of slavery; but the Chol words for male and female slaves, *pentac* and *mun*, are almost identical with the Maya, which are *ppentac* and *ah munil*, so it is to be suspected that the Chontal expression mentioned above was a euphemism. Judging by Mexican and Yucatecan analogies, we surmise that the free population was divided into nobles and commoners. We have found no specific term for the nobles unless, as is possible, the words nucalob and nuc uinicob refer to the ruling social class as well as to actual holders of office.

No description of the temples of Itzamkanac has come down to us, but a passage in the Text telling of the burning of the idols in 1550 gives us a better idea of religious organization than the equivalent section in the Spanish version. In the former we read: "Then they began to remove their devils: Cukulchan, the devil of the ruler, the devil of Tadzunun, that of Tachabte, that of Atapan, [that of] Taçacto, and the other devils. All these they carried before Fray Diego de Béjar and he burned them."[24] From this it would appear that the god of the head chief was housed in the principal temple and that each of the patron deities of the four quarters had its own sanctuary. This was the case at Tenochtitlan, where each of the four quarters had a special temple and was a religious as well as a military and administrative subdivision of the city.[25]

Cukulchan, who is to be identified with the Maya Kukulcan and the Mexican Quetzalcoatl, was closely associated with the wind god in Mexico. In

[23] Bandelier, 1880, p. 590; Fuentes y Guzmán, 1932–33, 2: 90; Roys, 1933, p. 142.
[24] Cf. p. 395, *infra*. Although the term devil (*cizin*) was probably a name given to the gods of the underworld, here it was piously applied to all the pagan deities.
[25] Bandelier, 1880, p. 685; Waterman, 1917, p. 276.

Yucatan he was the deified captain of certain former invaders from Mexico, the special god of the ruling class, and, strangely enough, a god of fevers. In both regions he was thought of as a famous culture hero, the feathered serpent, and apparently was associated with the planet Venus. At Cholula he was the god of commerce and special patron of the merchants. The Olmeca Uixtotin were called the children of Quetzalcoatl, and the Cocom rulers of Mayapan and Sotuta in northern Yucatan claimed descent from him. Consequently it seems logical to find him the particular deity of the Acalan ruler, who was the most prominent merchant in the land.[26]

Besides Cukulchan only four deities are named in the account of the destruction of the idols by the Spanish missionary. Although their idols were brought out from hiding at this time, we surmise that these were the patrons of the four quarters of the city. They were Ikchaua, Ix Chel, Tabay, and Cabtanilcab, or Cabtanilcabtan. The first three were prominent in the Yucatecan pantheon. Here Ikchaua was known as Ekchuuah, who was the god of the cacao planters and merchants; Ix Chel was a goddess of medicine and childbirth; and Tabay was a deity of the hunters.[27] We are unable to identify Cabtanilcab.

Ix Chel was evidently a very popular deity among the Chontal generally. Her shrine on Cozumel Island off the northeastern coast of Yucatan was visited by pilgrims from Tabasco, and the site of Tixchel, which was twice occupied by the Acalan, was apparently named for her. As Seler has pointed out, the names of Ciuatecpan ("palace of the woman") on the Usumacinta and of Ciuatan ("the place of the woman") in central Tabasco must refer to her worship. Landa notes that the Isla de Mujeres ("island of the women") north of Cozumel was named for the idols of goddesses which were found there. He names Ix Chel and three others, but Tozzer suggests that at least two of them were the same deity. In Tabasco on the Río Chico, a branch of the Usumacinta, is a site named Cuyo de las Damas, which may well refer to Ix Chel also. She was probably the goddess to whom, according to Cortés, the people of Teutiercas in Acalan dedicated their principal temple. In her "they had much faith and hope." In her honor "they sacrificed only maidens who were virgins and very beautiful; and if they were not such, she became very angry with them." For this reason they took especial pains to find girls with whom she would be satisfied and brought them up from childhood for this purpose.[28]

[26] RY, 1: 270; Acosta, 1880, bk. 5, ch. 9; Seler, 1902–23, 4: 431, 5: 375; Torquemada, 1723, bk. 6, ch. 24. Cf. Gann and Thompson, 1931, pp. 136–37.

[27] Landa, 1941, pp. 107, 155, 164. Ix Chel was also a mother of other gods and a goddess of the moon, illicit love, and weaving (Thompson, 1939, pp. 129–37).

[28] Roys, Scholes, and Adams, 1940, p. 5; RY, 2: 54; Seler, 1902–23, 3: 583–84; Landa, 1941, pp. 9–10 and note; Cortés, 1866, pp. 417–18.

Except for the Text, the principal source of information regarding the religion of the Chontal is the report from the Villa de Tabasco in 1579, which is scanty enough. Here we read:

They had idols of clay, wood, and the stones which they call chalchiuites [Aztec, *chalchiuitl*, a green precious stone]. These they worshipped and held as gods of various things; because they had gods of the sun, rain, maize, and the winds, so that for any thing or season they had its god, and likewise they had a god of battles. They worshipped these gods with great veneration and much respect, and they made sacrifices to them of human blood and game birds as well as domestic animals and whatever they hunted for the purpose. They observed with great vigilance and care their religious ceremonies and the rules which they had in this respect.

Herrera tells of their "sacrificing men, and eating them, wherein they followed the example of the Mexicans." [29]

In spite of its remote situation and the rapids and cataract on the Candelaria River, which lay between Itzamkanac and the Gulf of Mexico, the Acalan capital was an important commercial center. Its merchants traded with Potonchan, Xicalango, and the towns of the Chontalpa to the west and overland with the Cehache and Itza to the east. Their traffic extended to Nito near the mouth of the Río Dulce in what is now Guatemala. This town seems to have been the outlet for the commerce of the Sarstoon, Polochic, and Motagua valleys, all of which were rich in cacao; and from its location we may well infer that there was also much trade with Chetumal and the commercial centers of northeastern Yucatan.[30]

At Nito, Cortés tells us, one entire ward of the town was occupied by Acalan merchants, headed by a brother of Paxbolonacha, the Acalan ruler. Such an arrangement, as we have already noted, was not unusual, for at an earlier period the "lords" of Chichen Itza traded with northern Honduras by way of Ascension Bay, and at the time of the fall of Mayapan, about the middle of the fifteenth century, one of the sons of the Cocom ruler was absent in the land of Ulua on a trading expedition.[31] Like the merchants of Xicalango and Yucatan, those of Acalan no doubt reached the Ulua River, but of this we have found no direct evidence.

According to Cortés, the principal commodities in which the Acalan merchants traded were cacao, cotton cloth, dyestuffs, body paint, pitch pine for torches, pine resin for incense, and red shell beads. There was also an important slave trade. Whether their slaves were purchased and imported, or whether they were largely captured in their wars with their neighbors is hard

[29] RY, 1: 364–65; Herrera y Tordesillas (Eng. ed.), 1725–26, 3: 352.
[30] Cortés, 1866, pp. 417–30, *passim*; Roys, 1943, pp. 114–15.
[31] Ciudad Real, 1873, 2: 408; Landa, 1941, p. 39.

to tell. Since slaves were brought to Tabasco by the Aztec and to northern Honduras from Yucatan, it might well be inferred that the Acalan acquired most of their slaves by capture, employing some at home and exporting the surplus. They had a little gold, but it was heavily alloyed with copper. Gold and shell beads were of course imported.[32]

Some idea of the more important products of Acalan may be obtained from a list of articles which they gave the Spaniards as tribute. These consisted of canoes, paddles, honey, copal incense, fowl, cloth, beans, maize, squash seeds, chile, cotton, and tree gourds. Cortés tells us that Acalan was "very rich in food supplies and there was much honey"; and his statement is amply confirmed by the rapidity with which Bernal Díaz obtained a hundred canoe loads of grain and other food for the expedition. The canoes were probably made from large Spanish cedars. Although there has been little botanical exploration in the region, the copal gum, which was the principal native incense, was apparently a local product. In northern Peten *Protium copal* is one of the common smaller trees in the high forest; and at Tuxpeña, just northeast of the Candelaria drainage, Lundell reports it as a frequent large tree 10 to 20 m. high. Even after the Acalan were moved to Tixchel by the missionaries, they brought down copal and annatto from the neighborhood of the former capital, and their merchants carried these commodities to the Chontalpa for sale. Annatto, which has always been widely used for flavoring, is the fruit of *Bixa orellana* L., a shrub or small tree, which is also used for coloring matter, and the Maya are said to have employed it for painting pottery. In the Yucatan Peninsula, as far as we know, it has been found usually in a state of cultivation; possibly it continued to flourish around the former settlements after Acalan was abandoned.[33] Some cacao groves were reported in Acalan, but it seems doubtful that there was sufficient for exportation, since the Spaniards did not require it as tribute.

Cortés' encounter with some Acalan merchants between their country and that of the Cehache affords a little further information. These men were returning home loaded with cotton cloth, which they had received from the Cehache in exchange for salt. Since the nearest salt beds were on the west coast of Yucatan near Campeche, the latter commodity must have been brought down the Gulf coast and up the Candelaria, most of the way, if not entirely, by water, and the remainder of the journey overland.[34]

In spite of what is known of the extensive commerce with Nito, it is

[32] Cortés, 1866, pp. 421–22.
[33] García *v.* Bravo, *passim;* Díaz del Castillo, 1939, ch. 177; Lundell, 1934, p. 280; Standley, 1930, p. 359.
[34] Cortés, 1866, p. 423.

difficult to determine what route the Acalan merchants followed. Cortés obtained a map at Acalan, which probably showed approximately the route he followed through the Cehache country and to Lake Peten. Here the Itza ruler told him that the easiest route to Nito was "by sea." It was no doubt feasible, without horses, to go overland to the head of canoe navigation, down the Belize River, and south along the Caribbean coast by sea, but this seems a very roundabout route. Possibly what the Itza ruler really said was "by water," meaning to march south to the Río de la Pasión, ascend this river and the Río Cancuen by canoe, and cross the divide to the head of navigation on the Sarstoon, which flows into the Bay of Amatique not far from the mouth of the Río Dulce. Cortés, however, seems to have passed directly southeast to the Sarstoon, although he had much difficulty getting his horses across a spur of the Maya Mountains which intervened. Many merchants were accustomed to pass along this route, and Cortés found a number of buildings said to belong to the Itza ruler, apparently rest houses for the travelers; so it seems likely that much of the trade between Tayasal and the region around Nito followed this road.[35]

Of the Acalan who were later living on or near the Gulf coast Ciudad Real tells us that at Tixchel the Indians were "better featured and somewhat more refined and neater than the Maya." This refinement may have been due to their commerce and contact with foreign peoples. We are reminded of the commercial towns on the northeastern coast of Yucatan. Here the Indians were considered more polished and intelligent than those of the interior, whom the former called "Ah Mayas, despising them as mean and base people of low minds and propensities." It seems likely that Tabasco was at this time the cultural center of this commercial empire, which extended from Laguna Tupilco to the Ulua River; and if this is true, the Chontal may well have been considered models of elegance.[36]

Besides the eight Nahuatl-speaking towns in Tabasco which can be identified with certainty and a few which, like Xicalango, were probably partly Mexican, there can have been but few, if indeed any, others of importance. Nevertheless, as we have seen, they exercised a remarkable influence on the Chontal population, many of whom spoke Nahuatl as a second language.

From the sixteenth-century Spanish reports that have come down to us, it is difficult to make an adequate appraisal of the relations which existed be-

[35] *Ibid.*, pp. 422–54, *passim*. Another possible route, although it involved more land than sea travel, could have been from Lake Peten to San Luis and Pusilha and thence by river to the coast (communication from J. E. S. Thompson).

[36] Ciudad Real, 1873, 2: 452; RY, 2: 14, 23.

tween the Chontal- and Mexican-speaking populations of the area. If in northern Yucatan, where the Mexican intruders had been either driven out or absorbed by the Yucatecan Maya, the former had been able to effect permanent changes in the local religion and the social organization, we may well believe that the Chontal were still more profoundly affected by this intrusive culture in Tabasco, where a number of Mexican-speaking towns were in existence at the time of the Spanish conquest. About 1541 the Chontal inhabitants of Amatitan were, as we have already seen, persuaded by their cacique to desert the town with the intention of fleeing from Spanish oppression to Cimatan, which was still unconquered. Although the Spaniards were able to prevent them from going there and they later returned to their homes, it is significant that they were willing to move to a Mexican-speaking town.

With the exception of Potonchan few, if any, Chontal place names have come down to us in the area west of the Usumacinta River. These names are all Mexican. As far as we have been able to learn, this is true not only of the town names, but also of the native names of lakes, arroyos, and the rural districts on the river banks locally known as *riberas*. It was no doubt partly due to the Spanish conquerors and their highland Mexican allies, who have perpetuated Nahuatl names in non-Mexican areas in many parts of Middle America, but elsewhere the local native names have frequently survived or appear in the older Spanish reports. It is difficult to believe that among themselves the western Chontal did not employ their own place names at the time of the conquest, and it seems significant that we do find Chontal names, like Petenecte, Balancan, and Tenosique, on the upper Usumacinta. Here apparently Mexican influences, although by no means absent, were less marked than farther west.

The Nahuatl place names are either very similar to, or dialectal variants of, those found elsewhere in Mexico. Many are derived from those of flora or fauna and some are descriptive. Most of them have geographical suffixes such as *-tan* (Aztec, *-tlan*), *-co*, and *-can*, indicating various associations, or like *-apan*, which means that it is on a river.[37]

More important perhaps than these Nahuatl place names are the personal names of the Chontal of Tabasco proper that have come down to us. Strangely enough, they are Mexican, not Chontal. It is hard to believe that they would have given the Spaniards different names from those which they employed among themselves. These names have been culled from various early Spanish documents. Many of them were written by scribes who attempted to repro-

[37] Rovirosa, 1888, pp. 28–30; Díaz del Castillo, 1939, ch. 11; RY, 1: 361. Cf. Brinton, 1896, *passim*.

duce them as they would have been pronounced in the classical Aztec of the highlands, but others were recorded simply as they sounded to the writer of the document. In the Mexican dialects of the southern Gulf coast the most noticeable variations are that *t* replaces the highland *tl* and *o* usually becomes *u*. We also find these sound shifts in the few Mexican names that have survived among the Yucatecan Maya and in the Pipil language of Guatemala and El Salvador. For Aztec *ocelotl*, a certain leopardlike cat, in the Chontalpa we find the name Ucelo; in Acalan Çelut and Çelu; in Yucatan Zalu and Zulu; and in El Salvador occurs the Pipil place name, Usulutan, or "place of the ocelot."

Of twenty-four personal names from towns in the Chontalpa, eleven apparently correspond with Mexican day names. Sometimes among the Aztec, though perhaps more often farther south, children were named for the day on which they were born, but the numerical coefficient of the day was an essential part of the name. In these Tabasco names, however, the coefficient is lacking. The following names from the Chontalpa appear to be referable to Mexican day names. It will be noted that the Aztec *-tl* form was often retained by the Spanish scribe.

Chontalpa	*Mexican*
Çipaque, perhaps also Baçipaque	Cipactli ("Swordfish," Sahagún)
Coatle	Coatl ("Serpent")
Maçatle, Mazat	Mazatl ("Deer")
Tuxtl, Tustle, Tochin, Tochintli	Tochtli ("Rabbit")
Izquin	Itzcuintli ("Dog")
Malyna	Malinalli (a certain medicinal herb or grass)
Acatel, Hacatl	Acatl ("Reed")
Uzelotl, Oçelote, Uçelo	Ocelotl ("Jaguar")
Olin	Olin ("Movement"?)
Tequepal	Tecpatl ("Flint")
Suchil	Xochitl ("Flower")

Other personal names from the Chontalpa, which either are, or have the appearance of being, Mexican, are found written as follows:

Abase	Cuccacoatel	Ocoyel
Agto	Chicoase	Quipaque
Aoca	Mule	Tatuani
Ayoco	Oco	
Azucoatel	Ocoycocoltl	

Of these Chicoase evidently corresponds to the Aztec *chicuace* ("six");
Tatuani, probably to *tlatoani* ("speaker, *gran señor*"); and Oco may well refer
to a pine tree. It seems very possible that Cuccacoatel is an error of the Spanish
scribe for Cuçcacoatel and a corruption of some form of the Nahuatl day
name Cozcaquauhtli ("vulture"). Quipaque might be intended for Çipaque,
although a mistake of *qui-* for *çi-* would be somewhat unusual.[38]

The Zoque towns of Tabasco were also influenced by the Mexicans;
indeed, as we have seen, some of them are known to have been subject to
Cimatan. Ever since the conquest their official names have been Nahuatl, but
for at least one of them, Pichucalco, a Zoque name has survived. This is
Jomenas, which, according to Rovirosa, means "tierra nueva." Pichucalco
apparently is not the equivalent of this name, for the same writer derives it
from the Mexican *pitzotl* ("coati"), *calli* ("house"), and *-co* meaning "at." He
also identifies the Río Poana east of Tacotalpa as Poano, a Zoque name meaning
"río de los jolocines." Like the Chontal towns, the Zoque apparently made
their reports to the Spanish authorities in Nahuatl, for in a list of tributaries
from Teapa written about 1579 the names, which are Spanish, are occasionally
followed by Nahuatl notations, such as *ueuentzin*, "old man," and *cocosqui*,
which is evidently intended for *cocoxqui*, "sick."[39]

On the Usumacinta River above Jonuta we find both Mexican and Chontal
place names in use at the time of the conquest. Iztapa, Usumacinta, and Ciuatecpan are Mexican names; Petenecte, or Petenacte, Balancan and Tenosique
(Tanodzic) appear to be Chontal. Popane is difficult to classify. The Nahuatl-
speaking population doubtless had their own names for the Chontal towns.
Cortés and Bernal Díaz give only Mexican names for all the Usumacinta
towns which they mention, with the exception of Petenecte. On the modern
maps a number of other names appear which might be of Chontal origin, but
they could equally well be ascribed to the Yucatecan Maya or Chol who have
come into the region in more recent times.[40]

It is only from the long list of Acalan towns in the Chontal Text that we
are able to form a general idea of what Chontal place names were like, and it
may well be inferred that the original names of the Chontal towns of Tabasco
were very similar. Their meanings are not unlike those of the Nahuatl place

[38] Fiscal *v.* López; Información de servicios de Alonso Gómez de Santoyo . . . , 1565–66,
AGI, México, leg. 98. The suggested reading of *-quauhtli* for "-coatel" finds some support in the
Pipil dialect of Izcalco, where the name for the *guatusa* or *cotusa* is *kŭ-tŭš* and is considered to
be referable to the Aztec *quauh-tochtli* (Lehmann, 1920, p. 1047). Cf. Seler (1902–23, 1: 437),
who discusses the meaning of the Aztec day name Cozcaquauhtli.

[39] Rovirosa, 1888, pp. 23, 26–27; RY, 1: 328–29.

[40] Oviedo y Valdés, 1851–55, bk. 32, ch. 4; Alfaro map, 1579; Cortés, 1866, pp. 405–12; Díaz
del Castillo, 1939, chs. 35, 36.

names of Tabasco already discussed, but they seem to follow even more closely the pattern of Yucatecan place names. From the very tentative translations which will be found accompanying the English translation of the Text, many of them are referable to the local flora, especially trees (Chontal, *te*). A few are named for fauna; others for man-made features, like Tapib ("at the pit oven"), Çacmucnal ("white tomb"), Homolna ("sunken house"), Tamultun ("at the stone mound"), and possibly Tachimaytun ("at the stone deer"?). Still other names seem descriptive of the location, such as those containing the word for island (*peten*), Tahchakan ("at the savanna"), Tuholham ("at the edge of the open tract" or "swamp"), Kanlum ("yellow earth"), Taniuitz ("at the tip of the hill"), Tuxakha ("where the waters mingle"), and Tançut ("at the turn").

We are unable to translate Itzamkanac. Itzam, which means "lizard," was also an element of the name of the Yucatecan sky god, Itzamna, and in Maya art generally the sky is represented by a snakelike lizard monster with a band of astronomical symbols along its body. As yet, however, we have found no mention of Itzamna either among the Acalan or in Tabasco.

The Mexican traders from Tabasco evidently had their own names for some of the Acalan towns. As we have already noted, Itzamkanac was also known as Acalan or Gueyacalan ("great Acalan") to distinguish it from a smaller place of that name. Moreover, the towns called Tizatepelt and Teutier-cas in Cortés' Fifth Letter were apparently the same as Çacchute and Tuxakha respectively. The latter is also called Teotilac in Ixtlilxochitl's account of Cortés' entrada.

The Text contains many Acalan personal names, and we also have a ma-trícula, or tax list, from Tixchel and some baptismal records from Zapotitlan. Since a more detailed study will be found in Appendix C, this material will be only briefly discussed here.

The Acalan system of nomenclature is somewhat obscure, and most of the names are difficult to translate. Certainly they are not patronymics such as we find in Yucatan. This is readily seen by comparing the names of the Acalan rulers with those of their fathers. If they also had patronymics, none that we can recognize have been preserved. About a third of the persons listed in the Tixchel matrícula have names which appear to be Mexican, and a Nahuatl linguist could probably identify others. Some names are very similar to Yucatecan Maya patronymics, but it is difficult to determine the significance of these resemblances, since a number of the latter are Mexican and some appear to be of Chontal origin. The correspondence is what one might expect, if a number of people with Mexican and Chontal names had at some time settled among the Yucatecan Maya and some of their names had become patronymics in their new homes.

A very considerable proportion of the Acalan names, both Chontal and Mexican, have Chontal prefixes. For men's names these are Pa-, Pac-, Pax-, or Pap-, but the first three are probably elided forms of *pap*, which means "father." In the case of women's names, the prefix is either Ix- or Ixna-. *Ix* is simply a feminine prefix common in both Chontal and Maya, and *na* means "mother." The significance of these "father" and "mother" prefixes is doubtful. They are often absent from the names of persons who had children, notably a number of ancestors of Don Pablo Paxbolon, and among the married couples listed in the Tixchel matrícula frequently only one spouse bears the prefix. Such prefixes can hardly be associated with middle age, since Luis Paxmala was only fifteen years old, and Ursula Ixnauit was a girl of sixteen.[41]

Several Mexican day names are represented, although probably less than we found in the Chontalpa. So far, we have noted only one case which is certainly a Nahuatl day name accompanied by its numerical coefficient, although this was common practice in some parts of the highlands of Mexico. This was Martín Navycali of Tixchel, whose name corresponds to the Aztec day name Naui Calli (4 House). At least one Mexican numeral, Chicnau (9), appears as a name. Similarly the baptismal records from Zapotitlan for the year 1569 give the name Juan Bolonlamat, which is Maya day name with its coefficient, 9 Lamat. Lamat by itself is a fairly common name. Chanpel (4?), Bolon (9), Lahun (10), Boluch and Buch (intended for *buluch*, 11) are apparently Chontal numerals employed as names. One of the names in the Text, Buluchatzi, may well be a Chontal day name with its coefficient, although we cannot be certain of this. Not only does *buluch* mean 11, but *atzi* resembles the Cakchiquel day name Tzi, which means "dog." The Yucatecan and Tzeltal names for the corresponding day, which are Oc and Elab, are quite different. We are ignorant of their meaning, nor do we know what the Chontal day names were. *Tzi*, however, means "dog" in Chol and Tzeltal.[42]

Some of the Chontal personal names are referable to fauna, such as Bolay (an unidentified beast of prey), Chacbalam ("red jaguar"), Chacchan ("red snake"), Chan ("snake"), Ulun (Maya *ulum*, "turkey"), and probably Iquin (Maya *icim*, "owl"). We find many names extremely difficult to translate; probably more of them are of Nahuatl origin than we have been able to recognize as such. If transitional forms like Uçelo and Çelut had not been found,

[41] García v. Bravo, ff. 2116v–2128v.

[42] *Ibid.*, f. 1963v. Thompson also reports the name Bolon among the Mopan in British Honduras.

we should hardly have ventured to associate the Acalan Çelu with the Aztec *ocelotl*. It is quite possible that the name Çelu, or Çelut, which is very frequent in the Tixchel list, may have another association than with the day Ocelotl. The name means "jaguar," and it may be referable to one of the Nahua military orders, whose members wore the jaguar skin. Indeed, among the Aztec "eagles and jaguars" was the conventional designation of the brave warriors. However, since many women in this list bear the name Çelu, or Çelut, we have preferred to associate it with the day name. It should also be noted that Balam, a common Yucatecan patronymic which has the same meaning, is not a day name nor, in all probability, is it referable to one of the military orders.[43]

In both the Chontal Text and the Tixchel matrícula are a number of double, or hyphenated, names, like those of the rulers, Macua-abin and Paxbolon-acha, and Patzin-chiciua, one of the latter's principal leaders. As yet the reasons for such names is somewhat doubtful. Possibly it is significant that the mother of Don Pablo Paxbolon, whose full name after baptism was Pablo Antonio Paxbolon-acha, appears to have been Isabel Acha, although the evidence is somewhat conflicting.[44] If this is true, it could imply that descent was reckoned in both the female and male line, as in Yucatan, although there can be little doubt that in both regions the latter was the more important. So far as Don Pablo is concerned, however, another explanation is possible. Acalan culture was a mixture of Nahua and Maya traits, and among the Aztec they not only named a child for his birth date or for some animal, but they would also often "give the child the name of one of his ancestors, in order that it might bring the fortune and success of the person whose name they bestow." Perhaps Don Pablo was named in full after his famous grandfather, Paxbolonacha, who founded Itzamkanac and later received and aided Cortés. The

[43] Roys, 1933, p. 199, and 1940, *passim*. As explained in Appendix A, in the notation employed in the Chontal Text, *c* is always hard, even before *e* and *i*. The Spanish scribes who recorded the Tixchel list and that of Zapotitlan, however, write *qu* to indicate this sound before *e* and *i*.

[44] Information concerning the mother of Don Pablo Paxbolon, cacique of Tixchel and descendant of the rulers of Acalan, is found in a probanza formulated in 1612–14 by Paxbolon's son-in-law, Francisco Maldonado. This probanza, of which the Chontal Text forms a part, comprises Part I of the Paxbolon-Maldonado Papers. (Cf. Chapter 12 and Appendix A.) The probanza proceedings were instituted on June 8, 1612, when Maldonado presented various documents illustrating Paxbolon's services and a long interrogatory for the examination of witnesses. This interrogatory was evidently based, in part at least, on information Maldonado had obtained from his father-in-law. In two of the questions Isabel Acha is specifically named as Paxbolon's mother. Most of the witnesses were Spaniards, and although they gave affirmative answers to the questions relating to genealogy, they did not specifically mention Isabel Acha by name. In May 1614 certain Indians of Tixchel gave testimony in reply to the genealogical questions and named Isabel Acha as Paxbolon's mother. At the same time, however, they also gave affirmative replies to two additional questions, in one of which it would appear that the wife of Lamatazel, father of Paxbolon, was Catalina Ixnazelu. It is difficult to explain or reconcile these conflicting data. But the burden of the evidence, taking the probanza as a whole, favors Isabel Acha as the mother of the Tixchel cacique.

problem as to how the first Paxbolonacha came to have a double name would, however, still remain unsolved.[45]

It seems likely that many of the Acalan spoke Nahuatl as well as Chontal. We know that Acalan merchants attended the markets or fairs at Xicalango, which was at least partly Mexican-speaking. Moreover the first document of the report was written originally in Nahuatl by the town clerk of Tixchel in 1567 and later translated into Chontal by another clerk of the town in 1612. Juan Bautista Çelu, who wrote the original report and later signed the Tixchel matrícula, had a Mexican name, it is true, but we see no reason to believe that this circumstance has any connection with his ability to write Nahuatl, since his name was apparently not a patronymic at that time, and we find father and son or two brothers, one with a Mexican name and the other with a Chontal appellation.

The eastern neighbors of the Acalan were a Yucatecan Maya people known as the Cehache or Mazateca. Bernal Díaz tells us that they were so named because they worshipped the deer and did not kill them. Like the modern Maya, they no doubt believed in certain supernatural deer, but we doubt the chronicler's statement that they never hunted them. Possibly the name Cehache really refers to their country, since it might be translated as "an abundance of deer."[46] The Mexicans called the land Mazatlan, which means "the place of the deer."

The Cehache occupied the lacustrine belt lying between the rolling country covered by the rain forest, in which most of the Acalan towns were situated, and the hilly dry forest farther east. This is a large area of lakes and logwood swamps alternating with fertile low headlands which extends from Mocu and Cilvituk south into the Peten. During the rainy season the surplus waters from the northern part of this zone probably drain into arroyos leading to the Mamantel, and from the southern end, into some tributary of the San Pedro Mártir, but little is known of the hydrography of either region. In the center, however, for a distance of nearly 100 km. north and south, the country is drained by the widely spread tributaries of the Candelaria.[47]

The most prominent feature of the central zone is the great unexplored swamp known as Isla Pac. Andrews states that it drains southward into the Arroyo Caribe.[48] Various missionary reports of the seventeenth century indi-

[45] Roys, 1940, pp. 37–38; Sahagún, 1938, 2: 214. This use of the day name was somewhat rare among the Aztec but very frequent among the Mixteca.
[46] Redfield and Villa, 1934, pp. 117, 118; San Buenaventura, 1888, f. 20r; Díaz del Castillo, 1939, ch. 178.
[47] Andrews, 1943, p. 12; Lundell, 1934, p. 259.
[48] Andrews, 1943, p. 37.

cate, however, that in earlier times there was at least a seasonal drainage affording communication by canoe through this region west to the Mamantel.[49]

In this connection attention is called to data in a document of 1604 giving a list of Indian settlements, most of them inhabited by apostate fugitives from northern Yucatan, situated in the south-central part of the peninsula. The first name in the list is "Nacaukumil-taquiache." *Ukum* means "estero" or "river" in Yucatecan Maya, and *naca* may possibly mean "close to" the river in question. Although this was not a Cehache settlement, *taquiache* unquestionably refers to the land of the Cehache. Inasmuch as Nacaukumil-taquiache was only a few leagues east of Popola, situated on the upper Mamantel, the name apparently indicates that this stream led to the Cehache country.[50]

In 1526 Cortés crossed the southern part of the Cehache area on his way from the Acalan lands on the Candelaria to Lake Peten. The town of Yasuncabil, "last of the Cehache settlements," was five days' journey from the lake, apparently in the region of Chuntuqui in the northern Peten. Five years later Alonso de Avila passed through Cehache country en route from Acalan to Champoton, and Luján's narrative of the entrada describes a town named Mazatlan situated midway between these points. Such a location would place the settlement in the general area of Mocu and Cilvituk.[51] A probanza of Francisco de Montejo, Adelantado of Yucatan, formulated in 1531, stresses the proximity of both the province of Acalan and that of Mazatlan to the Gulf coast.[52] Thus it appears that at the time of the conquest the Cehache inhabited an extensive area north to south, with the southern limits in the neighborhood of Chuntuqui.

A number of these people were apparently still living near the northern end of the lacustrine belt in 1582. In that year an Indian of the Hecelchakan district told of a journey he had made into the interior of the peninsula and stated that after several days of leisurely travel, hunting along the way, he had come to a small settlement "called Cehach." From the nature of his testimony it would appear that he could not have traveled much farther south than some point in the Matamoros–Cilvituk–Chan Laguna region.[53] Although the pressure of numerous fugitives from northern Yucatan had already begun, the latter seem to have been in some fear of the Cehache. In the course of time,

[49] Paxbolon-Maldonado Papers, Part II; Sobre las diligencias que se han hecho sobre la reducción de los indios de Sahcabchen y otros pueblos, 1670, AGI, México, leg. 307. Cf. also pp. 276–77, *infra*.
[50] See Appendix E.
[51] Cf. discussion of the routes of Cortés and Avila in Appendix B.
[52] Sobre las provincias de Acalan y Mazatlan, 1531, *in* Montejo *v.* Alvarado. Cf. Appendix B, pp. 412–13, *infra*.
[53] Testimony of Pedro Che, Campeche, October 12, 1582, *in* Probanzas of Feliciano Bravo, AGI, México, leg. 109.

however, the northern intruders so increased in number that they appear to have absorbed some of the autochthonous inhabitants and to have driven others into the southern portion of the Cehache area. Missionary reports of 1605–15 place the major Cehache settlements southeast of the Mamantel and south of Tzuctok, located near the modern site of Concepción.[54]

There is some indication, however, that a few of the Cehache settlements continued to exist in the lakes and swamps in the northern part of the lacustrine belt until the end of the seventeenth century. Early in 1695 Alonso García de Paredes attempted to make a preliminary survey and begin opening a road from northern Yucatan to Lake Peten. After covering 8 leagues of road, which had been constructed several years before from Cauich to Sucte, he left his pioneers and proceeded with an armed force into the wilderness. Villagutierre tells us that "after traveling for some distance through the forest, they encountered some hamlets of many pagan and apostate Indians of the Cehache tribe." A fight ensued and some of the natives were taken prisoner. "They declared through interpreters that they were of the Cehache tribe and that many persons of that and various other tribes inhabited those forests." Although we are not told what distance the expedition had traveled, it seems plain that Paredes was still far to the north of the present Guatemala-Mexico boundary, where most of the Cehache tribe were living at this time.[55]

Later the same year, during the construction of the road, no Cehache towns were encountered until Paredes reached a lake called Chunpich, evidently the modern Aguada Cumpich.[56] Altogether a dozen of their settlements were found here, at "Ixban" (Paixban), Batcab, and along or near the road as far as Chuntuqui. Apparently the southern limit of the Cehache country at this time, as in that of Cortés, was in the region of Chuntuqui.

The Cehache appear to have been divided into subdivisions, which were named either for the ruling family or from the predominating lineage of the group. Near Batcab was a town of Indians, whom Villagutierre calls "Chocmoes," but the name evidently corresponds to the Yucatecan Maya Chacmo, which means "red macaw." In the Mopan Maya dialect the Yucatecan *chac* ("red") becomes *chuc*. Mo is a common patronymic in northern Yucatan. There was also a group of "Chanes," who lived at Pachechen 14 leagues from Chuntuqui. We do not know in which direction, but we are told that the trail

[54] Paxbolon-Maldonado Papers, Part II; Expediente formado a instancia del Capitán Pedro Ochoa de Leguízamo . . . , AGI, Patronato, leg. 20, núm. 5, ramo 25.
[55] Villagutierre Soto-Mayor, 1701, bk. 4, ch. 6; Molina Solís, 1904–13, 2: 340.
[56] Villagutierre Soto-Mayor (1701, bk. 5, ch. 8) records the distance by road from Chumpich to Batcab as 9 leagues, and the best modern maps place Aguada Cumpich 26 km. by airline north of Batcab. Since the present road is shown to wind through a large swamp, these distances seem to correspond.

to this town lay through swamps and bogs and that the Itza visited them to trade for iron tools. We infer that they lived in the lake country to the northwest and were probably in either direct or indirect communication with native merchants from the region of Sahcabchen, who were accustomed to carry Spanish goods to the unconverted tribes of the interior.[57]

Our only descriptions of the Cehache towns are those by the first explorers. They were all strongly defended, not only against foreign enemies, but also apparently against neighbors of their own nation. The first town visited by Cortés and Bernal Díaz was newly built upon a rock beside a lake. The previous homes of its inhabitants had been destroyed by invaders. It had a double fortification. The first was a ditch and wooden breastwork, and behind it was a palisade of heavy timbers twice the height of a man. The latter contained loopholes or embrasures (*troneras*), and at intervals it was surmounted by high protected platforms (*garitas*) for shooting arrows and hurling stones. Inside, the town was similarly defended with barricades (*traveses*) and embrasures. The ruler was a boy, and an uncle governed in his stead.[58]

Seven leagues away was another much larger town called Tiac, which was at war with the first. Not only was it surrounded by a ditch and palisade, but each of its subdivisions, or wards, was separately enclosed in much the same way. Bernal Díaz states that this place was on an island in a lake, which they reached by wading. A day's journey distant was a third town, which Cortés calls Yasuncabil. The name might be reconstructed as Yaxumcabil, or "town of the quetzal," although Ixtilxochitl calls it Xuncahuitl, a Nahuatl name. Cortés remarks on the handsome house of the ruler, but he adds that it was a thatched building. Bernal Díaz puts this town on a lake also, but it seems possible that he confused it with one of the others.[59]

Avila traveled from Itzamkanac in a northerly direction and reached one of the Cehache towns apparently in the region of Mocu and Cilvituk, although no lake is mentioned in the account of his journey. Like the others, this place was defended by a ditch crossed by a narrow bridge, and behind it was a palisade.[60]

Archaeologically the lacustrine belt, which formed a large part of, if not the entire, Cehache area, has been little explored. Andrews has made a reconnaissance of the Mocu-Cilvituk region, and his report gives us some idea of a still larger part of the area.

[57] Thompson, 1931, p. 204; Villagutierre Soto-Mayor, 1701, bk. 5, ch. 9, bk. 8, ch. 19; letter of Antonio Laynez to the governor of Yucatan, August 29, 1669, AGI, México, leg. 307.
[58] Cortés, 1866, p. 425; Díaz del Castillo, 1939, chs. 177–78.
[59] Cortés, 1866, pp. 425–26; Díaz del Castillo, 1939, ch. 178; Alva Ixtlilxochitl, 1891–92. 1: 421.
[60] Oviedo y Valdés, 1851–55, bk. 32, ch. 5.

South of the Guatemala boundary and west of Batcab and Chuntuqui no geographical account of the country is available and the maps are practically a blank. North of Guatemala, however, the lake country lying between the tributaries of the Candelaria has been exploited for chicle, and the ancient remains in this region appear to be much like those immediately to the west in what we believe to have been a part of the Province of Acalan. Here, as we have already noted, on the higher ground between the lakes and swamps were frequent ruined sites, but neither standing walls nor sculptures had been noted by Andrews' informants.

North of the Arroyo Caribe in the swampy region now called Isla Pac but formerly known as Bolonpeten ("nine islands") many surface pottery fragments were reported to Maler by the people of Chan Laguna.[61] The term Bolonpeten is recorded as early as 1605, and we also have several references to a settlement of this name in documents of the later seventeenth century relating to the history of what is now southeastern Campeche.[62]

Around Lake Mocu at the northern end of the lacustrine belt are various groups of mounds, one of them containing an extensive system of plazas. No standing architecture or sculptures were seen, but there were indications of fallen vaulted buildings. Between Mocu and Lake Cilvituk are many mounds and platforms of this sort, and on a hill near the latter lake is an acropolis composed of courts, plazas, and mounds. Although details are lacking, the description of these remains suggests that they antedate the Spanish conquest by a very considerable period; indeed, it seems possible that they lie beyond the horizon of Yucatecan historical tradition.[63]

More pertinent to our present inquiry are some remains in the same region which might be assigned to a much later time. At Las Ruinas, scattered among the older ruins, are low walls of unshaped stone blocks forming apsidal enclosures. Apparently these are the lower walls of thatched buildings, larger but similar in form to the modern houses with rounded ends which are so familiar in northern Yucatan today. Wauchope expresses a doubt that in Yucatan such a ground plan goes back even to the conquest, but we found among the older ruins at Calotmul the remains of a large apsidal structure like those described at Las Ruinas. Calotmul was occupied at the time of the conquest but disappears from history about the middle of the seventeenth century. Although a very early house foundation with rounded ends has been unearthed at Uaxac-

[61] Maler, 1910, p. 146; Andrews, 1943, p. 37.

[62] Fray Juan de Santa María to the governor of Yucatan, Ichbalche, January 31, 1605, *in* Paxbolon-Maldonado Papers, Part II; Sobre las diligencias que se han hecho para la reducción de los indios de Sahcabchen y otros pueblos, 1668–70, AGI, México, leg. 307. Cf. also p. 278, *infra*.

[63] Andrews, 1943, pp. 34–38.

tun, according to Wauchope, Lundell assigns apsidal or dumbbell-shaped foundations in central Peten to the period after 1450, and the well-preserved standing walls at Las Ruinas may also date from the century preceding the conquest. South of the city of Campeche modern houses with rounded ends are rare, but from the information available the possibility that these remains at Las Ruinas date from colonial times cannot be excluded.[64]

On an island in Lake Cilvituk are two other sites to which a fairly late date might also be assigned. The first was discovered by Maler nearly half a century ago and has recently been examined again by Andrews. Here are two temples faced with squared stone blocks. One certainly had a thick beam-and-mortar roof painted a bright red. The other, which was probably covered in a similar manner, has a row of square columns on each side, and on it are painted decorations and glyphs. At the other site is a building with well-preserved walls only a meter high. The lack of debris indicates that they were topped by a perishable structure and covered with a thatched roof like those described by Grijalva's chaplain on Cozumel Island and by Avendaño at Tayasal. The substructure beneath it has a painted façade on which is still preserved a somewhat damaged human figure rudely modeled in stucco relief. The head and shoulders are bent downward and hang over the molding below, not unlike the stucco ornaments on one of the friezes at Tulum, which suggests that the builders were influenced by the art of the east coast.[65]

It would probably be difficult to determine the precise age of the buildings on the island without excavation and ceramic studies. Surface sherds were found, including fragments of the coarse incensario ware usually ascribed to the last period preceding the Spanish conquest. On one of them is a sun symbol, which Andrews notes is similar to those in a fresco at Santa Rita, British Honduras, and he finds parallel forms in a Mexican codex and in frescoes at Mitla. These sherds seem to indicate worship on the island at a late date, but we cannot be certain that the temples were still in use at the time. Thompson notes that he found a late incensario just below the ground in front of an Old Empire stela. Nevertheless, although beam-and-mortar roof construction in the Maya area goes back to the Old Empire, the preservation of the color of the wall painting in exposed positions at Cilvituk and the resemblance of the stucco figure to those at Tulum would rather indicate that the buildings on the island were not extremely old. If the low stone walls were topped by a perishable structure, as has been assumed, it would suggest that some of these buildings may have been very late. This evidence, however, is not conclusive,

[64] *Ibid.*, p. 36; Wauchope, 1940, p. 234.
[65] Andrews, 1943, pp. 38–43; Juan Díaz, 1939, p. 22; Means, 1917, pp. 18–19.

since we do not know how old this style of architecture was at the time of the conquest.[66]

The culture of the Cehache was evidently similar to that of the other Yucatecan Maya. They were an agricultural people and probably manufactured some of the cotton cloth which we know they bartered for salt with the merchants from Acalan. At Tiac Cortés found a guide who had been in Nito and had seen the Spaniards there, so they were evidently in communication with the Bay of Honduras. As in Yucatan, the local chiefs were called batabs, and the priests had a voice in the government of their towns.[67]

[66] Andrews, 1943, p. 74.
[67] Cortés, 1866, p. 426. See also Appendix E.

4

Aboriginal History of Acalan

THE CHONTAL TEXT begins with an account of the ancestry of Don Pablo Paxbolon, which is of unusual interest. Not only does it constitute the only native historical source for pre-Spanish history that has come down to us from the extensive area lying between the highlands of Guatemala and northern Yucatan, but also it is the only connected narrative in a native language which deals with the history of the lowland Maya over any considerable period of time. As already noted, we have from northern Yucatan Indian manuscripts which furnish a large amount of historical information, but they were evidently compiled from various sources in the seventeenth century, and the attempts of the native recorders to fit these fragments of history into a single consecutive scheme are not entirely successful. A considerable number of episodes are recounted, but their historical significance in many cases remains to be determined. A consistent chronological framework into which they can be fitted will in all probability be reconstructed eventually largely from the archaeological evidence.

Yucatecan Maya historical tradition, as we have seen, probably does not go back of the advent of certain foreign invaders, who were the bearers of a Mexican culture and who established themselves in the country as a new ruling caste. Neither they nor their descendants were interested in the history of their predecessors. At the time of the Spanish conquest even the most erudite among them appear to have known as little of the Maya Old Empire, perhaps even less, as did the classical Greek historians of the pre-Hellenic Aegean civilization. This abrupt break in historical tradition is probably reflected in the local nomenclature of some of the archaeological sites in the hills of western Yucatan. Although the depopulation of two of these cities, Kabah and Uxmal, and the occupation of the latter by the Xiu are recorded in the Books of Chilam Balam, other imposing ruins are known to the natives by such names as Labna ("old ruined building"), Xlabpak ("old ruined wall"), and Mulultzekal ("heap of loose stone"). This seems the more strange because the Yucatecan Maya are on the whole conservative in the preservation of place names. Even now, four centuries after the Spanish conquest, many of the Indians still refer to Mérida and Valladolid by their old names, T'hoo and Saci.[1]

[1] Roys, 1943, pp. 58–59; 1933, p. 82.

In the Chontal Text we are told that an ancestor of the Acalan ruling family had come to the Chontal area with a group of followers from an island near the northeastern coast of Yucatan, and there is abundant evidence of Mexican influence in the personal nomenclature of the Acalan people, as well as similar indications in their religion and political organization. In view of these circumstances it seems pertinent to our present inquiry to consider briefly the intrusion into Yucatan of immigrants from continental Mexico. These people have left both Nahuatl and Chontal words in the Yucatecan Maya language. Probably most of them were bilingual, but of this we cannot be certain.

This phase of pre-Spanish history in Yucatan has been divided into two archaeological periods. The first covers the ·so-called Mexican period at Chichen Itza, during which art and architecture were superior to what followed later. In the second, architectural activity had ceased at Chichen Itza, but Mayapan in the west and Tulum on the east coast were now in their prime. Walled cities came into existence. Vaulted edifices were still being constructed, but flat beam-and-mortar roofs apparently became more frequent. The handsome stone veneer of Chichen Itza was now replaced by a masonry of rough stone blocks, and new sculptural forms appeared.[2]

In the west this period ended with the destruction of Mayapan about the middle of the fifteenth century. The belief has been expressed that the handsome structures at Tulum were still in use when the Spaniards arrived, owing no doubt to the account by the chaplain of Grijalva's expedition, which sailed past the site but did not land, and it is true that the village of Zama, or Tzama, still existed at the site. A report of the latter town, however, was written in 1579, and it would indicate that the stone buildings had long been abandoned. Here we are told that these edifices were constructed in ancient times, but "the natives who are living are unable to give an account of who made them or for what purpose they were made."[3]

The sequence of this reconstruction of pre-Spanish history is similar to the accounts of the Maya writers. In the latter the hegemony of Chichen Itza precedes that of Mayapan. If the city now known as Tulum ("enclosure") is mentioned in these sources, it is under some name which we are as yet unable to identify. The architecture and pottery of the site are believed to indicate that it was contemporary with Mayapan.[4]

According to the Maya Chronicles, the Itza ruled at Chichen Itza from A.D. 987 to 1204, when they were conquered by Mayapan, and there is some

[2] Andrews, 1943, pp. 77–78, 81–82.
[3] Juan Díaz, 1939, pp. 23–24; RY, 2: 197; Roys, Scholes, and Adams, 1940, p. 22.
[4] Andrews, 1943, pp. 77–78; Brainerd, 1942, p. 256.

evidence to support these dates, especially the latter. The native accounts, which place the end of the hegemony of Mayapan about the middle of the fifteenth century have been generally accepted and recently confirmed by the exploration of this site. During the latter period the Mexican intruders became more and more influenced by the autochthonous population, whose language and customs they adopted, although they retained many of their old traditions. It has long been believed that the Mexican domination of Chichen Itza did not begin until about 1200, but Thompson cites convincing evidence that one of the important architectural complexes of this period was already in ruins about the middle of the thirteenth century.[5]

The Yucatecan Maya accounts of the advent of peoples from continental Mexico are somewhat confusing, but it seems plain that there were several different waves of immigration at various times. The first of these was the invasion of the Itza, who are said to have entered Yucatan from the east coast and to have taken Chichen Itza. They were driven out but returned in larger numbers and from the southwest, after which they ruled the entire country from Chichen Itza for more than 200 years. Possibly other groups of invaders were also called Itza. In one of the Chronicles we read of the conquest of a number of northern cities by 100 valiant Itza captains from Mayapan, but recent investigations at the latter site indicate that the Mexican occupation of this city by any large body of people was later than that of Chichen Itza. The Itza were said to be foreigners; they came in great numbers, and made themselves thoroughly disliked until they were finally driven out.[6] The Spaniards found them living around Lake Peten in the south of the peninsula, where they still preserved traditions of their former sojourn at Chichen Itza.

Other smaller groups of foreigners who came later were headed by the Canul and Xiu lineages and are definitely known to have come from continental Mexico. The Cocom rulers of Mayapan, who moved to Sotuta after the fall of that city, asserted that they were the "natural lords" of the country, but their claim to be descended from Quetzalcoatl indicates that they believed themselves to be of Mexican descent. The Nahuatl name of the Iuit family, which ruled at Hocaba, is evidence of a similar origin. We know nothing, however, of how or when the last two came to Yucatan.[7]

[5] Brinton, 1882, *passim*; Roys, 1933, *passim*; RY, 1: 176; Thompson, 1941a, p. 103, and 1943, pp. 106–07. Brainerd's ceramic studies ascribe the architectural activity at Chichen Itza and that of Mayapan-Tulum to two successive periods, and Andrews does the same on architectural grounds. The latter places both stages between 1200 and 1450 (Brainerd, 1942, p. 256; Andrews, 1943, p. 89).

[6] RY, 1: 119, 269; Roys, 1933, pp. 83–84; Roys, Scholes, and Adams, 1940, p. 6; Holmes, 1895–97, 1: 66.

[7] Landa, 1941, p. 40; Roys, 1933, p. 194, and 1940, p. 36.

Since the Acalan rulers came from Cozumel, we are especially interested in the Mexican occupation of northeastern Yucatan. The native Maya literature tells us only of the Itza invasion of the region, but the proceedings of a lawsuit at Valladolid in 1618 state that the ancestors of Don Juan Kauil, including a certain Kukum Cupul, were prominent persons and "lords" from Mexico, who had founded towns "in these provinces." The account goes on to say "that those who came from Mexico were four kinsmen or relatives with their friends and the people they brought with them; one settled as heretofore said at Chichen Itza; one went to settle at Bacalar; one went toward the north and settled on the coast; and the other went toward Cozumel; and they founded towns with their people and were lords of these provinces, and governed and ruled them many years; and that he [the witness] had heard it said that one of them named Tanupolchicbul was a kinsman of Moctezuma, King of Mexico." Those who settled at Chichen Itza are said to have been the builders of "the sumptuous edifices which are in the said locality."[8]

Whether or not all these four settlements were contemporary, as stated above, seems rather doubtful, but two important facts stand out. One is that the Cupul, who ruled the region around Chichen Itza after the Itza had been driven out, claimed descent from the Mexican invaders. The other is that the Maya identified some of the lineage groups of the invaders with those still existing on the highlands of Mexico.

Of the history of Cozumel we know nothing. In the Merida museum is a stela which is attributed to the island and which has been ascribed to the time of the Old Empire on stylistic grounds, but no buildings of this period have as yet been found. The proceedings of the Valladolid lawsuit state that Cozumel was at one time subject to a Cocom who ruled at Chichen Itza, but since none of this family is known to have ruled at Chichen Itza, the statement might mean either Chichen Itza or Mayapan, where the Cocom did rule. Traces of Mexican influence are seen in the anthropomorphic roof supports, which are also found at Mayapan and Tulum, and the attributes of Ah Hulneb, the archer god of Cozumel, also suggest Mexican influence.[9]

As already noted, at the time of the Spanish conquest Cozumel was famous for the shrine of Ix Chel, the goddess who was so popular in both Yucatan and Tabasco, and her sanctuary was still visited by pilgrims from Potonchan and Xicalango as well as from the seaports of western Yucatan. The name of the principal cacique as well as that of the most numerous lineage on the island

[8] Brinton, 1882, p. 118.
[9] Ibid., p. 117; Andrews, 1943, p. 82; Roys, Scholes, and Adams, 1940, p. 6; Holmes, 1895–97, 1: 66.

was Pat, which means "dogfish." The Pat lineage was also important socially in the towns on the east coast and at Dzitnup near Valladolid. A census of the island taken in 1570 contains no names which we can recognize as being of Mexican origin, nor indeed any which are peculiarly Chontal.[10] Some of the people, we believe, were descended from foreign invaders but had been pretty well assimilated by the autochthonous population.

The history of the ruling family of Acalan begins with the arrival in the region of Tenosique on the Usumacinta River of a leader named Auxaual and four "great principal men." Needless to say, each of the latter was accompanied by a group of followers. As we have already seen, such an organization follows a familiar political pattern, which occurs on the highlands of Mexico and in other parts of Middle America.

No explanation is given for this migration, but judging by the conduct of their descendants we may well infer that the activities of Auxaual and his followers on the east coast of Yucatan had aroused the antagonism of their neighbors and that they had been driven out. Cozumel lay athwart the main trade route between northeastern Yucatan and the Gulf of Honduras and was easily defended since it could be attacked only by water. We do not know that Chetumal and the northeastern towns were already the large commercial centers which they later became, but if Tulum was contemporary with Mayapan, it must have been a large and important city when the Acalan leaders left the region.

The names of the five leaders of these immigrants are of considerable interest. *Xaual* could be either a Maya or a Nahuatl word. In Maya it means to stir or turn over something. In Aztec *xaualli* is defined as a certain face paint, probably red. According to Villagutierre, among the Itza *xagual* meant "galán," which suggests a Nahuatl derivation for the name Auxaual.[11] The latter also resembles that of Taxaual, a town near Potonchan in Tabasco.

Paxmulu appears to be of Mexican origin also. Pax- is a Chontal prefix not found in Yucatan, but *mulu* is probably referable to the Aztec *molotl*, which is defined as "sparrow" (*pardal o gorrión*). In the name Paxoc, *oc* means "leg" or "foot" in both Maya and Chontal, but if the name is merely a contracted form of Paxoco, which we also find in the Tixchel matrícula, it could be referable to the Aztec *oco*, or "pine." Chacbalam means "red jaguar." Balam is a common Maya patronymic, but we have found Chacbalam only among the Acalan. The name, however, reminds us of a foreign conqueror named Ek-

[10] Roys, Scholes, and Adams, 1940, p. 16; Roys, 1939, p. 291.
[11] Motul Dictionary, 1929; Molina, 1880, 2: f. 158v; Villagutierre Soto-Mayor, 1701, bk. 8, ch. 18. The so-called *xagual* was the lover of a certain witch and appeared in the form of a puma or jaguar. This was evidently a case of nahualism.

balam ("black jaguar"), who entered northeastern Yucatan from the east coast and founded a town of the same name north of Valladolid. He was also noted as a sorcerer. After ruling for forty years he and his captains became unpopular and were killed by the plebeians, but he was succeeded by another "who was of his lineage." We infer that Ekbalam and his followers, like the ancestors of the Acalan ruling class, were a Nahuatl-Chontal group, and that another group of similar origin put an end to their rule with the aid of the local population.[12] We are unable to suggest any derivation for Huncha, the fourth of Auxaual's "great principales."

The name Auxaual does not recur in any of our documents, but the four others are found in the 1569 matrícula of Tixchel. These names therefore appear to follow the general pattern of Tabasco-Acalan nomenclature rather than that of northern Yucatan, and it seems possible that the group had not been established in Cozumel over a very long period.

It would be of considerable interest to know the time of Auxaual's arrival in the Usumacinta valley. Morley has shown that the lives of six generations of heads of the Xiu family, from the estimated birth date of the first down to the last appearance of the sixth in their family papers, covered a period of 183 years.[13] According to our Text, Paxbolonacha, who represented the sixth generation of Acalan rulers, died about 1526, which on this basis would place the birth of Auxaual in 1343. From this it might be tentatively assumed that he left Cozumel and came to the Usumacinta basin toward the end of the third quarter of the fourteenth century. As we shall see, however, a single generation of rulers is said to have lived at Tixchel for sixty or eighty years. This statement suggests that one generation was omitted and that Auxaual may have lived a little earlier than the time reached by our calculation. The expulsion of Auxaual from the north may have been only the result of local conditions, but it is also possible that it was part of a political change of considerable historical significance.

Auxaual and his followers assembled the people living around Tenosique in a town and took over the government of the region. No struggle to accomplish this is indicated and it seems likely that there was none. The obvious implication is that the local population was living in scattered farms and hamlets. A similar procedure by aggressive groups of wanderers in northern Yucatan was not unusual. However they may have acted later, they were likely to conciliate the native inhabitants upon their arrival. At the time the Xiu entered Yucatan, they established themselves among the local rulers "more by

[12] Molina, 1880, 2: f. 58v; RY, 2: 160–61.
[13] Morley, 1941, passim.

strategy (*maña*) than by war." In another report we also read: "They were
subject to a lord called Tutulxiu, a Mexican name, who they say was a foreigner from the west; and when he came to this country the principal men of
it made him king by common consent in consideration of his worthy qualities."[14] Later, when nine members of the Canul lineage with their followers
sought homes in western Yucatan after their expulsion from Mayapan: "They
were not greedy for chieftainship, nor were they provokers of discord. . . .
They began to love the towns with their batabs, and they were also loved there
by the towns." Similarly Ekbalam and his captains at first "were valiant and
sagacious and they were chaste," although in course of time the ruler "became
arrogant and made himself hated, because he came to despise and disregard his
subjects and imposed excessive tribute upon them as well as treating them
badly in other ways, which was the cause of his death."[15] From other accounts
which the Indians related to the first Spaniards, this story was evidently not
an unusual one. The Xiu, on the other hand, were always careful to retain the
good will of their subjects.[16]

The new rulers of Tenosique exacted tribute, but it was probably moderate, as in northern Yucatan. In the latter area we know that military service
was an important obligation, and the same was no doubt true here as well.
Cacao was produced around Tenosique, and the town was in a strategic position commercially, since it lies just below a series of dangerous rapids which
extend upstream as far as Yaxchilan. Beyond the latter site river navigation is
described as good for a long distance to the southeast in the direction of the
Gulf of Honduras. Consequently there was water communication with the
areas where we find the Lacandon and Acala Chol in the sixteenth century
and almost to the edge of the Itza and Manche Chol territories. Even in the
latter part of the seventeenth century the Itza raided the town of Canizan
just below Tenosique.[17]

Auxaual's son, Pachimal, either was content to consolidate his father's gains
on the Usumacinta or did not long survive him. Chanpel, the third ruler, resumed the aggressive policy of his grandfather and seized positions at three
of the four passes leading from Laguna de Términos to the Gulf of Mexico.
These were Tatenam at Boca de Términos, Dzabibhah, or Dzabibkak, at Boca

---

14 RY, 1: 161, 287.
15 Crónica de Calkini, pp. 13–14; RY, 2: 160. In the prophecies lewd conduct was ascribed
to the Itza, possibly because of certain erotic ceremonies inspired by the Quetzalcoatl legend.
This finds some confirmation in two sculptured columns at Chichen Itza (Roys, 1933, pp. 83,
121, 151, 161).
16 RY, 1: 181; Landa, 1941, p. 36.
17 Roys, 1943, p. 61; Información de los malos tratamientos que los españoles hacen a los
indios de la provincia de Tabasco, 1605, AGI, México, leg. 369; Maler, 1901–03, 1: 40; Villagutierre Soto-Mayor, 1701, bk. 6, ch. 4.

Nueva, which formerly divided Isla del Carmen into two islands, and Holtun at Puerto Escondido. The name Tatenam reminds us of the Aztec *tenamitl*, which means the wall or enclosure around a town, although the first Spanish explorers found no permanent settlement on the island. In Yucatan Holtun means an opening in a rock and is the name of a cenote at Piste, but here it evidently means a port. On the east coast was a place named Holtun Itza. The seizure of these sites was a bold stroke, since they commanded the main trade route between Tabasco and Yucatan.[18]

Paxua, the fourth ruler, moved to Tixchel on the mainland. Whether the settlements on the islands were difficult to defend, or whether there was not enough agricultural land to support the group, is hard to tell. We do not know how large a population they comprised. In any case, the site of Tixchel lay on the same trade route. At the modern Hacienda Tichel are two groups of mounds, one on the east shore of Sabancuy estuary and the other on a savanna 4 km. inland. They are connected by an ancient paved road, which crosses the mangrove swamp lying between the two sites. Since there has been no archaeological exploration of the region, we know nothing of the age of these ruins, but in the light of the present narrative it seems probable that some traces of an occupation during the fifteenth century could be found there. It should be noted, however, that none of the paved roads or causeways outside the towns seem to have been in use when the Spaniards arrived in northern Yucatan. Cortés' expedition found a causeway extending across a low flooded stretch near Potonchan, but we do not know whether or not it was paved.[19]

Paxua and his followers are stated to have remained at Tixchel sixty or eighty years, but this seems hardly probable. Either, as we have suggested, the name of one of the rulers is omitted, or the length of their stay at this site is overstated. In any case they were attacked by their neighbors from Champoton on one side and by the people of three Tabasco towns on the other. In view of the situation of Tixchel it is difficult to escape the conclusion that they made themselves disliked by interfering with the canoe trade between Tabasco and the west coast of Yucatan.

The names which are given for the three Tabasco towns are of interest. They have a Chontal appearance. One is Apopomena, which we are unable to identify. The second is called Cactam[20] in the Text and Xicalan in the Spanish version, so we infer that the former was the Chontal name for Xicalango. The third is said to have been Acucyah, also known as Tabasquillo.

[18] Roys, 1933, p. 146.
[19] Herrera y Tordesillas, 1726–30, dec. 2, bk. 4, ch. 11.
[20] Near Chetumal was a town named Tiçactam, and Çactam may be the correct form of this name (DHY, 2: 63).

Tabasquillo was the Spanish name of an unimportant village south of Potonchan, or Tabasco, where a few surviving families from the latter town settled
after the conquest, and it seems probable that the reference is really to Potonchan. This city and Xicalango would be seriously affected by any interference
with the Yucatan trade.[21]

From Tixchel our group moved to Acalan, where they expelled the
Cehache from Tayel, which is named as one of the Acalan towns at the time
of the conquest. Its location is not known, but presumably it was in the eastern
part of Acalan toward the Cehache area. We are told nothing about the previous inhabitants of the Candelaria basin, but the Spaniards found such a large
Chontal-speaking population there only two generations later that it is difficult
to believe that they were all recent immigrants. What seems most probable is
that the region was already settled by people of this stock, but that there were
a number of Cehache intruders.

The descendants of Auxaual and his followers also returned to the Usumacinta valley. Very possibly the region around Tenosique had remained tributary to them during their stay in Tixchel. They now captured Ciuatecpan from
a people called the Dzul, and the Text claims that they controlled the river
down to Iztapa. Dzul means "foreigner" in Maya and the name is a common
patronymic in northern Yucatan. Since Iztapa and Ciuatecpan are Mexican
names and the Text seems to employ Chontal place names wherever possible,
the Dzul were probably a Nahuatl-speaking people living farther down the
Usumacinta. Apparently the ancestors of the Acalan were now in control of
the Usumacinta between Tenosique and Iztapa as well as a considerable part
of the Candelaria area.

Paxua was succeeded by his son Pachimalahix, who went to Chetumal
Bay on the east coast. Both the Text and the Spanish version are somewhat
obscure as to just what happened, but it is plainly stated that he and his warriors went to Chactemal, the native name for Chetumal, and exacted tribute
from the people of this town.

Chetumal was the capital of a province of the same name, which was ruled
by Nachan Can at the time of the first Spanish invasion of Yucatan. His principal captain was Gonzalo Guerrero, a Spaniard who had been shipwrecked
on the east coast in 1511. The story of this man's career seems incredibly
romantic, but it is on the whole well substantiated. He was at first enslaved.
He turned completely native, piercing his nose and ears and tattooing his
face and hands, rose to the position of war chief, and married an Indian
woman of rank. He refused to be ransomed by Cortés in 1519 and later re-

[21] RY, 1: 346.

jected Montejo's invitation to join him when he invaded the region. The Spaniards ascribed their failure here partly to Guerrero's opposition. Finally, he was killed when he took part in a native expedition to the Ulua River in northern Honduras to aid the natives there in their resistance to the Spaniards.[22]

Chetumal was a large town on the bay of that name, and according to Fray Bartolomé de Fuensalida it was situated between the mouth of the Río Hondo and that of the New River in what is now British Honduras. Here the Spaniards obtained so-called emeralds, turquoises, and a large quantity of gold.[23] Apparently it was a port of call for the trading canoes plying between the Gulf of Honduras and the group of commercial towns in northeastern Yucatan, since Cortés was told at Cozumel that some Indian traders had seen Guerrero only a few days before.[24] The province was the only important cacao-producing district known to exist in Yucatan.

Although Chetumal was still in existence in 1582, Cogolludo, quoting a report by Fuensalida, tells us that it had disappeared by 1618. At this time Fuensalida and Fray Juan de Orbita, who were on their way to Tayasal, stopped at a cattle ranch 3 leagues beyond the mouth of the Río Hondo and before they entered the New River. On this ranch, they were told, was the former site of the great town of Chactemal, or Chetumal. Dr. Thomas Gann explored the region thoroughly during his twenty years' residence at Corozal, and the only archaeological sites reported on or near the shore between the two rivers are Consejo, less than a league from the mouth of the Río Hondo, Santa Rita, about 4 leagues from this river following the shore, and at the town of Corozal, a very short distance farther on. Of these Santa Rita is the closest to the situation described in Cogolludo, although it appears to be about a league farther from the Río Hondo.[25]

Here, about 1.5 km. back from the swampy shore, is a large group of forty or fifty mounds, a number of which have been excavated by Gann. Some of these were erected over older buildings, and on the walls of one of the latter he found the remarkable frescoes for which the site has long been famous. In spite of the Maya glyphs and a number of faces which are recognizable as those of Maya gods, the pictures have a Mexican appearance. It is almost as though a Mexican artist had depicted a Maya ceremony. Spinden and Andrews compare the astronomical symbols in these frescoes with those at Mitla and in various

[22] Tozzer, 1941, p. 251; Roys, 1943, p. 116.
[23] Tozzer, 1941, p. 8. The Maya name of the Río Hondo was Nohukum ("large river"), and that of the New River was Dzuluinicob ("foreign men").
[24] Díaz del Castillo, 1939, ch. 27.
[25] López de Cogolludo, 1867–68, bk. 9, ch. 6; Gann, 1900, passim. If Fuensalida has overstated the distance between the mouth of the Río Hondo and Chetumal, the latter could have been situated on the opposite shore in what is now Quintana Roo.

southern Mexican codices, and the latter suggests that they were painted after the fall of Mayapan. It should be noted that since the building was artificially covered, a later structure was presumably imposed in pre-Spanish times, although that does not necessarily entail any great antiquity for it. It would be of considerable interest to our present study to know the age of the Santa Rita paintings. Obviously they are late, but in the absence of associated sherds, as Thompson notes, it is difficult to determine how late they are. Not only are there late incensarios at the site, but excavations have also revealed an occupation going back to an early Old Empire period.[26]

Emphasis has been laid on Fuensalida's location of Chetumal, not only because it is the only precise geographical description that has come down to us, but also because of Scholes' recent discovery of a document recording the existence of a town of that name in the region only thirty-six years before the missionary's visit. The situation of Chetumal, however, still remains a problem. Oviedo states that it was 2 leagues from the sea and "almost surrounded by water, for the sea is on one hand and the lagoon on the other,"[27] and modern archaeologists have located the town at various sites between Lake Bacalar and Chetumal Bay. Dr. Eduardo Noguera places it 2 km. west of the modern Ciudad Chetumal, formerly named Payo Obispo.[28] The Tulane-Carnegie archaeological map shows a ruined site named Chetumal some distance farther north and about 12 km. inland from the bay, which would no doubt correspond more closely to Oviedo's description than any of the other locations that have been suggested. We doubt, however, that it was as far from navigable water as this site appears to be. Gann ascribes the location to an important archaeological site locally known as Trincheras, which he discovered on the west shore of Chetumal Bay and to which he gave the name Ichpaatun ("stela within the walled enclosure"), possibly because Mayapan in the north was often called Ichpaa.

Except for the side along the sea, Ichpaatun is surrounded by a wall of roughly squared stone about 5 m. high in places. Although an early Old Empire stela bears evidence to the antiquity of the site, the presence of the wall, some large drum columns, and many late sherds suggest that it was an important city down to the fall of Mayapan. In the north such ceremonial centers

---

[26] Gann, 1900; Spinden, 1913, p. 209; Andrews, 1943, p. 79 and fig. 15; communication by J. E. S. Thompson.

[27] DHY, 2: 63; Oviedo y Valdés, 1851–55, bk. 32, ch. 6.

[28] Communication by J. E. S. Thompson. The first mention we have found of the name Payo Obispo is on the map of Yucatan by Juan de Dios González, 1766, MS. in British Museum. The name of the site, however, really goes back a century earlier, for in the account of Fuensalida's journey in 1641 "a port which they call el rancho del obispo" near the mouth of the Río Hondo is mentioned (López de Cogolludo, 1867–68, bk. 11, ch. 15).

had been abandoned for some time before the Spanish conquest, although a pole-and-thatch village sometimes still existed as at Tulum, near the site. A few kilometers north of Ichpaatun Gann found a colonial Spanish church, which he believes to have been built by Avila during his stay at Chetumal in the early 1530's, but it seems doubtful that a stone church would have been erected during this temporary occupation. To us Gann's photographs and description of this well-built structure, with its vaulted chancel, thick walls, and recessed doors and windows, would rather indicate that it was completed

THE RULERS OF ACALAN-TIXCHEL

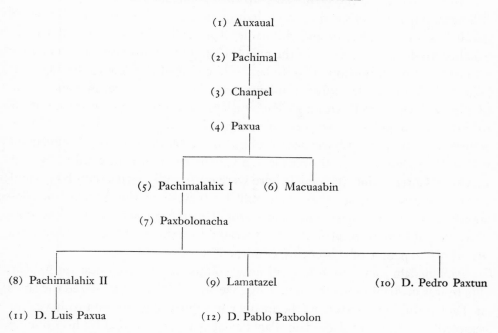

(1) Auxaual

(2) Pachimal

(3) Chanpel

(4) Paxua

(5) Pachimalahix I (6) Macuaabin

(7) Paxbolonacha

(8) Pachimalahix II (9) Lamatazel (10) D. Pedro Paxtun

(11) D. Luis Paxua (12) D. Pablo Paxbolon

after the end of the sixteenth century, especially at this remote place. Indeed, from his examination of some graves beneath the floor of the chancel Gann himself concluded that the church was in use for at least two centuries, and it is difficult to reconcile his findings with Fuensalida's account of Chetumal.[29]

In the 1582 list of colonial Indian towns in the parish of Bacalar we find one with the surprising name of Mayapan.[30] In view of the resemblance of the remains at Ichpaatun to those of the famous walled capital in northern Yucatan, the name of this village rather suggests that it was near the ruins discovered by Gann, but it would be highly conjectural to imply from this that

[29] Gann, 1927, pp. 26–27, 33–37; communication by J. E. S. Thompson.
[30] DHY, 2: 63.

Ichpaatun was actually called Mayapan during the period of its occupation. We are, however, inclined to believe that Ichpaatun was once the most important city on the bay and that Chetumal, although the town itself may have been an old site, became the capital of the district only after the city now known as Ichpaatun lost its power.

It is hard to believe that the Acalan actually conquered Chetumal. We know that their merchants occupied an entire quarter of Nito, and it seems likely that a commercial conflict with Chetumal had arisen, resulting in a raid on the latter and the collection of damages.

In the meantime the Dzul came up the Usumacinta to seize the town of Balancan. Their leader's name was Tzitzimit, which is Nahuatl and is variously defined as a certain insect and the name of a devil.[31] His demand of Pachimalahix "to divide the tribute of the pueblos" suggests a proposed joint occupation of the region, possibly a confederacy like that of the Aztec, although we believe the two peoples differed in language. The offer was refused and a war of eighty days ensued. Although Pachimalahix is said to have been supported by the local population, he was evidently defeated, for he and his followers returned to Acalan and we hear nothing more of them in the Usumacinta valley. The Dzul apparently recaptured Ciuatecpan and continued to govern it. When Cortés came, the people here were on friendly terms with Iztapa and the towns upstream, but they were still the enemies of the Acalan and constantly at war with them. The guides from Ciuatecpan, who were to accompany Bernal Díaz to Acalan, fled the first night on the road because they were afraid of the people of this enemy country.[32]

Pachimalahix and his followers now completed the conquest of Acalan. There was probably some resistance, for we are told that "they seized the lands at Tachakam," in contrast to the manner in which they are said to have "assembled" the town of Tanodzic. Pachimalahix was succeeded by his younger brother, Macuaabin, but the Text has nothing more to tell about him.

The sixth generation of rulers was represented by Paxbolonacha, son of Pachimalahix. He evidently completed the organization of Acalan, for it was

[31] One of the leaders of the Nahuatl-speaking Pipil was named Jucotzimit and his son was Pilecuautzimit. On the highlands of Mexico, if new fire could not be made at the end of the 52-year period, it was believed that the Tzitzimime would descend and the sun would not shine. These terror-inspiring demons were supposed to eat people (communication by J. E. S. Thompson). Tzitzimitl was also the name of a military device or symbol, which consisted of a representation of the monster made of gold and feathers (Sahagún, 1938, bk. 6, ch. 8; bk. 7, ch. 11).

[32] Possibly the Dzul were a Nahuatl-speaking people. Among the Maya the word meant foreigner and was employed to designate the Spaniards; but it was also applied to the Xiu, who were believed to be of Mexican origin, and to the Itza in Yucatan. Montejo's Mexican auxiliaries, however, were called Culua by the Maya (Redfield, 1938, pp. 527-28; Roys, 1933, p. 84; Brinton, 1882, pp. 142, 148; Crónica de Calkini, p. 16).

he who established the capital at Itzamkanac. It is difficult, however, to believe that this large and imposing city did not exist before the time of Paxbolonacha, although no doubt its importance was greatly enhanced under him. Possibly there were already a number of independent Chontal-speaking towns in the Candelaria basin, but we know as little of the previous history of this region as we do of Tabasco.

Paxbolonacha's hesitation and his subsequent conciliatory attitude toward Cortés was very much like the policy of the Xiu rulers in northern Yucatan in regard to Montejo and his son. In both cases it was consistent with the adaptability displayed by these groups in pre-Spanish times, and after all, it was only good sense. Some towns refused to contribute supplies, but on the ruler's advice Bernal Díaz was sent with canoes to requisition them and no resistance was offered. The execution of Cuauhtemoc undoubtedly had some effect on the attitude of the Acalan toward Cortés.

Nevertheless, the ruler's appeasement of the Spaniards aroused much resentment. Although no one was maltreated or killed and there was no destruction of property, there had been a large expenditure of provisions. Also Oviedo tells us that 600 carriers, who had been furnished to the Spaniards when they left, never returned to their homes.[33] Many of them, no doubt, were slaves, which would represent an additional loss of valuable property. The result was that a year after Cortés' departure Paxbolonacha was obliged to abdicate and leave the capital, and he went to Chakam. This was evidently not a revolution, for his body was returned in a canoe to Itzamkanac when he died, and his sons succeeded him.

Although it was some years longer before the Acalan were converted to Christianity and reorganized politically in the pattern which the Spanish administration devised for the government of the Indian pueblos, they were visited by other Spanish expeditions and placed in encomienda, and the period following the death of Paxbolonacha becomes a part of Spanish colonial history.

[33] Oviedo y Valdés, 1851–55, bk. 32, ch. 5.

5

The Coming of the Spaniards

IN 1517 Francisco Hernández de Córdoba, sailing from Havana on a westward voyage, discovered the peninsula of Yucatan and explored its northern and western coastlines from Cape Catoche to Champoton. In this new land the Spaniards found a native civilization superior to anything hitherto encountered in the New World. Stimulated by the news of this discovery, Diego Velásquez, lieutenant governor of Cuba, who had authorized Córdoba's voyage and had contributed part of the cost, helped to organize a second and more powerful expedition to continue exploration in the west and to trade with the Indians. Juan de Grijalva, a kinsman of Velásquez, was named commander.[1]

With four ships and some 200 men Grijalva sailed from Cape San Antón at the western end of Cuba on May 1, 1518. Four days later he landed on Cozumel Island and took possession in the name of his sovereign. From Cozumel the flotilla crossed to Yucatan, sailed south as far as Ascension Bay, then turned back and doubled around the peninsula. At Campeche, where the Spaniards went ashore to fill their water casks, one soldier was killed and many others, including Grijalva, were wounded in a fray with the Maya. Continuing the voyage southward along the coast, on May 31 Grijalva reached Puerto Deseado, a passage into the eastern end of Laguna de Términos. Here a leaky ship was careened for repairs, and exploring parties examined the adjacent shores and waterways.[2]

Puerto Deseado was near Tixchel, a former outpost of the Acalan people,

[1] The principal sources for Grijalva's voyage are Juan Díaz, 1858, and Oviedo y Valdés, 1851–55, bk. 17, chs. 8–19. Wagner (1942) gives English translations of these and other early accounts. Díaz del Castillo (1908–16 and 1939, chs. 8–16) gives what purports to be an eyewitness account, but it differs from other sources in various respects, and Wagner doubts that the author was actually a member of the expedition. Secondary accounts of the voyage are given by Orozco y Berra, 1880, 4: 25–58; Bancroft, 1883–88, 1: 15–31; Molina Solís, 1896, pp. 47–100. We follow the chronology as given by Oviedo y Valdés.

[2] Puerto Deseado is usually identified as Puerto Escondido, a passage into Sabancuy Inlet at the eastern end of Laguna de Términos. The Desceliers map of 1550 (reproduced in Jomard, 1854–62) actually shows a place named Puerto Deseado in the approximate location of Puerto Escondido. Antón de Alaminos, the chief pilot, stated the opinion that it was only 20 leagues from Puerto Deseado to Ascension Bay and that there was a waterway between these points separating the "island" of Yucatan from the mainland. (Oviedo y Valdés, 1851–55, bk. 17, ch. 12.) In short, such a passage marked the *términos*, "limits," between these lands; hence the term Laguna de Términos. In the early Spanish sources the Laguna is sometimes called the Bahía de Términos, and occasionally Puerto de Términos, although the latter term more specifically applied to the passage between the western end of Isla Carmen and the mainland. On the Alfaro map of 1579 (Map 2) the Laguna area is called "Lagunas de Xicalango."

but in 1518 this site and the nearby coasts were apparently uninhabited. According to Bernal Díaz, the Spaniards found masonry structures along the shore. These contained idols of wood, pottery, and stone, but, so the chronicler tells us, "the oratories were merely those belonging to traders and hunters who put into port when passing in their canoes and made sacrifices there."[3] The only Indians encountered in this region were four traders or fishermen in a canoe, whom the Spaniards seized to serve as interpreters.[4]

On June 5 Grijalva sailed west along the southern shores of the Gulf and three days later came to the mouth of a great river, the Río de Tabasco, which the Spaniards named the Grijalva in honor of the captain. Grijalva sailed up the river for about half a league, where the Indians came out in canoes to meet him. As the result of parleys with messengers of the ruler of Potonchan, the principal Chontal settlement in the region, peaceful relations were established and a certain amount of barter was carried on. On the morning of June 10 the cacique came out in person to visit Grijalva, and after a friendly interview the two leaders exchanged gifts. The cacique dressed Grijalva in a suit of wooden armor overlaid with gold leaf, and the latter gave his visitor a velvet jacket and cap and other articles of European dress.[5]

Oviedo lists many other pieces of rich native workmanship presented by the cacique on this occasion, for which he received knives, scissors, glass beads, and other trinkets in exchange. The list includes such items as wooden masks with mosaics of stone resembling turquoise, strings of hollow gold beads, gold earrings with pendants, necklaces of thin beaten gold on leather, and ornate featherwork. Bernal Díaz mentions jewels in the form of ducks and lizards.[6] It is not surprising that Grijalva's men, seeing such evidence of wealth, "desired to enter the lands of the said cacique." But their commander, who interpreted the instructions given him by Velásquez as authorizing only exploration and trade, refused their petition. Moreover, the Chontal, who were undoubtedly

[3] Neither Juan Díaz nor Oviedo mentions the finding of such structures near Puerto Deseado, and it is possible that Bernal Díaz, who calls the place Boca de Términos, had in mind the shrines found on the return voyage on Isla Carmen at Puerto de Términos, the western end of the Laguna. Cf. Oviedo y Valdés, 1851–55, bk. 17, ch. 17. It may be noted, however, that in 1939 Scholes and Roys found temple substructures on the shore of Sabancuy Inlet near the former Puerto Deseado.

[4] In 1517 Córdoba seized two Maya youths at Cape Catoche and took them to Cuba where they were taught Spanish. The following year one of them, named Julián, accompanied the expedition. When the Spaniards reached the Río de Tabasco, Julián was unable to understand the Chontal, and the language problem there was solved by using one of these Indians captured at Puerto Deseado, who apparently understood both Yucatecan Maya and Chontal (Oviedo y Valdés, 1851–55, bk. 17, ch. 13).

[5] Juan Díaz and Las Casas describe this ceremony. Oviedo does not mention it, but includes various items of wooden armor in the list of goods presented by the cacique.

[6] Wagner, 1942, pp. 111–12; Díaz del Castillo, 1939, ch. 11. Cf. the list of gold ornaments obtained by Alonso López from the Indians of the Chontalpa in 1541, p. 30, *supra*.

anxious to be rid of the intruders, asserted that they had no more gold, but if the Spaniards would sail to the west to Culua, or Mexico, they would find it in plenty.[7]

Resuming the voyage on June 11, Grijalva explored the Gulf coast as far as the Veracruz area and for some distance beyond. In the region to the south of Veracruz the Spaniards carried on profitable barter with the Indians of Aztec-dominated settlements, exchanging baubles for gold objects, textiles, and other native products. On June 24 one of the ships, under command of Pedro de Alvarado, was sent back to Cuba with the treasure and reports of the voyage.

On the return journey along the coast Grijalva spent some time at the Río de Tonala in western Tabasco. Here the soldiers petitioned that he establish a settlement, but to the disgust of all he again refused. Leaving the Río de Tonala on July 27, the flotilla encountered contrary winds and for several days made little headway. On August 17 the ships turned back toward the shore to obtain water and "came to a port between two lands," which was named Puerto de Términos. This was apparently the western entrance to Laguna de Términos, between Isla Carmen and the mainland. Once more the Spaniards were in a region dominated in former times by the Chontal of Acalan. A landing was made on the western end of Isla Carmen, but the island was now uninhabited, although shrines frequented by Indian traders were found along the shores.[8] The remainder of the voyage to Cuba was uneventful, except for skirmishes with the Maya at Champoton and Campeche.

The increasing evidence of the existence of highly advanced native states in the lands bordering on the Gulf of Mexico caused Velásquez to organize a third expedition, for which Hernán Cortés was chosen to serve as commander-in-chief. Sailing from Cuba in February 1519, Cortés spent some time at Cozumel and on the east coast of Yucatan before striking west and south into the Gulf. When he reached Tabasco he found the Chontal in a defiant mood. Driven from Potonchan after a sharp encounter, the natives assembled in force on the fields of Centla southwest of the city. Here a hard-fought battle took place in which the Spaniards, although greatly outnumbered, made effective use of their horses and superior weapons and inflicted a crushing defeat on the enemy. The Indian chieftains now sued for peace and promised obedience to the Spanish king. In celebration of the victory, said to have occurred on the day of Our Lady, the Spaniards gave the name of Santa María de la Victoria

[7] Juan Díaz, 1858, p. 295; Oviedo y Valdés, 1851–55, bk. 17, ch. 13; Díaz del Castillo, 1939, ch. 11.

[8] Oviedo y Valdés, 1851–55, bk. 17, ch. 17; Wagner, 1942, pp. 129–30. Oviedo describes certain idols of indecent form, one portraying the act of sodomy, found at this place.

to the settlement of Potonchan. During the remainder of Cortés' stay in Tabasco a certain number of Indians were baptized, and it was here also that he obtained the Indian woman, Doña Marina, who became his faithful interpreter during the conquest of Mexico.[9] From Tabasco, Cortés sailed on to the Veracruz district, where he eventually dismantled his ships and initiated the remarkable series of campaigns which culminated two years later in the destruction of the Aztec power.

As early as 1520 Cortés sent an expedition under Diego de Ordaz to explore the Gulf coast. Montezuma explained that his dominion did not extend as far as the Río Coatzacoalcos, but he kept garrisons of warriors on his frontier, who would give assistance if needed. These were encountered at a place which is not named, but it is said to have been near the town of Coatzacoalco, and the natives of the region complained to the Spaniards of the exactions of the Mexicans. Ordaz went on to the river, where he was well received and furnished with canoes to explore the stream. The country was found to be rich and thickly populated.[10]

At the town of Coatzacoalco the caciques also complained of Montezuma and his frontier garrison, which had apparently attempted to raid their country. They related that a short time previously they had defeated these troops in a battle at a small town. Bernal Díaz states that in his time the place was still called Cuylonemiquis, which meant "where they killed the Mexican homosexuals," and except for the omission of the name Mexican, the Molina Dictionary seems to confirm this definition. Blom and La Farge suggest that it may be Cuilonia, now a Popoluca town on the lower slope of the mountains to the northwest of the river.[11]

Sahagún gives us the impression that, for much of the time at least, Coatzacoalco was on friendlier terms with the Aztec confederacy than Ordaz' report would appear to indicate. The town was an important commercial center; here the Aztec merchants came by way of Tuxtepec, as they did to Cimatan and Xicalango, bringing gifts and greetings from the Mexican ruler to the local lords.[12]

The town of Coatzacoalco is known to have been Nahuatl-speaking at the time of the conquest. The same appears to have been true of most, if not all,

[9] Cortés, 1866, pp. 13–19; Díaz del Castillo, 1939, chs. 31–37.
[10] Cortés, 1866, pp. 94–95; Díaz del Castillo, 1939, chs. 102, 103.
[11] Díaz del Castillo, 1939, ch. 103; Blom and La Farge, 1926–27, 1: 68; Molina, 1880, 2: ff. 26v, 57r. J. E. S. Thompson has called our attention to a passage in Fuentes y Guzmán (1932–33, 1: 48) in which this event is compared with the story of Mexican intruders in El Salvador who were presumably Pipil, although the historian apparently considers them to be Aztec. These men were cast down some cliffs by the Quiche, Cakchiquel, and Tzutuhil rulers.
[12] Sahagún, 1938, 2: 354–55. Coatzacoalco was on friendly terms with Potonchan (Cortés, 1866, p. 95).

of the basin of the Río Coatzacoalcos for a considerable distance inland, but in a list of towns subject to Espíritu Santo in 1580 another idiom called Popoluca is also mentioned, although Mexican is said to be the principal language of the district. Like *chontalli, popoloca* is a Nahuatl word meaning a foreigner who speaks a different language, and the Popoloca of Puebla are not to be confused with the Popoluca of Veracruz. Linguistically the latter are related to the Zoque and Mixe, and it has recently been shown that they speak four distinct languages, which are mutually unintelligible. Three of these are still spoken around Texixtepec, Oluta, and Sayula near the edge of the Coatzacoalcos basin, and the fourth, by a much larger group on the southern and eastern slopes of the Tuxtla Sierra to the north. They are considered to be culturally less advanced than their Nahuatl-speaking neighbors, and the presence of these people between two such important centers of civilization known as Tres Zapotes and La Venta is of considerable interest.[13]

After the fall of Tenochtitlan in 1521 Cortés sent out military expeditions into the outlying areas north, south, and west of the Valley of Mexico. A force under the command of Gonzalo de Sandoval defeated the warlike Mixe in the southeastern highlands and then proceeded to the Gulf coast, where a new Spanish villa named Espíritu Santo was founded on the Río Coatzacoalcos. Bernal Díaz tells us that it was located on the right bank of the river 4 leagues from its mouth. He also refers to the villa as Coatzacoalco, so it was probably near the pre-Spanish town of that name. Blom and La Farge mention a tradition that Espíritu Santo was at the modern Paso Nuevo, but González places it at Tuzantepetl, where he reports burials accompanied by armor and spurs. These places are very near one another, and both appear on the Tulane-Carnegie map as archaeological sites.[14]

From Espíritu Santo the Spaniards sought to extend dominion over western Tabasco and the highlands of Chiapas. The Indians of the Chontalpa, Cimatan, and parts of the Zoque area were assigned in encomienda to citizens of the villa, including the soldier-chronicler Bernal Díaz del Castillo, but control over these frontier districts was precarious, and from time to time it was necessary to send out punitive expeditions to deal with actual or incipient revolt.[15]

Thus the initial contacts of the Spaniards with the Chontal area involved only the coastal region of Tabasco, the Chontalpa, and its environs. Penetra-

[13] Díaz del Castillo, 1939, ch. 37; Foster, 1943, pp. 531, 532, 535; Blom and La Farge, 1926–27, 1: 49–53. Thompson suggests that the low cultural rating in pre-Spanish times long ascribed to the Mixe-Zoque group has been undeserved; and he notes that some pottery of fine quality has been found in the Zoque area. Cf. Roys, 1943, p. 110.

[14] Díaz del Castillo, 1939, ch. 160; Blom and La Farge, 1926–27, 1: 77; González, 1940, p. 395.

[15] Díaz del Castillo, 1939, chs. 166, 169; Riva Palacio, 1888–89, 2: 41–104, *passim.*

tion of the interior, including the Acalan lands to the east, came about only as the result of the expedition of Cortés from Mexico to Honduras in 1524–25. Although the major purpose of this journey, one of the most famous in the history of American exploration, was to punish the defection of Cristóbal de Olid, whom Cortés had sent to Honduras early in 1524, a secondary motive, as indicated in Cortés' Fifth Letter, was the discovery of "unknown country" and the "many and divers provinces" that would be crossed en route.[16] One of the most important of these provinces was Acalan.

In October 1524 Cortés journeyed to Espíritu Santo, where he completed preparations for the Honduras expedition. According to the Fifth Letter, the army comprised 230 Spanish soldiers, including 93 horsemen. In addition, there were 3000 Mexican auxiliaries. The latter were under the immediate command of certain native chieftains, including Cuauhtemoc, last ruler of the Aztec, Cohuanacoch, lord of Tezcoco, and Tetlepanquetzal, lord of Tacuba, whom Cortés had brought from Mexico City as a precautionary measure to lessen the danger of an Indian revolt during his absence from New Spain. The Spanish force included veterans of the conquest of Mexico as well as a considerable number of recent comers. A secular priest and two Flemish Franciscans accompanied the army, and Doña Marina served as interpreter. Inasmuch as it was Cortés' plan to march along the coast or not far inland at least part of the way, the artillery, surplus arms and ammunition, and other stores were sent by ship to the Río de Tabasco, and arrangements were made for three other vessels to follow with food and other provisions.[17]

While at Espíritu Santo Cortés sent word to the caciques of Tabasco and Xicalango advising them of his proposed journey and ordering them to come to see him or to send trustworthy persons to receive his instructions. The cacique sent seven or eight persons of importance, evidently merchants, who gave Cortés a report concerning marauding Spaniards who were on the Caribbean coast. They also painted a map on cotton cloth showing the route to the coast, which the expedition apparently followed as far as Acalan.[18] There a new map was obtained, which contained more precise information for the remainder of the journey. Although these maps left much to be de-

[16] Cortés, 1916, p. 349.

[17] Cortés, 1866, pp. 395–99; Díaz del Castillo, 1939, chs. 174, 175; Bancroft, 1882–87, 1: 537–42. Díaz del Castillo gives the size of Cortés' Spanish force, including those enlisted at Espíritu Santo, as more than 250, of whom 130 were horsemen.

[18] Cortés, 1866, pp. 396–97; Alva Ixtlilxochitl, 1891–92, 1: 407. Ixtlilxochitl, who has much to say of the services of his famous namesake, states that the latter and Cuauhtemoc were sent on this mission to Tabasco and Xicalango, but it seems doubtful that Cortés would have trusted them to this extent, especially Cuauhtemoc.

sired, they proved very useful. They indicated a main objective for each stage of the journey, gave some idea of the rivers to be crossed, and, most important of all, led the expedition as far as possible through inhabited country where food supplies could be had. On the whole it seems remarkable that such serviceable maps could have been prepared by persons who, in all probability, did most of their own traveling by water.

The country through which the expedition traveled from the Río Coatzacoalcos to the Grijalva was familiar to the citizens of Espíritu Santo, who, it will be remembered, possessed encomiendas throughout the region and had been compelled to send out armed forces from time to time to enforce the payment of tribute. Only Cimatan was giving trouble at this particular time, but Bernal Díaz tells of two occasions when he had passed along the route now followed by Cortés to the eastern border of the Chontalpa.[19]

The first stage of the journey was to Tonala, also known as San Antón, 9 leagues distant. The settlement was about a league from the Gulf shore. Bernal Díaz was well acquainted with the place. Not only had he passed through it on several punitive expeditions, but he claimed that in 1518 he had stopped there with Grijalva and planted the first orange trees in New Spain. Coatzacoalco was evidently on good terms with Tonala, for its people came to the latter town to trade with Grijalva. On this occasion some ornaments of low-grade gold were obtained by barter, and in a temple on a pyramid one soldier found many idols, copal incense, flint knives, and a chest containing headbands, necklaces, hollow beads, and two idols of gold. Most of the men carried shining copper axes with painted wooden handles, and the Spaniards purchased many of these, thinking they were gold. Cortés' route probably lay close to the shore, for behind the sand banks is a wide mangrove swamp. Also the expedition crossed the river in canoes, swimming the horses. If they had passed behind the swamps, this would hardly have been necessary, since Dampier tells of a ford situated only 4 or 5 leagues inland.[20]

Leaving Tonala, they continued another 9 leagues to Ahualulco near the present Santa Ana. Grijalva did not land there, but one of his smaller vessels passed close to the coast, where the town could be seen, and on the shore were warriors with tortoise-shell shields. The Spaniards named the place La Rambla, which could mean either a gully or an expanse of sand, in this instance probably the latter. Later, after the founding of Espíritu Santo, the ship which brought Cortés' unfortunate first wife from Cuba had been forced by bad weather to land at this port, where Bernal Díaz with other citizens met her and her party

[19] Díaz del Castillo, 1939, chs. 166, 169.
[20] *Ibid.*, ch. 16; Stirling, 1940, p. 316. Cf. Dampier, 1906, 2: 215.

and escorted them to the villa. Here are two large lagoons, Laguna del Carmen and Laguna Machona, and near the eastern end of the latter is a ruined site now known as Ahualulco. Since Bernal Díaz and Cortés give the impression that the port and river were near the town, it seems a little doubtful that the last was at the archaeological site of that name. In any case Cortés probably passed along the shore and not through the swampy region south of the lagoons, for, as we shall see, he crossed the next river close to its mouth.[21]

La Venta, the most important archaeological site in this region, was once a great cultural center. From here, as we have seen, certain artistic features spread to the Maya Old Empire, and it is generally believed that by way of this region an intrusive Mexican culture was later carried to many parts of the Maya area. Nevertheless, little is known of the ethnography of western Tabasco at the time of the Spanish conquest or even in colonial times. A small group of Nahuatl-speaking Indians known as the Ahualulco are reported to be still living in the Santa Ana region. Seler describes their language as "a corrupt Mexican," but Lehmann notes that not enough is known about it to ascertain its relation to Aztec and Pipil. For the purposes of this inquiry a comparison of Ahualulco with the Nahuatl of southern Veracruz and that of the Mexican-speaking towns in Tabasco would be of considerable historical interest.[22]

Dampier, who was familiar with the coast of this district, gives a detailed description of the actual shore, but he does not mention any of the settlements in the region. Gil y Sáenz, however, relates that in 1680 four towns of "Aztec" Indians, called Ahualulco and living between Santa Ana and Tonala, were attacked by Laurent de Graff's buccaneers and were later moved to other places, some to the Coatzacoalcos region and others to the vicinity of Ocuapan, Mecatepec, Tecominoacan, and Huimanguillo in Tabasco. Villa-Señor y Sánchez, writing about the middle of the eighteenth century, tells us that Moloacan, which is still a Nahuatl-speaking settlement a short distance east of the Río Coatzacoalcos, was the principal town of one district of the Ahualulco and that San Francisco Ocuapa, presumably the modern Ocuapan, was the principal town of another. Subject to the church of the latter town were San Cristóbal Huimanguillo, San Pedro Ostitan, Mecatepec, and Tecominoacan. He also notes that at San Francisco Ocuapa twenty families of Indians were preached to in the Popoluca language. These towns were under the church of Acayuca, Veracruz, which, although it is Mexican-speaking, is close to three Popoluca towns. On the face of it, this would appear to suggest that some of

[21] Cortés, 1866, p. 399; Díaz del Castillo, 1939, chs. 12, 160.
[22] Cf. pp. 22–23, *supra;* Seler, 1902–23, 4: 431; Lehmann, 1920, 2: 995.

the Ahualulco from the region of La Venta spoke a language other than
Nahuatl. It should be noted, however, that the present site of Ocuapan is not
far from the Zoque area and that the Popoluca idioms of southern Veracruz
are Mixe-Zoquean. At the present time Nahuatl is spoken around La Venta,
but Blom and La Farge believe that the Indians here are recent settlers, presumably from the Coatzacoalcos region, for they mention one family that had
come from Jaltipan.[23]

Crossing the "river" at Ahualulco in canoes, Cortés continued east to the
Río Copilco, which was evidently at the west end of what is now Laguna
Tupilco, since the 1579 report states that it was 6 leagues west of the mouth
of the Dos Bocas. It was not feasible to swim the horses over this body of
water, and half a league from the sea a bridge 934 paces in length was constructed. Here an important linguistic frontier was crossed. Cortés now left
the Nahuatl-speaking area, through which he had been traveling, and entered
a Maya Chontal district, which he calls the Province of Copilco. It will be
recalled that this river was the western boundary of the vast lowland Maya
country, which Montejo claimed as far east as the Ulua River in Honduras.
Fifty-five years later a line only 2 leagues west of this stream still divided the
jurisdiction of Tabasco from that of Espíritu Santo.[24]

Cortés tells us little to define his route from the Río Copilco to Nacajuca,
the last town of the "province," but it seems very likely that he followed
approximately the road shown on the Alfaro map (Map 2), which may have
been an old native trade route, although most travel is said to have been by
water. It was apparently the one which Bernal Díaz had taken on two previous
trips through the Chontalpa, for he mentions Tonala, Ahualulco, Copilco-
zacualco, Ulapa, Teotitan-copilco, and Nacajuca. Cortés does, however, give
an account of the products of this rich country and tells us that there were
"ten or twelve good towns, I mean local capitals (*cabeceras*), in addition to
the villages." He goes on to say that the land was low and swampy and more
than fifty bridges were constructed over a distance of about 20 leagues. The
natives served him well, and indeed we know that they supplied the labor for
building the bridges.[25]

For a part of the journey Bernal Díaz furnishes a few more details. After

[23] Dampier, 1906, 2: 214–16; Gil y Sáenz, 1872, p. 127; Villa-Señor y Sánchez, 1746, ch. 28,
apud Blom and La Farge, 1926–27, 1: 49–50; Blom and La Farge, 1926–27, 1: 76, 86–87. In
Dampier's time (1676) Acayuca was the principal town of the Coatzacoalcos district. In 1746
Espíritu Santo had been abandoned because of attacks, presumably by buccaneers.

[24] Cortés, 1866, p. 399; RY, 1: 360. Among the various streams flowing into La. Tupilco the
Río Tortuguero seems most likely to have been the former Río Copilco. See maps in Maudslay,
1908–16, vol. 5, and González, 1940.

[25] Cortés, 1866, pp. 399–400; Díaz del Castillo, 1939, chs. 166, 169; Alva Ixtlilxochitl, 1891–92,
1: 408.

crossing the Río Copilco the expedition passed through some small towns before reaching the "river named Mazapa . . . which the sailors call the Río de Dos Bocas." From the Alfaro map and the accompanying report we know that the first three were Copilco-zacualco, Huimanguillo, and Iquinuapa, known as the Copilcos and situated about 4, 6, and 8 leagues inland from the mouth of the river. Beyond them lay Ulapa and Boquiapa. None of these towns remain at their former sites today, but three of them are still to be found where they were moved, farther inland.[26]

In the sixteenth century, it will be remembered, the Dos Bocas (the modern Río Seco) was a large and deep river and the main outlet of the Río de Chiapa, which drained a vast region to the south. This stream was crossed by means of a great number of canoes tied together in pairs. East of the river Cortés was joined by Bernal Díaz, who had been sent from Espíritu Santo with a force of thirty Spaniards and many Mexican auxiliaries to pacify Cimatan. The town submitted without any resistance, although it revolted again as soon as it was learned that most of the Spaniards at Espíritu Santo had gone to Honduras. Bernal Díaz states that the place, east of the river, where he joined Cortés was Iquinuapa, but we see no reason to believe it had not always been situated west of the stream, where we find it on the Alfaro map. From the Dos Bocas they passed on to Teotitan-copilco, which Díaz describes as a large place, and to Nacajuca, the last town of the district.[27]

After leaving the Chontalpa at Nacajuca the expedition marched in a southerly direction to the Grijalva, crossing what is now the Río González above the five Nahuatl-speaking towns, four of which lay at that time along its left bank according to the Alfaro map. Neither Cortés nor Bernal Díaz mentions this river, but the map and report state that the remains of the bridge constructed here by Cortés were still in evidence in 1579. The Grijalva was crossed, apparently a short distance below the present site of Villahermosa, by means of rafts and some canoes sent by the cacique of Tabasco. Cortés' map showed that he must next proceed to a place called Ciuatan. With some difficulty a road was opened along the right bank of the river formed by the confluence of the Teapa and the Tacotalpa and continued up the same shore of the latter river to Ciuatan. Cortés considered this to be a single town com-

[26] Díaz del Castillo, 1939, ch. 175; RY, 1: 360. The name was probably originally Huey-mango, or Huimango, and the Spanish suffix added to distinguish it from the larger town of that name. The name Copilco-Zacualco suggests that there was a pyramid-temple at the site since it seems referable to the Nahuatl *tzaquali* and could be translated as "Copilco, the place of the pyramid" (Sahagún, 1938, 2: 257).

[27] Díaz del Castillo, 1939, ch. 175. Because of its size and commercial importance, Cortés' "Province of Copilco" may have been named for Teotitan-copilco, the modern Copilco, rather than for Copilco-zacualco. Cf. p. 31, *supra*.

posed of three subdivisions. One, containing 200 houses, was on the right bank of the river, and the other two, on the left. In 1579 it was said to be three towns, Astapa, Jahuacapa, and Jalapa, also known as the three Ciuatans. At this time all three were on the left bank, but today they are again on the right, where Cortés found only one of them.[28]

Here the expedition remained twenty days. Food was brought up the river from the ship which had been sent to Tabasco, and further supplies were obtained from Bernal Díaz' encomienda at Teapa. Although the people of Ciuatan had assisted in constructing the road by which Cortés had come, they fled when he reached the place, which caused considerable difficulty. He knew from his map that his next objective was Chilapa, but the few Indians he could find told him they knew of no land route. They could only point to some mountains apparently 10 leagues distant and told him that Chilapa was on a great river in that vicinity. The modern village of Chilapa is on the lower Grijalva, and we are obliged to depend on the Alfaro map and Cortés' description to locate its former site. There can be little doubt that the natives were showing Cortés a spur of the Chiapas Mountains lying to the east of Ciuatan. Its northwestern outpost, the Cerro de Macuspana, is only a short distance to the south of the town of that name, and from that point it gradually increases in height as it extends to the southeast. We do not know whether the Macuspana mountain would be visible so far away. Cortés, however, was usually an excellent judge of distance, and we are inclined to accept his estimate and place Chilapa on the left bank of the Río Macuspana about 15 km. east of the town of Macuspana. Such a location would not be very far from the sierra. The Macuspana and Tepetitan Rivers are a continuation of the Río Chilapa, and they were formerly all known as the Río Chilapa. Rovirosa reports a modern hacienda of the same name in the jurisdiction of Macuspana, but he does not give its precise location.[29]

Cortés had much difficulty in finding a road across the swamp east of Ciuatan, but this obstacle was finally surmounted by building a bridge of long timbers; indeed, it was 300 paces in length. Although it was only a third as long as that over the Río Copilco, it was probably a much more serious undertaking, since all the local Indians had fled and the expedition was now obliged

[28] RY, 1: 324; Alfaro map (Map 2); Cortés, 1866, pp. 400–02. Huimango, Culico, Anta, and Pechucalco are now on the right bank of the Río Conduacan above Nacajuca. Like the Cimatans, they may have been moved because of inundations caused by the diversion of the waters of the former Río de Dos Bocas. Cf. Roys, 1943, pp. 99–100.

[29] Cortés, 1866, p. 402; Díaz del Castillo, 1939, ch. 175; RY, 1: 347; Blom and La Farge, 1926–27, 1: 137, 145, 154; Rovirosa, 1888, p. 17. There has been some confusion regarding this stage of the journey through mistaking the modern Chilapa for the town through which Cortés passed.

to supply its own labor. Later they were to become more accustomed to such emergencies. Beyond this swamp, which was probably the one which appears on the modern maps east of Jalapa, things went more easily. The ground was somewhat higher, and at a town which Cortés calls Ocumba a scouting party found considerable food. A few prisoners were also taken, who guided the expedition to Chilapa. Cortés had been told at Ciuatan that Ocumba was up the river from Chilapa. His scouts veered somewhat from the direction followed by the expedition and reached the town by crossing a body of water by swimming and in canoes. We find no mention of the town in colonial times, but Acumba is still the name of a lake to the south of San Fernando, of the stream which flows from it into the Río Macuspana, and of a hacienda at the mouth of the tributary. Strangely enough, Macuspana is not mentioned either by Cortés or by Bernal Díaz.[30]

Chilapa was a large and attractive town with many farms and orchards around it. Ixtlilxochitl tells us that "this province was subject to the city of Tezcoco." Although we doubt that the Aztec confederacy had conquered any part of Tabasco, this may indicate that Tezcoco had special commercial privileges here. Many of the people had burned their houses and fled, but two men were found who led the Spaniards to Tepetitan. A league and a half below Chilapa the large river was crossed by means of rafts, and Tepetitan was reached after a journey of two days covering 6 or 7 leagues through many swamps. Once it was necessary to construct a bridge, possibly over the Arroyo Tepecintila. Apparently they followed the general direction of the river, but it must have been at some distance from the stream, since we find no mention of the town of Tepecintila. This settlement has since disappeared, but we know from the Alfaro map and the accompanying report that it was on the right bank of the Río Chilapa, presumably close to the tributary which still bears its name.[31]

133701

The modern town of Tepetitan lies on the west bank of the river, but in 1579 it was on the opposite side. Some question has been raised as to its location in Cortés' time, since he states that it was "close to the lower part (la halda) of a great chain of sierras." Tepetitan could mean "in, near, or below the mountains," and Tamacaztepec, which Cortés gives as another name of the town, could be translated as "mountain or hill of the tlamacazque," the appellation of a class of priests and temple attendants. Tepecintila has much the same meaning as Tepetitan and is probably referable to the Nahuatl expression *tepetl itzintlan*, "at the foot of the sierra."[32]

[30] Cortés, 1866, pp. 402–03; Rovirosa, 1888, p. 11; 1931, pp. 129–30.
[31] Cortés, 1866, pp. 403–04; Alva Ixtlilxochitl, 1891–92, 1: 408; RY, 1: 347.
[32] Cortés, 1866, pp. 403–04; Molina, 1880, 2: f. 102v; 1886, p. 195; Sahagún, 1938, 1: 296.

We are inclined to believe that Cortés was referring to the low ridge northeast of the Río Tulija, which is known as "Los Cerrillos." Possibly he skirted these hills on his journey, but we do not know how far they extend to the north. The present site of Tepetitan is no doubt in sight of this elevation, but it must be 10 to 15 km. distant and perhaps farther. Various opinions have been expressed as to where the town was in Cortés' time. The most reasonable, we believe, are those of Maudslay and Morley, who place it near its present site, the former noting that it must have been on the right bank of the river and the latter, that the foothills of the cordillera are about 4 leagues distant. In Yucatan a large group of towns in the Province of Mani were considered to be in the "territorio de la sierra," although they extended from the base of the range to a distance of 5 or 6 leagues. So far as the meaning of Tepetitan is concerned, it does not necessarily imply that the town was actually at the base of the sierra. Tepetitlan is the name of one of the *calpullis*, or wards, of Tlatelolco, which was a part of the City of Mexico on an island in Lake Tezcoco.[33]

Tepetitan, like Chilapa, was found burned and deserted, which, as Cortés remarks, doubled the hardships of the journey. The Spaniards do not appear to have maltreated the natives, but they must have left famine in their wake, and by this time the Indians everywhere knew what it meant to open roads and build bridges for the invaders. Sufficient food was discovered, however, to relieve the more urgent necessities of the expedition.

Iztapa was the next objective indicated on Cortés' map, and a single prisoner was induced to act as guide, although he had never gone there by land. Laguna Catazaja, however, which is little more than halfway to the Usumacinta, was accessible by canoe, and since we believe that the route passed not far south of this lake, it is not unlikely that the guide had some general knowledge of the country. An advance party of thirty horse and as many infantry was sent on ahead, and two days later the entire army followed on their trail. They appear to have crossed the Sabanas de Maluco, which lie east of Tepetitan. Here no doubt were the first of the swamps where "the horses sank to their girths when riderless and led by hand," and beyond them are the extensive savannas lying between the drainage of the Río Tepetitan and that of the Usumacinta. Cortés must have traveled through this region to reach Iztapa.[34] For reasons which will be discussed elsewhere in this study, we be-

[33] Maudslay, 1908–16, 5: 336; Morley, 1937–38, 1: 10; Sahagún, 1938, 5: 74; López de Cogolludo, 1867–68, bk. 4, ch. 20. González (1940, p. 402) places Tepetitan 6 or 7 leagues east of the river at Hacienda Los Cerrillos near the hills of the same name.

[34] Cortés, 1866, pp. 404–05; González, 1940, p. 402.

lieve that this town was situated on the left bank of the Usumacinta at or near Montecristo (modern Emiliano Zapata).[35]

The intervening country is not very well known, but Stephens and Charnay, who traveled by land from Palenque to Laguna Catazaja and from there to Jonuta by water, have given us some idea of the region. On leaving Palenque, Stephens "entered immediately upon a beautiful plain, picturesque, ornamented with trees, and extending five or six days' journey to the Gulf of Mexico. The road was very muddy, but, open to the sun in the morning, was not so bad as we feared." Charnay, describing his journey in the opposite direction, tells us: "After Las Playas [on the southern shore of Laguna Catazaja], the landscape opens out into a noble perspective of fields and shady groves; now the eye wanders over the rich flora of the savanna, now it plunges into the unfathomable depths of the forest." Charnay's "charming ride" was on December 30; but Stephens made the trip in June, when the rainy season was well advanced, and we should expect the roads to be at their worst. Without attempting to belittle the difficulties, of which Cortés complains bitterly, the preceding accounts suggest that a very considerable part of the journey was over a favorable terrain. Indeed, the same conclusion might be drawn from the time in which it was performed.[36]

Immediately north of Laguna Catazaja are the swampy Lagunas de San Carlos, and the whole plain is a network of creeks and rivers. Stephens describes the Río Chico as "varying from two to five hundred feet in width, deep, muddy, and very sluggish, with wooded banks of impenetrable thickness." No such river is mentioned during this stage of Cortés' journey, and in any case it would seem most unlikely that his army could have reached the Usumacinta in three days from Tepetitan traveling through such a country.[37]

Cortés describes Iztapa as a large place with land suitable for a Spanish settlement. When the Spaniards approached the town, most of the inhabitants fled to the opposite (right) bank of the river, but in due course, after Cortés had made known his peaceful intentions, the cacique returned with forty of the fugitives. The cacique promised obedience and ordered his people to supply food for the army. He also sent Indians to open a road to Tatahuitalpan, the next town through which the expedition would pass, and subsequently he accompanied some of the Spaniards in canoes to the upstream towns.[38]

During his stay in Iztapa, Cortés sent three Spaniards to the Gulf coast with

[35] For a detailed discussion of the location of Iztapa and other towns on the Usumacinta, see Appendix B.
[36] Stephens, 1841, 2: 365; Charnay, 1887, pp. 215–16.
[37] Charnay, 1887, p. 212; Stephens, 1841, 2: 369, 375.
[38] Cortés, 1866, pp. 405–08.

instructions for the commander of the supply ships waiting there to proceed to
Ascension Bay in eastern Yucatan, where he would meet them or send word
what to do next. The messengers were also ordered to load their canoes and
any others they could obtain in Xicalango and Tabasco with provisions and
to take them "up a great river" to Acalan. It is evident, on the basis of data
now available concerning the location of this province, that the food was to
be transported across Laguna de Términos and up the Candelaria River to the
Acalan settlements. The person to whom Cortés entrusted these orders quar-
reled with the master of the ships on arrival in Xicalango. Bitter fighting
ensued, during which most of the men in the ships' crews, who divided into
factions, were killed. The Indians of the coastal towns finished off all the
survivors and burned the ships, with the result that the supplies Cortés expected to receive in Acalan never arrived.[39]

From Iztapa Cortés marched upstream along the road cleared in advance
by the Indians to Tatahuitalpan, 5 leagues distant. This was a small village on
the left bank of the Usumacinta, probably located near the present site of
Pobilcuc. The Spaniards found the place burned and abandoned, but they
soon rounded up about twenty of the inhabitants, who had fled to a shrine
half a league from the opposite shore, and brought them back to the town.
Cortés asked one of them, said to be the cacique, to show him the road to
Ciuatecpan, "as according to my map it was higher up the river and we should
have to pass through it." The cacique stated that the Indians did not know
the road by land, since they always traveled by river, but agreed to furnish
guides who would try to lead the army through the forest. Accordingly,
Cortés instructed some of the Spaniards, who had made the trip from Iztapa
to Tatahuitalpan by river, to proceed upstream to Ciuatecpan, "and try to
pacify the people there, and also of another pueblo named Ozumazintlan
[Usumacinta] which they would pass on the way." With the main body of
his troops and the Mexican auxiliaries he set out overland.

The march to Ciuatecpan was through very difficult country. On leaving
Tatahuitalpan the Spaniards encountered a great swamp more than half a
league wide, but with the aid of the auxiliaries, who covered the trail with
brush, the army managed to get across. "Then we came to a deep creek where
we had to make a bridge in order to carry over the saddles and baggage, the
horses swimming; and as soon as we were across we came upon another
swampy place, more than a league long, where the horses sank to their knees
and often to their girths, but as the ground underneath was hard we got across

[39] Cortés, 1866, pp. 407–08, and 1916, pp. 359–60; Díaz del Castillo, 1939, ch. 176. Díaz states
that Cortés sent the messengers from Ciuatecpan.

safely and entered the forest." After an arduous journey of two days through the forest, "so thick that, standing on the ground and looking up, one could not see the sky," the guides confessed that they were lost; whereupon Cortés ordered the army back to a small swamp where there was pasture for the horses. "There we passed the night suffering much from hunger. . . . Some of the men were more dead than alive, and almost gave up all hope." With the aid of a marine compass Cortés on the following day directed the march to the northeast, the direction in which he calculated Ciuatecpan should be; "and it pleased God that our calculations should turn out so well that by the hour of vespers we came in sight of the idol houses which stood in the middle of the pueblo."

Although the town had been burned and was entirely deserted, the army found a plentiful supply of maize and other foods. "Thus refreshed we began to forget our past troubles, although I was still very anxious for news of the canoes which I had sent up the river." Walking through the town, he found a crossbow bolt in the ground and realized that the canoes had arrived, but now his concern was all the greater, fearing that the men might have been killed.[40]

The Indians of Ciuatecpan had fled to a lagoon across the Usumacinta, where some of Cortés' men found them and brought back thirty or forty for questioning. The latter informed the commander that the Spaniards in the canoes, having waited two days in Ciuatecpan, had proceeded upstream to another settlement named Petenecte, 6 leagues away. Messengers were immediately sent to contact them, and the following day all returned, with news of three more villages (called Coatzacoalco, Taltenango, and Teutitan by Cortés) located above Petenecte. The very next day Indians from these upstream towns arrived, bringing provisions "and a little gold."

At Ciuatecpan, as at other places en route, Cortés told the Indians "that they must believe in God and serve your Majesty." They promised obedience to the Spanish sovereign and burned some of their idols in the commander's presence. The cacique of Ciuatecpan, who had not appeared before, now arrived, and Cortés gave presents to all the Indians, "on which they became well contented and satisfied."[41]

Although the exact location of Ciuatecpan is still somewhat uncertain, the available data indicate that it was in the region of Canizan. The village of Usumacinta was apparently situated below the junction of the San Pedro

[40] Cortés, 1866, pp. 408–11, and 1916, pp. 360–63; Díaz del Castillo, 1939, ch. 175. Díaz' account of the march to Ciuatecpan is somewhat confused, for he puts the story about getting lost in the forest in the first stage of the journey from Iztapa to Ciuatecpan instead of the second stage.

[41] Cortés, 1866, pp. 410–12, and 1916, pp. 363–64.

Mártir and Usumacinta Rivers not far from modern Balancan. Petenecte was a short distance below Tenosique, which was evidently one of the three towns farther upstream mentioned by Cortés.[42]

The next important point on Cortés' march was Acalan. He asked the Indians about the route he should take, and after some discussion it was agreed that he should cross the river at Ciuatecpan and follow a trail used by native merchants. Advance parties were sent out to explore the road and also to notify the caciques and people of Acalan of the impending arrival of the army and establish friendly relations with them. Bernal Díaz and Gonzalo Mexía were the leaders of one group, of whom we shall hear more later. Although Cortés intended to await reports of the advance parties, depletion of supplies gathered for the march forced him to set out before word was received from them. Bernal Díaz also states that the Indians of Ciuatecpan had again abandoned the town, evidence that the loyalty and obedience they had promised were mere expressions of temporary expediency.[43]

After crossing the Usumacinta, the army proceeded along a narrow trail through thick forest, and on the third day reached a great "estero" (Bernal Díaz calls it a river) more than 500 paces wide. This was a widened section of the Río San Pedro Mártir, apparently in the region of Nuevo León northeast of Canizan. Search up- and downstream for a ford was fruitless, and the native guides told Cortés that none would be found unless he traveled upstream for twenty days to the sierra (the elevated country that forms the divide between the Usumacinta and the San Pedro Mártir southeast of Tenosique).[44]

The army now faced a very grave situation which Cortés describes in these words:

This lagoon or creek (*estero ó ancón*) placed me in such difficulty that I cannot find words to express it; to cross it seemed impossible on account of its width and the want of canoes, and even if we had had canoes for the people and baggage the horses could not have crossed, for on both sides were great swamps with a network of tree roots. No other way could be thought of for getting the horses across. To turn back meant certain death on account of the bad roads which we had passed over and the amount of rain that had fallen, for we well knew that the flood in the rivers must have washed away all the bridges that we had made, yet to rebuild these seemed equally difficult when all the men were exhausted and the thought was pressing on our minds that we had consumed all the provisions prepared for the journey and should find nothing more to eat. . . .

[42] See Appendix B, pp. 442–48, *infra*, for a discussion of the location of these towns.
[43] Cortés, 1866, p. 413; Díaz del Castillo, 1939, ch. 176.
[44] For a discussion regarding this "estero" and the point of crossing, see Appendix B, pp. 448–57, *passim*.

I have already told your Majesty what difficulties there were in the way of our advance, so that no human brain could have suggested a remedy if God, who is the true help and succour of the afflicted and needy, had not aided us.[45]

By chance a small canoe was found in which the Spaniards who had been sent ahead to Acalan had crossed the stream, and Cortés had soundings made to test the depth of the water. It proved to be 4 fathoms deep with another 2 fathoms of mud at the bottom. "As a last resource I determined to throw a bridge across and at once I ordered wood to be cut to measure, that is nine or ten fathoms long, including that part which would remain above the water." The Mexican auxiliaries cut and hauled the logs, and the Spaniards, using rafts and three canoes (two more had been found) began to drive them in place. Cortés sought to inspire his men by actively participating in the labor, but the task seemed so hopeless that the soldiers began to grumble, saying that it would be better to turn back before hunger and exhaustion made it impossible. "As I saw them so greatly discouraged—and in truth they had good reason to be so, both on account of the nature of the work that we were undertaking, and because they had nothing to eat except such roots and herbs as they could find—I told them that they should not be employed on the bridge, for I would build it with the Indians alone."

Summoning the Mexican chieftains, the commander told them "that they could see to what extremity we were reduced and that we must either go forward or perish." He begged them to have their followers complete the bridge, assuring them that food in plenty would be available in Acalan. "In addition to this I promised them that when we got back to Tenochtitlan they would be handsomely rewarded by me in your Majesty's name." The chieftains immediately promised to have the work carried on, and it proceeded so rapidly that within four days the bridge was finished and the army crossed to the opposite shore. The completed structure contained more than 1000 posts, "the smallest of them almost as thick as a man's body," not counting the timbers of lesser size.[46]

The building of this bridge was undoubtedly a remarkable feat. It was another example of the leadership, resourcefulness, and driving energy more than once demonstrated by the great conqueror in the face of danger and adversity.

After crossing the bridge, the Spaniards encountered another hazard, a great swamp two crossbow shots wide, "the most terrible thing that man ever saw." The horses sank to their girths and at first it seemed impossible to extri-

[45] Cortés, 1916, pp. 365–66.
[46] Cortés, 1866, pp. 414–15, and 1916, pp. 366–67; Díaz dèl Castillo, 1939, ch. 176.

cate them. But the soldiers used brush and branches to support them, and
finally a channel was made through which the horses swam to dry ground.[47]

The advance party of Bernal Díaz and Mexía had meanwhile reached the
first Acalan town, despite the fact that their guides had fled the first night
after they left Ciuatecpan. At first the inhabitants, who apparently had no
news of the expedition, adopted a somewhat hostile attitude, and they were
little inclined to heed the Spaniards' request that they send supplies to the
army. But the following day they learned from native merchants that Cortés
had a large force, and they now indicated greater willingness to furnish provisions, although refusing to go to see Cortés because the people of Ciuatecpan,
where the army was assumed to be, were their enemies. At this juncture two
messengers arrived with letters from Cortés, stating that he had already set out
for Acalan and instructing Díaz and Mexía to bring him as much food as
possible. Collecting a large quantity of maize, fowl, and other supplies, the
Spaniards, with eighty Indian carriers, hastened back along the trail and met
the army after dark on the very day it got through the swamp on the east
bank of the Río San Pedro Mártir.[48]

The soldiers, hungry and exhausted, cast aside all discipline and seized the
food for themselves, leaving none for Cortés and the captains. When he heard
what had happened, the commander "cursed with impatience" and threatened
to investigate this act of insubordination, but, as Bernal Díaz remarks, "his
anger was useless and merely 'lifting up his voice in the wilderness.'" The
soldier-chronicler had evidently anticipated that there would be a wild
scramble for the food and had hidden some in the forest, which he agreed to
share with Cortés and Sandoval. He notes, however, that Sandoval went in
person to bring his share, trusting no one else.

So great was the army's need that Cortés ordered Díaz to return in haste
to Acalan "and impress strongly on the caciques that they should keep the
peace and should at once send provisions along the road This I did, and the
very day that I arrived at Acalá I sent by night three Spaniards who accompanied me with over one hundred Indians laden with maize and other things."
This second supply of provisions arrived during the march of the main force
to the first Acalan town. On this occasion, however, Cortés, Sandoval, and
Luis Marín went ahead of the army to receive the food and supervise its distribution.[49]

With the first supply party came "two persons of distinction" who brought

[47] Cortés, 1866, pp. 415–16, and 1916, pp. 367–68.
[48] Díaz del Castillo, 1939, ch. 176; Cortés, 1866, p. 416. Díaz states that the supply party arrived before the army crossed the swamp east of the estero.
[49] Díaz del Castillo, 1908–16, 5: ch. 176.

messages and gifts from Paxbolonacha, the ruler of Acalan. They told Cortés that for some time past their chieftain had known about him through reports of merchants from Xicalango and Tabasco and that he was "delighted at my arrival." Cortés expressed thanks for the good will of this ruler, gave them presents, and sent them back to Acalan with Bernal Díaz. He also states, "They marvelled greatly at the building of the bridge, and this went far to establish the security which we afterwards enjoyed among them, for as their country lies amid lagoons and creeks, they could easily have hidden themselves in them, but after seeing that wonderful work they thought that nothing was impossible for us to accomplish." [50]

The army now proceeded toward the Acalan border towns, evidently following the trail used by Díaz and the supply party. The first night was spent in the forest, and about noon of the second day they came to some planted fields. Later in the afternoon, after making a detour around a swamp, they reached the first settlement, called Tizatepelt by Cortés and recorded as Çacchute in the Chontal Text. This town could not have been far from the San Pedro branch of the Candelaria, if not actually on it. [51] In contrast with the situation all along the Usumacinta, where the natives had abandoned their towns because of reports spread by the cacique of Ciuatan, the Indians of Tizatepelt had remained peacefully in their village. The army also obtained enough food for the men and horses "to make us forget the want that we had suffered."

At this place one of Paxbolonacha's sons, accompanied by a considerable following, came to see Cortés "and placed his land and person at your Majesty's service." He informed the commander, however, that his father had died. Although Cortés realized that he was not telling the truth, he expressed his condolences and treated him with due respect. The youth and his company remained in Tizatepelt two days, evidently for the purpose of obtaining information concerning the size and strength of the expedition.

The cacique of Tizatepelt suggested to Cortés that the army would find better accommodations and more plentiful provisions at a larger and more populous town, also under his jurisdiction, that was close by. The commander accepted this obvious invitation to move on, and the cacique at once gave orders to have the trail cleared and lodgings prepared for the soldiers. A 5-league march brought the Spaniards to this second settlement, named Teutiercas in the Fifth Letter, and Tuxakha in the Chontal Text. (Gómara and Ixtlilxochitl record the Nahuatl name as Teuticaccac and Teotilac re-

[50] Cortés, 1916, p. 368.
[51] Cf. Appendix B, p. 459, *infra*.

spectively, and these forms are undoubtedly more exact.)[52] On the basis of a remark by Ixtlilxochitl and the meaning of the Chontal name, we infer that the town was located on the Río San Pedro, possibly near the junction with the Arroyo Esperanza.[53]

Cortés describes the place as "a very beautiful pueblo" with imposing temples, two of which the soldiers used as living quarters after casting out the idols. "At this the natives did not show much distress as I had already spoken to them and shown them the error in which they lived, for there was no other than the one God creator of all things, and all the rest that I could tell them at the time. Later on I spoke to them more fully on the subject of religion to both Chief and people."[54]

At Teutiercas, or Tuxakha, the cacique informed Cortés in great confidence that although Paxbolonacha had given instructions to spread the report that he was dead, he was alive and had ordered that the Spaniards should be led astray and diverted from the major Acalan settlements. Whereupon the commander sent for the ruler's son and expressed surprise at Paxbolonacha's conduct, in view of his own desire to do the ruler honor and reward him for the good treatment the Spaniards had thus far received from the Acalan people. He requested therefore that he should persuade his father to come, "for I felt sure that it would be greatly to his advantage to do so." The youth admitted the deception, with the excuse that his father had ordered it; but he expressed the belief that the ruler, "knowing, as he now did, that I [Cortés] did not come to do them any harm," would accede to the commander's request. So he went back to Itzamkanac, and the following day both father and son appeared before Cortés, who received them "with much pleasure." Paxbolonacha excused his conduct on the ground that he had been afraid to come until he was certain of the peaceful intentions of the Spaniards. It was true that

[52] López de Gómara, 1943, 2: 140; Alva Ixtlilxochitl, 1891–92, 1: 412. The latter also records the name Teotlycacac, which he seems to apply to another town, but from the nature of his narrative it evidently refers to Cortés' Teutiercas. In short, Ixtlilxochitl gives both Teotilac and Teotlycacac (evidently variants of the same name) for the second town.

[53] Cf. Appendix B, p. 460, *infra*.

[54] Cortés, 1866, pp. 416–18, and 1916, pp. 368–70.

MAP 3—THE CHONTAL AREA AND ADJACENT REGIONS

Based on the Tehuantepec and Belize sheets of the 1:1,000,000 map of Hispanic America issued by the American Geographical Society; the Tulane-Carnegie map of Archaeological Sites in the Maya Area (1940 edition); the map of Quintano Roo issued in 1937 by the Secretaría de Agricultura y Fomento, Mexico; and maps by Rovirosa (1880), Pacheco Blanco (1928), Morley (1937–38, vols. 4 and 5), González (1940), Aguilera Martínez (1942), Ruppert and Denison (1943), and Andrews (1943).

he had sought to divert the Spaniards from the Acalan settlements, but he now invited Cortés to accompany him to Itzamkanac, where the army would find all the facilities and provisions needed.[55]

The Chontal Text gives a somewhat different version of events leading up to the meeting of Paxbolonacha and Cortés. It contains no mention of the visit of the "two persons of distinction" to Cortés' camp near the famous bridge, nor does it give any account of the goings and comings of Paxbolonacha's son. The story in the Text begins with the statement that after the Spaniards arrived in Tuxakha, they sent word summoning the Acalan ruler, but since he could take no action without consulting his principal men, the latter assembled to consider what would be the best policy to follow. They advised that inasmuch as they did not know what the Spaniards wanted, it would not be fitting for Paxbolonacha to accede to the summons. In his place was sent a certain Chocpalocem Ahau, accompanied by three other chieftains named Patzinchiciua, Paxuanapuk, and Paxhochacchan.

When these men appeared before Cortés, the latter, learning that Paxbolonacha was not among them, said: "Let the ruler come, for I wish to see him. I do not come to make war nor to do him harm. I wish only to pass through to see the land [and] whatever there is to see. I will be very good to him if he receives me well." In this way Cortés made clear his firm purpose to see the Acalan ruler, and although his words were friendly enough, they unmistakably implied that the maintenance of peaceful relations depended on the ruler's actions. "Having understood it," the chieftains returned to Itzamkanac.

Paxbolonacha now informed his principal men that he wished to go in person to see Cortés, and without further delay he set out for Tuxakha, taking "a generous gift of honey, turkeys, maize, copal, and a great deal of fruit." Cortés and the Spaniards received him with courtesy, and the commander stated that he had come in name of "the lord of the world, the emperor who is on his throne in Castile," to see the land and its people. He reiterated his peaceful intentions, and stated that all he asked was that Paxbolonacha should facilitate his journey to the east coast. Paxbolonacha replied "that he would grant him passage with great pleasure," and he now invited Cortés to accompany him to Itzamkanac, where they would discuss the measures to be taken. But the Spaniard suggested that the ruler should rest a while in Tuxakha, "whereupon they spent twenty days taking their ease."

It is not surprising that the Text fails to mention the activities of Paxbolonacha's son, or the ruler's attempted deception and his efforts to direct the Spaniards away from Itzamkanac and other major settlements. This part of

[55] Cortés, 1866, pp. 418–19, and 1916, pp. 370–71.

the Text (Document III), written eighty-five years later, was designed to establish the services of Don Pablo Paxbolon, cacique of Tixchel, and his ancestors to the Spanish Crown. In this case, as in other parts of the record of Cortés' visit to Acalan in 1525, it naturally seeks to emphasize the loyalty of Paxbolonacha and the aid rendered the Spaniards at this time. The equivocal attitude of the ruler at first is discreetly passed over in silence. The account of the embassy of Chocpalocem Ahau and his retinue, which probably coincided with one of the visits by Paxbolonacha's son, has genuine value, however, for it illustrates the nature of political authority in Acalan and shows that the ruler by no means exercised free right of decision in local affairs.

The statement in the Text that Cortés and Paxbolonacha spent twenty days in Tuxakha (Teutiercas) is not confirmed by any other source. In the Fifth Letter Cortés relates that after his meeting with the Acalan ruler the latter immediately gave orders for a road to be cleared to Itzamkanac. The following day the army proceeded to the capital. Paxbolonacha accompanied it, riding one of the commander's horses.[56] We believe that Cortés' testimony should be accepted on this point, since the Fifth Letter is a more authoritative source than the Text. In addition, it seems more likely that Cortés would have spent any period of rest and ease in Itzamkanac than in one of the lesser towns.[57]

Cortés describes Itzamkanac, which we locate on the south side of the Candelaria near the junction of the Arroyo Caribe and the Río San Pedro, as a large place with many temples, and we have already noted that the Spaniards evidently considered it a more imposing place than the Itza capital at Tayasal.

[56] Cortés, 1866, p. 419.
[57] We also find it difficult to reconcile a twenty-day stay at Tuxakha or any other Acalan town with the chronology of the expedition as set forth in the Fifth Letter and other sources. Cortés (1866, p. 419) states that he left Acalan on his journey to the Cehache country on the first Sunday in Lent in 1525, i.e., March 5, 1525, O.S. (see note 61, infra). Although no date is recorded for the departure from Espíritu Santo, Chamberlain (1938, pp. 523-25) has published a copy of a Cortés document dated at Espíritu Santo on December 14, 1524. Wagner (1944, pp. 531-32, note 51) states that the original of this document, owned by the Rosenbach Company, is dated at Tupilco, also on December 14, 1524. Assuming that Cortés was actually in the Tupilco area on December 14, 1524, this would leave only eighty-one days (December 14, 1524—March 4, 1525) for Cortés' march to Acalan and his stay in the latter province. If we add up Cortés' stated time schedules for the march and also make reasonable estimates when specific time schedules are not recorded, we find that Cortés' entire stay in the province of Acalan could not have lasted twenty days. A twenty-day period in one of the Acalan towns, or indeed for the entire Acalan phase of the journey, can be worked out only by assuming (1) that Cortés left Espíritu Santo earlier than the documents mentioned above would indicate, or (2) that the time schedules recorded in the Fifth Letter for certain phases of the journey (such as the twenty-day stay at Ciuatan, six days at Tepetitan, eight days at Iztapa, etc.) are incorrect. The March 5 date for leaving Itzamkanac appears to be correct, since it fits in with recorded time schedules up to the next specific date, namely, Cortés' arrival at Tenciz on April 15, 1525, the day before Easter.

Although Paxbolonacha had his own residence in Itzamkanac, he remained with Cortés in the quarters occupied by the latter. We suspect, however, that this action was not entirely voluntary, and that Cortés kept him in his company as a precautionary measure for the security of the army.[58]

Although the major purpose of Cortés' expedition was to punish the treason of Cristóbal de Olid and to assert authority over the Honduras area, the commander, prior to his arrival in Acalan, lacked precise information concerning the whereabouts of the various groups of Spaniards on the Caribbean coast. At Espíritu Santo the Indians of Xicalango and Tabasco told him about depredations committed by foreigners on the east coast, and on the basis of these reports Cortés apparently concluded that the raiders (he was not sure whether they were Olid's men, soldiers of Francisco de las Casas, or followers of Alvarado) were operating in the region of Ascension Bay, which he seems to have confused with Chetumal Bay. It appears, therefore, that his actual objective when he set out from Espíritu Santo was the east coast of Yucatan, and the instructions sent from Iztapa to the commander of his ships on the Tabasco coast indicate that this was still his objective at that time. But as the result of his conversations with Paxbolonacha and the Acalan merchants, Cortés learned that a group of Spaniards were established at Nito, where the Acalan traders had warehouses and occupied an entire *barrio* of the town. Consequently he now made plans to march in that direction. It was only after he had traveled to within a short distance of Nito that he learned that these Spaniards were members of Gil González Dávila's expedition, of which he had no information at the beginning of his march.[59]

The Acalan chieftains made a new and detailed map of the route he should follow. On it were indicated the principal towns through which he should pass and also important geographical features, "even to the rivers and swamps and miry places." Paxbolonacha had a bridge built across a broad swamp between Itzamkanac and a nearby river (the Río San Pedro), and he also agreed to supply the necessary canoes for crossing the river and guides for the journey. But when Cortés asked for provisions for the march, the caciques told him that the natives of certain towns would not obey them and that it would be necessary to send soldiers to requisition the supplies. Perhaps they adopted this policy in order to escape responsibility for the seizure of the needed food. In any case, the commander sent out a force of eighty soldiers, who obtained 100 canoe-loads of maize, fowl, honey, salt, and other supplies.[60]

[58] Cortés, 1866, p. 419.
[59] Cf. discussion of this point in Appendix B, pp. 430–34, *infra*.
[60] Cortés, 1866, p. 419; Díaz del Castillo, 1908–16, and 1939, ch. 177.

It was during Cortés' stay in the province of Acalan that a famous episode occurred, namely the execution of Cuauhtemoc and one or more of the other Mexican lords who had been brought along on the expedition. Neither Cortés nor Bernal Díaz records the exact time or place of this incident. Cortés introduces the story after describing his arrival in Itzamkanac, his conferences there with Paxbolonacha, and his preparations for the next stage of his journey. This obviously suggests that the affair took place in the Acalan capital. Gómara specifically states that Itzamkanac was the scene of the execution, and most later writers have accepted his word on this point. Ixtlilxochitl, however, records that the incident occurred in Teotilac. The Chontal Text names Tuxakha as the place "where the head of the Mexican captain, Cuauhtemoc, was cut off." Teotilac and Tuxakha, as we have seen, were evidently the same place, the Teutiercas of Cortés' narrative. Although it is interesting to find Tezcocan and Acalan traditions in agreement on this point, we believe that the burden of the evidence indicates that the Mexican lords were put to death at Itzamkanac.[61]

Cortés tells us that "an honored citizen of this city of Tenuxtitan" named Mexicalcingo secretly warned him that the native lords were conspiring to regain their lands and power. This informer stated that the chieftains had often talked about the loss of their realms and had said "that it would be well to seek a remedy by which they might again rule and possess them." During the long overland journey they had discussed the matter and had concluded that a

[61] According to López de Gómara (1943, 2: 144), this incident occurred at Itzamkanac "during Carnestolendas," i.e., the three festival days before Ash Wednesday, in 1525. Alva Ixtlilxochitl (1891–92, 1: 416) states that the Mexican lords were hanged at Teotilac during the early hours of Tuesday of Carnestolendas, or the day before Ash Wednesday. Vetancurt (1870–71, 1: 363) gives the date as February 26, 1525, but Orozco y Berra (1938, 1: 139, note 232) notes that this is an error, since the Tuesday before Ash Wednesday fell on February 28 in 1525. Dr. Walter S. Adams of Mt. Wilson Observatory has informed us that Easter fell on April 16 in 1525 (O.S.), which would fix Ash Wednesday as March 1. This confirms Orozco y Berra's date for the execution and also Cortés' own date, April 15, for the eve of Easter (Cortés, 1866, p. 434). Wagner (1944, p. 444) gives March 1 as the date of the execution, but cites no reason for putting it on this date (Ash Wednesday) instead of the preceding day (Tuesday) as recorded by Alva Ixtlilxochitl. Cortés left Itzamkanac on the first Sunday in Lent, or March 5, 1525. If the Mexican lords were put to death in Teutiercas (Teotilac, Tuxakha) on February 28, this would leave a very short interval for the march to the Acalan capital and the preparations there for the next stage of Cortés' journey. It may also be noted that although the Chontal Text identifies Tuxakha as the scene of the execution, the Maldonado-Paxbolon probanza of 1612 places it in "the pueblo of Acalan," i.e., Itzamkanac (Paxbolon-Maldonado Papers, Part I, ff. 3v, 39r). Maldonado, who formulated the probanza, knew of the existence of the Text and was acquainted with its general contents, and he later succeeded in having it incorporated in the probanza proceedings as a substantiating document. It is rather significant therefore that the probanza evidence and the Text differ on this point. Moreover, it should be pointed out that although the Text statement as to the place of the execution finds confirmation in Ixtlilxochitl's narrative, these two accounts of the incident differ in every other respect. Everything considered, we believe that we should accept Gómara's statement that the Mexican lords were put to death at Itzamkanac.

THE COMING OF THE SPANIARDS

suitable plan would be to find a way to kill Cortés and his soldiers. Having done this, they would incite a similar movement against Olid in Honduras and also send word to the Indians in Tenochtitlan to kill the Spaniards who had remained there. The last part of the scheme could easily be carried out, so they believed, since most of the Spaniards in the city were newcomers inexperienced in warfare. When these plans had been executed, the chieftains would then convoke all the land and wipe out all other Spaniards wherever they might be found. Cortés promptly arrested the alleged conspirators and questioned them separately, telling each one that the others had already told him of the plot. They confessed that Cuauhtemoc and Tetlepanquetzal, lord of Tacuba, "had set the matter on foot, and also that it was true that the rest had heard of it, but that they had never given their consent to the plan."

Bernal Díaz also records that the Mexican chieftains "had been deliberating or had arranged to kill us all and return to Mexico, and when they had reached their city to unite all their great forces and attack those [Spaniards] who remained in Mexico." He identifies the informers as "two great caciques," named Tapia and Juan Velásquez, the latter having been Cuauhtemoc's "captain general" during the siege of Tenochtitlan. The testimony of these men and of the accused lords, which was taken down in writing, revealed that the Mexican leaders, having observed the exhaustion of Cortés' forces and the general discontent and lack of discipline, had agreed that there would be a favorable opportunity to attack when the army was crossing some river or swamp. "Guatemoc confessed that it was as the others had said, but the plot was not hatched by him, and he did not know if they were all privy to it or would bring it to pass, that he never thought to carry it out but only [joined in] the talk there was about it. The Cacique of Tacuba stated that he and Guatemoc had said that it were better to die once for all than die every day on the journey, considering how their followers and kinsmen were suffering famine."

Cuauhtemoc and Tetlepanquetzal were hanged without further trial. The others were released, so Cortés says, "as they did not seem to have been guilty of more than listening, although that was sufficient for them to have deserved death." Gómara, who repeats Cortés' story of the incident with few changes, records, however, that a chieftain named Tlacatlec was also hanged.[62]

Torquemada and Ixtlilxochitl, who based their narrative of the affair on Tezcocan sources and folk tradition, deny the existence of an actual conspiracy against Cortés. The former relates that at some point during the jour-

[62] Cortés, 1866, pp. 420–21, and 1916, pp. 372–73; Díaz del Castillo, 1908–16 and 1939, ch. 177; López de Gómara, 1943, 2: 143–45.

ney Cohuanacoch bitterly reminded his fellow chieftains that whereas they
had once been kings they were now slaves carried along by Cortés "and the
few Christians who came with him." And he also said: "If we were men of
another sort, unmindful of the promise we have given not to create trouble,
we might well make sport of them so that they would remember the past and
how they burned the feet of my cousin, Quauhtemoc." Whereupon Cuauhtemoc told him to abandon such talk, "lest it be misunderstood and [the
Spaniards] think that we were actually planning it." But as Torquemada remarks, "even the walls have ears, and there is nothing, no matter how secretly
it is mentioned, that does not leak out through some chink to the plaza."
A Mexican Indian, "a villainous commoner," reported the conversation to
Cortés, who readily believed that the chieftains were plotting against him.
That very night he hanged eight of them.[63]

Ixtlilxochitl gives a more elaborate and circumstantial defense of the native lords. He relates that during the stay at Teotilac the pre-Lenten festivals
(*carnestolendas*) were celebrated, and that the Indians, partly in imitation of
the Spaniards and also because they were accustomed to hold certain native
ceremonies at this time,[64] also spent the season in gaiety day and night. An
added motive for merriment, so the chronicler states, was the fact that Cortés
had told them they could now return home. "Thus they were all content, and
the kings engaged in pleasant conversation, jesting (or amusing themselves)
with one another." Among other scoffs and jests (*burlas y chocarrerías*) they
indulged in argument about their respective claims to lands they were going to
conquer. Cohuanacoch claimed prior rights since the city of Tezcoco, according to the laws of the great Nezahualcoyotl, always held first place; Cuauhtemoc asserted that he should be ruler; and Tetlepanquetzal insisted that the
rights of Tacuba should now be considered first. Finally, Temilotzin, "general
of the kingdom of Mexico," spoke up and chided them for talking in this vein.
How could they jest about such things, since the loss of their realms had resulted from rivalry and dissension in the past? "Our pride and discord delivered
us into the hands of these foreigners, to suffer the long and weary journeys,
the hunger, cold, and a thousand other calamities we now endure, dispossessed
of our kingdoms and lordships, forgotten by our cherished fatherland, as if
it were our enemy; but all this we can consider well employed since these our

[63] Torquemada, 1723, bk. 4, ch. 104.
[64] The period of these pre-Lenten festivals in 1525 would have been February 26–28, since
Ash Wednesday fell on March 1 in that year. In the Gregorian calendar these days would have
been March 7–9. Vaillant (1941, p. 196) lists various Aztec ceremonies for the period March
4–23 (Gregorian), such as "impersonation of Xipe by priests wearing skins of captives; dances
by priests wearing human skins; agricultural dances."

enemies, children of the sun, brought us the true light, the salvation of our souls, and eternal life." They should emulate Ixtlilxochitl, brother of Cohuana-coch and ancestor of the chronicler, who showed no signs of sadness and had wholeheartedly accepted the new faith. The chieftains (nine of them partici-pated in the discussion) thanked Temilotzin for his wise counsel, and some were prompted to recall how their "ancient philosophers" had prophesied their present fate.

Seeing that the chieftains spent much time in talk and storytelling, Cortés "misjudged them, for as the proverb says, 'The thief thinks all are of his condition.'" He summoned an Indian named Cotexmi (the Mexicalcingo of the Fifth Letter), who had already been serving him as a spy, and demanded to know what these lengthy harangues were about. The chronicler states that Cotexmi was later put to torture in Tezcoco, and that although he confessed that he reported the nature of the chieftains' discussions, he denied telling Cortés they were plotting against him. In short, it was Cortés who "manu-factured" the conspiracy in order to be rid of the chieftains, "so there would be no natural lord in the land." In the early hours of the following day (Tues-day before Lent) the commander started to hang the Mexican leaders one by one. Cuauhtemoc was the first, then Tetlepanquetzal and the others, and last of all, Cohuanacoch. But when Cortés saw that the brother of Cohuanacoch was rallying his forces, he hastily cut down the Tezcocan lord. Within two days, however, Cohuanacoch died of wounds and shock.[65]

The Chontal Text devotes a lengthy paragraph to this incident. Here we are told that during the time when Cortés and Paxbolonacha were "taking their ease" at Tuxakha, Cuauhtemoc proposed a joint attack on the Spaniards. Cuauhtemoc is reported to have said: "My lord ruler, there will come a time when these Spaniards will give us much trouble and do us much harm and they will kill our people. I am of the opinion that we should kill them for I bring a large force and you are many." To which the Acalan ruler replied: "I will con-sider it. Leave it for now and we will discuss it later." But Paxbolonacha, see-ing that the Spaniards committed no acts of violence against his people and asked for nothing except supplies of food, decided "that since they did him no evil he could not have two faces with them, nor show two hearts toward the Spaniards." Nevertheless, Cuauhtemoc "was always importuning him about this," and Paxbolonacha finally went to Cortés and warned him to watch out lest the Aztec "commit some treason against you, because three or four times he has talked with me about killing you." The commander immediately ar-

[65] Alva Ixtlilxochitl, 1891–92, I: 412–17.

rested Cuauhtemoc and put him in chains. "On the third day that he was a prisoner they took him out and baptized him. . . ."[66] After baptizing him they cut off his head, and it was spiked on a ceiba in front of the house of idolatry which was in the pueblo of Yaxdzan." The words "in the pueblo of" appear only in the Spanish version and not in the Text. Yaxdzan does not appear in the list of Acalan towns recorded in the Text, so we surmise that it refers to a subdivision of Tuxakha where the native author of the Text believed the execution occurred.

In the probanza formulated in 1612 to record the services of Francisco Maldonado and his father-in-law, Don Pablo Paxbolon, grandson of Paxbolonacha, we also find statements that Cuauhtemoc tried to induce the Acalan ruler to join a conspiracy against the Spaniards. But here a different reason is given for Paxbolonacha's refusal to participate in the plot. The Acalan chieftain is said to have advised the Aztec "not to exert himself in vain." Had it not been prophesied that their rule would last only until the coming of the white men, "children of the sun," who would wear clothing and shoes (*que vendrían vestidos y calzados*)? "And there could be no doubt about it, now that they had seen the Spaniards." The probanza then goes on to tell how Paxbolonacha, in keeping with the loyalty and obedience he had promised Cortés, warned the commander, who condemned Cuauhtemoc to death. "And he was beheaded, and his head was nailed to a ceiba in the pueblo of Acalan."

No other source that we have seen records that Paxbolonacha played any part in this affair. Indeed, Ixtlilxochitl states that it occurred before Cortés' meeting with the Acalan ruler. Although we believe that the Tezcocan historian is wrong on this point, we are also of the opinion that Paxbolonacha was not the informer who denounced Cuauhtemoc. Just as the Text narrative of the meeting of Cortés and Paxbolonacha describes that event in the most favorable light, so also we regard the Text and probanza versions of the Cuauhtemoc episode as obviously designed to provide further proof of the loyalty of the ruling house of Acalan to the Spanish Crown. It is also rather significant that these two accounts disagree concerning the scene of the execution and Paxbolonacha's motives for refusing to join the alleged conspiracy. The "pueblo of Acalan" mentioned in the probanza was undoubtedly Itzamkanac. It may be noted, however, that the statements that Cuauhtemoc was beheaded finds some confirmation in a sixteenth-century Mexican picture manuscript, the Mapa de Tepechpan, which, as Morley has pointed out, "portrays the *headless* body of Quauhtemoc *hanging* by his feet."[67]

[66] The Text account is obviously in error on this point, for Cuauhtemoc had been baptized soon after the fall of Tenochtitlan.

[67] Morley, 1937–38, 1: 15. Pérez Martínez (1945, pp. 283–86) gives a lengthy discussion of

It is unlikely that we shall ever know the entire truth about this incident. Although the testimony of the accused lords and of the person or persons who denounced them is said to have been taken down in writing, this document has not been found. The evidence recorded in the available sources, most of them secondhand, is fragmentary and conflicting. Cortés and Bernal Díaz, authors of the only eyewitness accounts, disagree concerning the identity of the informers and the extent of Cuauhtemoc's complicity and guilt. The secondhand accounts also record conflicting data concerning the informers,[68] the character and intent of the chieftains' conversations, the scene of the executions, the number of persons executed, and the manner in which they were put to death.

It is reasonable to assume that during the long march from Espíritu Santo to Acalan the Mexican lords had talked about their unhappy lot and their grievances against the Spaniards. Moreover, it was only natural that they should dream of regaining their lands and authority, and they may well have discussed how they might achieve this end. They could not fail to observe the increasing weariness and discontent among Cortés' soldiers, and it would not be surprising if they had considered the possibility of an attack on the army at some opportune time. A favorable moment, as Ixtlilxochitl points out, would have been at the great estero where the famous bridge was built, but Cortés leaves no doubt as to their loyalty on that occasion. On the other hand, if they were actually contemplating revolt, they may have reasoned that it would be better to wait until they reached Acalan and to seek the aid of Paxbolonacha. Torquemada and Ixtlilxochitl admit that the chieftains had discussed their situation and had made remarks that could easily be misjudged. The question is whether they had any plan to translate this talk into action. In view of the unsatisfactory character of the available evidence, we find it difficult to believe that their intentions were actually treasonable.

---

the question concerning the manner of Cuauhtemoc's execution. He notes that most of the available sources state that the Aztec was hanged, and consequently rejects the evidence of the Mapa de Tepechpan and the Chontal Text that he was beheaded. In his discussion of the alleged plot of Cuauhtemoc and the other lords, Pérez Martínez (*ibid.*, pp. 245–56) skillfully weaves together the traditional sources (Fifth Letter, Díaz del Castillo, Torquemada, Alva Ixtlilxochitl) and the Text version. He also makes some use of another source entitled "Unos annales de la Nación Mexicana," Mexican MSS. 22 and 22 bis, Bibliothèque Nationale, Paris, which has been translated into German by Ernst Mengin and published in Baessler-Archiv, vol. 23, parts 3–4 (Berlin, 1939–40). We have not been able to consult this item, but it would appear to add little to the other sources.

[68] A probanza of the grandson of Doña Marina, the famous interpreter, claims that she was the person who denounced the Mexican lords (Cuevas, 1915, p. 291). This probably means that she translated the statements of the actual informer. Pérez Martínez (1945, pp. 252–53) gives an account, apparently based on the manuscript entitled "Unos annales," etc. (see preceding note) of how Mexicalcingo reported the plot to Doña Marina, who in turn informed Cortés.

In a letter to the king in 1527, Luis de Cárdenas asserted that Cortés killed Cuauhtemoc and Tetlepanquetzal because they had refused to disclose where they had hidden their treasure.[69] But Cárdenas was an enemy of Cortés, and we may discount his accusations. Torquemada states the opinion that Cortés had found that holding Cuauhtemoc a virtual prisoner had become a heavy responsibility and that he did not wish to be burdened with him any longer. As we have noted above, Ixtlilxochitl also argues that the commander took advantage of the situation in order to get rid of the "natural lords" of the country. So long as Cuauhtemoc and his associates lived they might become the rallying points of a native insurrection, and there is evidence that the Spaniards were uneasy about the general security of the country.[70] That Cortés shared this uneasiness is indicated by the statement in the Fifth Letter that he had held Cuauhtemoc a prisoner since the fall of Tenochtitlan, "as I believed him to be a turbulent person, and whom I had brought with me on this journey together with all the other chiefs whom I thought to be the cause of all insecurity and revolt in this country."[71] He may have considered therefore that in order to ensure the permanence of his conquests and the success of the Honduras expedition it was necessary to rid himself of these native leaders. Another possible explanation is that Cortés was not sure of the loyalty of Paxbolonacha and the other Acalan caciques, since the former had adopted a rather equivocal attitude at first and the lesser caciques had shown no great willingness to cooperate in the requisitioning of supplies. Under these circumstances he may have decided upon a spectacular display of his power in order to frighten them into complete subservience.

But none of these explanations is entirely satisfactory. Moreover, no reader of the Fifth Letter can fail to be impressed by the fact that when Cortés found himself in dire straits at the great estero (Río San Pedro Mártir), with his own men openly critical of his leadership, he turned to the native chieftains for help, promising them a "handsome reward" if they would put their followers to work and finish the bridge. A short time later Cuauhtemoc, Tetlepanquetzal,

[69] Relación hecha por Luis de Cárdenas . . . , Sevilla, 30 de agosto, 1527, AGI, Patronato, leg. 16, núm. 2, ramo 6.

[70] At this time few of Cortés' veterans remained in Tenochtitlan. Some had gone to Honduras with Olid and Francisco de las Casas, others to Guatemala with Alvarado, and Cortés had taken many with him on the overland journey to the east coast. López de Gómara (1943, 2: 143-45) states that the Spaniards in the city were uneasy, telling how they began to go about armed because they heard the Indians making more noise than usual at night. Wagner (1944, p. 444) calls attention to Motolinía's statement that Cortés left only 50 horse and 100 foot soldiers to defend Tenochtitlan, and that the Indians were ready to rise whenever they should hear that Cortés had been killed. Wagner expresses the opinion, however, that Motolinía, being a newcomer, was "unduly nervous over the great disproportion between the numbers of Spaniards and Indians and was quite ready to believe such a story."

[71] Cortés, 1916, p. 372.

and possibly others were put to death. Unless Cortés had discovered some new, impelling reason to mistrust the Mexican leaders, his action can be characterized only as the grossest form of ingratitude. Bernal Díaz considered the execution unjust, and he suggests that Cortés soon regretted it. Most writers, colonial and modern, regard the incident a stain on the conqueror's character. The most that can be said in justification of it is that a combination of factors —a certain lack of confidence in the native lords, the stress of hardships recently endured, the discontent among his own soldiers, the equivocal attitude of Paxbolonacha, and preoccupation with the long march ahead—caused Cortés to act with undue haste without giving the accused men a proper trial.

Cortés did not tarry long in Acalan after this famous episode was enacted. According to the available evidence, the executions occurred on Tuesday, February 28, 1525.[72] On the following Sunday, March 5, the army left Itzamkanac on its march to the Cehache country and beyond. Cortés' plans may already have been well advanced before the chieftains were put to death. The short interval between the executions and the departure from Itzamkanac suggests, however, that the situation in Acalan had become tense and that Cortés deemed it wise to resume the march without delay. (See Appendix B for a discussion of the march as far as Tayasal.)

The coming of the Spaniards under Cortés marks a turning point in the history of Acalan, for although the province was not subjected to permanent occupation then or later, Cortés' visit was the first of a series of events by which the region was eventually brought within the orbit of Spanish colonial administration. Moreover, the arrival of the Spaniards in 1525, regardless of its immediate consequences, was certain to make a profound impression on the Acalan people. Prior to this time a few merchants may have had personal contacts with the Spaniards in Tabasco or on the Caribbean coasts, but most of the natives had known about the invaders only by report. Now they had seen them face to face. They had seen their horses and their exotic weapons; they had learned what it meant to provision a large and hungry force of soldiers and auxiliaries; they had seen their idols cast down from the temple sanctuaries; and they had witnessed the summary execution of Cuauhtemoc, lord of the proud and warlike Aztec. All this must have caused great searching of heart.

The equivocal conduct of Paxbolonacha during these fateful days does not inspire admiration, and if he had any part in the sordid drama that culminated in Cuauhtemoc's death, he deserves severe condemnation. It is only just to note, however, that the arrival of Cortés had created a situation the like of

[72] Cf. note 61, p. 112, *supra*.

which the ruler and his advisers had never faced before. To what extent Pax-bolonacha was influenced by the native prophecies about the coming of foreign invaders, it is impossible to say. Certainly the success already achieved by the Spaniards had more than justified the prognostications of the "ancient philosophers" of the Indians. In any case, he had long since learned of the crushing defeat of the Aztec, and now the commander who had destroyed their power had arrived in Acalan. In Cortés he saw the symbol of Spanish military prowess, and in Cuauhtemoc, the unhappy example of a defeated chieftain carried along as the virtual prisoner of his conqueror. Paxbolonacha's vacillating attitude reflects his anxiety and uncertainty at this critical moment. And when Cuauhtemoc was put to death in the ruler's own city, anxiety turned into fear. Gómara states that Paxbolonacha was terrified by this event, perhaps as Cortés had hoped, and that he hastened to give evidence of his loyalty and obedience, even burning many of his idols in the presence of the Spaniards.[73]

It is interesting to speculate what would have happened if Paxbolonacha had joined forces with the Mexicans in an attack on the Spaniards. In the Acalan towns Cortés occupied temple structures or other important buildings which provided a means of defense. If the Indians had laid siege to these places, the Spaniards could probably have cut their way out, if necessary, as they had done in Mexico on the Noche Triste. Moreover, the Chontal, who would have constituted the larger part of any attacking force, lacked experience in combat with opponents who had the advantage of sword, crossbow, and firearms. With skillful leadership, such as Cortés would have provided, the Spaniards might easily have crushed any revolt, inflicting heavy losses on the natives. But in case they suffered many casualties and were forced to retreat, where would they have gone to lick their wounds and recuperate? There were no Tlaxcalan allies in the Acalan country to succor them. Their only alternative would have been to withdraw to the Gulf coast, subject to attack as they struggled through bush, forest, and swamp. On the coast there would have been no loyal garrison to come to their aid, no ships in which to escape as a last resort. Under such circumstances Cortés' position would have been extremely precarious, and it is possible that his entire force would have been wiped out.

But Spain could not have permitted such a defeat to go unchallenged, and sooner or later a punitive expedition in force would have been sent to avenge it. In this new crisis the only hope of the native leaders would have been united

[73] López de Gómara, 1943, 2: 143–45.

action. There is no reason to believe, however, that any confederacy hastily arranged in Acalan would have been lasting. The internal discord and the spirit of local independence which had facilitated the conquest of Mexico were too deeply rooted to be overcome so quickly. Moreover, if the Spaniards attacked first in Acalan, in order to take vengeance in the land of Cortés' defeat, it is difficult to see how the chieftains in Mexico proper could have come to the defense of the country in time to provide much help. A campaign in force against Acalan would probably have resulted in the ravaging of the country, great loss of life, and the scattering of the surviving population.

Although Paxbolonacha's conduct may not have been courageous, it was realistic and sensible. His principal aim was to get rid of the Spaniards as quickly as possible and with the least trouble. At first he tried to divert the army from the major Acalan towns, but when this manoeuvre failed, he wisely offered to supply Cortés' needs and to facilitate his preparations for the next stage of the journey. In this way he avoided conflict with the Spaniards, who departed after a relatively short stay in the province. Cortés was not prepared at this time to occupy any of the lands through which he passed en route to the east coast. He was content to receive Paxbolonacha's promise of allegiance, leaving enforcement to a later time or to other Spaniards who might visit Acalan in future.

It was inevitable, however, that Cortés' visit should have created a certain amount of unrest and discontent among the Acalan people. They had seen their towns stripped of food, and they had been subjected to heavy demands for labor. Oviedo states that when the Spaniards left Acalan they impressed 600 Indians into service as carriers, none of whom returned.[74] Most of these carriers were probably slaves of the principal men and lesser caciques, and the loss of such valuable property was bound to create resentment among this group, which exerted a powerful influence in local affairs. The Maldonado-Paxbolon probanza records that the ruler's subservient attitude caused fear that the Spaniards would soon return and take possession of the land, and that many of the natives sought refuge in outlying areas. It is probably true that a large number withdrew into the forests during the Spaniards' stay in Acalan, but we doubt that many permanently abandoned their old settlements. A more significant development is recorded in the Chontal Text. Here we read that "a year after the Spaniards and the Capitán del Valle [Cortés] were in Acalan, Paxbolonacha, ruler, went to another pueblo which is called Tachakam, where he died." This laconic statement suggests that the ruler had

[74] Oviedo y Valdés, 1851–55, bk. 32, ch. 5.

abdicated and had left his capital city to reside in one of the lesser towns of the province.[75]

But the unrest which may have prompted this move was not of such serious character as to endanger the position of the entire ruling family. Paxbolonacha was succeeded by Pachimalahix, eldest of his three sons, and in later years the second and third sons also became rulers of Acalan. Further evidence that the discontent caused by Cortés' visit was not of serious proportions is provided by the fact that when Avila arrived in 1530 the ruler and lesser chieftains offered no resistance, reaffirmed allegiance to the Crown, and submitted to tribute. The coming of Cortés had paved the way for the establishment of permanent Spanish dominion in Acalan.

[75] The abdication of Paxbolonacha evidently occurred in 1526. The Chontal Text dates the coming of the second Spanish expedition three years after the ruler's death. Avila came in 1530, so it appears that Paxbolonacha lived for a year after his abdication and died in 1527.

6

Developments in Yucatan, Tabasco, and Acalan, 1526-1550

ALTHOUGH THE Cortés expedition remained in Acalan only a short time, the land and its people had made a lasting impression on the Spanish commander and his soldiers. In the Fifth Letter, written in 1526 after his return to Mexico City, Cortés describes the province as a very important place (*muy gran cosa*) with many towns and a numerous population, and in more than one passage he comments on the plentiful food supply and the far-flung commerce of the Acalan merchants. Cortés' companions also brought back favorable reports of the wealth and resources of the region. These accounts, as related to Francisco de Montejo, Adelantado of Yucatan, were the prime cause of the second Spanish expedition to Acalan.

In 1526 Montejo, a former associate of Cortés, obtained a royal contract, or *capitulación*, for the conquest and colonization of Yucatan, and the following year he sailed from Spain with a large force to undertake the occupation of the peninsula. Landing on the east coast, where he established bases near Xelha and at Pole, Montejo made an unsuccessful entrada through the northeastern part of the peninsula. Owing to the inhospitable character of the country, the hostility of the Maya in certain areas, and the prevalence of disease, which carried off many of his soldiers, he was finally obliged to return to his east coast bases. The Adelantado now turned his attention to the regions to the southward. With part of his force he sailed along the coast, first to Chetumal and thence to the Ulua River in Honduras. Alonso de Avila, his second in command, marched overland toward Chetumal but turned back before reaching his objective. Although the voyage to Honduras also produced no immediate results, it gave Montejo an opportunity to obtain some knowledge of the resources, commerce, and general ethnography of the coastal areas as far as the Ulua River country, on the basis of which he formed the idea that these southern districts properly formed part of his government of Yucatan. Soon after his return from Honduras Montejo decided to go to New Spain for supplies and reinforcements, leaving Avila in command at Xamanha, where a new base had been established.[1]

[1] Molina Solís, 1896, pp. 368-410; Chamberlain, 1936, pp. 93-133, 192-96, 199-201.

During the campaign in northeastern Yucatan the Spaniards had been handicapped by the lack of a good harbor. The Chetumal district, visited on the voyage to Honduras, seemed to offer better port facilities, and it was Montejo's intention when he arrived in New Spain in the autumn of 1528 to return to that area and to occupy the town of Chetumal as a base of operations for his next campaign. His preparations were well advanced when various factors caused him to make a radical change of plan.

In New Spain the Adelantado was reunited with his natural son, Francisco de Montejo the Younger, who had accompanied Cortés on the journey to· Honduras in 1524–25. From him and other veterans of that epic march he received reports about the vast interior region through which they had passed. These reports supplemented his own knowledge of Tabasco gained as a member of the Grijalva and Cortés expeditions of 1518–19, and he now learned about the province of Acalan, its general location, and the extensive trade carried on by the Acalan merchants with Tabasco and the Caribbean coast. On the basis of these accounts and his own recent activities in the Caribbean area, he now came to regard the *adelantamiento* of Yucatan, the limits of which had not been fixed by the contract of 1526, as comprising the entire region from western Tabasco to the Ulua River in Honduras, which he considered a geographic, economic, and ethnographic unit. The province of Tabasco occupied a key position within this larger area. With its many rivers and harbors and ease of communication with New Spain, Tabasco would provide a better base of operations for the conquest of northern Yucatan, Acalan, and adjacent areas than would the Chetumal district. Moreover, if Montejo could obtain control over the province of Tabasco, he would have taken the first step in the realization of his expanding territorial ambitions.

In 1525 Juan de Vallecillo, apparently acting on instructions from Cortés, founded the Villa de Tabasco (Santa María de la Victoria) on the left bank of the Grijalva River a short distance from its mouth. From the beginning the colony maintained a very precarious existence because of determined native resistance and the inhospitable climate. In 1527 Baltasar de Osorio, named to succeed Vallecillo as commander of the province, brought reinforcements from New Spain, but he was unable to make much progress in the reduction of the Indians. Toward the end of 1528 the colonists, torn by dissension and discontent and threatening to abandon the area unless prompt aid was forthcoming, appealed to the authoritities of New Spain for help.[2]

This turn of events was Montejo's opportunity. He petitioned Nuño de

2 Probanza concerning the province of Tabasco, 1530, *in* Montejo *v.* Alvarado; RY, 1: 361–62.

Guzmán and other members of the first audiencia, recently arrived in New Spain, to incorporate the province of Tabasco with Yucatan, stressing the advantages of such a move as a means of advancing the larger projects he had in mind. Guzmán and his associates had no authority to decide the territorial question involved, but prompted by the urgent necessity of the Tabasco situation they appointed him *alcalde mayor* of the province to succeed Osorio.[3] This action did not constitute formal governmental union of Yucatan and Tabasco, since Montejo would hold office as governor of Yucatan and alcalde mayor of Tabasco by virtue of separate appointments emanating from the Crown and one of its subordinate agencies. It provided, however, a temporary personal union of the two areas pending an appeal to the crown for formal incorporation of Tabasco as part of Yucatan. It also enabled the Adelantado to initiate the scheme of action by which he hoped to promote his territorial pretensions. The first step would be to complete the subjugation of Tabasco as a base from which future military operations could be conducted. The second step envisaged by Montejo was the occupation of Acalan. On the basis of the information received from Cortés' veterans he had apparently concluded that Acalan was a rich, populous region centrally located within his government of Yucatan.[4] He believed therefore that it could serve as an advance center for the conquest and colonization of the peninsula.[5]

In the spring of 1529 Montejo the Younger was sent to Tabasco with three ships carrying supplies and recruits, and shortly thereafter the Adelantado proceeded overland with horsemen and a herd of livestock. Upon arrival in Santa María he dispatched two of the ships to Yucatan to evacuate the soldiers who had been left there under command of Alonso de Avila and bring them to Tabasco. The situation in Tabasco had deteriorated to such an extent that with the exception of the area in the immediate vicinity of Santa María the entire province was in revolt. While waiting for the arrival of Avila's soldiers, the Adelantado undertook the pacification of the coastal areas, reducing the

[3] Montejo to the Crown, Veracruz, April 20, 1529, *in* Colección de documentos inéditos relativos al descubrimiento, conquista y colonización de las posesiones españolas en América y Oceanía (cited hereinafter as DII), 13: 86–91; Oviedo y Valdés, 1851–55, bk. 32, ch. 3.

[4] Oviedo y Valdés (1851–55, bk. 32, ch. 3) relates that Montejo met Cortés in New Spain and that the latter told him that when he went to Honduras in 1524–25 "avia passado por una hermosa cibdad que está en la gobernaçion del mesmo adelantado é tierra de Yucatan, que se diçe Acalan, rica é apropóssito suyo, é loósela en tanta manera que le hiço mudar de propóssito." Since we know that Cortés was not in New Spain at this time, Oviedo's statement undoubtedly refers to the reports given Montejo by Cortés' veterans. In any case, it gives indication of the Adelantado's ideas concerning Acalan and the influence of these ideas in the formation of his new plans.

[5] Chamberlain (1936, pp. 135–40) describes Montejo's plans, his territorial aspirations, and the jurisdictional status of Tabasco resulting from the Adelantado's appointment as alcalde mayor.

districts of Copilco, Gueyatasta, and Xicalango to obedience. When the ships arrived from Yucatan he organized a large force, with Avila as his lieutenant, to effect the subjugation of the interior. The district of the three Cimatans was pacified, temporarily at least, and from there Montejo and Avila moved southward into the highland areas occupied by the Zoque.[6]

When the Adelantado reached Teapa toward the end of 1529, he learned that another force coming from the south had arrived at the nearby settlement of Ixtapangoya. This group was commanded by Juan Enríquez de Guzmán, who had been sent by the authorities of New Spain to take charge of the province of Chiapas. Moving north from San Cristóbal, Enríquez had been engaged in operations similar in character to those of Montejo in central and southern Tabasco. The two commanders held a friendly meeting, agreed upon their respective spheres of influence in the Zoque country, and made arrangements for mutual aid.

Learning Montejo's plan to occupy Acalan, Enríquez not only offered any necessary assistance but also suggested that the Adelantado's force should proceed to San Cristóbal and march overland from there to Acalan. Ill health prevented the Adelantado from accompanying the expedition any farther, so he placed Avila in command of most of his men and returned with a few soldiers to Santa María de la Victoria. Avila now marched to San Cristóbal, where Enríquez, who had preceded him, generously supplied him with horses, arms, and cotton armor, and also arranged for Indian guides to lead his force part of the way from Chiapas. After a period of rest, Avila set out for Acalan in the early spring of 1530.[7]

After an arduous march across rugged, forested country, during which he visited certain lake towns in eastern Chiapas, Avila finally reached the town of Tanoche, or Tenosique, on the Usumacinta River. The town was deserted, because of raids by Spaniards from the Grijalva area, but Avila was able to capture a few natives, who guided him to the road Cortés had taken from Ciuatecpan five years earlier. The rainy season had now started, and the Spaniards found the estero where Cortés had crossed the Río San Pedro Mártir swollen to the size of "a very large lagoon" 2 leagues wide. All that remained of Cortés' bridge was some forked poles submerged in the water. Although Avila started to build another bridge, lack of the necessary laborers and the heavy rains made the task impossible. So he now decided to return to Tanoche, where he remained, so Oviedo says, four months until the rains abated. Canoes

---

[6] Probanzas concerning the province of Tabasco, 1530 and 1533, *in* Montejo *v.* Alvarado; Oviedo y Valdés, 1851–55, bk. 32, ch. 4.

[7] Oviedo y Valdés, 1851–55, bk. 32, ch. 4.

were then sent to the lagoon, evidently by way of the Usumacinta and lower San Pedro Mártir, by means of which a crossing was finally made.[8]

We now know that Avila reached Acalan prior to August 1, 1530, since we have an encomienda grant made at Salamanca de Acalan on that date. It is evident therefore that the expedition did not remain in Tanoche until the end of the rainy season. We infer that Avila returned to Tanoche to obtain supplies and to arrange for the canoes to be sent to the point of crossing on the lagoon, or Río San Pedro Mártir.[9]

After the crossing had been made, the expedition again picked up Cortés' trail. It appears, however, that Avila actually followed a route somewhat farther inland, north and west of the San Pedro branch of the Candelaria, since the Luján-Oviedo narrative contains no reference to the towns of Tizatepelt and Teutiercas visited by Cortés and records that the first Acalan settlements reached by Avila were some small villages only 3 leagues from Itzamkanac. From here the commander sent some Indians ahead to the capital to give notice of his coming and to tell the inhabitants to remain in the city, since he would do them no harm. Despite this appeal, the ruler and inhabitants hastily withdrew from the city to await further developments. Upon receipt of this news Avila immediately proceeded to Itzamkanac and set up camp there.

The following day several principal men came in the name of the ruler "to state that he wished to come as a friend to see the lieutenant Alonso Dávila, and [the latter] replied that certainly he and all the Indians might come back without misgivings. And so he came with some four hundred men, bringing a large quantity of fowl and provisions, all of which was presented to the lieutenant Alonso Dávila." The ruler here mentioned was Pachimalahix II, eldest son and successor of Paxbolonacha.

Although the ruler's attitude seems to have been friendly enough, the Spanish commander, who had a smaller force than Cortés, apparently decided to take no chances. "He immediately had the cacique and the other principal men who came with him put in chains in order to get information from him and them, and not with the intention of doing them any harm. He took them aside with the interpreter, and they informed him at once about the land and all the towns of the district. The lieutenant founded a villa there in the same [town of] Acalan, or capital, and called it Salamanca; and he divided the surrounding country and Indians [in encomienda] so that they might give service, and within six days all came peacefully to serve those Christian masters into whose charge they were given. And the cacique and the others were re-

[8] *Ibid.*, bk. 32, chs. 4, 5.
[9] Cf. Appendix B, p. 465.

leased, [having been] very well treated by the Spaniards." In this way Avila took steps to carry out Montejo's plans for the occupation of Acalan as an advance base of operations and also made sure of the ruler's loyalty and allegiance.[10]

Within a short time, however, he became convinced that the province was not suited for the purpose that Montejo had in mind. It was apparent that Acalan was isolated in relation to other major centers of population. By personal experience he had learned that an interior overland line of communications was not practicable, and reconnaissance of the province had undoubtedly revealed the existence of the rapids and falls on the Río de Acalan, or Candelaria, which would impede direct communication between the Gulf coast and the major Acalan settlements. Moreover, the Acalan population evidently was not so numerous as Montejo had been led to believe; at least, Avila did not consider it large enough to support a permanent Spanish colony of any size. And Oviedo significantly adds that the Indians had no gold to give the Spaniards, "nor any other thing except food." So within six weeks the commander disestablished the newly founded Villa de Salamanca de Acalan "and took the road for another province [the Cehache] which is thirty leagues from there."[11]

Accompanied by the ruler and other Indians of Acalan, Avila marched in a northeasterly direction through swampy country and came to the large moated town of Mazatlan (the Mexican name for the entire Cehache area) probably located somewhere in the general region of Mocu and Cilvituk. This town was deserted when the Spaniards arrived. Oviedo also relates that a few Cehache who were seized in the neighboring country refused, even under torture, to give information about their lands and people. From the probanza on Acalan and Mazatlan formulated by Montejo in 1531 we learn, however, that Avila established contact with some of the Cehache caciques and also made encomienda grants in this area to some of his soldiers. But the region, which Oviedo describes as poor and sparsely populated, was even less suited than Acalan to serve as a base of operations, and the chronicler's narrative clearly implies that the Cehache offered greater resistance than their Acalan neighbors. Consequently the expedition again moved on and eventually reached Champoton on the Gulf coast.[12]

[10] Oviedo y Valdés, 1851–55, bk. 32, ch. 5. The Chontal Text gives a similar account of the arrest of Pachimalahix during an expedition by Francisco Gil, Lorenzo de Godoy, and Julián Doncel, but the Text obviously confuses this expedition with that of Avila.
[11] Ibid.
[12] Ibid.; Montejo v. Alvarado.

Thus Montejo's scheme to make Acalan an advance center of conquest and colonization had come to naught. And in the meantime the Adelantado had also suffered a serious setback in Tabasco. Here he had become involved in controversy with his predecessor, Baltasar de Osorio, who brought action before the Audiencia of New Spain to regain his post as commander of Tabasco. This manoeuvre was successful, and the Adelantado was removed from office, probably in the summer of 1530. Osorio now set about to humiliate his rival, casting him into jail with little cause. Although the Adelantado was soon released, his future now seemed very uncertain, since he had lost control over the Tabasco area which he considered so essential to the realization of his plans. With his son, Montejo the Younger, and the few men still in his service, he withdrew to Xicalango, which he held in encomienda, to await further developments.

Sometime in 1530 the Adelantado established friendly relations with the natives of Champoton, and when he received news of Avila's arrival on the Gulf coast he immediately made plans to transfer his headquarters to Yucatan. The arrival of fresh reinforcements and supplies brought from the West Indies by Juan de Lerma, a loyal aide of the Adelantado in these early years, also raised new hopes. Early in 1531 the Adelantado moved to Champoton, where he joined forces with Avila, and shortly thereafter he occupied Campeche, which now became the chief base of operations for another attempt to conquer Yucatan.[13]

In the summer of 1531 Montejo sent Avila with fifty men to explore and pacify the Maya provinces in the central and eastern parts of the peninsula. The lieutenant carried on a long and difficult campaign in the cacicazgos of Cochuah and Uaymil-Chetumal, but at the end of a year native hostility and the gradual depletion of his force caused him to abandon these areas. In the autumn of 1532 the expedition set out in canoes along the eastern coasts and after a hazardous voyage finally reached Puerto Caballos. From here Avila entered the Ulua River country and eventually moved on to Trujillo in Honduras proper. In the spring of 1533 he returned by ship to Campeche.[14]

Although this expedition achieved no permanent conquests, it had other results of considerable significance. It had given Avila extensive knowledge of the ethnography and linguistic affiliations of a large area reaching from central and southeastern Yucatan to the province of Higueras on the Caribbean coast.[15] He had also received a favorable impression of the resources of the

[13] Molina Solís, 1896, pp. 442–45; Chamberlain, 1936, pp. 152–60.
[14] For Avila's report of this expedition, see DII, 14: 97–128.
[15] In June 1533, after Avila's return from Honduras, Montejo formulated a probanza to

Ulua River country, and he had apparently formed a tentative scheme, which he was unable to carry through, to occupy Puerto Caballos as a center of colonization in this region. Avila's report not only strengthened Montejo's idea that the southeastern areas as far as the Ulua River logically formed part of his adelantamiento, but also caused him to continue plans already being made in Campeche for an expedition to Puerto Caballos. Finally, during his stay in Trujillo, Avila obtained information concerning the chaotic condition of Honduras proper, and he may have encouraged an appeal made at this time by some of the colonists for Montejo to assume the governorship of that province.

During Avila's absence the Adelantado had extended control over the Ah Canul area north of Campeche. An expedition under command of Montejo the Younger was also sent by sea to the north coast of the peninsula, from which it moved inland through the districts of Ceh Pech and Ah Kin Chel. Having made alliance with the rulers of these provinces, Montejo the Younger advanced into the Cupul lands and established the municipality of Ciudad Real at Chichen Itza. Although the Cupul lords at first opposed this intrusion into their territory, the cacique of Chichen Itza and others now gave nominal allegiance. The commander also succeeded in obtaining promises of obedience from the Xiu chieftains and possibly also from the lords of Hocaba and Tazes. By the end of 1532 a considerable part of northern Yucatan had apparently accepted Spanish suzerainty, and the Adelantado had cause to believe that at last he had achieved a notable success. The time also seemed ripe to seek royal approval of his larger projects.[16]

In a letter to the king, dated April 20, 1529, Montejo had already outlined his territorial aspirations and had requested jurisdiction over an area extending from western Tabasco to the Caribbean coast. This dispatch was prompted in part by reports that Pedro de Alvarado, governor of Guatemala, had been

substantiate the following major point: "that from this said Villa de Salamanca, which is at the port of Campeche, to the Ulua River it is all one language and one commercial area, and that the Indians of this pueblo of Campeche and of all this land maintain houses in the said Ulua River for their trading operations, for there is the boundary of these provinces and from the River of Copilco-çaqualco to there is all one language, which are the limits of these said provinces." On this point Avila testified that the Yucatecan Maya interpreter whom he took along on the expedition of 1531–33 talked to the Indians along the east coast as far as the Ulua River and was able to understand them, although their languages differed in some ways. He also stated "that from the pueblo of Campeche and the provinces of Guaymyll and Tutuxio and Cochuah all trade in cacao and [other] merchandise in the said Ulua River, and he also learned that the said Indians of the said provinces maintain houses there where they trade with the said Indians of Ulua; and he learned and they told him that all the trade of this land is in the said [Ulua] River." Sobre lo del Río de Ulua, 1533, *in* Montejo v. Alvarado.

16 Avila's expedition of 1531–33 and its results and the campaigns of the Adelantado and Montejo the Younger in northern Yucatan are described at length by Chamberlain, 1936, pp. 162–200. Cf. also Molina Solís, 1896, pp. 446–88.

granted authority over certain districts, including Acalan, which the Adelantado considered part of his own government.[17] Between 1530 and 1533 Montejo or his agents also formulated a series of five probanzas to substantiate his claims to Tabasco and Acalan and to prove that the entire region from the Copilco River (Río Tortuguero?) on the west to the Ulua River on the east constituted a linguistic, economic, and geographic unit. For the present study the most important is one which deals with Acalan and Mazatlan.[18]

The Acalan-Mazatlan probanza, drawn up in Campeche in September 1531, recorded certain facts pertaining to or revealed by the Avila expedition of the preceding year. Avila was absent at this time, having already set out on his journey across the Yucatan Peninsula, but twelve of his soldiers who had accompanied him on the entrada of 1530 gave testimony. The major points set forth in this probanza were: (1) that Avila, acting as Montejo's lieutenant, had "conquered and pacified" the provinces of Acalan and Mazatlan and had granted encomiendas to his soldiers in these areas; (2) that Acalan and Mazatlan were close to the Gulf of Mexico and centrally located within the province of Yucatan; (3) that there were no settlements between the province of Acalan and the Gulf coast; and (4) that the Indians of Acalan carried on extensive trade with the coast towns of Tabasco and made the journey down the Río de Acalan (Candelaria) and thence to Xicalango in three days' time. In short, it was the purpose of this document to establish once and for all Montejo's claim to Acalan and Mazatlan as part of the government of Yucatan.

One copy of this probanza contains a supplementary statement dated at Campeche on June 1, 1533. Here we read that four or five months after the probanza was formulated, i.e., early in 1532, the Adelantado sent a Spaniard with the chieftains of one of the Yucatan pueblos to summon the lords of Acalan to appear before him. These messengers made the journey to Acalan by canoe and visited Itzamkanac and other towns of the province. Upon their return they brought with them "certain lords and principal men and Indians said to be from the aforesaid province of Acalan." "These Indians brought their tribute, and the said governor [Montejo] received them and ordered them to bring their tributes from that time on. They went away, and up to the present time [i.e., June 1533] they have always given service in this villa [of Campeche] and have brought their tributes here, as the said governor ordered." Thus we see that Montejo, not content with assembling evidence that Acalan formed part of the government of Yucatan, had also taken practical measures to affirm his jurisdiction and control over that region.

[17] Montejo to the Crown, Veracruz, April 20, 1529, *in* DII, 13: 86–91.
[18] These probanzas comprise the expediente frequently cited as Montejo *v.* Alvarado.

In the summer of 1533 Alonso López, brother-in-law of Montejo, was sent to Spain to serve at court as agent of the Adelantado and the colonists of Yucatan. In a petition to the Council of the Indies he set forth in some detail the Adelantado's governmental and territorial pretensions, in support of which he submitted the above-mentioned probanzas and other supplementary documents. This petition made a number of specific requests, of which the most important are stated in the following items.

1. It was requested that the limits of Montejo's government of Yucatan should be defined as the area extending "from the Ulua River, which is in the region of Higueras, to the River of Copilco-çaqualco, which is between Guaçaqualco and the Grijalva [River], since from the Ulua River to the River of Copilco-çaqualco it is all one language, and they all trade with one another and consider themselves to be the same, and all the Indians of those parts say that those are their boundaries. . . ." Although this statement of the linguistic situation was not accurate, it gives expression to the fact, which we have noted in Chapter 2, that most of the Indians within this area spoke the closely related Chontal-Chol-Chorti and Yucatecan Maya languages.

2. López asked for restoration of Montejo's authority over Tabasco, since this province was included within the Copilco-Ulua limits mentioned above and had been pacified by the Adelantado at great effort and expense prior to his removal from the office of alcalde mayor by the Audiencia of New Spain.

3. López called for recognition of Montejo's jurisdiction over Acalan and challenged Alvarado's right to authority in this region. Whereas Acalan was situated close to the Gulf coast and centrally located within the government of Yucatan, it was "very far from Guatemala." Moreover, it had now been pacified under Montejo's auspices. Alvarado had merely heard about it from Cortés' soldiers, had decided that it was a rich area, and in order to obtain jurisdiction over it had falsely claimed to have conquered it.

4. The petition also claimed Chiapas as part of the government of Yucatan and asserted that the grant of authority to Alvarado over this area (made by the Crown in 1528) violated Montejo's rights.

5. Request was made that the region of Puerto Caballos, which López represented as already occupied by Montejo, should be joined with the government of Yucatan.[19]

Although López failed to achieve all that Montejo hoped for, his mission produced very important results. On December 19, 1533, a royal cedula was issued which confirmed Montejo's rights and privileges as adelantado and governor of Yucatan proper and also named him royal governor at the will of the

19 Petition of Alonso López, Madrid, October 25, 1533, *in* Montejo v. Alvarado.

Crown over "all the lands and provinces from the River of Copilco-çaqualco inclusive to the Ulua River which is toward the east." Over this larger area he was given complete civil and criminal jurisdiction regardless of any capitulations and decrees previously granted in favor of other persons. A separate cedula issued on the same date placed Puerto Caballos under Montejo's jurisdiction and authorized him to colonize that area and the Valley of Naco.[20]

The first cedula of December 19, 1533, requires some explanation. By virtue of the royal contract of 1526 Montejo had received appointment as governor and captain general of Yucatan for life and also the title of adelantado to be handed down to his heirs and successors in perpetuity. He had evidently hoped that the Crown would define the province and adelantamiento of Yucatan as the Copilco-Ulua area, thus giving him hereditary rights as adelantado and life tenure as governor over the larger region. Instead, the first cedula of December 19, 1533, limited his privileges under the contract of 1526 to Yucatan proper, which was now roughly defined as extending from the north coast of the peninsula "to the shoals and passage (*entrada*) which is formed between two rivers which flow into the northern sea." The meaning of this passage is not clear. It probably reflects, to some extent at least, the old belief that Yucatan was an island, although the various expeditions of Montejo and Avila had demonstrated the falsity of that idea. In any case, it is evident that the Copilco-Ulua limits comprised a much more extensive area than this ill-defined province and adelantamiento of Yucatan. Over the larger region Montejo was to serve only as royal governor at the will of the crown, without the hereditary rights, life tenure, and other special privileges conferred by the contract of 1526.

But the two cedulas of 1533 constituted a major triumph for the Adelantado. Although Tabasco was not incorporated with Yucatan proper, as Montejo had hoped, the provision giving him jurisdiction as governor at will over the Copilco-Ulua area automatically restored his control over that province. Although Acalan is not specifically mentioned in the first cedula, it was also included in the Copilco-Ulua limits. It is doubtful whether it could also be regarded as comprising part of the area roughly defined as Yucatan proper, although the Adelantado always considered it part of the Yucatan jurisdiction. The second cedula of December 19, 1533, authorizing Montejo to occupy Puerto Caballos and the Valley of Naco, gave him an additional claim to districts also included within the Copilco-Ulua area. During López' negotiations with the Council an agent of Alvarado filed a counter-petition challenging the Adelantado's right to jurisdiction over Chiapas, Acalan, and

[20] AGI, México, leg. 2999, libro D-1.

Puerto Caballos,[21] but succeeded only in the case of Chiapas, which was retained as part of the government of Guatemala. As a result of the cedulas of 1533 the Adelantado had, in effect, been given authority over the entire lowland Maya area.

Alonso López returned from Spain in the latter part of 1534 only to find that Montejo had suffered a reverse of fortune in Yucatan., A revolt of the Cupul lords, in coalition with the chieftains of Sotuta, Cochuah, and Ecab, had forced Montejo the Younger early in 1534 to abandon Chichen Itza and withdraw to the Chel province on the north coast. The municipality of Ciudad Real was temporarily reestablished at the port of Dzilam, but within a short time a critical situation developed at this new center of operations. Unrest among the soldiers, disappointed by the lack of mineral wealth in Yucatan and wearied by the campaign against the Maya, rapidly increased, and the flames of discontent were fed by news of Pizarro's success in Peru and the fabulous wealth of this new conquest. Singly and in groups the soldiers began to desert in order to seek fortune in South America or elsewhere. By the summer of 1534 the position of Montejo the Younger at Dzilam had become so insecure that he decided to evacuate his depleted force and march overland to join his father at Campeche. But the situation there was no better. Continued desertions, lack of discipline among the soldiers who remained, and the failure of an appeal to the Audiencia of New Spain for aid finally forced a decision to abandon the peninsula. Toward the end of 1534 or early in 1535 the Adelantado evacuated Campeche and withdrew to Tabasco.

Thus by the time Montejo received the cedulas of 1533 he was in no position to take full advantage of the opportunities offered by these decrees. The plans for an expedition to Puerto Caballos had been suspended when the situation in Yucatan became acute. Moreover, the campaigns of 1531–34 had depleted the Adelantado's financial resources, and the colonial authorities were reluctant to provide aid for any new venture. Receipt of the cedulas of 1533 enabled Montejo, however, to resume authority over Tabasco at a time when control of the province was again essential to his projects. The grant of jurisdiction over the Copilco-Ulua area and authority to occupy Puerto Caballos also raised new hopes. So it was not long before the Adelantado began to make plans for another effort, although it is not clear whether he intended to return to Yucatan or to move first into the richer region of Puerto Caballos and the Ulua River.[22]

Whatever Montejo's plans may have been during the months following

---

[21] Petition of Fernán Ximénez, *in* Montejo *v.* Alvarado.
[22] Molina Solís, 1896, pp. 488–512; Chamberlain, 1936, pp. 194–212, *passim.*

the withdrawal from Yucatan, receipt of another royal decree, dated March 1, 1535, naming him governor of the provinces of Higueras and Honduras,[23] caused a new turn in his career. The chaotic state of Honduras proper had long demanded a remedy, and prior to 1535 the Crown had received many representations on the subject from the colonial authorities and colonists. We have also noted that when Alonso de Avila returned from Trujillo in 1533, he brought the news that a faction in Honduras desired that Montejo should assume the governorship of the province. Moreover, in the report on his expedition of 1531–33 Avila informed the Crown that some of the citizens of Trujillo had stated that the appointment of Montejo as governor of Honduras would bring them great favor. Although Alonso López' petition to the Council in the autumn of 1533 made no representations on this matter, one argument cited in support of Montejo's request for jurisdiction over Puerto Caballos was that the citizens of Honduras desired it, since the occupation of that district would have a stabilizing effect on the neighboring province. In 1534 Juan de Lerma, probably with Montejo's approval, actually proposed that Honduras should be added to the other lands under the Adelantado's authority. In view of the foregoing and also of the fact that the cedulas of 1533 had already given Montejo jurisdiction over most of Higueras, it is not surprising that the Crown should now name him royal governor of both Higueras and Honduras proper. At the time the cedula of March 1, 1535, was issued the king and Council had no knowledge of Montejo's reverse in Yucatan and undoubtedly believed that he possessed adequate resources to assume this new responsibility.

After some delay Montejo accepted the appointment and proceeded to Honduras in 1537. Two years later (1539), having pacified the greater part of Higueras, he became involved in bitter controversy with Alvarado, who claimed Honduras-Higueras as part of his own government. The latter, supported by a considerable faction of the colonists who had been antagonized by some of Montejo's policies, finally forced the Adelantado to relinquish control over these provinces in exchange for Chiapas. But in 1542, a year after Alvarado's death, Montejo was recalled to Honduras-Higueras by the local authorities, and he again served as governor, with certain interruptions, until the Audiencia of Confines (Guatemala) took office in 1544. This new administrative agency had been granted governmental powers over Honduras-Higueras and Chiapas, and these areas were now permanently removed from Montejo's jurisdiction. This development, which involved loss of control over Puerto Caballos and the Ulua River area, also restricted the Adelantado's

[23] AGI, Guatemala, leg. 402, libro T-1.

authority under the cedulas of 1533 and had the effect of limiting his jurisdiction to Tabasco and Yucatan proper. And within a few years, as we shall
see in the succeeding pages, he was also removed as governor of these
provinces.[24]

After Montejo's withdrawal from Yucatan in 1534–35, the province of
Tabasco became the center of operations from which a third and, as it turned
out, successful attempt was made to occupy the peninsula. But first it was
necessary to restore order in Tabasco, where many of the Indian towns had
rebelled against Spanish authority during the preceding years. Second, new
recruits had to be found, supplies and munitions assembled. All this took time,
and five years elapsed before Montejo the Younger, who governed Tabasco as
his father's lieutenant, was ready to move in force against the Maya. In the
meantime, however, certain events occurred which gave him an opportunity
to establish an advance base at Champoton. During the course of this operation
another Spanish expedition passed through Acalan.

In 1536 Francisco Gil, a lieutenant of Alvarado, undertook the pacification
of Tila, Pochutla, and other districts in eastern Chiapas. Finding no place
suitable for a permanent settlement, he moved on to the Río de Tanoche, or
Usumacinta, where he founded the town of San Pedro at or near Tenosique,
within the jurisdiction of Tabasco. From here he made entradas into the surrounding country. When Montejo the Younger learned of Gil's activities, he
promptly advanced up the Usumacinta with a small force to defend his
father's rights. By this time Gil's position had become precarious because of
native hostility and lack of supplies, and he readily agreed to recognize the
Adelantado's jurisdiction and to transfer authority over the settlement to
Montejo the Younger. The latter now formed the plan to move most of the
colonists of San Pedro to Champoton as a preliminary step toward final occupation of Yucatan. Lorenzo de Godoy, Gil's *maestre de campo* and *alcalde
ordinario* of San Pedro, was placed in charge of this move, and some time in
1537 he marched overland with about thirty men to Champoton.[25]

On this journey, which lasted two months, Godoy traveled through low,
forested country, crossing rivers and lagoons en route. A witness who gave
testimony in a probanza of Godoy's services made in 1562 also mentions
"Acala" in connection with this march. This could not be the region of the
Chol Acala, since the latter area was south or southeast of Tenosique, whereas

[24] Chamberlain, 1936, pp. 222–23.
[25] López de Cogolludo, 1867–68, bk. 3, ch. 2; Molina Solís, 1896, pp. 547–51; Chamberlain,
1936, pp. 223–25.

Godoy must have followed a northeasterly direction to Champoton. There can be little doubt therefore that the place mentioned by Godoy's witness was Acalan in the Candelaria drainage. The Chontal Text also mentions an expedition to Acalan in which Godoy participated, although the author of this part of the narrative evidently confused this entrada with Avila's expedition of 1530. It seems likely that Godoy followed much the same route as Cortés and Avila to Acalan. From Acalan to Champoton the route is less certain. Godoy's witness mentions the crossing of lagoons in canoes "between Acala and las Alunas," but we are unable to identify the latter place.[26]

Unfortunately the documents record no data whatever concerning Godoy's stay in Acalan. If he had encountered any serious trouble, his probanza would probably have had something to say about it. We infer therefore that his visit was uneventful, that the natives received him in peace, probably supplying him with food and guides, and that his entire stay in Acalan was short.

During the next three years (1537–40) the new settlement at Champoton maintained a very uncertain existence. Although Montejo the Younger sent his cousin, Francisco de Montejo, nephew of the Adelantado, to take charge of the base in 1538, it was not yet possible for him to provide adequate supplies and reinforcements. The natives of the region became increasingly restive, and by 1540 the colonists had become thoroughly disheartened and threatened to leave unless immediate help was sent. By this time, however, Montejo the Younger was at last in a position to carry on operations on a larger scale. Moving to Yucatan with some sixty men, he joined forces with his cousin and initiated the final conquest of the peninsula. The settlement at Champoton was removed to Campeche, where, toward the end of 1540 or early in 1541, the first permanent European town in Yucatan was established. A year later (January 6, 1542) Mérida was founded, and from here the forces of occupation, strengthened by many new recruits, moved into the northern, central, and eastern parts of the Maya country. A serious native revolt flared up in 1546, but the Montejos were now in strong enough a position to crush it, and thereafter Spanish supremacy was never seriously challenged.

In 1546 the Adelantado, having lost control over Honduras-Higueras and Chiapas and having submitted to residencia investigation of his government in these areas, returned to Yucatan to take personal charge of the provincial government. During the next three years he took effective measures to stab-

[26] Testimony of Gonzalo Tirado, Santiago de Guatemala, November 26, 1562, in Probanza of the merits and services of Lorenzo de Godoy, 1562, AGI, Guatemala, leg. 111. Data supplied by R. S. Chamberlain.

ilize local administration, promote the internal development of the colony, and foster the missionary program. These years were also characterized by prolonged dispute with local factions in Yucatan and Tabasco and with the Audiencia of Confines, which now exercised supervisory authority over these provinces. Complaints of maladministration, conflicts of jurisdiction resulting from the cedulas of 1533 and later decrees, and litigation over removal of the encomienda holdings of the Adelantado and members of his family in accordance with provisions of the New Laws of 1542 were the major sources of trouble. As the result of residencia proceedings instituted in 1548–49, the Adelantado was finally removed from office in both Tabasco and Yucatan. In 1550 he went to Spain to plead his case before the Council of the Indies and to seek restoration of authority under the terms of the contract of 1526. But his health had been undermined by long years of strenuous activity in the New World, and he died in his native city of Salamanca in 1553.[27]

The removal of Montejo from office opened the way to the establishment of royal government in Yucatan and Tabasco under the ordinary norms of colonial legislation and administration. In 1550 alcaldes mayores were appointed for both provinces, but in 1561 Tabasco was subordinated to the government of Yucatan. Four years later (1565) the chief executive in Yucatan received the title of governor, and subsequently the title of captain general with a wide measure of military authority was also conferred. In 1560 the provinces of Yucatan and Tabasco, which had been subject to the jurisdiction of the Audiencia of Confines after its creation in the 1540's, with the exception of a brief period in 1548–50, were permanently transferred to the district of the Audiencia of Mexico.[28]

The documents contain few specific references to Acalan for the period from Avila's expedition in 1530 to the end of Montejo's government two decades later. We have seen how the Adelantado took action in 1532 to reaffirm the obligation of the Indians to give service and tribute. We have also taken note of Godoy's visit during the march from Tenosique to Champoton in 1537. From time to time other Spaniards, singly or in small groups, undoubtedly entered the province to arrange for the delivery of tribute and to recruit native labor. Franciscan friars are reported to have made occasional

[27] Molina Solís, 1896, bk. 3, chs. 16–24; Chamberlain, 1936, pp. 224–25.
[28] Yucatan and Tabasco were originally subject to the jurisdiction of the Audiencia of Mexico but were transferred to the district of the Audiencia of Confines when it was established in the 1540's. The provinces were reassigned to the Mexico jurisdiction in 1548, again transferred to the Audiencia of Confines in 1550, and finally, in 1560, were permanently subjected to the Audiencia of Mexico.

trips to Acalan in the late 1540's. There is no evidence, however, that any expedition in force entered the country between 1537 and the end of the Montejo period. So far as we know the Chontal chieftains at no time made any attempt, either by passive resistance or open acts of revolt, to repudiate the promises of allegiance given in 1530 and later reaffirmed at Montejo's summons. Spanish dominion in Acalan was achieved and maintained without resort to the military campaigns that ravaged other areas.

This was probably due in part to the original impression of Spanish power received at the time of Cortés' visit in 1525 and strengthened by the firm measures of Avila five years later. We might ask, of course, how the Acalan would have reacted if any serious effort had been made to colonize the country. But the Indians never had to face such a situation. The Spaniards established dominion over Acalan as a by-product of a larger movement involving other areas that were more suitable for European settlement. Indeed, Montejo's scheme to make Acalan an advance base of operations was only a means to a more important end—the conquest of northern Yucatan and the greater adelantamiento he hoped to achieve. And when the Adelantado learned, on the basis of Avila's reports, that the province was not so rich and populous as Cortés' soldiers had led him to believe and that it was isolated from other centers of poulation, he directed his major efforts to other lands.

It is evident, however, that even after receiving Avila's reports Montejo thought it worth while to maintain control over the Acalan country. It had no gold, as Oviedo pointedly remarks, so the Spaniards had to seek for treasure elsewhere. Its population was small in comparison with northern Yucatan and could not support many encomiendas of the size often granted at the time. Nevertheless, the amount of tribute and labor levied in Acalan before the population declined must have had considerable value, which was appreciated the more as the hope of finding precious metals in Yucatan faded.

Jurisdiction over this province, centrally located between Tabasco and Yucatan, was also essential to Montejo's larger projects, if only to forestall the claims of a grasping rival like Alvarado. In retrospect it seems very doubtful that Alvarado would have made any serious attempt to occupy Acalan, at least for many years, for he had more important fish to fry in regions closer to Guatemala. Moreover, the geographical obstacles to any colonizing effort based on Alvarado's outposts in Chiapas and northern Guatemala would have been almost insuperable, since direct contact with any settlement established in Acalan could have been maintained only by way of an overland route across some of the most difficult terrain in Central America. In Montejo's time, however, when the Spanish conquerors were engaged in a wild scramble for territory, and accurate knowledge concerning distances and geographical barriers was lacking, it would have been dangerous to take chances. The prospect, immediate or remote, that Acalan might be occupied by an unfriendly rival constituted a threat which the Adelantado could not neglect. The prompt action by Montejo the Younger to assert authority over the Villa de San Pedro founded at Tenosique by Francisco Gil shows that the Montejos were on the alert to prevent infringement on the area which they regarded as their rightful sphere of action.

Montejo's interest in Acalan must also be considered in the light of his ambition for a greater adelantamiento. It is easy now to characterize his scheme as an impossible dream, to point to the fact that Tabasco, Yucatan, and Higueras are separated by great stretches of swamp and jungle and mountain. The exploits of the Spaniards in the first century of discovery and conquest show, however, that geographical obstacles were lightly regarded by men in feverish search for wealth and glory. Nor could the Adelantado know, until taught by bitter experience, that he had drawn one of the lesser prizes in the grand lottery of conquest in Middle America. The Copilco-Ulua area actually contained natural resources of great value. Even the Acalan country with its log- and dyewood and the chicle-producing zapote, has proved to be richer than Montejo supposed. But the gold and silver prized above all else by the sixteenth-century conquerors were lacking in most of the lands over which the Adelantado received jurisdiction. The agricultural possibilities of the Copilco-Ulua region, in terms of colony economy and exportable staples, were also less extensive than those of Cortés' Mexico and Alvarado's Guatemala. Geographical barriers, an inhospitable climate, and a dearth of precious metals, to say nothing of personal rivalries and interminable jurisdictional conflicts, spelt the failure of Montejo's ambition for a vast colonial state in the home of the lowland Maya. But he never gave up all hope that at some time or place he would find a reward for all his efforts. And long after his name was only a memory other venturesome Spaniards sought the pot of gold in lands he hoped to incorporate in the adelantamiento of Yucatan. Ironically enough, in modern times the extensive cultivation of sisal hemp in stony Yucatan and of bananas in the tropical lands of Higueras has made men rich beyond Montejo's dreams.

The cedula of December 19, 1533, by which the Adelantado was made royal governor of the Copilco-Ulua area, gave him unchallenged jurisdiction over Acalan and its environs. After the withdrawal from Yucatan in 1534–35 control was maintained by his agents in Tabasco, but when the peninsula was finally conquered Acalan was again administered from Yucatan. The Adelantado always considered Acalan to be part of the Yucatan jurisdiction, and so it remained, except possibly for a brief period in 1553–55, after he was removed from office.

In regard to the internal history of Acalan during the quarter-century after the coming of Cortés we know very little. We have already related that Paxbolonacha abdicated in 1526 and was succeeded by his eldest son, Pachimalahix. We do not know how long the latter lived. He was the ruler whom Avila held in chains in 1530, while arrangements were made for the founding of the town of Salamanca de Acalan and the introduction of the encomienda system. When Pachimalahix died, probably during the following decade, he left a young son named Paxua, but the succession passed to Lamatazel, brother of the deceased ruler, and the second son of Paxbolonacha. Lamatazel governed until about 1549–50. At his death he also left a son, Don Pablo Paxbolon, of whom we shall have much to tell in later chapters of this volume. But again the rulership went to a brother, Paxtun, third son of Paxbolonacha, during whose time the Acalan were converted and baptized.

This uninterrupted succession of the members of Paxbolonacha's family would seem to indicate that the internal history of the country was peaceful and undisturbed by any serious factional rivalries. Although Spaniards probably came and went oftener than we know, for many years the Acalan continued to enjoy virtual independence in the conduct of their local affairs. In the chapter that follows we shall see, however, that the conquest of Middle America and the establishment of foreign dominion over Acalan wrought great changes in this isolated region in the Candelaria drainage.

7

The Impact of the Conquest in Acalan

SUBSEQUENT TO 1530, when Alonso de Avila founded the Villa de Salamanca in Itzamkanac and then disestablished it within the short space of six weeks, no further attempt was made to occupy and colonize Acalan. The adjacent lands of Tabasco and Yucatan were not only more accessible but also offered superior attractions as areas of settlement. In these areas the Spaniards found greater opportunities for economic enterprise, more numerous native populations to serve as a source of tribute and labor, and, in the case of northern Yucatan, a more favorable climate. Moreover, although Acalan formed part of the province of Yucatan for administrative purposes, no resident Spanish official was named to direct local affairs. The native rulers enjoyed virtual autonomy, subject to the supervisory jurisdiction of the provincial authorities. It was by means of the encomienda system[1] and the missionary program, rather than by colonization and direct governmental intervention, that effective Spanish dominion was maintained in Acalan.

The first encomienda grants in Acalan were made in 1530 by Alonso de Avila in connection with the temporary establishment of the Villa de Salamanca in Itzamkanac. In making these grants Avila acted on authority from his superior officer, Montejo the Adelantado, and in accordance with the plan discussed in the preceding chapter to make Acalan an advance base of conquest and colonization. The encomenderos, or recipients of the encomienda grants, were soldiers in Avila's company, who, it may be assumed, had enrolled as citizens of the newly founded villa. A partial list of them, compiled from Montejo's Acalan-Mazatlan probanza of 1531 and other sources, follows: Alonso de Arévalo, Pedro Galiano, Blas González, Jerónimo de Alvarado, Fernando de Escobar, Pedro González, Hernán Muñoz, Gonzalo Sánchez, Cristóbal de Sotelo, and Alonso de Torres. The first three were loyal associates of the Montejos during the conquest of Yucatan and became prominent citizens of Mérida and Valladolid. We assume that Avila also made grants to Montejo and to himself.

A copy of one of these early Acalan grants has been preserved. It reads:

---

[1] For a discussion of the encomienda system by two famous colonial authors, see León Pinelo, 1630, and Solórzano Pereira, 1648, bk. 3. The best modern study is by Zavala, 1935. Cf. also Simpson, 1929; Chamberlain, 1939; and Zavala, 1940 and 1943.

Por la presente se deposita en vos, Pedro Galiano y Alonso de Arévalo, el pueblo y señores de Teçacab para que os sirváis de él en tanto que el señor adelantado hace el repartimiento general conforme a las ordenanzas que S. M. le tiene dadas. Que es hecho en esta villa de Salamanca hoy lunes, el primero de agosto de 1530 años. Alonso de Avila. Por mandado de su merced, Gonzalo Fernández de Herrera.[2]

The town of Teçacab here mentioned was undoubtedly the same as Tah-çacab included in the list of seventy-six Acalan towns in the Chontal Text. It was evidently a large town since it was assigned to two encomenderos. From the Acalan-Mazatlan probanza of 1531 we learn that Fernando de Escobar and Pedro González were assigned the towns of "Cithute" and "Estela" respectively.[3] The first was probably Çacchute, or Tizatepelt, but we are unable to identify Estela. No information is available concerning the towns assigned to the other encomenderos, nor do we know to whom Itzamkanac was granted. The capital city may have been reserved for the king as a Crown town, or Avila may have assigned it to Montejo or to himself.

The document quoted above indicates that the grants made by Avila were of temporary character, to have force until the Adelantado should make a general allotment of encomiendas (*repartimiento general*), presumably for the entire Yucatan area. There is ample evidence, however, that the encomenderos made use of them to obtain service and tribute, in accordance with general encomienda practice, during their stay in Acalan. Eight of the encomenderos listed above testified in 1531 that the towns assigned to them had given service, tribute, or both. Only one of them, however, gives any indication of the kind of tribute received, and this witness (Cristóbal de Sotelo) merely states that the Indians of his encomienda "gave him slaves and other articles of service." This reference to the giving of slaves as tribute is interesting for two reasons. First, it confirms other evidence that the Acalan merchants trafficked in slaves and that the caciques and principal men of the province owned a considerable number of bondsmen. Second, it suggests that slaves constituted the most valuable kind of property the natives had to offer as tribute. It is well known that in other areas the Spaniards often demanded slaves when the Indians lacked other items of value or could not fulfill their tribute obligation. Moreover, we again call attention to Oviedo's remark that the Acalan had no gold "nor any other thing except food" to give the Spaniards.[4] A certain amount of food and other staples of local produce would have been useful, indeed welcome, after the long march to Acalan, but Avila's men probably expected a

[2] *In* Isabel Sánchez, hija de Pedro Galiano, difunto, con Francisco Manrique, vecino de Yucatán, sobre los indios de Yobain y Tixcacal, 1557, AGI, Justicia, leg. 1012, núm. 2, ramo 3.
[3] Sobre lo de Acalan y Mazatlan, *in* Montejo v. Alvarado.
[4] Cf. p. 128, *supra*.

richer harvest of tribute in the form of treasure, such as gold, jewelry, and other luxury items. In lieu of treasure, slaves would be most acceptable, but how many of the encomenderos received tribute in this form is a matter of conjecture. In any case, it is evident that Avila and his companions were disappointed in Acalan. The place did not measure up to the stories told by Cortés' soldiers. And Avila soon realized also that the region, isolated by forest and swamp from other centers of population, was not suitable as an advance base of operations. After a stay of only forty days in Acalan he left the country and proceeded overland to Mazatlan and thence to Champoton.

For about a year and a half after Avila withdrew from Acalan the Indians apparently enjoyed temporary relief from the obligation to give tribute and labor that was inherent in the encomienda grants of 1530. But early in 1532, after Montejo had moved his forces from Tabasco to Yucatan and the early campaigns of the second phase of the conquest of the peninsula were proceeding satisfactorily, the Adelantado took action to reaffirm authority over Acalan. In the preceding chapter we have told how he summoned some of the Acalan chieftains to Campeche and made arrangements for the regular payment of tribute and service. The document recording this action is dated June 1, 1533, and it certifies that the payments had been maintained up to that time.[5]

This move was apparently one phase of a general plan to impose tribute and service in all of the government of Yucatan—to carry out the general allotment, or repartimiento, envisaged by Avila in 1530. In the spring of 1532 Montejo made grants of encomienda in northern Yucatan, and the system was extended to the various native provinces as rapidly as they were subjected to Spanish authority. This raises a question as to the status of the original Acalan grants, which, as we have seen, were of temporary character. There is reason to believe that most, if not all, of the encomenderos named by Avila in 1530 exchanged their Acalan holdings for new assignments in northern Yucatan. We have a copy of a document dated April 8, 1532, by which Montejo assigned to Pedro Galiano and Alonso de Arévalo, two of the Acalan encomenderos listed above, the town of Yobain in the cacicazgo of Ah Kin Chel and the town of Taxaman in Uaymil.[6] It is possible, of course, that Galiano and Arévalo retained their Acalan encomienda in addition to this new grant, but we doubt that such was the case. The available data concerning the enco-

[5] Certification by Antonio de Castro, notary of Villa de Salamanca de Campeche, June 1, 1533, *in* Montejo v. Álvarado. Cf. also p. 131, *supra*.

[6] Isabel Sánchez . . . con Francisco Manrique . . . , 1557, AGI, Justicia, leg. 1012, núm. 2, ramo 3.

mienda history of Acalan in the later 1530's contain no reference to these men or to any of the original encomenderos of 1530. Moreover, it seems obvious that Galiano, Arévalo, and the others would have preferred to exchange their Acalan grants for new encomiendas close at hand in northern Yucatan.

If this reasoning is correct, then the Acalan encomiendas were available for reassignment to other soldiers in Montejo's army. Whether new grants were actually made prior to 1534–35, when the Adelantado was forced to abandon Yucatan a second time, or whether the Acalan towns remained "vacant" for a time, it is impossible to say. If we assume the latter, this would have had no effect on the obligation of the Acalan to give tribute and service reaffirmed by Montejo in 1532. In the case of vacancy, the tributes would have constituted Crown revenue, although it seems likely that Montejo would have used the payments, which probably consisted to a great extent of food, to help provision his soldiers. Whatever the situation may have been, the document of June 1, 1533, mentioned above, and other sources indicate that the tribute payments were consistently maintained.

After the Spaniards withdrew from Yucatan in 1534–35 the Acalan paid tribute for several years in the Villa de Tabasco, but when the permanent occupation of the peninsula was finally achieved in the 1540's, the payments were again made in Campeche, as had been the case in the early 1530's.[7] Although the Acalan encomiendas may have been vacant for a time subsequent to 1532, new grants were evidently made as early as 1537, since the documents record that in the latter year Ginés Doncel was an encomendero of Acalan and received tribute in Tabasco.[8] The Chontal Text also mentions as encomendero a certain Palma, probably Hernando de la Palma, listed in other sources as a resident of Tabasco.[9] In the 1540's the entire Acalan area was held in encomienda by Diego de Aranda and Gonzalo López in equal shares.[10] This suggests a rapid decline of the population subsequent to 1530, when at least ten persons held encomiendas in Acalan. Further evidence of a sharp falling-off of the population will be presented in the last section of this chapter.

Diego de Aranda served in Yucatan under Montejo the Adelantado in 1533. Subsequently he held office as alcalde ordinario of the Villa de Tabasco

[7] The payments in Campeche were resumed not later than 1548, when two citizens of Campeche held a half share in the Acalan tributes. There is reason to believe, however, that the change occurred at an earlier date.

[8] García v. Bravo, passim.

[9] Fiscal v. López.

[10] The Chontal Text indicates that Aranda succeeded Palma, but it does not mention Gonzalo López. The case of García v. Bravo, however, contains references to López as encomendero of Acalan, as does the letter of Fray Lorenzo de Bienvenida to Prince Philip, February 10, 1548, in Cartas de Indias, 1877, p. 75.

in 1540 and as regidor in 1541, and in later years he appears to have resided in Yucatan.[11] Gonzalo López, a relation of Montejo's brother-in-law, Alonso López, was a prominent citizen of Mexico City, where he acted as agent of the Adelantado for several years. In 1547–48 he also served as Montejo's representative at court in Spain.[12] Although Gonzalo López held other encomiendas in New Spain and, so far as we know, never resided in Tabasco or Yucatan, Montejo gave him a half share in the encomienda of Acalan, presumably as a reward for services rendered.[13] Aranda died about 1547–48. The Chontal Text (which does not mention Gonzalo López) implies that the next encomendero of Acalan was Antón García, who married Aranda's widow, Francisca de Velasco. Although García was later assigned the entire encomienda of Acalan, the immediate successors to Aranda's half interest were two citizens of Campeche, who apparently received a quarter share each in 1548.[14] Five years later (1553), however, the full half-interest formerly possessed by Aranda was held by Antonio Ponce of Campeche, who may have been one of those who received quarter shares in 1548.

In 1552 Lic. Tomás López Medel, judge of the Audiencia of Guatemala, was appointed *visitador* of Yucatan and Tabasco with authority to make sweeping reforms in the local government of these provinces. During his stay of some eight months (June 1552–February 1553) in Yucatan the visitador introduced many changes in the structure of Indian government and administration. He revised the schedules of tribute payments, reassigned various encomiendas, and initiated the policy of concentrating the native population in larger towns in order to facilitate the work of the missionary clergy. He also formulated a series of ordinances, famous in Yucatecan history, regulating the government of Indian towns and other phases of native life.[15]

Among other changes in encomienda holdings made by the visitador, the entire encomienda of the "pueblo and province" of Acalan, held in half shares

[11] Montejo v. Alvarado; Fiscal v. López, *passim;* Cartas de Indias, 1877, p. 81.

[12] In 1540–41 Gonzalo López served as legal agent of Montejo the Adelantado in a lawsuit with Pedro de Alvarado over the encomienda of Xochimilco (AGI, Justicia, leg. 134, núm. 3), and he appears to have acted as Montejo's agent in the viceregal capital in later years. In 1547 Montejo sent him to Spain to represent his interests before the king and Council.

[13] Aranda apparently served as collector of López' share of the tributes, since later documents record that he received the tributes "for himself and for Gonzalo López" (García v. Bravo).

[14] In a letter to Prince Philip, dated February 10, 1548, Fray Lorenzo de Bienvenida records that the encomenderos of Acalan were Gonzalo López and two citizens of Campeche (names not given) who had received half of the encomienda "this very year." Bienvenida also refers to the death of Aranda, so we infer that the two Campechanos had been given his half interest in the encomienda, each receiving a quarter share (Cartas de Indias, 1877, pp. 75, 81).

[15] The decrees defining López' authority as visitador of Yucatan and Tabasco have been published in DHY, 1: 13–25, and in Rubio Mañé, 1942, 1: 115–42. The López ordinances on Indian affairs are set forth in López de Cogolludo, 1867–68, bk. 5, chs. 16–19.

by Gonzalo López and Antonio Ponce at the beginning of 1553, was re-assigned to Antón García of Campeche. The visitador made the change effective by two decrees dated February 4 and 26, 1553.[16] This new development was apparently the result of questions raised as to the legality and justice of the holdings of Gonzalo López and Ponce.

By various decrees, dating from 1527, the Crown had ordered that encomenderos should live in the province where they held encomiendas and maintain residence (*casa poblada*) in the city or villa designated as the *cabecera* (administrative center) of the district to which their encomienda belonged.[17] In the case of the Acalan encomenderos, this meant that they should reside in Campeche, inasmuch as Acalan was included in the limits and jurisdiction of the Campeche subdivision of the province of Yucatan. But Gonzalo López, as we have seen, was a resident of Mexico, where he also held other encomiendas. Consequently he was not entitled to hold a share in the Acalan encomienda.

In the case of the share held by Antonio Ponce, a resident of Campeche, the question at issue was of another kind. According to the law of encomienda succession promulgated in 1536 and clarified by later royal cedulas, the wife inherited a husband's encomienda in second life if there were no surviving children.[18] Since Diego de Aranda apparently died without issue, his half interest in the Acalan encomienda should have gone to his widow, Francisca de Velasco, who later married Antón García. Instead, Montejo the Adelantado reassigned it to other persons, one of whom was probably Antonio Ponce, who, by 1553, had come into possession of the entire share. There is reason to believe that García brought action to establish his wife's claim, although such a move, if successful, meant that he would have to choose between the half share of Acalan and the encomienda of Pocboc in Ah Canul, which he had held since 1546.[19] Pocboc had 250 tributaries, and there were now only 500 in all of Acalan.[20] Consequently, there would be no advantage in giving up the encomienda of Pocboc, a town located northeast of Campeche, in order to

[16] García v. Bravo, ff. 1943–44v, 1946–49.

[17] Encinas, 1596, 2: 250–53; Solórzano Pereira, 1648, bk. 3, ch. 27.

[18] Encinas, 1596, 2: 200–03; Solórzano Pereira, 1648, bk. 3, chs. 22–23.

[19] On January 24, 1546, Montejo the Younger granted García the encomiendas of Pocboc in Ah Canul and Yaxkukul in Ceh Pech (García v. Bravo, ff. 1941–41v; AGI, Indiferente General, leg. 1382B). Montejo the Adelantado later took away the encomienda of Yaxkukul, and in 1549 this town was held in the name of the Crown (AGI, Guatemala, leg. 128, f. 320v). According to the rules of encomienda succession, when a wife succeeded to an encomienda held by a deceased spouse and later remarried, the second husband, in case he already held an encomienda, had to choose between his original holding and the encomienda inherited by his wife.

[20] The number of tributaries for Pocboc and Acalan is indicated by the tribute assessments for these places drawn up in 1549 and 1553 respectively (AGI, Guatemala, leg. 128, f. 363; García v. Bravo, ff. 1959v–60).

obtain a half interest in the tributes and services of faraway Acalan, unless García could obtain additional tributaries. Moreover, it was not likely that Ponce would willingly abandon his claims to the Acalan holding without recompense of some kind.

These problems seem to have been ironed out in the following manner: (1) the visitador revoked Gonzalo López' half share in the Acalan encomienda on the grounds cited above; (2) Ponce abandoned his claim to the other half share in return for another encomienda in the Campeche district; (3) López' and Ponce's shares were reassigned to Antón García, on condition that he give up the encomienda of Pocboc. Although the decrees recording these transactions do not name the encomienda Ponce was to receive, there is evidence that it was Pocboc, which García renounced. In other words, Ponce and García apparently agreed to exchange their encomienda holdings, and the visitador made the deal worthwhile to García by granting him the other half of Acalan, formerly held by Gonzalo López. In this way García became sole encomendero of Acalan.

It appears, however, that in the later 1550's García attempted to reassert his title to Pocboc. This resulted in prolonged litigation before the Audiencia of Guatemala, but in the end García was defeated and forced to make formal renunciation of all claim to Pocboc under the grant of 1546 by which it was originally assigned to him. Whereupon the audiencia, by decree of January 31, 1560, officially confirmed his title to the entire encomienda of Acalan.[21]

For more than two decades after the introduction of the encomienda system in Acalan there was no fixed schedule (*tasación*) regulating the amount of tribute and service to be paid by the Indians to their encomenderos. In this respect the situation in Acalan was similar to that which prevailed in other areas. The encomenderos everywhere demanded as much tribute and labor as they could get, with the result that many abuses existed. Examples of excessive tribute payments and the uncontrolled exploitation of encomienda labor could be cited in the case of Mexico and other major colonies. For our present purpose it will be more pertinent, however, to note some of the complaints recorded in documents from Tabasco and Yucatan, where the encomenderos of Acalan (except Gonzalo López) lived.

A document of 1541 reveals that the Tabasco encomenderos made unreasonable demands for cacao, the staple item of tribute in that area, native jewelry made of gold and precious stones, and slaves. The Tabasco Indians were also subjected to the usual forms of service as farm laborers and house-

---

[21] This litigation is summarized in the decree of January 31, 1560 (García v. Bravo, ff. 1937–59v).

hold servants; in 1540–41, when Montejo the Younger moved his forces to Yucatan to begin the final conquest of the peninsula, the sierra towns of southern Tabasco were called upon to furnish canoes, and many Indians from other settlements were rounded up to serve as carriers (*tamemes*) in Yucatan. We also learn that the natives were freely moved from town to town and that some of the encomenderos sold the services of their Indians to other Spaniards. Acts of violence were frequent, and there is some evidence of the branding and sale of encomienda Indians as slaves. In 1541 Diego de Aranda, who held an encomienda in Tabasco and later had a half share in the encomienda of Acalan, was arrested on charges of unlawful seizure of Indian property, of selling the services of his encomienda Indians, and of forcibly transporting others from Tabasco to Campeche.[22]

In the case of Yucatan, we also have many complaints of abuses committed by encomenderos. Fray Lorenzo de Bienvenida, writing in February 1548, denounced the excessive tribute burden and the widespread exploitation of native labor. "There is no assessment of tribute," he said, "except that each person makes his own assessment as he wishes."[23] Two years later (1550) Fray Luis de Villalpando wrote a scathing letter to the king in which he accused some of the Spaniards of barbaric acts of violence against Indians of their encomiendas.[24]

For the Acalan area the Chontal Text is the most important source of information concerning the tribute burden during the period of unregulated assessments. The Text states that payments were made "every six months and every two months." This evidently means that certain items of tribute were paid at more frequent intervals than others. Maize, for example, would be paid after harvest, whereas other produce could be delivered more frequently. The Text also adds: ". . . when they (the encomenderos) wished, they came for what they wanted, such as canoes, paddles, honey, copal, hens, mantas, beans, maize, squash seeds, chile, cotton, [and] calabashes." The narrative has nothing to say about the giving of labor, and in view of the fact that the Acalan towns were distant from the Villa de Tabasco and Campeche, where the encomenderos lived, the amount of service demanded was probably less than in the case of Tabasco and Yucatan. There is no reason to believe, however, that the Acalan were exempt from the obligation to give labor on demand. As in the case of the Tabasco Indians, they were probably called upon to furnish canoes, paddlers, and carriers during the final conquest of Yucatan,

[22] Fiscal *v*. López, *passim*.
[23] Cartas de Indias, 1877, pp. 70–82.
[24] Villalpando to the king, Mérida, October 15, 1550, Archivo Histórico Nacional, Madrid, Cartas de Indias, caja 2, núm. 54.

and we have no doubt that groups of Acalan Indians were summoned to both Tabasco and Yucatan from time to time to help in the construction of buildings and on farms. Nor is it likely that Diego de Aranda, for example, showed greater consideration in the treatment of the Indians of his Acalan encomiendas than in the case of those assigned to him in Tabasco.

The flood of complaint about excessive levies of tribute and labor caused the Crown as early as the 1530's to formulate legislation designed to remedy the situation. An important cedula of 1536 instructed the colonial authorities to make fixed assessments, and the order was repeated in 1540 and in the New Laws of 1542. The formulation of the tasaciones, or assessments, was a slow process, however, and in some areas was not carried out until the late 1540's or early 1550's. The abuses resulting from the exploitation of Indian labor finally caused the Crown in 1549 to send out a decree prohibiting the giving of service as part of the encomienda obligation. In case the schedules already made included provision for stated amounts of labor, it was now necessary to revise them and eliminate the service items. Henceforth the Indians were obliged to give only tribute and in fixed amounts annually to their encomenderos.[25]

Although the elimination of service eased the burden imposed on the Indians by the encomienda, it also made the problem of an adequate labor supply more acute. The encomenderos, like other Spaniards, now had to employ Indian laborers on a wage basis. But it soon became evident that under a system of free contract the natives would not hire out in sufficient numbers to meet the labor demand, and the Crown had to authorize forced labor for pay. It should be emphasized, however, that this method of recruiting Indian workers (known in Peru as the *mita*, in New Spain as the *cuatequil*, and generally designated as the *repartimiento*[26] or personal service) was legally and institutionally separate from the encomienda system as now constituted.[27] It is well known, however, that the encomenderos in many areas continued to exploit the labor of their Indians by extra-legal devices.

The first schedules of fixed annual tribute payments in Yucatan were drawn up in 1548, apparently after the date of Bienvenida's letter mentioned above, by Montejo the Adelantado and the Franciscan missionaries. The assessments were confirmed by the Audiencia of Guatemala in the following year (1549).[28] The staple items of tribute listed in these schedules were *mantas*,

[25] Cf. Zavala, 1935, chs. 2–5, *passim*.

[26] The term *repartimiento* had also been used for the encomienda system.

[27] Cf. Zavala, 1943, ch. 9.

[28] The Yucatan tribute schedules of 1548–49 are in AGI, Guatemala, leg. 128, ff. 307–402. They have also been published in Paso y Troncoso, 1939–42, 5: 103–181; 6: 73–112. There are many errors in the spellings of the town names in the printed version.

gallinas (turkeys or hens of European variety), maize, beans, beeswax, and honey. Some of the towns located near the coasts also gave salt and fish. The tribute manta consisted of four lengths (*piernas*) of cotton cloth, each four *varas* long and three-fourths of a vara wide, making a total of about 10 square yards (English measure) per manta.[29] In general, the schedules were based on the number of tributaries, or married men, in each town, with exemptions for the aged and infirm, members of the native ruling families, and certain town officials. For example, the number of mantas to be paid by a given town was equal to the number of tributaries. The proportions of gallinas to mantas varied considerably, but the average payment called for five-eighths to two-thirds as many gallinas as mantas. The maize and bean assessments were made in terms of plantings (a stated number of *fanegas* of maize and beans to be planted annually) instead of measures of harvested produce as was the case in later tribute schedules. Beeswax, honey, salt, and fish were assessed in terms of *arrobas* (the arroba being approximately 25 pounds by weight and four gallons as a liquid measure). The size of the plantings of maize and beans and the quantities of wax, honey, etc., were also fixed according to the size of the towns, although some variation may be noted in the case of towns with an equal number of tributaries.

In 1550 Fray Luis de Villalpando, the celebrated missionary and Maya linguist, reported that the tribute manta was worth 6 *reales* (.75 silver peso) and that the total value of the tribute paid by each tributary was 9 reales (1.125 pesos).[30] There is evidence, however, that Villalpando's valuation for the manta is too low. We have record of a sale of 100 mantas for 250 pesos, or 2.5 pesos each, in 1555, and other data also indicate an average price of 20 reales (2.5 pesos) during the 1560's.[31] Although we also have prices for maize, gallinas, beans, beeswax, etc., it is difficult to check Villalpando's 3-real valuation for each tributary's share of these items, inasmuch as the maize and bean assessments were in terms of plantings rather than harvested produce. If we accept his estimate as fairly accurate, the total value of the tribute paid by each tributary during the 1550's was at least 23 reales. It may have been as high as 24 or 25 reales.

In 1561 the Yucatan tribute schedules were revised by Lic. García Jufre de

[29] The Castilian vara measured about 33 inches (.835 meter). Consequently the tribute manta of 12 square varas of cloth was the equivalent of about 10 square yards (English measure).

[30] Villalpando to the king, Mérida, October 15, 1550, Archivo Histórico Nacional, Madrid, Cartas de Indias, caja 2, núm. 54.

[31] García v. Bravo, ff. 1983v–84; Cuentas de real hacienda dadas por los oficiales reales de Yucatán, 1540–1606, AGI, Contaduría, leg. 911A. The tax schedules of 1548–49 give the value of the manta as two tomines, or reales, but we find no evidence whatever to substantiate this very low valuation.

Loaisa, *oidor* of Guatemala. At this time each tributary was assessed three-fourths of a manta, one-half fanega (the fanega was about 1.6 bushels) of harvested maize, and one turkey or hen. In addition each town paid small amounts of other articles, such as wax, honey, beans, chile, kitchen pottery, and rope. The treasury accounts kept for the first nine years (1562-70) after the new schedule went into effect show that the tribute revenues of certain Crown towns[32] (Mani, Tacul, Telchac, Tecoh, and Yaxkukul) averaged about 20 reales annually for each tributary.[33] Inasmuch as Loaisa's assessments were intended to reduce the tribute burden to some extent, this figure confirms the conclusion stated above that the minimum value of the tributes in the 1550's was 23 reales per tributary.

The record of the Yucatan assessments of 1548–49, as we now have it, does not include an entry for Acalan. The first tribute schedule for the latter area was apparently made in 1553 by the visitador, Lic. Tomás López Medel. The Chontal Text states: "This Tomás López released us from giving canoes, and also hens, mantas, maize, honey, copal, beans, squash seeds, chile, cotton, calabashes, paddles, and other items which we, the Chontal of Acalan, gave." This statement would cause the reader to wonder what kind of tribute the Acalan actually gave as the result of López' assessment. Fortunately we have a copy of the tribute schedule formulated by the visitador at Campeche in February 1553. It provided that the pueblo and province of Acalan should make an annual payment of 500 mantas of the customary size, 500 gallinas (half of them to be turkeys and the other half hens of European variety), and 30 cakes (*panes*) of copal.[34] Thus the articles of tribute were limited to three staples, in contrast with the variety of items the encomenderos had previously demanded.

The manta assessment was evidently at the rate of one manta per tributary, as in the case of Yucatan schedules of 1548–49. This would indicate a total of 500 tributaries in all of Acalan in 1553. Inasmuch as the Acalan schedules did not provide for payments in maize, beans, wax, and honey, standard items in the Yucatan assessments, we infer that Acalan did not have large exportable surpluses of these products. The elimination of these items was apparently offset by the copal payment and a larger quota of gallinas (equal to the number of mantas or tributaries, instead of the five-eighths to two-thirds proportion that was average for the Yucatan schedules).

Lacking prices for copal, we are unable to make an accurate estimate of

---

[32] Crown towns were those which paid tribute to the king instead of to encomenderos. The tributes for Crown towns and encomienda towns were assessed on the same basis.
[33] Cuentas de real hacienda . . . , 1540–1606, AGI, Contaduría, leg. 911A.
[34] García v. Bravo, ff. 1959v–60.

the annual value of the Acalan tributes. A sum of 1350 to 1400 pesos would seem, however, to be a reasonable figure. Although some of the larger holdings in northern Yucatan produced greater revenue, the value of the Acalan tributes was considerably higher than that of the average Yucatan encomienda. In this connection it may be noted that the provincial governors of Yucatan in the sixteenth century received an annual salary of only 1000 pesos gold, or about 1655 pesos silver, in which the tribute values have been calculated. It is evident therefore that Antón García's income as encomendero of Acalan represented a substantial living.

On the basis of 500 tributaries, the value of the Acalan tributes represented an annual tax of some 22 reales (2.75 pesos) per tributary, or about the same as the minimum payment already indicated for northern Yucatan in the 1550's. The question arises as to how much of a burden this imposed on the Indians. The answer depends, of course, on many factors, some of which it is difficult to evaluate, but there can be little doubt that the Yucatan and Acalan tribute assessments were excessive. Perhaps the best method of measurement is to determine the wage equivalent of the tax, since wages for Indian labor remained fairly stable during the second half of the sixteenth century. The maximum pay for unskilled Indian labor during this period was apparently 3 reales (.375 peso) per week. On this basis the annual payment of 22 reales per tributary in Acalan represented the earnings of an unskilled worker for 7.33 weeks, or slightly more than 14 per cent of his gross wages for an entire year. In the same way the total annual value of the Acalan tributes represented the wage equivalent of at least 3600 weeks of labor, or the earnings of about seventy unskilled workers for a year. The excessive burden of the tributes is also indicated by evaluating the tax in terms of maize consumption, although in this case the bases of calculation are probably less exact. However, if we estimate the amount of maize that could be purchased for 22 reales at current prices in the 1550's and 1560's and also take into account Steggerda's figures concerning the daily maize consumption of a present-day Yucatecan family of five persons,[35] we find that the Acalan tax of 22 reales per tributary would have supplied the maize ration of a family for something like sixty days. Further evidence that the Yucatan and Acalan assessments were burdensome is provided by tribute schedules promulgated in New Spain in the early 1560's which called for an annual payment of 10 or 11 reales per tributary.[36]

The visitador, Lic. Tomás López Medel, also made a change in regard to

[35] Steggerda, 1941, pp. 127–30.

[36] In these New Spain schedules each tributary was assessed one peso (8 reales) and half a fanega of maize. The current price of maize was 4 reales the fanega. Indians who gave cash instead of maize were assessed 3 reales in lieu of the produce payment.

the place of delivery of the Acalan tributes. During the period immediately preceding 1553 the payments had been made in Campeche, but apparently on petition of some of the Indians of Acalan the visitador decreed that delivery should again be made in the Villa de Tabasco, as had been the case during the interval between the second and third phases of the conquest of Yucatan. The reason cited for making this change was that it was more convenient for the Indians to make payment in Tabasco.[37] Actually the distance would have been about the same in either case. We surmise therefore that the Acalan wished to combine the delivery of the tributes with their trading operations in Tabasco and the Chontalpa area, which were probably more extensive than the trade carried on with northern Yucatan. As the result of López' decree, the encomendero, Antón García, temporarily transferred his residence to the Villa de Tabasco. The Chontal Text refers to tribute payments made to García in Chilapa in the Tabasco province. This may be an error, or it is possible that García owned farms in the Chilapa area, where delivery of the tributes was occasionally made. But the change introduced by the visitador was evidently of short duration, for as early as July 1555 the payments were again being made in Campeche, where García resided permanently thereafter.[38]

The Text also states that the visitador established rates of pay for the Indians who transported the tributes to the place of delivery. Hitherto labor of this kind had apparently been considered a part of the services owed by the Indians to their encomenderos. Now that the Crown had prohibited the giving of labor as part of the encomienda obligation, the encomendero had to pay for this service. The documents record, for example, that in 1554 Indians of Acalan received the sum of 19 pesos for the transportation of 100 mantas to Tabasco, or about 7.5 per cent of the value of the mantas. That García also occasionally employed his encomienda Indians as day laborers is indicated by record of a payment of 59 pesos for the building of a house in the Villa de Tabasco during the time the encomendero resided in that place.[39]

Encomenderos were under obligation to provide religious instruction for the Indians of their encomiendas. In actual practice, however, this obligation was usually discharged by the payment of salary to a missionary priest and by sharing in the cost of building and equipping the local church. Inasmuch as effective missionary work in Acalan was started only in 1550, most of the encomenderos who preceded Antón García were not called upon to fulfill their duties in this matter. In García's case, however, we have evidence that

[37] García v. Bravo, ff. 1946–47v.
[38] Ibid., ff. 1984v–85.
[39] Ibid., ff. 1983v–84.

he paid the usual fees to the Franciscan missionaries and facilitated their work in Acalan prior to the removal of the Chontal to Tixchel in 1557.

On more than one occasion during his stay in Acalan in 1525 Cortés harangued the native chieftains on the subject of the Christian faith and "the error in which they lived." The commander also tells how Paxbolonacha and other chieftains "burned many of their idols in my presence and said that from that time forward they would pay them no honour."[40] But this act was obviously prompted by mere expediency, or by fear inspired by the summary execution of Cuauhtemoc. Although missionary clergy accompanied the Cortés expedition—and it may be assumed that they as well as the commander talked to the Indians on the subject of religion—there is nothing in the narratives of Cortés and Bernal Díaz to indicate that any true converts were made at this time. When Avila imposed Spanish sovereignty and introduced the encomienda system in 1530, he undoubtedly explained that in due time these measures would be followed by the introduction of Christianity and that the encomenderos were under obligation to provide instruction in the new faith. The withdrawal of the Spaniards from Acalan within six weeks after the founding of the Villa de Salamanca, however, caused the postponement for many years of any effective effort to indoctrinate the Indians. It was only after the successful occupation of northern Yucatan and the coming of the Franciscan missionaries to that area that the conversion of the Acalan people was finally achieved.

In 1545 two groups of Franciscans, one from Guatemala and the other from Mexico, arrived in Yucatan. A third group came from Spain in 1549, and in succeeding years other friars were recruited for service in the province. Among these early missionaries were several who became famous in Yucatecan history as teachers, linguists, and Church leaders, notably Fray Luis de Villalpando, Fray Juan de la Puerta, Fray Lorenzo de Bienvenida, and Fray Diego de Landa. The first monastic houses were established in Campeche and Mérida, but within a few years the Franciscans also founded mission centers in Mani, Conkal, Izamal, Valladolid, and other important towns. The reforms and administrative policies introduced by Lic. Tomás López Medel during his stay in Yucatan in 1552-53 assisted the progress of the missionary program. The López ordinances on Indian affairs contained many provisions designed to combat the influence of the native priests and to break down aboriginal customs regarded as inconsistent with Christian standards of moral conduct and social life. The visitador also facilitated the concentration of the Indians in

[40] Cortés, 1916, pp. 369, 374.

larger settlements or their removal to sites nearer the mission centers. During these early years the Franciscans exerted increasing influence in provincial affairs. They carried forward the visitador's policies as rapidly as possible; they actively intervened in the government of the Indian towns; and they freely denounced abuse and exploitation of the natives by the encomenderos and imposed ecclesiastical censures on Spaniards who set an evil example by immoral or irreligious conduct. Although some of the encomenderos and colonists opposed the growing power of the friars, the latter were able to enlist support from the colonial authorities, especially the Audiencia of Guatemala, which had jurisdiction over Yucatan in the 1550's. The Franciscans continued to dominate the local scene until the coming of the first bishop, Fray Francisco de Toral, in 1562. The new prelate immediately assumed general direction of the missionary program. Although Toral himself was a Franciscan, the introduction of episcopal authority necessarily involved the limitation of the influence and power of the Order.[41]

The Chontal Text is the sole source of information concerning the conversion of Acalan. According to this narrative, the first missionaries visited the country when Lamatazel, second son of Paxbolonacha and successor of Pachimalahix, was ruler. The Text reads:

> During his time and government the first Franciscan fathers arrived, Fray Luis de Villalpando, Fray Juan de la Puerta, [and] Fray Lorenzo de Bienvenida.[42] At this time they were still in their pagan and idolatrous state, and the Spaniards and the above-mentioned friars who came entered the land and began to teach them the true way and the true God. They went about teaching everyone that our gods were already finished and had already come to an end, [saying]: "You will never see them worshipped again, and he who worships them is deceived in his way of life and he who does so will be punished, for their time is now over. See that no one deceives the people, for that age is now gone by." All the principal men and the ruler and all their pueblos heard what the father priests said.
>
> Then Lamatazel, their ruler, died, and before he died he ordered all the principal men summoned. When they had assembled he said to them: "Now I am dying, and I bear sorrow in my heart that I have not attained to being a Christian and living with faith instead of as we live. As my life draws to a close, I beg you to

[41] For the early history of the Franciscan missions in Yucatan, see López de Cogolludo, 1867–68, bks. 5, 6; Molina Solís, 1896, bk. 3, ch. 22, and 1904–13, vol. 1, chs. 1–2; Scholes and Adams, 1938, 1: i–cvii; Scholes and Roys, 1938.

[42] We have no positive evidence to substantiate this statement that Villalpando, Bienvenida, and La Puerta visited Acalan. In his letter to Prince Philip, February 10, 1548, Bienvenida gives a brief account of conditions in Acalan and describes the hazards of the journey from Yucatan to the Acalan area. Although the account may well have been based on personal experience, the author does not state that he or any other friars had actually visited Acalan (Cartas de Indias, 1877, pp. 75–76). It is entirely possible, however, that the Text refers to a journey made by one or more of the friars late in 1548 or in 1549.

give yourselves to the service of another God, because I see and have heard that the father priests will come to baptize and preach, and [the new faith] will not be destroyed, nor will the end [of it] be seen. Now the truth comes, and the good of which they tell, and therefore I charge you to seek it and bring the father preachers to teach you and set your feet on the true road." After this speech this ruler Lamatazel died.

Lamatazel was the father of Don Pablo Paxbolon, who later served for many years as cacique and governor of Tixchel. Don Pablo was educated by the Franciscans, and during his career as governor of Tixchel he established a reputation as a loyal servant of the Church. The Text narrative quoted above was obviously designed to show that his father, although a heathen, had been sympathetic to the new faith and had urged his people to accept it. The Maldonado-Paxbolon probanza of 1612 went even further and definitely implied that Lamatazel actually became a Christian.[43] There is no evidence, however, to substantiate this. The Text clearly indicates that he died a heathen. Moreover, neither the Text nor the Paxbolon-Maldonado Papers record a Christian name for the ruler.

When Lamatazel died, probably in 1549 or early in 1550, the succession passed to his brother named Paxtun, third son of Paxbolonacha. The new ruler "heard the news of the preaching and baptism which the fathers were engaged in and took the matter under consideration with all his principal men. They summoned the whole pueblo in order that they might go to seek the fathers in Campeche, and thus ruler Paxtun set out for Campeche with his people in search of the fathers." On the way they met Fray Diego de Béjar, who was traveling from Tabasco to Yucatan. He expressed great pleasure that the Indians desired to become Christians and agreed to visit their lands after he had disposed of certain business in Yucatan. A month later the Indians came with canoes to Campeche and took the missionary to Acalan. The Text records the date of his arrival as April 20, 1550.

Although the account of Father Béjar's visit is brief, it provides interesting clues concerning missionary methods and also as to the manner in which the Indians received the new religion. In his talks with Paxtun and other chieftains the friar stressed the fact that acceptance of Christianity meant that they would have to abandon belief in their old gods. "The first thing I have to say to you is that it is impossible to serve two lords or two fathers. . . . I come to tell you that [there is] only one God in three persons, God the Father, God the Son, God the Holy Ghost, who created heaven and earth and all there is to be seen today." Having emphasized this fundamental point, he then told

[43] Paxbolon-Maldonado Papers, Part I, f. 1.

the Indians to come and display their idols. They brought him first "the idol of the ruler which bears [the name of] Cukulchan," evidently Kukulcan, and then "the devil [of] Tadzunum, and [those of] Tachabtte, Atapan, and Taçacto." The latter phrase probably refers to the idols of the four quarters of Itzamkanac. "They brought all these before Father Fray Diego de Béjar, who burned them."

After these preliminaries the friar instructed the Indians in the elements of Christian faith and doctrine. He taught them to recite "the Paternoster, the Ave María, the Credo, and the Salve, and the articles of the faith. And then he began to give them their [Christian] names," i.e., to baptize them. The ruler Paxtun received the name of Pedro, a native priest called Kintencab was named Mateo, and Caltzin, another chieftain, was named Francisco.

The Text, as amplified by the Spanish version, implies that on this first visit Father Béjar made many other converts. The remainder of the narrative deals, however, with the measures taken to stamp out idolatry. "The idols hidden in their secret places by the Indians . . . were sought out in all of the pueblos. The custodians of the idols went for them and brought them and burned them. Those who retained them were imprisoned and whipped before the eyes of the people. In this way the idols perished and came to an end among the natives, some of whom [conformed] willingly, others through fear of punishment."

In such manner Fray Diego de Béjar initiated the missionary program in Acalan. In due course a church was built, probably a very modest structure, in Itzamkanac, where most of the population was now concentrated, and a few simple ornaments were provided by the encomendero, Antón García.[44] The new mission area was attached to the district served by the Franciscans of the Campeche convent, from which friars came from time to time to administer the sacraments, baptize new converts, and supervise the routine religious instruction carried on by native teachers trained for this purpose. Father Béjar made a second visit, probably in 1551, and in later years Fray Miguel de Vera, Fray Juan de Escalona,[45] and Fray Diego de Pesquera also served as missionaries in Acalan. But due to the long and hazardous journey from Campeche, especially the arduous passage up the rapids and falls of the Río de Acalan, or Candelaria, the visits of these friars and others who may have assisted them were necessarily infrequent.

It appears, however, that the friars succeeded in making at least nominal

[44] García v. Bravo.
[45] The Text does not mention Escalona, but several documents in the case of García v. Bravo indicate that he served in Acalan prior to 1557, when the Indians were moved to Tixchel.

converts of most of the Acalan people. One or more of the chieftains and an undetermined number of the common people remained heathens, but most of the unconverted were evidently slaves. Although the López ordinances of 1552 decreed that "all the Indians of this province who may have slaves at the present time . . . shall set them free and give up control over them"[46] the slave owners resisted enforcement of this order as long as possible. In an isolated area like Acalan, where there was no resident official or priest, enforcement was practically impossible. Slaves who became Christians were, of course, automatically emancipated, but it was easy for the Acalan slave owners to prevent their bondsmen from seeking baptism by hiding them in the forests or on farms whenever the friars visited the country.

The account of Father Béjar's visit to Acalan in 1550 clearly shows that the use of force was necessary to compel some of the Indians to give up their idols and that many of the converts were inspired by fear of punishment if they refused to conform to the new order. The introduction of the Christian religion, with all that it implied in relation to established thought and custom, was bound to create a conflict of loyalties which could be overcome only by careful instruction and by close supervision of native life over a long period of time. This was impossible, however, in the case of Acalan, located many days' journey from the nearest mission center. The problem was finally resolved in 1557 by the forced removal of the surviving population to Tixchel. This event, the most important in the postconquest history of Acalan, was the direct and logical result of the missionary program.

Although Acalan was not subjected to the ravages of a military conquest, with its inevitable depredations, destruction of property, and loss of life, the population of the province rapidly declined during the quarter-century after the coming of the Spaniards. The decrease cannot be measured accurately, but the fact that the population fell off sharply is beyond question.

Cortés describes Acalan as prosperous and well populated. The list of seventy-six towns in the Chontal Text also suggests a fairly numerous population. Statements in Montejo's probanza of 1531 that it was only a day's journey from Acalan (apparently referring to the borders of the province) to Laguna de Términos would indicate that some of the settlements were located along the rapids and falls of the Río de Acalan, or Candelaria. Most of them, however, appear to have been situated above the rapids and along the upper tributaries of the river.[47]

[46] López de Cogolludo, 1867–68, bk. 5, ch. 18.
[47] Cf. Appendix B, pp. 426–27, *infra*.

Unfortunately the chroniclers give no estimates of the total population of the province at the time of the conquest. Itzamkanac was evidently a fairly large place, at least for so remote a region. Teutiercas (Tuxakha), with its two large temples used by the Spaniards as living quarters, probably ranked second to Itzamkanac. We also infer that Tizatepelt (Çacchute), Chakam, and Tahçacab, which had two encomenderos in 1530, were settlements of larger than average size. There is reason to believe, however, that the total population of Acalan was not so large as might be expected on the basis of seventy-six inhabited localities. As already noted, one reason cited by Oviedo to explain why Avila withdrew from Acalan within such a short time was the fact that he regarded the population as too small to support a colony. Moreover, Bernal Díaz, who apparently saw more of the country than Cortés, twice refers to the existence of "more than twenty settlements,"[48] by which he probably meant places large enough to be considered towns or villages. This suggests that many of the "pueblos" listed in the Text were small hamlets of only a few families each. In other words, the situation in Acalan was similar to that in Yucatan, where the principal towns or villages (called *cabeceras* by the Spaniards) had one or more adjunct settlements of smaller size.

If Itzamkanac had 900–1000 houses, as Oviedo states, its total population would have been 4000–4500 on the basis of 4.5 persons per family and only one family to a house.[49] If there were many multiple-family houses, the figure would have been considerably larger. It is impossible, however, to estimate the number of such houses. Moreover, this factor may well be offset by the probability that Alonso de Luján, from whom Oviedo obtained his information, overestimated the size of the town. In order to keep our own estimates on a minimum basis, we shall assume a population of 4000 for Itzamkanac, a conservative figure in terms of Cortés' description of the capital as a large place with many temples.[50]

We have no data for estimating the population of the twenty-odd lesser towns and villages mentioned by Bernal Díaz, or of the small hamlets and subsidiary settlements which apparently comprised about two-thirds of the seventy-six places listed in the Text. If the 75 settlements outside the capital averaged only 100 persons each, this would give an additional 7500, making a total of 11,500 for the entire province. For the purposes of the present dis-

[48] Díaz del Castillo, 1939, chs. 176, 177.
[49] Late eighteenth-century census reports, the earliest we have for the entire province of Yucatan, indicate a ratio of about 4.5 persons per family. It may be noted, however, that counts of certain towns made during the visita of Lic. García de Palacio in 1583 reveal a somewhat lower number of persons per family. Consequently a 4.5 ratio is probably the maximum that can safely be used for making an estimate of population based on the number of families.
[50] Cortés, 1866, p. 419.

cussion, however, we shall reduce this figure to 10,000, which would appear to be the absolute minimum consistent with the fact that in 1525 the Acalan provisioned Cortés' soldiers and some 3000 auxiliaries. Although an estimated population of 10,000 probably errs on the side of understatement, we shall see that even on this basis the decrease prior to 1553 amounted to at least 60 per cent.

Attention has already been called to the fact that whereas there were at least ten encomenderos of Acalan in 1530, the number was reduced to two by the 1540's. Although this may have been due, in part, to the consolidation of the earlier holdings into larger grants, declining population was probably the major factor. And in 1553, as we have seen, the entire province of Acalan was assigned to a single encomendero, Antón García.

Evidence of a rapid decrease in the population subsequent to the coming of the Spaniards is also found in the letter of Fray Lorenzo de Bienvenida to Prince Philip, dated February 10, 1548. According to this dispatch, the pueblo of Acalan (Itzamkanac) now comprised only 200 houses. Although Oviedo's statement that Acalan-Itzamkanac had 900–1000 houses in 1530 may be an exaggeration, the testimony of Bienvenida shows that a marked change had taken place within the short space of eighteen years. The friar also reported that "there is only one pueblo," evidently meaning that there was only one settlement of any size in the entire province.[51]

Further evidence that the population had rapidly melted away is provided by the tribute assessment of 1553, which was based on a total of 500 tributaries, or married couples. In addition, there was undoubtedly a certain number who were exempt from tribute, such as persons of noble blood, village officials, and the aged and infirm. This group may have represented an additional 10 per cent, or 50 heads of families. Moreover, the counts on which tribute assessments were made were often inaccurate owing to carelessness on the part of the officials who made them and to the fact that the Indians used every device possible to conceal or hide out potential tributaries. In the case of Acalan the person sent to make the count could not know the location of every hamlet on the creeks and bayous of the Candelaria drainage, and the native officials of Itzamkanac naturally would not have volunteered more information than necessary. There is no way of determining the number who were not counted, but for purposes of estimate we shall assume that it was as high as 40 per cent of the total actually listed, or 200 potential tributaries. If the number of families was 750, then we have a total of 3375 persons, counting 4.5 persons per family. We also learn from the Chontal Text that some 600

[51] Cartas de Indias, 1877, p. 75.

slaves later fled to Chakam, presumably during the disorders that occurred as
the result of the transfer of the Acalan to Tixchel in 1557. This would increase
the estimated population in 1553 to 3975. In short, the total for the entire
province was about equal to the conservative estimate for Itzamkanac in 1530.
On the basis of the minimum estimate of 10,000 for the province at the time
of the conquest, the population had declined by 60.25 per cent within three
decades. The actual decrease was undoubtedly greater, since we have pur-
posely held the preconquest figure to a minimum and have made a generous
estimate for the population in 1553.

Northern Yucatan comprised a larger area than Acalan and was more
densely populated, but for purposes of comparison it is interesting to note that
in 1548–49 it had more than 57,000 tributaries. Moreover, there were 28 towns
with their adjunct settlements (some of them being fairly important villages)
which had 500 or more tributaries each, and there were 17 with 400–500 each.
As we might expect, Hocaba-Homun (2400 tributaries), Conkal (1450),
Telchac (1030), Mani (970), and Tekax (940) were centers of considerable
population, but even in such towns as Tixkokob (530), Dzidzantun (600),
Chancenote (600), Dzilam (580), and Mocochi (500) the number of tributaries was equal to or greater than the total for the entire Acalan area in 1553.[52]

What were the causes of the rapid decline of Acalan subsequent to the
conquest? The Maldonado-Paxbolon probanza of 1612 asserts that many of
the Indians, seeing the "benevolence" with which Paxbolonacha received
Cortés and fearing that he would return and make himself master of the land,
fled from their towns and went away to live in the forests.[53] It is probably true
that some of the natives withdrew into the surrounding forests during Cortés'
stay in 1525. The historical allusions in the prophecies seem to indicate, however, that although the Maya often took refuge in the bush when some disturbance occurred, most of them returned to their homes when the crisis was
past. The Chontal probably did the same. Although Avila was disappointed
in the size of the Acalan population in 1530, this was probably due to the
over-enthusiastic reports given to Montejo by Cortés' soldiers, and we doubt
that there had been any marked decrease in the population within the short
space of five years. According to the Luján-Oviedo narrative, Itzamkanac was
still a sizable place in 1530. Moreover, the above-mentioned statement in the
probanza of 1612 was clearly intended to support Don Pablo Paxbolon's claim
that the forest Indians whom he pacified and reassembled in the Tixchel area
in later years were former Acalan subjects. As we shall see in Chapters 10 and

[52] AGI, Guatemala, leg. 128.
[53] Paxbolon-Maldonado Papers, Part I, f. 3v.

11, many of these Indians were actually apostate fugitives from northern Yucatan. It is quite possible, of course, that a certain number of the Chontal left the Acalan area in 1525 and thereafter, never to return, but we are of the opinion that they were not numerous and that their withdrawal from the old homeland was at best a minor factor in the decrease of population after the coming of the Spaniards.

According to Bienvenida, the population of Acalan had declined "por no aver justicia entre ellos." This phrase is somewhat ambiguous. It may refer to actual injustice, or to the lack of a Spanish magistrate to administer local affairs and enforce justice. But the implications are the same in either case. Bienvenida evidently attributed the sharp decrease of population to the abuses and exploitation suffered by the Indians at the hands of the Spaniards. This is also made clear by the friar's suggestion that the king should revoke the encomiendas and take charge of the Indians as royal tributaries "because being under his protection they will be better treated."[54]

Although the missionaries were severely critical of the encomenderos and may have exaggerated the amount of mistreatment encomienda Indians received, the history of Mexico, Yucatan, and Tabasco offers ample proof that grave abuses existed. In an isolated area like Acalan, where there was no resident colonial official, the encomenderos and other Spaniards who visited the country from time to time may have acted with even greater impunity than in regions closer to the centers of governmental authority. On the other hand, there was no Spanish colony in Acalan so that mistreatment of the natives could not have been so constant as in other areas. That abuses existed in the case of Acalan may be taken for granted, although we have little specific evidence. The Chontal Text indicates that the encomenderos made heavy demands for food and other local products as tribute. If it is true, as we believe, that the Acalan did not raise exportable surpluses of maize, then the tribute levies prior to 1553, when maize and other food products, except fowl, were eliminated as items of tribute, may have caused a certain amount of scarcity. To the extent that this resulted in actual want, the population would necessarily suffer. There is also reason to believe that Acalan Indians summoned to Yucatan or Tabasco to serve their encomenderos as laborers were held in service for longer periods of time than the natives of encomienda towns closer to the centers of Spanish population, and some of them may never have returned to their homes.

It is difficult, however, to form an accurate judgment concerning the effects of abuse and exploitation on the native population. Bienvenida obviously

[54] Cartas de Indias, p. 75.

stressed the lack of justice and close governmental supervision in order to make a strong case for his major recommendation, the removal of the Acalan to a more accessible site in Yucatan where the missionary program could be carried on effectively. But there were also other reasons for the decline of Acalan, and we doubt that Bienvenida put his finger on the primary cause.

A more important factor was probably the disruption of native commerce resulting from the conquest and occupation of adjacent areas. As early as 1524 the Indians of Tabasco and Xicalango complained to Cortés of the effects of the depredations of the Spaniards on the Caribbean coast. To quote from Cortés' Fifth Letter:

> . . . they also told me that on the sea coast on the other side of the land called Yucatan, towards the bay which is called "La Asuncion," there were certain Spaniards who did them much injury, for, besides burning many villages and killing the people so that many places were laid waste and the people had fled to the forests, they had done even greater damage to the traders, and the whole trade of that district, which was very considerable, had been lost.[55]

During the succeeding two decades conditions in the Higueras-Honduras area can be described only as chaotic. Bitter personal rivalries, ruthless exploitation of the Indians, a series of Indian revolts and military campaigns to suppress them, and jurisdictional conflicts characterized the history of the area. These conditions resulted in great loss of life and constituted a serious blow to native economy in an area formerly rich and prosperous. Trade declined and the old commercial centers suffered accordingly.[56]

The campaigns of the Pachecos in Uaymil-Chetumal in 1544, resulting in the conquest of these areas, were conducted with great severity. The Indians suffered heavy losses, and many of the survivors fled into the interior of the peninsula. Consequently the Chetumal district, which had formerly been prosperous and an important center of trade on the east coast, was to a large extent depopulated. The Golfo Dulce area, of which Nito was the most important trade outlet, naturally suffered from the chaotic conditions in nearby Higueras-Honduras. Moreover, the activities of Montejo's lieutenants, sent to found the colony of Nueva Sevilla in the Golfo Dulce region, caused many of the Indians to rebel or to abandon their homes, with the result that the population measurably decreased.[57]

Although the early history of Tabasco was not characterized by the same

---

[55] Cortés, 1916, pp. 348–49.
[56] For an account of conditions in Higueras-Honduras, see Bancroft, 1882–87, vol. 1, ch. 21; vol. 2, chs. 9, 17.
[57] Molina Solís, 1896, pp. 751–57.

degree of violence and internecine rivalry which produced such chaos in the Higueras-Honduras, a strong, orderly government was not established for many years. We have already alluded to the lack of stability during the period from 1525 to 1535. Although Montejo the Younger introduced a degree of peace and security in the later 1530's, the history of the province during the following decade, after Montejo moved to Yucatan, was characterized by personal rivalries and jurisdictional conflicts. The flagrant excesses committed by the Spanish officials and colonists also created chronic unrest among the Indians, and certain areas were not permanently pacified until the decade of the 1560's.

It was inevitable that these conditions should interfere with the native commerce that had made the region from Tabasco to the Ulua River a prosperous economic unit in preconquest times. It should not be assumed, of course, that the old trade was entirely destroyed. The natives continued to trade by canoe along the coasts and river systems, and a certain amount of overland commerce was undoubtedly carried on. But the volume of business decreased; the wars and rebellions disrupted the trade routes and the continuous flow of commerce; and many of the old commercial centers, such as Potonchan, Xicalango, and Nito, declined in size and importance. Spanish merchants now entered the field in competition with the Indians. They controlled the major trading centers and markets and, by use of seagoing vessels, were able to take over a large part of the coastal commerce.

The trade between the Acalan and the Cehache and other interior tribes was probably little affected by these developments. The major operations of the Acalan merchants had been carried on, however, in Tabasco and Yucatan and on the Caribbean coast, areas in which the coming of the Spaniards had caused the greatest disturbance. Although the merchants undoubtedly continued to trade by canoe with Tabasco and Yucatan and by land with Nito and other east coast towns, the volume of business with these areas must have been sharply curtailed. The decline of trade was bound to have an adverse effect on the flourishing prosperity of the province which had so favorably impressed Cortés and his followers. The population of areas that were primarily agricultural had a better chance of survival than the inhabitants of regions like Acalan in which a far-flung commerce played such an important part in local economy. In the latter the effects of the conquest were more immediate and far-reaching. In the course of time the Acalan could readjust their life to changed conditions, but during the period of transition there would inevitably be suffering, want, and loss of life.

Although no information is available concerning the introduction of

European diseases in Acalan, we believe that this was another cause, probably the most important one, of the rapid decrease of population in that area. Throughout the Indies the natives suffered heavy losses during the first decades of conquest and colonization as the result of diseases imported by the Spaniards and their followers. It is well known, for example, that small-pox was introduced into Mexico as early as 1520 by a negro in the Narváez expedition. The disease spread rapidly among the Indians, assuming epidemic proportions. Bernal Díaz states that the natives died in great numbers, and Herrera records that the loss of life was so heavy that it was an important factor in weakening the resistance of the Aztec to the armies of Cortés.[58] From the Valley of Mexico the pestilence spread to other areas and apparently reached as far as Guatemala.[59] During the sixteenth century other epidemics of major proportions scourged the Indian population of New Spain, notably in 1545 and 1575–76. The cause of these later outbreaks is still a matter of some debate, but it was evidently some disease for which the natives had no acquired immunity.[60]

The ravages of disease in the Tabasco area are described in a significant passage in the *Relación de la Villa de Tabasco* written in 1579. A translation follows:

This province of Tabasco has scarcely three thousand Indians. The population has diminished greatly since its pacification, for it was formerly inhabited by thirty thousand Indians. It has declined to this point because of great illnesses and pestilences which have occurred, both those characteristic of this province and those of general character throughout the Indies, such as measles, smallpox, catarrh (*catarros*), chronic coughs (*pechugueras*), and nasal catarrh (*romadizos*), hemorrhages, bloody dysentery, and high fevers, which are prevalent in this province. And when [the Indians] have them, they bathe in cold water in the rivers, and many have taken chills and died.[61]

Here we find specific reference to certain diseases imported from Europe, viz. measles and smallpox. The chronic coughs (*pechugueras*, which the dictionaries define as "toz pectoral y tenaz") suggest tuberculosis, and Shattuck is of the opinion that the pulmonary form of this disease was not indigenous in America.[62] The "high fevers . . . prevalent in this province" could have been caused by certain intestinal infections, but it seems more likely that the phrase refers primarily to malaria. This raises important questions. Did any form of

---

[58] Díaz del Castillo, 1939, ch. 124; Herrera y Tordesillas, 1726–30, dec. 2, bk. 10, ch. 20.
[59] Shattuck, 1938, p. 41.
[60] Bancroft, 1883–88, 2: 529, 657–58.
[61] RY, 1: 350.
[62] Shattuck, 1938, p. 46.

malaria exist in America prior to its discovery? Was the malignant form of the disease brought from the Old World? Recent writers have shown considerable caution in dealing with these questions, reflecting the dearth of reliable information on the early history of malaria in America. Perhaps a more careful analysis of documentary data concerning the decrease of Indian population in other low swampy regions of Spanish America in the sixteenth century may help to resolve the problem (cf. discussion in Chapter 14, pp. 323–27, *infra*). Whatever the final conclusion may be on this subject, the *Relación* of 1579 bears witness to the fact that the rapid decline of the native population of Tabasco was caused in part at least by new diseases imported by the Spaniards.

In the case of Acalan European diseases could have been introduced by the Spanish expeditions which passed through the country from 1525 to 1537. Moreover, groups of Acalan Indians visited Tabasco and Yucatan at fairly frequent intervals to carry on trade, to serve as laborers, or to deliver tribute to their encomenderos. Some of them undoubtedly contracted smallpox or other epidemic diseases and carried the infection back to the Candelaria country. Thus there was ample opportunity for the introduction of the "illnesses and pestilences" that decimated the Indian population of Tabasco and other areas. It is impossible to make any estimates of the loss of life caused by the new diseases in Acalan, but they must have taken a heavy toll. Pestilence would also have caused many Indians to abandon their homes and seek refuge in the forests. Some probably failed to return, thus increasing the losses caused by deaths.

If the native economy had been seriously disturbed, as there is reason to believe, the possibility of resisting the ravages of disease would be reduced. Severe pestilence, in turn, would further disrupt native economy. These two forces, working together, were probably the major causes of the rapid decline of Acalan in postconquest times.

8

The Pueblo of Tixchel

IN THE LETTER to Prince Philip, dated February 10, 1548, in which Fray Lorenzo de Bienvenida described conditions in Acalan, the author stated that the situation worsened daily and predicted that as things were going the population would be wiped out within ten years. He also called attention to the isolation of the province and the hazards of the journey from Yucatan, referring specifically to the rapids and falls of the Río de Acalan, or Candelaria. Consequently the friars were reluctant to undertake the conversion of the natives, "because it will never be possible to provide permanent instruction, for there is only one pueblo and in a remote region where only the birds can go without danger." In order to save the surviving population and to facilitate the missionary effort, Bienvenida recommended that the Acalan should be moved to a site near Campeche or Champoton. He also suggested that the Crown should take them under its protection, revoke the encomiendas, and grant exemption from tribute for ten years.[1]

Although Bienvenida volunteered to undertake the task of moving the Indians to Yucatan, the Crown, so far as we know, never replied to his letter. In 1550, as we have seen, Fray Diego de Béjar initiated the missionary program in Acalan, and the work was carried forward in succeeding years by Fray Miguel de Vera and other friars who visited the province from time to time. But as Bienvenida had foreseen, the permanence of the conversions could not be assured so long as the Chontal remained in their old homeland. The number of friars in Yucatan was so small that none could be spared for service as a resident priest in Acalan. There would also have been considerable risk in sending a friar to serve alone for any length of time in an area where he would not have the protection of Spanish colonists and soldiers. Routine instruction was undoubtedly carried on by native teachers, but the effectiveness of this method of indoctrination depended upon more careful and more frequent supervision by the missionary clergy than was possible in the case of an isolated area like Acalan. It was inevitable therefore that sooner or later the Franciscans should seek to carry out the proposal made by Bienvenida in 1548 for the removal of the Acalan to a more accessible site. Now that the visitador, Lic. Tomás López Medel, had introduced the policy of concentrat-

[1] Cartas de Indias, 1877, p. 75.

ing the Indians of Yucatan in larger and more conveniently located centers there was ample precedent for it.

The person who effected the transfer of the Acalan to a new location was Fray Diego de Pesquera, one of the friars who came from Spain in 1549. He rapidly achieved prominence in Yucatan, serving as master of novices, *defini-dor*,[2] and guardian (administrative head) of various monastic houses. In 1556–57 he was apparently one of the friars assigned to the convent in Campeche, which had jurisdiction over the Acalan area. The Chontal Text is the chief source of information concerning his activities in Acalan, although a few details have been gleaned from other sources.

Plans for the removal of the Indians to a new site were apparently made sometime in 1556. The ruler of Acalan at this time was Don Luis Paxua, son of Pachimalahix II, who had succeeded his uncle, Don Pedro Paxtun, at some unspecified date subsequent to 1550. The Text states that Pesquera discussed the expediency of the proposed move with the Indians and it outlines the arguments he evidently employed in favor of it. The reasons cited are (1) that it would facilitate the religious instruction of the Indians, and (2) that they would enjoy greater protection from the colonial authorities if they were established at a more accessible location. It seems clear, however, that Pesquera was determined to force the move regardless of the desires of the Indians, for there is ample evidence, as we shall see farther on, that Paxua and a considerable number of the people opposed it. Although the Text records that Antón García, the encomendero of Acalan, favored the scheme and agreed to relieve the Indians of tribute for four years, García later testified that he was in Guatemala at the time and that Pesquera took advantage of his absence to carry out the plans without his knowledge and consent.[3] The four-year exemption from tribute was evidently granted but probably on orders from the provincial authorities. In short, it would appear that the Franciscans planned and carried out the transfer of the Acalan to a new location with the consent of the alcalde mayor of Yucatan but in the face of opposition from the Indians and their encomendero. The incident serves as another example of the powerful influence enjoyed by the missionary friars during these early years.

The site of Tixchel on the Estero de Sabancuy, which empties into the northeastern corner of Laguna de Términos, was chosen as the new home for the Chontal. Several reasons evidently prompted this choice. In the first place,

[2] A member of the governing committee which, together with the prelate, directed the local affairs of the Order between the triennial chapter meetings.

[3] García v. Bravo.

Tixchel had been occupied by the Chontal for some sixty to eighty years in preconquest times, and Pesquera probably believed that they would be more willing to reoccupy this site than to move to a place in no way connected with their past history. Second, it was strategically located on the route of canoe travel from Tabasco to Yucatan and would be visited frequently by officials, traders, and clergy traveling back and forth between these areas. Consequently it would be possible to exercise fairly close supervision over the new settlement. Third, a site on Sabancuy estuary would offer the Acalan a greater opportunity to share in the coastal trade, and it would also serve as a convenient base from which they could carry on trade with Indian tribes in the interior of Yucatan.

There appears to be little reason to doubt that the new town of Tixchel, or Tichel, was situated at the site of the modern hacienda of the same name. It lies on the left bank of the Estero de Sabancuy opposite Las Palmas, a large coconut plantation located on the barrier beach between the estuary and the Gulf of Mexico. The site is about 20 km. from the mouth of the estuary, which is narrow at this point.

The hacienda building is on a low wooded ridge a few hundred meters in width, behind which is a mangrove swamp half a kilometer wide and running parallel to the estuary. Beyond the swamp extends a savanna flanked on either side with low scrubby bush. Near the swamp the savanna has the appearance of being inundated during the rainy season. A few mounds, one fairly large, lie on the shore of the estuary, and there is another somewhat larger group in the bush beside the savanna about 4 km. inland. The two groups are connected by a road, paved with flat stones, which crosses the swamp.

The ridge along the shore appears to be better soil than that farther inland, and there was no doubt a settlement where the canoes were kept. The ridge is not wide, however, and a Maya or Chontal town of the size of colonial Tixchel usually covered a considerable area, since it was customary to have large yards or gardens around the houses. It seems very probable therefore that the town founded by Pesquera followed the pattern of the preconquest settlement represented by the two groups of mounds and the paved road connecting them.

A visit to Tixchel gives the impression that the site has never been occupied by a rich agricultural community. Although some of the land, as already noted, seems good, none of the savanna could have been cultivated by the milpa system, and much of the wooded area does not have a very promising appearance. It is obvious, of course, that maize, squash, and beans could be raised at Tixchel, but most of the better milpa land, which made possible the exportation of a certain amount of maize toward the end of the sixteenth century, was evidently located farther inland. Like some thickly populated parts of northern Yucatan, whatever prosperity the region enjoyed was apparently due to commerce and fishing.

In January 1557, Indian laborers were sent from Campeche and Champoton to clear land for the new town and probably to build some houses for the first group of settlers. Later in the year Pesquera began to move the Acalan to their new home. The narrative in the Chontal Text mentions July 10, 1557, in this connection, and we surmise that this was the date of the formal establishment of the town or of the dedication of the mission.

Within less than two weeks after the founding of Tixchel a significant incident occurred. On July 22, 1557, so the Text says, Don Luis Paxua, ruler of the Acalan, "ran away" and went to Chiuoha, a Chontal site southeast of Tixchel. Here he is said to have died of an illness sometime during the following year.[4]

Although the Text gives no reason for the flight of Paxua, there can be little doubt that it was inspired by opposition to Pesquera's activities and plans. The history of northern Yucatan provides evidence that the natives in certain areas resisted the policy of concentrating them in larger and more conveniently located settlements, and it would have been surprising if the Chontal of Acalan had not shown some opposition to being moved from their old lands. The move to Tixchel would inevitably result in economic losses, temporarily at least, and it would also bring about greater control over all phases of native life than heretofore. It was natural, moreover, that the greatest resistance should come from the ruling class. In Acalan, even after the acceptance of Spanish suzerainty, the ruler and chieftains had continued to enjoy a wide measure of autonomy. At Tixchel their freedom of action would be limited to the extent that the clergy and colonial authorities would be able to maintain more effective supervision over local affairs. Removal to a new site would also involve the abandonment of valuable property in the form of houses, lands, and orchards and the freedom of their slaves. If the slaves

[4] The Text states that in 1558 Don Pablo Paxbolon went to Chiuoha where he learned that Paxua had died. It may well be true that some of the older men at Tixchel made a journey to Chiuoha at this time to find out what had happened to Paxua, and Paxbolon may have accompanied them, although he was then only fifteen years old. We are inclined to believe, however, that the author of this part of the narrative confused this journey with another entrada made by Paxbolon to Chiuoha in 1574. The fact that the author records the same month and day (April 25) in each case argues in favor of this supposition. Other documentary evidence shows that the 1574 entrada was made in the spring of the year. The Text statement that it was well known that Paxua had died of an illness was evidently intended to silence any suggestion that the former ruler had met with foul play and to dispel any doubts as to Paxbolon's rightful claim to the caciqueship.

were taken to Tixchel, it would be more difficult to hide them out, and their emancipation would be only a matter of time. If they were left behind in Acalan, they would probably run away and find freedom in the forests. In short, the move to Tixchel was a serious threat to the vested interests of the ruling class as then constituted, and the flight of Paxua was merely the most striking example of its opposition to Pesquera's plans.

It is evident, of course, that some of the native leaders accepted the change without much resistance. After the disappearance of the ruler an elder chieftain apparently assumed control at Tixchel and directed local affairs under Pesquera's guidance. Moreover, the death of Paxua eventually resulted in the strengthening of missionary influence, for the person who was next in line of succession was a youth, Don Pablo Paxbolon, who had been educated by the Franciscans. Paxbolon turned out to be a very able ruler, who skillfully made use of religious motives to advance his own interests. It was several years, however, before he took personal charge of local affairs. In the meantime, especially during the years 1557–61, conditions in Tixchel and the old Acalan area were characterized by instability and recurrent unrest.

Persons who witnessed the removal of the Chontal to Tixchel in 1557 later testified that some of the Indians had to be taken by force in chains and collars (*prisiones y colleras*). There is also evidence that Pesquera had the cacao and copal trees cut down at Acalan-Itzamkanac in order to compel the abandonment of the old capital and to discourage desertions from Tixchel.[5] But despite these drastic measures the transfer of the Chontal to their new home was a slow process. In the Text we read, "The years 1558 and 1559 had passed and as yet the people . . . had not completely abandoned . . . Acalan." Moreover, one of the chieftains, named Don Tomás Macua, had apparently assumed leadership in the Acalan country and "detained" the Indians who remained there. The main group controlled by Macua was at Chanhilix, one of the towns listed in Document II of the Text. Others were scattered in small hamlets at various sites in the Candelaria drainage.

For those who had moved to Tixchel the change caused serious property loss and privation, especially among the common people. The families of merchant-chieftains who owned large trading canoes could transport at least part of their movable belongings from Acalan, but the common people probably had to abandon most of their personal possessions as well as their lands, fruit trees, and orchards. Although the wealthier Indians apparently left their slaves behind to tend the milpas and cacao trees, the disorders and general

[5] García *v.* Bravo.

weakening of authority in Acalan provided ample opportunity for the slaves
to run away and seek freedom in the forests. According to the Text, 600
bondsmen, including women and children, owned by the ruler and principal
men fled to the region of Chakam on the San Pedro branch of the Candelaria.

The people at Tixchel also suffered from a shortage of food. The first
groups of settlers left Acalan during the growing season in 1557, so that adequate crops could not be raised that year. Subsequently maize and other
produce could be planted in good season, but new arrivals from Acalan
apparently caused a shortage of supplies despite increasing harvests. When
some of the Indians returned to Acalan for food that had been left behind,
probably to harvest crops planted before their departure, they became involved in "disputes and trouble" with those who had refused to leave. The
followers of Don Tomás Macua "seized them there, tied them up and whipped
them, and took away their canoes," thus preventing the transportation of
needed supplies to Tixchel.

By 1559 the situation had become critical. Rebellion and apostasy reigned
in Acalan. The survival of native religion is indicated by a brief but significant
sentence in the Text: "They worshipped their idols." At Tixchel hardship
and privation caused increasing unrest. "By this time," the narrative says, "all
the Indians were about to flee." At this juncture Pesquera received support
from an unexpected source.

In 1559 the Audiencia of Guatemala, on orders from the Crown, organized a campaign against the Lacandon Indians who had been causing
depredations on the frontiers of Chiapas and Verapaz. Lic. Pedro Ramírez
de Quiñones, a member of the audiencia, was given command of the expedition, which set out from Comitan in Chiapas and made war on the major lake
stronghold of the Lacandon and the towns of Topiltepec and Pochutla.[6] Before setting out, Ramírez apparently sent orders to the alcalde mayor of
Yucatan, Bachiller Juan de Paredes, to send another force from the north.
Accordingly, Paredes dispatched forty soldiers under command of Capt.
Francisco Tamayo Pacheco with instructions to advance overland to join
Ramírez.

According to the Acalan narrative, Tamayo's force had not proceeded
farther than Tixchel when news was received that Ramírez had already
finished his campaign and had returned to Chiapas. Whereupon Pesquera
proposed that Tamayo should go to Acalan "and bring down all the Indians
who had remained there and rebelled." This plan met with Tamayo's ap-

[6] Remesal, 1932, bk. 10, chs. 10–12; Villagutierre Soto-Mayor, 1701, bk. 1, chs. 9–11.

proval, and he proceeded with his soldiers to Acalan where they seized Don Tomás Macua and other chieftains and rounded up the inhabitants of various settlements. "They brought them down to Tixchel in the year 1560."

Other sources, which record the testimony of soldiers who accompanied Tamayo, give no indication that Pesquera had any part in this affair, and we get the impression that Tamayo's force had proceeded as far as Acalan en route to the Lacandon country, but turned back at that point because it was impossible to go any farther. Some of the witnesses mention Acalan by name; others merely refer to the difficulties encountered in going up a great river with many rapids (the Candelaria). Only one of the witnesses (Juan Vela, also mentioned in the Text as a member of the expedition) has anything to say about the Indians, but his testimony is rather significant. He states that they found the natives in tumult (*alborotados*), and this is not surprising, since the Indians undoubtedly assumed that the soldiers had come to punish them or to take them to Tixchel. Vela continues, "The matter having been considered by this witness and the other soldiers, we set about removing them from their land (*asiento*)".[7] Thus Vela's testimony confirms the Acalan narrative on the major point involved: that the Tamayo Pacheco expedition of 1559–60 brought about the forced removal to Tixchel of the Indians who had held out in the Candelaria area for more than two years.

The arrival of this large group apparently aggravated the problem of food supply, for the Acalan narrative, having recorded the episode, adds, "On this account there was a very great famine." Consequently it was not long before desertions began to take place, amounting all together to about seventy families who returned to the Acalan area.[8] No effort appears to have been made at this time to bring these deserters back. In the next chapter we shall see, however, that they were not permitted to remain permanently in the old homeland.

Subsequent to 1560–61, when this group abandoned Tixchel, a few more families may have deserted, but we have no evidence of any major withdrawal. During the decade of the 1560's local governmental affairs were stabilized by the coming to power of a new cacique; the Tixchel mission was placed on a firm basis; and economic conditions slowly improved, as evidenced by an

---

[7] Información de los méritos y servicios del Capitán Francisco Tamayo Pacheco, 1568, AGI, Patronato, leg. 82, núm. 2, ramo 1; Probanza of the merits and services of Nuño de Castro, 1569–75, AGI, México, leg. 100; testimony of Juan Vela, May 8, 1571, *in* García *v.* Bravo, ff. 2087v–2089v. López de Cogolludo (1867–68, bk. 1, ch. 15) and Villagutierre Soto-Mayor (1701, bk. 1, ch. 7) also have brief references to an expedition by Tamayo Pacheco to Acalan. The latter author clearly confuses the Acalan with the Chol Acala, who were neighbors of the Lacandon.

[8] Testimony of Gómez de Castrillo, May 8, 1571, *in* García *v.* Bravo, f. 2085v.

increasing population. By the end of the decade the permanence of the new settlement was assured.

As we have already noted, an elder chieftain took charge of local affairs at Tixchel after the flight of Don Luis Paxua in 1557. This man, named Don Gonzalo, had been one of the principal men of Acalan. He served as governor of the town until 1566 when Paxua's cousin and successor, Don Pablo Paxbolon, assumed control as cacique and governor of the Chontal. The coming to power of Paxbolon was an important event in Tixchel history, for the new ruler was destined to become one of the most respected Indian leaders of his time in Yucatan.

Don Pablo Paxbolon (his full name was Pablo Antonio Paxbolonacha[9]) was born about 1543.[10] He was the son of Lamatazel, the last heathen ruler of Acalan, and Isabel Acha. Both Don Pablo and his mother were probably baptized in 1550 on the occasion of Fray Diego de Béjar's first visit to Acalan. There is some evidence that Isabel Acha was still living when Father Pesquera moved the first group of the Chontal to Tixchel seven years later.[11]

Soon after his baptism Paxbolon was taken to Campeche where he lived for several years in the Franciscan monastery. There he received instruction in Christian doctrine, music, Spanish, and the manual arts. He learned to play the organ and the guitar, and we are told that in later years, after he became governor of Tixchel, he occasionally served as organist in the village church. Although he undoubtedly learned to use the Spanish language with considerable facility, it is interesting to note that his reports to the provincial authorities, even those made in the 1560's soon after he took office, were written in Chontal. Another accomplishment which he acquired during the years he spent in Campeche was wood carving, a skill which he later put to good use by carving images for the Tixchel church.[12]

Don Pablo probably returned to his people when they were brought to Tixchel in 1557. He was then fourteen years old, and we surmise that he gave Father Pesquera valuable assistance in the founding of the new mission and in the religious instruction of the Indians. After the death of his cousin, Don Luis Paxua, he became head of the ruling family of Acalan-Tixchel, but

[9] The compound form of Don Pablo's surname is seldom used in the documents.

[10] In a sworn statement made at Tixchel on December 24, 1573, Paxbolon gave his age as thirty years (Probanzas of Feliciano Bravo, AGI, México, leg. 109).

[11] The Maldonado-Paxbolon probanza of 1612 states that the reason why the Chontal moved to Tixchel was that his mother and the principal men wished to be near the young cacique, who was then at Campeche (Paxbolon-Maldonado Papers, Part I). This statement is obviously incorrect, but it suggests that Isabel Acha was still alive in 1557.

[12] Paxbolon-Maldonado Papers, Part I, ff. 2–3.

because of his youth he was not permitted to take charge of local affairs for several years. Don Gonzalo, whom we have already mentioned, governed in his place, and from this elder chieftain of the Chontal Don Pablo undoubtedly received instruction in the history of his people and in the customary procedures of local government. And as time went on, he probably exerted an increasing influence in the actual conduct of village business.

When the alcalde mayor of Yucatan, Don Diego de Quijada, passed through Tixchel early in 1565 on his return from a trip to Tabasco, Don Gonzalo, who had now grown old, asked to be relieved of his duties and to have Paxbolon take his place. Although the latter was now about twenty-two years old, Quijada decided that he should wait a while longer before being installed in office. By a decree of January 13, 1565, the alcalde mayor ordered that Don Gonzalo should serve for another year, at the end of which Paxbolon should then assume "the government and lordship of the pueblo as its principal lord to whom [such authority] belongs by law." The decree continues, "and after the said year [the Indians shall obey] the said Don Pablo as governor and natural lord . . . and in regard to him they shall observe the privileges and preeminences which it is customary to observe in the case of such natural lords, caciques, and governors, under penalty of punishment according to law."[13] The following year (1566) the young cacique entered upon his duties, and for a half-century thereafter he served as leader of the Chontal of Acalan-Tixchel.

Quijada's action in conferring the "government and lordship" of Tixchel on Don Pablo Paxbolon was in accordance with a basic principle of Spanish colonial policy. Throughout the Indies the Spaniards recognized the hereditary rank and status of the descendants of former native ruling families and granted them various privileges, such as exemption from tribute and forced labor and the right to receive services and support from their former subjects. It was also a fairly general practice, at least in the sixteenth century, to retain native rulers or their descendants at the head of the local government in Indian towns, subject, of course, to the control and supervision of the superior colonial authorities.

The term natural lord (*señor natural*), which Quijada's decree employed in referring to Paxbolon, "implied a rightful lord, who was obeyed by his subjects and acknowledged by other lords and their peoples." The concept was derived from mediaeval Spanish law, and after the conquest of America

---

[13] Título de gobernador del pueblo de Tixchel, Campeche, 13 de enero, 1565, in *ibid.*, ff. 8–8v.

the Spaniards applied it in the case of important native rulers.[14] A more common term was that of cacique, which has been used rather loosely to designate the governors, or chief administrative officers, of Indian towns. Strictly speaking, the term cacique implied hereditary rank or status, whereas the governor was an elective or appointive official. In many cases the cacique was also the governor, but we have cases of towns, in Mexico at least, which had both a cacique and a governor. It is difficult, on the basis of present knowledge, to make a clear distinction between the functions of each, but it is apparent that the cacique enjoyed a superior status.

For northern Yucatan we have numerous examples of former native rulers and their descendants who became caciques and governors of Indian pueblos after the conquest. Don Francisco Montejo Xiu of Mani and Don Melchor Pech of Motul also enjoyed a certain authority over wider areas. In the course of time more and more of the governors were recruited from outside the ruling families, but the term cacique continued to be applied to such officials, although they had no hereditary rank. Roys notes that hereditary caciques like the Xiu continued to be called "caciques and natural lords" until the mid-seventeenth century. Subsequently they were variously designated as "natural lords," "hidalgos and natural lords," "hidalgos and descendants of natural lords," and finally only as "hidalgos." In Mexico hereditary caciques kept the title until the end of the eighteenth century.[15]

As natural lord, cacique, and governor of Tixchel, Paxbolon enjoyed the hereditary status of a descendant of a former native ruling family and exercised governmental functions as the head of local pueblo administration. We shall see later on that some of Quijada's successors gave Paxbolon authority over a wider area than the pueblo of Tixchel, so that he became a sort of native territorial ruler, subject to the provincial colonial authorities. As governor of Tixchel, he was responsible for the maintenance of public order, the collection of tribute, and the execution of laws and ordinances governing the administration of Indian settlements. It was also his duty to see that the Indians of Tixchel attended religious services and remained faithful to the doctrinal and moral teachings of the Church. He was assisted by a native cabildo, or town council, consisting of two alcaldes, or petty magistrates, and four regidores, or council men, annually elected by the pueblo. The documents also speak of certain principales, or principal men of the Chontal. Some of these were

[14] Roys, 1943, p. 141. For a discussion of the concept of the señor natural in Spanish law, see Chamberlain, 1939a.

[15] Roys (1943, pp. 129–71) gives a general discussion of the cacique system in Yucatan and New Spain.

probably men of noble status, although others may have been heads of barrios, or subdivisions, of the town. There was also a town clerk (*escribano*), and probably other lesser officials, such as *alguaciles* (bailiffs) and *mayordomos*.

In his personal conduct Paxbolon set a good example to his people, and we have no evidence that he ever faltered in his loyalty to the Christian faith. His administration of local office was characterized by good judgment, energetic leadership, and ability to inspire the confidence of the provincial authorities, governmental and religious. Although he accepted the changes wrought by the conquest and shrewdly identified his own interests with those of the new regime, he did not adopt a passive role, as did many of his Indian contemporaries in northern Yucatan. He was aggressive and ambitious, and he sought to extend his influence beyond the limits of the pueblo of Tixchel. The unpacified areas south and east of the new Chontal settlement gave him a wide field of action, and, as we shall see farther on, most of what is known about his later career deals with his activities in that region.

The Tixchel mission founded by Fray Diego de Pesquera was administered for several years as a visita of the convent of Campeche. During the early years Pesquera probably spent a good deal of time at the new mission, but later on native teachers (*maestros de doctrina*) took charge of routine religious instruction and conducted the daily prayers in the village church. From time to time friars came from Campeche to say mass, baptize infants, perform marriages, and supervise the work of the native instructors.

About 1568 the missions of Tixchel and Champoton (the latter was also a visita of the Campeche convent) were removed from the jurisdiction of the Franciscans. This change was effected by Fray Francisco de Toral, first resident bishop of Yucatan, who secularized several other missions founded by the Franciscans. Fray Juan de Santa María of the Mercedarian Order (Orden de Nuestra Señora de la Merced) was placed in charge of Tixchel and Champoton, and he was succeeded in 1570 by Father Juan de Monserrate, a secular priest.[16] Toral's successor, Fray Diego de Landa, later restored the secularized missions to the Franciscan Order, and Tixchel once more became a visita of the convent of Campeche. This status was maintained until 1585, when the provincial chapter voted to create a separate *guardianía*, or mission district,

---

[16] According to Ayeta (*ca.* 1693, pt. 2, f. 95) Toral appointed Pedro de Acosta y Rueda as *vicario* (curate and delegate ecclesiastical judge) for Champoton and Tixchel. The Chontal Text also mentions a priest named Gabriel de Rueda. Both are mentioned in the first volume of the Libro de bautismos y matrimonios of the Archivo Parroquial de la Catedral de Mérida, but the documents of the 1560's and 1570's relating to Tixchel and the Acalan area do not refer to them. It is possible that Gabriel de Rueda succeeded Monserrate as curate of Champoton and Tixchel in 1571.

for Tixchel and the adjacent area to the southeast, where new Indian settlements and missions had been established in the preceding decade (see Chapter 10).[17]

The documents do not record a description of the Tixchel church. It was probably a modest building, consisting of a masonry *capilla*, or altar space, and a pole-and-thatch structure for the nave. In later years the nave may have been enclosed with masonry walls and a vaulted roof. The priest who served the mission in 1569 received an annual stipend of about 90 pesos from the encomendero of the pueblo.[18] The Indians gave services of various kinds and made gifts of food and local produce on the celebration of church festivals. The mission founded by Father Pesquera was dedicated to Santa María, but in later years the appellation of the church was changed to La Pura Concepción de Nuestra Señora.

During the first few years after the founding of Tixchel the Franciscans undoubtedly exerted great influence in the direction of local affairs. They also intervened to protect the Indians from abuse and exploitation by outsiders. It appears that the natives frequently received maltreatment from the travelers who passed through the pueblo, but justice in such cases was often delayed because of the fact that complaints had to be filed before the colonial authorities in Campeche. In order to remedy this situation the Franciscans obtained a decree from the Audiencia of Guatemala, dated February 5, 1560, which authorized the native officials of Tixchel to arrest any Spaniard, mestizo, or mulatto who committed an offense in the pueblo, receive evidence against him, and send him to the nearest Spanish judge for sentence.[19] The decree was probably the result of representations made by Father Pesquera, who was responsible for the removal of the Chontal to Tixchel. Such action in behalf of the natives undoubtedly helped to temper their resentment against being forced to leave their old homeland and to reconcile them to changed conditions. Cogolludo cites the case as one of many examples of the zeal shown by the friars in promoting the temporal and spiritual welfare of the Indians of Yucatan.

Some measure of the success of the missionary program at Tixchel is found in the fact that we have no evidence of the recurrence of idolatry among the Chontal who became permanently established there. Undoubtedly many of the Indians continued to practice some of their old religious customs in their daily life, and others probably withdrew into the nearby forests from

[17] López de Cogolludo, 1867–68, bk. 7, ch. 9, bk. 8, chs. 5–7; Ayeta, *ca.* 1693, *passim*.
[18] García *v.* Bravo, ff. 1972–73.
[19] López de Cogolludo, 1867–68, bk. 6, ch. 8.

time to time to worship the old gods, but it would appear that the Chontal of Tixchel maintained a greater degree of loyalty to the Christian faith than was true of the Indians in certain parts of northern Yucatan.

This was probably the result of two major factors. First, although the pueblo was situated on the southwestern frontier of the province, it was frequently visited by officials, merchants, and clergy traveling from Tabasco to Yucatan and vice versa. This meant that any signs of backsliding would have been noted and reported before the situation became serious. Second, Don Pablo Paxbolon, who served as cacique and governor for so many years, apparently gave the clergy loyal and effective support. This was due in part to the training he had received from the Franciscans in Campeche. He was also motivated by a desire to enhance his own authority and prestige as an Indian leader, and this could best be achieved by gaining a reputation for service to the Church and the missionary program.

According to the tribute assessment made in 1553 by Lic. Tomás López Medel, the Indians of the province of Acalan were under obligation to pay their encomendero 500 mantas, 500 gallinas, and 30 cakes of copal annually.[20] This assessment remained in effect until 1557, when the Acalan were granted a four-year exemption from tribute in order to facilitate their resettlement at Tixchel. At the end of this period a new assessment was made by Lic. García Jufre de Loaisa, oidor of Guatemala, who revised all of the Yucatan tribute schedules during his visitation of the province in 1560–61.

The new levies formulated by Loaisa were based, as in the case of those formerly in effect, on the number of married men in each pueblo, with exemption for the aged and infirm, the widowed, those of noble rank, and certain local functionaries. The annual tribute levied on each tributary consisted of three-fourths (three piernas) of a tribute manta, half a fanega of harvested maize, and one gallina (a turkey or a European hen). In addition, most of the pueblos were also assessed small amounts of beans, chile, beeswax, honey, and household utensils. The new schedules represented a certain reduction of the tribute burden, since the assessments previously in force in Yucatan had called for the payment of one entire manta per tributary.[21]

The Tixchel assessment was set forth in a decree dated February 27, 1561,

[20] See p. 152, *supra*.

[21] The new tribute schedules formulated by Loaisa are not available for all of the pueblos of northern Yucatan, but a sufficient number have been preserved to illustrate the character of the assessments. These are found in Cuentas de real hacienda . . . , 1540–1606, AGI, Contaduría, leg. 911A; and El fiscal con los oficiales reales de la provincia de Yucatán sobre . . . varias ayudas de costa que pagaron, 1567, AGI, Justicia, leg. 209, núm. 4.

to be effective on May 1 of that year. According to the matrícula, or official count, of the pueblo, there were 253 married men, of whom 23 were exempt, leaving 230 liable to tax. But in contrast with the schedules formulated for northern Yucatan, the Tixchel assessment called for payment in mantas only at the rate of one manta per tributary, or a total annual payment of 230 mantas. This would seem to indicate that maize and poultry were not being raised in sufficient quantity to warrant payments in such produce. At current prices the extra one-fourth of a manta levied on the Tixchel tributaries was worth about as much as half a fanega of maize and one turkey or hen. The elimination of copal as an item of tribute is not surprising, in view of the fact that the Indians were no longer living in an area where it was plentiful.

Antón García, the encomendero, objected to the new assessment on the ground that many of the Indians belonging to his encomienda were not included in the count. Some were fugitives in Acalan, and García also claimed that the Indians had hidden others at Tixchel. Loaisa took note of the encomendero's complaint and decreed that in case future governors of Yucatan made a new count and found more than 253 heads of families the excess should be taxed one manta each.[22]

Comparison of the Tixchel assessment of 1561 with that for the province of Acalan made by López Medel in 1553 shows a decrease of 270 tribute payers, or 54 per cent, in the short space of eight years. The tribute schedules for northern Yucatan indicate that the population had declined to some extent since 1548, when the last count had been made in that area. There would probably have been some decrease in the case of Acalan, but a decline of 54 per cent in such a short time calls for special explanation. The hiding out of potential tribute payers when the 1561 count was made can be disregarded as a factor in the situation, since it is probably true that a considerable number were not included in the 1553 count for the same reason. We have already noted that seventy families are said to have fled after the Tamayo Pacheco expedition brought to Tixchel the groups who had been holding out in Acalan since 1557. Even if the refugee families numbered 100 or more, this would not account for all of the decrease since 1553. It seems clear therefore that the disorders of the period 1557–61, the shortage of food at Tixchel during these early years, and the general disruption of native life and economy resulting from the forced removal of the Indians to a new settlement had caused considerable loss of life. From the standpoint of Antón García, encomendero of Acalan-Tixchel, the tribute assessment of 1561 represented a heavy loss of

[22] Copy of Loaisa's assessment is in García v. Bravo, ff. 1960v–1962.

182 ACALAN-TIXCHEL

income, and it is not surprising that he was bitterly critical of Pesquera for having moved the Chontal to Tixchel without his knowledge.

In 1565 Don Gonzalo and other local officials of Tixchel petitioned for a reassessment of tribute on the ground that since 1561 many tribute payers had died and that consequently the Loaisa assessment had become an excessive burden. Quijada, the alcalde mayor, gave orders for a new count of the pueblo, but it does not appear to have been made.[23]

Four years later the Indians of Tixchel again complained that Loaisa's assessment of tribute was burdensome and asked for relief. In accordance with this request the provincial governor, Don Luis Céspedes de Oviedo, instructed his brother, Juan Céspedes de Simancas, who was serving as his lieutenant in Campeche, to make a count of the pueblo and to report on conditions in the Tixchel area. This order was dated February 1, 1569. Despite protests by Antón García, the lieutenant governor proceeded to Tixchel, where a matrícula was drawn up with the assistance of Don Pablo Paxbolon on February 14–16, 1569.[24]

A copy of this matrícula, included in the manuscript record of the case of García v. Bravo, gives the names of 275 married couples or heads of families.[25] Accompanying the report is a supplementary statement listing thirty-five persons to be exempted from tribute for various reasons. These persons included five widowers, nine old men, seven heads of families who were exempted because of some infirmity or because their wives were ill, crippled, or blind, eight *cantores* (singers in the village church), and six married men aged thirteen to fifteen years, who were apparently excused as being too young to pay tribute.[26] When Governor Céspedes made the formal assessment of tribute on the basis of these lists, he stated that the total number of married men was 280 and that those who were exempt for the reasons stated above were 36. It appears therefore that our copies of the lists are not entirely accurate. Unfortunately we do not have record of the persons who were exempted from tribute because of noble birth. It would have included Don Pablo Paxbolon, cacique and governor of the pueblo, but it would be interesting to know the names of others who enjoyed noble status.[27]

[23] García v. Bravo, ff. 2107v–11v.

[24] *Ibid.*, ff. 2112–16v.

[25] *Ibid.*, ff. 2116v–28v. For a special study of the matrícula in relation to various phases of Chontal ethnology, see Appendix C.

[26] García v. Bravo, ff. 2135v–36v. On the basis of statements in later Yucatan documents it would appear that men became liable for tribute at the age of eighteen and women at sixteen.

[27] Don Gonzalo, if still living, would probably have been exempt. Other documents of the 1560's mention principal men named Don Francisco Montejo, who was alcalde of Tixchel in 1565, and Don Juan Pacua (1567).

By decrees of March 3–4, 1569, Governor Céspedes formulated a new tribute schedule on the basis of his brother's reports. From the total of 280 married men said to have been counted, the governor deducted the 36 who were exempt because of old age, widowed status, illness or infirmity, youth, and service as *cantores*. This reduced the total to 244. Then by reference to Loaisa's count and assessment of 1561, he deducted 23 more, the number who were exempted from tribute at that time, so that the net total liable to the annual tax of one manta each was 221.[28] This procedure would seem to imply that all of those who were reserved in 1561 enjoyed noble rank or some official position that would make them exempt. It may be doubted, however, that this was the case, since there must have been some persons in 1561 who were exempt because of old age and infirmity, if for no other reason.

As noted above, Loaisa had decreed in 1561 that in case a new count of Tixchel showed a greater number of persons than were listed in that year, the total tribute should be increased accordingly. Despite the fact that the 1569 matrícula, according to Céspedes' official statement, listed 280 heads of families as compared with 253 in 1561, the total annual tribute had been reduced by nine mantas. The encomendero called attention to this fact, but to no avail.

A short time before the 1569 count was made Don Pablo Paxbolon had visited the settlement of Tixchel fugitives who had fled to the old Acalan area about 1560–61 and had reported that they were now willing to submit to Spanish authority. For this reason the encomendero had objected to the making of a new count at this time, pointing out that a matrícula that did not include the fugitives would be prejudicial to his interests. Although the new count was made despite this protest, Governor Céspedes, in the official schedule of tribute formulated on March 4, 1569, decreed that the assessment might be revised at a later date, "whenever [the fugitives] should appear." This rather vague statement disregarded, however, the encomendero's claim that the Indians of the settlement recently visited by Paxbolon were actually tributaries of Acalan-Tixchel. About two and a half months later (May 1569) the governor placed this settlement under the protection of Feliciano Bravo, chief governmental notary of Yucatan, and in January 1570 he formally appointed Bravo as its encomendero. This action resulted in prolonged litigation, which will be described in the following chapter.

In 1569, as on former occasions, a certain number of married men probably were not listed. The official count shows, however, an increase of 10.6

28 García *v.* Bravo, ff. 2138–39*v.*

per cent in the number of families since 1561. This indicates that the Indians had finally surmounted the difficulties and hardships resulting from their removal from old Acalan and that they were successfully adapting themselves to their new environment and to changed conditions. Counting 4.5 persons per family, we find that Tixchel had a population of at least 1260 in the year 1569. The actual population was probably somewhat greater, since some of the families may not have been counted.

A brief report which the lieutenant governor filed with the matrícula of 1569 throws some light on economic conditions in the new settlement. The Indians evidently had a poor opinion of the site, for they told the lieutenant that it was not healthy, that the soil was poor, and that the sea winds consumed the crops. Some small cacao groves had been planted, but they pointed out that the trees were young and would not bear much fruit for many years. The pessimistic report of the Indians is not surprising, for the coastal area where they were now settled was undoubtedly less productive than the lands along the Candelaria where they had formerly lived. On the other hand, the lieutenant governor, who evidently compared the Tixchel region with the stony country of northern Yucatan, regarded the land as fertile and reported that good crops of maize and cotton were being raised. He also noted that every household possessed a number of turkeys and hens. But the fact that the tribute schedule of 1569, like that of 1561, did not call for payments in maize and poultry provides evidence that the Indians were not yet producing any considerable surplus of food.

The increasing prosperity of Tixchel was apparently based to a great extent on trade, for the lieutenant governor stated that "the people of the said pueblo appear to be traders and are wealthier than the Indians of these provinces [of northern Yucatan]." Although inter-provincial commerce was now largely dominated by Spanish merchant-colonists, the location of Tixchel enabled the Indians to share in the canoe trade between Tabasco and Yucatan. Their principal operations at this time appear to have been carried on with the Chontalpa in Tabasco. But there is also some evidence that they were already trading with the unpacified tribes in the interior of Yucatan, and as time went on this commerce apparently became more profitable. The later activities of Paxbolon in the region south and east of Tixchel were undoubtedly prompted in part by economic motives.[29]

[29] *Ibid.*, ff. 2136v–38.

9

The Zapotitlan Episode

ALTHOUGH MOST of the Acalan people who had survived the shock of the Spanish conquest were now firmly established in their new home on Sabancuy estuary, a certain number still remained in the Candelaria area, where they practiced the old native customs and religion. Some of the latter were apostate fugitives from Tixchel; others were unconverted Indians who had never left the old homeland. This chapter deals with the final pacification of these remnants of the Acalan people and their eventual resettlement at sites nearer Tixchel.

Most of the apostates were apparently members of the group who fled from Tixchel about 1560–61 after the Tamayo Pacheco expedition had brought out the "rebel" Chontal who had resisted Pesquera's efforts to move them from Acalan.[1] According to the Acalan narrative, the leaders of these apostate fugitives were Diego Paxcanan, Francisco Ahcuz, Baltasar Paxcanan, Martín Paxtun, and a certain Achachu.[2] The unconverted Indians were the survivors and descendants of former slaves who had fled during the period of disorder following the removal of the Chontal to Tixchel and had taken refuge at Chakam.[3] We have no definite information concerning events in the Candelaria area for several years subsequent to 1560–61. It would appear, however, that the Tixchel fugitives also settled in the region of Chakam and that in the course of time the two groups merged to form a settlement which in 1568–69 came to be known as Zapotitlan. This place, located at or near Chakam, was not far from the former site of Acalan-Itzamkanac, and on the basis of data recorded in various sources we infer that it was situated near the San Pedro branch of the Candelaria in the region of Mundo Nuevo.[4]

The Tixchel fugitives originally comprised about seventy families.[5] The slaves, young and old, are said to have numbered 600 persons,[6] but this

---

[1] See pp. 173–74, *supra*.

[2] The fact that Achachu had no baptismal name indicates that he was still a heathen.

[3] See p. 173, *supra*. Document IIIb of the Acalan narrative (p. 399, *infra*) lists the leaders of this group, none of whom had Christian names.

[4] Cf. discussion of the location of Zapotitlan and related topics in Appendix B, pp. 427–29, *infra*.

[5] Document IIIb of the Acalan narrative (p. 399, *infra*) merely states that "there must have been a great number." In 1571, however, Gómez de Castrillo, testifying concerning the removal of the Acalan to Tixchel and the Indians who fled about 1560–61, stated that the latter numbered "setenta indios," by which he obviously meant heads of families (García *v.* Bravo, f. 2085v).

[6] Cf. p. 399, *infra*.

figure, if correct, obviously refers to the size of the group which had settled at Chakam in years past. Both the apostates and the slaves, especially the latter, suffered heavy losses before their final pacification. Various sources indicate that in 1569 Zapotitlan had about eighty married couples, with a total of some 300 persons, although one document contains evidence that the actual figure may have been even lower. At this time the apostates formed the majority of the population, and one of their chieftains, Diego Paxcanan, was apparently the leader of the entire community.[7]

Some distance from Zapotitlan, evidently to the northeast, were two small villages named Puilha[8] and Tahbalam with a total population of about 125 persons. The Acalan narrative refers to the inhabitants of these settlements as "indios cimarrones," a term usually employed to designate apostate fugitives from northern Yucatan, and we have other evidence that most of them were Yucatecan Maya, although a small minority were apparently Chontal.[9] There is also some indication that the population of Zapotitlan may have included a certain number of Maya fugitives, but the great majority (at least 80 per cent) were undoubtedly Chontal or had Chontal names.[10]

The pacification of the Indians of Zapotitlan was accomplished by Don Pablo Paxbolon, the young cacique and governor of Tixchel, who made three entradas into the interior for this purpose in 1566–68. The major source of information concerning these journeys is a memorial written by Pax-

[7] In a letter to Governor Céspedes in January 1569, Don Pablo Paxbolon stated that there were eighty heads of families (*casados*) in Zapotitlan, and in two petitions, one presented in May 1569 and the second in August of the same year, he estimated the total population as about 300 persons (Paxbolon-Maldonado Papers, Part I, ff. 13, 17v, 19). The figure given in the Acalan narrative is evidently based on copies of these papers in Paxbolon's possession. However, one copy of the Zapotitlan baptismal document of 1569, lists only 57 couples and a total of 254 persons, including those who had been previously baptized and those who received baptism on that date (García v. Bravo, ff. 1962–70).

[8] Also spelled Puhilha and Puytha.

[9] Lists of personal names recorded for Puilha and Tahbalam contain a certain number of names that appear to be Chontal, but the great majority are Yucatecan Maya. What is more significant, the principal men in Puilha were Juan and Francisco Ku, and in Tahbalam, Lorenzo Can and Marcos Balam. Moreover, these villages apparently contained relatively few women, another sign that most of the inhabitants were fugitives (García v. Bravo, ff. 2155, 2169–70, 2206). Whether the small number of Chontal had come from Tixchel, old Acalan, or Zapotitlan is uncertain.

[10] The baptismal list drawn up at Zapotitlan in 1569 (García v. Bravo, ff. 1962–70, 2158v–67) contains a number of names which are also found in northern Yucatan. Some of them may also have been in use among the Chontal of Acalan. Comparison of the Zapotitlan list with the matrícula of Tixchel drawn up in February of the same year (García v. Bravo, ff. 2117–28v) reveals, however, that a high percentage—perhaps 80 per cent—of the Zapotitlan names were Chontal. Many names, such as Acat, Çelut or Çelu, Lahun, Lamat, Macua, Patzin, Paxbolon, Paxcanan, Paxmulu, Paxoc, etc., are found in both lists. Cf. discussion of Chontal names in Appendix C.

bolon and presented to Governor Céspedes for certification on May 27, 1569.[11] This narrative is supplemented by letters of the cacique and the testimony of Indians of Tixchel and Zapotitlan relating to the third and successful journey of December 1568.[12] Document IIIb of the Acalan narrative also gives a brief account of the Zapotitlan episode.

In January 1566 Bishop Toral passed through Tixchel on his return from Mexico City, where he had attended the Second Council of the Mexican Church. During the bishop's stay in the pueblo, an Indian woman whose husband had fled about five years earlier, probably in the group who abandoned Tixchel about 1560–61, sought permission to remarry. The bishop naturally refused her request, since it was possible that the fugitive might some day return. This incident caused Toral to ask Paxbolon if he knew the whereabouts of any "forest Indians" who might be converted. The cacique replied that there might be some from "the pueblo of Acalan." He asked permission "to go in search of them in the fields and forests, for it might be possible to find them," and the bishop agreed that he should do so, for if he should have success, "it would be a great service to God our Lord and his Majesty."[13]

Such was Paxbolon's version of the origins of his first entrada, as related in his memorial of 1569. Because of his early education by the Franciscans, Paxbolon was undoubtedly inspired by a certain zeal to serve the Church and to advance the missionary program. It is also apparent, however, that he was eager to enhance his own prestige as head of the ruling house of Acalan-Tixchel. Toral's visit, which occurred in the very month in which Paxbolon took office as governor of Tixchel, gave the young chieftain an opportunity to obtain the prelate's approval of an enterprise which, if successful, would win him the favor of the provincial authorities and at the same time enable him to assert jurisdiction over the Tixchel fugitives and other Chontal still living in the old homeland. Thus the expedition had a double purpose, but in his *post factum* report Paxbolon shrewdly stressed the religious motive.

Paxbolon probably discussed the proposed expedition with Antón García, encomendero of Acalan-Tixchel, and he also wrote a letter to a certain Fray Alonso[14] saying that he wished "to go to the said pueblo of Acalan in search of the Indians." This passage in Paxbolon's narrative and the refer-

---

[11] Paxbolon-Maldonado Papers, Part I, ff. 13–17.

[12] *Ibid.*, ff. 17v, 20–24v; García v. Bravo, ff. 2152–57v; Probanza of the services of Don Pablo Paxbolon, 1569–76, AGI, México, leg. 97.

[13] Memorial of Paxbolon, May 27, 1569, *in* Paxbolon-Maldonado Papers, Part I, f. 13.

[14] Probably Fray Alonso Toral, who is mentioned in other sources as serving in the Campeche-Tixchel area in the 1560's.

ence to the pueblo of Acalan in the account of his conversation with Bishop
Toral clearly indicate that it was the cacique's plan to go to the site of Acalan-
Itzamkanac, the former Chontal capital, evidently expecting to find the
fugitives at that place or nearby. Paxbolon asked Fray Alonso to commend
him to God in his prayers, "since it was always my intent to bring [the
Indians] to the knowledge of our Holy Catholic Faith," and the friar replied
"that I should go ahead with my journey and that God Our Lord would
go with me and give me victory."[15]

With a picked group of Indians Paxbolon set out from Tixchel on April
25, 1566. Traveling by canoe, he passed down Sabancuy estuary, crossed
Laguna de Términos, and then proceeded up the Río de Acalan, or Candelaria. Toward the end of the third day (April 27), he encountered the
first rapids and falls. Paxbolon and his men slowly made their way through
these obstacles, removing many logs and rocks from the channel and in places.
dragging the canoes through "with ropes by the sheer strength of [our]
arms." Finally, on the morning of the sixth day (April 30) they reached the
sluggish upper course of the river with its swamps and overflow areas.

In Paxbolon's narrative, the account of the arduous passage through the
rapids and falls is followed by this significant statement: "And after this we
came to certain lagoons, along which it was necessary for me and my people
to travel two days." This statement indicates that Paxbolon's original destination, the site of Acalan-Itzamkanac, was located two days' journey above
the falls of the Río de Acalan. It is on the basis of this evidence, together
with data from other sources, that we place Itzamkanac near the junction of
the Caribe and San Pedro branches of the Candelaria.

After reaching the lagoons on the morning of April 30, Paxbolon and
his men spent the remainder of the day fishing in order to replenish their
food supply, and while thus engaged some of them came to a place where it
appeared that canoes had recently been taken from the river. Scattered
maize and baskets were also found along the shore. Realizing that some of
the "forest Indians" could not be far away, Paxbolon now decided to go inland in search of them instead of proceeding upstream to the site of Acalan-
Itzamkanac, as he had originally intended. On the morning of May 1 the
party started overland, advancing cautiously along the trail, in which the
fugitives had planted pointed sticks of *chulul* wood, and about midday
reached some milpas where supplies of maize, beans, and chile were found.
Here Paxbolon decided to make camp and wait to see whether any of the
Indians would come out of the forest.

[15] Memorial of Paxbolon, May 27, 1569, *in* Paxbolon-Maldonado Papers, Part I, f. 13*v*.

On May 3, after Paxbolon's men had set fire to some fields, two young men appeared and were promptly seized. They wore their hair long in accordance with heathen custom and their bodies were painted black.[16] In reply to friendly words by the cacique, who asked whether they were Christians and where they had their homes, one of them, named Francisco Patzin, said: "I was a Christian . . . and this companion of mine, named Baltasar, was also [a Christian]; and as to what you ask concerning the location of our homes, we have no homes except the forests, and we are no longer your comrades." After further parley Paxbolon asked them "to go and inform the other Indians who were in those forests that I, the said cacique, was there, and that I came in peace and friendship as a son of their house and as lord to seek them." As a token of his friendly attitude, he sent a gift of salt for the principal men of the settlement, "so that they would see by this that I did not come to do any harm." He warned, however, that if he did not receive a reply within six days, he would go where they were and seize them.

Three days later (May 6) the messenger returned, bringing with him three other Indians, Diego Paxcanan, Francisco Ahcuz, and Baltasar Patzin, "who had been baptized." Paxbolon made them a pious speech, pointing out the error of their ways and urging them to return to a Christian mode of life. But they replied: "You no longer have the right to command, nor are we your comrades; allow us to live according to the customs in which we live, for we are very satisfied and content; return to your home." Having listened attentively to their words, the cacique told them that the devil had made them say such things, and he protested that he came to them for their own welfare. Whereupon the apostates responded that they wished to have nothing to do with anyone from Yucatan, and that if the cacique should again visit them he should bring no one with him except those who had accompanied him on this occasion. "And so I, the said cacique, took my leave and returned to my pueblo." Paxbolon gives no account of the return journey, merely stating that he reached Tixchel on May 14, 1566.[17]

This account of Paxbolon's first entrada, based on his narrative of May 1569, indicates that little had been achieved, except to establish contact with some of the fugitives, including two of their chieftains, Diego Paxcanan and Francisco Ahcuz. But Paxbolon was not easily discouraged, and soon after his return to Tixchel he got in touch with Fray Antonio Verdugo, probably one of the Franciscans assigned to the missions of Champoton and

[16] "Enbijados de negro."
[17] Memorial of Paxbolon, May 27, 1569, in Paxbolon-Maldonado Papers, Part I, ff. 13v–15v.

Tixchel, to whom he gave a report of his journey. The friar immediately wrote a letter to the apostates, urging them to return to the Christian faith; "and he gave me, the said cacique, this letter, which I later delivered to the said savages, and I read it to them and explained what it contained." Upon receipt of this message, the Indians expressed displeasure that Paxbolon had told the friar about them and they said that they had no desire to see the missionary or any other Spaniard. If the cacique wished to visit them and trade with them, such dealings must be between him and them only. Under such conditions they would also do his will and in time pay tribute to him, but Paxbolon piously told them that he desired only "to promote the law of God and his Majesty."

The remainder of Paxbolon's account of this second entrada, for which he gives no date, is rather obscure, and the language suggests that certain words or phrases of the original (our manuscript version is a copy) have been omitted. It appears, however, that before Paxbolon returned to Tixchel fifteen of the fugitives had started to build houses "on the site of Acalan," undoubtedly a reference to the former capital. Here they remained for a time "and were halfway converted." But later on "they repented [of their conversion] and went away again into the forests to practice idolatry."[18]

The brief account of the pacification of Zapotitlan in Document IIIb of the Acalan narrative helps to clarify the situation. Here we are told that in the year (1566) in which Paxbolon assumed office as governor of Tixchel he "brought out" the fugitives after finding them at a place called Sucte. "They fled again in the year 1568 and again he found them" with the former slaves in Zapotitlan. This version apparently telescopes the first two entradas. The place named Sucte was probably the milpas where Paxbolon met some of the apostates, including two of their principal men, Paxcanan and Ahcuz, in May 1566. But the statement about bringing out the fugitives obviously refers to what happened on the second entrada, when a small group began to resettle at the site of the former capital. Since it is unlikely that Paxbolon would have returned to the interior in the rainy season of 1566, his second journey probably took place in the spring of 1567. The abandonment of the new settlement, according to the narrative, occurred in the following year.

The milpas of Sucte were apparently located about midway between the upper course of the Candelaria above the falls and the site of Zapotitlan, which as we have already noted, was on or near the Río San Pedro somewhere in the region of Mundo Nuevo. Paxbolon did not visit Zapotitlan in 1566, and there is no evidence that he did so on the occasion of his second journey. Indeed,

[18] *Ibid.*, ff. 15v–16.

the statement of Francisco Patzin quoted above may imply that in 1566 many of the apostates were still living in scattered groups in the forest. It is evident, however, that by the end of 1568 most of them had joined with the former slaves and were living at or near Zapotitlan.

Although the fugitives whom Paxbolon had contacted on the first and second entradas had recognized him as their legitimate lord and ruler, they were unwilling to submit to Spanish authority or return to the Christian faith. But the cacique, although anxious to assert jurisdiction over them, refused the terms they proposed. He desired recognition of his rights by the provincial authorities of Yucatan, and he realized that this could be obtained only after the Indians had been pacified in the name of the king and the Church. The temporary and partial success achieved on the second entrada was a step in this direction, but complete submission of the Indians was the only means of attaining his major purpose. With this end in view he made plans for a third expedition, this time determined to secure permanent results.

With sixteen experienced and trusted companions from Tixchel, Paxbolon set out again for the interior on December 10, 1568, and after a journey of seven days approached the settlement at Zapotitlan. In accordance with a pre-arranged plan, Paxbolon and his followers rushed into the village, surprising its inhabitants who were unaware of their approach. Some offered a feeble resistance, but most of them took to their heels and fled into the surrounding forests. Paxbolon's men gave chase and seized six of their leaders, whom they brought before the cacique. By friendly words Paxbolon made them understand that he meant no harm, and they agreed to round up the others. Within three or four days all those who had fled returned to the village, bringing their wives and children.

During his subsequent parleys with the Indians Paxbolon explained that they were deceived in putting trust in their idols (*quiçines*), "for there was only one God, Creator of all things, and they should believe in Him and in His Blessed Mother." He also told them that it would be better for them to live under the protection of the king and his governor in Yucatan, from whom they would receive favor and good treatment as did all the other Indians who had submitted to Spanish rule. With such words he finally persuaded them to give obedience and abandon their heathen ways, but apparently they agreed only on condition that they be permitted to live in their present location and not be moved to another site. To this Paxbolon agreed, promising to intercede for them with the provincial governor and to see that a missionary was sent to instruct them in Christian doctrine.

In token of their submission the Indians handed over their bows and arrows, lances, shields, and other weapons. At Paxbolon's command they also brought out all their idols "and other things which they had in a devil house," all of which the cacique destroyed and burned in their presence. Such objects, he told them, were things to laugh at and scorn, and not to worship and venerate.

After a stay of nine days in Zapotitlan, Paxbolon returned to Tixchel, taking with him six of the principal men, including Diego Paxcanan. In Tixchel the cacique gave these men religious instruction, clothed them, and sought to show them the advantages of living like the Indians of his own pueblo, under the protection and guidance of the provincial authorities and the missionary clergy. He also urged them to go to Mérida to see the Spanish governor, perhaps with the idea of obtaining formal recognition that he was their cacique and lord. But they were unwilling to make the trip, saying that the governor might find them strange because they wore their hair long and that they would be ashamed. So after two weeks Paxbolon sent them back to their homes, instructing them to open a road and promising to bring a priest to baptize their people. In order that they might have some religious teaching in the meantime, he sent with them two native teachers from Tixchel "to preach to them and teach them their prayers in the language of Chontalpa, which is the same as ours of Tixchel, and it is also their native language." One of these native teachers, named Miguel Huncha, remained in Zapotitlan for about two years.[19]

Toward the end of January Paxbolon dispatched reports to Governor Céspedes and Bishop Toral in which he described the results of his recent journey to Zapotitlan. He told how he had persuaded the Indians to abandon their heathen ways and to submit to Spanish rule, having assured them that they would be received under the royal protection and that provision would be made for their baptism and religious training. Paxbolon also petitioned the governor to permit the inhabitants of Zapotitlan to remain where they were, at least for the present, "for they have good land, and they have cacao groves, large forests, and wood for making canoes." He suggested, however, that in the course of time they might be moved to the Río de Acalan, where they would be only three days' journey from Tixchel. What Paxbolon evidently had in mind was a site on the Candelaria above the falls, and the time schedule refers to the trip downstream to Laguna de Términos and thence to Tixchel.[20]

In one of his letters Paxbolon also announced the discovery of the two smaller villages of Puilha and Tahbalam, whose principal men he had brought

[19] Paxbolon-Maldonado Papers, Part I, ff. 16–26, *passim;* García *v.* Bravo, ff. 2152–52*v;* Probanza of the services of Don Pablo Paxbolon, 1569–76, AGI, México, leg. 97.
[20] Paxbolon-Maldonado Papers, Part I, ff. 17–17*v;* García *v.* Bravo, ff. 2154–55.

to Tixchel. Since this letter does not state that Paxbolon had visited these settlements, we infer that the principal men came to Zapotitlan during his stay in that place, and that they then accompanied him to Tixchel. The cacique referred to the inhabitants of Puilha and Tahbalam as "heathens," but it is evident that they were actually apostates, most of them from northern Yucatan.[21]

On January 31, 1569, these reports were reviewed by Governor Céspedes in the presence of Francisco Palomino, defender and protector of the Indians in Yucatan, and Feliciano Bravo, the chief governmental notary (*escribano mayor de gobernación*). The same day two Indians from Tixchel, who had brought the letters, gave testimony which confirmed the cacique's reports. On petition of Palomino the governor formally received the inhabitants of Zapotitlan under his protection as vassals of the king and agreed to consult Bishop Toral in regard to their instruction in the Christian faith. Céspedes also accepted a recommendation by Palomino that for the present Paxbolon, "as the person whom the Indians will most willingly obey," should be instructed to look after them and supervise their local affairs. It may be noted, however, that in the documents recording these proceedings there is no reference to Paxbolon's rights in the matter as cacique and natural lord of Acalan-Tixchel.[22]

In letters dated January 31 and February 16 Céspedes thanked Paxbolon for his loyal services and expressed satisfaction with what had already been accomplished. He told the cacique to continue the good work, to seek out any other Indians who might be living in the forests, and to offer all of them favor and protection in the governor's name, especially in the case of the two settlements of Puilha and Tahbalam. The governor also agreed that the Indians of Zapotitlan should continue to live in their present location and advised Paxbolon that it was not a suitable time to discuss their eventual transfer to another site. Such a proposal, if the Indians should hear of it, might cause unrest and hinder the missionary work to be carried on among them.[23]

Bishop Toral, to whom these decisions were notified, immediately agreed to send a missionary to Zapotitlan to supervise the religious instruction of the Indians. The person chosen for this task was Fray Juan de Santa María of the Mercedarian Order, who had been serving for several months as curate and *vicario* of the missions of Champoton and Tixchel and had probably acquired

---

[21] García *v.* Bravo, f. 2155. The principal men of Puilha and Tahbalam and all other Indians listed for these settlements had Christian names. Cf. also note 9, p. 186, *supra*.

[22] Paxbolon-Maldonado Papers, Part I, ff. 17v–18; García *v.* Bravo, ff. 2152–57; Probanza of the services of Don Pablo Paxbolon, 1569–76, AGI, México, leg. 97.

[23] Paxbolon-Maldonado Papers, Part I, ff. 18v–19, 24v–25.

some knowledge of the Chontal language.[24] In a letter to Paxbolon, written a few days later, the bishop expressed pleasure over the happy outcome of the Zapotitlan affair and promised to visit the new mission at some later time. This letter indicates, however, that the cacique's motives had not been entirely disinterested. In his report to the bishop, Paxbolon had apparently suggested that the Indians of Zapotitlan might soon begin to pay him tribute.[25] In rather outspoken terms Toral disapproved of the proposal and told the cacique that the Indians should be favored in every way possible in order to facilitate the missionary program. He also called attention to royal legislation which provided that Indians who accepted Christianity freely and without the use of force should be exempt from tribute for a term of years, and he informed Paxbolon that he had already brought this point to the attention of Governor Céspedes.[26]

In accordance with Bishop Toral's instructions Father Santa María, accompanied by Don Ambrosio de Montejo, cacique of Champoton, and by Paxbolon and other Indians of Tixchel, went to Zapotitlan a few weeks later. Prior to his arrival the native teachers sent by Paxbolon had already given the Indians some instruction and had probably made arrangements for the baptism of those who had not previously received the sacrament. The latter would have included children of the apostate fugitives born after their parents had fled from Tixchel in 1560–61 and the adult survivors of the unconverted slaves and their families. The document recording Santa María's visit states that the friar entered Zapotitlan on March 18, 1569, and dedicated the new mission to Nuestra Señora de los Remedios. This record also lists the Indians of the settlement in five groups: (1) married couples baptized by the missionary, with the names of their sponsors; (2) married couples previously baptized, presumably in old Acalan or in Tixchel (the names of Diego Paxcanan and his wife appear at the head of this list); (3) unmarried adults including some who had already been baptized (no sponsors are listed for them) and others now baptized by Santa María (the sponsors are listed); (4) children baptized by the missionary, with the names of their parents and sponsors; and (5) widows previously baptized.[27]

24 García v. Bravo, f. 2157.

25 This was a rather unusual suggestion, for subsequent to the conquest the Indians paid formal tribute only to the Crown or to encomenderos. It should be noted, however, that the colonial authorities authorized the giving of services and certain payments in cash or kind to caciques and descendants of natural lords (cf. Roys, 1943, pp. 146–47), and it is possible that this was what Paxbolon had in mind. It is evident, however, that Bishop Toral believed that the cacique wished to receive formal tribute from Zapotitlan.

26 Toral to Paxbolon, n. d., in Paxbolon-Maldonado Papers, Part I, ff. 25–26.

27 Two copies of this document are included in García v. Bravo, ff. 1962–70, 2158v–67.

During the friar's stay in Zapotitlan (March–April 1569) a small church was built, probably a pole-and-thatch structure with an enclosed altar space. It was furnished with a bell, image, frontal, and candlesticks sent from the church at Tixchel. During this time Santa María also obtained a list of Indians living in Puilha and Tahbalam. It is not clear, however, whether he actually visited these settlements or received the information from some of their inhabitants who came to Zapotitlan.[28]

Upon his return to Yucatan Father Santa María proceeded to Mérida, where he presented the baptismal lists to Bishop Toral. The latter in turn handed over the lists to Feliciano Bravo, the governmental notary, and requested that the original or a copy should be filed with other papers relating to Zapotitlan in the notary's possession. Santa María also gave testimony before Bravo concerning his recent activities in Zapotitlan. These proceedings were recorded in a document of May 10, 1569, formulated by Bravo, to which the notary added a copy of the baptismal lists. The original was returned to the bishop, who apparently gave it back to the missionary for future use at Zapotitlan.[29]

The document of May 10 contains two important statements attributed to Father Santa María: (1) that the Indians of Zapotitlan were settled "in a new land"; (2) that they were ignorant of Christianity and had never had dealings with Christians. In view of the Zapotitlan data already presented, it is evident that these statements were inaccurate, and we doubt that the friar ever made them, at least in the form recorded by Bravo in the May 10 document. Santa María had served as curate of Champoton and Tixchel since the autumn of 1568, and it seems likely therefore that prior to his journey to the new mission he already knew that it was located in the old Acalan area and that the people were former subjects of Acalan and Tixchel. In any case, as the result of his recent visit to Zapotitlan he had certainly learned that the Indians spoke the Chontal language of Acalan-Tixchel, that most of them had Chontal names like those of the Tixchel Indians, and that many of the adults were Tixchel fugitives who had previously been converted and baptized. In testimony before Bravo the missionary may have described the Zapotitlan country as a remote region distant from northern Yucatan, and he undoubtedly reported that the Indians had been living according to heathen customs. It is difficult to believe, however, that he regarded the Zapotitlan area as a "new land" hitherto unknown, or that he described the Indians as a people who were completely ignorant of Christianity and had never had contacts

[28] The Puilha and Tahbalam lists are in García v. Bravo, ff. 2169–70.
[29] Ibid., ff. 2157v–67.

with Christians. We are convinced that in recording Santa María's testimony Bravo misrepresented it or rephrased it in such a way as to facilitate a scheme of action that was soon revealed.

The Zapotitlan papers, including the document of May 10, were now laid before Governor Céspedes. The latter, "having seen the *autos*," issued a decree on May 20, 1569, in which he declared that the Zapotitlan people were "vacant" Indians and that as such they could be granted in encomienda to a suitable person, subject to the provisions of royal laws granting tribute exemption for a term of years to Indians who voluntarily submitted to Spanish authority and agreed to accept Christianity. This decree was communicated to Francisco Palomino, defender of the Indians, who voiced no objection. Accordingly, on May 25, 1569, the governor placed the Indians of "the pueblo and province of Zapotitlan" under the care and protection of Feliciano Bravo, who was charged with fostering their religious instruction. Although this procedure did not constitute a formal grant of encomienda, it was a step in that direction. Bravo promptly accepted the obligation and paid Father Santa María 20 pesos as an advance toward expenses he might incur in future work at Zapotitlan. About eight months later, January 15, 1570, Governor Céspedes made formal grant of encomienda of the pueblos of Zapotitlan, Puilha, and Tahbalam to Bravo, on condition that the Indians should pay no tribute until after the expiration of the exemption period provided by law.[30]

The decrees of May 20 and 25, 1569, precipitated a bitter dispute concerning the encomienda status of Zapotitlan which dragged on for more than two years. As encomendero of Acalan-Tixchel, Antón García protested that the Indians of Zapotitlan were his tributaries and that consequently Governor Céspedes had no right to declare them vacant and place them under the protection of another party. The controversy was intensified when the governor, by decree of January 15, 1570, granted the towns of Zapotitlan, Puilha, and Tahbalam in encomienda to Bravo. That García had a valid claim to Zapotitlan as part of his encomienda of Acalan-Tixchel there can be no doubt. It is evident, however, that from the beginning Céspedes and his governmental associates adopted a policy designed to deny this claim and to defraud the encomendero.

This policy can be traced back to January 31, 1569, when Paxbolon's reports of the 1568 entrada were reviewed by the governor in consultation with Feliciano Bravo and the defender of the Indians, Francisco Palomino.

[30] *Ibid.*, ff. 2167–69, 2171–72. The period of tribute exemption for Indians who voluntarily accepted Christianity was ten years.

It is interesting to note that the various petitions and decrees formulated on this occasion contain only vague statements as to the location of Zapotitlan with no mention whatever of Acalan,[31] and refer to the Zapotitlan people as Indians who had now agreed to accept Spanish authority and Christianity for the first time. For example, Palomino's petition asking Governor Céspedes to accept the offer of obedience made by the Indians described them as people who "have never had the light or knowledge of our holy Catholic faith." Moreover, the defender's request that Paxbolon should be instructed to take charge of local affairs in the Zapotitlan area and the governor's decree accepting this suggestion contain no reference to Paxbolon's rights in the matter as cacique and natural lord of Acalan-Tixchel.

It may be argued that at this time the provincial authorities lacked adequate information concerning Zapotitlan and its people. In this connection it is only fair to state that Paxbolon's January reports do not record explicit evidence as to the location of the settlement and the identity of its inhabitants. The cacique's long memorial describing his three entradas to the Acalan-Zapotitlan area beginning in 1566, which is the major source for our own narrative, was not presented to Céspedes and Bravo for certification until May 1569. On the other hand, in one of the January letters Paxbolon made the significant statement that in the course of time the Indians of Zapotitlan might be moved to a site on the Río de Acalan where they would be only four days' journey from Tixchel. Moreover, one of the Indian messengers who delivered the January reports testified before Palomino and Bravo that the purpose of the 1568 expedition to Zapotitlan was to search for Indians who had fled from Tixchel.[32] These statements, which obviously provided important clues as to the location and status of the Zapotitlan settlements, were apparently disregarded by the governor and his associates. Although it is possible that they did not appreciate the full significance of this evidence, it is difficult to believe that such was the case. By virtue of their respective offices, Céspedes, Palomino, and Bravo were obviously in a position to obtain full and complete information concerning developments in all parts of the province. Moreover, Palomino and Bravo had lived in Yucatan for many years, and we doubt that they could have been ignorant of the basic facts in the Acalan-Tixchel-Zapotitlan situation.

Whatever the facts may be as to the extent and accuracy of the informa-

---

[31] One of these documents refers to Zapotitlan as being located "toward the region of Mazatlan." Another describes the Zapotitlan area as bordering on the Tixchel district (*ibid.*, ff. 2152v, 2157). These vague statements would obviously apply to the old Acalan area, but as noted above, these papers contain no explicit reference to Acalan.

[32] García *v.* Bravo, f. 2155v.

tion possessed by the provincial authorities at the end of January 1569, the major issue relating to the status of Zapotitlan was brought to their attention during the succeeding months. In the preceding chapter we have told how Governor Céspedes by a decree of February 1, 1569, authorized a new count of the tributaries of Tixchel. Antón García, the encomendero, promptly filed objection on the ground that the Tixchel fugitives had recently been reduced to obedience and that a count which failed to include them would be prejudicial to his interests. Despite this protest, the governor's lieutenant made a matrícula of Tixchel, on the basis of which Céspedes formulated a new tribute schedule on March 4, 1569. In this document the governor stated, however, that in view of García's objection that "certain Indians who are at present fugitives from the said pueblo were not counted" the assessment could be revised at a later date "whenever [the fugitives] should appear."[33] This statement can be regarded only as deliberately vague and evasive, inasmuch as García's protest obviously referred to the Indians settled at Zapotitlan, not to a group whose whereabouts was still unknown. If the governor had reason to doubt the encomendero's claim that the Indians of Zapotitlan were former subjects of Acalan-Tixchel, or if he had been motivated by a sincere desire to do justice, he could easily have postponed action pending an investigation of the facts. Instead, he proceeded with evident haste and resorted to a tactic which evaded the major issue of the case. In subsequent litigation García also called attention to the fact that the official decrees relating to the count and assessment of Tixchel studiously avoided any reference to Acalan.

The document of May 10, 1569, which records certain proceedings in Mérida after Father Santa María's return from Zapotitlan, marks the next stage in the evolution of a policy resulting in the denial of Garcia's claims. As we have seen, this document attributes to the missionary two inaccurate statements about Zapotitlan which we doubt that he made, at least in the manner recorded by Bravo, the governmental notary. At this point we call attention to the fact that the second statement, viz., that the Indians of Zapotitlan were ignorant of Christianity and had never had dealings with Christians, expressed the same idea already set forth in Palomino's petition of January 31, 1569, as quoted above. The obvious purpose of the May 10 document was to provide grounds for the decree of May 20, 1569, in which Governor Céspedes declared that the people of Zapotitlan were "vacant" Indians and subject to encomienda grant. Five days later (May 25) the governor, with the tacit consent of the defender of the Indians, placed "the pueblo and province of Zapotitlan" under the care and protection of Feliciano Bravo.

[33] *Ibid.*, f. 2139v.

Further evidence of fraud is provided by comparison of the two copies of the Zapotitlan baptismal list included in the record of the García v. Bravo litigation. One version (to be described as Copy A) is evidently the original drawn up at Zapotitlan by Father Santa María.[34] The other (to be designated as Copy B) is the copy made by Feliciano Bravo and attached to the document of May 10, 1569. Although Copy B is obviously based on the first version, it differs from the latter in many respects. Some of the differences may be ascribed to carelessness on the part of the copyist, but others cannot be explained on this basis. For the purpose of the present discussion it will be sufficient to call attention to two significant points.

1. The preamble to Copy A is a brief statement recording the entry of Fray Juan de Santa María in Zapotitlan, "pueblo de Acalan e sujetos," on March 18, 1569. In Copy B the preamble is much longer and records data not mentioned in Copy A. But what is most important, the former contains no reference whatever to Zapotitlan as being a pueblo of Acalan.

2. In Copy A the various name groups (see p. 194, supra) are identified by marginal notations or subheadings. In Copy B most of these notations and subheadings are omitted. Although the different groups in Copy B can be identified by comparison with Copy A, the former, standing alone, does not give clear indication that some of the Indians listed had previously been baptized.

It is our opinion that these changes and omissions in Copy B, as well as others that might be mentioned, were the result of deliberate intent on the part of Bravo, who made this copy or supervised the work. The reason for this fraud is clear. If the copy certified by Bravo had contained reference to Zapotitlan as a pueblo of Acalan, or if it had indicated that some of the Indians had previously been baptized, such evidence would have disproved the thesis set forth in the document of May 10, 1569, to which Copy B was attached, that Zapotitlan was located in a new land and that its people had never had contacts with Christians.

Finally, we call attention to the memorial, or relación, in which Don Pablo Paxbolon gave account of his three entradas from Tixchel to the Acalan-Zapotitlan area in 1566-68. This document indicates (1) that the purpose of the first entrada was to search for Acalan fugitives and that the original destination of Paxbolon on this trip was the site of Acalan-Itzam-

[34] This version (García v. Bravo, ff. 1962–70) was in the possession of Fray Juan de Santa María until January 24, 1571, when it was introduced as evidence in the lawsuit proceedings at the request of Antón García. There can be no doubt that it is the original. It contains no certification of copy. Moreover, the record of Santa María's testimony given on January 24, 1571, refers to it as "el mismo" which the friar had made in Zapotitlan (ibid., f. 1970v).

kanac, (2) that the fugitives whom he met at the deserted milpas in May 1566, after half a day's march inland from the Río de Acalan, were apostate Christians, among whom was Diego Paxcanan, one of the principal men of Zapotitlan, (3) that on this occasion Paxbolon addressed these men as their ruler and lord and that they recognized him as such, although they refused his appeal to submit to Spanish authority, (4) that as the result of Paxbolon's second expedition (probably made in 1567) some of the fugitives were temporarily resettled at the site of the former Acalan capital, (5) that the pueblo of Zapotitlan was not far from this place, and (6) that the Indians of Zapotitlan spoke the Chontal language of Acalan-Tixchel. These facts, already noted in our own narrative, clearly prove that Zapotitlan was located in the old Acalan lands and that its inhabitants were former subjects of Acalan-Tixchel.

On May 27, 1569, a Spanish translation of the memorial was presented to Governor Céspedes and Feliciano Bravo, the notary. In a joint petition Paxbolon and Francisco Palomino, defender of the Indians, asked the governor to certify the document, to which should be added a statement setting forth the official action that had been taken in regard to Zapotitlan. By order of the governor Bravo prepared such a statement, in which he described the proceedings of January 31, 1569, the decision to send Fray Juan de Santa María to Zapotitlan, and the presentation of the Zapotitlan baptismal lists on May 10, 1569. This record and the Spanish translation of Paxbolon's memorial received formal certification in a decree of May 29, 1569, signed by Céspedes and countersigned by Bravo.[35]

Having given official sanction to these documents, the governor and his associates could no longer honestly deny the essential facts concerning the location of Zapotitlan and the identity of its people. Nevertheless, in all subsequent proceedings they sought to maintain the fiction that Zapotitlan had been discovered in a land hitherto unknown ("tierra no sabida ni conocida"),[36] and that the Indians were all heathens who had been newly converted to Christianity. Moreover, they took action to thwart Antón García's efforts to prove his claims to Zapotitlan and to obtain justice. These facts, together with evidence presented in preceding paragraphs, leave little doubt that Céspedes, Palomino, and Bravo were guilty of a deliberate scheme to defraud the encomendero and to give Bravo control over Zapotitlan.

[35] Paxbolon-Maldonado Papers, Part I, ff. 12–18v.
[36] This phrase appears in a petition of Feliciano Bravo, dated March 29, 1571 (García v. Bravo, ff. 1988–90v).

As a first step toward vindication of his rights, Antón García summoned to Tixchel certain chieftains of Zapotitlan, including Diego Paxcanan, now recognized as leader of the settlement. On July 8, 1569, these men made a sworn statement in the presence of Fray Juan de Santa María, Don Pablo Paxbolon, and the regidores of Tixchel in which they "freely" declared that in years past they had paid tribute to Diego de Aranda and Gonzalo López, former encomenderos of Acalan. Furthermore, they now "gave obedience in sign of possession" to Antón García as their present encomendero.[37]

From Tixchel García hastily returned to Campeche, where Governor Céspedes and Feliciano Bravo were temporarily residing at this time. On July 13, 1569, García filed a petition before the governor and notary in which he set forth his legal rights as encomendero of "the pueblo and province of Acalan with all its subject settlements (*sujetos*)." As supporting evidence he presented the decree of January 31, 1560, in which the Audiencia of Guatemala confirmed his titles as encomendero of Acalan,[38] and the Tixchel document of July 8 described above. The petition also reviewed the proceedings of February–March 1569, resulting in a new count and tribute assessment for the encomienda of Acalan-Tixchel. García pointed out that that Céspedes had authorized the count "at a time when the Indians who had fled during the removal to Tixchel were being reassembled, and others who had remained in the said province [of Acalan] were about to become Christians." He had filed protest on these grounds, but despite the objection the governor's lieutenant "counted the Indians who were settled in Tixchel, and he did not count the Indians of the subject settlements," i.e., the fugitives in old Acalan. Moreover, although the new matrícula of Tixchel listed more families than had been counted in 1561, the tribute schedule formulated by Céspedes called for an annual payment of only 221 mantas as compared with the assessment of 230 mantas fixed by Lic. García Jufre de Loaisa on the basis of the 1561 list. In view of these facts the encomendero asked to have the Loaisa assessment restored until such time as it would be suitable to count and tax all the Indians of his encomienda; otherwise he would receive "evident injury," and he would appeal to the Audiencia of Mexico.[39] For purposes of record García also asked for a copy of the present petition and for copies of the papers relating to the count and assessment of Tixchel in February–March, 1569.

[37] *Ibid.*, ff. 1973v–74.
[38] See p. 148, *supra*.
[39] The Audiencia of Mexico was again given jurisdiction over Yucatan in 1560 (DHY, 1: 8–9).

In his reply to the petition Governor Céspedes resorted to a legal formula often employed by the colonial authorities when they wished to evade a troublesome issue. The reply reads: "[This writing] having been seen by the said governor, his lordship states that he has already disposed of the matter (*ya tiene proveído en el caso*)." In short, the governor refused to reopen the question of the count and assessment of Tixchel, or to examine the validity of García's claim that the Indians of Zapotitlan were his tributaries. Céspedes agreed, however, that García might have copies of such documents as he wished, but when the encomendero asked for them Bravo put him off by saying that the papers relating to the count and tax of Tixchel were in Mérida.[40]

García apparently made no further effort to continue the litigation until the spring of 1570. In the meantime, however, he neglected no opportunity to strengthen his case. In September 1569 and again in the following April (1570) he paid Fray Juan de Santa María the salary due him as curate of Tixchel, and he saw to it that the friar's receipts contained statements indicating that the payments were for the religious instruction of all the Indians of his encomienda, including both Tixchel and Zapotitlan.[41] Likewise, García purchased an image and other ecclesiastical ornaments for the Tixchel church to replace those sent to Zapotitlan. It also appears that during the early months of 1570 García and Paxbolon began to make plans for the removal of some of the Zapotitlan people to Tixchel. As we shall see later on, this move was promptly challenged by Francisco Palomino, defender of the Indians.

On January 15, 1570, Governor Céspedes gave Feliciano Bravo a formal encomienda grant for the pueblos of Zapotitlan, Puilha, and Tahbalam. This action left no doubt as to the policy of the governor and his associates, and it obviously called for some countermeasure by García. It is evident, of course, that García's claim to Puilha and Tahbalam was less valid than in the case of Zapotitlan, since a majority of the Indians of Puilha and Tahbalam were Maya fugitives from northern Yucatan. These settlements were located, however, in the general area of Acalan and some of the Indians, at least, were Chontal. Moreover, as the result of the encomienda grant to Bravo the question of legal title to these towns was linked with that of Zapotitlan in all subsequent litigation.[42]

---

[40] García *v.* Bravo, ff. 2105*v*–07*v*.

[41] *Ibid.*, ff. 1972–73.

[42] Bravo, of course, had even less claim to the encomienda of Puilha and Tahbalam than García. Legally, the Maya fugitives were tributaries of the encomenderos of the towns from which they had fled, and most of the Chontal were probably Acalan-Tixchel fugitives.

For some reason García was unable to press the case in person, and he authorized a certain Juan González to act as his agent. In a petition to Governor Céspedes filed on April 10, 1570, González reiterated the complaint that the Tixchel tribute assessment of 1569 was unjust, since all of the Indians of García's encomienda had not been counted. Although this action did not directly challenge the validity of the encomienda grant to Bravo, it served the same purpose. If the governor admitted the plea, it would be necessary to reopen the entire question of the identity and status of the Indians of Zapotitlan and adjacent settlements, for they were the people who had not been counted. But now, as before, Céspedes had no intention of facing this issue. "The said governor did not admit [the petition] and he tore it up, saying that it contained things contrary to customary procedure and disrespectful to a judicial officer; besides, his lordship had long since disposed of the matter." The governor decreed, however, that if González asked for copies of the assessment proceedings, the notary should give them.

The notary, of course, was Feliciano Bravo, who was an interested party in the case. We have seen that when García filed his first action in Campeche in July 1569, Bravo evaded his request for copies of the assessment documents on the plea that the papers were in Mérida. Now that he was encomendero-designate of Zapotitlan, Puilha, and Tahbalam Bravo had even greater reason for not wishing to furnish a record that could be used by García in an appeal to a higher tribunal. In subsequent litigation García claimed that the notary now refused González' request for copies of the Tixchel count and assessment proceedings, but the actual facts seem to have been somewhat different. It appears that Bravo offered to furnish copies of such papers as were in his possession on payment of the usual fees but protested that he could not make a complete record to date since Governor Céspedes had torn up the petition of April 10. González in turn refused to accept an affidavit without a copy of this document. The reason for his refusal is obvious, for a record of the case that contained no evidence that formal protest had been made against the 1569 assessment would have little value for García's purposes. The result of this legal farce was that García again failed to obtain the documentary data needed for an appeal in proper form on the merits of the case. The chief responsibility for this situation rested with Céspedes, who destroyed González' petition of April 10, but we suspect that Bravo, as an interested party, also had a hand in this tactic which could only have the effect of delaying formal litigation before a higher court.[43]

[43] This version of the April 10 hearing before Governor Céspedes and the controversy

Realizing that further action before the Yucatan authorities was futile, García now turned to the audiencia in Mexico City. His attorney gave the tribunal a factual review of the history of the case, called attention to the obstructionist tactics of Céspedes and Bravo, and filed intention of appeal on the major issues involved if the necessary papers could be obtained. By decree of May 27, 1570, the audiencia directed Bravo to furnish copies of any documents García might need for this purpose within four days after notification of the said decree.[44] There was evidently some delay in transmitting this order to Yucatan, for it was not communicated to Bravo until the following November (1570). In the meantime Bravo had taken effective measures to strengthen his own position as encomendero-designate of Zapotitlan.

Little is known concerning the course of events in the Zapotitlan area for several months after Fray Juan de Santa María's visit in March–April 1569. Acting on instructions from Bishop Toral, the friar apparently made other trips to the new mission from time to time to supervise the work of the native teachers, but we have no reports for these journeys. For the year 1570, however, more information is available. This is very largely due to the fact that Feliciano Bravo, after receiving formal appointment as encomendero in January 1570, actively intervened in Zapotitlan affairs.

On February 28, 1570, Bravo wrote a letter to the chieftains of Zapotitlan, Puilha, and Tahbalam to inform them that he was now their encomendero and that henceforth they should direct all their requests for help to him. At some length he described his interest in their general welfare and his desire that they should become good Christians. He also claimed credit for the decision of the governor and bishop to send a missionary to baptize and indoctrinate them. He charged them to heed Santa María's teachings and to accept the counsel of Don Pablo Paxbolon, "a good man who loves you much." In this letter Bravo also announced that he was sending an image of Our Lady and an altar covering for the Zapotitlan church and presents of hats, shirts, knives, scissors, and other articles for the caciques.[45]

The notary made arrangements with a certain Juan Nieto to take this message and the gifts to Zapotitlan. Nieto set out sometime in March but

---

concerning the furnishing of copies of the Tixchel assessment proceedings is based on later evidence introduced in the García v. Bravo case, especially ff. 2104–05v.

[44] Two copies of the audiencia decree of May 27, 1570, are recorded in García v. Bravo, ff. 1925v–28v, 1974v–78.

[45] Probanzas of Feliciano Bravo, AGI, México, leg. 109.

got no farther than Tixchel. It seems that Paxbolon refused to supply canoes and provisions for the remainder of the journey and indicated in other ways that he had no desire to cooperate with Bravo or his agent. Antón García undoubtedly had a hand in this affair, for he and Paxbolon had now joined forces to promote their own interests in Zapotitlan.[46]

Toward the end of March 1570, Fray Juan de Santa María gave up his post as curate of Champoton and Tixchel. It appears that he had supported García's claims,[47] and we suspect that Bravo had something to do with his withdrawal from service in the Champoton-Tixchel district. In any case there is evidence that the notary exerted some influence in the appointment of Santa María's successor, a secular priest named Juan de Monserrate. The latter, whom the bishop instructed to take charge of the Zapotitlan mission, promptly sponsored Bravo's cause and took measures to combat the projects of García and Paxbolon.[48]

In April Father Monserrate went to Tixchel to make preliminary arrangements for his first trip to Zapotitlan. In talks with Paxbolon, who agreed to accompany him on the journey, he learned that the cacique and Antón García were scheming to move the Zapotitlan people to Tixchel. Returning to Champoton, the priest reported this news to the provincial authorities, with the result that Francisco Palomino promptly filed action before Governor Céspedes to prevent execution of the plan. Palomino's petition, dated May 18, 1570, called attention to the fact that the governor had given his word that the Indians of Zapotitlan should not be moved from their present location. But now Paxbolon and García proposed to take them to Tixchel on the pretext that it would facilitate their religious instruction and because García, by virtue of various titles and decrees, "pretended" that they belonged to his encomienda. "These are frivolous reasons and of no value in this case." Consequently García should be punished and charged to maintain "perpetual silence" on the encomienda issue. Moreover, the governor should take action to prevent the removal of the Indians from Zapotitlan to any other place. In response to this appeal Céspedes decreed that there should be no

---

[46] García v. Bravo, ff. 2179v–81v.

[47] In May 1571, Don Ambrosio de Montejo, governor of Champoton, who accompanied Santa María on his first visit to Zapotitlan, testified that the friar told the Indians that Antón García was their encomendero. Similar testimony was given by Diego Paxcanan and Baltasar Patzin of Zapotitlan (*ibid.*, ff. 1893, 1897, 2092v).

[48] Although there is no evidence that Bishop Toral actively intervened in the encomienda dispute, he appears to have maintained a friendly attitude toward Bravo. Moreover, his letter to Paxbolon (see p. 194, *supra*) indicates that he was anxious to obtain tribute exemption for the Zapotitlan people for a term of years as a means of facilitating the missionary program. For this reason he may have favored Bravo's cause, since the encomienda grant to Bravo provided for such exemption, and consequently he may well have welcomed the opportunity to appoint the notary's friend as curate of Champoton and Tixchel and missionary to Zapotitlan.

innovation in regard to the status of Zapotitlan and dispatched an order to Paxbolon forbidding him to move any of the Zapotitlan people from their present location. It was not until July 6, however, that his order was received in Tixchel.[49]

In the latter part of May Father Monserrate, accompanied by a young Spaniard named Juan Vázquez Tirado, who was in Bravo's service, and Don Ambrosio de Montejo, governor of Champoton, set out for Zapotitlan. They took with them the gifts Bravo had previously tried to send by Juan Nieto and another letter from Bravo to the chieftains of Zapotitlan, Puilha, and Tahbalam. This dispatch, dated May 20, 1570, was framed in language similar to that of the notary's February letter. It is not surprising, however, that it contained no admonition for the Indians to heed Paxbolon's counsel.[50]

When Monserrate and his party reached Tixchel they learned that Paxbolon had already set out with seventy men with the express intention of moving the Indians from Zapotitlan. The missionary pushed on rapidly and caught up with the cacique before he had gone very far. After lengthy argument Paxbolon and his group apparently turned back to Tixchel, and Monserrate continued the journey to Zapotitlan. During a stay of nine days at the mission in the first and second weeks of June, Monserrate baptized several infants, laid out streets near the church, and instructed the Indians to bring in scattered families from the forests in order to form a compact settlement. To the principal men of Zapotitlan and those summoned from Puilha and Tahbalam he read Bravo's letter and presented his gifts. The governor of Champoton, who served as interpreter on this occasion, certified that the chieftains promised to obey Bravo's commands. Monserrate also saw to it that the Indians wrote letters of thanks to Bravo, "our encomendero."[51]

Upon his return to Champoton the missionary sent a report of his journey to Governor Céspedes. In this dispatch he recommended that Diego Paxcanan should be named governor of the pueblo of Zapotitlan and that Francisco Ku and Marcos Balam should be appointed to the same office in Puilha and Tahbalam respectively. The obvious purpose of these recommendations was to limit the influence and authority of Paxbolon in the Zapotitlan area. The cacique was evidently determined to assert his rights in this region as native ruler of Acalan-Tixchel, and the scheme to move the Zapotitlan people to Tixchel was inspired in part by this ambition. During his stay in

[49] García v. Bravo, ff. 2174v–79v, 2187.
[50] *Ibid.*, ff. 2182–84v.
[51] Probanzas of Feliciano Bravo, AGI, México, leg. 109; García v. Bravo, ff. 2184v–88.

Zapotitlan Father Monserrate also learned that the Indians were raising cacao and maize for Paxbolon and that they were sending timber to Tixchel on orders from the cacique. It may be assumed that they performed these services in recognition of Paxbolon's status as their natural lord. The appointment of local governors in Zapotitlan, Puilha, and Tahbalam, as recommended by the missionary, would in effect deny the cacique's rights by giving these towns full autonomy, subject only to the superior jurisdiction of the provincial authorities in Yucatan. It would also be a logical development of the fixed policy of Céspedes and his aids, who had consistently refused to admit that the Indians of Zapotitlan were former subjects of Acalan-Tixchel. It is not surprising therefore that within a short time after receiving Monserrate's report Céspedes issued commissions to Diego Paxcanan, Francisco Ku, and Marcos Balam as governors of their respective settlements.[52]

From the standpoint of the Indians of Zapotitlan the situation that had developed since the spring of 1569 must have been perplexing, to say the least. Although the promise of Governor Céspedes to leave the Indians in their present location had thus far been kept, they were undoubtedly aware of the fact that Paxbolon and García wished to move them to Tixchel. Paxbolon had also taken measures to impose his authority as cacique of Acalan-Tixchel in the Zapotitlan area. As the result of Father Monserrate's intervention, however, Paxbolon's authority had been curtailed by the appointment of local governors with autonomous authority for Zapotitlan, Puilha, and Tahbalam. Most confusing of all were the conflicting claims of García and Bravo. As we have seen, in the summer of 1569 García summoned the principal men of Zapotitlan to Tixchel, where they formally recognized him as their encomendero. But now Bravo had informed them that he was their encomendero by virtue of appointment by Governor Céspedes and that henceforth they should look to him as their protector and address all their communications and requests to him. Moreover, both García and Bravo claimed credit for support of the missionary program initiated by Fray Juan de Santa María. Consequently it was probably true, as Bravo claimed, that the Indians were "disturbed and upset" and wished to have this situation clarified. This "unrest," for which the provincial authorities were largely responsible, now served Bravo as a pretext for other moves to promote his own interests.

Toward the end of October 1570, Bravo informed the *provisor* of the diocese of Yucatan that Father Monserrate was making preparations for a second trip to Zapotitlan. The notary also presented a bell, images, and other

[52] García v. Bravo, ff. 2188v–90.

ornaments which he had purchased for the Zapotitlan church and requested
the provisor to certify that they were suitable for the purpose intended and
to send them to the missionary. The provisor acceded to this request.[53] Although Bravo alleged that he had received a letter from the Indians of his
encomienda asking for the bell and ornaments, no such document is found
in the papers which constitute Bravo's defense in the litigation with García.
The real purpose for sending these articles to Zapotitlan at this time will be
revealed in the succeeding paragraphs.

Before Monserrate set out for Zapotitlan an important event occurred.
On November 14, 1570, when Bravo was in Campeche on official business,
García presented the decree of the Audiencia of Mexico described above (see
p. 204, *supra*). By this action García served notice that he intended to press
his claims and to carry an appeal to the audiencia as soon as he obtained copies
of the necessary papers, which Bravo, by the terms of the decree, was ordered
to provide without delay. The notary realized therefore that prompt action
was necessary to strengthen his own position and to oppose his rival's claims.
So instead of giving an immediate reply he hurriedly made plans to accompany Monserrate to Zapotitlan. His alleged reason for going to Zapotitlan at
this time was to "tranquilize" the Indians and quiet their unrest. There can
be little doubt, however, that his actual purpose, as García later protested, was
to take personal possession of Zapotitlan as encomendero.[54]

Early in December Bravo went to Tixchel, where Father Monserrate, Juan
Vázquez Tirado, and others were already waiting. Paxbolon's services were
also enlisted for the trip to Zapotitlan, although we suspect that the cacique
consented to accompany the expedition because it would enable him secretly
to protect his own interests. Leaving Tixchel on December 8, 1570, Bravo and
his party rapidly crossed Laguna de Términos and proceeded up the Río de
Acalan, or Candelaria. That the notary was in great haste is indicated by the
fact that he traveled day and night and reached the sluggish upper course of

[53] *Ibid.*, ff. 2190–90v.

[54] Copies of the audiencia decree in the García *v.* Bravo papers contain a supplementary
statement dated November 10, 1570, which purportedly describes the notification proceedings
on that date (ff. 1928v–30v, 1978–80). This record states that Bravo gave obedience in the usual
form by kissing the decree and placing it upon his head and promised to make copies of the
documents requested by García as soon as he returned to Mérida, where the original papers
were on file. But the record does not end here. It goes on to state that Bravo protested that
his own interest in the Zapotitlan affair was entirely unselfish and that he had incurred heavy
expense in support of the new mission. Moreover, at great hardship and risk he had made a
personal visit to Zapotitlan to quiet the unrest of the Indians. But this trip occurred after November 14, 1570, and not before. In other words, the notification record, although dated November 14, was subsequently added by Bravo and was not made by the attesting notary whose
name appears at the end of the record. This means that Bravo not only failed to make immediate reply to the decree but kept possession of it until after his return from Zapotitlan in
December 1570. García did not fail to call attention to this fact in subsequent litigation.

the Candelaria above the rapids and falls on the afternoon of December 10. The following day he covered the 5-league overland stretch to Zapotitlan.[55]

On December 12 Bravo made a lengthy speech to the Indians assembled in the village church. He told how Governor Céspedes, as soon as news had been received of their "discovery," had placed them under his care and protection and had later named him as their encomendero. In fulfillment of his obligations he had sent priests to baptize and teach them and had provided ornaments for their church. In addition he had sent gifts of clothing and other articles for their principal men. Now he had come in person to visit them and "to undeceive them" concerning certain things they had been told and which had caused unrest among them. He assured them that the governor's promises that they would not be moved from their present location and that they would be exempt from tribute for a stated period would be scrupulously observed. He also wished them to know and understand that his sole interest as their encomendero was to promote their general welfare and to help them to save their souls by facilitating the work of the missionaries.

This harangue was recorded in a document signed by Father Monserrate, Juan Vázquez Tirado, Paxbolon, and Miguel Huncha, the *maestro de doctrina* serving in Zapotitlan. A copy was later filed with other papers in Bravo's defense in the encomienda litigation.[56] Although this document was intended to prove Bravo's unselfish motives, it is significant, as an indication of the notary's true purpose, that the record is entitled "Possession." It also states that after Bravo made his speech the principal men "embraced him" and promised to do his will. Moreover, although there is no mention of García in this document, Diego Paxcanan, governor of Zapotitlan, subsequently testified that Bravo explicitly told the Indians that they had no obligation to give tribute to García.[57]

Further evidence of Bravo's actual motives is provided by another incident of December 12, concerning which no reference is made in the document described above. We have already noted that in the spring of 1569 a bell and various ecclesiastical ornaments were sent from Tixchel for the Zapotitlan church and that García later purchased others for the Tixchel church to replace them. Consequently the items sent from Tixchel were in effect gifts by García as encomendero of Acalan-Tixchel. Monserrate and Bravo now in-

[55] For a detailed account of Bravo's trip to Zapotitlan, see Appendix B, pp. 421–24, *infra*.
[56] García v. Bravo, ff. 2193v–96v. Another copy of this document is found in the Probanzas of Feliciano Bravo, AGI, México, leg. 109.
[57] Testimony of Diego Paxcanan, Campeche, March 28, 1571, *in* García v. Bravo, f. 1894. Baltasar Patzin, another Indian of Zapotitlan, confirmed Paxcanan's testimony on this point (*ibid.*, f 1898).

formed the Indians that these ornaments actually belonged to the Tixchel church and should be returned, for it was illegal for them to possess the property of another church. In their place the provisor of the diocese had sent a new bell, images, and ornaments. It is evident, of course, that these new ornaments were those which Bravo had purchased and presented to the provisor in the preceding October. At first Paxcanan and the other chieftains refused to give up the bell and furnishings from Tixchel, but they finally consented to their removal under threat of excommunication by the priest and a warning by Bravo that a fine of 200 pesos would be imposed if they persisted in their opposition. This sordid affair clearly reveals Bravo's purpose to impose his will as encomendero of Zapotitlan and to undermine García's claims.[58]

On December 14 Bravo and Monserrate set out on the return trip to Tixchel, where they arrived on the 16th. The short stay in Zapotitlan and the evident haste of the journeys both going and returning also prove that some great urgency, viz., the recent developments in the encomienda controversy, had prompted Bravo's expedition. From Tixchel Bravo immediately proceeded to Campeche and thence to Mérida in order to report to Governor Céspedes and the provisor. Monserrate apparently remained for a time in Tixchel. In a letter to Lic. Cristóbal de Miranda, dean of the cathedral church of Yucatan, he gave account of his trip, describing the hardships encountered in passing through the rapids and falls of the Río de Acalan en route to Zapotitlan. He petitioned the dean to obtain his removal from the "banishment" area where he now served, an obvious reference to the isolation of the Champoton-Tixchel district.[59] The documents contain no further reference to Monserrate's missionary services, and we surmise that his removal as curate of Champoton and Tixchel was not long delayed. His active support of Bravo's cause was probably a major factor, however, in his transfer to a new post.

During his stay in Zapotitlan Bravo sent out a summons to the governors of Puilha and Tahbalam. He also instructed his servant, Juan Vázquez Tirado, to remain in the country until these men arrived and to arrange for the transfer of their people to Zapotitlan, where lands and house sites had

---

[58] The story of this incident is based largely on the testimony of Diego Paxcanan and Baltasar Patzin, Indians of Zapotitlan, and Bravo's servant, Juan Vázquez Tirado (García v. Bravo, ff. 1893v–94, 1897v–98, 2012–14). Although Bravo evidently tried to have Monserrate take the leading part in demanding removal of the Tixchel bell and ornaments, he later testified that it was done on his own authority in the name of the governor and bishop. His testimony carefully avoids any mention, however, of the threat of a 200-peso fine if the Indians refused to permit removal of the bell and ornaments (ibid., 2020v–23v).

[59] Monserrate to Miranda, Tixchel, December 16, 1570, in García v. Bravo, ff. 2199v–2201v.

been set aside for them. The Indians from Puilha and Tahbalam finally appeared a day or two before Christmas and agreed to the plan for moving the people of their settlements to Zapotitlan. They informed Vázquez that this would require a few weeks' time, but promised to bring their followers not later than Ash Wednesday of the succeeding year. Vázquez in turn promised that the missionary would return at that time to supervise the transfer.⁶⁰ It appears, however, that because of later developments in the encomienda litigation this plan for the consolidation of the three settlements in the Zapotitlan area was not carried out.

Having finished his business with the chieftains of Puilha and Tahbalam, Vázquez now returned to Yucatan. On this journey he was accompanied by Diego Paxcanan and three other chieftains of Zapotitlan. Antón García subsequently asserted that Vázquez compelled the Indians to accompany him, telling them that Governor Céspedes and Bravo had ordered them to do so, and that it was Bravo's purpose to obtain from them formal recognition in the presence of Céspedes that he (Bravo) was their encomendero. Both Bravo and Vázquez denied that any pressure had been imposed to force the Indians to make the trip and said that they came of their own accord to consult Céspedes on certain points that troubled them. Inasmuch as the Indians later stated that Vázquez insisted that they should accompany him, threatening to impose a heavy penalty if they refused, we are inclined to accept García's version of this affair.⁶¹

Although Bravo had apparently tried to make the trip to Zapotitlan with as much secrecy as possible, the news soon leaked out. Suspecting the intentions of his rival, García immediately took action to protect his own legal rights. On December 9, 1570, García filed an action before the lieutenant governor in Campeche in which he reviewed the history of the encomienda case and called attention to Bravo's failure to fulfill the provisions of the audiencia decree presented on November 14. Instead, Bravo had secretly gone to Zapotitlan "to take possession" and to defraud the petitioner. Consequently García, who was ill and unable to travel to Zapotitlan to contradict such

⁶⁰ *Ibid.*, ff. 2203v–09v.

⁶¹ Information on this incident is scattered through the García v. Bravo record. Vázquez testified (ff. 2014–14v) that the Indians wished to consult the governor because they were perplexed by conflicting statements by Monserrate and Paxbolon, the latter claiming authority as their chieftain. Bravo (ff. 2024v–25v) stated that before he left Zapotitlan the Indians had indicated a desire to go to see the governor and bishop, and that he told them they might come with Vázquez if they wished. On the other hand Paxcanan and his companions testified that Vázquez forced them to make the trip, telling them Bravo had ordered it. A letter from the Indians to García also states that Vázquez threatened a fine of 200 pesos if they refused (ff. 1894, 1914v, 1996–96v).

possession in person, made formal protest in writing against any proceedings
of Bravo in violation of his claims as encomendero of Acalan-Tixchel. A week
later García reiterated this protest in a similar petition before the lieutenant.[62]

Early in January 1571, Juan Vázquez Tirado, accompanied by Diego
Paxcanan and the other Indians from Zapotitlan, arrived in Campeche. When
García learned of their coming and that Vázquez was taking the Indians to
Mérida, he protested to the lieutenant governor, charging that this was another
move to serve Bravo's "pretensions." The lieutenant immediately ordered that
the Indians should be detained pending an investigation. On examination Paxcanan and his companions stated that they had received no orders from Governor Céspedes to come to Yucatan and that they had made the trip on
Vázquez' demand. In the meantime Vázquez hurried on to Mérida, where
Palomino and Bravo obtained orders from Céspedes that the Indians should be
permitted to continue the journey if they wished to do so. Although Vázquez
hastily returned to Campeche with these orders, the Indians apparently had
no desire to proceed to Mérida and soon thereafter returned to Zapotitlan.[63]

Having scored on this point, García now took action to prove that he had
given full support as encomendero to the missionary program in Zapotitlan
and to clarify the situation regarding the ecclesiastical ornaments recently
removed from the Zapotitlan church by Bravo and Monserrate. To this end
he presented as a witness Fray Juan de Santa María, founder of the Zapotitlan
mission. In testimony before one of the alcaldes of Campeche on January 24,
1571, the friar stated that he had received aid and assistance from García
during the time he had served as missionary in Zapotitlan, citing receipts for
salary paid by the encomendero. He also presented the original copy of the
Zapotitlan baptismal lists of 1569 as evidence of his own activities at the new
mission. With regard to the ornaments that had been removed from the
Zapotitlan church, the friar testified "that the citizens of the said pueblo of
Tixchel, being one with those of the said pueblo of Zapotitlan, had consented
that the said ornaments should be sent" to Zapotitlan. García had later purchased others for the Tixchel church.[64] The most significant item of this
testimony from the standpoint of the encomienda controversy is the state-

[62] García v. Bravo, ff. 1905–11.
[63] Ibid., ff. 1911–23. Paxcanan later testified (f. 1894) that Vázquez had not wished to enter
Campeche and tried to take the Indians around the town by way of a savanna trail. This maneuver failed, for García learned of their coming and had them summoned before the lieutenant.
Palomino later sought to prove that García exerted pressure on Paxcanan and his companions
and was responsible for their decision to return to Zapotitlan (ff. 2221–28v). We have no doubt
that García urged them to return home. The burden of the evidence, however, shows that fraud
and threats had been employed by Vázquez to induce the Indians to accompany him as far as
Campeche.
[64] García v. Bravo, ff. 1962–73v.

ment that the Indians of Tixchel and Zapotitlan were one people. This remark also provides additional evidence that Santa María could not have made the statements attributed to him in the document of May 10, 1569, by virtue of which Governor Céspedes placed the Indians of Zapotitlan under the care and protection of Feliciano Bravo.

Further action in the case was suspended until the arrival of Don Diego de Santillán, successor of Céspedes as provincial governor, who took office in Mérida on March 12, 1571.[65] Bravo evidently realized that with the coming of a new governor García would press his claims with increased vigor and that his own position, now that he would no longer have Céspedes' support, had become untenable. On March 10, only two days before Santillán assumed authority, Bravo resigned the encomienda of Zapotitlan in favor of the Crown.[66] By this maneuver Bravo apparently hoped to remove himself as a party in subsequent litigation and to embarrass García by forcing him to fight out the case with the treasury officials, who had charge of the administration of Crown towns.

Toward the end of March García started proceedings before Santillán to substantiate the claim that the Indians of Zapotitlan were his tributaries and to prove that without being defeated at law he had been deprived of his rights as encomendero. As part of the proceedings García also filed an accusation against Bravo on the following charges: (1) that Bravo, as governmental notary, had failed to furnish copies of the necessary papers for an appeal to the audiencia; (2) that he had not complied with the audiencia's decree of May 27, 1570, of which he had received notification on November 14, 1570; (3) that the visit of Bravo and his companions to Zapotitlan in December 1570, which was characterized by false statements to the Indians, the forced removal of the bell and ornaments from the village church, and threats of punishment if the Indians disobeyed orders, constituted trespass on García's rights as encomendero. Juan Vázquez Tirado and Father Monserrate were also made defendants on the third charge.

As supporting evidence García presented numerous documents, including his titles as encomendero of Acalan, the 1560 decree of the Audiencia of Guatemala confirming these titles, the tribute assessments for Acalan in 1553 and for Tixchel in 1561, and copies of the proceedings in Campeche in November–December 1570 and January 1571. During the trial Bravo was finally obliged, on order of Santillán, to furnish copies of the Tixchel assessment documents of 1569 and available papers relating to the protests subsequently

[65] Molina Solís, 1907–13, 1: 120.
[66] García v. Bravo, ff. 2231–33v.

filed by García and his agent, Juan González. At García's request sixteen witnesses were summoned for examination on the basis of a lengthy interrogatory in which the complainant set forth the major points he wished to prove. These witnesses included Diego Paxcanan and Baltasar Patzin of Zapotitlan, Don Pablo Paxbolon and two other Indians from Tixchel, Don Ambrosio de Montejo, governor of Champoton, Lucas García Caltzin, a Spanish-speaking Indian from San Román near Campeche whose knowledge of Acalan affairs was said to extend over a period of thirty years, and prominent citizens of Campeche, Mérida, and Valladolid. Among the Spaniards were Juan Vela, Gómez de Castrillo, Blas González, and others who had personal knowledge of the Acalan country.

These witnesses gave ample testimony to establish the following points: (1) that the Indians of Zapotitlan were former Acalan subjects and spoke the language of Acalan-Tixchel; (2) that in years past the Zapotitlan people had paid tribute to García and to other encomenderos of Acalan; (3) that during the disorders resulting from the forced removal of the Acalan many of the Indians had fled to the old homeland where they reassembled at Zapotitlan; (4) that the count and assessment of Tixchel in 1569 had been made despite García's protest that a revision of tribute which failed to take into account the fugitives would be prejudicial to his interests; (5) that Céspedes had subsequently refused to recognize García's claims to Zapotitlan and had obstructed his efforts to obtain justice. The testimony also substantiated García's charges against Bravo, Vázquez Tirado, and Monserrate.[67]

The declarations of the Indian witnesses have special importance in relation to the origins and tribute status of the Zapotitlan people. Lucas García Caltzin, who had gone to Acalan in 1557 with Fray Diego de Pesquera and had accompanied Bravo to Zapotitlan in December 1570, stated that he had known many of the Zapotitlan Indians when they lived in Acalan and that "they are all of one language with those of Tixchel, born and raised in and proceeding from Acalan and its subject settlements." Diego Paxcanan, governor of Zapotitlan, testified that he had known García since his appointment as encomendero of Acalan, that in earlier years the Zapotitlan refugees had paid tribute to him, and that the Indians of Zapotitlan and Acalan "are all one people and of one language."[68] Similar testimony was given by Baltasar Patzin, who also stated that he had lived in Acalan when Pesquera forced the Indians

---

[67] The testimony of García's witnesses comprises ff. 1890v–1904v, 2061–80v, 2083–98 of the García v. Bravo record. The Zapotitlan and Tixchel witnesses testified on March 28, 1571, and the others in the second week of May.

[68] Paxcanan, said to be sixty years old, also stated that he knew these facts to be true because "since childhood he had lived and resided in the said pueblos of Acalan and Zapotitlan."

to move to Tixchel and that he was one of those who later ran away. The
Tixchel witnesses and several of the Spaniards also made explicit statements
in support of the Acalan origin of the Zapotitlan people and their former
status as tributaries of García.

Bravo summoned no witnesses in his own defense, resting his case on
various petitions of objection, a lengthy personal statement in reply to the
charges,[69] and documents recording his Zapotitlan activities. He made excuses
for his failure to provide copies of the Tixchel assessment papers and played
for further delay on this point during the trial. An order of Santillán in
answer to repeated demands by García finally forced him to furnish them.
Bravo denied that selfish interest had motivated any of his Zapotitlan activities. On the contrary, he had merely acted in accordance with Céspedes' instructions to aid and protect the Indians and to assist the missionary program.
To this end he had spent a considerable sum of money without any material
reward. He was forced to admit, however, that removal of the bell and ornaments from the Zapotitlan church had been carried out on his initiative and
authority, although he sought to justify it on the ground that these items had
belonged to the Tixchel mission and had been sent to Zapotitlan without consent of the Tixchel Indians. This was an obvious misstatement of fact, as Santa
María's testimony proves. During the trial García also charged that receipts
of salary paid by Bravo to Monserrate were fraudulent, to which Bravo gave
no satisfactory answer.[70]

During the entire proceedings Bravo stubbornly maintained the old line
of argument that Zapotitlan was located in a new and unknown land and that
the people had all been heathens. With regard to the encomienda issue he
insisted that he was no longer an interested party and that the treasury officials
should assume responsibility for litigation on this point. Although these officials
went through the motions of demanding possession of Zapotitlan in the name
of the Crown, it was evident, as García took pains to point out, that they
realized that they had no case. They summoned no witnesses and based their
demand for possession on Céspedes' grant of encomienda to Bravo, the papers
illustrating Bravo's support of the Zapotitlan mission, and his resignation of
the encomienda to the Crown. No attempt was made to challenge García's
claims on the major issue, viz., that the Zapotitlan people were former tributaries of Acalan-Tixchel.

Governor Santillán finally pronounced his decision in the case on June

[69] This declaration, made on May 2, 1571, constitutes the most comprehensive statement of
Bravo's defense (García v. Bravo, ff. 2018–31).
[70] Although García submitted no proof of this charge, evidence that Bravo had tampered
with other documents lends some support to the accusation.

18, 1571. He declared that Céspedes had unlawfully dispossessed García of his encomienda rights in Zapotitlan, Puilha, and Tahbalam, and that consequently the grant of these towns to Bravo was null and void. Since Céspedes had no right to make this grant, Bravo in turn could not resign it to the Crown. Therefore García should be placed in possession and he should not again be dispossessed without being defeated at law in accordance with royal decrees regulating procedure in encomienda disputes.[71] Moreover, since Céspedes had exceeded his legal authority in this case, it should be made a charge against him in his residencia and the García v. Bravo record should be incorporated in the proceedings as evidence. Bravo was fined 30 pesos gold and forbidden to enter the Zapotitlan area for ten years. His servant, Vázquez Tirado, was fined 120 pesos and condemned to perpetual banishment from Zapotitlan.[72]

Upon notification of the decision Bravo made formal protest and gave notice of an appeal to the audiencia. There is no record that such an appeal was actually made. Among other points listed in his petitions of protest Bravo complained that he had spent a considerable sum of money in behalf of the Zapotitlan mission and called attention to the fact that he had resigned the encomienda to the Crown on condition that if it were regranted to another party the latter should repay him. According to the terms of the decision the resignation was declared null and void inasmuch as Bravo never possessed a valid title to Zapotitlan. It is quite possible, however, that in imposing a light sentence on Bravo the new governor took into consideration what the notary had spent on the Zapotitlan mission. In any case the heavier sentence imposed on Vázquez seems unjust, for he was a youth of only eighteen years and as Bravo's servant had merely carried out orders. The charge against Céspedes was formulated as Article 39 of the residencia indictment to the effect that the former governor illegally granted the Indians of Zapotitlan to Bravo without proper investigation as a personal favor to the notary. Santillán found Céspedes guilty on this charge and imposed a penalty of six months' banishment from Mérida.[73] The complaints against Father Monserrate were referred to the ecclesiastical authorities, but we have no record of their action.

[71] On this point the decision evidently refers to the Law of Malinas of 1545, confirmed and clarified by a royal decree of 1550. This legislation provided that in the case of an encomienda dispute resulting from conflicting claims or titles, the parties involved should submit *informaciones*, or evidence, of their respective claims to the audiencia within a prescribed period of time. The audiencia should then close the record and transmit it to the Council of the Indies for final decision. In the meantime there should be no dispossession of the party holding the encomienda by virtue of prior claim or title. At García's request copies of these decrees were introduced into the García v. Bravo record (ff. 2143v–50v) a few days before Santillán handed down his decision.

[72] García v. Bravo, ff. 2238–40v.

[73] Residencia of Don Luis Céspedes de Oviedo, AGI, Justicia, leg. 250, f. 604, leg. 251, f. 750v.

Although Bravo must have suffered a certain loss of prestige as a result of the Zapotitlan affair, his position as chief governmental notary, which he had purchased a decade earlier, was in no way threatened. This office gave him great influence in provincial administration and most of the governors worked in close cooperation with him to their mutual benefit. Céspedes evidently gave Bravo the encomienda of Zapotitlan, as well as another grant in Tabasco, as reward for the notary's support in other phases of local government. We shall see that Santillán and his successors employed Bravo in various commissions and offices of trust.

Palomino's office of defender of the Indians was also an important post. In later years Palomino carried on a long and bitter campaign against the encomenderos, seeking to reduce the tribute burden, to alleviate the evils of forced labor, and to effect other reforms. We are of the opinion that his role in the Zapotitlan affair was inspired by a desire to relieve the Indians of tribute for a term of years, as Céspedes decreed. There is also some evidence, at least for later years, that Palomino found it expedient to maintain friendly relations with Bravo in order to facilitate litigation in behalf of the Indians.[74]

The decision of June 18, 1571, gave García unqualified possession of Zapotitlan, Puilha, and Tahbalam as part of his encomienda of Acalan-Tixchel. So far as we know his rights were never again challenged. In the case of Zapotitlan the decision was obviously called for by the evidence presented. Although García had a less valid claim to Puilha and Tahbalam, in view of the fact that most of the Indians were evidently Yucatecan Maya fugitives, he had a stronger case than Bravo, for some of the Indians were Chontal and the settlements were apparently located within the confines of the Acalan area. By order of Santillán the pueblos of Zapotitlan, Puilha, and Tahbalam were counted and taxed on the same basis as those of Tixchel, but when García sought to collect the tribute the Indians protested on the ground that the former governor had promised them exemption from tribute for ten years. As we should expect, Palomino supported the Indians on this point. Appeal was made to the audiencia, but the decision of this tribunal is not known.[75] Inasmuch as García's claim to encomienda rights in Zapotitlan, Puilha, and Tahbalam was not involved in this appeal, a decision favorable to the Indians would merely have postponed the payment of tribute until 1579, when the ten-year period of exemption would have expired.

Santillán's findings in the encomienda case were forecast by an earlier

[74] Palomino to the king, Mérida, October 2, 1572, AGI, México, leg. 99.
[75] Paxbolon-Maldonado Papers, Part I, ff. 6–8.

decree of March 30, 1571. This document confirmed Don Pablo Paxbolon's title as cacique and governor of Acalan-Tixchel and provided that he should have charge of local administration in the Zapotitlan area, exercising such authority as the successor of former rulers of Acalan. Thus the cacique finally obtained recognition of his own claims and achieved the end he had sought from the beginning of his Zapotitlan activities in 1566.[76]

Now that García's encomienda claims had been upheld and Paxbolon had been placed in control of local affairs in Zapotitlan, the encomendero and cacique were in a position to carry out their earlier plan to move the Indians to Tixchel or to sites in the Tixchel district. Although Céspedes had promised that the Indians should remain where they were, their transfer to another location could easily be justified on the ground that the old settlements were far away and that the difficulty of travel from Tixchel hampered the missionary effort. The removal of the Indians to new sites took place sometime between 1571 and 1573. Most of the inhabitants of Tahbalam and Puilha were apparently congregated in a single settlement called Xocola and later known as Mazcab or Mahazcab. In one report it was also called Puhila (Puilha). The Indians of Zapotitlan were resettled in a village known for many years by the same name but later called Tiquintunpa. The position of these new settlements, which were not far apart, cannot be accurately determined, but the available evidence indicates that they were located in the Mamantel area southeast of Tixchel. Xocola (Mazcab) was probably situated on the river near the modern settlement of Mamantel. Zapotitlan (Tiquintunpa) was evidently closer to the Gulf coast.[77] (See locations on Map 4, where the town names are given as Tiquintunpa and Mazcab.)

[76] Ibid., ff. 8v–9v.

[77] The Spanish version of the Acalan narrative states that the Indians were brought to a place called Hunlucho, and then adds: "And thus the people of Zapotitlan and Xoquelha were settled." A document of 1604 (Paxbolon-Maldonado Papers, Part II; AGI, México, leg. 359) records a site named Chumluchu or Chunlucho some distance in the interior, probably somewhere in the region of modern Matamoros. In describing the events of 1583–84, resulting in the founding of Popola, the Acalan narrative refers to a site called Puila near Chunuitzil. Since Chunuitzil, or Chacuitzil, was apparently in the same general region as Chunlucho, this may indicate that some of the Puilha people settled in this area. It is quite clear, however, that most of the Indians from Puilha, Tahbalam, and Zapotitlan were moved to sites closer to Tixchel and to the Gulf coast. A report of 1582 (DHY, 2: 62) indicates that the new village of Zapotitlan was some 8 leagues from Tixchel. The town of Puilha (evidently Xocola and not the place called Puila near Chunuitzil) was said to be in the same locality as Zapotitlan. Although the Mamantel River is more than 8 leagues from Tixchel, other evidence points to a location in the Mamantel area for Zapotitlan and Xocola. The name of the latter town appears as both Xocola and Xoquelha in the Acalan narrative. Xocola means "river" in Maya, and Xoquelha is the Hispanicized form of the Chontal word xocelhaa, which has the same meaning. Thus a river location is indicated for this town. In 1584 the settlement of Popola was founded near the "embarcadero" of the Mamantel, evidently toward the end of permanent canoe navigation on the upper course of the river. This site was apparently halfway betwen Xocola and Chiuoha, the latter being located farther inland than the modern site of Chivoja on A. Chivoja Grande.

The reasons for resettling the Indians of Zapotitlan, Puilha, and Tahbalam at sites on or near the Mamantel instead of moving them to Tixchel are not entirely clear. Lack of sufficient farmland close to Tixchel to accommodate an increased population may have been one factor. The Indians may have consented to leave the Candelaria area on condition that they should occupy separate villages. We are of the opinion, however, that choice of sites in the Mamantel region was largely prompted by Paxbolon's desire to extend his influence and authority over an expanding area south and east of Tixchel. The Mamantel provided an easy route of communication to the interior country occupied by the Cehache and by an increasing number of Maya fugitives from northern Yucatan.[78] During the latter part of the sixteenth century a flourishing trade developed between the frontier settlements of western and northern Yucatan and these unconverted and apostate Indians in the south-central part of the peninsula. The Mamantel settlements of Zapotitlan (Tiquintunpa) and Xocola (Mazcab) would give the cacique control over the river trade and communications between the Gulf coast and the interior country and would also serve as convenient outposts from which he might extend his control over a larger area. In Chapter 10 we shall describe Paxbolon's activities as a frontier leader and his efforts to enlarge his political and administrative authority in the region southeast of Tixchel.

The removal of the Zapotitlan people from the Candelaria country brings to an end our narrative of events in the old Acalan homeland. Small groups of Indians apparently occupied sites in this area from time to time in later years, but the region as a whole was now very largely unpopulated. In the seventeenth and eighteenth centuries the Términos district was exploited for dye- and logwood and occasional expeditions undoubtedly penetrated to the upper

---

Thus Xocola was evidently situated downstream from Popola, probably in the region of the modern site of Mamantel. We also know that the new village of Zapotitlan was somewhat nearer the coast, since Paxbolon traveled first to this place, thence to Xocola, and on to Chiuoha, when he pacified the Chiuoha people in 1574. The 1582 report, cited above, indicates, however, that Zapotitlan and Xocola were not far apart. In the seventeenth century Zapotitlan (then always called Tiquintunpa) and a town called Mamantel were joined to form a single mission (López de Cogolludo, 1867–68, bk. 4, ch. 19). This place called Mamantel was probably the earlier Xocola, or Mazcab. Other seventeenth-century sources also indicate a closer geographical relationship between Tiquintunpa (Zapotitlan) and Popola than between Popola and sites to the north such as Chekubul and Chiuoha (which by this time had been moved to the present site of Chivoja or nearby). Note that on Map 4 the towns of Zapotitlan and Xocola are recorded as Tiquintunpa and Mazcab respectively.

[78] Modern maps extend the Mamantel inland for only a short distance, i.e., about 30 km. Earlier maps carry its tributaries far into the interior. Although these older maps are probably inaccurate, it is interesting to note that the documentary sources of the early seventeenth century indicate that it was possible to travel by canoe from the Bolonpeten, or Isla Pac, area to Popola on the upper Mamantel, at least at certain seasons of the year. Thus the Mamantel evidently served as a route of communication and trade from the Gulf coast into the interior as far as Isla Pac and beyond. Cf. pp. 276–77, *infra*.

reaches of the Candelaria and its tributaries. Eighteenth-century maps also show a trail known as the "camino de la provincia" crossing the Candelaria country from Yucatan proper to the Usumacinta, a route which approximates that followed by the recently constructed standard gauge railroad from Campeche to Tenosique. In the nineteenth century enterprising individuals established estancias along the lower Candelaria. One of these modern pioneers was an American named Henry Pawling, who accompanied J. L. Stephens from Central America to Carmen in 1840. As we have noted in Chapter 3, it was Pawling who first blasted channels through the rapids and falls of the Candelaria. In recent times the chicle industry has been responsible for increased traffic on this river and for exploration of the lands drained by its two major branches, the Caribe and San Pedro. For the history of Acalan-Tixchel, however, the Candelaria country has no importance after 1571–73. Henceforth the Tixchel district is the center of activity for the history of the Acalan Chontal.

10

Developments in the Tixchel Area, 1574-1604

THE PRESTIGE of Don Pablo Paxbolon was greatly enhanced as a result of the events described in the preceding chapter. By effecting the
pacification of the Zapotitlan people he had demonstrated his ability as an
Indian leader and established a reputation for loyal service to king and Church.
He had also succeeded in extending his own authority as cacique of Acalan-
Tixchel. Governor Santillán's decree of March 30, 1571, gave him jurisdiction
over Zapotitlan, Puilha, and Tahbalam,[1] and his control over the Indians of
these settlements was made more effective by their transfer to new sites in
the Mamantel region. On February 15, 1573, Santillán also named Paxbolon
military captain of the Tixchel district with authority to organize detachments
of native warriors and to lead them into the interior to effect the reduction of
unsubdued Indians.[2] By virtue of these commissions, which were granted as a
reward for his services and in recognition of his hereditary rights as lord of
the Acalan Chontal, Paxbolon achieved the status of a native territorial ruler
within the framework of provincial administration and became the outstanding Indian figure in southwestern Yucatan.

The record of Paxbolon's frontier activities subsequent to the Zapotitlan
affair begins with the year 1574 when he made a journey to Chiuoha located
southeast of Tixchel. In Chapter 8 we have already mentioned this site as the
place to which Don Luis Paxua, Paxbolon's cousin and his predecessor as lord
of the Acalan people, fled in 1557. The Chontal Text states that in the following year Paxbolon "discovered" the pueblo of Chiuoha, where he learned
that Paxua had died as the result of illness.

Document IIIb of the Spanish version of the Text gives an account of the
1574 entrada. Here we are told that in April 1574 Paxbolon obtained information concerning a settlement of idolatrous fugitives in the interior from two
Indians of Xocola (Mazcab). Although his informants had visited the place,
they professed ignorance of its name and the size of its population. The
narrative relates that when Paxbolon received this report "he wanted to go
there at once, by virtue of the commissions he held from the governors who

[1] Cf. pp. 217–18, *supra.*
[2] Paxbolon-Maldonado Papers, Part I, ff. 9v–10.

ruled this province [of Yucatan] for the purpose of bringing out such idolatrous wild Indians."

With a force of 100 Indians from Tixchel, Paxbolon proceeded to the new
settlement of Zapotitlan (Tiquintunpa) near the Mamantel, from there to
Xocola (Mazcab), and then went on to a place called Tachunyupi. From
here he advanced toward the settlement of the "idolaters" and came upon
them unaware. At first they were hostile, and one of their warriors, named
Pazelu, attempted to shoot Paxbolon with an arrow. But when the principal
men of the village, named Paxmulu and Paxtun, "saw that it was Don Pablo,
they went to him and said: 'Lord, whether you come for war or come for us
or come to kill us, here we are, do what you like.'" Paxbolon explained that
he did not come to make war or to seize them but to preach the word of God
and to urge them to live as Christians under the rule of the Spanish sovereign.
In this way he overcame their fears, and within two or three days the women
and children who had fled into the forest at his approach were brought back
to their homes.

Some of the Indians were persuaded to return to Tixchel, where they
were instructed in Christian doctrine and eventually baptized. In the course
of time a church was built in the settlement and vestments and other ecclesiastical ornaments were sent from the mission at Tixchel. The narrative ends
with the statement that "this pueblo mentioned above is now Chiua (Chiuoha)."

This version of the Chiuoha incident was written about 1610. As we
might expect, it magnifies the role played by Paxbolon and stresses the religious motive. It also raises important questions concerning the location,
origin, and status of the Chiuoha settlement. Discussion of these points is
postponed for the present in order to give another version of the affair based
on a contemporary account recorded in the probanzas of Feliciano Bravo.[3]

Early in 1573 Governor Santillán sent Bravo to Tabasco to organize an
expedition for the pacification of certain groups of heathen Indians living in
the region southeast of Tenosique. The story of this expedition, made in
April–May 1573, is told in Appendix D. On December 2, 1573, Santillán's
successor, Don Francisco Velásquez de Gijón,[4] appointed Bravo, who by
this time had returned to Mérida, to the post of lieutenant governor of Tabasco
with instructions to investigate local administration in that area. Velásquez
also authorized him to take suitable action to bring about the conversion of
heathen Indians in the interior between Yucatan and Tabasco.

[3] Probanzas of Feliciano Bravo, AGI, México, leg. 109.
[4] Velásquez de Gijón succeeded Santillán in the autumn of 1573.

On his way to Tabasco Bravo stopped in Tixchel for a conference with Paxbolon, the results of which are recorded in a decree issued by Bravo at Puerto Escondido on December 28, 1573. In this document Bravo stated that "having heard and understood that toward the region of Taquichel Maçatlan [Cehache-Mazatlan] there are a certain number of heathen Indians in settlements who might be easily converted," he had gone to Tixchel to discuss with Paxbolon the best means to achieve this end. It was agreed that Paxbolon, "as a person who knows the language of the said Indians and is accustomed to have dealings with them," should go to visit them and ascertain whether they would become Christians and submit to Spanish authority. For this purpose Paxbolon was authorized to take as many Indians as might be necessary. On his return from Tabasco Bravo would take appropriate action on the basis of Paxbolon's report.

In accordance with this agreement Paxbolon, in April–May 1574, "went to where the Indians were at the site of Chiuoha, where he found and assembled more than fifty persons," who voluntarily agreed to become Christians and to give obedience to the king. This journey is undoubtedly the one we have described above on the basis of the account in the Spanish version of the Acalan narrative. This account, however, does not mention the preliminary discussions with Bravo and makes it appear that Paxbolon had acted entirely on his own initiative. In August 1574, when Bravo returned from Tabasco and received Paxbolon's report, he sent a message to the Indians at Chiuoha asking them to come out to meet him at some place nearer to Tixchel. His excuse for not going all the way to Chiuoha was that the rainy season would make the journey too difficult and hazardous.

Accompanied by Paxbolon and two Spaniards, Bravo started inland toward the end of August and after an arduous journey, partly by canoe and partly on foot through swampy country, he met his messengers and five Indians from Chiuoha at some milpas called Tacalha. The Chiuoha men wore their hair long in accordance with heathen custom and were clothed only in loincloths. At first they were afraid, "because they had never seen or spoken to other Spaniards." With Paxbolon serving as interpreter, Bravo explained that he had come to tell them about the Christian way of life and that they should promise obedience to the Crown, whose representatives in Yucatan would guarantee the freedom of their persons and property. If they voluntarily accepted Christianity, they would be exempt from tribute for a term of years and would subsequently be royal tributaries. At the end of this harangue he asked if they wished to be baptized and become vassals of the king, and they replied in the affirmative. Whereupon Bravo assured them of the royal protection and promised to tell the governor and bishop about them. As a sign of friendship he presented gifts of mantas, hats, pieces of colored cloth, and scissors. The Indians in turn gave him a cake of copal and a little copper idol (*idolillo de cobre*) "as a sign that they wished to abandon their idols and sacrifices and become Christians."

At the end of the document describing this parley we find the following statement: "And these Indians spoke in the language they call *manac chontal*,[5] and they said that their chieftain (*el más principal de ellos*) is named Apaxmulo-Apaxtian-Nachacquilnitzachan-Amaquaçelu." What the Indians probably said was that their principal men were named so-and-so, etc. The names as recorded by the scribe are obviously garbled, but it is possible to identify at least three of them: Apaxmulu, Apaxtun, and Amacua-çelu. Paxmulu and Paxtun, as we have seen, are mentioned in the Acalan narrative of this incident. Amacua-çelu may possibly be two names, Amacua and Çelu. Although it is something of a conjecture, the long combination, Nachacquil-nitzachan, may record the names Acha, Quiuit, and Chacchan, or possibly Acha-quiuit and Chacchan. In any case the identifiable names are Chontal and were in common use in Acalan, Tixchel, and Zapotitlan. The lack of Christian names indicates that the persons listed had not been baptized.

On December 15, 1574, Bravo made a full report of this affair to Governor Velásquez de Gijón. The latter formally received "the settlement and land of Chiuoha" under the protection of the Crown and promised to see that the Indians received religious instruction. A few days later the matter was brought to the attention of Lic. Cristóbal de Miranda, dean of the cathedral church of Mérida and administrator of the diocese in the absence of Bishop Landa.[6] Miranda announced that he would instruct the priest stationed nearest to Chiuoha to take charge of missionary work there.

The data recorded in the Bravo papers and in the Spanish version of the Chontal Text definitely prove that Chiuoha was a Chontal settlement. The Indians spoke the Chontal language and their names were Chontal. The burden of evidence also indicates that they were unconverted heathens. Although the Text narrative describes the Chiuoha people as "cimarrones," which usually means fugitives who had reverted to a heathen state, the contem-

---

[5] This name for the language is of considerable interest, since *manac*, unlike the term Chontal, does not appear to be a Mexican word. The usual Maya name for this language was Putunthan. *Manac* is defined in the Motul dictionary as meaning "something distant or removed." In the Yocotan dialect of Chontal *muhnaat* has almost the same meaning, although we doubt that it is from the same root. The name Manac Chontal might be derived from either of these words, but it is largely a matter of conjecture (Ciudad Real, 1873, 2: 452; Motul dictionary, 1929, p. 604; Blom and La Farge, 1926–27, 2: 474).

[6] Landa was in Mexico City at this time.

porary Bravo documents call them "salvajes" and "infieles," terms normally employed to designate unconquered heathens rather than apostate fugitives. It is also significant that neither the Text narrative nor the Bravo papers record Christian names for any of the Indians. Moreover, we have the statement that the men who met Bravo at Tacalha had never before seen or spoken to Spaniards.

Although Bravo's decree of December 28, 1573, suggests that he may have known about the Chiuoha settlement prior to his meeting with Paxbolon earlier in the month, we are inclined to believe that he merely had a general knowledge about groups of unconverted Indians living in the south-central part of the Yucatan peninsula and that it was Paxbolon who directed his attention to the Chontal of Chiuoha. It seems clear from Bravo's account of the conference at Tixchel that Paxbolon had already established contact with this group. This may have been as early as 1558, although we are of the opinion that the alleged discovery of Chiuoha by Paxbolon in that year actually refers to the entrada of 1574.[7] Whatever the truth may be on this point, the cacique evidently had knowledge of the settlement and doubtless desired to bring this remnant of the Chontal people under his jurisdiction. Bravo's visit offered the opportunity to achieve this end under the guise of a missionary enterprise, and Paxbolon shrewdly took advantage of it. The native chronicler who wrote the *post factum* account of the Chiuoha episode in the Acalan narrative naturally stressed the religious motive and gave Paxbolon entire credit for its success.

The new mission at Chiuoha was made a visita of the Franciscan convent at Campeche and was served by the friar assigned to the Tixchel district.[8] The Text narrative mentions a certain Fray Bartolomé Garzón as the person who baptized some of the Chiuoha people in 1575. For administrative purposes Chiuoha was placed under the jurisdiction of Paxbolon, governor and cacique of Tixchel.

The evidence that Chiuoha was a settlement of unsubdued and unconverted Chontal is of considerable significance for the ethnography of the Yucatan Peninsula. It is a matter of some importance therefore to determine the location of the site and, if possible, to form some conclusion whether or not it was occupied at the time of the conquest. Definite answers on these points would help to define the linguistic frontier between Maya and Chontal in preconquest times.

---

[7] See note 4, p. 171, *supra*.

[8] The missions of Champoton and Tixchel, secularized by Toral, were reassigned to the Franciscans by Bishop Landa soon after his arrival in Yucatan. Cf. pp. 237, 238–39, *infra*.

Modern maps record a site named Chivoja on the Arroyo Chivoja Grande about 30–32 km. airline southeast of Tixchel. We doubt, however, that this was the place visited by Paxbolon in the spring of 1574. The report of the cacique's journey in the Bravo papers give no indication of the route from Tixchel to Chiuoha, nor does it record a time schedule for the journey. Likewise, we have no data to fix the location of Tacalha, where Bravo met the Chiuoha men in the following summer. The Acalan narrative states, however, that Paxbolon traveled by way of the new settlements of Zapotitlan (Tiquintunpa) and Xocola (Mazcab) and a site named Tachunyupi. From this last place it was about a day's journey to Chiuoha. If we are correct in locating Zapotitlan (Tiquintunpa) and Xocola (Mazcab) in the Mamantel region, then such a route would have been roundabout in case Paxbolon's destination was the modern Chivoja. A direct overland route would have been shorter, and since the cacique made the trip in the dry season it probably would have offered no great difficulty. Although Bravo visited the country in the rainy season of 1574, he undoubtedly could have traveled by canoe from Tixchel to modern Chivoja by way of Sabancuy estuary, Laguna de Términos, and the Arroyo Chivoja Grande, and it would not have been necessary to ask the Indians to meet him at some point closer to Tixchel. Finally, the story of the founding of Popola, to be related below, indicates a location for this settlement on the upper course of the Mamantel halfway between Xocola (Mazcab) and Chiuoha. Such a location would not make sense if Chiuoha were situated at or near Chivoja. Everything considered, it would appear that the site visited by Paxbolon in 1574 was located farther inland east of the headwaters of the Arroyo Chivoja Grande. (See Map 4.) In later years, however, the settlement was apparently moved closer to the coast, probably at or near modern Chivoja. This is indicated by various data concerning Chiuoha in the seventeenth century. documents. The statement in Document IIIB of the Acalan narrative, written about 1610, that "this pueblo . . . is now Chiua (Chiuoha)" suggests that the removal to a new site had already taken place.

The Maldonado-Paxbolon probanza of 1612 implies that Chiuoha was settled by Acalan refugees who fled into the forests as the result of Cortés' visit in 1525.[9] We have already expressed doubt, however, that many of the Acalan permanently abandoned their homes and lands at that time.[10] Some may have done so, but the site of Chiuoha was a long way from the Itzamkanac area. There was plenty of inaccessible forest country nearer at hand with good soil and living conditions similar to those in the old homeland to

[9] Paxbolon-Maldonado Papers, Part I, *passim.*
[10] Cf. p. 121, *supra.*

which they could have withdrawn. Moreover, in view of the fact that the Text goes to so much trouble to explain the Acalan origin of the Zapotitlan people, we should certainly expect that it would also give clear indication that the Indians of Chiuoha were Acalan fugitives, if such were the case.

It also seems very unlikely that Chiuoha was founded as late as 1557 by Don Luis Paxua and other fugitives from Tixchel. Although Paxua was probably accompanied by a few faithful followers, the Text narrative, which is the sole source that records the ruler's flight to Chiuoha, contains no evidence that any sizable group abandoned Tixchel at that time. This is in striking contrast with the Text statement that a large number fled in 1560–61 with Diego Paxcanan and associates. It is evident, of course, that Chiuoha was not a large place, for the Bravo report of Paxbolon's entrada in 1574 states that the cacique assembled about fifty persons. It adds, however, that there were other Indians, presumably Chontal, in the surrounding bush and forest. The most convincing evidence that Chiuoha was not founded by Tixchel fugitives in 1557 consists of two facts: (1) less than twenty years later the principal men were unconverted heathens without Christian names; (2) the positive statement that the men who met Bravo at Tacalha had never before seen Spaniards.

In view of the foregoing we are of the opinion that the people of Chiuoha had lived in the region southeast of Tixchel since preconquest times. That such was the case is nowhere specifically stated, but it would not be surprising if a group of Chontal continued to live in that area after the Acalan leaders abandoned Tixchel in the fifteenth century. Since all other known Chontal villages, so far as we can recall, were found on or near canoe-navigable water, we surmise that Chiuoha was originally located on some stream or bayou tributary to Laguna de Términos. If they were living farther inland in 1557 and thereafter, it must have been because they had retired from the proximity of Spanish activities on the Gulf coast. The site of Chivoja on Arroyo Chivoja Grande, to which they probably moved sometime subsequent to 1574, may have been the original location of the village.

Whether or not Chiuoha was subject to the rulers of Itzamkanac is a matter of conjecture. The fact that Don Luis Paxua took refuge there in 1557 might possibly suggest that the Chiuoha people recognized his authority and lordship. On the other hand, the omission of Chiuoha from the list of seventy-six towns in Document II of the Chontal Text implies that it was not one of the subject settlements. We are inclined to believe that it was an autonomous village, although the people may possibly have given a nominal allegiance to the Itzamkanac rulers as leaders of the Chontal in the Candelaria area.

As a result of the Chiuoha episode Paxbolon further increased his prestige as an Indian leader and strengthened his control over the frontier area southeast of Tixchel. The history of his later activities deals very largely with his efforts to effect the pacification and resettlement of various groups of Yucatecan Maya who had fled to the swamp and forest country adjacent to the Tixchel district.

The flight of Indians from the mission towns of northern Yucatan to the unpacified regions in the eastern, central, and southern parts of the peninsula began within a few years after the conquest and continued at an accelerated rate during the last quarter of the sixteenth century and throughout the seventeenth. Some of the fugitives abandoned their homes to escape the burden of tribute and labor imposed by the Spaniards; others, including native priests and their followers, fled in order to practice the old religious cult without interference from the missionary clergy; a certain number were fugitives from justice; and others journeyed to the interior to hunt, to obtain beeswax and other forest products, or to barter with the forest Indians, and never returned. In some cases they left in small groups with their families, but there were many who abandoned their wives and children and formed new family ties in the interior country.

Although these Indians came from all parts of the province, the majority were refugees from the frontier towns, where flight was easiest. In the east many fled from the Valladolid-Tizimin-Chancenote area to the east coast and south toward Bacalar and beyond. From the Campeche, Ah Canul, and Xiu districts a larger number migrated to the central regions of the peninsula southeast of Champoton and Tixchel. At first the fugitives settled in small *rancherías* of a few families each scattered through the swamp and forests, but later on larger settlements were formed under the leadership of one or more chieftains. A report of 1604 lists more than a dozen such settlements in the central southern part of the peninsula. In the interior the Indians reverted to pagan customs, and the 1604 report indicates that the ah kins, or native priests, exerted considerable influence in the government of the villages.[11]

The fugitives in the region southeast of Champoton and Tixchel penetrated into the northern part of the lacustrine belt occupied by the Cehache, and at first they seem to have stood in some fear of the latter. In the course of time, however, as the refugees increased in number, they exerted increasing pressure on the old residents of the area, possibly absorbing some of them and pushing most of the others into the southern district where the Cehache were more numerous. A few Cehache rancherías appear to have survived

[11] See Appendix E.

in the northern part of the lacustrine belt as late as 1695, but the seventeenth-century sources reveal that the fugitives dominated the region west, north, and east of Isla Pac and that the major Cehache villages were then located near the present Mexico-Guatemala boundary and southward toward Chun-tuqui in the Peten.[12]

The withdrawal of an increasing number of tribute-paying Indians from the towns of northern Yucatan meant a loss of revenue for both the encom-enderos and the Crown.[13] The freedom of the fugitives to practice the native religion in the interior settlements also tended to undermine mission discipline and hindered the efforts of the clergy to stamp out idolatry and pagan ceremonial. Moreover, the refugees threatened to some degree the stability and security of the frontier districts. From time to time they made raids on border towns, carrying off women, children, and, occasion-ally, adult men. We also hear of attacks on Indians who journeyed from northern Yucatan to the interior to obtain forest products or to barter with the apostates and heathens of the unconquered areas. The operations of these raiding parties sometimes extended as far west as the Gulf coast, where they robbed traders on the trails between Campeche and Tixchel.

The provincial authorities viewed this situation with increasing con-cern, and during the last two decades of the sixteenth century and the early years of the seventeenth various measures were adopted to reduce the fu-gitives to obedience. It is interesting to find that for some years the authorities relied to a considerable extent on certain Indian leaders to achieve this end. In northeastern Yucatan the most prominent Indian chieftain was Don Juan Chan, cacique of Chancenote, who was authorized to make expeditions to the east coast country in search of heathens and apostates. As the result of his efforts a certain number of Indians were pacified and settled at various places in the Chancenote district. In southwestern Yucatan Don Pablo Paxbolon played a similar role.

The Spanish version of the Chontal Text describes Paxbolon's first efforts in the resettlement of Yucatecan fugitives.[14] Here we are told that a group of Indians from Hecelchakan, who had migrated to the interior

---

[12] Cf. p. 69, *supra*.

[13] As an example of this phase of the problem, we may cite the case of Francisco Sánchez Cerdán, citizen of Campeche. About 1575 fifty Indians of his encomienda fled to the interior. With the permission of the provincial governor, Sánchez set out with a force of friendly Indians to round up the fugitives, whom he eventually found at a site in the forests several days' journey from Campeche. At first the refugees offered resistance, but the encomendero overpowered them and took them back in chains to their pueblo (Paxbolon-Maldonado Papers, Part II, ff. 257v–62v).

[14] The Chontal original of Document IIIb of the Spanish version, in which this episode is recorded, is missing.

country, were attacked by another band of fugitives at a place called
Chunuitzil. This site was apparently located some distance east of Tixchel
toward Isla Pac.[15] In this attack the Hecelchakan group were defeated, several of their leaders being killed in the fray. Some of those who escaped
returned to Hecelchakan; others scattered through· the forests, where they
wandered about "without knowing where." One of the refugees, named
Pedro Chan, who was badly wounded, finally made his way to the Gulf coast
and thence to Paxbolon's estancia near Tixchel, where he told the story of the
defeat and rout of his companions.

Paxbolon sent out search parties from Zapotitlan (Tiquintunpa) and
Xocola (Mazcab) to round up those who had scattered through the forests,
and eventually sixty persons, including a chieftain named Juan Cauich, were
reassembled and brought to Xocola. The narrative relates that Cauich and
his followers informed Paxbolon that they wished to settle "near the embarcadero of Mamantel," apparently a site at the end of deep water on the
upper course of the Mamantel River. This place, said to be halfway between Chiuoha and Xocola (Mazcab), was called Popola. Paxbolon assigned
the Indians lands at this site, "and there Cauich and his companions settled."

Other sources throw additional light on this episode and illustrate the
manner in which Paxbolon made use of it for his own purposes. It would
appear that the cacique, after hearing Pedro Chan's story, journeyed to
Mérida to obtain permission to search for the Hecelchakan refugees and
to settle them at a new site in the Tixchel area. It is interesting to find, however, that the grant of authority issued on this occasion took the form of a
general contract, or capitulación, setting forth terms and conditions under
which the cacique might undertake the pacification of any group of fugitives or heathen Indians in the region bordering the Tixchel district. This
document, dated June 7, 1583, was signed by Dr. Diego García de Palacio,
oidor of Mexico, who served as visitador of Yucatan in 1583–84, and by the
provincial governor, Don Francisco de Solís.

This contract authorized Paxbolon to employ suitable measures to effect
the reduction of apostates and heathens in the interior country and to resettle them in new villages where they might receive adequate instruction in
Christian doctrine. The document also mentioned plans for opening a road
from Champoton to the Usumacinta River that would pass through the
region controlled by the cacique, and it stipulated that any new settlements
should be located near this route in order to facilitate the religious instruc-

15 The general location of Chunuitzil, later called Chacuitzil, is indicated by various documents of the period 1604–15. Cf. discussion of the Chacuitzil mission in Chapter 11 and Map 4.

tion of the Indians and to provide convenient stopping places for travelers on the road. All Indians, heathen or apostate, reduced to obedience by virtue of this agreement should henceforth have the status of royal tributaries and should never be granted in encomienda to any Spaniard. The heathens should also be exempt from tribute for ten years; apostate fugitives were promised tribute exemption for one year and a general pardon for their disloyalty to king and Church. The contract guaranteed to Paxbolon certain privileges and rewards, as follows: (1) that all the Indians pacified and resettled by his efforts should recognize and obey him and his descendants as their caciques and give them the services and aid customarily paid by other Indians of Yucatan to their hereditary caciques and lords; (2) that he should hold office for life as governor of all new settlements founded by virtue of the agreement and that no corregidor or other Spanish official should exercise local jurisdiction over them; and (3) that he and his heir should receive an annual gratuity of .20 peso for each Indian brought to obedience, this sum to be paid from the tributes levied on such Indians.[16]

The resettlement of the Hecelchakan refugees at Popola was evidently carried out under authority granted by this contract. In the autumn of 1583 Pedro Martín de Bonilla, encomendero of Hecelchakan, tried to intervene and establish contact with the fugitives, doubtless with the intention of forcing them to return to their pueblo. Paxbolon promptly opposed this move on the ground that it would antagonize the Indians and create difficulty in reassembling them at a new site in accordance with the agreement of June 7. As a result of this protest the visitador, García de Palacio, gave an order, dated October 29, 1583, forbidding the encomendero or any other Spaniard to interfere with Paxbolon's activities.[17] The Acalan narrative states that the search for the refugees lasted eight or nine months, so we may date the actual founding of Popola in the first half of 1584.

The contract of 1583 is a rather remarkable document, in view of the fact that one of the contracting parties was an Indian. On various occasions the colonial authorities entered into agreements with Spanish colonists who proposed to undertake the pacification of unsubdued areas or peoples in the Yucatan Peninsula, but so far as we know this is the only case of a formal contract with an Indian authorizing the reduction of rebellious and heathen groups. None of the commissions granted to Paxbolon's contemporary, Don Juan Chan, cacique of Chancenote, were in the nature of a contract

[16] Copy of the agreement of June 7, 1583, is in Paxbolon-Maldonado Papers, Part I, ff. 27v–30.
[17] Ibid., ff. 10v–11.

nor did they confer such extensive privileges and rewards, although Chan, by virtue of his many services, his descent from a pre-Spanish Maya lord, and his marriage with a noble woman descended from a chieftain of Mayapan, might well have claimed similar consideration.[18] The contract of 1583 and the supplementary decree issued by the visitador in the autumn of the same year clearly demonstrate that Paxbolon was able to enlist powerful support in governmental circles and that he enjoyed the respect and confidence of the provincial authorities. The Popola episode also serves as further evidence of the cacique's skill in making use of the missionary and political motives of Spanish conquest to advance his own interests.

In 1587 Paxbolon informed the provincial governor, Don Antonio de Vozmediano, that another opportunity to effect the pacification of "forest Indians" had now presented itself and requested confirmation and renewal of the contract of 1583. This petition was granted.[19] Under this new grant of authority Paxbolon subsequently made an entrada into the interior, concerning which the only available report is a document filed before the lieutenant governor of the province in 1591 by Francisco Maldonado, son-in-law of the cacique.

This source states that Paxbolon, having learned that a large number of fugitive Indians had settled in the bush and forest country of Mazatlan (the Cehache area), set out with a group of his own people for the place where they were living. After a long and difficult journey, "through thick bush, lagoons, and swamps," he finally reached the settlements only to find that the fugitives had been warned of his coming by Indian traders from Campeche and that many had fled farther into the interior. He rounded up those who remained, gave them presents, and quieted their fears, explaining that if they submitted they would be well treated and received under the royal protection. In this way he succeeded in bringing out seventy-nine persons, part of whom he settled at Popola and the others at Tixchel, "where they are now being indoctrinated." Although most of these Indians were evidently apostates from northern Yucatan, it appears that some were unconverted pagans, for Maldonado reported that "those who are heathens are being taught and instructed in the things of our holy Catholic faith preparatory to baptism and admission into the fraternity of our holy mother Church." The unconverted may have been Cehache or descendants of apostate fugitives born in the interior. To all of these Indians Paxbolon had given food and supplies; he had had them build houses; and he had assigned them farmland,

[18] Probanza of the merits and services of Don Juan Chan . . . , AGI, México, leg. 140.
[19] Paxbolon-Maldonado Papers, Part I, ff. 11-11v.

"so that they may remain permanently [where they are] and pay that [tribute?] which your Grace may order and command."[20]

Maldonado presented a list of the Indians who had been resettled (this document is now missing) and requested fulfillment of the contract terms in reward of Paxbolon's services on this occasion and his earlier frontier activities. The phraseology of the document suggests that no action had hitherto been taken to confirm the cacique's rights in regard to Popola, although the Indians settled there had doubtless accepted him in fact as their cacique and governor. It appears therefore that Maldonado now sought formal recognition and confirmation on behalf of his father-in-law of all rights, privileges, and rewards that were due for past services under the contract originally issued in 1583 and renewed in 1587.

Although the lieutenant, by decree of June 17, 1591, expressed approval of Paxbolon's services and ordered fulfillment of the contract, he ruled that its provisions applied, in the case of fugitives, only to those who had fled to the interior prior to the date of the original agreement. This limitation would not affect the status of the people settled at Popola in 1584, but in the case of apostates more recently brought to obedience it meant that those who had run away subsequent to 1583 could be returned, on orders by the provincial governor, to their encomenderos. The lieutenant decreed, however, that all the Indians who had been brought in from the Cehache area should remain where Paxbolon had settled them, pending further orders by the governmental authorities. If any of them were later returned to their original settlements, the encomenderos should pay Paxbolon one peso per head for his labor in bringing them out of the forests.[21]

This decree formally confirmed Paxbolon's rights as cacique and governor of the Hecelchakan refugees living at Popola. It also confirmed any claim he might have made for an annual gratuity from the tributes of these Indians, although any such sum would have been small. Later documents contain no specific reference to the second group, pacified subsequent to 1587 and settled at Popola and Tixchel. The converted heathens would, of course, have remained under Paxbolon's jurisdiction, since the lieutenant governor's interpretation of the contract of 1583 had no application in the case of such Indians. Eventually some of the apostates may have been sent back to their encomenderos; others, who had fled to the Cehache country prior to 1583, doubtless remained permanently in the Tixchel area where Paxbolon had settled them.

[20] Ibid., ff. 26–27v.
[21] Ibid., ff. 30–30v.

Nothing more is known concerning Paxbolon's frontier activities until the year 1599, when events occurred which resulted in the founding of another new settlement in the Tixchel district. For this episode Document IIIc of the Chontal Text is the only source available.

This narrative relates that a group of apostates from northern Yucatan under the leadership of a certain Pedro Tzakum-May terrorized the country south and southeast of Champoton, where they "roamed in all directions" and committed various acts of violence. At a place called Holha, probably near the modern site of Holail, they killed a number of peaceful Indians from Campeche and other frontier settlements who had gone to the interior to hunt and to collect beeswax. On another occasion they attacked Indian traders on the coastal trails south of Champoton and robbed them of the goods they were carrying. When Paxbolon learned of these developments, he petitioned the provincial governor, Don Diego Fernández de Velasco, for permission to search for the raiders and seize them. The governor promptly authorized him to use as many men as might be necessary for this purpose. Accordingly, the cacique recruited a force from all the villages under his jurisdiction and set out toward Usulaban, a site northeast of Tixchel frequented by Tzakum-May and his followers. In the meantime the Indians of Champoton had organized a similar expedition and had dispersed the raiders at a place called Kinacanal.[22] The latter now fled south to Usulaban, where Paxbolon and his men seized them. "In all there were about four score [or] five score with their women and children. We took them to Tixchel." Here the children and three or four adults were baptized by Fray Diego Mejía de Figueroa, who had charge of the Tixchel mission.

Paxbolon questioned these people about the land through which they had wandered, and they informed him "that it was suitable for houses, milpas, [and] cacao groves." Whereupon Fray Joseph del Bosque, Mejía's assistant, was sent out to inspect the country, presumably to select a site where the fugitives might settle. After a tour through the region east and north of Tixchel, Bosque brought back a favorable report and informed his superior that it contained ample milpa land for all of the Indians of the Tixchel district. The friars now proposed to Paxbolon that all the existing villages— Tixchel, Zapotitlan (Tiquintunpa), Xocola (Mazcab), Chiuoha, and Popola —should be consolidated into a single town at a new site in this area, where "religious instruction [and] the Holy Gospel could be administered to all of them together." After some discussion the cacique and his principal men

---

[22] We are unable to locate this site, although it was evidently somewhere between Champoton and Usulaban.

agreed to the plan, and the matter was also taken up with the encomendero of Tixchel, Mateo de Aguilar. Subsequently the defender of the Indians, acting on behalf of the interested parties, presented the proposal to the provincial governor, who eventually gave his consent. The site of Usulaban, located a short distance inland from the upper reaches of Sabancuy estuary, was chosen for the new settlement.[23]

The preliminary discussions and the legal formalities must have taken considerable time, for the governor's decree approving the plan was not issued until some time in 1602. In the same year the Crown ordered the secularization of the Tixchel mission, thus removing it from the jurisdiction of the Franciscans.[24] The secular priest, Father Juan Rodríguez, who was assigned to Tixchel in 1603, evidently opposed the location of a new mission center at Usulaban on the ground that its inland location would make travel to it difficult in the rainy season. It also appears that he lacked the leadership and missionary zeal of the friars, who had sponsored the scheme for the founding of a new concentration settlement as a means of facilitating the religious instruction of the Indians in the Tixchel area. In any case, the plan was now abandoned, and the Chontal Text cited the removal of the Franciscans from the Tixchel mission as the primary cause.

This suggests that Paxbolon and his principal men had never been enthusiastic about moving from Tixchel and had agreed to do so only because they had been subjected to considerable pressure by the friars. Although the concentration of the Indians in a single town would have strengthened Paxbolon's control over them, it would also have meant the abandonment of outposts in the Mamantel area that served as points of contact for trade with the Cehache and other unpacified groups and for extending the cacique's influence in the interior country. Moreover, Tixchel occupied a more advantageous location than Usulaban in relation to the coastal trade between northern Yucatan and Tabasco. Finally, we doubt that Paxbolon and his advisors would willingly have abandoned a site so long associated with the history of their people.

Although the plan to establish a large settlement at Usulaban was never carried out, a certain number of Indians actually settled there in a village under Paxbolon's jurisdiction. A church was built and dedicated to San

[23] The name of this site is recorded in the Chontal Text as Uzulhaban. The tentative location given on Maps 3 and 4 is based on data of various kinds in the seventeenth-century sources. The most explicit statement we have places Usulaban three leagues from a site called Cucmiz, which in turn was said to be one league from Sahcabchen. (Paxbolon-Maldonado Papers, Part II, f. 246v.) Other evidence clearly indicates a location north of Tixchel and a short distance inland from Sabancuy estuary.

[24] Cf. p. 239, infra.

Felipe and San Diego, and the new mission was formally inaugurated by Father Rodríguez on April 20, 1604. Most of the people who moved to Usulaban were probably members of the band of apostate Maya fugitives who had followed a marauding career under the leadership of Pedro Tzakum-May until they were routed by the Indians of Champoton and finally brought to obedience by Paxbolon in 1599. A few Chontal-speaking Indians may have settled at the new village of Usulaban, but the predominant element was Yucatecan Maya, as evidenced by the fact that in 1615 both of the local alcaldes had Maya names.[25]

At the beginning of the period under discussion in this chapter the Tixchel district comprised three settlements: the town of Tixchel, which was the cabecera, or administrative center, and the two villages of Zapotitlan (Tiquintunpa), and Xocola (Mazcab) located on or near the Mamantel River. Each settlement had its own local government, consisting of annually elected alcaldes, regidores, and other officials, but they were all subject to the authority and jurisdiction of Don Pablo Paxbolon as cacique and governor of Acalan-Tixchel. Between 1574 and 1604 three more villages were added: Chiuoha (1574), Popola (1584), and Usulaban (1603–04). These were also subject to the supervisory control of Paxbolon, although they had their own local officials. The Indians of Chiuoha recognized Paxbolon as both cacique and governor. In Usulaban he exercised governmental authority, and we surmise that he also enjoyed cacique status, although the documents do not provide explicit evidence on this point.

Thus an extensive area on the southwestern frontier of the province of Yucatan had been brought under the control of this able Indian leader, descended from the lords of Acalan. As a local territorial ruler he was subject only to the superior jurisdiction of the Spanish provincial authorities. An interesting phase of this development is the fact that the Indians under Paxbolon's control were not all Chontal but also included a contingent of Yucatecan Maya. Tixchel, Zapotitlan (Tiquintunpa), and Chiuoha were Chontal settlements, although at the beginning of the seventeenth century a few Maya may have settled permanently at Tixchel and possibly in the other two villages. In Xocola (Mazcab) the population was part Maya and part Chontal, the former comprising the predominant element. Popola and Usulaban were Maya settlements, with perhaps a small number of Chontal in the latter town.[26] There is also a possibility that a few Maya-speaking

25 Paxbolon-Maldonado Papers, Part II.
26 Ciudad Real (1873, 2: 452) reports that in 1588 the guardianía of Tixchel included four

Cehache, pacified by Paxbolon on the occasion of his trip to the interior sometime between 1587 and 1591, lived at Popola or at Tixchel. In 1604 the Chontal still comprised a large majority of the total population of the towns under Paxbolon's jurisdiction. However, the Maya contingent was steadily increasing, and this trend continued throughout the seventeenth century.

The town of Tixchel, which served as governmental headquarters for the entire district, also became the administrative center of a separate missionary unit prior to 1604. In Chapter 8 we called attention to the fact that about 1568 Bishop Toral removed the towns of Champoton and Tixchel from the jurisdiction of the Franciscan convent of Campeche and placed them under a secular priest nominated in accordance with the royal patronage.[27] This new curacy was served at first by Fray Juan de Santa María, a Mercedarian, and subsequently by Father Juan de Monserrate, a secular priest, both of whom have been mentioned in connection with the Zapotitlan episode (Chapter 9). Monserrate was probably succeeded in 1571 by Father Gabriel de Rueda. Soon after Fray Diego de Landa took office as Toral's successor in 1573, the Franciscans were again given control over the missions of Champoton and Tixchel, which reverted to their former status as visitas of the Campeche convent. The new settlements of Zapotitlan (Tiquintunpa), Xocola (Mazcab), Chiuoha, and Popola were also served as visitas by the Franciscans in Campeche. This administrative organization continued until 1585, when the provincial chapter of the Order voted to establish a convent in Tixchel as headquarters for a separate guardianía comprising the entire Tixchel area. Under this new arrangement the four interior missions became visitas of the Tixchel convent.[28]

When the next provincial chapter convened three years later (1588) under the presidency of Fray Alonso Ponce, Commissary General of the Franciscans of New Spain, there was some debate whether the Tixchel convent should be maintained. The isolated location of Tixchel and the relatively small population of the new guardianía, as compared with the size of other mission units in northern Yucatan, were apparently questions that came up for discussion. The failure to provide adequate living quarters for the two friars assigned to Tixchel may have been another factor. Ciudad

---

lesser settlements, two of which were Chontal, one was Maya, and the fourth, part Maya, part Chontal. He does not give the town names in each case, but we are now able to identify them on the basis of the data presented in Chapter 9 and the narrative of Paxbolon's activities subsequent to 1574 as related in the present chapter.

[27] Cf. p. 178, *supra*.

[28] DHY, 2: 62; López de Cogolludo, 1867–68, bk. 7, ch. 9.

Real relates that in 1588 the Tixchel convent was "merely a straw house," evidently a pole-and-thatch structure of the native type. Before the meeting of the chapter in 1588 the principal men of Tixchel, probably headed by Paxbolon, came to see the Commissary General and urgently petitioned that the friars should not be withdrawn, offering to build a suitable dwelling for them. This plea was repeated during the chapter sessions, and after some argument the assembled friars voted to maintain the new guardianía set up in 1585, thus assuring a permanent convent status for the Tixchel mission to be served by resident friars. Ciudad Real, who regarded the Chontal as more diligent than the Yucatecan Maya, doubtless exerted his personal influence in favor of this decision.[29]

Although later sources record no specific data on the subject, there is no reason to doubt that the Indians kept their word and built a new convent structure as a residence for the missionaries. At the same time the village church was probably enlarged or rebuilt. The story that Paxbolon carved images for the Tixchel church, related in the Maldonado-Paxbolon probanza of 1612, may well record another phase of this activity. That the church was also equipped with musical instruments is confirmed by the story that the cacique occasionally served as organist. Prior to 1585 the mission was known as Santa María de Tixchel, but when the convent was established the advocation was changed to La Pura Concepción de Nuestra Señora.[30]

Ciudad Real states that in 1588 there were only two Chontal-speaking friars in Yucatan. One had served as guardian of the Tixchel convent during the preceding triennium, and the other was elected to the office in 1588.[31] The latter was probably Fray Diego Mejía de Figueroa, mentioned above, who had charge of the mission for several years prior to 1600. During Mejía's term of office the bishop made use of his linguistic ability by sending young priests to Tixchel for instruction in Chontal in preparation for assignment as missionaries in the Chontalpa and other Chontal-speaking districts in Tabasco.[32] Fray Joseph del Bosque, who assisted Mejía for a time, succeeded him as guardian about 1600 and was the last friar to hold the post.

The action of Bishop Landa in restoring Champoton, Tixchel, and other missions to the Franciscan Order aroused considerable feeling among the secular clergy, of whom there was an increasing number in the province.

[29] Ciudad Real, 1873, 2: 452–53.
[30] Paxbolon-Maldonado Papers, Part I, f. 3; López de Cogolludo, 1867–68, bk. 4, ch. 19; bk. 7, ch. 9.
[31] Ciudad Real, 1873, 2: 453.
[32] Información de los servicios de Fray Juan de Izquierdo, obispo de Yucatán, 1595, AGI, México, leg. 369.

Many of the latter were natives of Yucatan, the sons of Spanish conquerors and colonists, and they resented the fact that relatively few appointments were open to them, inasmuch as the Franciscans, the majority of whom came from Europe, controlled most of the missions, including the most lucrative posts. Moreover, since the native-born priests usually had a complete mastery of Maya, which they had spoken since childhood, they naturally felt better fitted to serve the Indian population than the Franciscans from Spain, who had to learn the language after their arrival in Yucatan. Consequently there was increasing pressure for the secularization of some of the Franciscan missions, especially after the death of Bishop Landa in 1579. Although the Franciscans resisted any change as long as possible, the Crown finally issued orders in 1602 transferring the missions of Hocaba, Tixkokob, Ichmul, and Tixchel to the secular clergy. This action was the result of urgent representations by Bishop Izquierdo and of negotiations carried on in Spain by Father Pedro Sánchez de Aguilar, a brilliant young priest of Yucatecan birth.[33]

Thus the Franciscans, who had converted the Acalan people and had brought about their removal to Tixchel in 1557, permanently lost jurisdiction over the Tixchel mission area. Henceforth it had the status of a benefice, or curacy, served by a secular priest appointed in accordance with the rules of the royal patronage governing ecclesiastical affairs in the Indies.[34] The subject settlements of Zapotitlan (Tiquintunpa), Xocola (Mazcab), Chiuoha, and Popola, as well as the new village of Usulaban founded in 1603–04, were administered as visitas by the priest at Tixchel.

The first secular priest named to the new curacy of Tixchel was Father Juan Rodríguez, already mentioned in our discussion of the plan to congregate the Indians at Usulaban. Rodríguez received only a temporary appointment and was removable at will (*amovible ad nutum*) by the bishop and provincial governor. In 1605 he was removed for "just cause," and the benefice was declared vacant. Only two candidates applied for appointment as Rodríguez' successor. One was Father Hernán Sánchez Tinoco, who had a knowledge of Nahuatl, Chontal, and Maya and had served as curate of the Villa de Tabasco. On April 27, 1606, Bishop Vázquez de Mercado nominated both candidates, listing Sánchez Tinoco in first place. A few days later the provincial governor, Don Carlos de Luna y Arellano, acting as vice-patron in the

[33] DHY, 2: 129–32; Ayeta, *ca.* 1693; López de Cogolludo, 1867–68, bk. 8, chs. 5–7; Carrillo y Ancona, 1895, 1: 341–52.

[34] For an excellent short account of the royal patronage in the Indies, see Mecham, 1934, ch. 1.

name of the king, presented the preferred candidate for the vacant benefice. Formal installation (*colación*) of Sánchez Tinoco as the new curate of Tixchel occurred on September 30, 1606.[35]

The decision of Governor Santillán in the García *v.* Bravo litigation, described in the preceding chapter, confirmed Antón García's claim to the pueblos of Zapotitlan, Puilha, and Tahbalam, later moved to new sites near the Mamantel, as part of the encomienda of Acalan-Tixchel. After the pacification of Chiuoha in 1574 the Indians of this settlement also became tributaries of García. Although it seems clear that these Indians had never paid tribute to any of the Acalan encomenderos, a claim could be made that they belonged to the encomienda of Acalan, since they were Chontal-speaking and may possibly have given nominal allegiance to the rulers of Itzamkanac. The Maya fugitives settled at Popola and Usulaban evidently became royal tributaries. In later years, however, after the Tixchel people moved to Usulaban, the Maya inhabitants of this town were added to the Tixchel encomienda, probably as a means of simplifying the tribute situation.

The most important development in the history of the encomienda during the period covered in this chapter was the formulation of a new tribute schedule in accordance with regulations introduced by Dr. Diego García de Palacio during his visita of Yucatan in 1583–84.[36] The last general revision of the Yucatan tribute assessments had been made by Lic. García Jufre de Loaisa in 1561. As noted in Chapter 8, these levies called for an annual payment of three-fourths of a tribute manta, half a fanega of harvested maize, and one gallina by each tributary. In addition, stated quantities of beans, chile, beeswax, honey, and household utensils were furnished by most of the towns. The new schedules introduced by García de Palacio in 1583–84 required an annual payment of half a manta, one fanega of maize, and two gallinas (one turkey and one European hen) by each tributary unit. The assessment of other items of produce formerly paid by most of the towns was abolished. Thus the schedules formulated by García de Palacio called for payments in only three staples, mantas, maize, and gallinas. A town with 100 tributary units would now give 50 mantas, 100 fanegas of maize, and 200 gallinas annually, and nothing more.

The visitador also introduced an important change with regard to the

[35] Nombramiento del obispo de beneficiados a los partidos de Tichel y Tepetitlan, 1606, AGI, México, leg. 2606.

[36] During a stay of several months in Yucatan in 1583–84, García de Palacio visited many of the Indian towns, investigating abuses in the encomienda system and revising the tribute schedules. In the eastern areas he uncovered evidence of widespread idolatry and the practice of native religious ceremonial. Before leaving Yucatan the visitador promulgated a new series of ordinances regulating Indian affairs which superseded those issued thirty years earlier by Lic. Tomás López Medel (Molina Solís, 1904–13, 1: ch. 7).

persons subject to tribute. Heretofore the amount of tribute payable by a given town had been based on the number of married couples, with exemption for persons of noble rank, the aged and infirm, and certain local functionaries. Widowers, widows, and unmarried adults had not been subject to tax. In formulating the new tribute schedule, the visitador counted all adults of both sexes, married, widowed, or unmarried as half-tributaries. Thus a married couple was counted as one tributary unit and widowers, widows, and unmarried adults as half-units.[37] Exemption was granted as before to Indian nobles, the aged and infirm, and certain local officials. A town with eighty married couples and forty widowers, widows, and unmarried adults, none of whom were exempt for other cause, would now comprise 100 tributary units. In short, the number of tributary units in a given town would now be equal to one-half the total number of adults, married, widowed, or unmarried, subject to tax.

The Chontal Text implies that the visitador visited Tixchel, although the year is incorrectly recorded as 1586. A document of 1606 lists the amount of tribute then paid to the encomendero of Tixchel, and the items of tribute and proportions of each are in accordance with the schedules introduced by the visitador in northern Yucatan.[38] We conclude therefore that the new assessment for the Tixchel encomienda was made by García de Palacio or by one of his agents in 1583–84.

This new schedule of tribute called for an annual payment from the encomienda of Tixchel (comprising the towns of Tixchel, Zapotitlan, Xocola, and Chiuoha) of 160 mantas, 320 fanegas of maize, and 640 gallinas (320 turkeys and 320 European hens). The number of tributary units was evidently 320. On the basis of current prices in 1606 of 5 pesos per manta, 1 peso for a fanega of maize, 2 reales (.25 peso) for a turkey, and 1 real (.125 peso) for a European hen, the total value of the annual tribute was 1240 silver pesos.[39] The value of the assessment for a married couple, or one tributary unit, was 31 reales (3.875 pesos); half-tributaries (widowers, widows, and unmarried adults) paid at the rate of 15.5 reales (1.9375 pesos).[40] These figures show that the value of the levy for each tributary unit had increased since the mid-

[37] For some time widowers, widows, and unmarried adults had been counted as half-tributaries in Mexico proper. Thus the visitador, who held office as a member of the Audiencia of Mexico, applied to Yucatan the system with which he had been familiar in New Spain.
[38] Minuta de los encomenderos de la provincia de Yucatán y la renta que cada uno tiene, 1606, AGI, México, leg. 1841. A printed text of this document, containing many errors, is found in Paso y Troncoso, 1939–42, 15: 26–41.
[39] The report of 1606 lists the tributes on a semiannual basis. The entry for the encomienda of Tixchel gives the semiannual payment as 80 mantas, 320 cargas of maize, and 320 gallinas. A carga of maize at this time was half a fanega. The prices cited above are taken from this report.
[40] For the value of the tributes in the 1550's and 1560's, see pp. 151–53, *supra*.

sixteenth century, the increase being due to rising prices for mantas and maize.

The encomendero of Tixchel in 1606 was Mateo de Aguilar, a citizen of Campeche, who held the encomienda in third life. The Chontal Text refers to Aguilar as encomendero in 1599, and we surmise that he had possessed the encomienda for several years prior to that time, although the exact date when he succeeded Antón García is not known. The fact that Aguilar held the grant in third life obviously suggests that he had married the eldest daughter and heir of García, who had apparently possessed the encomienda of Tixchel in second life.[41] In other sources we find reference to Aguilar as late as 1615, when he was alcalde ordinario of Campeche.[42] At his death the encomienda was reassigned to another citizen of Campeche (see Chapter 13).

The tribute assessment of 1583–84, which required annual payments of mantas, maize, and fowl, may be regarded as evidence of increased agricultural production in the Tixchel area during the last decades of the sixteenth century. The tax schedules for the pueblo of Tixchel formulated in 1561 and 1569 had called for payments in mantas only, indicating that in these earlier years the Indians were not raising maize and other food products in sufficient quantity to warrant the export of such items for tribute purposes. In 1583–84, for the first time since the Acalan were moved to Tixchel, they were assessed on the same basis as the Maya of northern Yucatan, who had always given food as tribute. This means that the taxing authority, after a visit to Tixchel or on receipt of reports from that area, concluded that stated quantities of maize and fowl could now be exported annually as tribute without disturbing local economy. Further evidence of improved agricultural conditions is also provided by the fact that in 1597, when there was a serious shortage of maize in the public granary of Campeche, supplies sent from Tixchel helped to ease the emergency.[43]

Increased maize production by the Indians of Tixchel was made possible by the exploitation of bush and woodland areas located some distance inland that were better suited for cultivation by the milpa system than the sparsely forested country in the immediate vicinity of Tixchel. In the region east of Sabancuy estuary and extending north toward Usulaban and beyond, there was ample milpa land for all their needs and for the production of an exportable surplus of maize. Both Paxbolon and his son-in-law, Francisco Maldonado, owned estancias in this region, and no doubt many other persons, lesser chieftains and commoners of Tixchel, cultivated tracts of good land scattered through this same area. At the close of the sixteenth century the lands in and

[41] Cf. p. 147, *supra.*
[42] Paxbolon-Maldonado Papers, Part I.   [43] Paxbolon-Maldonado Papers, Part I, ff. 39v-40.

around Usulaban apparently marked the northern limits of this expanding area exploited by the people of Tixchel. The Chontal Text records that one of Francisco Maldonado's estancias was located near Usulaban in 1599, but also indicates that this district was occasionally used as a place of refuge by the marauding Maya fugitives who followed the leadership of Pedro Tzakum-May. After the pacification of this group the Franciscan missionaries of Tixchel proposed the establishment of a large concentration settlement in this northern area where "forested country" suitable for cultivation by the milpa method was plentiful. Although this scheme failed, the founding of a small village at Usulaban in 1603–04 marked the beginning of more intensive use of the agricultural resources of this region. The new village of Usulaban prospered, and it was to this place that most of the Tixchel people moved when their own town was destroyed in later years (see Chapter 13).

The lieutenant governor's report of 1569, to which reference was made in Chapter 8, stated that each household in Tixchel owned a number of turkeys and hens, but the supply evidently was not great enough to permit payments of fowl as tribute. The annual levy of 640 gallinas (half in turkeys and half in hens) included in the tax schedule of 1583–84 obviously suggests therefore a certain increase in production during the preceding decade and a half. The report of 1569 also tells of good crops of cotton, which would have been necessary to meet local needs and to provide a surplus for the manufacture of the tribute mantas.[44] It is possible, however, that part of the cotton supply was obtained by trade. In any case, the reduction in the number of mantas to be paid as tribute, as provided for in the assessment of 1583–84, would have decreased demand for this staple, whether it was met entirely by local production or in part by import from northern Yucatan.

In Ciudad Real's account of Tixchel in 1588 we read of the abundance of tropical fruits, but cacao is not mentioned. Groves of cacao trees had been planted after the founding of the town, so we infer from the chronicler's silence in regard to this product that the trees had not flourished and that most of the cacao needed for local consumption was imported. Ciudad Real states that much copal was grown at Tixchel, but we doubt this. It seems likely that people either made expeditions to the interior to gather it or obtained the gum by trade.[45]

It would be of interest to know to what extent livestock was raised in the Tixchel area during this period, but unfortunately the sources record no

[44] García v. Bravo, f. 2137v.
[45] Ciudad Real, 1873, 2: 452.

specific data on this point. Paxbolon probably kept some cattle at his estancia northeast of Tixchel, and some of the lesser chieftains may have owned a few animals. But here, as elsewhere, the common people do not appear to have engaged in cattle raising, although the savannas near Tixchel would have furnished pasturage. In Yucatan at this time few Indians owned horses. Most of the owners were chieftains or persons of noble descent, for whom the right to ride horseback with saddle and bridle, granted by special license, was a mark of honor and prestige.[46] The use of horses as pack animals was a luxury only the wealthier Indians could afford. As an outstanding Indian leader who had rendered service to the Crown, Paxbolon had doubtless received permission to ride horseback in Spanish style. In the Tixchel area, however, the canoe served as the ordinary means of transportation, so there was less use for pack animals than in northern Yucatan.[47]

Although there is unmistakable evidence of improved agricultural conditions in Tixchel and its dependent area subsequent to 1569, the importance of this trend prior to 1600–10 should not be overemphasized. Food production had increased to some extent, permitting a certain amount of export, but the major upward swing evidently occurred after the founding of Usulaban in 1603–04. The cumulative effect of increasing maize production in the Usulaban area would not be felt, however, for a good many years. Moreover, both before and after 1600 fishing and commerce continued to be important factors in local economy and contributed much to the prosperity of the entire region.

Turtle fishing was a lucrative industry. Ciudad Real reports that the inhabitants of Tixchel manufactured tortoise-shell objects, including spoons, rings, reels, and boxes for the Host. The handsome feather fans, for which the town was also noted, presumably had carved shell handles.[48] Strangely enough, there is little if any mention in the accounts of Tixchel of the famous fishing grounds along this part of the coast, but there can be little doubt that the Indians engaged in this industry.

The canoe trade between Yucatan and Tabasco was also an important source of revenue for the people of Tixchel. Salt, cotton cloth, honey, and beeswax were carried from Yucatan to Tabasco to be exchanged for cacao and for products from the Chiapas highlands and from Mexico. The lieutenant

[46] Roys (1943, pp. 153–54) discusses the regulations on this point and the system of licenses granting Indians the right to ride horseback with saddle and bridle.

[47] It is interesting to note that in 1615 when the Indians of Usulaban agreed to furnish forty fanegas of maize to help provision the new town of Sahcabchen founded southeast of Champoton they lacked horses for transporting the grain and that animals had to be brought from Siho for this purpose (Paxbolon-Maldonado Papers, Part II, ff. 302v–04).

[48] Ciudad Real, 1873, 2: 452.

governor's report of 1569 relates that the Indians also brought out copal and annatto from the Acalan country, which they sold in the Chontalpa, their chief market in Tabasco.[49] Supplies of these products had doubtless been obtained by Paxbolon and his companions during their expeditions of 1566–68 in connection with the pacification of the Chontal refugees settled at Zapotitlan. The founding of a mission at Zapotitlan provided occasion for numerous visits to the upper Candelaria in succeeding years during which additional supplies could have been obtained. After the removal of the people of Zapotitlan, Puilha, and Tahbalam to new sites near the Mamantel such trips probably became less frequent. We have no doubt, however, that for many years the Tixchel traders journeyed to the Candelaria area from time to time to collect forest products for sale in Tabasco and Yucatan.

Barter with the Cehache and the settlements of apostate fugitives in the interior of the Yucatan Peninsula provided another source of profit for the traders of Tixchel. The inhabitants of the interior needed various articles, such as salt, cloth, knives, machetes, and axes, which could be obtained only by trade with Indians of the towns under Spanish control. In exchange they gave beeswax, honey, copal, and other products of the bush and forest for which there was a ready market in northern Yucatan, Tabasco, and New Spain. Despite the fact that the colonial authorities frowned on this trade, which assumed a contraband character, the volume of business sharply increased during the latter part of the sixteenth century and the early decades of the seventeenth, due very largely to the increasing number and size of the fugitive settlements. From Oxkutzcab and other towns of the Xiu province, from Hecelchakan in the Canul area, and from Campeche and Champoton Indian traders followed the trails southward and eastward to the interior to barter with the fugitives and the Cehache, and in some of the documents we read of occasional trips as far south as the Itza country.[50] For the commercially minded Tixchel chieftains this inland commerce offered special opportunities in view of the strategic location of the pueblo of Tixchel.

The overland trails from Tixchel to the interior settlements were much shorter than the north-south routes which the traders of Oxkutzcab and Hecelchakan, for example, had to travel. But what was more important, the Tixchel traders could travel by canoe to the upper reaches of the Mamantel River, from which a few days' journey would take them to the northern part of the lacustrine belt dominated at first by the Cehache and in later times by apostate Maya from northern and western Yucatan. Finally, the settlements

[49] García v. Bravo, f. 2137v.
[50] See testimony of Pedro Uc of Hocaba in Appendix D, pp. 495–96, *infra*.

at Zapotitlan (Tiquintunpa), Xocola (Mazcab), Popola, and Chiuoha provided convenient points of contact with this inland country.

The sources at our disposal actually have little to say about trade between Tixchel and the Indians of the interior. This is not surprising, for most of the available documents were designed to prove the disinterested services of Paxbolon to king and Church. Occasionally, however, we find statements which leave no doubt that frequent communication was maintained between Tixchel and the unpacified area east of the frontier settlements. Francisco Maldonado's report of the journey made by Paxbolon to "the forests of Mazatlan" sometime between 1587 and 1591 clearly implies that this was no mere search expedition but was directed toward a definite area where apostate and heathen Indians were known to be settled. In 1606 Bishop Vázquez de Mercado, in a dispatch to the king describing the recently founded Montañas missions (see Chapter 11), characterized Paxbolon as "an Indian of great intelligence with whom the forest Indians are well acquainted and also, so it is said, carry on trade."[51] Repeated statements in the Maldonado-Paxbolon probanza of 1612 that the cacique enjoyed universal respect among the Indians of the interior also suggest frequent contacts between these groups and the Tixchel area.

Evidence of this kind and the obvious advantages enjoyed by the Tixchel traders lead us to believe that inland commerce constituted an important phase of economic activity in the Tixchel area during the last quarter of the sixteenth century and for many years thereafter. Of course, we have no way of estimating the annual volume of this trade or the profits derived from it. The same is true of the canoe traffic along the Gulf coast. It seems clear, however, that commerce and local industry gave Tixchel a greater measure of prosperity than it would otherwise have enjoyed.

The bishop's letter quoted above implies that Paxbolon personally shared in the inland trade. Indeed, we suspect that he actively controlled a large part of this traffic and of the canoe trade between Yucatan and Tabasco. As the dominant figure in Tixchel he was obviously in a position to direct the commerce of the entire district dependent on this seacoast town, and as the wealthiest person in the community he possessed the necessary capital to carry on trading operations on a fairly extensive scale. The Maldonado-Paxbolon probanza of 1612 gives the impression that the cacique was poor, but this does not make sense. He not only owned an estancia northeast of Tixchel but also had other property with which to dower his elder daughter in marriage to a Spaniard. Although Paxbolon probably was not wealthy

[51] Vázquez de Mercado to the king, Mérida, October 12, 1606, AGI, México, leg. 369.

according to the standards of many Yucatan colonists of the time, there is reason to believe that this descendant of the Acalan merchant-rulers became something of a capitalist engaged in agriculture and commerce.

A mission report of 1609 states that the curacy of Tixchel then contained "over 800 Indians under religious instruction."[52] This phrase obviously refers to the number of adults, married and unmarried, under confession. Although it is impossible accurately to calculate the actual population of the curacy on this basis, we estimate that the total was in the neighbourhood of 1600 persons, young and old.

According to the estimate given in Chapter 8, the town of Tixchel in 1569 contained at least 1260 persons. The various groups of Indians settled at Zapotitlan (Tiquintunpa), Xocola (Mazcab), and other sites in the Tixchel area numbered about 700 persons.[53] Adding these figures, we have a total of 1960. Thus the estimate of total population for the year 1609 represents a loss of some 360 persons for the entire curacy.

The major cause of this decrease was probably a sharp drop in the population of the new villages during the process of resettlement. In northern Yucatan the resettlement of Indians at new sites usually resulted in loss of population, and the same was true in the case of the Acalan moved to Tixchel in 1557. Disease may have been another factor, although we have no specific evidence of epidemics in the Tixchel area for the period from 1569 to 1609.

Since we have no separate data for the town of Tixchel subsequent to 1569, it is impossible to determine the trend of population at this place. In view of increasing food production and other favorable economic conditions, we might expect the population to show some increase, provided, of course, that no major losses due to disease had occurred. It is evident, however, that if the inhabitants of Tixchel in 1609 exceeded the earlier total of 1260 persons, we should have to assume losses of more than 360 persons in the other towns. For example, a postulated 10 per cent gain for Tixchel would necessitate raising these losses to 486 persons, or almost 70 per cent, which would be very high. It is evident therefore that any increase in the population of Tixchel

[52] Vázquez de Espinosa, 1942, p. 126.

[53] The population of the towns of Zapotitlan, Puilha, and Tahbalam, moved to Zapotitlan (Tiquintunpa) and Xocola (Mazcab) in 1571–73, did not exceed 425 persons, and the actual figure may have been lower, since one report for Zapotitlan indicates a lower figure than the usual estimate of 300 persons for this town (cf. p. 186, *supra*). "More than fifty" persons were pacified at Chiuoha in 1574, and others may have been brought in from the forests in later years. Sixty persons were settled at Popola in 1584, and a group of seventy-nine were brought in from the Cehache area between 1587 and 1591, although some of the fugitive Indians in this group may have been returned to their original towns. The fugitives pacified in 1599, most of whom were later settled at Usulaban, numbered "four score [or] five score." Thus it is impossible to form an exact estimate of the total number of persons settled in the Tixchel area subsequent to 1569, but a round figure of 700 is probably accurate enough.

prior to 1609 must have been at a moderate rate, and it is quite possible that the population remained more or less stationary.

Paxbolon's success in expanding his sphere of action and influence on the southwestern frontier of the province of Yucatan was due in part to his skill in dealing with the fugitive and unpacified Indians of the interior country. But equally important were his knowledge of European ways, gained during his youth when he lived for several years in the Franciscan convent of Campeche, and his frank acceptance of and collaboration with the aims of colonial administration. His personal loyalty to the Christian faith and his active support of the missionary effort won the lasting respect of the clergy. The repeated approval of his frontier projects by the provincial authorities also indicates that he enjoyed the confidence of influential persons in governmental circles.

Marriage alliances with Spanish colonists strengthened his ties with the ruling class. After the death of his first wife, a native woman of Tixchel,[54] the cacique married Mencía de Orduña, daughter of Diego de Orduña, a long-time resident of Yucatan and Tabasco. Orduña served with the Montejos in the 1540's and later lived for several years in Tabasco, where he learned the Chontal language. He took part in Feliciano Bravo's expeditions from Tenosique to the Peten in 1573 and 1580 (see Appendix D), and he appears to have had rather extensive knowledge of all the Tabasco country and its environs. Since he is not listed as one of the encomenderos of Tabasco in 1579,[55] we surmise that he was a trader, carrying on barter in the Chontalpa and other parts of the province. This would suggest that Paxbolon's marriage to Mencía de Orduña was prompted by business considerations. Orduña's knowledge of Chontal and his contacts in Tabasco would have made him a useful aid in the cacique's trading operations in that area.

Paxbolon had no sons by either marriage. His first wife gave birth to a

[54] Document I of the Chontal Text states that Paxbolon's first wife was a certain Doña Isabel but gives no surname. In the Paxbolon-Maldonado Papers, Part I, the name is given as Isabel Acha. The Tixchel matrícula of 1569 lists María Yxnaçe[lu, or -lut?] as the cacique's wife (cf. p. 470, infra). This suggests that Paxbolon may have had three wives: (1) María Yxnaçelu, (2) Isabel Acha, and (3) Mencía de Orduña. However, both the Text and repeated statements in the Paxbolon-Maldonado Papers refer only to two, the first an Indian woman and the second the daughter of a Spaniard. Although most of Document I of the Text was written in 1567, the data concerning the cacique's family was evidently added in 1612, when a copy of the Text was made to be filed in the probanza of services formulated by Francisco Maldonado. The Paxbolon-Maldonado Papers, Part I, are dated 1612–14. It is possible that in these later documents the names of Paxbolon's mother and his first wife were somehow confused. This is not a very satisfactory explanation, but the only other alternative is to assume that the cacique had three wives.

[55] The Tabasco encomenderos are listed in RY, 1: 330–41.

daughter, Catalina Paxbolon, who married Francisco Maldonado, a young Spaniard of Campeche. By his second wife the cacique had another daughter, María Paxbolon, who was unmarried as late as 1612. The Maldonado-Paxbolon probanza of 1612 asserts that María remained single because her father was poor and could not give her an adequate dowry. Although the cacique may have given his elder daughter such a large amount that he could not make similar provision for her half-sister, we doubt that he was a poor man in 1612. Paxbolon probably hoped that María would also marry a Spaniard, but the fact that she was a mestiza, as well as any lack of means to dower her, may have been an obstacle to such an alliance.

Francisco Maldonado, an immigrant just out from Spain, settled in Campeche about 1590. He was then about twenty-one years old. His marriage to Catalina Paxbolon, which occurred sometime prior to June, 1591, was probably a union of convenience on both sides. For the Paxbolon family it offered another opportunity to enhance their prestige and to consolidate their ties with the ruling class. For Maldonado, who apparently had little money, the dowry of the cacique's daughter provided welcome financial assistance at the beginning of his career in a new country. The dowry probably consisted of land in the Tixchel area. As already noted, Maldonado owned an estancia near Usulaban in 1599, and five years later (1604), when he was asked to declare his occupation during certain legal proceedings, he stated that he made his living "from the operation of farms in the province of Tixchel."

In 1593 Catalina Paxbolon had a son, Martín Maldonado, who now became next in line for the headship of the ruling house of Acalan-Tixchel. Catalina died four years later in March 1597. Thereafter Martín apparently spent most of his time in Tixchel under the tutelage of his grandfather. In 1612, at the age of nineteen, he was described as "a youth of good countenance, courteous and kind, of good judgment and demeanor."

About 1600 Francisco Maldonado married again, this time the daughter of a Spanish colonist. By this second marriage he had another son, of whom we shall hear more later. As a citizen of Campeche Francisco Maldonado took part in defensive operations against English corsairs who harassed the western coasts of the peninsula and eventually rose to the rank of captain of artillery in the local garrison. On one occasion he served as lieutenant captain general for the entire Campeche jurisdiction. In 1616 he was elected alcalde ordinario of the villa, and during the succeeding decade and a half he was twice re-elected to the same office. Prior to 1631 he also held appointment as an official of the royal treasury for the port of Campeche.[56]

[56] Most of our information concerning the Maldonados is derived from the Paxbolon-

From the beginning Paxbolon apparently relied on his son-in-law to represent his interests before the provincial authorities. We have already discussed
Maldonado's petition in behalf of the cacique in 1591. Other examples could
also be cited. The Spaniard in turn made use of Paxbolon's prestige as an
Indian leader to advance his own interests. In 1603–04 a group of colonists,
of whom Maldonado was one, formed a plan to effect the pacification of the
inland country east and south of Tixchel in which the cacique was to play a
leading part. The story of this enterprise and its later developments forms
the topic of the following chapter.

Maldonado Papers, Parts I and II. Additional details are found in Expediente concerning confirmation of Capt. Nicolás Fernández Maldonado as encomendero of Calkini, 1628–31, AGI,
México, leg. 242.

11
The Missions of Las Montañas

IN BOOK 8, Chapter 9, of his *Historia de Yucatán* Cogolludo gives an interesting account of the founding of four new missions in the interior of the peninsula during the first decade of the seventeenth century. These missions are listed as San Francisco de Sacalum, Santos Reyes de Ichbalche, San Juan de Chunhaz,[1] and San Jerónimo de Tzuctok.

The chronicler introduces the story after describing the disastrous expedition of Capt. Ambrosio de Argüelles to the east coast of Yucatan in 1602. The major purpose of this expedition, made by sea from Río de Lagartos, was to pacify the Ascension Bay area occupied by Indians who had never been subjected to effective Spanish control. If successful in this enterprise, the commander was also authorized to undertake the conquest of the Itza lands in the Peten. But Argüelles and his companions never reached Ascension Bay. Near Cape Catoche their ship was attacked and captured by a more heavily armed English vessel, and they were cast ashore on a nearby beach. Three months later they straggled home bearing the news of their unfortunate voyage.[2]

Although the expedition ended in complete failure it had unexpected results, so Cogolludo says, "for Divine Providence used it as the means for the conversions of other heathens." He goes on to tell how reports of Argüelles' plans, presumably carried by traders from northern Yucatan, caused alarm among the Indians "of the forests (*montañas*) called Saclum, which lie to the west of Ascension Bay and south of the city of Mérida and villa of Campeche between this land and that of Vera-Paz and Guatemala." These Indians, apostate fugitives and heathens, feared that if the Spaniards achieved success in the Ascension Bay area they would then try to subjugate the remainder of the peninsula. Among the fugitives were many who had been taught Spanish by the missionaries and had served as sacristans and singers in the mission churches. It was this group who were most apprehensive, fearing punishment for their apostasy in case the Spaniards occupied the interior country by force. "These persuaded the heathens and agreed among themselves that the best means of avoiding the severity of arms and the disasters war would bring to them and to their wives and children was to offer submission, giving obedience to the

---

[1] The chronicler records this name as Chunhaas, but most of the contemporary documents have the form used above.

[2] López de Cogolludo, 1867–68, bk. 8, ch. 8.

governor and asking for missionaries to teach them how they should live according to our Holy Catholic Faith."

The fugitives did not dare publicly to proclaim their submission, so great was their fear. Instead, they felt that it would be safer to establish contact with some friar whom they knew and to ask him to intervene in their behalf with the colonial authorities. Accordingly, nine of them went in secret to see Fray Juan de Santa María, guardian of the Franciscan convent of Campeche,[3] who promised to arrange matters to their satisfaction. The friar took them to Mérida, where the provincial governor, Don Diego Fernández de Velasco, received them "with courtesy and love" and accepted their offer of obedience. The governor then conferred with the bishop and the provincial of the Franciscan Order, and arrangements were made to send missionaries to the interior settlements, as the Indians had requested. "These events and the decision as to who should go took up the year 1603."

Early in the following year Fray Juan de Santa María, who was a proficient Maya linguist, was named superior (*comisario*) of the new mission area, and shortly thereafter he set out for the interior, accompanied by "his new spiritual sons." He spent all of the year 1604 traveling through the forests, visiting the settlements and gently bringing the Indians to obedience. "So great was his diligence that in that year he reduced and settled three provinces, which were made guardianías the following year." These were the missions of Sacalum, Ichbalche, and Chunhaz, mentioned above, to which resident friars were now assigned. Subsequently a fourth mission was established at Tzuctok.

Not content with this success, Father Santa María now wished to undertake the conversion of the Itza lands to the south. However, a new governor, Don Carlos de Luna y Arellano, who had taken office in 1604, refused permission, with the result that the friar, disheartened by the governor's opposition, left the new mission field and returned to northern Yucatan. Cogolludo states that he had not been able to ascertain the true motive for the governor's stand, and then adds: "What is known for certain is that this gentleman wished to conquer the Itzas and neighboring lands by force of arms and soldiers, and to this end he wrote to the royal council of the Indies asking permission and the title of Adelantado for his son, D. Tristan." The Council denied this request and dispatched a decree that the conversion should be carried out by apostolic means "without the clangor of soldiers." The chronicler also states that this decision probably was the result of representations by the Franciscan provincial.[4]

[3] This priest should not be confused with the Mercedarian friar of the same name who founded the Zapotitlan mission in 1569 (see Chapter 9).
[4] Cogolludo quotes a royal cedula of August 22, 1609, to Fray Hernando de Sopuerta, pro-

In 1607 Fray Pedro de Beleña, by order of the provincial of the Franciscans, made an inspection of the new mission area and on his return gave a favorable report of the progress that had been achieved. Guardians of the interior convents were regularly appointed up to the year 1614. Subsequently the missions were "lost," but Cogolludo has nothing to say about the circumstances that caused their abandonment.

Such, in brief, is the historian's story of the "misiones de las montañas," or missions of the forests. Part of his information was obtained from Fray Juan de Santa María, who helped to found them. Other data apparently came from the provincial records of the Franciscans. But the story as we have it is circumstantial and inaccurate on various points, as evidenced by contemporary records concerning the founding of the Montañas missions and their later history preserved in the Paxbolon-Maldonado Papers and other manuscript sources recently come to light. The following narrative is based on these new materials.[5]

In 1599 Gregorio de Funes, *procurador general* of the province of Yucatan, filed a petition in the Council of the Indies calling attention to the seriousness of the fugitive problem and the urgent need for a remedy. He informed the Council that Indians were leaving the mission towns of northern Yucatan in increasing numbers to live in the forests of the interior country, where they reverted to idolatry and other heathen customs. The forest settlements menaced the security of the frontier districts, for the apostates were growing bolder daily, making raids on the more isolated villages and attacking Christian Indians who ventured into the forests in search of beeswax, honey, and other forest products. Moreover, traders from the mission towns frequently spent from four to six months among the fugitives, from whom they learned "many and diverse idolatries" which they subsequently introduced in their own pueblos. Funes recommended therefore that the governor of Yucatan should be instructed to take immediate action to bring the fugitives to obedience and to settle them "in open country" where they could be kept under surveillance and taught Christian doctrine. If it seemed best to au-

---

vincial of the Franciscans in Yucatan, which acknowledges receipt of a letter from the provincial dated July 13, 1608. Sopuerta had apparently given a favorable report of missionary progress in Yucatan, and the Crown charged him to continue the good work, corroborating the provincial's opinion that the conversion should be carried on "solely by preaching of the Gospel by means of its ministers, without the noise of arms and soldiers."

[5] The Paxbolon-Maldonado Papers, Part II, deal almost entirely with the history of the Montañas missions from their founding in 1604 to their abandonment in 1615. There is a copy of ff. 1–75v in AGI, México, leg. 359, and in AGI, Patronato, leg. 231, núm. 4, ramo 16, we have a copy of ff. 146r–204v. The Paxbolon-Maldonado series alone will be cited.

thorize some colonist to organize an expedition for this purpose, he should be guaranteed suitable rewards and favors.[6]

On June 28, 1599, the Crown sent a copy of Funes' petition to the provincial governor, Fernández de Velasco, with a covering decree asking for a full report on the situation. At the same time the governor was instructed to take suitable action to stamp out the practice of idolatry.[7] Although this decree did not specifically authorize a formal expedition against the fugitives for this purpose, Velasco evidently concluded that this was the best way to deal with the problem. Funes, who doubtless had some definite project in mind when he reported to the Council, may have influenced the governor's decision. In any case, in December 1601 Velasco entered into an agreement with him for an armed entrada to bring the fugitives to obedience. Funes submitted certain conditions, some of which the governor refused to confirm without royal approval. The most important of these was a request for a loan from the Crown to be used for the purchase of arms and supplies. Execution of the contract was suspended pending decision by the Council on this and other points. The Council apparently failed to reply, and the project was never carried out.[8]

Less than a month before the tentative agreement with Funes was made, Velasco had authorized Argüelles' plan for an expedition to Ascension Bay. Argüelles had received permission to make the journey as early as 1595, but Velasco's predecessors had not granted adequate concessions and rewards, so that the commander had encountered difficulty in arousing interest in the scheme. Velasco now promised Argüelles and his men encomiendas in the lands to be conquered (Argüelles made no demand for a loan), and preparations for the entrada were rapidly completed.[9] As already noted, the expedition sailed early in 1602 but met disaster off the east coast.

These incidents indicate that interest had been aroused in the possibility of bringing the unconquered regions of the peninsula under Spanish control and that local colonists could be enlisted for such an enterprise provided certain rewards were guaranteed. They also show that Governor Velasco, whom Cogolludo praises for aiding a purely missionary effort among the Montañas settlements, was actually committed to the use of force to reduce the Indians to obedience. We shall see that it was Luna y Arellano, not Velasco, who ac-

---

[6] AGI, México, leg. 2999, libro D-4.

[7] The viceroy of New Spain and the bishop of Yucatan were also instructed to file reports (*ibid.*).

[8] Copy of the contract with Funes, dated December 9, 1601, is found in Paxbolon-Maldonado Papers, Part II, ff. 100v–108.

[9] For the terms of Argüelles' contract, dated November 23, 1601, see López de Cogolludo, 1867–68, bk. 8, ch. 8.

cepted the Franciscan point of view that the Indians of the interior should be pacified by apostolic means alone. Velasco was also willing to grant reasonable concessions and rewards to contracting parties, although he could not agree to the use of royal funds, as Funes requested, without consent of the Council. Funes' project had been suspended; Argüelles' expedition came to an unhappy end. But there were other Spaniards who also sought permission to make expeditions to the interior country and the rewards Velasco was willing to offer.

In 1603 Francisco Maldonado and four other Spaniards of Campeche and Mérida entered into negotiations with Velasco for a contract authorizing the pacification of fugitive and heathen settlements in the montañas, or forests. Maldonado's associates were Lic. Alonso Fernández Maldonado, Iñigo de Sugasti, Cristóbal de Arzueta, and Cristóbal Ruiz de Ontiveros. Fernández Maldonado, who served as lieutenant governor in 1601, was probably the father of Francisco Maldonado's second wife. The second partner, Iñigo de Sugasti, was also a prominent citizen of Campeche, who had achieved distinction in defensive operations against foreign corsairs on the Campeche coast and had served as alcalde ordinario of the Villa de Campeche.[10] Arzueta, a resident of Mérida, had served in the royal fleets and in reprisals against English pirates who had attacked the port of Sisal. Ruiz de Ontiveros was a soldier of Campeche.

The project of this group was probably formulated originally by Francisco Maldonado and Lic. Alonso Fernández Maldonado. Because of his close personal relations with Don Pablo Paxbolon, cacique of Tixchel, Francisco Maldonado must have possessed considerable information concerning conditions in the interior of the peninsula. He was familiar with Paxbolon's success in resettling a certain number of fugitives in the Tixchel district, and there is evidence that for several years he had been promoting some sort of scheme for bringing the forest settlements to obedience.[11] Having served as lieutenant governor, Fernández Maldonado doubtless had an intimate knowledge of Velasco's plans and aims in dealing with the fugitive problem and the nature of the negotiations carried on with Funes and Argüelles. Thus he was in a position to exert considerable influence in governmental circles and also to frame a project in terms that would be likely to receive the governor's ap-

[10] Probanza of the merits and services of Iñigo de Sugasti, 1598–1615, AGI, México, leg. 242.
[11] Some of the documents contain vague statements indicating that Francisco Maldonado, apparently in conjunction with Paxbolon, had sponsored "explorations" in the interior country over a period of five or six years prior to 1604, when Governor Velasco made a formal contract with the five associates. Moreover, we have a statement that the forest Indians had sent word to Paxbolon many times that they wished to be converted, but we are inclined to doubt this.

proval. Sugasti was probably brought in as an associate because of his prominence in Campeche. Arzueta and Ruiz de Ontiveros would be useful because
of their military experience. But the two Maldonados were evidently the prime
movers in the enterprise now proposed. Fernández Maldonado is always listed
first among the associates, and we shall see that he was promised the largest
reward. Francisco Maldonado conducted the final negotiations for a contract
in the spring of 1604.

Although Paxbolon was not included as one of the partners, it is clear
that he was expected to have an important part in the plans that were being
made. The Spanish associates intended to use him as a means of establishing
contact with the forest settlements and to exploit his influence among the
fugitives and heathens to facilitate the submission of these groups. The cacique
willingly collaborated in the project, probably hoping to extend his jurisdiction as a native ruler over some of the settlements.

Preliminary discussions with Governor Velasco in 1603 resulted in authorization for a reconnaissance expedition to obtain more exact information
concerning conditions in the interior and to ascertain whether the Indians
would be inclined to submit peacefully. On December 21, 1603, the governor
dispatched a commission for this purpose to Paxbolon, who had been chosen
for the task.[12] It appears that the cacique had advised that it would be well to
make the Indians certain promises, such as exemption from tribute for a term
of years and a guarantee that they could continue to live in the region they
now occupied, as means of inducing them to offer obedience and to accept
religious teaching. Velasco authorized Paxbolon to give them such assurances
in his name.

Paxbolon set out from Tixchel in February 1604. After a journey of six
days he reached a district called Nacaukumil a few leagues east of Popola.
Here were two foci of settlement about a league apart containing eighty
families of fugitives. From these Indians the cacique obtained information
concerning more than a dozen other settlements located in the interior country
to the east, north, and southeast. This information was later set forth in a
memoria, or report, submitted to the provincial governor. A translation of
this document is presented in Appendix E.

This report begins with a brief account of the two settlements of Nacaukumil. The first was named Nacaukumil-taquiache. As we have noted elsewhere, the first half of this name apparently means that the settlement was
located close to a river or stream.[13] Since the Nacaukumil district was a short

[12] Paxbolon-Maldonado Papers, Part I, ff. 11v–12.
[13] Cf. p. 68, *supra*, and note 3, p. 505, *infra*.

distance east of Popola, situated on the upper course of the Mamantel, we infer that the two sites visited by Paxbolon were near the headwaters of this river or some affluent leading into it.[14] The term *taquiache* evidently refers to the lands of the Cehache, indicating that the Mamantel led toward the northern part of the Cehache country. The report does not give the name of the chieftains who governed the first settlement. In the second, also named Nacaukumil, a certain Pedro Zeque (Tzek) was the leader. Later in 1604, when Francisco Maldonado and associates made a formal entrada into the region, these two settlements were apparently consolidated into a single mission village with Pedro Zeque as governor.

The report lists six settlements located toward the east from Nacaukumil. In the order named these were Ixkik, Chunluch, Zapebobon, Tibacab, Ixtok, and Chunpich. Ixtok, governed by two chieftains named Francisco Canche and Antonio Pech and by six other principal men, was evidently the place later known as Tzuctok, where a mission was established in 1605 by Fray Juan de Santa María. We tentatively locate this place near the modern site of Concepción on the upper reaches of the Arroyo Caribe southeast of Isla Pac. Chunpich, said to have 200 houses, was evidently a heathen settlement. At the end of the seventeenth century a village of the same name, located 8 leagues from Tzuctok on the route to Batcab and Chuntuqui, was inhabited by Cehache.

North and northeast of Nacaukumil were seven more settlements named Tixchalche, Çucmiz, Ichmachich, Ichbalche, Coobziz, Ixchan, and Chekubul. Ichbalche, which we locate between L. Mocu and L. Cilvituk, later became the most important of the Montañas missions, with a visita in Ichmachich. Ixchan may be the place listed in documents of 1609–15 as Xan or Texan, a visita of one of the Montañas missions. Modern maps record a site named Taschan between L. Mocu and Pixoyal. Chekubul was doubtless the place where a mission subject to the curate of Tixchel was founded subsequent to 1615 and probably before 1639. The modern site of this name is located southeast of Tixchel.

Southeast of Nacaukumil was a settlement named Tazul or Tajul, governed by "fifteen captains and principal men." The report states that the people of this settlement, having heard that Spaniards were coming to them, had scattered because they did not wish to be Christians. They had migrated toward Tayza, but had been attacked and routed by the Itza warriors. This had occurred only recently, and although the people of Tazul had not reassembled, it was reported that they were now ready to accept Christianity.

[14] Cf. discussion of the Mamantel and its affluents, pp. 276–77, *infra*.

We are unable to work out even a tentative location for Tazul, for the documents contain no further reference to this place. Moreover, it is not clear whether it was a settlement of apostate fugitives or of heathen Indians.

Beyond Tazul was a place called Petox. This was a Cehache village, and as we might expect, all of its chieftains had pagan names. It was evidently located in the southern part of the Cehache area which extended into northern Peten.[15] The last place mentioned by the memoria of 1604 is "the famous town of Tayza [Tayasal] and other settlements subject to it, the names of which are not known."

Although Chunpich, Petox, Tayza, and possibly Tazul were settlements of heathen Indians, in most of the other places apostate fugitives comprised the dominant element. This is indicated by the preponderance of Christian names for the leaders of these places. It should be noted, however, that in two cases, Ixkik and Tixchalche, there was one chieftain with a Christian name and another with a pagan name, and in Ixchan the only chieftain named was a pagan. These men with pagan names may have been unbaptized descendants of apostates who had fled from northern Yucatan in earlier times, or they may have been autochthonous inhabitants (Cehache) of the region.

During his stay in Nacaukumil Paxbolon informed the Indians that Governor Velasco had promised that if they gave obedience and returned to the Christian faith he would receive them under his protection, pardon any crimes they had committed, and permit them to remain in the region they now occupied, where friars would be sent to them. The Indians agreed to submit under these conditions. On February 29, 1604, they wrote a letter to the governor to this effect and asked him to confirm the promises Paxbolon had made.[16]

After his return to Tixchel Paxbolon wrote an account of his journey for Governor Velasco, with which he sent the report of villages in the interior country and the letter from the Indians of Nacaukumil. Toward the end of March these papers were presented to the governor by Francisco Maldonado, who now requested formal permission in the name of his associates to undertake the pacification of the interior settlements. On March 30, 1604, Velasco signed a capitulación, or contract, authorizing an expedition for this purpose.

The preamble of this document refers to the earlier negotiations carried on by the "discoverers" with Governor Velasco and then sets forth the immediate purpose of the proposed entrada, which was to begin the reduction of the settlements in the region east and southeast of Tixchel, as listed in

[15] Modern maps do not record any site named Petox in this area. A manuscript map of British Honduras, dated 1783, shows a place called Aguada Petach just to the south of Paixban on the route from central Yucatan to Lake Peten (AGI, map no. 390, Mexican series).
[16] Paxbolon-Maldonado Papers, Part II, ff. 5-16v.

Paxbolon's report. If this area was subjected to Spanish authority, it would no longer be a place of refuge for discontented elements from northern Yucatan. The preamble goes on to state that success in this enterprise would serve other important ends. It would facilitate the opening of communications from Yucatan to Tabasco, Chiapas, and Verapaz; and it would offer an opportunity for the eventual pacification of the Itza and Lacandon lands, "concerning which his Majesty had issued various cedulas." Therefore the governor authorized the associates to proceed with their plans under the following conditions:

1. The reduction of the interior settlements was to be effected without expense to the Crown.

2. "As requested by the Indians," two or three Franciscan friars should accompany the expedition as missionaries. The associates should furnish them necessary supplies and ecclesiastical ornaments.

3. The entrada should be carried out in a peaceful manner without bloodshed and without maltreatment of the Indians.

4. The fugitive Indians should remain in the region they now occupied, except that men who had wives by Christian marriage in the towns they had abandoned should be sent back to their respective settlements.

5. All Indians brought to obedience under this contract should be exempt from tribute for four years. At the end of this period of exemption, heathen groups and also fugitives who had lived in the interior for more than six years should pay tribute to the Crown or to the contracting associates. Fugitives who had lived in the forests less than six years should then resume payments to their former encomenderos, but such Indians should not be returned to their old settlements, "since experience shows that once Indians have fled and are brought back, they will flee again."

6. As reward for their services, the associates should receive encomiendas in the pacified settlements after expiration of the period of tribute exemption. By a supplementary decree Governor Velasco authorized a grant of 800 tributaries to Lic. Alonso Fernández Maldonado for his son, Jerónimo Maldonado; Sugasti and Francisco Maldonado were granted 600 tributaries each; Arzueta and Ruiz de Ontiveros were promised 500 tributaries and 300 tributaries respectively.

7. In case the governor decided to establish a Spanish settlement in the province of Nueva Ocaña, the name proposed for the region to be pacified, the associates would be under obligation to live there.

On March 30 Velasco also named Sugasti as commander of the expedition authorized by the contract. Arzueta was subsequently appointed notary. On March 31, Francisco Maldonado, in the name of his partners, requested that the Franciscan provincial, Fray Antonio de Ciudad Real, should be instructed to name two friars to take charge of the missionary phase of the enterprise. After some delay the provincial chose Fray Gregorio González and Fray Rodrigo Tinoco for this task.[17]

The project for a semi-military expedition to the inland country soon aroused the opposition of Fray Juan de Santa María, guardian of the Campeche convent, who had served for many years in the Yucatan missions. Apparently acting on his own initiative without communicating with the provincial, he sent a letter to the village of Auatayn, one of the interior settlements of which we shall have much to say in other parts of this chapter, in which he denounced the proposed entrada as a scheme designed to advance the selfish interests of Maldonado and his associates and of the cacique of Tixchel, Don Pablo Paxbolon.

This letter, addressed to "all my sons who dwell in the forests toward the south in the direction of the pueblo of Ahyza [Tayasal]," begins with the statement that it is not surprising that many of them had abandoned Christianity and had fled to the forests, in view of the "many labors and abuses" they had received at the hands of the Spaniards. "But you, my sons, know well . . . that we are not among those who do you harm, for we are ministers of God, Minor Fathers of the habit of St. Francis; rather we and you suffer merely because we defend you, seeking the will of his Majesty that you should be favored and protected." Reminding the Indians that some of them doubtless knew him, since he had come to Yucatan more than twenty years ago, Santa María assured them that he shared their suffering and was grieved that there was no priest among them to administer the sacraments and to teach them doctrine and the road to salvation.

The letter continues: "Be attentive, my sons, to what I wish to tell you. . . . You should not permit any Spaniards to come to seize you and molest you. The cacique of Tixchel, called Paxbolon, is he who has recommended that Spaniards should go to the forest where you are settled . . . saying that Maldonado, his son-in-law, should go and take with him some Spaniards, and that they should take arms, so that you will more easily give in to the Spaniards —merely because Paxbolon wishes and seeks the tribute you will some time have to give for his grandchild." Santa María warned that negotiations regarding such an expedition were now being carried on with Governor Velasco (the friar apparently had not learned that the contract had already been issued). "And there are many Spaniards who wish to go to do you evil and

---

[17] The contract of March 30, 1604, and various supplementary decrees are in Paxbolon-Maldonado Papers, Part II, ff. 11v–26v, 34v–36, 56–60.

again drink the blood of all of you and have you serve in their houses, as they have done and do with all the other Christian Indians." In order to forestall the expedition, the Indians should immediately seek royal protection and ask for a friar to teach them. "I am your father . . . and I am ready and prepared to endure any labor in your behalf, and I desire to go to indoctrinate you and to teach you the holy Catholic faith. . . . As for my support, so long as there is bread to sustain me, that will be sufficient, for I have nothing more to ask than to suffer for Our Lord Jesus Christ . . . and I am ready to die in His service, freeing you from the hands of the Spaniards, who wish you no good."

The friar urged the Indians to circulate the letter among other people in the forests and to let him know what they wished to do, sending their reply by Indians from Campeche, who were going out to collect beeswax. "If you wish me to come to administer the sacraments and to teach you the doctrine of the holy Catholic faith, do not fail to write to me and to advise where you wish me to be, and to this end you will send me four competent Indians to guide me. . . . For this purpose I send you blank paper so that you will reply."

Before the friar's messengers set out for the interior Francisco Maldonado returned from Mérida with news that an expedition had been authorized and would soon be carried out. In a short note, which he enclosed with the letter of April 24, Santa María notified the Indians of this development, and then added: "You surely know that they have no other purpose than to have you give tribute." And again he assured the fugitives of his desire to aid them and his willingness to visit their settlements if they would send guides.[18]

In one part of the letter of April 24 Santa María tells how at some earlier time he had gone to New Spain to seek a remedy for the "vexations and calamities" which caused the Indians of the mission towns of northern Yucatan to seek refuge in the forests; also how he had recommended that resident missionaries should be sent to the interior settlements and that no other Spaniards should be permitted to visit these villages. Thus his opposition to the Maldonado expedition reflected a sincere interest of long standing in the fugitive problem. Although the outburst against Paxbolon may have had some justification, at least to the extent that the cacique doubtless had some personal interest in the enterprise and had cooperated with the contracting associates, the friar probably would have opposed any other expedition of similar character. Like many of his Franciscan brethren in Yucatan, Santa María believed that oppression by the Spanish colonists was the principal factor in alienating the Indians from the missionary program, that an expedition of soldiers and colonists, inspired by the hope of reward, would merely intensify the hos-

[18] *Ibid.*, ff. 27v–33.

tility of the apostates, and that the pacification of these Indians should be effected by purely missionary methods. We have no doubt of the friar's zeal, his earnest desire to protect the Indians against abuse and exploitation, and his disinterested ambition to play some part in bringing the fugitives back to the Christian faith. However, the language of his letter was intemperate and could hardly have had other effect than to cause unrest in the interior country on the eve of the entrada now being organized. It is easy to understand the bitterness it aroused among the Maldonado associates, who naturally regarded the friar's letter as an unwarranted attempt to thwart their own plans and as a deliberate challenge of colonial authority.

After Francisco Maldonado's return to Campeche toward the end of April, the organization of the expedition was rapidly completed. On May 14, 1604, the "discoverers," accompanied by Fray Gregorio González, Fray Rodrigo Tinoco, and Cristóbal de Interián, who was to serve as official interpreter, set out from Campeche "for the province of Nueva Ocaña which borders on Bacalar and Verapaz." They traveled first to Tixchel, where Paxbolon joined them, and then proceeded to Popola, "last pueblo of Christians," where they arrived on May 23.[19]

On May 25 the expedition left Popola for Nacaukumil, "first pueblo of the heathens and idolaters." Paxbolon and Interián, who went ahead to notify the Indians and to prepare for the arrival of the soldiers and friars, apparently arrived in Nacaukumil the same day. The main party, commanded by Captain Sugasti, spent the night in the forest 2 leagues from Popola and the following day (May 26) covered the remainder of the journey to Nacaukumil, where the Indians came out to receive them with gifts of *pozole*.

The expedition remained in Nacaukumil until May 30. During this time the friars celebrated mass in a hut (*jacal*) built by the Indians for a church and preached to them in Maya. Many of the Indians confessed and received pardon for their apostasy; ten infants were baptized; and two adults were married to women "whom they had taken [as wives] in their heathenism." A certain number of unconverted adults accepted the faith, but the friars postponed the baptism of these persons until they should learn the prayers and the elements of Christian doctrine. The new mission was dedicated to Our Lady, and an image of the Virgin was placed in the church.

On May 28 the Indians, having promised obedience to the Crown, elected Pedro Zeque as their governor and named other village officers. The election was confirmed by Captain Sugasti, who gave them staffs of office, and Paxbolon explained their respective duties and obligations. Inasmuch as the journal

[19] The journal of the expedition kept by Cristóbal de Arzueta is in *ibid.*, ff. 36–48.

of the expedition and later documents mention only one settlement named Nacaukumil, we infer that the two settlements of this name listed in Paxbolon's earlier report were now consolidated into a single mission village.

On May 30 the expedition left Nacaukumil and marched through the forests, passing through some swamps en route, to another settlement of fugitives named Auatayn. This place is not listed in Paxbolon's report. It was evidently a well known settlement, however, for it was to this village that Fray Juan de Santa María had sent the letter described above. Although few of the Indians came out to receive the Spaniards as they approached the settlement, the people soon promised obedience and asked forgiveness for their apostasy. A chieftain named Miguel Queb (Keb) was elected governor and other village officers were appointed, all of whom Sugasti installed in office. Between May 30 and June 3 the friars confessed more than 100 persons, baptized eleven infants, and married four adults. A bell and other ornaments were placed in a *ramada* structure that served as a church and the mission was named San Francisco de Auatayn.[20]

At Auatayn the Indians handed over to the Spaniards the letter from Fray Juan de Santa María, explaining that the message had caused considerable fear and unrest and that this was the reason why they had not received the expedition with a greater show of friendship. News of the friar's letter had also spread rapidly throughout the forest country. It appears that the Indians of Nacaukumil had shown some alarm at the coming of the Spaniards, although Paxbolon had evidently quieted their fears in advance of the arrival of the main party.[21] "Spies" sent out from Auatayn to nearby settlements now reported that the letter had caused such fear that the Indians of five villages had fled into the surrounding forests. Consequently Sugasti and his companions decided that it would be unwise to continue the entrada at this time and that they should return to Campeche, leaving Fray Gregorio González and Fray Rodrigo Tinoco to carry on their missionary labors at Auatayn and Nacaukumil. In

[20] The name Auatayn (the name also appears as Tauatain, Tahuatayn, Aguatayn, and in other variant forms) apparently means "place where the crocodiles roar." It is possible that this may have been another name for the settlement of Ixkik mentioned in Paxbolon's report and said to be a day's journey from Nacaukumil, although we should expect in such case to find one of the chieftains of Ixkik named as governor of Auatayn. The chieftains of Ixkik, according to Paxbolon's report, were Napol Couoh and Juan Tuyu. Couoh, being an unconverted heathen, would not have been eligible for election as governor of a mission settlement, but the apostate Juan Tuyu, after receiving pardon for his apostasy, could have held office, as did Pedro Zeque in Nacaukumil. But we find no person named Tuyu among the Indians elected as officials of Auatayn on May 28 and again later in the year. The only chieftain named Queb listed in Paxbolon's report was one of the leaders of Chunpich, but this place could not possibly be the same as Auatayn.

[21] The journal of the expedition reports that the Indians of Nacaukumil gave Santa María's letter to Sugasti, but this is probably an error, unless a copy of the original had been made in Auatayn and sent to Nacaukumil.

view of the contents of Santa María's letter, it is not surprising that the Indians were alarmed at the coming of the Spaniards, and there may have been considerable justification for Sugasti's decision to return home. But there was also another reason, for the journal of the expedition significantly states that "the rains were heavy."

On June 4 the soldiers left Auatayn on the journey back to Campeche. The two friars remained in the interior a few weeks longer, and during this time they apparently established contact with the settlement at Ichbalche, located beyond Auatayn, and obtained a promise of obedience from its chieftains.[22] By early autumn, however, the missionaries also returned to Campeche.

An interesting sidelight on the entrada of May–June 1604 is provided by the Maldonado-Paxbolon probanza of 1612. Here we are told that the Indians of Nacaukumil and Auatayn built a "casa principal" in their towns for Paxbolon's use whenever he should come to visit them. This was done, so the probanza states, because of their great respect for the cacique and in recognition of his status as their natural lord.[23] It is obvious, of course, that Paxbolon had no right to claim such status among the fugitive Maya, since he was not their hereditary ruler, and we doubt that they actually recognized him as their lord, although they may have been willing to submit to his influence and direction in local affairs. The probanza clearly shows, however, that the cacique, like the Spanish associates, hoped to use the project for the pacification of the province of Nueva Ocaña for the advancement of personal ambition.

Fray Juan de Santa María's letter of April 24 had caused intense resentment on the part of Captain Sugasti and his companions, and soon after their return to Campeche they took prompt action designed to prevent such interference in future. On June 24 Sugasti published an order forbidding any person to send messages to the interior settlements. Whereupon the cabildo of Campeche, probably on demand by Santa María, nullified the decree and ordered Sugasti to make no further use of his commission as commander of the expedition. The captain immediately appealed to Governor Velasco, who renewed his commission and revalidated the decree of June 24. The governor also instructed him to verify the authorship of any letters that had been sent to the

---

[22] In a petition dated July 27, 1604, after the friars had returned, Arzueta, notary of the expedition, implied that the pacification of a third settlement, unnamed but doubtless the village of Ichbalche, occurred before the soldiers set out on the return journey on June 4. But the notary's journal of the entrada contains no entry to this effect, and it seems clear that he had reference to some activity of the friars before their return from the interior.

[23] Paxbolon-Maldonado Papers, Part I.

fugitives, seize the guilty parties, and send them to Mérida for trial. Although this order provided authority for legal proceedings against Santa María, Sugasti wisely refrained from such action. Instead, he sent Cristóbal de Arzueta, notary of the expedition, to Mérida to present the friar's letter to Governor Velasco. In this way he established proof of Santa María's activities and avoided procedure that would have involved a serious violation of ecclesiastical immunity.[24]

In Mérida Arzueta also filed a brief report on the expedition of May–June, noting that definite results had been achieved despite the fact that Sugasti had suspended the entrada until a more favorable occasion because of the unrest caused by Santa María's letter. He informed the governor that the associates were ready to fulfill their obligations under the contract of March 30 and intended to make another journey at the earliest opportunity. Within a short time, however, their plans were completely upset. On August 11, 1604, Don Carlos de Luna y Arellano took office as governor of the province. Six weeks later he suspended the contract with the Maldonado associates and placed the Franciscans in sole charge of the pacification of the fugitive settlements.

When the new governor arrived in Campeche en route to the provincial capital the controversy inspired by Fray Juan de Santa María's activities was brought to his attention. After conferences with Sugasti and Francisco Maldonado and also with Santa María, he apparently decided that before coming to any decision on the major issue involved, viz., the manner in which the pacification of the interior country should be carried out, he wished to hear from the Indians themselves. Consequently he framed a letter to the Indians, assuring them of his friendship and inviting them to send representatives to Mérida for a personal conference. Copies of this dispatch were given to Maldonado and to Santa María for transmission to the interior settlements.

Maldonado delayed, perhaps intentionally, in sending out the message entrusted to him, but Santa María quickly got in touch with the Indians and doubtless repeated his offer to help them in every way possible. Early in September leaders of the three settlements of Nacaukumil, Auatayn, and Ichbalche arrived in Campeche, where they conferred with Santa María. Shortly thereafter the friar accompanied them to Mérida. Learning of this development, Sugasti and Maldonado also hastened to the capital to be on hand to defend their interests.

On September 17 the Indians were received by the new governor, to whom they presented a lengthy petition in the name of their own people and

[24] Paxbolon-Maldonado Papers, Part II, ff. 26v–27v, 33–34v, 48–51v.

other Indians in the forests. For three years, so the document states, they had intended "to come and manifest themselves" to the Franciscan friars who had baptized them and instructed them in Christian doctrine; for although they had fled to the forests because of maltreatment by the Spaniards and the excessive burden of labor and tribute, they realized their "grievous fault" in abandoning the true faith and in going to live where their children could not receive religious instruction. Therefore they now asked forgiveness and begged the governor to receive and protect them as vassals of his Majesty. They requested, however, that henceforth no Spanish colonists or soldiers should be permitted to visit their settlements because of the harm such visits caused among the common people and also because other "shy" Indians now being assembled in the forests would be unwilling to live "where the Spaniards plan to go." Finally, they asked that after a period of tribute exemption they should have the status of royal tributaries.[25]

This document is dated August 4 and presumably had been drawn up some time before the Indians left their settlements on the journey to Campeche and Mérida. However, it clearly reflects Santa María's influence and was doubtless inspired by the letter of April 24 or by some later communication from the friar. If the date is a scribe's error for September 4, the petition may actually have been based on a draft sent by Santa María when he transmitted Governor Arellano's letter from Campeche. The statement that the Indians had planned for three years to establish contact with the friars was obviously designed to prove that their present offer of obedience was not inspired merely by the May–June entrada of Sugasti and his companions. To this same end the petition stated that they submitted "of their own free will." Moreover, the request that no Spanish colonists should visit their settlements in future and that they should eventually have the status of royal tributaries, another way of asking not to be granted in encomienda, clearly implied opposition to the project of the associates for the pacification of the interior country. In short, the petition bears the mark of Santa María's ideas, whatever the facts may be as to its date and the circumstances under which it was formulated.

The governor assured the Indians that their petition would receive due consideration and that he would confer with the bishop, the Franciscan provincial, and other experienced friars as to the best means of providing religious instruction for their settlements and "to reach a decision concerning the people who should accompany [the missionaries]." Meanwhile the Indians should remain in his house, where they would receive food and every favor.[26]

25 *Ibid.*, ff. 1–3v, 67–75, *passim.*
26 *Ibid.*, ff. 3v–4v.

On September 17, after receiving the petition of the Indians, Arellano ordered Captain Sugasti to present all the papers in his possession relating to the expedition of May–June. During the succeeding days the governor conferred with Bishop Vázquez de Mercado, the provincial, Fray Antonio de Ciudad Real, and three definitors of the Order, Fray Francisco de Bustamante (a former provincial), Fray Alonso de Ortega, and Fray Antonio de Villalón. The decision of this group was announced in a decree of September 22.

This document states that the governor and churchmen, having considered ways and means of dealing with the Indians living in the unconquered area between Yucatan, Chiapas, and Guatemala, had agreed that the first need was to bring the fugitive settlements to obedience, after which plans could be made for the conversion of the heathen groups in lands farther south. The conferees had also found that the expedition of May–June had failed to achieve satisfactory results, "as is proved by public knowledge of the affair, the reports of some persons, and the *autos* formulated in the case." Therefore it was their unanimous decision that the pacification of the fugitives should now be entrusted to four friars, competent Maya linguists, to be chosen by the provincial. It was also agreed that the fugitives who submitted to Spanish authority should be exempt from tribute and forced labor for six years and that they should not be moved from the region they now occupied. Finally, in view of the fact that the Indians recently come to Mérida had asked that no soldiers or colonists should be permitted to visit their settlements because of the unrest such visits caused, and since the presence of such persons was not necessary for the security of the friars, the governor and his advisors decreed that Sugasti, Maldonado, and associates should take no further part in the enterprise, at least until the matter was referred to the Crown for decision.[27]

Francisco Maldonado immediately filed objections on behalf of his partners. In a petition of September 23 he called attention to the fact that the original offer of submission by the Indians of Nacaukumil was made as the result of Paxbolon's journey of February 1604 sponsored by "the discoverers." During the subsequent entrada of May–June other Indians had also promised obedience, and missions had been founded in the forest settlements. Moreover, the associates had furnished supplies for the friars who accompanied this expedition and had provided ecclesiastical ornaments and bells for the mission churches. Although they had returned to Campeche within a short time, for reasons that were well known, it was not their intention to abandon the project for the pacification of the interior country. Nor was it just that others

[27] *Ibid.*, ff. 63–65v.

should now reap the reward of their labors. Consequently the governor should conserve their rights under the contract of March 30. In the name of his companions Maldonado offered to pay the expenses of the four friars to be sent out to the fugitive settlements by virtue of the decree of September 22. He also requested permission for the soldiers to accompany these missionaries on their journey in order to perform any necessary tasks to facilitate their work among the Indians; "for such is the obligation of my associates until [the region] is pacified and placed under the royal crown and dominion."[28]

The Franciscans promptly challenged Maldonado's claims by presenting evidence to prove that most of the vestments and other ecclesiastical ornaments taken by the friars on the expedition of May–June had been furnished by the Order and that Maldonado and his companions had actually incurred little expense for missionary purposes on that occasion.[29] The Indians from Nacaukumil were also called in to testify that during the entrada Maldonado had forced them to purchase a quantity of axes and machetes for which they had no need. Without further investigation of this charge, which was clearly intended to show that the project of the Campeche associates was inspired by selfish motives, Governor Arellano gave orders forbidding them to carry on trade with the fugitive settlements under penalty of exile from the province.[30]

On September 30 the Franciscan provincial called the governor's attention to certain remarks Maldonado was said to have made during a conversation with Fray Antonio de Villalón, one of the churchmen who participated in the conferences on the fugitive problem. According to the provincial's report, Maldonado expressed the opinion that in case missionaries were sent to the forest settlements without escort the Indians would rebel against them within a year's time. The prelate characterized this statement as "somewhat dangerous," since it might cause the friars to refuse to serve among the apostates. For this reason he asked the governor to consider carefully its import.

Summoned by the governor to answer these charges, Maldonado freely

---

[28] *Ibid.*, ff. 53–56.

[29] On September 25 the provincial presented a list of vestments and ornaments supplied by the Order. A month later (October 22) Fray Gregorio González made a statement to the effect that the associates gave nothing for the missions except a medium-sized bell for the church of Auatayn and a few pieces of cloth for the altars. He also stated that most of the food consumed on the expedition was furnished by the Indians of the towns through which they passed (*ibid.*, ff. 61–63, 85–86).

[30] Maldonado later testified that the axes and machetes were taken along to open the roads and for use in building churches and that they were left with the Indians for the latter purpose. The natives asserted, however, that Maldonado demanded payment for the tools at the rate of ten pounds of beeswax each (*ibid.*, ff. 60–61, 82v–83).

admitted that he had engaged in sharp dispute with Father Villalón. He testified that the argument was precipitated by a discussion of the activities of
Fray Juan de Santa María, whom he characterized as a meddlesome person.
Villalón promptly took exception to this remark and accused Maldonado and
his partners of being the troublemakers. The friar also stated that he opposed
sending soldiers with the missionaries "because the Spaniards interfered with
the preaching." Regarding this statement as an unwarranted slur on the conduct of his associates, Maldonado warned him not to say such things, and then
ventured the opinion that any attempt to pacify the fugitives by missionary
methods alone would fail because of the fickle character of the Indians. He
denied, however, that he had said anything to cause fear among the missionaries to be chosen for service in the interior settlements.

The governor evidently regarded Maldonado's reply as unsatisfactory,
for he placed the Spaniard under arrest and authorized an investigation that
dragged on for several weeks. During the hearings Maldonado stubbornly held
to his own version of the affair, as stated above. The proceedings were finally
suspended, having achieved no result except to publicize an unseemly controversy.[31]

This incident, which revealed the bitterness engendered by the events of
the preceding months, clearly indicated that effective cooperation of the Maldonado group and the Franciscan friars was no longer possible. Governor
Arellano, who had favored the Franciscans from the beginning, now issued
strict orders forbidding Sugasti and Maldonado to maintain any contact with
the forest settlements. In a dispatch to Spain, with which he sent copies of
all the documents in the case, he called attention to "the meager results" of
the expedition of May–June and the controversy it had aroused. For these
reasons he had agreed to the new arrangements outlined in the decree of
September 22. "I make this report so that your Majesty may take such action
as you think best." After some delay the Council approved the governor's
action in suspending the contract with Maldonado and associates for the
pacification and conquest of the province of Nueva Ocaña. Moreover, by
virtue of a royal cedula dated March 25, 1607, the six-year period of tribute
exemption promised the fugitives who offered submission was extended to
ten years.[32]

The decree of September 22, 1604, which gave the Franciscans entire
responsibility for the reduction of the fugitive Indians, constituted a major
triumph for Fray Juan de Santa María. His victory was complete when, a few

[31] Ibid., ff. 65v–95, 99–99v, 116–17v.
[32] AGI, México, leg. 359; Paxbolon-Maldonado Papers, Part II, ff. 192v–193.

weeks later, he was named one of the four missionaries to serve in the forest settlements. It is not surprising that the bishop and the Franciscan provincial and definitors supported Santa María in his controversy with Sugasti and Maldonado, or that they cast their votes in favor of a plan to pacify the fugitives by apostolic methods, without the aid of soldiers and colonists. The motives which prompted Governor Arellano to adopt a similar policy are not entirely clear. If we accept his report to the Crown at face value, he evidently had little confidence in the aims and methods of Maldonado and his associates. There can be little doubt that he also regarded the conflict of interest between this group and the Franciscans as irreconcilable. On the other hand, if it is true that Arellano hoped to organize an expedition for the conquest of the Itza lands, he may have voted to suspend the Nueva Ocaña project in order to have a free hand to develop his own plans. It should be noted, however, that Cogolludo is the sole source of information concerning Arellano's ambition to conquer the Itza. We find no reference to any such scheme in the governor's unpublished letters to the Crown.[33]

In November 1604 Fray Antonio de Ciudad Real, the Franciscan provincial, named the four friars who were to serve as missionaries in the fugitive settlements. Fray Gregorio González, who had accompanied the Sugasti-Maldonado expedition of May–June, was appointed *comisario*, or superior, of the missions already founded in Nacaukumil and Auatayn. Fray Juan de Santa María received a similar appointment for the Ichbalche district. Fray Juan García and Fray Francisco Matías were named as their respective assistants.[34] In December the friars set out in two groups for the forest country. Two months later (February 1605) a serious illness forced González to return to Campeche, where he died on April 13, 1605. In his place the provincial appointed Fray Joseph del Bosque, who had served as guardian of the Tixchel convent from 1600 to 1603.[35]

On his return from the interior González made an encouraging report on the progress of the missionary effort in Nacaukumil and Auatayn. It appears, however, that the friar had a poor opinion of the area in which these settlements were located, doubtless because of the swampy, unhealthful character of the country, for he had already made plans for the removal of the Indians to a new site about 12 leagues southeast of Champoton. The people of Auatayn

[33] The available correspondence of Arellano (AGI, México, leg. 359) comprises a relatively small series, and it is quite possible that some of his letters are missing.

[34] Paxbolon-Maldonado Papers, Part II, ff. 95–99, 112v–14v.

[35] Ciudad Real to Fray Diego de Castro, May 1605, *in* Expediente formado a instancia del Capitán Pedro Ochoa de Leguízamo . . . , 1604–05, AGI, Patronato, leg. 20, núm. 5, ramo 25.

had agreed to the scheme, although evidently with some misgivings, as evidenced by a letter of the village officials to Governor Arellano in which they asked for assurance that the Spaniards would not molest them at the new settlement. The leaders of Nacaukumil actively opposed the plan and sent word to Fray Juan de Santa María that rather than move to a place where they would be in frequent contact with soldiers and colonists their people would scatter through the forests. Santa María sent on this message to the governor.

There was considerable merit in González' proposal, since the new location would have been more healthful and also more accessible, and we shall see that ten years later the majority of the Indians of the forest missions were actually resettled at a site a few leagues from Champoton. But in view of the fact that the governor and churchmen, by virtue of the decree of September 22, 1604, had promised that the fugitives should remain in the region they now occupied, it was obviously necessary at this time to avoid any innovation that would cause them to lose confidence in the pledged word of the provincial authorities. It is not surprising, therefore, that Governor Arellano vetoed González' plan and issued an order forbidding the removal of the Indians to new locations against their will.[36]

Santa María and his companion. Fray Francisco Matías, had arrived in Ichbalche on December 23, 1604, after an arduous journey from Campeche. Received by the Indians in friendly fashion, the friars immediately set to work assembling the people of the surrounding forests at the new mission. In a letter to Governor Arellano, dated December 27, Santa María remarked that this task would require considerable time and effort "because the forests are full of people" scattered in small rancherías of a few houses each. He predicted, however, that eventually at least 200 families would be under instruction at Ichbalche.[37] Although we have little information concerning the activities of Santa María and Matías at Ichbalche during the following months, they evidently succeeded in gathering in many of the scattered Indians at this site. Statistical data for later years reveal that Ichbalche had the largest population of all the Montañas missions. In 1615, after missionary discipline had declined and some of the people had drifted away, the town still numbered more than 800 persons, young and old. This figure did not include the visita at Ichmachich, probably founded by Santa María and Matías. Cogolludo gives the advocation of the Ichbalche mission as Santos Reyes. The contemporary sources usually record the name as San Antonio de Ichbalche.[38]

[36] Paxbolon-Maldonado Papers, Part II, ff. 121–22, 133–37.
[37] *Ibid.*, ff. 117*v*–121.
[38] The town name is sometimes recorded as Ichçayab, which has the same meaning as Ichbalche. Cf. note 19, pp. 506–07, *infra*.

At Ichbalche Santa María received information concerning the village of Tzuctok located four days' journey toward the south. This place, aptly described in one of the friar's letters as "the gateway to all heathendom," was on the route of travel to the southern Cehache towns and the Itza lands of the Peten. Most of the people of Tzuctok were apostate Maya from northern Yucatan, but there were also many rancherías of unbaptized Indians in the same vicinity. Some of the latter were doubtless Cehache, although the major Cehache settlements were located farther south.

Realizing the strategic importance of Tzuctok as a point of contact with Cehache and Itza "heathendom," Santa María promptly sent messages to its chieftains, "exhorting them to be Christians." At first these Indians were wary of his friendly advances, for they feared that the founding of the forest missions was merely the first step in the occupation of the interior country by Spanish soldiers and colonists. However, in mid-January four "caciques" of Tzuctok came to Ichbalche to see the friars, who quieted their fears and assured them that no Spaniards other than missionaries would be permitted to enter the interior settlements. Whereupon the Indians offered obedience and invited the friars to visit their village.[39]

In March 1605 Santa María and Matías journeyed to Tzuctok, where they founded the mission dedicated to San Jerónimo.[40] The coming of the friars is briefly described in an interesting letter of the principal men of the pueblo to Governor Arellano dated March 31. This letter, probably written at Santa María's direction, begins with the usual offer of submission and then goes on to state that the people of Tzuctok wished "to serve one God and Lord called Hunabqu in their language, which means all powerful God."[41] Therefore they had now abandoned the pagan rites and ceremonies they had practiced and had built a church and dwelling for the missionaries. In accordance with the custom in villages under Spanish control they had also elected a local governor (Francisco Canche, mentioned in Paxbolon's report of February 1604 as one of the eight chieftains of Ixtok) and a town council. Confirmation of this election by the provincial governor was requested. The Indians also asked Arellano to reaffirm the promise of tribute exemption for a term of years and to give assurance that no Spaniards, negroes, or mulattoes would

[39] Paxbolon-Maldonado Papers, Part II, ff. 117v–21, 128v–30.
[40] In this case we rely on Cogolludo (1867–68, bk. 4, ch. 20), for the contemporary sources do not record the advocation of the Tzuctok mission.
[41] Here we find use of the name Hunabku, said to be a preconquest deity, for the Christian deity. Hunabku ("only God") is described in the Motul Dictionary (1929, p. 404) as "the only living and true God, the greatest of the people of Yucatan, of whom there was no image, because, they said, there was no conception of his form, since he was incorporeal." Translation from Roys, 1943, p. 73. Cf. also Landa, 1941, note 707, p. 146.

be allowed to visit the forest settlements. In a reply dated May 9, 1605, the governor accepted the promise of obedience and granted their requests.

In a letter of April 16 Santa María gave a personal report on developments at Tzuctok, describing the friendly attitude of the Indians and their apparent willingness to abandon their idolatrous customs and to receive instruction in Christian doctrine. He also reported satisfactory progress of the missionary effort in the other fugitive settlements and expressed the hope that within a year "all of these Indians will be in the fellowship of the Church." This dispatch and the letter of the chieftains of Tzuctok were delivered to Governor Arellano early in May by Fray Francisco Matías, sent by his superior to make a more detailed report on conditions in the forest country.[42]

It is evident that from the beginning of his work among the fugitives Fray Juan de Santa María hoped to extend his activities to the unconverted Cehache and Itza. In a lengthy section of his first report to Governor Arellano, written at Ichbalche on December 27, 1604, he told how these groups, having heard about the Sugasti-Maldonado expedition, had adopted a hostile attitude and had taken measures to shut off trade and communications with settlements visited by the Spaniards. He expressed the opinion, however, that they would be more friendly on learning that soldiers and colonists were now forbidden to enter the forest towns, and he gave notice of his intention to establish contact with the Cehache as soon as possible.[43]

This letter brought a prompt reply from Arellano reminding the friar that the decree of September 22, 1604, limited the missionary program for the present to the apostate fugitives from northern Yucatan. Consequently no attempt should be made at this time to enter any of the heathen settlements, although the missionaries should obtain all the information possible concerning them on the basis of which plans could be made for the eventual conversion of such groups. Santa María received this message before setting out for Tzuctok and accordingly abandoned any project he may have had to visit the Cehache towns. But during his stay in Tzuctok some Cehache chieftains came to see him and apparently indicated willingness to be baptized. It appears, however, that the major reason for their visit was to complain about raids on their settlements made a few weeks earlier by a group of Spaniards from the Usumacinta area in Tabasco. If they also consented to become Christians, they probably hoped that acceptance of the missionary program, which now involved no contacts with soldiers and colonists, would serve as a guarantee of protection against such raiding attacks in future.

[42] These letters are found in Expediente formado a instancia del Capitán Pedro Ochoa de Leguízamo . . . , 1604–05, AGI, Patronato, leg. 20, núm. 5, ramo 25.
[43] Paxbolon-Maldonado Papers, Part II, ff. 117v–21.

Santa María reported these developments in his dispatch of April 16 and expressed regret that he was not permitted to visit the Cehache towns, since the occasion seemed so propitious. His companion, Fray Francisco Matías, gave Arellano a more detailed account on his arrival in Mérida early in May. Although the governor ordered an investigation of the recent raids on the Cehache settlements and the arrest of the guilty parties, he again refused to authorize expansion of the missionary effort at this time to include the heathen tribes.[44]

In his dispatches to Santa María the governor emphasized the point that although recent royal cedulas (the decree of 1599, already mentioned, and a later order of December 31, 1601[45]) had instructed the provincial authorities to take measures to stamp out idolatry and to deal with the related fugitive problem, these decrees contained no provisions authorizing expeditions, missionary or otherwise, to the pagan Cehache and Itza. Therefore any scheme for the pacification of these groups would have to be referred to the Crown for approval. It is possible, as Cogolludo implies in his version of this incident, that the governor refused permission for Santa María to begin the conversion of the Cehache and Itza because he hoped to organize an expedition of his own for the conquest of the Itza country and that his citation of the royal cedulas merely served as an excuse to gain time for the presentation of this project in the Council of the Indies. We have already noted, however, that the governor's correspondence contains no reference to any such plan. Moreover, there is evidence that Arellano's decision was influenced to some extent by representations by the Franciscan provincial, who called attention to the fact that the death of many veteran friars in recent years had left the Order without adequate personnel for an expanding missionary program in the interior country.[46]

[44] Expediente formado a instancia del Capitán Pedro Ochoa de Leguízamo . . . , 1604–05, AGI, Patronato, leg. 20, núm. 5, ramo 25.

[45] The cedula of December 31, 1601 (AGI, México, leg. 2999, libro D-4) was prompted by a report on the fugitive problem presented to the Council of the Indies by Fray Alonso de Ortega, then serving as representative of the Yucatan Franciscans at court. In this report Ortega suggested that the situation might be remedied if an agreement were made with some colonist to organize an expedition at his own cost for the purpose of pacifying the fugitive settlements. The cedula of December 31, 1601, summarized this report and instructed the provincial governor, Fernández de Velasco, to take steps to bring the Indians back to their pueblos. It contained no reference to the heathen tribes. It is interesting to note that Ortega, who suggested the possibility of a formal expedition for the reduction of the fugitives, was a member of the group of churchmen who shared in the decision to suspend the contract with Maldonado and associates in September 1604.

[46] According to missionary reports of this period, twenty-six friars had died within a period of five years (1600–05), greatly reducing the number available for service in the missions administered by the Franciscans. In 1602 twelve new recruits were sent out from Spain, six of whom died in a shipwreck off Jamaica. The following year Fray Diego de Castro was sent to Spain to make an appeal for thirty additional missionaries. The Crown eventually agreed to

Arellano's refusal to authorize the conversion of the heathen tribes doubtless caused Santa María great disappointment. In 1611 the friar testified that
because of the governor's "interference with the said reduction and conversion" he decided to withdraw from the forest missions and return to northern
Yucatan.[47] We doubt, however, that this action was prompted entirely by the
governor's policy. From the beginning of his service in the interior Santa
María had been in poor health, and we suspect that illness was an important
factor in causing him to give up his work among the fugitives. He probably
returned to northern Yucatan in the latter part of 1605.[48]

We interrupt the narrative at this point to review the evidence on which
we have based the tentative locations for the Montañas missions shown on
Map 4.

As already noted, Nacaukumil was located a short distance (about 4
leagues) east of Popola, probably on or near the Mamantel or one of its
affluents. Auatayn occupied a site 6 or 7 leagues east of Nacaukumil, or 10-11
leagues from Popola. From one of Fray Juan de Santa María's letters we also
learn that Auatayn was situated about halfway between Nacaukumil and
Ichbalche.

For the village of Nacaukumil the sources also employ other names, viz.,
Ichcun, Yscuncabil, and Chacuitzil (also recorded as Chunuitzil). In the documents of 1605 et seq. Chacuitzil is the name most frequently used. Moreover,
sometime during the year 1605 the people of Nacaukumil moved to another
site about 2 leagues west of Auatayn. On Map 4 the name Nacaukumil shows
our tentative location for the original settlement and the name Chacuitzil indicates the new location.

---

send out eighteen. It was while these negotiations were in progress that the governor and
churchmen decided, by virtue of the decree of September 22, 1604, to send four friars to the
fugitive settlements. Although the provincial, Fray Antonio de Ciudad Real, shared in this
decision, he showed some reluctance, when the time came to execute the decree, to name missionaries for this project, because of the shortage of friar personnel. It was only after the governor and bishop exerted pressure that the provincial finally appointed Santa María, Matías,
González, and García for service in the forest settlements. In 1605, when the question of the
heathen tribes came up, the provincial informed the governor that in case he decided to expand
the missionary effort in the interior country he should petition the king for more friars. "We are
so few," the provincial wrote, "that we cannot serve in so many places" (Paxbolon-Maldonado
Papers, Part II; AGI, México, leg. 294; Expediente formado a instancia del Capitán Pedro Ochoa
de Leguízamo . . . , 1604–05, AGI, Patronato, leg. 20, núm. 4, ramo 25).

[47] López de Cogolludo, 1867–68, bk. 8, ch. 9.

[48] It is interesting to note that Santa María's letter of April 16, 1605, although expressing
regret that he was not permitted to visit the Cehache settlements, clearly indicates that he
planned to continue his work among the fugitives. References to his poor health are found in
most of his letters and also in those of his companion, Fray Francisco Matías. On one occasion
Matías expressed doubt whether Santa María would be able to make the journey from Ichbalche
to Tzuctok.

Early in 1609 the Indians of Auatayn and Chacuitzil petitioned Governor Arellano for permission to combine into a single settlement and to move to a new site about 6 leagues east of Popola (or about halfway between Nacau-kumil and Chacuitzil), where they already had their milpas and had cleared ground for their church and houses. This new location, also known as Chacuit-zil, or Cheuitzil, was described as the site of "an old pueblo depopulated because of wars." The main reason cited by the Indians for desiring to make the move was to obtain a better water supply. At their present locations both villages depended on rain water that collected in an aguada located between the two settlements. In the dry season this source of supply sometimes failed. The place where they wished to resettle was on a stream connecting with Popola, evidently the Mamantel or one of its tributaries. Although Arellano granted the petition, the plan was not carried out for reasons to be described farther on.[49]

The chief interest of this incident is that it raises a question as to the extent and character of the Mamantel drainage in which the site of the proposed consolidation settlement and also that of Nacaukumil were located. On Map 4 we have shown the Mamantel as a short stream without northern affluents, in accordance with recent cartographical data. The tentative location indicated for Nacaukumil lies beyond the headwaters of the river as drawn, although this settlement was apparently on or near this stream or one of its tributaries. Nineteenth-century maps and also some published since 1900 show the Mamantel as extending much farther inland with affluents coming in from the north. For example, the Hübbe–Aznar Pérez map (Berendt revision of 1878) and the Espinosa map (*ca.* 1910) carry the main stream inland to a point a short distance beyond San Antonio. However, the former uses a broken line for the eastern section of the river, possibly indicating a seasonal drainage in this area. This dotted line section crosses through the northern part of the great unexplored swamp called Isla Pac (formerly known as Bolonpeten), which is not shown on the map, nor on any other maps, old or recent, prior to the publication of Andrew's study in 1943.

Although these earlier maps were based on inadequate reconnaissance, it is interesting to note that seventeenth century sources indicate that it was possible, at least at certain seasons of the year, to travel by canoe from Bolon-peten, or Isla Pac, to the Mamantel. Thus a document of 1669, describing a fugitive settlement called Bolonpeten, reads: "This Bolonpeten is surrounded by nine small islands (*islotes*), and [the Indians] are settled on the largest, about half a league in extent; and by canoe they travel to the river that goes to

---

[49] Paxbolon-Maldonado Papers, Part II, ff. 146-54*v.*

Popola, and the canoe will accommodate five or six persons."[50] This statement obviously indicates that some sort of drainage, possibly of seasonal character, existed between Isla Pac and the Mamantel. Whether any connection of this kind still exists, we do not know. The only line of drainage from Isla Pac shown on Andrews' maps is to the south toward the Arroyo Caribe, a tributary of the Candelaria, which we have copied on our own maps.[51]

The Hübbe–Aznar Pérez map also shows two small affluents, separated by a distance of about 10 km., entering the Mamantel from the northeast a short distance above the village of Mamantel. These are the Arroyo Xotkukun and the Arroyo Cheucil. The same tributaries are shown on the Espinosa map without names. We are informed that a reconnaissance map of the Ferrocarril del Sureste, which crosses this region, also shows these affluents, with the names recorded as Arroyo Xalkukun and Arroyo Chaucel.[52]

The names for the eastern affluent (Chaucel, Cheucil) bear considerable resemblance to the names (Chacuitzil, Cheuitzil) recorded for the site of the proposed consolidation settlement of 1609, to which reference is made above. This site, as we have seen, was on a stream. The resemblance is much closer in the case of the site named Cheusih, located two or three days' journey east of Tiquintunpa, to which the Indians of Ichmachich, Chacuitzil, and Chunhaz (to which Auatayn had been moved) were permanently resettled in 1615.[53] We are of the opinion therefore that Cheusih and probably the proposed consolidation site of 1609 were located on or near the Arroyo Cheucil, or Chaucel. Moreover, in view of the fact that Nacaukumil was closer to Popola, we also suggest that it was on or near the Arroyo Xotkukun, or Xalkukun.

Ichbalche was located in a southeasterly direction from Campeche and south-southwest of Cauich, where another new mission was established in 1605.[54] Fray Juan de Santa María estimated the distance from Campeche

[50] Sobre las diligencias que se han hecho para la reducción de los indios de Sahcabchen y otros pueblos, 1668–70, AGI, México, leg. 307.

[51] This point was referred to Sr. Pedro Sánchez, Director of the Instituto Panamericano de Geografía e Historia, Tacubaya, D. F., Mexico, for an opinion. Sr. Sánchez kindly sent back a report made by the cartographer of the Office of Geography, Sr. Arnulfo de la Llave. This report states that although all recent maps show the Mamantel as a stream of short length, it is possible that a "corriental" proceeding from the east is linked up with the Mamantel and serves as a drainage in the rainy reason for part of the area east of the Mamantel. However, it seems probable (this is our own suggestion) that the blasting of channels through the rapids and falls of the Candelaria has resulted in more rapid drainage of the surplus waters from the region of Isla Pac through the Arroyo Caribe–Candelaria system. This in turn would tend to reduce the amount of drainage from the northern part of this district westward toward the Mamantel. In short, present day freshet streams in the latter area probably were navigable for a much larger part of the year in earlier days.

[52] Report transmitted by Sr. Pedro Sánchez (see preceding note).

[53] Cf. p. 289, infra.

[54] About 1596–97 a group of Indians from Ticul, Pustunich, and other towns in the Xiu area migrated to a forest site called Tiytz some 20 leagues east of Campeche. Their leader was

as 35 leagues. The friar's letters also place Ichbalche some 14 leagues from Nacaukumil and a shorter distance from Bolonpeten (Isla Pac).[55] We also find that in 1615, when the people of Ichbalche were moved to Sahcabchen, the journey between these two places could be made in two or three days. On the basis of these data we tentatively locate Ichbalche in the region between L. Mocu and L. Cilvituk. Ichmachich was apparently closer to Nacaukumil, as evidenced by the order in which the towns are listed in Paxbolon's report of 1604 (Appendix E). Consequently we place Ichmachich west of Ichbalche in the area on the opposite side of L. Mocu.

The location of Tzuctok has special interest in view of the fact that sources of the later seventeenth century contain numerous references to a place of the same name and apparently located in the same area.[56] The most explicit locational data concerning this later site are recorded in the narratives of the expeditions of Capt. Alonso García de Paredes and Fray Andrés de Avendaño to the Peten in 1695-96. These accounts place Tzuctok 45-50 leagues south of Cauich and about 17.5 leagues from Temchay, an important point en route.[57] The Cauich-Tzuctok distance compares well with earlier estimates in the documents of 1605-15 which place Tzuctok 55-60 leagues from Campeche. In each case, of course, the figures doubtless exceeded the airline distance. Avendaño's account of his first entrada in 1695 states that Tzuctok was "eight long leagues" from Chunpich (evidently

---

a certain Juan Ucan of Ticul. In mid-January 1605 Ucan and other members of this fugitive group came to Campeche and notified the local authorities that they wished to resettle at the site of Cauich, east of Champoton. The matter was referred to Governor Arellano, who promptly authorized the plan and named Ucan as governor of the new settlement. The removal of the Indians to Cauich was carried out a few weeks later. The Cauich mission became a visita of the Campeche convent, of which Fray Alonso de Guzmán was guardian at this time. This place is occasionally described in the contemporary sources as one of the Missions of Las Montañas, although this designation, as used in the present chapter, applies more specifically to missions in the fugitive settlements located farther south (Paxbolon-Maldonado Papers, Part II, ff. 122-26v, 130-31, 136-38v, 140v-43).

[55] In 1605, when Fray Gregorio González proposed the removal of the Indians of Nacaukumil and Auatayn to a new location southeast of Champoton, Santa María made an alternative proposal, suggesting that the people of Nacaukumil might resettle "near here [Ichbalche] at an old site called Bolonpeten, where it would be possible to administer them from this pueblo" (ibid., f. 134).

[56] The name of this settlement appears in various spellings, e.g., Çuctok, Zuctoc, Tzuctoc, Tzuchhok. The last form appears in Avendaño's account of his journeys to the Peten. According to the interpreters who accompanied the Paredes expedition of 1695, the name indicates a flint deposit (Villagutierre Soto-Mayor, 1933, bk. 5, ch. 2). Tzuc is occasionally a prefix indicating a locality where the plant or other natural feature which follows is found; tok means "flint."

[57] Documents of the year 1669 describe Temchay, then said to have a population of 300 warriors, as a site north of Tzuctok. This place and other interior villages inhabited at the time, including Tzuctok, were subsequently abandoned (Sobre las diligencias que se han hecho para la reducción de los indios de Sahcabchen y otros pueblos, 1668-70, AGI, México, leg. 307). Cf. also pp. 306-07, infra.

located near Aguada Cumpich),[58] the first important town of the southern Cehache. Moreover, both Avendaño and Villagutierre place Tzuctok on or near a stream of seasonal character. These facts point to a location for Tzuctok near the site of Concepción on the headwaters of the Arroyo Caribe, a branch of the Candelaria.[59]

We have already noted that the settlement where Fray Juan de Santa María founded the mission of San Jerónimo de Tzuctok in 1605 was located four days' journey to the south of Ichbalche on the route to the southern Cehache towns and the Peten. We have also quoted Santa María's statement that it was "the gateway to all heathendom." Other reports of 1605 describe Tzuctok as "the last pueblo of the outlaws" (fugitives) on the frontier of heathendom. Paxbolon's memorial of 1604 places it next to the last in the group of settlements in an easterly direction from Nacaukumil, the last in this group being Chunpich. In the letter of the Indians of Tzuctok to Governor Arellano, March 31, 1605, Chunpich is listed as one of the border settlements surrounding the Tzuctok area. Documents of 1615 record that the journey from Tzuctok to Sahcabchen took one week. In 1669 the site of Tzuctok, subsequently visited by Avendaño, was said to be eight days' journey from Sahcabchen. Finally, the mission records of 1609 indicate that it was possible to travel by canoe from Tzuctok to Chunhaz, a site southwest of Ichbalche and near the western borders of Isla Pac, in two days. This clearly shows that Tzuctok was near the Isla or on some stream connecting with it. A location at or near Concepción on the Arroyo Caribe would answer this requirement.

Thus there can be little doubt that the mission settlement of 1605–15 and the place called Tzuctok mentioned in later sources were located in the same area and probably at the same site.

Prior to 1609 the friars established missions in three other forest settlements: Texan, Petcah, and Sacalum. Texan, apparently administered as a visita of Ichbalche, may have been near the modern site of Taschan southeast of Pixoyol. For the location of Petcah we have no information, except that it appears to have been a visita of Tzuctok.

In regard to Sacalum, the sources state (1) that it was southeast of Cauich in the direction of Bacalar and (2) that it was 50 leagues (an excessive estimate, but indicating a long distance) from Ichbalche. Thus we can safely place it in southern Quintana Roo, although the approximate site is still a matter of considerable doubt. Cogolludo relates that the mission of Sacalum

[58] Avendaño describes a "lake" lying to the west of Chunpich (Means, 1917, p. 119).
[59] Villagutierre Soto-Mayor, 1933, bk. 5, chs. 1–2; Means, 1917, pp. 105–20.

founded in 1622 by Fray Diego Delgado was at the same place as the earlier settlement of this name. If this is true, then the location must have been south of any direct route from Cauich to Bacalar. The original mission founded as a result of the Mirones-Delgado expedition of 1622 was at a place named La Concepción de la Pimienta. The journal of the entrada does not permit an accurate location of this site, but the name indicates that it was in a region where allspice trees (*pimienta*) were found. This would seem to place it in the rain-forest belt that extends from the Bacalar area south-westward into northern Peten. According to Cárdenas Valencia, this mission was later moved to Sacalum located "farther on," i.e., farther south. We also know that Delgado subsequently traveled overland from Sacalum to Tipu and thence to Lake Peten without going to Bacalar.[60] In view of this evidence, we tentatively locate the settlement on Map 4 in the region of Lagunas Om and Acon. It should be stressed, however, that this location is less certain than any other indicated on the map.

In 1606, or thereabouts, the Franciscans established three guardianías in the Montañas area with headquarters at Ichbalche, Tzuctok, and Cha-cuitzil.[61] Fray Francisco Matías, the former companion of Fray Juan de Santa María, served as superior of the Ichbalche district, which also included Ichmachich and probably Texan. Fray Joseph del Bosque, who had been sent to the Chacuitzil-Auatayn district after the death of Fray Gregorio Gon-zález, became guardian of Tzuctok. This mission subsequently had two visitas, evidently at Petcah and Sacalum. Fray Juan de Buenaventura took charge of the mission at Chacuitzil and its visita at Auatayn after the transfer of Bosque to Tzuctok. Another friar who served in the Montañas area prior to 1609 was the lay brother, Fray Juan Fernández.

In 1607 Fray Pedro de Beleña was sent out on a tour of inspection of the forest missions. According to Cogolludo, he made an encouraging report on the progress thus far achieved by the friars. It appears, however, that Bishop Vázquez de Mercado held a less favorable view of the situation, as evidenced by a letter to the Crown, dated June 16, 1606. In this dispatch the bishop briefly outlined the events leading up to the promulgation of the decree of September 22, 1604, which gave the Franciscans sole responsibility for the pacification of the fugitive settlements, and then stated that the Indians

[60] López de Cogolludo, 1867–68, bk. 10, ch. 2; Scholes and Adams, 1936; Cárdenas Valencia, 1937, p. 76.

[61] We suggest the year 1606 as the date when the guardianías of Ichbalche, Tzuctok, and Chacuitzil were established because of the fact that the provincial chapter of the Franciscan Order met in that year.

had not shown so great an inclination to accept religious instruction as had
been expected. Experience had also shown that the missionaries would need
the aid and protection of soldiers and colonists in order to achieve lasting
results. The bishop recommended therefore that a settlement of about twenty
Spanish families should be established at a suitable location in the Montañas
area. Otherwise he feared that the Indians might seize a favorable opportunity to rebel against the missionaries and flee into the forest.[62]

Despite this pessimistic report, the Council instructed the provincial
authorities to continue the pacification of the fugitives by missionary
methods, without resort to force of any kind or the intervention of any persons other than the friars. This statement of policy, issued in 1607, gave
full support to the views of the Franciscans, who still held that soldiers and
colonists should be excluded from the forest settlements. Two years later the
same policy was reaffirmed in a letter of the king to the Franciscan provincial,
Fray Hernando de Sopuerta.[63]

Various statements formulated early in 1609 leave no doubt, however,
that conditions in the Montañas area were far from satisfactory. A prominent citizen of Campeche, Francisco Sánchez Cerdán, described as a person
having a wide knowledge of the interior country, reported that missionary
discipline in the fugitive settlements had rapidly deteriorated and that many
of the Indians continued to practice idolatry and other heathen customs.
The protests and admonitions of the friars merely evoked threats by the
offenders to abandon the missions and withdraw into the forests. Cerdán
warned that the inability of the missionaries to curb "the very great liberties"
of the Indians had created a serious situation that would steadily grow
worse unless corrected by prompt and effective action. To illustrate the open
contempt of certain Indian leaders for the religious, he cited the case of a
chieftain of Tzuctok who had used violent and abusive language against
Fray Joseph del Bosque when the latter went out to serve as guardian of
the Tzuctok convent. From other sources, including a decree of Governor
Arellano, we learn that some time during the latter part of 1608 Fray Francisco Matías narrowly escaped death at the hands of a group of fugitives,
apparently from Tzuctok.[64]

In February–March 1609 the governor and provincial conferred on measures to remedy the situation. They agreed to send Fray Juan de la Cruz,

[62] López de Cogolludo, 1867–68, bk. 8, ch. 9; Vázquez Mercado to the king, Mérida, June
16, 1606, AGI, México, leg. 369.
[63] AGI, México, leg. 359; López de Cogolludo, 1867–68, bk. 8, ch. 9.
[64] Paxbolon-Maldonado Papers, Part II, ff. 155–56v, 163–66v, 170–73v; López de Cogolludo,
1867–68, bk. 8, ch. 15.

a former guardian of the Hecelchakan convent, to make a general investigation of conditions in the interior settlements, on the basis of which appropriate action might be taken to improve mission administration and strengthen the disciplinary authority of the friars. It was also proposed that a new convent should be established at Cauich to serve as general headquarters for the Montañas area and as a place of refuge for the friars in time of danger. This scheme was later abandoned, however, as impracticable.[65]

Fray Juan de la Cruz spent the months of April–July 1609 in the Montañas area. At this time only two friars were in residence at guardianía headquarters: Fray Francisco Matías at Ichbalche and Fray Juan de Buenaventura at Chacuitzil. Fray Joseph del Bosque had apparently gone to Sacalum some months earlier, and the Tzuctok mission was being administered temporarily by the friar at Chacuitzil. During his inspection of the missions Fray Juan de la Cruz relied to a great extent on Matías for advice and counsel, which was only natural in view of Matías' four years of service in the interior and his position as guardian of Ichbalche, the largest of the forest settlements.

It appears that prior to 1609 there had been some debate among the friars concerning the advisability of consolidating the pueblos of Chacuitzil, Auatayn, and Tzuctok at a new location near Chacuitzil as a means of simplifying mission administration. The proponents of this plan apparently included Fray Juan de Buenaventura and Fray Pedro de Beleña, who had served as visitador of the missions in 1607. Fray Francisco Matías strongly opposed it, evidently on the ground that if any reorganization were made it would be better to concentrate the missions in a more restricted district in the region of Ichbalche. Because of this difference of opinion the provincial and his advisers had taken no action in the matter. But early in 1609, as we have seen, the Indians of Chacuitzil and Auatayn actually petitioned Governor Arellano for permission to unite and to form a new settlement about 2 leagues from Chacuitzil. On the advice of Buenaventura and Beleña the petition was approved, but the project apparently encountered renewed opposition, with the result that the governor and provincial agreed to refer the matter to Fray Juan de la Cruz for further investigation.

Thus the instructions received by Fray Juan de la Cruz for his visita of the Montañas district specially charged him to determine whether it would be advantageous from the standpoint of the missionary program to move some of the settlements to other sites, "since the friars who have been there hold different opinions [on the subject]." He was not authorized, however, to carry out any reorganization on his own initiative without prior approval

65 Paxbolon-Maldonado Papers, Part II, ff. 158–68v.

by the governor and provincial. Nevertheless, after consultation with Fray Francisco Matías, he decided to move the villages of Tzuctok, Chacuitzil, Auatayn, and Ichmachich to a new site called Chunhaz. This place, located only 5 or 6 leagues southwest of Ichbalche, occupied a fairly central position in relation to the towns to be consolidated. The chief disadvantage of the site was its proximity to extensive swamps, evidently on the western fringes of Isla Pac.

The friar's plan met with some opposition, especially in Tzuctok. Two chieftains of this pueblo hastily journeyed to Mérida to file protest before the governor, who promptly issued an order that the Indians should not be forced to abandon their settlement without his consent. But Fray Juan ignored this instruction, and during the month of May most of the people of Tzuctok were moved to Chunhaz. The houses at Tzuctok were burned in order to discourage dissident elements from returning to their old homes. The friar's action in this case apparently quieted resistance in the other towns, for by early June the Indians of Chacuitzil, Auatayn, and Ichmachich had also assembled at Chunhaz.

Arellano received news of these developments in a letter from the governor and alcaldes of Ichbalche delivered in Mérida in mid-June. This message also contained a report of an unfortunate incident that had occurred in Ichbalche. It appears that Fray Juan de la Cruz ordered the village bailiff (*alguacil*) to arrest a group of fugitives recently arrived from northern Yucatan whom he proposed to send back to their respective towns. The order was carried out, but within a day or so most of the Indians escaped into the forests. Whereupon the friar accused the bailiff of negligence and had him whipped. This affair, so the letter stated, had created considerable unrest among the people of Ichbalche, who also feared that the friar would force them to move to Chunhaz, as he had already done in the case of the other towns.

The report that Fray Juan had moved the Indians of Tzuctok and other settlements to a new location without permission and in disregard of orders naturally aroused Arellano's displeasure. The governor also regarded the friar's actions at Ichbalche as entirely unwarranted.[66] Consequently he filed

[66] Arellano had already engaged in argument with the Franciscans concerning the case of a friar who had imposed corporal punishment on a cacique of Dzonotake in northern Yucatan. The governor held that the friars had no authority to impose punishments of this kind and that in doing so they infringed the civil jurisdiction (López de Cogolludo, 1867–68, bk. 8, chs. 12–13). He evidently regarded the Ichbalche case as of similar character, for he now dispatched orders to the officials of the Montañas villages to the effect that in case the friars issued orders in matters pertaining to the "royal jurisdiction," such as the moving of a town, imprisonment, or corporal punishment, they should suspend execution of such orders until the provincial au-

demand with the provincial for the immediate recall of the missionary to
Mérida. The provincial expressed doubt concerning the accuracy of the
information at hand but agreed to summon both Fray Juan de la Cruz and
Fray Francisco Matías for questioning. Arellano in turn dispatched an order
to the interior instructing the Indians to send him an exact account of what
had occurred.

On receipt of this message the officials of the various towns met in Ichbalche and drew up letters of report as requested. These papers described in
some detail the arbitrary manner in which Fray Juan had forced the removal
of the settlements to Chunhaz and the consequent hardships suffered by
the Indians. The governor and regidores of Tzuctok testified that when
the two chieftains of their pueblo returned from Mérida with Arellano's order
forbidding the transfer of the town to a new location without his consent
the friar took possession of the decree and misrepresented its true import.
Moreover, in order to prevent the messengers from making a further appeal
to the governor, he had them arrested and held in jail until the removal of
the settlement to Chunhaz was completed. Many families had suffered hunger
at Chunhaz because they had been forced to abandon accumulated supplies
of food in their old villages. During the burning of Tzuctok a large number
of fowl and several pigs had been destroyed, as well as a considerable quantity
of maize and beans in storage. The letters also complained that Chunhaz,
situated near mosquito-infested swamps, was an unhealthy place and that
many people were ill with fever. Finally, the governor and alcaldes of Ichbalche confirmed their earlier account of Fray Juan's actions in their own
pueblo.[67]

On July 27, 1609, after receipt of these letters, Arellano issued orders
authorizing the Indians to return to their old settlements. Accordingly, most
of the people of Tzuctok, Chacuitzil, and Ichmachich abandoned Chunhaz
within a short time. We suspect, however, that some of the Indians, including
many from Tzuctok, drifted away into the forests instead of returning to
their villages. The Indians of Auatayn chose to remain at Chunhaz, probably
because there was a better water supply at this site. Earlier in the summer
Fray Juan de Buenaventura had also moved his residence to Chunhaz, which

thorities had been notified. In spiritual matters, however, the village officers should obey the
friars under penalty of loss of office (Paxbolon-Maldonado Papers, Part II, ff. 179v–80v).

[67] It should be noted that we also have letters of the Indians of Tzuctok and Chacuitzil
written in early June which indicated their approval of the new arrangements and gave a
favorable report on the location of Chunhaz. It seems clear, however, that these letters were
written at the direction of Fray Juan de la Cruz and did not reflect the true sentiments of
most of the Indians.

served henceforth as headquarters for the guardianía of Chacuitzil-Auatayn.[68]

Unfortunately we do not possess the testimony given by Fray Juan de la Cruz and Fray Francisco Matías after their arrival in Mérida on summons by the provincial. However, the fact that Fray Juan was not permitted to return to the interior suggests that the authorities, both civil and ecclesiastical, regarded his conduct as worthy of censure. Fray Francisco Matías, who had served as his counsellor, was also relieved of his post as guardian of Ichbalche.

The plan for the consolidation of four of the smaller towns at a site in the region of Ichbalche had obvious merit, for it would have greatly facilitated the instruction of the Indians. There is ample evidence that Arellano favored reorganization of the missions, but it is not surprising that he disapproved of the methods employed by Fray Juan de la Cruz. The forced removal of the Indians to a new location against their wishes violated the promises made in the decree of September 22, 1604. Moreover, the governor naturally expected to share in a decision involving the shift of so many Indians to another site. If Fray Juan had acted with less haste and if he had used greater tact in dealing with the Indians, his plan might well have succeeded. As things turned out, he merely antagonized the governor and aroused unrest in the interior settlements.

The sources record only a few facts concerning the history of the forest missions during the next five years. Fray Buenaventura Valdés succeeded Matías as guardian of Ichbalche in the autumn of 1609, but he soon became discouraged because of his inability to enforce discipline and withdrew from the mission before the end of the year.[69] He was replaced by Fray Juan Roldán, who served in Ichbalche for about a year and a half. Subsequently Fray Juan de Buenaventura, who had spent several years in Chacuitzil and Chunhaz, was assigned to Ichbalche. A mission report of December 1610 indicates that Tzuctok had a resident friar at that time,[70] and there is some evidence that a convent was temporarily established in Sacalum in 1611–12.[71] Prior to 1614, however, both Tzuctok and Sacalum were reduced

[68] The major sources for the Chunhaz episode are in Paxbolon-Maldonado Papers, Part II, ff. 175–204v. A few additional items are in Autos hechos a instancia del defensor de indios . . . , 1609, AGI, Patronato, leg. 231, núm. 4, ramo 16.

[69] In a letter to Governor Arellano, dated November 18, 1609, Valdés made a long and bitter complaint concerning the sexual freedom practiced in Ichbalche. Neither public nor private admonitions had been of any avail, for the "caciques" tolerated the practice and protected the offenders. Because of his inability to remedy conditions, the friar had already asked the provincial for permission to return to northern Yucatan. Soon thereafter he withdrew from Ichbalche, ostensibly because of illness, and did not return (Paxbolon-Maldonado Papers, Part II, ff. 204v–08v).

[70] DHY, 2: 160.

[71] In 1609 there was talk of founding a convent in Sacalum, but action was apparently postponed for a year or more, for the mission report of December 1610 does not mention a guardi-

to the status of visitas of Ichbalche. Although the mission at Chunhaz retained convent status until 1615, when the settlements were finally moved to new sites, it frequently lacked a resident missionary after Fray Juan de Buenaventura was transferred to Ichbalche. In 1614–15 Buenaventura was the only friar actually in residence in the entire Montañas district.

An interesting commentary on conditions in the forest settlements in these later years is found in a letter of Fray Juan de Buenaventura to the provincial governor, dated September 7, 1614. The friar related that he had encountered considerable difficulty in getting the Indians of Ichbalche to build a new church to replace the one constructed when the mission was founded ten years earlier. "The [new] building is not a Santa Maria Maggiore but only a *ramada* for which the wood is available in the village. . . . But [the Indians] are great idlers and enemies of work." Buenaventura also reported that a group of malcontents had withdrawn from the town and had established a small settlement in the forests a few leagues distant, "where they are drunk with *balche* the year round and live in idolatry. My lord governor, I do not speak passion but only the truth, for a short time ago I took a basketful of idols from them." The leaders of this settlement had recently gone to Mérida to file certain complaints before the governor, and the friar begged that they should be detained there until the truth of their accusations was verified. He pointed out that on other occasions the provincial authorities, without verifying the facts, had taken action on the basis of false charges made by the Indians. "Favoring their mischief," Buenaventura wrote, "is the cause of their losing respect for us; it puts our lives in danger and it imperils the salvation of this whole land."[72]

Other documents of 1614–15 also reveal the lack of discipline in the interior settlements. Friars who had served in the missions in preceding years testified that many of the Indians continued to practice idolatry and other heathen rites. One missionary told how he had destroyed numerous idols of clay and stone in the town where he had been stationed. Sexual freedom was prevalent in most of the villages, and cases of incest had been noted. The efforts of the friars to correct these conditions had been unavailing, for the Indians refused to obey their orders even in spiritual matters. An increasing number of people had drifted away from the missions to live "in freedom" in the forests, and some had migrated to the region of Tipu.[73]

anía in Sacalum at that time. However, a document of 1612 refers to Fray Joseph del Bosque as guardian of Sacalum. López de Cogolludo (1867–68, bk. 8, ch. 9) also states that Bosque had charge of the convent of San Francisco de Sacalum.

[72] Paxbolon-Maldonado Papers, Part II, ff. 221v–24v.

[73] *Ibid.*, ff. 228v–38v, *passim*.

The Franciscans now realized that a drastic change was necessary to prevent the complete loss of all they had achieved during the preceding ten years. It was impossible to expect one or two friars effectively to administer all the missions at the sites now occupied. Tzuctok, for example, was four days' journey from convent headquarters at Ichbalche, and Sacalum was still farther away. Moreover, in view of the rapid deterioration of missionary discipline it was doubtful that conditions could be remedied by the assignment of additional friars for service in the various settlements. The obvious solution of the problem was to move the missions to a new location near Champoton or Campeche, where the Indians could be subjected to closer supervision and where the missionaries could have easy communication with other Franciscan houses in the area under Spanish control. Although this move would also mean bringing the Indians into frequent contact with Spanish colonists, the friars apparently concluded that this would be better than to risk the complete abandonment of the missions in the near future.

In the autumn of 1614 the proposal to resettle the Indians at a new site was submitted to the provincial governor, Don Antonio de Figueroa, who had succeeded Luna y Arellano in 1612. Figueroa took no action until early in the following year when he visited the Campeche-Champoton district during an official inspection of the province. At Calkini, on January 13, 1615, he issued orders summoning the officials of the interior settlements to Champoton, where the plan to found a new mission would be discussed. He also asked Fray Juan de Buenaventura and other missionaries who had served in the Montañas area to come to the conference.

The meeting at Champoton, attended by the governors, alcaldes, and other officials of Ichbalche, Ichmachich, Tzuctok, and Sacalum, was held January 31–February 2. Buenaventura and the other friars present made lengthy statements describing the urgent need for more effective instruction of the Indians and unanimously recommended the consolidation of the settlements at a new location near Champoton. After some discussion the Indian leaders agreed to the plan on one condition. The period of tribute exemption guaranteed to the Indians when the Montañas missions were founded had now expired. On behalf of their people the chieftains expressed willingness to begin payment of a moderate tribute after the transfer to a new site had been effected. They asked the governor, however, to promise that they would have the status of Crown tributaries and not be assigned in encomienda to Spanish colonists. Figueroa granted this request and also promised that during his term of office the Indians would not be subjected to forced labor.

The friars suggested two sites for the new settlement. One was at Ulumal

on the Champoton River, but the Indians objected to this location on the
ground that it was swampy, mosquito-infested, and unhealthy.[74] The other
site, named Sahcabchen, was situated about 8 leagues southeast of Champoton
in the savannas of Chunal. In this region there was plenty of woodland for
milpas, grazing land for livestock, and ample water supply provided by wells
and cenotes. On February 3–4 the Indians made a thorough inspection of
the country around Sahcabchen and agreed to settle there.[75]

From Champoton Figueroa returned to Mérida, where he conferred with
Bishop Salazar[76] and the Franciscan provincial and made final arrangements
for the removal of the Indians to Sahcabchen. The governor appointed
Francisco de Villalobos Cárdenas, a citizen of Valladolid, as special commissioner in charge of the resettlement, to be assisted by Fray Joseph del Bosque,
then resident in Hecelchakan, and Fray Juan de Buenaventura. The Franciscans also named Fray Joseph as guardian of the convent to be established
in Sahcabchen. The commissioner was authorized to recruit laborers in La
Ceiba, Champoton, and neighboring villages to bush the site of the new
settlement, build a church and a house for the friar, and clear lands for
planting. In these villages he could also requisition horses to transport valuable property from the forest settlements to Sahcabchen and purchase food
for the sustenance of the Indians until the first crop of maize was harvested.[77]

Early in March Cárdenas and the two friars journeyed to Sahcabchen and
marked out sites for the village church and houses for the new settlers. Indian
laborers who had been recruited en route were immediately put to work
building the church and clearing milpas for planting. Leaving Fray Joseph
del Bosque to supervise these operations, Cárdenas and Fray Juan de Buenaventura set out for the interior to begin the arduous task of moving the
Indians to their new home.

The events of the succeeding months will be summarized briefly. The
Indians of Tzuctok were brought to Sahcabchen at the end of March. In
the case of Ichbalche the transfer was made in three groups. The first two,
comprising the greater part of the population, reached Sahcabchen April
23–25; for various reasons the removal of the third contingent was delayed
until August. In accordance with Governor Figueroa's instructions the fruit
trees at Tzuctok and Ichbalche were cut down and the houses burned to dis-

---

[74] Sometime between 1609 and 1615 Ulumal was settled by other Indians from the forests,
but they had also found the place unhealthy and had moved away to Champoton and neighboring villages.
[75] Paxbolon-Maldonado Papers, Part II, ff. 228v–47v.
[76] Fray Gonzalo de Salazar, an Augustinian, succeeded Vázquez de Mercado as bishop of
Yucatan in 1610 (Carrillo y Ancona, 1895, 1: 375).
[77] Paxbolon-Maldonado Papers, Part II, ff. 247v–82.

courage the Indians from returning to their old locations. In June Cárdenas learned that the inhabitants of Ichmachich, in agreement with those of Chacuitzil and Chunhaz, now wished to settle at Cheusih, a few leagues east of Popola.[78] This request was forwarded to the governor, who gave approval. The removal of the three villages to Cheusih occurred sometime in July or August.[79]

Although the Indians of Sacalum had agreed at Champoton to settle in Sahcabchen, we have no evidence that any of them did so. It is possible that a few families later moved to Cauich.[80] In any case the Franciscans now abandoned the Sacalum mission, and the people who remained there eventually dispersed into the forests. The documents of this period contain no account of the settlements at Texan and Petcah, formerly administered as visitas of Ichbalche and Tzuctok respectively.

After the resettlement of the Indians at Sahcabchen and Cheusih was completed, Cárdenas made a matrícula of each town for tribute purposes. The list for Sahcabchen records 940 persons, old and young, of whom 828 had come from Ichbalche and 112 from Tzuctok. The population of Cheusih numbered 364 persons, as follows: 173 from Chacuitzil, 128 from Chunhaz, and 63 from Ichmachich. Each tributary unit (married couple) was assessed at the rate of 12 reales (1.5 pesos) annually.[81] This levy was much lower than the amount currently paid by the Indians of northern Yucatan. The governor of Ichbalche was named as the new governor of Sahcabchen, and other leaders of the old settlements also received appointments to office in Sahcabchen and Cheusih. These arrangements and the low rate of tribute doubtless helped to ensure the permanence of the new towns.

The mission at San Antonio de Sahcabchen (the advocation was the same as for Ichbalche) had convent status from the beginning. In later years the guardian of Sahcabchen also served a visita at Holail, located a short distance to the southwest. There is reason to believe that this place was settled by Indians from Tzuctok.[82] Although the Franciscans had some part in the

[78] Probably the same site to which the Indians of Chacuitzil and Auatayn wished to move in 1609. Cf. p. 276, *supra*.

[79] Paxbolon-Maldonado Papers, Part II, ff. 282–312.

[80] Figueroa's instructions to Cárdenas and the friars stated that in case the Indians of Sacalum wished to settle at Cauich they should be permitted to do so and that he would arrange for the assignment of a resident friar for the Cauich mission. It seems unlikely that many Sacalum families actually moved to this place. In Cogolludo's time (1656) Cauich was still a visita of the Campeche convent (López de Cogolludo, 1867–68, bk. 4, ch. 20).

[81] Paxbolon-Maldonado Papers, Part II, ff. 312–37v.

[82] At the time of their removal to Sahcabchen in March, 1615 the Indians of Tzuctok told Cárdenas that they wished to settle at Çucmiz about a league from Sahcabchen. This site, located near the Río Holha, was evidently near the place later known as Holail. It is also interesting to note that the advocation of the Holail mission was San Jerónimo, the same as for Tzuctok.

founding of the mission at Cheusih, this settlement was subsequently administered as part of the curacy of Tixchel.

The town of Sahcabchen became a center of trade and economic development in southwestern Yucatan. In this area Spanish colonists established farms and cattle ranches; others found the cutting of logwood a profitable business. The coastal region east of Sahcabchen was frequented by merchants engaged in commerce between Yucatan and Tabasco. In all these operations the Indians had a part, serving as laborers, messengers, and carriers. Sahcabchen also served as a convienient outpost of trade with the Indians in the interior of the peninsula, and there is some evidence that its inhabitants manufactured certain articles for sale to the fugitives. For about half a century the Indians of Sahcabchen enjoyed a measure of prosperity. In the 1660's, however, the population of this settlement and others on the southwestern frontier rapidly decreased as the result of conditions to be described in Chapter 13.

12

The Pretensions of Francisco Maldonado

THE EXPEDITION which Don Pablo Paxbolon made into the interior in 1604 with his son-in-law, Francisco Maldonado, and associates was the last recorded service of such nature performed by this able descendant of the ruling house of Acalan-Tixchel. Although he lived for at least another ten years, he no longer had the strength and energy to make such arduous journeys.

For almost half a century, perhaps longer, Paxbolon directed the affairs of his native people at Tixchel, apparently with general approval. During a period of thirty-eight years (1566–1604) he made numerous trips into the swamp and forest areas beyond Tixchel to seek out fugitive and heathen Indians in order to reduce them to submission to the king and the faith. He enjoyed the confidence and respect of governors and bishops, Spanish colonists and Franciscan missionaries. As an Indian leader he was undoubtedly the outstanding figure of his time in Yucatan.

By virtue of his position as cacique and governor of Tixchel Paxbolon enjoyed various privileges, such as exemption from tribute and forced labor and the right to receive service from the natives of the pueblo. In recognition of his services and ability the provincial governors gave him commissions of trust and responsibility. There is no evidence, however, that Paxbolon ever received financial reward for his labors as an explorer and frontier leader. In 1576 he petitioned the king for an *ayuda de costa,* or pension, of one hundred ducados[1] annually in recompense for his services during the Zapotitlan episode, but this request was apparently unsuccessful, and we have no record that it was repeated.[2]

In 1612 Francisco Maldonado instituted proceedings in the usual manner to draw up a probanza of the merits and services of Paxbolon, his father-in-law, and of his own as a citizen of Campeche. Although documents of this kind were partly for purposes of record, they were also intended, in most cases, to serve as evidence in support of a petition for office, a grant of encomienda, a pension, or some other form of reward for services rendered. In this case it was Maldonado's purpose to assemble evidence (1) to record the history and

---

[1] Approximately 138 silver pesos of 8 reales each.
[2] Probanza of the services of Don Pablo Paxbolon, cacique of Acalan-Tixchel, 1569–76, AGI, México, leg. 97. In response to Paxbolon's petition a royal cedula was issued instructing the colonial authorities to report on Paxbolon's activities and services (AGI, México, leg. 2999, libro D-2). The reports, if they were ever made, have not been found.

services of the ruling house of Acalan-Tixchel, (2) to establish the hereditary rights of Martín Maldonado, his son and the grandson of Paxbolon, and (3) to support his own claim to a grant of encomienda under the terms of the agreement of 1604 by which Governor Fernández de Velasco had authorized him and his associates of Campeche to undertake the reduction and indoctrination of the fugitive Indians in the interior of Yucatan. The documentary record, drawn up between 1612 and 1615, constitutes the Paxbolon-Maldonado Papers which have been cited so frequently in the preceding chapters.[3]

The first step in the formation of the probanza was taken at Mérida on June 28, 1612, when Maldonado presented a lengthy petition to Don Antonio de Figueroa, governor and captain general of the province. In this document, in which he acted as spokesman not only for himself but also for his father-in-law and his son, he set forth the essential facts concerning Paxbolon's descent from the ruling house of Acalan, Paxbolon's services as cacique and governor of Tixchel, his own activities since his arrival in Yucatan, and his marriage alliance with Paxbolon's daughter, Doña Catalina. With this petition he filed a series of supporting documents which he asked to have incorporated in the record. These included Paxbolon's titles of appointment as cacique and governor of Tixchel, the commissions and agreements issued by various governors of Yucatan authorizing Paxbolon to bring about the submission of heathen and fugitive Indians of the interior, and other papers illustrating the services of both Paxbolon and Maldonado. Finally, Maldonado asked to have witnesses examined on the basis of a long interrogatory which he presented. By a decree of Governor Figueroa the petition and supporting papers were formally accepted, and Maldonado was authorized to present his witnessses.

Between June 30 and July 6 five witnesses were examined. The interrogatory, which consisted of twenty-two questions, covered a wide range of topics, such as the lineage of Paxbolon, the coming of Cortés in 1525 and the Cuauhtemoc episode, the founding of the missions in Acalan, the removal of the Indians to Tixchel, the education of Paxbolon by the friars in Campeche, his services after becoming governor of Tixchel in 1566, and the activities of Maldonado as a citizen of Campeche and as an associate of his father-in-law. The witnesses included two leading citizens of Mérida and three Franciscan friars. Their testimony in general supported the facts as set forth in the interrogatory.

By a decree of August 23 Governor Figueroa authorized transfer of the probanza proceedings to Campeche, where Maldonado wished to have other

[3] The remainder of this chapter is based on these Papers, except as otherwise indicated in note 7, *infra*.

witnesses examined. Alonso Pérez, alcalde ordinario of Campeche, was named as the governor's delegate to conduct the hearings. In September Maldonado went to Campeche and presented three substantiating witnesses who gave testimony on the basis of the interrogatory mentioned above.

On September 24 Maldonado petitioned the alcalde to incorporate in the record a narrative in the Chontal language describing the history of Acalan-Tixchel from preconquest times to 1604. The originals of this document, or series of documents, which we have cited as the Chontal Text, were in the possession of Don Pablo Paxbolon. It is apparent that Maldonado had had access to them prior to the initiation of the probanza in June, for part of the interrogatory presented at that time was based on information recorded therein. Moreover, it was undoubtedly his intention from the beginning to incorporate a copy in the proceedings, because toward the end of June, or early in July, his son, Martín Maldonado, appeared in Tixchel and made the following petition to Paxbolon.

I, Martín Maldonado, citizen of the villa of San Francisco de Campeche, residing at present in this pueblo of Tichel, state that it has come to my attention that Don Pablo Paxbolon, governor and natural lord of this said pueblo and those subject to it, my grandfather, has in his possession some papers in the Chontal language which record my great-grandparents and great-great-grandparents and the descent and genealogy of my aforesaid grandfather and of my mother. It is stated by these papers that they were natural lords whose dominion was acknowledged by the majority of the subjects, and they governed and administered as its lords. And because in support of my legal rights it is fitting that you, as the person who has [this account], should produce it and hand it over to the notary of this said pueblo in order that one or two authorized copies may be made for me by the said notary and in the presence of the cabildo of this said pueblo so that it may carry weight and be capable of proof before a royal notary and a competent judge as stronger proof and corroboration of a probanza I intend to make *de perpetua rei memoriam* (*sic*)[4] in order to ask for favors in consideration of the services which my aforesaid ancestors rendered his Majesty: I therefore beg you to do as I have said, for in so doing you will perform a good office in my behalf. And you will order the aforesaid notary to give me a copy of the said papers in the language of these natives; and let the original be returned to you. And I ask justice, etc. Martín Maldonado.

In accordance with this request, Paxbolon authorized the clerk of Tixchel to make a copy of the papers, which Martín Maldonado delivered to his father in Campeche. In his petition of September 24, Francisco Maldonado not only requested formal acceptance of the document as part of the probanza

[4] This phrase should read: *ad perpetuam rei memoriam*.

record, but also asked that a Spanish translation be made by Father Gaspar
de los Reyes, cura of Campeche, who was said to have a better knowledge
of Chontal than anyone else in the province. By order of the alcalde the narrative was incorporated in the proceedings, but action on Maldonado's request
for a Spanish translation was postponed.

At this point Melchor Bonifacio, *alguacil mayor* of Campeche, filed a
petition to have the hearings suspended on the ground that the probanza was
not being made in the manner prescribed by law. Despite protest from Maldonado, who accused Bonifacio of personal malice and enmity, the alcalde
granted the request and referred the matter to Governor Figueroa for decision.
After litigation lasting two months, during which Maldonado accused Pérez
of partiality and succeeded in having him removed as the governor's delegate,
the hearings were resumed on December 19 before Mateo Aguilar, the second
alcalde of Campeche. Two citizens of Campeche were named as interpreters
to make a Spanish translation of the Chontal narrative and to receive the
declarations of certain Indians of Tixchel presented by Maldonado to give
testimony concerning Paxbolon's ancestry and to verify the accuracy of the
Chontal narrative. Bonifacio once more raised objections and succeeded in
preventing examination of the Indian witnesses, but a translation of the Chontal Text, made by the two interpreters, was filed on December 22 and accepted
as part of the record.

After a delay of more than a year a third delegate, or *juez de comisión*,
was appointed. In May 1614 the Indian witnesses were examined, this time
without opposition from Bonifacio. On petition of Maldonado, June 13, 1614,
the probanza record was closed and sent under seal to the governor in Mérida.
On October 15 Figueroa added to it a statement in which he certified that
Maldonado and his son were men of trust and honor who had served the
Crown in a faithful manner. He also stated that Paxbolon possessed all the
merits attributed to him in the probanza and that he had no equal among the
Indians of the province. Finally, on October 17, 1614, certified copies of the
entire record, made by a notary of Mérida, were delivered to Maldonado to
be used as he saw fit in support of his claims for reward for his services. One
of these copies constitutes Part I of the Paxbolon-Maldonado Papers.

After the successful completion of the probanza proceedings in Campeche, Maldonado went to Mérida where he presented a formal claim for an
encomienda in the region where the Montañas missions had been founded. In
a petition dated September 2, 1614, he reviewed the essential facts concerning
the contract of 1604 by which he and his associates had agreed to bring about
the reduction and indoctrination of fugitive Indians in the interior, in return

for which the partners had been promised a certain number of tributaries (600 in the case of Maldonado) after expiration of a four-year period during which the Indians were to be exempt from tribute. Although Governor Luna y Arellano had suspended the contract in the autumn of 1604 and had placed the Franciscan friars in charge of the project, it was Maldonado's contention that the latter had merely completed the work which he and his associates had started and that the contract had not been formally abrogated. The period of tribute exemption, increased to six years by Luna y Arellano and subsequently to ten years by a royal cedula of 1607, had now expired, and Maldonado asked to have the Indians counted in order that his share of the total might begin paying tribute to him. He offered to pay half of the salary of an official to make the count, and to pay the cost of religious instruction of the Indians to be assigned to him in encomienda. At the same time he expressed his desire to make new entradas to the bush and forest areas under the terms of the original contract.

Governor Figueroa referred the petition to his lieutenant, Damián Cervera de Acuña, and one of the alcaldes ordinarios of Mérida, Lic. León de Salazar, for opinions on the legal questions involved. Their reports were filed on September 25 and October 14 respectively. Cervera stated that the governor was under obligation to reward the partners in accordance with the terms of the 1604 agreement. He also recommended that Maldonado should be permitted, even compelled, to resume explorations in the interior as soon as possible, "before the death of Don Pablo Paxbolon." It was the opinion of León de Salazar that Maldonado and his associates, as the persons who had initiated the missionary project in the Montañas area, should receive the reward stipulated by the contract, but they should repay the royal treasury all that had been expended in support of the friars subsequent to the suspension of the contract in 1604. Moreover, before making the encomienda grants, the governor should take suitable action to prevent the Indians from abandoning the settlements where they had been congregated in the interior of the peninsula east and southeast of Tixchel. Salazar feared, with justice, that the Indians would object to being brought within the scope of the encomienda system. Although these reports were favorable to Maldonado's claims, the governor made no decision at this time.

Early in 1615 Governor Figueroa took action to move the Indians of the Montañas missions to sites nearer Champoton, and in order to induce them to make the change he agreed not to impose tribute on them until they were well established in their new settlements. As one of the interested parties, Maldonado accepted this agreement, partly to facilitate the move, partly because he believed that if the Indians were resettled where they would have good farm lands they would eventually be in a better position to pay tribute. The resettlement of the Indians at Sahcabchen and Cheusih has been described in the preceding chapter. In November 1615 Maldonado renewed his encomienda claim and petitioned the governor to make a formal grant in fulfillment of the contract of 1604, to become effective on the expiration of the period of tribute exemption. Figueroa ordered his notary to assemble all the pertinent documents relating to the history of the Montañas missions, and after these had been compiled he issued a decree, dated November 28, 1615, remitting the case to the Council of the Indies. He also authorized preparation of certified copies of the papers for Maldonado's use in an appeal to the Council. Part II of the Paxbolon-Maldonado Papers comprises one set of these copies, the certification being dated May 13, 1616.

Early in 1618 Pedro de Toro, Maldonado's agent, presented the Paxbolon-Maldonado Papers, Parts I and II, to the Council with a covering petition asking for execution of the agreement of 1604. After a delay of more than two years, the *fiscal* of the Council filed an opinion, dated at Madrid, October 6, 1620, to the effect that Maldonado had not proved that he had fulfilled his part of the original contract and that his claim for an encomienda should not be granted. But in view of the various services which Maldonado had performed, he recommended reward in some other form. Further action was suspended for more than seven years. At long last, on February 22, 1628, the Council voted to send the case back to the governor of Yucatan for final decision. This action was made the basis of a royal cedula issued on March 9 of the same year.

On March 14, 1629, Governor Juan de Vargas Machuca decreed that Maldonado had fulfilled his obligations under the terms of the 1604 agreement and authorized him to file action for an encomienda in the Montañas area or in any other part of Yucatan. Accordingly, Maldonado asked for a grant of 600 tributaries in the towns where the Montañas Indians had been resettled, of whom 200 should be granted to Martín Maldonado, and 400 to Capt. Nicolás Fernández Maldonado, a younger son by a second marriage. Inasmuch as the Indians in question had become royal tributaries after the expiration of the period of tribute exemption agreed upon in 1615, the treasury officials raised objections. The case was in litigation until December 1629, when an event occurred which made possible a solution satisfactory to all parties concerned.

On December 15, 1629, the encomienda of Calkini became vacant by the death of the encomendero, Juan Rosado Mosquera. Maldonado applied for the vacancy in the name of his younger son, Nicolás Fernández Maldonado.

offering to abandon further claim to an encomienda under the terms of the 1604 contract. Governor Vargas accepted Maldonado's offer, and by decree of February 22, 1630, Calkini was granted to Nicolás Fernández Maldonado in first life. The Indians of the Montañas settlements were also declared to be perpetual tributaries of the Crown.[5]

The tributes of Calkini were valued at 366 pesos, 6 reales annually, by no means a generous reward after so many years for the many and varied services of Don Pablo Paxbolon and his son-in-law. In some respects, however, Maldonado and his family made a better settlement than if they had obtained 600 tributaries in the Montañas district, for during the succeeding decades this area was the scene of increasing unrest and many of the Indians abandoned the settlement at Sahcabchen where most of them had been congregated in 1615.

The appointment of Maldonado's younger son by a second marriage as encomendero of Calkini also deserves some comment. Maldonado's probanzas had stressed the services of Paxbolon, and his earlier petitions, including the one filed by his agent in Spain, had cited these services as well as his own in support of his claim for reward under the terms of the contract of 1604. It is somewhat surprising, therefore, that Martín Maldonado, the grandson and heir of Paxbolon, received no share in the final settlement. Apparently the elder Maldonado, who by 1630 was growing old, was now more interested in providing for his family than for himself. Paxbolon was now dead and Martín Maldonado had probably inherited most of his property, which included lands near Tixchel. Consequently, his father may have decided that he was already well provided for and that any reward obtainable under the contract of 1604 should go to the younger brother. It should also be noted that Nicolás Fernández Maldonado, who received the encomienda of Calkini, had performed services in his own right and was a captain of artillery in the Campeche garrison, as his father had been in earlier years. Moreover, his mother was probably the daughter of one of Francisco Maldonado's associates in the 1604 expedition to the Montañas area, and in such case he would have had an additional claim to the reward.[6]

The sources at our disposal at the present time do not provide any infor-

[5] The later history of the case, including the litigation in 1629 and the final settlement, is found in Expediente concerning confirmation of Capt. Nicolás Fernández Maldonado as encomendero of Calkini, 1628-31, AGI, México, leg. 242.

[6] Although positive evidence is lacking, Francisco Maldonado's second wife, the mother of Nicolás Fernández Maldonado, was probably the daughter of Lic. Alonso Fernández Maldonado, citizen of Campeche, who was one of the partners with whom the governor made the contract for the reduction of the Montañas area in 1604. Francisco Maldonado's second marriage apparently took place about 1600.

mation concerning the later years of Francisco Maldonado. He was sixty-two
years old in 1631, and his death probably occurred sometime during the succeeding decade and a half. Martín Maldonado was only thirty-eight in 1631,
but the documents are also silent concerning his subsequent career. Although
he was next in line to succeed his grandfather as cacique of Tixchel, the fact
that he was a mestizo made him ineligible for such office under colonial law.[7]
Likewise, nothing is known concerning Doña María, daughter of Paxbolon
and Mencía de Orduña.

[7] Recopilación, bk. 6, tit. 7, law 6.

13

Decline of the Tixchel Area in the Seventeenth Century

VERY LITTLE is known concerning the history of Tixchel subsequent to 1604, when Don Pablo Paxbolon participated in the founding of the first Montañas missions. In that year the cacique was about sixty years old and his health was failing. The last years of his life were probably spent in quiet administration of local affairs and in the management of his farms and trading interests, but this was not the kind of activity that would be recorded in the documents of the time. In his youth a pride in his ancestry and the desire to justify his own rights and privileges as a native ruler had prompted the formulation of Documents I and II of the Chontal Text, which date from the year 1567. These papers were evidently jealously guarded as proofs of his noble descent, and toward the end of his life they were supplemented by Document III, which records the story of the conquest period, the conversion of the Acalan, the removal of the people to Tixchel, and the achievements of Paxbolon as a servant of king and Church. But this later record, written about 1610, stops short with the founding of Usulaban in 1603–04. Curiously enough it contains no record of the cacique's part in the founding of the Montañas missions, possibly because his role was overshadowed by the activities of his Spanish son-in-law and associates. The lack of any reference to later events indicates that Paxbolon's work was done. His death, which occurred some-time after September 25, 1614, rang down the curtain on the last of the Acalan chieftains.[1]

With the passing of Don Pablo the administration of local affairs may have lacked the effective guidance provided in years past by the old cacique. Paxbolon had set out to achieve definite aims and he possessed the qualities of leadership necessary to attain them. He had maintained firm control over the Indians of his jurisdiction, and apparently they accepted his authority without question. It is unlikely that his successors had equal ability or commanded the same respect. The absence of strong leadership may explain in part the fact that the sources record so little information about local events in the Tixchel area during the period subsequent to Paxbolon's death.

[1] Paxbolon is mentioned in a document of September 25, 1614, but the reference suggests that he did not have long to live. Cf. p. 295, *supra*.

The first specific reference to Tixchel during these later years is found in the *Relación historial eclesiástica* of Bachiller Francisco de Cárdenas Valencia, completed in 1639.[2] Here we learn that Tixchel was still the head of a missionary district served by a secular priest. This person was evidently Father Ambrosio de Figueroa, who had been appointed curate of Tixchel in 1636.[3] According to Cárdenas Valencia, the curacy now comprised seven towns. These are not listed, but they certainly included Tixchel, Chiuoha, Popola, Usulaban, and Cheusih, where the Indians of Ichmachich, Chacuitzil, and Chunhaz were settled in 1615 (See Chapter 11). The others were probably Chekubul and a merger settlement of Tiquintunpa-Mazcab (now known as Mamantel).

The first reference to Chekubul occurs in Paxbolon's report of settlements of fugitive Indians in the interior of Yucatan in 1604, where it is listed as one of the pueblos in the area north of Nacaukumil.[4] It was probably located at or near the modern site of the same name southeast of Tixchel. The Chekubul mission, first mentioned by Cogolludo writing in 1656, was apparently founded by the priest of Tixchel, but we have no record of the exact date. For reasons cited below we believe, however, that it was established prior to 1639.

Tiquintunpa is frequently mentioned in the seventeenth century documents. The last specific reference to Mazcab (originally called Xocola) is in Document III of the Chontal Text, i.e., for the year 1610. We find, however, that Cogolludo and other later sources mention a place called Mamantel, often in association with Tiquintunpa. A site of this name is shown on modern maps in the area where Mazcab was apparently located, and there can be little doubt that Mamantel was the old settlement of Mazcab under a new name. Sometime prior to Cogolludo's time Mamantel and Tiquintunpa were "joined" for mission purposes, although they may not have been immediately consolidated into a single settlement.[5] In view of Cárdenas Valencia's statement that the curacy of Tixchel comprised seven towns, which probably included Chekubul, we surmise that the missionary merger of Tiquintunpa and Mamantel occurred prior to 1639.

Cárdenas Valencia also reports that the seven towns of the curacy contained 1710 persons seven years of age or older.[6] Although an exact estimate of the total population cannot be made on this basis, the actual figure probably did not exceed 2500 persons. In Chapter 10 we estimated the total

[2] Cárdenas Valencia, 1937, p. 102. For a recent account of the author's life and work, see Adams, 1945.
[3] López de Cogolludo, 1867–68, bk. 11, ch. 12.
[4] See Appendix E.
[5] López de Cogolludo, 1867–68, bk. 4, ch. 19.
[6] Cárdenas Valencia, 1937, p. 102.

population of the curacy in 1609 as some 1600 persons. To this number should be added 364 persons settled at Cheusih in 1615, making a total of 1964. This means that we must account for an increase of 536 persons for other causes between 1609 and 1639. This would be at the rate of 33.5 per cent for the towns occupied in 1609.

The cumulative effects of increasing maize production, especially in the Usulaban area, might well explain a sharp rise after 1609. We doubt, however, that the population of all the older towns would have increased more than 30 per cent in as many years. For this reason we believe that another town, viz., Chekubul, was added to the curacy prior to 1639. If we assume that its population equaled that of Cheusih (an arbitrary estimate and probably too high), this would still leave room for an increase of 172 persons, or 10.75 per cent, for the towns occupied in 1609. The rate of growth would be higher if Cheusih suffered losses during resettlement, as we might expect.

Whatever the facts may be as to the population of the various towns in the Tixchel area in 1639, Cárdenas Valencia's report leaves no doubt that the region as a whole was in a prosperous condition at this time.

Within a few years, however, the town of Tixchel was abandoned. For this event we have only the laconic statement by Cogolludo (1656) that Tixchel had been destroyed and that the capital of the curacy had been transferred to Popola. According to the chronicler, the curacy now comprised the towns of Popola, Usulaban, Chekubul, Cheusih, and Tiquintunpa, to which had been joined the village of Mamantel.[7] Chiuoha is not mentioned as one of the visitas, but we know from other sources that it was still in existence and part of the curacy of Popola.

Although the date of the abandonment of Tixchel cannot be definitely fixed, it apparently occurred sometime between 1639, when it was still the head of the mission district, and 1643. In the latter year the bishop of Yucatan made a report concerning the secular clergy in the diocese, in which he lists Father Ambrosio de Figueroa as curate of Popola, As already noted, Figueroa had served as curate of Tixchel since 1636, so it would appear that the transfer of the capital of the curacy from Tixchel to Popola had occurred prior to the bishop's report, dated March 8, 1643.[8]

Lacking other information concerning the abandonment of Tixchel, we can only speculate as to its causes. We doubt that it was due to economic reasons. Although the land near Tixchel was poor from the standpoint of

[7] López de Cogolludo, 1867-68, bk. 4, ch. 19.
[8] Memorial de la clerecía de la ciudad de Mérida y obispado de Yucatán hecho por su Señoría el Dr. Don Juan Alonso Ocón, obispo de dicho obispado . . . , Mérida, 8 marzo, 1643, AGI, México, leg. 369.

milpa agriculture, we have seen (Chapter 10) that in the latter part of the
sixteenth century and early seventeenth the Indians had established farms
farther in the interior where better land was available and that food production had increased, making possible the occasional export of maize to other
areas. Although these farm lands were evidently some distance from Tixchel,
this fact probably would have had little effect in prompting abandonment
of the town, for the Indians of northern Yucatan in colonial and modern
times have been accustomed to farm lands located 20 or 30 km. and more
from their villages. Some of the best land in the Tixchel district was apparently
in the region of Usulaban, where a settlement of Maya fugitives was established in 1603–04. Although this town increased in population, there is no
evidence of a sizable migration from Tixchel to Usulaban prior to the 1640's.
The Tixchel people may have had farms in the Usulaban area, but it was
a relatively easy matter to transfer the harvested crops to Sabancuy estuary
and thence to Tixchel by canoe.

Although the Tixchel people obviously were not so well off agriculturally as the Maya of northern Yucatan, local commerce, tortoise-shell
manufacturing and export, and good fishing would have made up for bad
farming. Moreover, there is little reason to doubt that Tixchel continued to
share in the coastal trade between Yucatan and Tabasco. The buccaneer
menace may have interfered with the trade in seagoing craft, but this fact
probably would have increased the volume and profits of business by canoe
along routes which followed inland waters in many places, such as Sabancuy
estuary. After the British established a piratical base in the Laguna de Términos region, the canoe trade would of course have suffered, but this apparently occurred after the abandonment of Tixchel. It also seems likely that
the Tixchel people were able to retain their share of the trade with the fugitive
Indians of the interior of the peninsula. In fact, the increasing number of these
Indians would have enlarged the volume of business, at least until the 1660's
when conditions in the interior became chaotic.

Cogolludo's statement that Tixchel was destroyed obviously suggests
a sudden abandonment rather than slow decay. Although there is no positive
evidence to prove it, we surmise that the destruction of Tixchel was the
result of a piratical attack. Beginning with the 1560's the coasts of Yucatan
had been subjected to periodic attacks by foreign corsairs. The first raids
were made by French pirates, but toward the end of the sixteenth century
the British began to appear, and during the first half of the seventeenth century both British and Dutch corsairs scourged the coasts of the peninsula
and made shipping unsafe in Yucatecan waters. It was during this later period

that we have record of raids by well-known corsairs, such as Diego the Mulatto, Peg Leg (Pie de Palo), and Jacob Jackson. Inasmuch as Campeche was the leading port of Yucatan, the pirate menace was most serious on the west coast.[9]

Tixchel was located near Puerto Escondido, a sheltered and undefended harbor opening into Sabancuy estuary. Here the corsairs probably took refuge from time to time and landed to obtain water and replenish their supplies. The nearby town of Tixchel could hardly have escaped raiding attacks for food and booty. Even if the raiders did not treat the Indians badly, they probably would have sacked the church and principal buildings; and if the Indians, under the leadership of their priest and village officials, offered resistance, then the corsairs undoubtedly would have taken vengeance on the town, putting the pole and thatch houses to the torch. That such an event actually took place is supposition, but it seems the most reasonable explanation for the sudden abandonment of the town, as implied by Cogolludo's account.

The Indians would now have withdrawn not only to a safer spot farther inland but also to a place where better land was available. That most of them moved to Usulaban is indicated by three kinds of evidence: (1) documents of the 1660's show that the town was now predominately Chontal; (2) the advocation of the town in this later period was La Concepción de Nuestra Señora, the same as that of Tixchel after 1585; (3) the Tixchel encomienda is subsequently listed as the encomienda of Usulaban.

Thus by 1643 the site of Tixchel, which had been occupied by the Acalan in preconquest times and again for more than eighty years in colonial days, was once more abandoned. There is no evidence that it was ever again reoccupied as a village site. Today only a few hacienda buildings stand along the shore of Sabancuy estuary. The preconquest ruins along shore are being torn down and converted into lime for export to the Usumacinta area, and the mounds east of the mangrove swamp are covered with bush. The remains of a paved road, or sacbe, also bear witness to earlier occupation in pre-Spanish days. There is no recognizable trace of the colonial town.

The encomienda of Tixchel, comprising the towns of Tixchel, Tiquintunpa, Mazcab, and Chiuoha, was held in third life in 1606 by Mateo de Aguilar (see Chapter 10). At the death of Aguilar, sometime after 1615, the encomienda became vacant and was reassigned to Joseph Ortiz of Campeche. At the same time Doña María Centeno was granted an annual pension of 250

[9] Molina Solís, 1904–13, vol. 2, *passim*; Pérez Martínez, 1937, chs. 2, 3.

pesos, 125 fanegas of maize, and 250 gallinas as a charge against half of the encomienda. On the basis of the value of the encomienda in 1606, this would have reduced the encomendero's annual revenue to about 818 pesos. In 1648 Ortiz died, apparently without heirs, and the encomienda was now granted to Alférez Pedro Hernández of Campeche, who also received half of the encomienda of Pocmuch in the Ah Canul area.[10]

Documents recording the grant to Hernández describe the Tixchel encomienda as now comprising the towns of Usulaban, Tiquintunpa, Mamantel, and Chiuoha. As noted above, this constitutes one line of evidence that the Indians of Tixchel moved to Usulaban when their town was destroyed between 1639 and 1643. It also implies that the people of Usulaban, who may have been granted the status of royal tributaries when the town was founded in 1603–04, had now been included within the encomienda in order to simplify the collection of tribute in the consolidated settlement of Usulaban-Tixchel. Reference to Mamantel as part of the encomienda clearly shows that this was the old settlement of Mazcab under another name.

A new tribute assessment made in connection with the transfer of the encomienda to Hernández reveals that it now contained only 168 tributary units as compared with 320 units in the year 1606. This indicates a decline of population of 47.5 per cent. Such a rapid decrease can be attributed to two major factors. (1) The people of Tixchel doubtless suffered losses as a result of the destruction of their town and their removal to Usulaban. (2) In 1648 a severe epidemic swept the province of Yucatan, causing the death of hundreds of Spaniards and thousands of Indians. Cogolludo describes the pestilence at some length. He states that although the "illnesses" were not the same in all cases, most of the victims suffered from "intense pain in the head and in all the bones of the body," followed by a high fever causing delirium. Some of the sufferers also vomited blood, "and of these few lived;" others had a form of dysentery. These symptoms obviously suggest an epidemic of yellow fever. Contemporary documents record that between July and October inclusive more than 700 Spaniards died, and in some of the Indian towns of northern Yucatan the losses apparently ran as high as 50 per cent, as indicated by revised tribute schedules. The death of Joseph Ortiz, former encomendero of Usulaban-Tixchel, was evidently caused by the epidemic, and there can be little doubt that it also swept through the villages of the Tixchel area, although the documents do not explicitly state this.[11]

[10] Confirmation of a pension granted to Juan de Ribera y Garate on half the encomienda of Pocmuch, 1648–1660, AGI, México, leg. 243.

[11] López de Cogolludo, 1867–68, bk. 11, chs. 12–15; AGI, México, leg. 243.

Some time prior to 1688 the encomienda was reassigned to Fernando Alvarez Magaña, but on March 24 of this year it was declared vacant because the encomendero-designate had failed to obtain royal confirmation of the grant within the time specified by law. Alvarez' lack of interest is not surprising, in view of the fact that the value of the holding was now only 112.5 pesos annually.[12] This sharp reduction in the encomienda revenues resulted from continued population losses caused by conditions described in the succeeding paragraphs. The 1688 entry is the last recorded item in the encomienda history of Acalan-Tixchel.

The destruction of Tixchel sometime between 1639 and 1643 and the ravages of disease in 1648 marked the first stages of the rapid decline of the entire Tixchel district that continued throughout the remainder of the seventeenth century. In later years, however, the major cause of decline was increasing chaos on the southwestern frontiers of Yucatan due to oppression by the Spaniards, corsair raids, and the growing power and influence of the fugitive settlements in the interior of the peninsula.

During the seventeenth century an increasing number of Maya from northern and western Yucatan fled into the central and south-central parts of the peninsula. The causes of this movement were in general the same as had prompted the flight of fugitives in earlier times, beginning in the second half of the preceding century. Some fled to escape the religious and administrative controls established by the conquerors; others abandoned their homes to escape the burden of tribute and forced labor and maltreatment by the Spaniards. During the seventeenth century, however, the chief cause of unrest resulting in increased emigration from the frontier towns and from others farther north appears to have been the *repartimiento* system practised by the provincial governors and lesser officials. Under this system advances of money or raw materials were made to the Indians in return for which they were forced to supply stated quantities of beeswax, honey, cochineal, cotton, cotton cloth, and other products. The officials also forced the Indians to buy various kinds of manufactured goods for which they often had no need. The prices charged for goods sold to the natives were usually in excess of current market values, and the prices paid for beeswax and other articles supplied by the Indians were normally lower than actual market value. If the Indians failed to supply the amounts of produce or cloth called for under these forced contracts, or repartimientos, they were often subjected to severe punishment and

[12] AGI, Contaduría, leg. 920.

maltreatment by the governors' agents.[13] To escape the repartimiento burden
and its attendant abuses many Indians abandoned their homes and took refuge
in the forest and swamp country of the interior. From documents we have
seen, it appears that Governor Flores de Aldana, who held office in 1664–65
and again from 1666 to 1669, was one of the worst offenders in this business,
and toward the end of the 1660's a very critical situation developed on the
frontiers of the province and in the interior country.

Reports for the years 1666–70 record considerable data concerning settlements of fugitives in the central and south-central regions of the peninsula.
In the areas north and east of Isla Pac were the settlements of Thub, Chunputit (or Chunpuct), Temchay, Tanlum, Kukuitz, and Sayab, some of which
were said to have as many as 300 warriors each. Farther south were Bolonpeten and Tzuctok, with 300 and 200 warriors respectively. The inhabitants
of these towns came from the Maya settlements all along the western and
southern frontiers of the province. Each group had its local batab, or chieftain,
and in some of them we hear of native priests who had charge of the heathen
and idolatrous rites practised by the apostates in these interior towns. The relations of the fugitives with the inhabitants of the frontier mission settlements
were at times friendly, at other periods hostile. But as time went on the
fugitives made more frequent raids on the frontier towns, carrying off men,
women, and children and threatening the peaceful inhabitants with dire punishment unless they joined forces with the "rebels." Bolonpeten and Tzuctok
appear to have been the most consistently hostile of the interior settlements
and exerted an increasing influence over other fugitive groups and the border
towns of the peaceful area.[14]

[13] As we have noted elsewhere, the term *repartimiento* was also employed in colonial times
to describe the encomienda system and the forced employment of the Indians for pay. In these
instances, as in the system of forced contract described above, the term refers to an allotment,
i.e., an allotment of Indians for tribute or for labor, or, in the case of the forced contracts in
Yucatan, an allotment of goods for sale or of produce to be supplied. The exactions of the
Yucatan officials were similar in many respects to the abuses committed by the alcaldes mayores,
corregidores, and other governmental agents in other parts of Spanish America. Although the
appointment of alcaldes mayores and corregidores in Yucatan was prohibited by law, the provincial governors evaded this legislation by the appointment of *jueces de grana, capitanes de
guerra,* and other subordinate officials who served as their agents in carrying on the repartimiento business. The activities of these persons were the subject of innumerable complaints by
the Indians, and the residencias of the seventeenth-century governors contain a mass of information concerning such activities.

[14] The most important sources describing the status of the interior settlements and the
chaotic conditions on the frontiers of the province at this time are: Contra Antonio González
por malos tratamientos a los [indios] de Sahcabchen . . . de que resultó ausentarse los indios de
aquel partido a las montañas, 1666–70, AGI, Escribanía de Cámara, leg. 317C, pza. 4; Autos
hechos por Pedro García de Ricalde . . . sobre la reducción de los indios de Sahcabchen y otros
pueblos, 1668–70, AGI, Escribanía de Cámara, leg. 317B, pza. 8; Sobre las diligencias que se han
hecho para la reducción de los indios de Sahcabchen y otros pueblos, 1668–70, AGI, México, leg.

The settlement at Bolonpeten has special interest in view of the fact that it was located in the Isla Pac region, the great swampy area between Cilvituk and the Arroyo Caribe to which Maler called attention in 1910 and more recently described by Andrews.[15] The leader of Bolonpeten was a certain Francisco Puc, native of Cauich (the town of this name southeast of Campeche).

The most important data for this period relate to the settlement at Tzuctok, apparently located at or near the place where the Montañas mission of the same name was established in 1604–05 and from which the Indians were moved to the Sahcabchen area a decade later (see Chapter 11). In later years the site was reoccupied by fugitive Indians, and their leader in the 1660's was a certain Juan Yam, said to be recognized as "king" by all the forest Indians of the interior. In a 1669 report by Fray Cristóbal Sánchez, then stationed at Sahcabchen, we read: "[Batab Yam is the one] whom all those in the forests hold as their king, and the Cehache Indians have given him the appointment as such king; and thus all of the forest Indians from one end of the province to the other obey and venerate him as such king." Although this statement is probably an exaggeration, we shall see that Batab Yam did exert great influence in the interior country and its environs. The remark that the Cehache had named him as "king" is also interesting. Other reports of this period indicate that the Cehache at times maintained fairly close relations with some of the fugitives, at least in the southern district in and around Isla Pac.

The same causes which prompted the flight of Indians from northern and northwestern Yucatan also operated in the region from Sahcabchen south to Popola. In all of the towns of this region (Sahcabchen, Holail, Usulaban, Chekubul, Chiuoha, Cheusih, Tiquintunpa-Mamantel, Popola) the Indians were subjected to the repartimiento system described above. This area was also exploited for logwood, and we have numerous complaints by the Indians concerning Spaniards who made excessive use of Indian labor in the logging operations. Similar complaints—excessive use of labor, failure to pay just wages, acts of violence, and maltreatment—were directed against Spanish traders and estancieros in the region. For the 1660's we also have reports of raiding attacks by English corsairs, who followed the trails inland from the Gulf coast, robbed the Indians, and plundered their towns. The villages of Usulaban and Chiuoha, for example, were robbed and sacked four times by

---

307. The remainder of this chapter is based on these sources except as otherwise indicated in the following notes.

[15] Maler, 1910, p. 146; Andrews, 1943, p. 37. Maler called it Bolonpeten.

the English prior to 1668. Popola had also been sacked, and the corsairs had carried off the church furnishings.

These conditions caused a considerable number of Indians of the Sahcab-chen-Popola area to abandon their homes and to take refuge at sites farther inland. Another factor in creating unsettled conditions in this area was the growing power of the fugitives in the interior settlements, especially those of Tzuctok and Bolonpeten. These groups not only exerted increasing influence within the frontier towns but also made frequent raids on Holail, Sahcabchen, Tiquintunpa, Popola, and other villages, carrying off men, women, and children and forcing others to migrate against their will.

One of the most interesting features of the reports describing these events is the frequent reference to the fact that the fugitives went about proclaiming that the time had come when, according to the "ancient prophecies," the Indians should withdraw from contact with the Spaniards and go to live in the forests. Prophecies of this sort figure prominently in the native Books of Chilam Balam in northern Yucatan. It is possible that the reference might be to one of the year, or *tun*, prophecies, of which only a limited number have been found, although none of these would apply to the particular time in question. It seems more likely that the *katun* prophecies are meant. The latter were very popular throughout the colonial period and continued to be copied by the Maya scribes down to the latter part of the eighteenth century.[16]

The katun was a period of a little less than twenty years. It was designated by the coefficient and name of the day on which it ended, and one of the same designation recurred approximately every 256 years. Each had its own prophecy, which was based, in part at least, on events which had occurred during some similar katun in the past.

It is a little difficult to reconcile such a proclamation with the years 1668–69, which was not a time when we should expect much concern about such a prophecy. The current Katun 12 Ahau had begun in 1658. Not only did it have eight more years to run (i.e., until 1677), but its prognostic is one of prosperity on the whole. All the versions of it predict kind chiefs, good rains, and abundance of bread, and it is a time when people return from the forests to the towns. Some of the longer versions, however, cautiously state that part of the katun will be bad and refer to six favorable years and six unfavorable. For the succeeding Katun 10 Ahau it is a different story. Drought and famine are freely predicted, and the people are to live on the breadnut and the *jícama cimarrón*, which means that they must seek their food in the forests.

---

[16] Roys, 1933, p. 187, and 1943, p. 89; Book of Chilam Balam of Tizimin, pp. 1–13.

But so far as the actual prophecies are concerned, these misfortunes would not occur for some time to come.[17]

This anticipation of calamity to come, so long in advance, might be explained by some of the details of the katun cult in pagan times. Ten years before Katun 10 Ahau began, the idol of its patron deity was placed in the temple as the guest of the god of the current Katun 12 Ahau, and the latter began to lose some of his power. We infer that this idea extended to the observance of the prophecies. Whether or not the drought and famine predicted for 10 Ahau were expected to begin ahead of time is doubtful, but the exactions of Governor Flores de Aldana did not augur well for the remainder of the current katun, and it would be of advantage to have established a home and milpa in the forest area before the drought began. We have a vivid description of such a calamity in a well-populated region in the eighteenth century. People fled to the forests with their children, but were obliged to leave the aged and infirm at home to starve.[18]

The influence and power of the forest fugitives of the interior country reached a high point in 1669. Early in this year Batab Yam of Tzuctok sent word to all of the towns in the Sahcabchen-Popola area directing them to build a house at the entrance of each town where he or his representative should reside whenever they might come to visit the settlements. Orders were also sent to plant fields of maize, beans, and calabashes for the overlord. In March 1669, Batab Yam sent his chief priest, Ah Kin Kuyoc, to Holail and Sahcabchen to impose his authority in these towns. During a stay of ten days Kuyoc completely dominated local affairs. He held court as local judge, hearing and sentencing numerous lawsuits, and promulgated various orders for the government of the settlements. At the end of his visit he carried off the governor of Sahcabchen, naming in his place a certain Antonio Pix as lieutenant of Batab Yam. The former governor, Don Cristóbal Baz, was later put to death in the interior.

Throughout the remainder of 1669 conditions in the Sahcabchen area and its environs were chaotic. The pueblos of Holail and Sahcabchen were constantly visited by bands of Indians from the interior who carried things with a high hand. In the autumn of 1669 Batab Yam himself came to Sahcabchen accompanied by a troop of 300 followers. Later in the year a group arrived from Bolonpeten, and early in 1670 Holail was raided by another band of fugitives. During these troubled times Fray Cristóbal Sánchez,

[17] Book of Chilam Balam of Tizimin, pp. 1–13; Roys, 1933, pp. 158–60; Thompson, 1927, p. 21.

[18] Roys, 1943, p. 81, and 1939, p. 291.

guardian of the convent of Sahcabchen, remained at his post despite considerable personal risk. His reports tell of the complete disruption of mission discipline and the public practice of heathen rites at "mosques" in both Sahcabchen and Holail.

In November 1669, a new governor, Don Frutos Delgado, took charge of provincial administration and immediately turned his attention to the urgent problem of finding a remedy for the situation in the interior of the peninsula. He sent letters to the leaders of the interior settlements urging them to give obedience before it would be necessary to use armed force. The caciques of Thub, Tanlum, Kukuitz, and other towns made friendly reply, but they also made it plain that they had no desire to abandon their present settlements. Batab Yam and the leader of Bolonpeten apparently made no answer to the governor's appeal. In the late spring of 1670 Delgado held consultations with the bishop, the cabildo of Mérida, and other prominent persons as to the best method of dealing with the situation. Most of his advisors counseled the use of force, and tentative plans were made for an expedition to the interior during the dry season of 1671. The governor decided, however, that before resorting to military measures he would send some Franciscan missionaries to the fugitive settlements to see whether the Indians could be pacified by apostolic means.

In July 1670, Fray Cristóbal Sánchez and two other friars set out from Chekubul to the interior country. In a letter written at a place called Nacab Sánchez informed the provincial that some of the fugitives had received them in friendly manner and that a message had been received from the Indians at Tzuctok asking them to proceed to the latter settlement. The cacique of Bolonpeten remained hostile.[19] Unfortunately the contemporary documents record no further information concerning the friars' journey. The report of Fray Andrés de Avendaño's expedition to Peten in 1695 relates, however, that Fray Cristóbal Sánchez in former times, doubtless a reference to his activities in 1670–71, had brought Tzuctok to obedience, "though afterwards the people became rebellious." The same account also refers to the abandoned town of Tzuctok, "which the said Captain [Alonso García de Paredes] . . . had destroyed fifteen years since."[20] It appears therefore that Sánchez and his companions achieved at least temporary success in pacifying some of the interior settlements, including Tzuctok, and that for a few years the general situation was somewhat improved. But not later than 1680 it was evidently

[19] Letter of Fray Cristóbal Sánchez to the provincial, Nacab, August 5, 1670, AGI, México, leg. 308.
[20] Means, 1917, pp. 113, 115–16.

necessary to send a military expedition into the interior, resulting in the destruction and abandonment of Tzuctok and most of the other villages.

The result of the events and conditions described above was a rapid decline in the population of the towns in the area from Sahcabchen south to Popola. This can best be illustrated by citing a few figures and specific incidents.

A report of May 1668 states that the pueblo of Sahcabchen, which formerly had a population of 700 adults, had now been reduced to 200 or less. Similar conditions prevailed in Holail, visita of the Sahcabchen mission. During the summer and autumn of 1668 efforts were made to reassemble the fugitives from these towns, resulting in a temporary increase in the population. However, many of the Indians who were brought in from the forests at this time were fugitives from northern Yucatan, and we also have reports that a considerable number of the Sahcabchen people had fled northward, where they had settled at Hol, northeast of Champoton. The events of 1669 caused further withdrawals from Sahcabchen and Holail both to the interior and to the north, and as a result of the attack on Holail early in 1670 about half of the remaining population of this town fled toward Campeche. Reports of March 1670 indicate that in Sahcabchen the original inhabitants of the town now numbered only 129 persons, young and old, and in Holail the number was only fifty-nine persons. These towns also contained a contingent of fugitives from frontier settlements of the Campeche, Ah Canul, and Xiu areas, but the total population of each was smaller than it had been at the beginning of the 1660's.

Our chief interest, however, is in the curacy of Popola to the south, which comprised the old Tixchel district. Subsequent to the abandonment of Tixchel this curacy, or *partido*, included the towns of Usulaban, Chekubul, Chiuoha, Cheusih, Tiquintunpa-Mamantel, and Popola. The merger of Tiquintunpa and Mamantel probably occurred as early as 1639, and there is evidence that subsequently Popola was also included in this merging process.

All of the towns in the curacy were affected by the unsettled conditions described above. All of them suffered losses due to the flight of Indians to the interior, attacks by English corsairs, and raids by the followers of Batab Yam and the chieftain of Bolonpeten. Reports of 1668 refer to withdrawals from Usulaban, Chekubul, and Chiuoha, but the heaviest pressure was apparently exerted on Cheusih and Tiquintunpa-Mamantel-Popola. Various documents of May 1668 tell how the Indians of the Popola district, with the consent of the curate, had withdrawn to a place called Sosmula in order to escape the fury of the corsairs and the exactions of the Spaniards. A letter of the priest, Bachiller Nicolás de Loaisa, written about the same time, relates that the

Indians of "the pueblo of Popola, Tiquintunpa, and Mamantel" had all abandoned their homes but were now assembling "in a regular town (*pueblo en
forma*)" and had asked him to visit them. This is evidently a reference to the
site of Sosmula mentioned above. The priest also reported that the people of
Cheusih, who likewise had fled from their pueblo, were living near those of
Popola. In all later documents, however, the curacy of Popola is recorded as
containing only three towns, Usulaban, Chekubul, and Chiuoha, with the
administrative center at Chekubul. We hear no more about Sosmula. It seems
clear therefore that Tiquintunpa-Mamantel-Popola and Cheusih ceased to
exist as organized settlements and that the movement to reassemble the Indians
at Sosmula failed to materialize. In later years many of the Indians probably
settled in Usulaban, Chekubul, and Chiuoha; others apparently remained scattered in the forests.

Toward the end of 1668 Father Loaisa abandoned his curacy, and in the
spring of 1669 he was replaced by Father Antonio de Sarauz with headquarters
at Chekubul. Reports of the new curate indicate that conditions in his district,
like those in Sahcabchen and Holail, were chaotic. In a letter of July 27, 1669,
he wrote that during the preceding two weeks the towns under his jurisdiction
(Usulaban, Chekubul, and Chiuoha) had been visited by more than 100 of
the interior fugitives, who had committed great outrages. The daring of these
Indians, he said, increased daily. The priest also testified to the decline of
mission discipline, stating that "mosques" had been established outside the
towns, where the visiting fugitives engaged in idolatry and drunkenness, "accompanied by all those of the villages and assisted by the officials and principal men." The Indian women were not safe even in the churches, for a week
before, in the pueblo of Chiuoha, "they snatched a young girl (*muchacha de
doctrina*) from under my very eyes." Many other persons had been carried off.

As already noted, the population of the curacy of Tixchel in 1639 was
probably in the neighborhood of 2500 persons. Within nine years a sharp
drop occurred due to the destruction of Tixchel and the epidemic of 1648.
By 1650 the total was probably somewhere between 1300 and 1400. Later
statistical data illustrate the continued decline resulting from chaotic conditions on the frontier. Reports for the year 1670 give the following figures:

Usulaban	81 adults
Chekubul	117 "
Chiuoha	66 "
	264 "

In 1688 Father Sarauz transmitted matrículas for the three towns of his partido of "Popola."[21] These were Santo Domingo Chekubul, San Cristóbal Chekubul, and Concepción de Usulaban. The heading for the second is probably an error for Chiuoha. We have no other evidence of a second town named Chekubul at this time. Moreover, the advocation of Chiuoha was San Cristóbal. These matrículas of 1688 were partially burned in a fire in the Archivo General de Indias several years ago, and some of the names are now missing at the top and bottom of the lists. From the copies as they now exist we are able to count names for the three towns as follows:

Concepción de Usulaban	100 adults
Santo Domingo Chekubul	165 "
San Cristóbal Chekubul (Chiuoha)	155 "
	420 "

The missing names probably would not increase the totals by more than 10 per cent. These figures indicate an increase of at least 60 per cent since 1670. This was doubtless largely due to the return of fugitives scattered in the forests in 1670. The increase was naturally greater in Chekubul and Chiuoha, which were located farther inland, than in Usulaban. Many of the returning fugitives were probably from Cheusih and Tiquintunpa-Mamantel-Popola, which no longer existed as organized towns. In any case the reports of 1688 indicate a total population of some 850 persons, or about one-third the total a half-century earlier.

The figures for Usulaban are especially interesting, for it was to this place that most of the Tixchel people evidently moved when the pueblo was abandoned subsequent to 1639. In 1569 Tixchel had 280 families.[22] In 1688, almost 120 years later, Usulaban had about 50 families, and less than half of these were Chontal.

The decline of the Chontal element in the towns of the curacy of Tixchel-Popola is illustrated in numerous documents. Of these Usulaban naturally had the largest Chontal contingent, for although it started as a small settlement of Maya fugitives in 1603–04, the removal of the Tixchel people to Usulaban later gave it a heavy Chontal majority. As late as 1670 it had a Chontal governor, Don Miguel Acha, who had served in this capacity since at least 1657. On the other hand, of twenty-three lesser officials recorded for the years 1657–70, at least eight had Maya names.[23] Moreover, in the document of 1670, which

[21] Matrícula de los pueblos de la provincia de Yucatán con certificaciones de sus vicarios, 1688, AGI, Contaduría, leg. 920, exp. 1.

[22] Cf. p. 182, *supra*.

[23] This statement is based on data in the sources listed in note 14, pp. 306–07, *supra*, and Residencia of the officials of the pueblo of Usulaban, 1667, AGI, Escribanía de Cámara, leg. 318A, pza. 8.

lists the names of eighty-one adults in the town, only fifty-one can be positively identified as Chontal. Of the remainder, twenty-eight names are Maya, one is uncertain, and one person had a Spanish surname. Eighteen years later the Chontal element constituted a minority, for of 100 names that can be read in the Usulaban matrícula of 1688, only forty-three can be certainly identified as Chontal.

At the time of its pacification in 1574 Chiuoha was inhabited by unsubdued and unconverted Chontal. By 1670 the Chontal element had been reduced to a very small group. For the period 1657–68 we have the names of thirty local officials. Of these only four have names that are probably Chontal[24] Likewise, in the Chiuoha matrícula of 1670, which lists the names of sixty-nine adults, only nine names appear to be Chontal, four are uncertain, and there is one Spanish surname. The 1688 list for Chiuoha (designated as San Cristóbal de Chekubul) contains only one name certainly Chontal out of a total of 155.

In Santo Domingo Chekubul, a Maya town from the beginning, we find only two Chontal names in a total of 117 for the year 1670 and the same number in a total of 165 for 1688.

Tiquintunpa, to which the Zapotitlan people were moved in 1571–73, had a Chontal batab as late as 1667, and three of the other town officials for that year also had Chontal names. It is evident, however, that the merger settlement of Tiquintunpa-Mamantel-Popola must have had a large Maya contingent. Popola was founded in 1583 as a settlement of Maya fugitives, and if we are correct in identifying Mamantel as the earlier Mazcab, or Xocola, it also had a Maya majority. No data are available for Tiquintunpa-Mamantel-Popola for the years 1670 and 1688, since this merger settlement, as already noted, had ceased to exist. The same is true for Cheusih, originally a Maya town.

Finally, if we consider the total population of the three existing towns in the old Tixchel district in 1688, we find that out of 420 names that can be read in the matrículas of that year only forty-six are certainly Chontal. In short, the Chontal, who had comprised a majority of the population in this region prior to 1600, now comprised about 11 per cent of the total and were outnumbered eight-to-one by the Maya.

The foregoing facts speak for themselves. The population of the Tixchel area had declined very sharply since 1639, and the Chontal were being swamped by a predominately Maya element. During the eighteenth and nine-

---

[24] Statement based on data in sources listed in note 14, pp. 306–07, *supra*, and Residencia of the officials of the pueblo of Chiuoha, 1667, Escribanía de Cámara, leg. 318B, pza. 9.

teenth centuries this process continued, resulting in the disappearance of the Chontal as a separate, identifiable element in the population. The town of Usulaban, last stronghold of the Acalan Chontal, was eventually abandoned, and the site is not recorded on modern maps. In recent census reports all of the native villages in the old Tixchel district are listed as Maya settlements. At the present time there appears to be no trace of the Chontal language in the region to which the Acalan people who survived the shock of the Spanish conquest were moved in 1557.

14
Conclusion

I T HAS LONG been known that the people of northern Yucatan traded
with their neighbors in Tabasco to the west and on the Caribbean coast as
far east as the Ulua River and that they imported cacao from both regions as
well as handsome feathers from the latter. At the turn of the century (1898–
1900), when the *Relaciones de Yucatán* were published together with early
reports from Tabasco and Honduras, more details of this commerce were
brought to light. It was now learned that the chief exports from Yucatan were
salt, cotton cloth, and slaves, which were exchanged for some copper tools
and many articles of luxury. The latter consisted largely of the cacao and
feathers already mentioned and gold, semiprecious stones, red shell beads, and
skeins of dyed rabbit hair for embroidery.

From a few accounts by the early explorers we had also learned of the
Acalan, an important trading nation, who lived somewhere east of the Usumacinta River between Tabasco and the Yucatecan Maya area. Cortés passed
through their country and was befriended by the ruler. He reported that
these people carried on an extensive commerce across the base of the Yucatan
Peninsula to the Caribbean coast, where they had a large trading post at Nito
near the mouth of the Río Dulce. It still remained a little uncertain, however,
just what language they spoke, and even the location of their country has
remained a matter of debate down to the present time.

Cortés and Bernal Díaz tell us something about the Itza living on Lake
Peten at this time. But the other more important nations in the lowlands between Laguna de Términos and the Gulf of Honduras, such as the Chol
Lacandon, the Acala, and the Manche Chol, are known to us chiefly from
later observations, when intertribal commerce had shrunk to a fraction of its
former size and they were living on the basis of a self-contained subsistence
economy. By this time their external activities were largely confined to raids
on the peoples subject to Spanish rule or sometimes even on one another.

The historical and ethnological importance of this trade between the Gulf
of Mexico and the Caribbean is obvious. Little was known about how it was
organized, and it has been regarded simply as intertribal commerce, which
indeed it was, but it was something more than that. Recently discovered documents relating to the early history of Tabasco and Acalan in both pre- and
postconquest times now enable us to fill many of the gaps in our previous
information. The area extending from Laguna Tupilco in western Tabasco

to the Ulua River in northern Honduras emerges as an economic bloc, which, in spite of its political diversity, can be considered a single commercial empire.

Recent studies of Chontal, Chol, and Chorti, which were spoken continuously from the western to the eastern end of the area, have shown that they are no more than dialectical variants of the same language and that the Yucatecan Maya to the north, although a different language, is sufficiently similar in vocabulary and sentence structure not to constitute a very serious bar to communication. Moreover, the Acalan trading post at Nito on the Gulf of Honduras was not an isolated case. Not only did the merchants of Xicalango and Potonchan in Tabasco and of Campeche and Champoton in southwestern Yucatan maintain similar stations on the Ulua River in northern Honduras, but a number of the Maya peoples in the interior of the peninsula also had their own factories on this stream. Indeed, Chetumal on the southeast coast at one time sent a force of fifty war canoes to help defend its commercial interests on the Ulua against Spanish aggression. As Montejo himself claimed, before the heavy hand of the Spanish conqueror had severed the commercial ties which united it, the entire region could well be considered one country and one language.

The newly discovered historical sources we have mentioned make it possible to enlarge our previous knowledge of the Chontal-speaking area. Except for a limited addition extending west of Comalcalco to Laguna Tupilco, it remains as we had already known it as far east as the lower Usumacinta. Along this stream from Emiliano Zapata (formerly Montecristo) to Tenosique the Indian population has been Maya-speaking for so long that this condition was believed to go back to the period of the Spanish conquest. We now know, however, that in early colonial times petitions from these towns were written in Chontal and the names of the chiefs and other village officials who appear in them can be identified as referable to Tabasco and not Yucatan. Linguistic conditions were altered by converts from the pagan Maya-speaking tribes to the east, whom the missionaries brought in and settled on the Usumacinta. For a while there was a mixed population, but in course of time the Chontal language disappeared from the region leaving only the Maya.

The most important addition to our ethnographical knowledge, however, is the discovery from the Text and other related documents that the Chontal Acalan occupied the large basin of the upper Candelaria and its tributaries. Moreover, for the first time we learn something of the political and social organization of this important branch of the lowland Maya. Here we find resemblances to the Yucatecan Maya on one hand and Mexican features on the other, but the strong Acalan tendency toward matrilocal residence, which seems characteristic of neither, remains somewhat of a problem. The place names of Acalan were all Chontal, but the personal names of more than a third of the population were Nahuatl. In Tabasco almost all the place names and all the personal names were Mexican; and in Yucatan none of the place names and only a sprinkling of the personal names were of Nahuatl origin. Mexican influence was evident in all three areas, but it was strongest in Tabasco, somewhat less in Acalan, still more attenuated in Yucatan.

Although the great majority of the population of Tabasco was Chontal, two important minorities were of another stock. One consisted of six Zoque towns situated on the southern border. These people brought farm products and fine fabrics down the rivers in their canoes to the cacao growers and merchants, who were too busy with their own more profitable pursuits to be self-sufficient economically.

The other foreign element was the population of eight Nahuatl-speaking settlements, five of them lying in the very heart of the Chontal area. Locally they are sometimes called Ahualulco, and we are inclined to believe that they are referable to the builders of the ruined city now known as La Venta in western Tabasco. We also believe they were representative of the invaders who spread a more or less modified Nahua culture, originally from the highlands of Mexico, over a great part of the Maya area. Strangely enough, they did not appropriate the rich cacao lands of the Chontalpa, but left this lucrative business largely in the hands of the Chontal. They were active traders. Cimatan was the most powerful of the eight Mexican towns and an important commercial center. It exercised a certain control over the trade with the highlands of Mexico and Chiapas, which was accomplished partly through its own strategic position and partly by means of its political conquest of several of the Zoque towns. Xicalango on the coast, although mainly Chontal-speaking, was apparently ruled by an important Mexican element of its population, and the widespread use of Nahuatl personal names leads us to infer that many of the other Chontal towns were governed by a ruling class of similar origin.

Little is known of the ancient history of Tabasco. Scarcely any local historical traditions exist apparently, and archaeological investigations in the Chontal area have been so few that no ceramic or architectural sequences for this region from the end of the "Old Empire" down to the Spanish conquest have as yet been made available to the historical student. Consequently any speculation concerning the course of events in pre-Spanish times rests largely on our rather scanty knowledge of the relations of Yucatan with this country.

According to the historical traditions of the Yucatecan Maya, "At one time all this land was under the dominion of one lord, when the ancient city of Chichen Itza was in its prime, to whom all the lords of this province were tributaries. And even from without the province, from Mexico, Guatemala, Chiapas, and other provinces, they sent them presents in token of peace and friendship."[1] This suggests that Chichen Itza at this time was not only the capital of the Yucatecan Maya and a famous center of pilgrimage, but also the most important market of a commercial empire not unlike the one existing at the time of the Spanish conquest. The Indians told the Spaniards how the "lords" of this city used to travel overland to Ascension Bay, where they embarked for Honduras to trade for cacao and feathers.[2] Also, fragments of cloth recovered from the Sacred Cenote have been identified by textile experts as being typical of the fabrics manufactured by the Zoque in Chiapas. In the ruins of Chichen Itza archaeologists have found fine orange pottery believed to emanate from the Gulf coast in southern Veracruz or adjoining territory in Tabasco, also plumbate presumably from the Pacific slope of Guatemala or Chiapas, turquoise probably from the Veracruz region, and metates carved from lava, which could have come only from the highlands of Guatemala or Mexico.[3]

For the period covering the subsequent hegemony of Mayapan we have as yet less evidence of the external commerce of northern Yucatan. J. E. S. Thompson has called our attention to evidence of trade in a fresco at Tulum, which flourished at this time. Here a goddess is pictured kneeling at a metate, one leg of which is shaped as an animal head.[4] He suggests that although some metates of the effigy type have been found in the Maya area, it seems unlikely that they were manufactured by the Maya. Landa's account of the so-called "Mexican mercenaries," who were brought to Mayapan from Xicalango and Tabasco at various times, is perhaps not to be taken literally, but it does indicate that Mayapan maintained close relations with Tabasco. Moreover, the fact that the son of the Cocom ruler is known to have been absent on a trading expedition to Honduras at the time of the fall of the city

[1] RY, 1: 120.

[2] Ciudad Real, 1932, p. 325.

[3] Foreign commerce of this character evidently preceded the hegemony of Chichen Itza. A. V. Kidder has drawn our attention to several pottery spindle whorls found by Thompson at San José in British Honduras and associated with the latest period of occupation at that site. Some are painted, apparently with asphaltum, and others bear an incised design, but both are very similar to spindle whorls from the Huaxtec region of Veracruz. Thompson notes that those decorated with asphaltum are almost certainly of Veracruz origin (Thompson, 1939, pp. 153–54).

[4] Lothrop, 1924, p. 57, pl. 7. Lothrop considers this form to be typical of the Pacific coast of Nicaragua and northern Costa Rica.

shows that Yucatecan commerce continued to be active in that direction.

Thompson has noted several striking analogies, apparently dating from the last period prior to the Spanish conquest, between the art of the east coast and that of Tabasco and the southwestern part of the peninsula. In the Peabody Museum at Harvard University are two incensarios, one from Jonuta and the other from the east coast, probably British Honduras. Both figures have heads in the beaks of birds and are so similar that they might well be ascribed to the same region, if it were not that each appears to be of the normal ware of the area to which it is attributed. In the case of other effigy incensarios found near Chetumal Bay the figure bears on its breast and stomach a rectangular object with a laced or herringbone pattern. This closely resembles a similar element of dress on an incensario from Cilvituk in the Cehache area northeast of Acalan.[5] These resemblances, as a whole, are perhaps general rather than specific, but they suggest an exchange of artistic ideas corresponding to the intertribal trade indicated by the historical sources.

This carries us down to the eve of the conquest, and commercial conditions along the coasts of the Gulf of Mexico and the Caribbean at the time of the arrival of the Spaniards might be summarized as follows: Potonchan and Xicalango were the most important ports of Tabasco. Acalan was accessible to canoe traffic, but it could hardly be considered a port. Closely associated with these cities were Champoton and Campeche in southwestern Yucatan. In the northwest the towns were somewhat farther from the coast, but close enough to supply the people of the interior with salt and dried fish. We do not know, however, whether they engaged to any great extent in foreign commerce. In the provinces of Chikinchel and Ecab on the northeastern coast was a group of large and important commercial towns, which included Chauaca, Cachi, Conil, and Ecab. Here agricultural conditions were generally poor, but they were situated near productive salt beds, so their size and prosperity were evidently due chiefly to their trade. Chetumal produced cacao and was the principal Maya town on the southeastern coast. For Nito, near the mouth of the Río Dulce, we have no ethnological information, except that it was either in or very close to the eastern Chol area, but its commercial importance is well established. In the lower Ulua basin the principal trading center was Naco, located in a rich, thickly settled valley of the Omoa Mountains near the Río Chamelcon. Presumably it was in a Chorti-speaking region, but the archaeological evi-

---

[5] Communication from J. E. S. Thompson; Gann, 1900, pl. 22, fig. 2; 1918, pl. 20; Andrews, 1943, pl. 21e.

dence suggests that it was a colony of Nahua traders.[6] Like Nito, it lay on the principal land route from Acalan to the Ulua River.

The Ulua was not only the eastern boundary of the economic bloc, or commercial empire, covered by this discussion, but also an ethnic frontier. Beyond it lived the Jicaque and Paya and farther south, the Lenca, whose cultures were derived from southern Central America and eventually from South America. Large quantities of cacao were produced in the Ulua basin, but we may well believe that the merchants from Tabasco also traded, directly or indirectly, with the tribes to the east and south.[7]

Since many of the Chontal were bilingual, speaking both their own language and Nahuatl, it is of interest to consider whether the latter could have been a lingua franca for the traders, whose activities extended across the lowland Maya area from west to east. This was possibly true in parts of the south, but the apparent absence of a knowledge of Nahuatl in northern Yucatan would indicate that it was not generally the case.

On the other hand, we do find some evidence of Chontal influence on the Yucatecan coast, particularly in the Maya dialect spoken at Campeche, which was called the "Canpech" and not the "Maya" language, although it was understood by the other Maya. In Uaymil, a region near Bacalar and Chetumal, they also spoke a dialect similar to that of Campeche.[8] Pilgrims from Potonchan and Xicalango, presumably traveling merchants, visited the famous shrine of Cozumel Island, but we have as yet no direct evidence of relations between Tabasco and the large commercial towns in the provinces of Chikinchel and Ecab on the northeast coast. Although they spoke the same language as did the rest of northern Yucatan, the people of Chikinchel evidently did not consider themselves to be Maya, since they applied the name to the Cupul and Cochuah of the interior as a term of reproach.[9]

The record of the Acalan rulers and their followers in the Text is the only report of the activities of any of the Chontal in pre-Spanish times that has come down to us. It reads somewhat like a heroic saga and is the history of an adventurous group, who moved from one locality to another seeking to establish themselves at some strategic site where they could dominate the trade between Tabasco and the countries to the east and north. During five generations they were dislodged from one place after another, apparently by the peoples whose commerce was affected by their presence, until at last they founded what promised to be a permanent government. This was in

[6] Ximénez, 1929–31, bk. 4, ch. 69; Isagoge histórica, 1935, p. 226; Roys, 1943, p. 117.
[7] Roys, 1943, pp. 118–20.
[8] Ciudad Real, 1932, pp. 347, 352; Motul dictionary, 1929, p. 464.
[9] RY, 2: 14, 23.

Acalan in the Candelaria basin. It comprised seventy-six settlements alto-gether, and at least two of them were towns of some importance. It was rich country agriculturally, and we have already mentioned its extensive commerce. It is a startling revelation of the rapidity with which such a state could rise to importance, when we consider that the capital and its government were founded by Paxbolonacha, who was still living and ruling over the land at the time of Cortés' arrival.

The history of Acalan no doubt represents an extreme case of political instability. In northern Yucatan we also find indications of a similar tendency during the century immediately preceding the Spanish conquest, and it is probable that this was an important factor in the cultural decline which occurred in the latter country during this period.

The conciliatory policy of the Acalan toward the Spanish invaders was very similar to that of the provinces of Tutul Xiu, Ceh Pech, and Ah Kin Chel in northern Yucatan. In some respects we find a fairly close parallel in the Xiu ruling class. They were of Mexican origin and had been in the Maya area for a considerable time; but they had moved from one place to another, and only since the fall of Mayapan apparently had they dominated the region where their towns were located at the time of the Spanish conquest. Like the Acalan, the Xiu attempted at first to maintain a benevolent neutrality, but when they were convinced of the military strength and determination of the Spaniards, they became their allies and later, their docile subjects. In neither case was there a real military conquest.

After the middle of the sixteenth century, when large numbers of the natives under Spanish rule fled to the forests, it was the Xiu and Acalan leaders who were especially noted for their activity in aiding the friars to establish missions in the southern central part of the peninsula or, when these were unsuccessful, in bringing many fugitives back under Spanish authority.

This attitude stands out in strong contrast to that of the provinces of Sotuta, Cupul, Cochuah, and Chetumal, which fiercely resisted the invasion, subsequently revolted, and for a long time afterward were occasionally on the verge of insurrection. Indeed, a century after the conquest a large part of Chetumal apostatized, threw off the Spanish yoke, and remained inde-pendent for some twenty-five years. The Chontal of Tabasco, once their early opposition was overcome, gave comparatively little trouble, but the Nahuatl-speaking town of Cimatan, although it was temporarily subdued from time to time, continued to resist the Spaniards until 1564.

Not only did the Acalan by their voluntary submission avoid the rigors of a military conquest, but their country was so isolated and difficult of access that they also escaped the discomfort of close supervision by either the Spanish officials or the missionaries, whose visits to the region were infrequent. They were not even nominally converted to Christianity until 1550, and even after that there was little change in their local government, so we may well infer that so long as they remained in the homeland, conditions were not unlike those found on the island of Cozumel in 1570. Here, in exchange for a rather heavy tribute and a certain amount of personal service, there was little interference with the natives, provided they maintained a decent semblance of Christianity in their towns and confined their pagan rites to the farms and forests. It will be recalled that soon after the Acalan were moved to the coast and put under the control of a resident priest, the cacique fled with a group of followers to a village of unconverted Chontal in the interior.

The postconquest history of the Acalan, like that of almost every other native group in Middle America, is one of decline. But the population decreased with surprising rapidity, considering the comparatively favorable circumstances which accompanied their first quarter-century under Spanish rule. During this time, as we have seen, the population diminished from a minimum estimate of 10,000 in 1530 to a maximum of 4,000 in 1553. This represents an estimated shrinkage of 60 per cent, and in all probability it was actually greater.

The principal causes of this decrease were the falling-off of the commerce, which was so important a factor in the economic life of the Acalan, and the introduction of new European diseases.

They did, however, produce enough food and other essentials for a subsistence economy, and commerce did not cease entirely. In spite of the heavy tribute, some surplus was apparently available for export, such as copal and annatto, which enabled them to import salt and other commodities they needed most. They were still able to trade with Tabasco, southwestern Yucatan, and their pagan Cehache neighbors to the east, although little, if indeed anything, remained of their former extensive commerce with the Caribbean coast.

Consequently it is difficult to avoid the conclusion that although the disruption of their commerce was a potent factor in the rapid decrease of population, the most important direct cause was probably the introduction of new diseases. The latter would not necessarily imply a shrinkage due entirely to deaths. Great numbers of the Yucatecan Maya fled from their homes to escape the epidemics which swept their country from time to time during the colonial period. Some of these returned when the danger seemed past but would flee again at a recurrence of the calamity, and many of them never returned at all.

The decrease of 60 per cent among the Acalan from 1530 to 1553 seems large, but even considering the longer period of time involved, it appears to have been still greater in Tabasco, where the population was reported in 1579 to have diminished 90 per cent since the time of its pacification. This country was self-sustaining as a whole. Commerce suffered greatly and the Spaniards oppressed the natives outrageously, but the people continued to produce a surplus of cacao, which was still in demand everywhere. The 1579 report ascribes the falling-off of the population to certain diseases, especially measles, smallpox, disorders of the respiratory tract, hemorrhages, dysentery, and fevers (*calenturas*). Calenturas is a term which covers the symptoms of both malaria and some of the intestinal infections, but although no doubt both of these complaints were serious, we surmise that the former was the more prevalent. In the Department of Izabal, Guatemala, where conditions are somewhat similar to those in Tabasco, far more deaths have occurred from malaria than enteric affections.[10]

With the exception of Campeche, Champoton, and possibly Cimatan, the population of the commercial centers of the lowland Maya faded away with almost incredible rapidity. These towns were mostly in low swampy regions near the coast and rarely close to any agricultural area large enough to support them after their commerce fell off. The land where Nito is reported to have been located is good, and Chetumal was in a cacao-producing region, but owing to the ruthlessness of the Spanish conquerors the former was soon abandoned and most of the inhabitants of the latter were dispersed, although a few remained at the site until some time after 1582.

The large towns on the northeast coast of Yucatan suffered less from actual conquest, but a decline soon set in. At Chauaca 3,000 Indian men were reported in 1528. In 1543 their number was variously estimated to be from 600 to 1,000; in 1549 we find 200 tributaries, and in 1579 only about 18. Similarly, Sinsimato, which was both large and important commercially in 1528, still had 600 male adults at the time of its conquest, but these decreased to 90 tributaries in 1549, and 8 in 1579. There were swamps, lagoons, and large savannas, but comparatively little agricultural land, around these towns; but they were not far from the salt beds and fisheries of the coast, and near Sinsimato were large and profitable groves of copal trees. Around Conil better farming land was reported. This town was said to contain 5,000 houses,

[10] Shattuck, 1938, p. 31.

which is no doubt a very considerable exaggeration. In any case it had shrunk to 80 tributaries in 1549 and was a small port in 1579. Of Ecab and Cachi we know only that they were unimportant towns in 1579 and 1582.[11]

Both colonial writers and modern travelers describe the entire north-eastern region as very unhealthy, and we infer that dysentery and malaria either did not exist or were mild diseases in pre-Spanish times, when the area was thickly populated. The falling-off of commerce would have caused a very considerable decline in any case, and losses were probably sustained when the inhabitants of some of the towns were moved to other sites by the missionaries. We are inclined, however, to ascribe the greater part of the enormous decrease of population to disease.

Campeche and Champoton were the two important coast towns that held up the best after the conquest. Luján, who came to Champoton from Acalan in 1530, reported that it was a walled city containing 8,000 houses and that Campeche was no smaller. It is hard to tell on what he based these estimates, which seem to be greatly exaggerated, but we are no doubt safe in inferring that both were populous commercial centers and larger than Itzamkanac.

Subsequent to 1530 these towns were occupied by the Spaniards and were bases for the military operations which resulted in the final conquest of northern Yucatan. During this time there was a great decrease of population, but it is hard to tell how much of it is to be attributed directly to deaths from the new diseases, how much to disturbed economic conditions, and to what extent it can be ascribed to desertions to escape the exactions or bad treatment by the Spanish invaders, which were especially burdensome at this time.

In 1549 Campeche together with the smaller towns around it had 630 tributaries, and 324 in 1583–84. Champoton and the surrounding villages contained 420 tributaries in 1549, and there were 180 in 1583–84. This was of course a great shrinkage, but it was nothing like what occurred in the trading pueblos of the northeast. Potonchan in Tabasco and Campeche were both important commercial centers which became Spanish villas after the conquest, but the former had shrunk to 25 tributaries in 1549. Campeche and Champoton, however, had certain advantages. Not only was there still a very considerable trade between Tabasco and Yucatan in colonial times, much of which passed through these towns, but also the adjoining country,

---

[11] RY, 2: 13, 48, 74, 154, 172–74, 205; Oviedo y Valdés, 1851–55, bk. 32, ch. 31; Landa, 1941, p. 49; Libro de tasaciones . . . , 1548–51, AGI, Guatemala, leg. 128; DHY, 2: 61. The figures mentioned above need further study and interpretation and are cited here only to give a general idea of the decline of population.

on which they depended for food, is mostly good agricultural land, much of it being hilly or rolling and well drained.[12]

In the thickly populated interior of northern Yucatan conditions were, generally speaking, the most favorable for the survival of the population and made possible the great recovery, which finally came in later colonial times. This was a fairly dry agricultural country, where the rains came at the time when they were most needed for the crops. The drainage was underground; there were no rivers or swamps and few surface ponds; and the drinking water, which was obtained from either artificial wells or the natural ones called cenotes, was considered good, which indeed it was, when the people did not pollute it themselves.

Here also there was a great decrease in population. According to native accounts it had begun not long after the fall of Mayapan about the middle of the fifteenth century. It was ascribed to internal wars and to two great epidemics, the last of which was smallpox and occurred some time before Montejo's first invasion in 1527. After the Spanish withdrawal in 1535 drought and a plague of locusts caused severe famines. If we add to this the rigors of the final conquest, it seems plain that the country was already badly weakened by 1543. In the neighborhood of Valladolid, which was considered one of the healthiest parts of Yucatan, the Spanish encomenderos reported that between this time and 1579 the population diminished by about two-thirds in a number of towns, although in a few of them decreases of only 20–40 per cent were noted. This decline was ascribed partly to the policy of the Franciscans, who moved a considerable portion of the population from their scattered villages and hamlets and concentrated them in towns near the various missionary headquarters, causing extreme poverty in many cases.[13]

Another important reason given for the decline was smallpox and "other pestilences." The latter included respiratory complaints and presumably measles and intestinal infections. There was no doubt some malaria, as there is today, but dysentery and other gastro-intestinal disorders are very prevalent at the present time, and the same was probably true in the sixteenth century. It would appear that many deaths were due to diseases to which the natives had acquired no immunity. These could be both European diseases and new and more virulent forms of those which had already existed. Yellow fever, it is now generally believed, was imported from Africa and did not become a menace until about the middle of the seventeenth century.[14]

[12] Oviedo y Valdés, 1851–55, bk. 32, ch. 5; Libro de tasaciones . . . , 1548–51, AGI, Guatemala, leg. 128; Ciudad Real, 1932, p. 346.

[13] Landa, 1941, pp. 41–42, 54–55; RY, 2: 14, 52, 68.

[14] Shattuck, 1933, pp. 335–36, 392, 481, and *passim*.

Nevertheless, the interior of northern Yucatan suffered less than most of the other regions which we have discussed. Its principal advantages appear to have been that it was an agricultural area, where economic conditions were less disturbed by the conquest, there was better drainage, and the climate was healthier.

The rapid depopulation of low-lying swampy areas as contrasted with those of higher levels or better drainage is of considerable interest. Since the centers of population in the former depended more on commerce than in the latter, it is obvious that the disruption of the canoe trade by the Spaniards played a very substantial part in this shrinkage. It may well be significant, however, that a sudden decrease of population was most noticeable in regions where malaria is especially prevalent at the present time. We have hesitated to draw positive conclusions from this, but it does suggest either that the disease was introduced by the Spaniards or that no malignant form of it was endemic in preconquest times. In any case it would appear that the historical sources, if properly analyzed and interpreted, would throw very important light on the presence or absence of malaria in pre-Columbian America.

The decrease of the Acalan population from disturbed economic conditions and disease was bad enough, but the greatest catastrophe occurred in 1557, when the Spanish authorities sought to remedy the trouble by attempting to deport the entire nation and settle them at Tixchel on the Estero de Sabancuy near Laguna de Términos on the Gulf coast. The idea was that here they could be protected from oppression and more closely supervised by the colonial officials and missionaries. A similar policy had been inaugurated in 1552 in northern Yucatan and was being carried out extensively with disastrous results to the people involved.

It is not surprising that this policy was also applied to Acalan. From the standpoint of the missionaries conditions here were extremely unsatisfactory. That the conversion of the natives was superficial is evident from the readiness with which those who evaded the removal reverted to paganism. The people were indoctrinated by permanent Indian teachers, but Acalan was so isolated that the missionaries could visit the country only rarely, and the friars were so few in number that a resident clergyman could not be spared. As things turned out, we know that it was most unlikely that Acalan would ever have constituted a political danger, but it is uncertain whether the colonial authorities realized this at the time.

The disadvantages of the move seem to have far outweighed any material benefits. The new site with its fisheries and commercial opportunities may have appealed to some of the old merchant class; but the region is as malarial as the Candelaria area, the land was much poorer, and it was a severe hardship for the people to leave their homes, farms, cacao groves, and orchards. They were exempted from tribute for four years, it is true, but it seems obvious that when the exemption period expired, the per capita tax would be higher than ever, since at Tixchel it would no longer be possible to conceal the existence of a considerable proportion of the population. Worst of all, the nation was divided by the bitter dissension between the submissive element and those who resisted removal.

To discourage resistance Pesquera, the missionary who effected the transfer, had the cacao and copal trees cut down at Itzamkanac, and some of the Indians were seized and carried away in chains. Only a few days after the arrival of the first contingent at Tixchel the Acalan ruler fled in disgust, apparently with a few followers, to Chiuoha, an unconverted Chontal village farther inland. During the following three years the removal of the population continued, and conditions were deplorable. The first move took place in the growing season, and the scarcity at Tixchel was aggravated by the arrival of more people from time to time. The men who returned to Acalan for food they had left there were molested and detained by those who had refused to leave. Conditions also were chaotic in the homeland, where the political organization had broken down and the people were reverting to paganism.

By 1560 the state of affairs at Tixchel was such that the population was about to desert the town, but at this time a belated Spanish force, which had been on its way to join in a campaign against the Lacandon, went to Acalan, where the soldiers apprehended as many people as they could find and brought them to Tixchel. This caused another famine. A number of recalcitrant leaders with about seventy families deserted the town and returned to the homeland, but no attempt was made to bring them back to Tixchel for some years to come. In 1561 the Spanish authorities made a count for taxation purposes of the married men at Tixchel. Only 253 were found, of whom 230 were liable for tribute. A few families may have been missed, but there was much less opportunity for evasion than in Acalan, where about 500 tributaries had been recorded in 1553. Taken at their face value, these figures represent a decrease of about 54 per cent in eight years, and it was probably considerably larger. We can account for this partly by the undetermined number of people who escaped apprehension in Acalan; some may have fled from Tixchel to more prosperous communities under Spanish rule; but there is little doubt that there were many deaths due to insufficient housing, disease, and malnutrition, such as occurred in northern Yucatan when the population of a town was moved to a new site.

During the years subsequent to 1561 things appear to have taken a turn for the better, since an enumeration of the adult population in 1569 shows an increase of 10.6 per cent. By this time the external trade was reorganized and no doubt the housing situation had improved. More was known about the better agricultural tracts in the region, and the technique of salt-water fishing was developed. In 1588 Ciudad Real remarked on the polish and diligence of the Tixchel Indians and reported that they had much copal, many fruit trees, and were noted for their manufacture of tortoise-shell objects, which included articles suitable for the Spanish market.

An important factor in this modest recovery was the ability, energy, and diplomacy of the young cacique, Don Pablo Paxbolon, who succeeded to the governorship of the town in 1566. After the death of his cousin, the cacique who had fled to Chiuoha in 1557, he was the only legitimate heir to the cacicazgo. He had been well educated in the Franciscan convent at Campeche and was a devout Christian, familiar with the ways and aims of the Spaniards. At the same time he knew the traditions of his own people and thoroughly understood their psychology. Life was hard for the ordinary plebeian Indian, but its rigors could be mitigated by a cacique who was able to induce his subjects to cooperate willingly with church and state and to conciliate the clergy and colonial officials. Don Pablo evidently had the ability to accomplish this, for we find no record of local insubordination or idolatry, and the native municipal officials were granted authority to apprehend any Spaniard, mestizo, or mulatto who misbehaved in the town, take the evidence, and send him to the court at Campeche for sentence.

Paxbolon's ambitions were by no means confined to the establishment of an efficient local administration and the economic recovery of his community. It would seem probable that early in his career he foresaw the possibility of populating the unoccupied region southeast of Tixchel with a group of villages, over which he might acquire a certain territorial authority, although under Spanish supervision, like that enjoyed by the caciques of Motul and Mani in northern Yucatan.

In any case, shortly after his accession to office the young cacique began to take steps to establish his authority over the remainder of the Acalan, who were still living in the upper Candelaria basin, and restore them to the Christian faith, apparently with the idea of transferring them eventually to the Tixchel area. These people included the families who had fled from Tixchel about 1560, a number of slaves who had escaped at the time of the removal to Tixchel, and presumably some freemen who had evaded deportation, although the last are not mentioned in the records. These groups had merged and retired to the neighborhood of the old Acalan town of Chakam on or near the Río San Pedro some distance above its junction with the main Candelaria. Here in course of time they formed a settlement which was known as Zapotitlan. They were less numerous than might be expected, for in 1569 the population seems to have been only about 300. Some distance away in the same region, however, were two villages of Maya refugees from northern Yucatan, who had entered the country after the bulk of the population had been moved to Tixchel. They were called Puilha and Tahbalam and had a combined population of about 125 persons. A small minority of them had Chontal names and some of these had intermarried with the Maya intruders.

In 1566, after consulting with Bishop Toral, Paxbolon made a journey to the neighborhood of Zapotitlan with a few followers. He did not enter any settlement but conferred with two of the local chieftains at an outlying farm. These men, who were apostates, at first repudiated any allegiance to the cacique and asked to be left alone. Friendly relations were established, however, and there was some suggestion of another visit in the future. The following year Don Pablo returned with a letter from Fray Antonio Verdugo urging them to become Christians. Possibly the choice of this friar was not a happy one, since only five years before he had taken an active part in Landa's inquisition and had gained such a reputation for severity that the Zapotitlan people could very well have heard of him from the Yucatecan fugitives. In any case, the apostates were displeased and did not wish to meet the missionary. They did express a willingness to trade with Paxbolon and even to pay him tribute, but they would have nothing to do with any Spaniard. Also a few families were persuaded to move to the more accessible site of their former capital on the main Candelaria, but they did not stay there long.

On the occasion of a third visit in 1568 Paxbolon entered Zapotitlan with sixteen followers, and the mission was more successful. The Indians agreed to submit to Spanish rule, they allowed the cacique to destroy their idols, and six of the leaders came back with him for Christian instruction. When these men returned to Acalan, they were accompanied by two native teachers from Tixchel.

Early in 1569 Don Pablo reported to the governor of Yucatan and Bishop Toral on the results of these visits. The governor formally declared the inhabitants of the Zapotitlan region to be subjects of the Crown, and he agreed to recommendations that they should remain where they were for the time being and that Paxbolon should supervise them. The bishop sent a missionary to Zapotitlan, where the latter dedicated a church, baptized the children and other unconverted persons, and made a record of the baptismal status of the people generally. He also procured a list of the inhabitants of Puilha and Tahbalam.

Although the adults were largely apostates, and, as such, still legally subject to their former encomenderos, the governor treated them as new converts and in 1570 gave them in encomienda to the governmental notary, Feliciano Bravo. This was contested by Antón García, the old encomendero of Acalan-Tixchel, and gave rise to a lawsuit, in which Paxbolon sided with García. By now the cacique had already begun to exploit the people of Zapotitlan for his own personal benefit. He even started with a force of seventy of his townsmen on a journey to bring the inhabitants to Tixchel, but he was turned back because of a decree by the governor at Mérida. Later local governors were appointed in all three towns, which would tend to curtail Don Pablo's hereditary rights over them. The details of the litigation, which lasted until 1571 and resulted in Bravo's defeat, furnish an interesting example of sordid rivalry between individual Spaniards for exploitation of the Indians.

Governor Santillán, who decided the case in favor of García, also confirmed Don Pablo as cacique and governor of Acalan-Tixchel and placed him in charge of local administration of the disputed area. Sometime between 1571 and 1573 the inhabitants of the three villages were moved to two locations on or fairly near the Río Mamantel in the Tixchel area. Their situation would give Paxbolon control over any commerce on the Mamantel between the Gulf coast and the interior, including the northern Cehache and the refugees from northern Yucatan. The upper Candelaria apparently remained deserted for a long time, for we have no evidence of any Indian settlements in that region during the seventeenth and eighteenth centuries.

With this beginning of a territorial district subject to Tixchel, Paxbolon's next step was to Christianize the pagan Chontal village of Chiuoha, where his late predecessor had fled in 1557 to escape the supervision of the Spaniards. In December 1573 Feliciano Bravo, who had now become lieutenant governor of Tabasco, visited Tixchel and discussed with the cacique the project of converting some of the Indians living in the interior. It was agreed that Don Pablo, who had recently been appointed military captain of the district, should visit certain of these heathen and see what could be done. Accordingly, the following spring he went to Chiuoha accompanied by 100 of his Indian militia. The precise location of this village would be of considerable interest, since apparently it marked the frontier between the Maya and Chontal linguistic areas. It was not at the modern site of the same name on the Arroyo Chivoja Grande near the eastern end of Laguna de Términos, and we can only infer that it was farther east but not very far north of the Río Mamantel. Here Paxbolon found a little over fifty people in the village, and there were some others in the adjacent forests. Although the force from Tixchel greatly outnumbered them, Paxbolon employed his usual tact and diplomacy to win them over, and in spite of some signs of hostility at first, they finally agreed to become Christians and submit to Spanish rule. Later in the year Bravo himself traveled part way from Tixchel to Chiuoha, met a delegation from the latter place, and accepted their submission. The result was that a mission was established there, and the village was placed under the jurisdiction of the cacique of Tixchel. Some time later, probably before 1610, the inhabitants moved to what is now Chivoja. Chiuoha was the last unsubdued Chontal community within the jurisdiction of Yucatan, and henceforth any similar activities on the part of Don Pablo were to be concerned with Maya-speaking peoples.

It was some years before another village was added to the district of Tixchel. The occasion was the result of a fortuitous occurrence, but the cacique was quick to take advantage of the opportunity. In 1583 a wounded Indian named Pedro Chan came with his children to Don Pablo at the latter's ranch near Tixchel and applied for aid. He was one of a group of fugitives from Hecelchakan, who had attempted to settle near a place called Chunuitzil, or Chacuitzil, some distance to the southeast. There they were attacked by another refugee group of considerable size living in the same region. A few of the assailants were killed, but a considerable number of the Hecelchakan people, including their leaders, lost their lives. Some returned to Hecelchakan, but more than sixty men, women, and children were dispersed in the forests.

Hecelchakan was in the province of Ah Canul in western Yucatan. Although the apostates in the southern forests had come from many parts of the north, the mention of fugitives from this district seems rather frequent. Besides the refugees, many of the men of this region were accustomed to make long trips into the interior gathering the wax of wild bees and trading with the apostate villages. Ciudad Real, in his report of a visit at Hecelchakan in 1588, describes the inhabitants of the town and district as being "somewhat addicted to the mountains and forests (*algo serranos y montaraces*)."[15]

Paxbolon ordered a search for the scattered fugitives by the inhabitants of the two towns on the Mamantel whom he had brought down from Acalan a decade before, and in the course of eight or nine months about sixty were found and brought to Xocola. They were finally settled halfway between this village and Chiuoha at a site called Popola. This would seem to account for the last of the four pueblos subject to Tixchel reported by Ciudad Real

[15] Cf. Chapter 10, p. 228, *supra*; Ciudad Real, 1932, p. 344.

in 1588. He states that two were Chontal-speaking, one at which both Chontal and Maya were spoken, and one Maya. Apparently the first two were Zapotitlan (Tiquintunpa) and Chiuoha, the third was Xocola (Mazcab), and the fourth, Popola.

Notwithstanding their small size, the founding of these settlements did much to establish the prestige of Paxbolon. This was the beginning of an extensive effort to bring the apostate refugees in the interior back to the Christian faith, which was to result in the settlement of a considerable number of them in villages on the coastal plain between Laguna de Términos and Champoton.

The grant of authority under which Paxbolon collected the Maya fugitives from Hecelchakan and settled them within his own jurisdiction was perhaps more significant than the recovery of this comparatively small group. Under certain terms it permitted him to accomplish the reduction of any group of fugitives living in the region bordering on the Tixchel area and resettle them in suitable locations. The conditions were very favorable both to the cacique and to the Indians. The latter were to pay tribute, after a certain period of exemption, to the Crown and not to an individual encomendero, and the apostates among them would be forgiven their past disloyalty to Church and state. They would, however, immediately become subject to Don Pablo as their cacique.

For some years Paxbolon engaged only in modest enterprises in pursuance of this policy, but as time went on he came to take an increasingly important part in coping with a problem, which, for a long time to come, was to be a serious threat to the Spanish administration of Yucatan.

This was the flight in large numbers by the inhabitants of the more thickly populated northern portion of Yucatan, especially from the southern edge of this area. In spite of its sparse population at the time of the Spanish conquest, south-central Yucatan was a reasonably healthy country, and the many ruined stone cities in the region bear evidence to a climate and a soil which would permit agriculture. The scarcity of water during the dry season must have always been a problem, and no doubt artificial reservoirs or improvements of the natural sources were necessary for the large population in ancient times, but there were still enough ponds and water holes to supply a very considerable number of refugees. In many parts of New Spain fugitives from Spanish rule were in danger of starving before they could produce a crop in their new homes, but here the breadnut was fairly abundant, and there is reason to believe that many, if not all, of the other forest trees and plants, which furnished food in time of famine in northern Yucatan, were also available. Besides the breadnut, the most important were the *baatun* (possibly *Anthurium tetragonum* Hook.), sapodilla, *jícama cimarrona* (*Calopogonium coeruleum* Benth.), ear tree, and bonete (*Pileus mexicanus* A. DC.), which, according to Maya belief, had the greatest food values. These, together with game, wild honey, and some fish from the ponds, made it possible to sustain life in the forests until the first harvest.

The fugitives comprised various classes of people. Probably all of them had found the rule of the Spanish officials and the strict supervision of the missionaries irksome and wished to escape the burden of tribute and forced labor as well as the other exactions of the conquerors. There were many fugitives from justice, but these included not only ordinary misdoers and heathen priests, but also the ordinarily well-behaved person who went to church but still secretly practiced some of the old pagan domestic rites. Moreover, there was a strong native tradition of easy divorce, which was anathema to the missionaries but extremely hard to eradicate. This led to the flight not only of men who were determined to leave their wives, but also of those who, according to the new dispensation, were living in sin and in constant danger of severe castigation.

People also fled to the forests because of epidemics and the famines caused by drought or locusts. Some of them later returned voluntarily to their homes, but many remained in the south. Practically all these fugitives promptly relapsed into paganism.

At first they lived in scattered hamlets, but even in these there were recognized leaders, often called ah cuchcabs. Later, as they became more numerous, larger settlements were formed and municipal governments were organized headed by a batab. Pole-and-thatch temples were constructed and the heathen priests again became influential in local affairs as in pre-Spanish times.

As time went on these independent native groups became more and more disturbing to the colonial authorities. Not only did the encomenderos resent the loss of profitable tributaries, but the apostasy of the fugitives set a very bad example to the subject population. For a long time, generally speaking, the refugees feared to provoke the Spaniards to such an extent that a military expedition would be sent against them, and for the most part they attempted to avoid bloodshed. Acts of violence did occur, however, and there were occasional raids on the border pueblos largely with the object of carrying off men, women, and children, especially women, who were always in the minority among the outlaws. During the second quarter of the seventeenth century there was an insurrection among the pueblos of the Bacalar district, and still later, in the southwest, large bands of the independ-

ents came openly into Sahcabchen and other neighboring villages and interfered in municipal affairs.

Although the independent population in the interior was constantly
recruited by newcomers from the north, it was possible to check the increase
from time to time, chiefly through the efforts of the missionaries and the loyal
native leaders. Of the latter, Paxbolon was the most prominent during the
earlier phase of this movement, but Don Juan Chan of Chancenote in northeastern Yucatan also recovered many Indians who had fled to the forests on
the Caribbean coast. In later times Don Francisco Camal of Oxkutzcab and
Don Juan Xiu of the adjoining town of Yaxakumche were also to take an
important part in such activities.

Some time about the year 1587 Don Pablo headed an expedition of
native militia into the Cehache area, where a large number of Maya fugitives
from northern Yucatan had settled. The precise location is uncertain, but
since he is reported to have made a long and difficult journey through thick
forests, lagoons, and swamps, we can only surmise that it was in the northern
part of the lacustrine belt, possibly between L. Mocu and Isla Pac. These
people had been warned, however, by Christian Indian traders, and many of
them had fled, but Paxbolon was able to collect seventy-nine of them, bring
them out peaceably, and settle them at Popola and Tixchel. Some of them
are said to have been unconverted heathen, but it is hard to tell whether they
were Cehache, who were mixed with the refugees, or unbaptized children
of the latter.

Since pre-Spanish times a large part of the country northeast of Laguna
de Términos had apparently been a sort of no man's land between the Chontal
and Maya areas, and much of the region between Tixchel and Champoton
was still unsettled. In 1599 a large group of marauding apostates from the
north were roaming about this country and committing depredations. Not
only did they kill a number of Indians from Campeche and other towns, who
were hunting or gathering wild beeswax, but they even attacked and robbed
travelers along the coast near Chencan and Uxkakaltok. Paxbolon was authorized to raise a force of native militia from his villages and restore order.
He encountered the outlaws at a site called Usulaban, where he seized eighty
or a hundred of them, including their families. These people were brought
to Tixchel, and during the discussion about where they should be settled the
fugitives gave a very favorable account of Usulaban. This was confirmed by
one of the Franciscan missionaries, who went to examine the locality, and
it was now proposed that all the people of Tixchel and its four subject
villages should be moved there. The plan was not carried out, but in 1604

a predominantly Maya-speaking village was established at Usulaban, which seems to have been largely composed of the reformed marauders.

It was good policy to settle a surplus Maya-speaking element of the population at Usulaban and thereby add another village to the jurisdiction of Tixchel. It seems evident, however, that the plan to move the entire population of the district to this inland site would have impaired the canoe trade and the fishing and tortoise-shell industries as well as resulting in many hardships and a falling off of the population. As it was, the appointment of a secular priest to Tixchel in 1603 appears to have checked the efforts of the Franciscans to concentrate the population in a single town, where they could be more closely supervised. During the first four decades of the seventeenth century agriculture improved somewhat, while commerce and the industries we have mentioned continued to flourish. There had evidently been some loss of population in the process of resettling the new villages subject to Tixchel, for in 1609 the total population of the district was only about 1600. Economic conditions were now basically sound, and by 1639 this figure increased to about 2500.

The menace of an unconverted heathen population, to which was added an ever-increasing body of apostate fugitives in the interior and eastern coastal areas of the peninsula, was a serious problem, and the efforts of the colonial administration and the Franciscan missionaries, as well as some attempts by groups of individual colonists, to deal with this situation have been followed in considerable detail in the preceding chapters. Anxiety had been growing for some time, and by the end of the sixteenth century the interest of the Spanish colonists generally had become aroused in subduing the uncontrolled portions of the Yucatan Peninsula, converting the pagan peoples, and restoring the apostates to the Christian faith.

A number of refugees and unbaptized Indians had been recovered in northeastern Yucatan and settled in the region of Chancenote, but a further effort in that direction had failed miserably. The success of Paxbolon in the southwest, as we have seen, had been much more promising, and a small group of Campeche colonists enlisted the cacique's aid in a similar enterprise, possibly intended to be on a larger scale. In 1604 Don Pablo explored the Mamantel basin above Popola in behalf of his son-in-law, Francisco Maldonado, and four other Spaniards, and the latter group obtained a contract from the government to pacify the interior settlements. After several years of exemption the Indians whom they recovered were to pay them tribute.

The Franciscans saw little merit in a project which would simply subject these fugitives to new encomenderos. In course of time the old abuses would recur, and the Indians would again flee to still more remote regions and revert to paganism. The missionaries wished to keep the Spanish colonists out of the region and carry out their own policy without interference. Consequently they resisted this semimilitary enterprise, and one of them, a Fray Juan de Santa María, even wrote a letter to the refugee villages advising them not to submit. Nevertheless the Campeche associates went on with their plans and sent an expedition up the Mamantel basin accompanied by Paxbolon and two friars. Missions were founded at Nacaukumil and Auatayn, and a third village, Ichbalche, seemed friendly, but other neighboring settlements had been disquieted by the friar's letter, and their inhabitants fled to the forests. The two missionaries remained for a time, but the expedition returned to Campeche. It is plain, however, that Don Pablo was highly respected by the refugees, for the people of the two new missions are said to have recognized him as their natural lord and erected a house in each village for his use and service. They were evidently glad to trade with him, and this new allegiance would serve to cut them off more completely from their old homes in northern Yucatan and their former caciques. Their desertion from the jurisdiction of the latter was probably a very serious matter from the native point of view.

It seems not unlikely that the Maldonado associates might have enjoyed some measure of success, at least as long as they had the aid of Paxbolon and were guided by his advice, but later in the year a new provincial governor arrived in Yucatan and was evidently convinced by the arguments of the Franciscans. The result was that he suspended the contract with the Campeche associates and entrusted the pacification of the interior settlements to the missionaries. No other Spaniards were to visit these villages nor were their inhabitants to be transferred elsewhere.

The two missions already established in the Mamantel basin were continued, and Santa María, who had been active in promoting this missionary enterprise, founded a mission at Ichbalche, which was successful for some years to come. Four days' journey to the south and not far from the unconverted Cehache was another refugee settlement named Tzuctok. Here Santa María overcame the fear of the inhabitants that his presence was merely the preliminary to a military occupation, and he succeeded in founding another mission. The position of the missionaries was further strengthened by a formal assurance from the provincial governor that the people should be exempt from tribute for a term of years and that no Spaniards except the missionaries would be allowed to visit them. At this time the Cehache also showed signs of being friendly. If Santa María had been permitted to attempt their conversion, even a partial success would have helped stabilize the Forest Missions, since the presence of these pagan Indians apparently had a disquieting effect on the refugees.

Nacaukumil was later moved to Chacuitzil farther to the east, and a mission was founded at Cauich to the north. Other missions were also established, among them Ichmachich, west of Ichbalche, and Sacalum, which was situated at an inconveniently long distance to the east. For a time the Franciscans seem to have been fairly well pleased with the progress of the missions, but any such feeling was not shared by Bishop Vázquez de Mercado, who had at first encouraged the enterprise. He now advocated settling a group of Spanish colonists in the interior, who would help keep the natives in order and discourage any inclination to rebel. The Crown, however, continued to support the policy of the friars.

In 1609 the Spanish colonists claimed that discipline had relaxed and that idolatry was rampant among the mission Indians. There was no doubt a good deal of truth in this assertion, but the Spaniards were less critical when somewhat similar conditions occurred in their own encomiendas, so long as the natives paid their tribute regularly. Nevertheless, it must be admitted that the Tzuctok people showed signs of getting out of hand. One of the chieftains became insubordinate, and conditions were aggravated by disquieting rumors among the Indians generally. The result was that a zealous friar named Juan de la Cruz was sent to investigate conditions.

The Franciscans had already considered moving some of the mission villages to a place where they could be more conveniently supervised, and indeed, two of the communities had favored some such plan, although no final agreement had as yet been reached on a location. The friar had not been authorized to act independently, but he soon began to take measures to transfer four of the settlements to an unhealthy site near Isla Pac named Chunhaz.

Most of the Indians did not want to go there, and those of Tzuctok even obtained a letter from the governor countermanding the friar's order. This was suppressed by the latter, who burned the houses in the town, destroyed livestock and provisions, and moved the population. The inhabitants of the other three villages then came to Chunhaz without resistance, but when this and other harsh acts were reported to the governor, he repudiated the course taken by the Franciscan and authorized the people to return to their former homes. The great majority of them did so, only those of Auatayn electing to remain at Chunhaz at this time. Although the governor had kept his original promise not to move the fugitive groups from their homes, the whole affair did not improve the morale of the Forest Missions. The most interesting feature of the episode is that, in spite of the unrest among the Indians, the friar was able arbitrarily to destroy property and move so many unwilling people from their homes without the support of any military force. We can only infer that there was little immediate danger of a rebellion.

For the next five years we have little detailed information about the Forest Missions. The action of Fray Juan de la Cruz had caused considerable hardship, but he was soon recalled from the field, and after his retirement conditions appear to have been more satisfactory to the Indians than to the missionaries. The Franciscans were able to keep the Spanish colonists out of the area, and when the natives felt that their spiritual guardians were unduly severe, they appealed directly to the provincial authorities, who, on several occasions, at least, took the part of the Indians. This of course weakened the authority of the missionaries, whose reports contain accusations of disobedience, immorality, and idolatry. Another important reason for the lack of discipline was the distance from the convents to many of the scattered villages, which could be visited only at fairly long intervals. Moreover, it was evidently difficult to find competent missionaries willing to undertake these arduous duties. The Chunhaz convent was often without a friar, and in 1614 Fray Juan de Buenaventura at Ichbalche was the only one resident in the entire district.

The fundamental problem of the missionaries was of course to prevent, or at least to curb, pagan worship. About all they could do apparently was to confine it to a more or less secret practice and destroy whatever idols they were able to discover from time to time. Another very serious difficulty was presented by the numerous sexual irregularities among the Indians. Even at Ichbalche, according to one report, many people were openly dispensing with Christian marriage, and the native authorities were lax in punishing the delinquents, some of whom were to be found even in the families of the local leaders.

Under the existing circumstances the problem was almost unsolvable. The fugitives generally represented the least stable element in the population of Yucatan. Many of them had fled from the north with women who were not their legal wives, and others who had come alone had either found new mates after their arrival in the south or did not dare return to bring their families for fear of punishment. A missionary could not conscientiously give most of these people absolution, and consequently there was an embarrassingly large number of noncommunicants. As time went on, more people deserted the mission towns, and in 1614 we find Father Buenaventura com-

plaining bitterly that people made light of him and would not obey his
orders and that the provincial authorities were not supporting his authority.

The Franciscan heads finally realized that the only solution was to move
the Indians to a new mission area nearer the coast, where they could be more
easily controlled. This was proposed to the provincial governor, who came
in person to Champoton early in 1615 and held a conference with the friars
and the local officials of the mission towns. After some deliberation it was
agreed that the people should be transferred to Sahcabchen, a fertile and well-
watered site south of Champoton and only about 5 leagues from the Gulf
coast. The Indian leaders said their people were willing to pay tribute, but
they insisted on a written promise from the governor that it should be to the
Crown and that they should not be subject to any individual encomendero.
These leaders were probably no more anxious for the proposed transfer than
were their subjects, but they realized that a refusal to comply might well
result in an armed expedition being sent against them. Under the conditions
agreed to by the governor the people would be better off than if they were
compelled to flee and scatter in the forests, and it is possible that the native
officials were also influenced by a desire to retain their positions.

The transfer from Ichbalche and Tzuctok to Sahcabchen was accomplished with fewer mishaps than might have been expected, and this was
largely due to the precautions which were taken to avoid hardship so far
as possible. Men from the villages near the coast were hired to clear the new
site, build a church and friars' house, and prepare fields for planting. Maize
was supplied for the new arrivals, and pack horses were sent to Ichbalche
and Tzuctok to assist in the moving. The towns of Ichmachich, Chunhaz, and
Chacuitzil were unwilling to go to Sahcabchen, and the governor permitted
them to settle at a site named Cheusih near a tributary of the Río Mamantel.
The people of Sacalum did not move to Sahcabchen as they had promised.
A number of them may have gone to Cauich, but others remained at Sacalum
when the mission was abandoned, and, like some of those of the more distant
smaller villages, subsequently scattered to the forests.

About 1300 men, women, and children were moved to the vicinity of
Sahcabchen and to Cheusih, but many others remained in the forests, and as
time went on they were joined by a stream of new fugitives from the north,
which continued throughout most of the seventeenth century. Flight was the
one effective protest that could be made against oppression, and in course of
time it must have exercised a restraining influence on the Spanish colonists,
especially the encomenderos, who lost many of their tributaries in this manner.

A remarkable aspect of the history of the Forest Missions is the apparent willingness with which so many of the refugees received the friars and that they obeyed them even to the extent they did. On the whole the Indians appear to have regarded the Franciscans as their friends in spite of the severe disciplinary measures imposed by the latter in northern Yucatan. It is true that when left to themselves the fugitives relapsed into open paganism, but the success of the missions, incomplete as it was, suggests strongly that even at this early period Christianity had made a deep impression on the people generally, notwithstanding that so many of them continued surreptitiously to worship the old gods.

The accounts of these early missions, fragmentary as they are, give us some idea of the refugee villages and how their inhabitants behaved during the decade they were under the control of the friars. As communities they were subject to little more than moral restraint. The missionaries were not in a position to take such measures as they did except through the native author-ities, and the latter could enforce this discipline only as long as it was tol-erated by a very considerable and influential part of the local population. It is of interest to compare conditions at this time with those which now exist among the independent villages in the forests of Quintana Roo.

Here, although time and new surroundings have worked inevitable changes, we find a conservative tendency to preserve a pattern of life as similar as possible to that which existed when the ancestors of the present inhabitants revolted and subsequently retired to the forests nearly a century ago. The old idolatry had by this time disappeared, but among the Santa Cruz Indians we find it replaced by the personification and worship of the cross. Certain crosses have been regarded as oracles, which give commands, instructions, and messages to the people. In 1860 a large masonry church was built at Chan Santa Cruz, and in the villages today many of their religious ceremonies are mainly Catholic in form, though they are mostly performed by local native priests or under their direction. Other observances are essen-tially pagan and directed toward the old Maya guardian deities of forest and field, but there is no conflict between the two. Christian and pagan rites may be performed simultaneously at different altars in the same place of worship. This reconciliation of Christianity with certain phases of the old pagan religion is not uncommon among many of the natives of northern Yucatan at the present time, and it seems not unlikely that in spite of the admonitions of the friars to the contrary, very much the same attitude of mind toward religious matters was already prevalent among the Indians of the Forest Missions in the early seventeenth century.[16]

[16] Villa, 1945, pp. 97–99, 105–07.

During the decade following the transfer to Sahcabchen and Cheusih an attempt was made to reestablish a forest mission in what is now the Territory of Quintana Roo, but it was largely incidental to a military project. In 1622 Francisco de Mirones Lezcano led an expedition to the south with the object of conquering the Itza living on Lake Peten. His force consisted of twenty soldiers and a larger number of native auxiliaries, and he was accompanied by Fray Diego Delgado. After collecting a number of apostate fugitives in the course of the expedition, these people, who had been reconciled with the Church, were finally settled at Sacalum, the site of the former mission of that name, and Mirones with his men remained there for a considerable time awaiting reinforcements before advancing against the Itza. Here the soldiers treated the natives badly, and Mirones followed the time-honored custom of exploiting them economically. Unable to check this behavior, Delgado left the place in disgust and made his way to Tayasal, the Itza capital, where he lost his life.[17]

Early in 1624 the Indians of Sacalum became so exasperated with the actions of the Spaniards that they organized an insurrection, took the members of the expedition by surprise while they were at church, and murdered every one of them. The villagers had not wished to take the life of the missionary who had taken Delgado's place, but their leader, an unbaptized heathen priest, killed him before he could be rescued. The rebels then burned the town and fled to the forest, but they were later pursued by a company of loyal native militia from Oxkutzcab. Twenty of the malefactors were killed, and twelve others, including the heathen priest, were captured and brought to Mérida for punishment.[18]

In connection with this uprising and massacre it is of interest to recall the proposal of Bishop Vázquez de Mercado in 1609 to settle twenty families of Spanish colonists in the area of the Forest Missions, the idea being that their presence would restrain the Indians and keep them from rebelling. If the project had been put into execution, it is not difficult in the light of the Sacalum episode to surmise what would have been the probable outcome. The policy of the Franciscans from 1604 to 1615 did not achieve the success which they anticipated, but their moderation would appear to have had much to do with avoiding a long period of guerrilla warfare and savage raids on the frontier settlements such as occurred during the period following the War of the Castes in the nineteenth century.

For many years after the failure of the Sacalum mission and the massacre

[17] Scholes and Adams, 1936, pp. 158–59; Means, 1917, pp. 76–81.
[18] López de Cogolludo, 1867–68, bk. 10, ch. 3; Scholes and Adams, 1936, pp. 272–73.

of the friar and Spanish soldiers stationed there, we find little evidence of concerted effort by the colonial administration to control the southern interior of the peninsula. The success of the native punitive expedition under Don Fernando Camal of Oxkutzcab, which apprehended the murderers and brought them to justice, no doubt exercised a restraining influence on the other groups of fugitives. This effect wore off in course of time, especially after the uprising in the Bacalar district, which culminated in 1639 and which the Spaniards were unable to subdue for a good many years. Moreover, in the latter year Philip III confirmed the policy of the crown to reduce pagans and apostates to the faith through missionary enterprises rather than by force of arms.[19]

There was little natural increase in the refugee population, but their numbers were constantly recruited by newcomers from the north and west. This movement was accelerated by the great epidemic of yellow fever in 1648. If, as Bequaert believes, *Aëdes aegypti* was not native to the New World, the yellow fever carrier must have been introduced into Yucatan considerably earlier for the pestilence to have spread so rapidly in 1648. In any case the forest dwellers probably suffered less from the epidemic than the people nearer the coast.[20] Besides the grievances discussed elsewhere in this study in connection with the flight of the Indians to the forests in earlier times, other vexations became more onerous. Merchants, cattle men, and logwood operators obliged people to work for inadequate pay, and it has been noted that some governors compelled the natives to accept advances of money or raw materials and furnish various products at a low valuation as well as to buy unwanted goods at a high price. These practices became so widespread and vexatious that many Indians fled to the forests on this account.

It has been shown that by 1666 such desertions were so numerous that a number of the interior settlements had become organized towns, each with a batab and other officials including an influential pagan priest, and some of them with forces of armed warriors. The most powerful appear to have been Tzuctok, the site of the former mission, and Bolonpeten on an island in the swamp now called Isla Pac. According to reports discussed in the preceding chapter, the batab was acknowledged as leader by other settlements and even by the unconverted Cehache. His prestige attracted many of the fugitives, who were now passing in considerable numbers through Sahcabchen. This was the last frontier town in this direction, and its inhabitants had long carried on an extensive trade with the interior. These people had always

[19] Villagutierre Soto-Mayor, 1701, bk. 2, ch. 10.
[20] López de Cogolludo, 1867–68, bk. 12, ch. 12; Shattuck, 1933, p. 336.

been somewhat difficult to control. Although they were the descendants of scattered fugitives from various parts of northern Yucatan, they appear to have been tenacious of the old traditional social system, for the head of the Dzul lineage was accompanied by his relatives of the same name when he deserted the town about this time because he failed to be elected cacique.[21]

Later, large bands of the independents visited the frontier towns of the Sahcabchen and Tixchel areas, where they robbed and carried off many persons. They even proclaimed a Maya prophecy that the time had come for all the Indians to desert the Spaniards and flee to the forests. Many did so, while others sought safety in the neighborhood of Champoton and Campeche, and by 1688 Sahcabchen had lost over two-thirds of its population.

In 1669 Batab Yam of Tzuctok assumed what was not unlike the position of a territorial ruler over the frontier towns. As Paxbolon had formerly done in Nacaukumil and Auatayn, he required at each the construction of a large house for his use or service, and he also ordered them to cultivate a field of grain and garden truck for him and to manufacture arrows for his warriors. On the eve of Palm Sunday a pagan priest came to Sahcabchen as his representative and accompanied by over 200 forest Indians. During Easter week the priest was feted by the local magnates. He presided over the drunken heathen festivals by night and held court by day; and when he fined anyone for harming another, he divided the amount between the injured party and a number of the latter's relatives, even though it was a case of a husband maltreating his wife.[22] We do not find this detail recorded from northern Yucatan, but it accords with the general principles of Maya justice, according to which an offense against an individual was one against the kin. The latter could even recover legal damages against the husband or wife of one of its members for a provocation which had led to suicide. There is some evidence of Cehache influence among the independents, since all the local men were ordered immediately to make what is called a Cehache garment. It is said to be a *kub*, which is the Maya name of a certain woman's garment, but it suggests the poncholike robe of the modern Lacandon more than it does any secular male costume reported from northern Yucatan.[23] The account of the

[21] Autos hechos por Pedro García de Ricalde . . . sobre la reducción de los indios de Sahcabchen y otros pueblos, 1668–70, AGI, Escribanía de Cámara, leg. 317B, pza. 8.

[22] Sobre las diligencias que se han hecho para la reducción de los indios de Sahcabchen y otros pueblos, 1670, AGI, México, leg. 307.

[23] Roys, 1943, p. 31. *Kub* is variously defined as a *huipil* and something like a huipil, which is a long loose blouse worn by women (Nahuatl, *huipilli*). The Lacandon, however, call their robelike garment *xicul*, a term applied by the Maya to a short sleeveless jacket and obviously referable to the Nahuatl *xicolli* (Motul dictionary, 1929, p. 93; San Francisco Dictionary, Maya-Spanish; Tozzer, 1907, p. 29; Sahagún, 1938, 1: 144, 4: 33).

kub is of considerable interest also because we have no positive information as to the origin of the Maya-speaking Lacandon, but this suggests that at least some of them came from the Cehache area.[24]

During the next twelve months the situation grew worse. Large groups from the interior accompanied their leaders to Sahcabchen and other frontier towns. Many of the independents came principally to trade, but there were a good many robberies as well as some beatings and abductions, and the village of Holail was sacked. Nevertheless, in view of the fact that these towns were completely in their power at various times, the refugees seem to have shown more restraint than might have been expected, especially if we compare their actions with the savage atrocities which the insurgents committed in the loyal Maya villages during the War of the Castes in the nineteenth century. It is true that two Spaniards were murdered on a ranch in 1668, and the following year the Indian governor of Sahcabchen was carried off to the interior, where he afterward lost his life, but few killings are reported by the Spanish accounts of the episode, which apparently did not understate matters. The friar in charge of the church at Sahcabchen was not personally molested, although he was no doubt in considerable danger at times.

In the meantime a new governor of Yucatan was making efforts to relieve the situation. He wrote letters urging the chiefs of the independents to submit and not compel him to send an armed expedition against them. Although Bolonpeten and Tzuctok do not appear to have replied, other settlements took a conciliatory attitude. As in 1605, they were willing to receive a friar, if unaccompanied by other Spaniards, and they wished to remain where they were. Many of the governor's advisers urged him to use force, but he rejected this counsel. He was only interim governor, and he probably felt that just then the buccaneers were a greater danger than the Indians. Finally Fray Cristóbal Sánchez, the priest stationed at Sahcabchen, was sent in July with two other missionaries to pacify the forest villages. The immediate results of this enterprise were apparently more favorable than the governor's advisers had anticipated. An early report from Sánchez stated that some of the apostates had already received them kindly and that they had been invited to come to Tzuctok.

At this point the contemporary accounts of Sánchez' mission come to an end, and it is only from a few allusions in the reports of the final conquest of the interior a quarter of a century later that we learn something of the outcome. The people of Tzuctok were temporarily pacified, and a church

[24] Cf. Thompson, 1938, p. 588.

was built there. Afterward they became insubordinate, and the town was destroyed about 1680 by Alonso García Paredes, who was later to take an important part in the campaign against the Itza on Lake Peten. We do not know what other towns were pacified by Sánchez, but Thub, or Nohthub, located 13 leagues north of Tzuctok, was no doubt one of them, for it was one of the settlements which had sent a conciliatory letter to the provincial governor. Subsequently this town also rebelled and was destroyed by Paredes.[25]

Sánchez' initial success with the fugitives was probably due in part to a fear that a military expedition would be sent against them, and this would be difficult to resist, because the natives had almost no firearms. By receiving the missionaries they might well expect to be left where they were, and we surmise that in spite of their reversion to paganism, many of them had a desire to be reconciled with the Church. Another incentive for restoring friendly relations with the Spaniards would be the prospect of freer trade with the outside world. Most of these people had grown up under Spanish rule, and by this late date they must have considered metal tools a necessity. An order by Chief Yam requisitioning a large quantity of arrows from Sahcabchen suggests that iron for arrowheads was at a premium in the interior.[26] An important factor also was the esteem which the natives obviously had for Father Sánchez, who had been able to remain at his post in Sahcabchen during the disturbances.

It would be of considerable interest to know more about the religion practiced by these apostates after the middle of the seventeenth century. There can be little doubt that it reflected openly the surreptitious worship of the old gods, as it was carried on in the Christian villages at this time. Features inspired by Christian teaching were constantly creeping into the idolatrous ceremonial. Within twenty years after the Spanish conquest crucifixion sometimes became a part of the human sacrifices, which were still being performed secretly in northern Yucatan at that time. By 1641 the rebellious Indians of the Bacalar district had introduced into their heathen ceremonies an improvised mass service, in which tortillas and maize gruel were substituted for the wafer and wine.[27] Idol worship has been recorded among Yucatecan Maya apostates almost until the end of the seventeenth century, and we infer that it was still clandestinely practiced in some of the Christian villages until this time. We do not know when it was generally abandoned

---

[25] Villagutierre Soto-Mayor, 1701, bk. 5, ch. 2; Means, 1917, p. 111.
[26] Sobre las diligencias que se han hecho para la reducción de los indios de Sahcabchen y otros pueblos, 1670, AGI, México, leg. 307.
[27] Scholes and Roys, 1939, *passim*; Roys, 1933, pp. 201–03.

nor when the cross took the place of an idol as an oracle. So far, the first known instance of a speaking cross was about 1850, among the insurgents during the War of the Castes. The personification of the cross is implied in an Ebtun document dated 1814, where we read of "our Lord the Holy Cross," but the concept may be considerably older.[28]

We are ignorant of what led to the insubordination of the interior towns, which were destroyed by Paredes, and can only surmise that the missionaries may have been unduly severe or that possibly they might have made an unsuccessful attempt to move the people nearer the coast. Moreover, among a population of fugitives from various parts of the country there would be lacking the stable native leadership which aided the missionaries to maintain order in the older communities. In 1678 it was reported from Sahcabchen that certain Indians had allied themselves with rebellious natives of Petenecte on the Río Usumacinta in Tabasco. It seems not unlikely that this was a factor in the situation which finally resulted in dispatching a military expedition into the interior in 1680.[29]

After this time the fugitives ceased to be a menace in the regions we have discussed. The expedition against the Itza in 1695 encountered little resistance and they did not compare in numbers with the refugee population reported in 1668–70. We hear nothing more of Bolonpeten. The location must have been an unhealthy one, but Maler, who was in that neighborhood in 1894, tells us that it had been the site of a settlement of free Maya families about the middle of the nineteenth century.[30]

The encomienda history of Acalan-Tixchel has been described in some detail in the preceding chapters. Considerable emphasis has been given to this phase of Acalan-Tixchel developments for various reasons. For many years the encomienda system constituted the chief means by which Spanish jurisdiction was made effective in Acalan. The data concerning tribute payments recorded in the Chontal Text and in the various tax schedules available for Acalan and Tixchel formulated in 1553 and later years provide valuable information concerning the economic life of the Chontal in postconquest times, especially with reference to agricultural production and surplus goods available for export. These tribute schedules, as in the case of those formulated for northern Yucatan and other areas, also contain data on the basis of which estimates of population may be made. Finally, the encomienda lawsuit of

[28] Villagutierre Soto-Mayor, 1701, bk. 5, ch. 9; Tozzer, 1941, p. 116; Roys, 1939, p. 363; Villa, 1945, pp. 20–22. A rare case of modern idolatry at Pustunich, southeast of Champoton, is recorded by Andrews (1943, pp. 26–29).

[29] Molina Solís, 1904–13, 2: 292.

[30] Means, 1917, pp. 107–16; Maler, 1910, p. 146.

García *v.* Bravo (see Chapter 9) is one of the most important sources for the history of Acalan-Tixchel in the sixteenth century.

The history of the encomienda in Acalan-Tixchel also serves to illustrate various trends in the evolution of this important institution of colonial Hispanic America. The encomienda was introduced in the island colonies at an early date as a means of providing the Spaniards with an adequate supply of native labor. In the mainland colonies, where the conquerors found more advanced civilizations and well-developed systems of tribute, they demanded the payment of tribute as well as labor from the Indians assigned to them in encomienda. For some years the encomenderos levied labor and tribute on the Indians more or less at will, but this resulted in numerous abuses, eventually causing the Crown to order the formulation of fixed annual assessments of tribute, payable in money or in kind, and the elimination of the labor phase of the encomienda obligation. These changes, introduced in most of the colonies in the mid-sixteenth century,[31] had the effect of making the encomienda a form of pension for the reward of deserving conquerors and their descendants and also for the support of local militia for the defense of the colonies, since the encomenderos were under obligation to maintain arms and horses and to answer call to military service in time of danger. The use of the encomienda for pension purposes is further illustrated by developments in the second half of the sixteenth century and in the seventeenth, when the Crown or colonial officials frequently made grants of money or produce in kind to non-encomenderos on the revenues of the larger encomiendas, thus providing rewards for a larger number of deserving colonists.[32]

The early encomenderos of Acalan required payments in labor and tribute and in such amounts as they wished or were able to collect. In 1553 Lic. Tomás López Medel, oidor of Guatemala, eliminated the labor obligation and formulated the first fixed annual assessment of tribute. After the removal of the Acalan people to Tixchel the tribute schedule was revised in 1561, in 1569, and again in 1583. On the last occasion the assessment was made on the same basis as for the towns of northern Yucatan. The assessment of 1553 and also that of 1583 gave the encomendero a gross revenue consid-

---

[31] These changes were put into effect in New Spain, Yucatan, and most of the other colonies. But some exceptions were made, notably in the case of Chile, where the Indians continued to give labor to their encomenderos.

[32] This practice was common in Yucatan. It should also be noted that the income from the Montejo encomiendas, declared vacant in the late 1540's in accordance with provisions of the New Laws of 1542, was used to pay pensions to deserving colonists, some of whom also held encomiendas, and the revenues of other vacant encomiendas were sometimes used for this purpose. Some of the larger encomienda grants held by conqueror families were eventually broken into smaller holdings for reassignment to several persons. And the Crown occasionally made encomienda grants in the Indies to Spanish nobles for pension purposes.

erably in excess of 1,000 pesos annually, a sizable income in terms of other grants of moderate size in Yucatan. In the seventeenth century (sometime between 1606 and 1648) the governor assigned part of the encomienda revenues as a pension to a person other than the encomendero of Tixchel. The falling-off of the population in the Tixchel district in the later seventeenth century caused a sharp decline in the encomienda revenues. As late as 1688, however, the Tixchel people, most of whom now resided at Usulaban, continued to be held in encomienda, although the gross revenue of the holding was now less than 200 pesos annually.

Various writers on colonial administration and land systems in Spanish America have regarded the encomienda as a kind of land grant. Recent investigations have shown, however, that such views are no longer tenable;[33] and it may be noted here that the Acalan encomienda documents, none of which record any reference to a grant of land, confirm the findings of these recent studies. It is necessary therefore to revise the thesis stated by earlier writers that many of the colonial haciendas evolved directly from encomienda holdings. Although there is evidence that encomenderos did obtain possession of lands within the territorial limits of their encomienda towns, study of the pertinent documents clearly proves that title to such land was not based on the encomienda grants but on separate procedures and instruments, such as specific grants of land, purchase, or unlawful occupation (often subsequently legalized by the process of *composición*). As Zavala has stated, an hacienda could be formed "under the cloak of an encomienda, but independently in the matter of juridical title."[34] This writer also calls attention to the need for detailed regional studies to determine the frequency of this process. Such investigations will involve "a scrupulous comparison of encomienda titles with those which define territorial property in the same zone, also an inquiry into the relationship between the encomienda families and those of the hacienda owners."[35]

Although labor was eliminated as an element of the encomienda system

[33] Zavala, 1940; 1943, pp. 80–84; 1945, pp. 56–61; Kirkpatrick, 1942.
[34] Zavala (1945, pp. 58–61) describes certain documents showing how the son of Bernal Díaz del Castillo by means of a separate grant of vacant land, purchase, etc., obtained title to lands within the limits of the old conqueror's encomienda in Guatemala. Commenting on these documents, the author makes two significant statements. The first, quoted in part above, reads: "Así iba naciendo una hacienda so capa de la encomienda, pero con independencia en cuanto a la titulación jurídica." The second reads: "La realidad es que la hacienda llegó a constituirse en aquellos términos, representando la irrupción—legal o abusiva—del propietario europeo y sus descendientes en medio de las posesiones de los pueblos de indios. La encomienda no influía directamente en este proceso, pero ya se ha visto que el encomendero que no se ceñía a su función específica, podía por otros medios convertirse en propietario de tierras y crear una hacienda dentro de la encomienda."
[35] *Ibid.*, p. 61.

by royal legislation of 1549, many encomenderos continued to exploit the labor of their encomienda Indians by extralegal devices. We have ample evidence of this for northern Yucatan in the documents of the sixteenth and seventeenth centuries, and we have no doubt that the encomenderos of Acalan-Tixchel did the same. But the major method of making use of Indian labor for many decades subsequent to 1549 was by means of the repartimiento, or forced labor for wages. Under this system a certain percentage of the Indians of each town were obliged to hire out to Spaniards (encomenderos and others) for stated periods and at fixed wages. This procedure was attended by many abuses, resulting in various reform laws and edicts in the early seventeenth century. It should be emphasized that this method of employment of native labor was separate from the encomienda, which now involved only the payment of stated amounts of tribute annually.

It is sometimes assumed that the repartimiento evolved into the system of debt peonage which characterized the history of Mexico in later colonial times and the nineteenth century. It should be noted therefore that recent studies by Zavala, based on extensive documentary evidence, prove that debt peonage actually .grew out of a system of voluntary labor for wages which gradually took the place of the repartimiento as the principal method of recruiting native workers in the seventeenth and eighteenth centuries.[36] Whether or not any of the Indians of the Tixchel area became debt peons we have no information.

In our discussion of the Acalan tribute assessment of 1553 we have stated that the payments called for imposed a heavy burden on the Indians, especially in terms of a wage equivalent. The schedule for Tixchel formulated in 1583 sharply lowered the manta requirement per tributary and correspondingly reduced the amount of labor required to produce the stated levies but the value of the annual payment remained high because of increasing prices. In fact, a document of 1606 shows that the value of the tribute paid by each tributary exceeded that of the 1553 levy. Although wages for unskilled labor may have increased to some extent since 1553, the 1606 valuation still constituted a heavy burden in terms of wages. We also find that the amount of tribute paid by the Indians of Yucatan in the sixteenth century was greater than that paid by natives of Mexico proper. This may be explained in part by the fact that the encomenderos of Yucatan enjoyed fewer opportunities for profitable enterprise than those of New Spain and so had to depend to a greater extent on the encomienda tributes as a source of income.

[36] Zavala, 1943, ch. 9, and 1943a. Zavala has in preparation a comprehensive study of Indian labor in the Spanish colonies.

Little information has come down to us concerning the history of Tixchel after the founding of the first Forest Missions in 1604. We last hear of Don Pablo Paxbolon in 1614, when he was seventy years old, but we do not know how much longer he lived, and there is some uncertainty as to whether or not his mestizo grandson would have been allowed to succeed to the caciqueship. This was wisely forbidden by the Laws of the Indies, which aimed to keep the office in Indian hands. It is true that there were mestizo caciques in Mexico in later times, but we have found none recorded from Yucatan. Paxbolon was closely associated with his Spanish son-in-law, Francisco Maldonado, who filled various civil and military offices in Campeche. After the death of his Acalan wife, the cacique married the daughter of a Spaniard named Diego de Orduña. The latter's knowledge of the Chontal language and his wide experience with Indian affairs in Tabasco suggest that he may have been a trader and a business associate of Don Pablo. Indeed, it seems very possible that the daughter's mother was a Chontal Indian woman. By this wife Paxbolon had a second daughter, who was still unmarried in 1612. If she later married an Indian of rank, according to political traditions in Tabasco and other parts of the mainland her son could have succeeded to the caciqueship, in default of any surviving son, brother, or nephew of the deceased cacique, but such a procedure would have been most unusual among the Yucatecan Maya. The tendency to matrilocal residence, however, suggests the possibility of inheritance of the office through a daughter among the Acalan.[37]

By 1639 the curacy of Tixchel comprised seven towns. The population of the district was now about 2500, and the revenue of the curacy was such as to indicate favorable economic conditions. Consequently it is surprising to learn that the town was destroyed some time between this date and 1643. No details of the destruction have come down to us, but the town was so close to the undefended harbor of Puerto Escondido as to suggest strongly that the disaster was due to a piratical raid. In any case it seems unlikely that Tixchel could have remained tenable later on, when the English buccaneers established a base on Isla del Carmen for the cutting and exportation of logwood. Popola now became the head of the curacy, but many of the inhabitants apparently moved to Usulaban, which was still predominantly Chontal in the 1660's. There was, however, a very considerable loss of population. Some of the Tixchel people no doubt settled in other villages of the region, and we surmise that a number of them fled to the interior.

After the abandonment of Tixchel the population of the district de-

[37] Roys, 1943, p. 108.

creased greatly. Following the death of the encomendero in 1648 there was a readjustment of tribute for the encomienda, which now comprised the villages of Usulaban, Chiuoha, Tiquintunpa (the former Zapotitlan), and Mamantel (originally known as Xocola and later renamed Mazcab). This new assessment does not cover the entire Tixchel area, but it discloses that the tributary units of these settlements, which had numbered 320 in 1606, had now shrunk to 168, indicating a loss of almost half of the population. We ascribe this rapid decline both to the hardships attending the destruction of Tixchel and the move to Usulaban and to the epidemic of yellow fever which swept the country in 1648 and caused enormous loss of life.

During the succeeding decades the population of the Tixchel area continued to diminish. This was partly due to the increasingly vexatious exactions of the Spaniards, and perhaps even more to attacks by the buccaneers, for Usulaban, Chiuoha, and Popola were repeatedly robbed and sacked by English raiders. If the latter had displayed any political acumen, it seems likely that by conciliating the local Indians and allying themselves with the fugitives in the interior they might have effected a more permanent occupation of the region. Indeed, some of the Spanish colonists envisaged such a possibility with no little apprehension. Moreover, the refugee groups demoralized the Christian villages here, as they did around Sahcabchen. They visited these settlements also in considerable numbers and were joined by the local inhabitants in their idolatry and drunken festivals, and many of the latter were carried off or persuaded to flee to the forests.

As a result of these unsettled conditions a number of the towns were deserted. In 1668 the people of Popola, Tiquintunpa, and Mamantel had withdrawn to an unidentified site named Sosmula, and those of Cheusih were now living in the same neighborhood. No permanent town was established here, however, and some of them appear to have resettled later in Usulaban, Chekubul, and Chiuoha. These were the only remaining villages in the district in 1688, and at this time they had a combined population of 420 adult inhabitants. The Chontal-speaking element was fast disappearing, for in the matrículas of this year only forty-six of the names can be identified as Chontal. All but a very few, and a majority of them are of women, are recorded from Usulaban, which contained about 100 adults all together. Even the site of this town has since disappeared from the maps. Consequently it is not strange that the Chontal language has now become extinct in the region. With the exception of the name of the Río Mamantel and possibly a few others of doubtful origin, hardly a trace of it is to be found there at the present time.

We have already remarked on the tendency for Chontal names to disappear, and if it were not for the Acalan Text and matrículas we would
know practically nothing of the nomenclature of this important branch of the
Maya stock. There is some evidence of a similar weakness in the language
generally. It is true that a good many Indians in Tabasco still speak Chontal,
but they are few compared with the large number of people who spoke it
in pre-Spanish times. Strangely enough, however, the small Nahuatl-speaking
element of the population, who occupied only eight towns and villages in
1579, still preserves its language at the present time. It would be of more than
ordinary interest to know whether this difference in language was reflected
in their religion and material culture at the time of the conquest, and whether
their manner of living varies from that of their Chontal-speaking neighbors
today. Unfortunately neither archaeological reports nor modern ethnological studies are available that would cast any light on the subject.

A still more notable example of this linguistic weakness is to be seen in the
closely related Chol. The latter was formerly spoken from the Chontal area
across the base of the Yucatan Peninsula to the Caribbean, but today this
language survives only in a small part of northern Chiapas.[38]

The very similar Chorti, however, is still spoken in the mountainous
region of eastern Guatemala and across the Honduras frontier.

In strong contrast to the instability we have noted, Yucatecan Maya
stands out as a startling example of linguistic strength and persistence. It has
held its own against Spanish to a remarkable degree in northern Yucatan,
where not only is it spoken as a secondary language by many persons of
European descent, but it is the language of the home among a large class
of people of mixed blood who are not considered Indians. Even in a town
as large as Peto the teachers say that the great majority of the children entering school are unable to speak any Spanish. Certainly, as Redfield remarks,
"Yucatec Maya is the most-used language of the peninsula and one of which
everyone has some knowledge and awareness."[39]

In addition to replacing Chontal in the Tixchel region and on the Usumacinta River, Maya has also superseded Chol in the Lacandon country in
eastern Chiapas and in parts of the former Manche Chol area in southern
British Honduras and the adjoining Peten. In the last named region, however, there are also Kekchi-speaking groups, who are partly of Chol descent.[40]
Recently a number of Kekchi from Alta Verapaz have been settling near

[38] Thompson, 1938, pp. 585–90; Roys, 1943, p. 111.
[39] Redfield, 1941, p. 2.
[40] Thompson, 1931, pp. 35–36; 1938, pp. 588–90.

the mouth of the Río Dulce opposite Livingston in a district that had long been Hispanicized. It seems evident that the Yucatecan Maya and the Kekchi have a pioneering spirit and a facility for adapting themselves to changed conditions which have enabled them to survive and preserve their language in regions where other native peoples have either disappeared or lost their ethnic identity.

The Acalan were a people of mixed origin who traded and made war over a widely extended area, and the pre-Spanish history of this nation emphasizes the importance of considering Middle America as a whole in the study of any particular phase of its culture. A signal example of this attitude is to be found in Kidder's report of the archaeological investigations at Kaminaljuyu near Guatemala City, which have achieved startling results. Here are shown not only the cultural relations of the inhabitants of this site with the lowland Maya and other peoples of southern and eastern Mexico during the first half of the Initial Series period, but also such close resemblances between Kaminaljuyu and Teotihuacan in central Mexico as to indicate some thing more than commercial intercourse. Indeed, an actual invasion and subsequent occupation by people from the latter region is strongly suggested.[41] Thompson has published a series of important comparative studies showing analogies in the art of Veracruz and western Tabasco with that of the classical Maya, and for a later period he traces similarities indicating significant relationships in the sculptures and ceramics of the Gulf coast, central Mexico, Chichen Itza, and the southern Maya area.[42] The native historical traditions are often confused and sometimes contradictory, so it would seem obvious that any satisfactory interpretation can hardly afford to neglect the archaeological evidence.

Our history of the Acalan is principally a chronicle of their ruling class, and a large part of it is concerned with the activities of two of their rulers. One was Paxbolonacha, whose friendly relations with Cortés had much to do with determining the destiny of his people in colonial times; the other was his grandson, Don Pablo Paxbolon, who reunited the remnants of his people in the Tixchel area, augmented the population of the district by bringing in Yucatecan Maya fugitives from the interior of the peninsula, and made himself the most important Indian leader of his time among the lowland Maya under Spanish rule.

It is true that Don Pablo was educated by the missionaries and cooperated with the colonial authorities and the clergy, but he was by no means merely a

[41] Kidder, 1945, pp. 241–60.
[42] Thompson, 1941, 1941a, 1943.

Hispanicized Indian. Under changed conditions his policy was very much like that of his grandfather, who had organized the Candelaria basin politically under Acalan rule and established an important commercial state there in pre-Spanish times. Consequently Paxbolon's career furnishes us with a sound basis for an appraisal of the methods and motives of his forebears, whose activities are recorded in the Chontal Text.

The history of the Yucatan Peninsula in colonial times abounds with instances of Spanish oppression on one hand and of evasion or flight from the rule of the conqueror on the other. This, however, is only one side of the picture. Equally significant was the cooperation between the native leaders and the Spanish authorities and clergy, such as we find recorded in the Xiu Chronicle, the Titles of Ebtun, and now in the Acalan-Tixchel documents.[43] Such cooperation, we believe, was a most important factor in the wide survival of the Yucatan Maya population and the preservation of their language with much of the native culture. The result was the development of a Hispano-Indian civilization, such as we find existing in Yucatan at the present time.

[43] Roys, 1939, pp. 44-45 and *passim;* 1941, *passim;* 1943, pp. 143-45, 178; Morley, 1941, *passim.*

APPENDICES

APPENDIX A

The Chontal Text

INTRODUCTION

IN THE PRECEDING chapters frequent reference has been made to the Chontal Text, which is the most important single document in the mass of new source material relating to the history of Acalan-Tixchel. It is the purpose of this appendix to make the Text available to both the specialist and the interested reader by means of facsimile reproduction, the Spanish version, and an English translation.

As indicated in Chapter 1, the Text is found in the Paxbolon-Maldonado Papers, which contain the probanzas of the merits and services of Don Pablo Paxbolon, cacique and governor of Tixchel, and of his son-in-law, Francisco Maldonado. These Papers comprise a lengthy manuscript which forms part of legajo 138 of the Audiencia de México section of the Archivo General de Indias in Seville.[1] An account of the legal proceedings of Francisco Maldonado which resulted in the compilation of these documents has been given in Chapter 12.

The Papers begin with the petition of Pedro de Toro, Maldonado's agent, who presented the probanzas to the Council of the Indies in Madrid in 1618. The probanzas are in two parts, each with unnumbered and numbered folios, as follows: Part I, ff. [i–ix], 1–112; Part II, ff. [i–ix], 1–340, [i]. Our photographs of the manuscript, which have recently been deposited in the Library of Congress, are numbered consecutively 1–939.

The main body of Part I (ff. 1–112, ph. 18–241)[2] consists of a certified copy, dated October 17, 1614, of the probanza formulated by Maldonado in Mérida and Campeche in 1612–14. The Chontal Text is found in ff. 69r–77r, ph. 154–170. The Spanish version is in ff. 89v–102r, ph. 195–220.

Part II (ph. 242–939) contains a long series of documents relating to

[1] The manuscripts in the Archivo General de Indias are kept in *legajos*, or bundles, each containing an extensive file of documents. The Audiencia de México section comprises the bulk of the correspondence and administrative reports for the district of the Audiencia of Mexico City, which included the province of Yucatan. The general title of legajo 138 of this section is: *Cartas y expedientes de personas seculares del distrito de esta Audiencia [de México]. 1620.*

[2] Photos 1–17 reproduce Pedro de Toro's petition to the Council of the Indies and the unnumbered folios [i–ix] of Part I. The latter contain (a) an undated petition of Maldonado summarizing his services and requesting reward for same, (b) a brief table of contents of the documents in f. 1–112, and (c) a petition of Maldonado in 1615 asking for additional copies of the probanza in Part I.

the history of the missions of Las Montañas, 1604–15. These documents constitute the major source for our discussion of the missions in Chapter 11. They were added to the probanza record to support Maldonado's claim to an encomienda, based on the agreement made by the governor of Yucatan with Maldonado and his associates when the missions were started in 1604. The series is in the form of a certified copy, dated May 13, 1616.[3]

The Chontal Text as we have it is not an original document, but a copy made by a Spanish scribe in 1614 from the version written by the native clerk of Tixchel in 1612. Moreover, most of the latter version was also a copy made at Martín Maldonado's request from the originals in the possession of his grandfather, Don Pablo Paxbolon. The Spanish version is also a 1614 copy of the original translation made at Campeche in December 1612.

The following notation appears on f. 69v, ph. 155, of the Text:

Después de esta petición[4] va escrito en la lengua de los naturales de Tichel el proveimiento y relación y conforme al pedimento que va por cabeza de esta probanza no se saca lo que así está en la lengua, sino la trasuntación que de ello se hizo por intérpretes vuelta en castellano a la letra, que va adelante, a que remito.[5]

This note will be meaningless to persons who do not have the complete copy of Part I of the Paxbolon-Maldonado Papers at hand.

In 1615 Francisco Maldonado petitioned the alcalde ordinario of Campeche to authorize the scribe of the cabildo to make one or more copies of his probanza of 1612-14 "sin que en los traslados se saque lo que está escrito en lengua chontal, sino la trasuntación de ello hecho como está por dos intérpretes en la lengua castellana, con todo lo demás procesado." The alcalde so ordered. Following this is a statement by Juan Martín Blanco, scribe of the cabildo, that he had made a copy of the probanza presented by Maldonado and in the form requested "sin sacar en él lo escrito en la lengua chontal, sino su trasuntación en la castellana . . . que sacada a la letra es como se sigue." These documents immediately precede our copy of the probanza in Part I of the Paxbolon-Maldonado Papers.[6]

Blanco's statement might appear to mean that our copy is the one he made in 1615. Actually it is the one presented by Maldonado to be copied

---

[3] In AGI, México, leg. 359, we have another copy of the materials in ff. 1–75v, ph. 259–549, and a copy of the documents in ff. 146r–204v, ph. 549–666, is contained in AGI, Patronato, leg. 231, núm. 4, ramo 16.

[4] This is a reference to the petition of Martín Maldonado (f. 69r, ph. 154), which precedes the Text, in which he asks for a copy of Paxbolon's papers. For an English translation, see p. 293, *supra*.

[5] The Spanish is here modernized.

[6] Paxbolon-Maldonado Papers, Part I, ff. [viii–ix], ph. 15–17.

by Blanco. Maldonado's petition to the alcalde, the latter's decree, and Blanco's statement were attached to it to record the fact that a new copy, omitting the Chontal documents, had been made. Fortunately for us Maldonado sent to Spain the first copy instead of the one made in 1615, for otherwise the Chontal Text would have been lost.

The marginal note on f. 69v, in the handwriting of Blanco, is merely the scribe's notation that, according to Maldonado's petition, he was omitting the Chontal material in the new copy he was making at that time.

The Chontal Text begins with a paragraph of six lines (last line of f. 69r, ph. 154, to line 5, f. 69v, ph. 155) which apparently contains the authorization of Paxbolon to have made copies of his original papers, as requested by Martín Maldonado. This preliminary paragraph was not translated in the Spanish version.

The main body of the Text consists of three separate documents. These are indicated by Roman numerals inserted in the printed text of the Spanish version and the English translation.

Document I begins with line 6, f. 69v, ph. 155, and runs to line 4, f. 71r, ph. 158. Most of this part, running to line 12, f. 70v, ph. 157, contains a brief account of the generations of rulers of Acalan from preconquest times to the mid-sixteenth century. This account was recorded in 1567, the year after Don Pablo Paxbolon took office as cacique and governor of Tixchel, and was written "in the Mexican language."[7] In 1612 a Chontal translation of the Mexican version was made for Martín Maldonado by the native clerk of the town.

Following this story of the early rulers are two short paragraphs (lines 13–22, f. 70v, ph. 157) recording (a) the marriage of Don Pablo Paxbolon to Doña Isabel, (b) the marriage of their daughter Catalina to Francisco Maldonado, and (c) the death of Doña Isabel and Paxbolon's subsequent marriage to the daughter of Diego de Orduña. These paragraphs were apparently added by the native clerk when he translated the 1567 account into Chontal in order to bring the genealogy up to date.

Document I ends with a paragraph (line 23, f. 70v, ph. 157, to line 4, f. 71r, ph. 158) dated July 21, 1612, in which the clerk records that the foregoing "descent and genealogy" of Don Pablo Paxbolon had been read to certain principal men and officials of Tixchel, who certified that it was true.

Document II runs from line 5, f. 71r, ph. 158, to the middle of f. 71v, ph.

[7] We have already seen that Mexican was almost a second language for many of the Chontal of Tabasco proper, and we know that Spanish officials communicated with these people in Mexican. It is a little more doubtful to what extent the Chontal of Acalan spoke Mexican, but the Text clearly shows that Juan Bautista, the clerk of Tixchel in 1567, was able to write the language. It is also obvious that more of the Spanish officials would be able to read Mexican than Chontal.

159. It begins with the statement that on July 5, 1612, "I [probably the native clerk] copied the names and count of the pueblos of the Mactun, who are the Chontal of Acalan, written by the principal men, our fathers, who died old men." There follows a list of seventy-six towns. At the end of the list in a design is written "67 pueblos," probably an error on the part of the copyist in 1614 for "76 pueblos." The date of the original, which was in the possession of Don Pablo Paxbolon, is not known, but it was probably drawn up in 1567 or soon thereafter as a supplement to Document I.

Document III gives an account of Acalan-Tixchel from the time of Cortés to 1604. It was apparently written in 1610, but it is impossible to identify the author. The Chontal Text of this part is incomplete. This is made clear by the Spanish version, which we have divided into three sections, IIIa, IIIb, and IIIc, in order to facilitate comparison with the Text.

The Text equivalent of IIIa begins immediately after the design on f. 71v, ph. 159, and runs to line 4, f. 76r, ph. 168. At this point the story breaks off in the middle of the account of Francisco Tamayo Pacheco's entrada of 1559. IIIb, which is entirely missing in the Text, completes the story of this episode and carries the narrative on through the visit of Dr. García de Palacio, oidor of the Audiencia of Mexico. The Text begins again with IIIc, which records events from 1599 to 1604 (line 5, f. 76r, ph. 168, to the end at line 5, f. 77r, ph. 170).

The break in the Text and the ommission of a Chontal equivalent for IIIb may be ascribed to carelessness on the part of the scribe who made our present copy in 1614. The only other alternative would be to assume that section IIIb was added to the Spanish version by the translator of the Text in 1612, but this possibility would seem to be ruled out by the fact that the break comes in the middle of the Tamayo Pacheco episode, which the Spanish version carries on and completes.

The reliability of the Text as a historical source is naturally a matter of considerable importance. The account of the early rulers recorded in 1567 was based on oral tradition, for we are told in the first paragraph that the information was given by two old men of Tixchel, Alonso Chacbalam and Luis Tutzin. The early Spanish chronicles, which mention a certain "Apaspolon" as the ruler of Acalan in Cortés' time, confirm the reference to Paxbolonacha of the sixth generation, but for the account of Paxbolonacha's predecessors we have no means of checking the veracity of the two informants. We are very fortunate to have this story of the early rulers, however, for it is all that we know about the preconquest history of Acalan, except for what may be inferred from archaeological evidence. The main outline gives the impression of being authentic, but, as is true of all native sources, the details should be used with caution.

The "list and count" of the pueblos in Document II presents many problems. The names are in Chontal, but some of them may be garbled. It should be remembered that the list as we have it is twice removed from the original in Don Pablo Paxbolon's possession. The copy made by the clerk of Tixchel in 1612 was probably fairly accurate because Chontal was his native language. There is no evidence, however, that the scribe who made our present copy in 1614 from the clerk's copy knew Chontal, although it would appear that he had considerable knowledge of Yucatecan Maya. The spellings in the Spanish version are often different from those in the Text. But regardless of any inaccuracies in the list, it constitutes a valuable addition to our fund of information, in view of the fact that the traditional sources for the history of Acalan record only a few place names and most of these in Mexicanized forms.

Document III, which tells the story of Acalan-Tixchel in postconquest times, appears to be based very largely on oral tradition, although at one point it refers to certain documents recording the services of Don Pablo Paxbolon. The main outline of events is fairly dependable, but in various details the story is inaccurate or conflicts with other evidence. For example, Cortés is said to have arrived in Acalan in 1527 instead of 1525. The Avila expedition is apparently confused with that of Lorenzo de Godoy. The statement that Antón García, encomendero of Acalan, favored the removal of the Indians to Tixchel is contrary to what García had to say on this point in 1571. Consequently, it is necessary to check the Text against contemporary sources on the events recorded, and in case of conflict the latter should be given greater weight.

On certain points, however, we are obliged to rely almost entirely on the story as told in the Text. Other documents contain only casual references to the conversion of the Indians of Acalan, which is described in some detail in the Text. Although the story as told in the latter is undoubtedly circumstantial in certain respects, it provides an interesting and plausible account of this important event. For other incidents, such as the gathering-in of heathen and apostate Indians and their settlement near Tixchel in 1583–1604, the Text is the only source available.

In various places the story is obviously colored by later developments and by the desire of the author to exalt the services of the rulers of Acalan-Tixchel. In the account of the death of Cuauhtemoc we are told how the Mexican leader tried to induce Paxbolonacha to join in the alleged plot to destroy Cortés and his army, and how the ruler revealed the scheme to Cortés. Other accounts, such as Cortés' Fifth Letter and the *True History* of Bernal Díaz, do not mention Paxbolonacha's role at this time. Whatever the facts may be, the author of the Text was obviously seeking to win favor with the Spaniards by stressing the loyalty of Paxbolonacha. In the same way the pious speeches attributed to Lamatazel and Paxtun in the story of the conversion of Acalan were doubtless intended to give the impression that these rulers deserved chief credit for inducing the Indians to abandon paganism and adopt the Christian faith.

The foregoing comments are not intended to minimize the historical and ethnological importance of Document III. It contains invaluable data relating to the political organization and native religion of Acalan and to historical events, not available elsewhere. It tells the story of postconquest developments from the native point of view, and the colored and circumstantial passages unconsciously reflect native psychology and the conflict between European and aboriginal cultures. From this standpoint the narrative is more valuable than if it had given only a factual résumé of events which could be verified at all points by other sources.

The Chontal Text is written in the European script which the Spanish missionaries adapted to the language of the Yucatecan Maya. In the latter most of the letters have approximately their Spanish sounds. When *v* is found in colonial Maya manuscripts, it represents the sound of *u*, either as a vowel or as a semivowel. La Farge, however, records a number of modern Chontal words containing a *v* sound.[8] *C* is always hard, even before *e* and *i*, and is pronounced much like the English *k*; and *x* has a sound somewhat like the English *sh*. According to the Motul dictionary, Coronel, and San Buenaventura, in the sixteenth and seventeenth centuries *h* could represent either of two sounds. One was the "strong *h*" (*h recia*) and the other, the "plain *h*" (*h simple*) which was said not to be aspirated. Beltrán, writing in the eighteenth century, no longer makes this distinction but tells us that "the *h* is pronounced with aspiration, since the language [*idioma*] employs it instead of the *j*, which it does not have."[9] Some letters represent sounds which do not occur in Spanish. These are *pp*, *tħ*, *ɔ*, *cħ*, and *k*, on which Andrade comments:

These sounds are very familiar to those who have studied the Indian languages of North America, where they are at present represented respectively by the phonetic symbols p', t', ts', tc', and k'. They are the so-called glottalized or fortis sounds. It is difficult to convey an idea of the acoustic effect of these sounds to those

---

[8] Blom and La Farge, 1926–27, 2: 470–79, 497.

[9] Motul Dictionary, 1929, pp. 358, 418; Coronel, 1929, p. 4, and *passim*; San Buenaventura, 1888, f. A2r, and *passim*; Beltrán de Santa Rosa, 1859, p. 4. Coronel and San Buenaventura in their discussion of this sound distinguish between *ħ* and *h*, but they do not observe this distinction in the examples they give farther on.

who have never heard them. Roughly speaking, it may be said that the Maya pp and th are emphatic articulations of Maya p and t, and that a similar correspondence exists between the series ɔ, cħ, k, and tz, ch, c. A careful enunciation of the k-sound, however, does not affect our ears as a mere emphatic articulation of the Maya c, but that is also the case in other Indian languages in which this sound occurs. In Maya these fortis sounds are not articulated as energetically as in many North American languages, particularly in those of the Pacific coast. On the whole they may best be compared with the corresponding sounds of the Dakota Sioux, although with many Maya speakers they are so weak that the untrained ear can not distinguish them from the unemphatic sounds.[10]

All these glottalized or fortis sounds are represented in our Chontal Text, although the pp and cħ occur only rarely.

It is hard to tell how closely this notation, which had been devised for Yucatecan Maya, corresponded to the spoken language represented by the Text. An approximate idea might be gained from a study of the phonetics of the modern Chontal still spoken in Tabasco. Unfortunately the Acalan dialect seems to have disappeared completely.

The Text is reproduced in facsimile because it would be extremely hazardous, in view of the lack of grammatical and lexicographical material relating to the Chontal language, to make a transcription. Although the Text was evidently copied rapidly by a professional scribe, it is sufficiently legible for linguistic study. Nevertheless, an examination of the first page, nearly all of which is written in Spanish, will give some idea of the difficulties which would be encountered in attempting an accurate transcription of a little-known language written in such a hand. Here, except for our knowledge of what letters are called for, it would be difficult to distinguish between e and l and between s and b. Not only does such confusion occur occasionally in the Text, but we also sometimes find u and h where we should expect b and k. For these reasons it would be premature to attempt to establish an authoritative version at this time, and it has seemed wise to reproduce the Text in facsimile. In this way the specialists in Maya linguistics will have access to it exactly as it has come down to us.

The Spanish version printed here has been transcribed by Miss Eleanor B. Adams from the 1614 copy in the Paxbolon-Maldonado Papers. The spelling and punctuation have been modernized, because many persons who know Spanish would probably encounter certain difficulties in reading a strictly paleographic transcription. In the case of Indian names, however, the original spelling has been retained. The original Spanish translation, dated December

[10] Andrade, letter of January 12, 1932, *apud* Roys, 1933, p. 10.

12, 1612, was the work of two citizens of Campeche, who were said to be well versed in the Chontal language. This version is frequently a very free translation, especially in the case of purported quotations of speeches. As far as we can tell from the Chontal original, it seems to be fairly reliable in the narration of actual events, although interesting details are sometimes omitted and occasional explanations are interpolated, as will be seen from a comparison with the English translation. The spelling of personal and place names in the Spanish version is often unsatisfactory, but it falls short chiefly in its faulty rendering of a number of ethnological details, matters in which the Spanish translators took little interest and which they probably did not understand. It may be noted, however, that the discrepancies in the Spanish version are not unlike those frequently found in official Spanish translations of colonial Maya documents from Yucatan.

The English translation is based on the Spanish version and to some extent on the Chontal Text itself. As the first step Miss Adams made an English rendering of the Spanish. This was later revised by Mr. Roys and Mr. Scholes. During the process of revision Mr. Roys checked the translation sentence by sentence against the Text in order to make the choice of words and phrases conform more closely to the meaning of the Chontal, in so far as he was able to read and understand it on the basis of his knowledge of Yucatecan Maya. In the case of longer passages in which the Spanish appears to deviate markedly from the Chontal, the translation is based on the Spanish and a suggested reading of the Chontal is given in the notes. Section IIIb is necessarily based entirely on the Spanish, as we do not have a Chontal equivalent for this section.

It was also decided to indicate, as far as possible, words and phrases found in the Spanish version but not in the Text, and vice versa. This has been done by the use of different kinds of type. Small capitals have been used for words in the Spanish version but not found in the Text, and italics for words in the Text but not in the Spanish. Parentheses indicate explanatory material introduced by the translators. Interpolation of words and phrases in the translation is shown by square brackets.

With the exception of certain names for which modern spelling has become standardized, Indian names are spelled as in the Chontal. The letter ɔ has been transcribed as dz.

The English translation is offered as a tentative rendering of the Text, and by no means as an accurate version in all respects. Study of the Text by specialists in the Maya languages will undoubtedly result in corrections and emendations, and in different interpretations of various passages.

FACSIMILES OF THE CHONTAL TEXT

El juramento que eso tiene en lo qual se afir=
mo e Ratifico e lo firmo de su nombre e cedho alcalde
Alonsso perez = francisco sanchez escrivan ante mi
Jhoan martin escrivano muy publico

Martin maldonado vecino e alcalde de semejante de camino
estante ael presente en este pueblo de tige y digo que
a mi noticia es venido que don pablo pareblo conve...
do señor natural deste pueblo y sus sujetos
a que eso tiene en su poder unos papeles de cierta
voluntad en que por ellos hace declaracion de mis vis...
pueblos y tara pueblos y de su descendencia y genealogia del
do homia pueblo y madre de como por ellos de tara fueron
señores naturales a quien los mas sujetos les conocieron
señorio y governando y administrando como se no... de
ella y porque a mi derecho conviene a uno como a persona
que le atiene haga demostracion de ella y sea entregu...
a mi muy deste ho pueblo para que de ellos me saque
un traslado o dos autorizados por el dho muy jurante
e alcaldes deste ho pueblo para que a gasee y apara
da comprobar mis muy reales que conpetente para
mayor abundamiento y conservacion de una prueba
za que pretendo hazer de perpetua y rey memoria para
pedir mercedes de los servicios que ellos dhos mis antepa-
sados hizieron a su magestad por tanto

...ndo su pedro asi como haga segund como lo ren
... no que en ello se me hara buena obra y man
dar al dho muy mere una tanto de los dhos papeles
en calendua de los naturales de una se le vuel...
va el original y eso jus la sexta Martin maldonado

auto y ha exausida una e don pablo gain cane permientos a

despues desta
peticion bac
crito en le-
gua de la na-
tural y esti-
que el prou.
ymº con este
lacion y con
forme a lo q
di m mayor.
cabeça desto
pº u nosoda
ca. Lo q ansi
esta la escriua
sino la traduc
tacion que ellos
segibo por ynter
pº co. Buelta
en castellano
a ca letra. Cha
a delante ap
mezeremito.

Vtzani ah lechuca Vxkiuanol caça Vcicinal Vha
Çem Vhalzoy lectayun ah lechuca martin macdonca
do tilua Vigelen audoricar Çupam Vcauedoilaça
Vhal Vyame Vtyae tzan iÿeix Vhaçi Vfirma. don
Pabco paxbolon

Ça don paxbolon Çuy Vubeico Viriaçtixyel Vixaça co
Ço ge Çibicta mexico tzan Vhal Çuan Çaptista Çuy cg
Mi oniÿi Vnacaçibae Çuay

Viriaçº Vhaua santamaria tixyel Vpaçotel Vhaba
Çuicca yl sam francisco cem Pel Ser Vprouinzia il ÿucatn
tulaçum Pel Vkinie V. genero de 1567 años ÿainob
francisco efecipe Çitÿoe luis garcia. Al cacdesob ÿayitÿo
Çob alonssomiartin pedro nava hernando hanan
mronqui vir Secidortesob tu Vaynal canoaÿaulea
Çumaç Çaracpabri. Ça don Çuan Çaprista Çuy Viriabº
Çain don pabco paxbolon gouernadoz Viracaÿai,
ÿ maÇi Vpakibae Vharmñel tucanue Xi Viccanob
Vhae yoe aeÿuobinÿol yunilm Zbaÿecaÿi Zbaÿoen
Çi Vmamob Vpaÿoob. aÿauanisobi ÿainob Vÿectce
Vtzaniob Vhabâ alonsso ÿacbaeam Çitÿoe luistuÇim
Nuexibiebaob Vnacaçibae aÿautaana Laÿ

N acahibae auxaual talicuaumil tali Vÿuaça
bie cabob Vÿ hoñ Vmole cag. tanodie yitÿoe Vnuca
Çob - Çunga = Çitÿoe = Çaxoe = Çitÿoe = çacbaeam = Vym
tucib = paxmucu = ÿainix Vbcob. Çeaçÿvaeabob ÿai

tali tuekadie ahau Çaçimal Vhaba Vppeñelacob
Aual Çibiel Vhaba Çagamay

tali Vÿux Çac aÿauob Vhaua Çampel Vpeñelÿva
Çimae acatÿaniÿi ÿaingampeti ÿainxaÿ ahauÿu
ual Çuei Çeÿu ce cabob Fareniam ÿatupaf Bolon lamat
Çermino Vtzamaeliÿebee Çuei Çabib Ïraÿa

ya del boca nueva ꝯ el ꝫ uei sol tun bueytos contiro
tzemeeli — tali vyam yac ahau vhaua pax
va vppenel gan pel acatzanizi gain agau uexe va
zagueei vinie trixg el tamae vxcal izin hal gao cage
gob tixg el cagi vtacei gobona b vkatunino b yebaxan joo
ton yitzoc cae tam yitoc apop omena zitza acueyeg tabes
cielo vhaua vaeecay vyacti obixca b tix g el bixio b tama
tun acaeon yaain veagi cia go b tayel ya la caga la agua
tecpano b tuxah gaa gaino b vpa yo lei vuinci lee yb
tapamne cato b gain xaug ahau paxua hainix vyue
vca b eiag mazate cat yitzoc vulo b eix vta va gio vab
yataa taeon — vho ya c ahau vhaua pagi
ma eagix zitzoc mae vaadin yidin penel paxua b
hain xag me agau yuual bixitagac temae yatu vat
vahgacae ꝫ opel vacpel abisa b vkotelo b yuual ta
yuual vyoyel vatun tuba ya koroba li yulo bagae
abal veeon cae bizimit avi haua veapirno b ca
gix abi vhata vae tuba pagima eagix agau vchepa
tan tuba cavilcae vhaeix abinamag yo lya heagix
vlota vel cavilcea vo b vpetel cagi vkatun alo b tamal
abvegan kae kin yuual vkatuno b talio b cuvano b
tu ꝫ aeuo hoko b aaeon vo ꝫ uci ca vo b tagae hern
yum vanix taagaulee mae va abin yiyi pagi ma eagix
acatzanizi — vuac yac ahau vhaua vaxo b
on aga vppenel pagima laꝫix gainix agau yu ual
vyue ꝫicas yꝫom hanae acaeon gaix cahalo b yuual
ꝫ ueca stieean vinie cajoirem mai que ꝫ del valee
gaina hau vaxbolonaga acatzanizi ayan vxtuli
vppenelo b pagima eagix vhava don luis paxua
vhaua vppenel gaix nix came vu yiyi vgatulib
vppenel — alamatuze l gainix vpa y don pablo
vyixtulie vppenel don pedro paxtun vyiha ꝫ

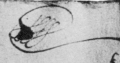

tlacamacaz ani yppenel ———— Vue dacdon
Vasco paxColon aça goueinadoz Vacca yppenel
Alamataz Lacasioksi ————————

Viaçidi axupi Vkarinteli Vrcanos çatul nucXibi L
Caos. Alonssol sacbalam zitsoc huis tuzincocoxcagaui
A hautitsanos gaindaga. Ti vcanonti Cellcasos ycu
tzani dupamos Sernandogenani antonquiuit alonso
May testigos sos aototnalcos tutogal zutualcatie
Firmaos Alcalexsos zitsoc ca filma nadon
Felipe = Luis garcia = Alonssumartin = pedro na Va=
Kernando Kanan = antonquiuit. = dae vamautitsan
nay nadon = Zuen Captista. Escriuano ————

Sain don Paolo Vax Colon gouernadoz Vaccea nup
ti zitsoc donaysauel ani Vppenel dona cataeina Vka
Casamix Menupti zitsoc francisco maldonado. cadra
CCan Uinie ————— from maldonado zitsoc dona cata
=ina acatzani ani Vppeneloos Martin maldonado sain
ayan Vaceeay u ————————

Faeuzann donaysauel aca tsamiz genupti don paolo
Vax Colon gouernadoz zitsoc doña menzia Vppenel
Dicos deorunti ani Vppeneloos maria Vkaba gaina m
Vaeeeay ——————

Fu. 22. Ukinie V. Zueuo de 1612 als nadon paolo
Vax Colon. Buiy tubacaça tate celos Unucae Vinicos
marcos Sacbalam alcaede Zuan Sacegan francisco
tuzin Reoidoresso os zitsoc ye Celos aous tin pax Uo
Lon aeonsopazinColon Carrassaz paptu cun a ca
Kici dupamos zubinos Utsuntel ypazolee Uuir
ci lee donpablo vaxColon gouernadoz ygeutzanios
tuxagaui malabayan mato Kitsanobi egeix Uzan
Uthaniobs dayuualçaos Kaba Vfirmaobi egenae

ta don Juan Zunal cabeça firma = marcos Baçbalin
Juan Baççan = françisco tuxin = agustin vax Colon
Alonso patzin Colon Baltasar pastilcan = tacpa
mauti = Pablo vax Colon Escriuano
Au. S. Ultinil v. Juecio 1612 as acasocsi vkaba vhicol
v cazil amal tun acalan dibil vkaçob vue vinico
capapob alsin Laulol vnacaçibal casibtipam çob çu
caguani v Sau vax Colon aga vkaba yn dibla

Acalan Zhçan Konae	cas	tomcut	cas
tahobo	cah	kançicix	cas
tapio	cas	Fauentuppoltun	cas
tabacau	cas	gomocria	cas
cacmuenal	cas	Haocabal	cas
Hanauibcas	cas	tahuli	cas
tauicabal	cas	cacçute	cas
tazkakalaez	cas	Hauiviz	cas
tavacauizcas	cas	tappottelal	cas
tixkomulim	cas	tapaxtok	cas
temacomcgutte	cas	tascgaccgauac	cas
tascczxutz	cas	tahucaycas	cas
takimelal	cas	Dacibperette	cas
tatok	cas	tasicilia	cas
temauibc	cas	tayaxttelal	cas
Detenmax	cas	tayaxakcas	cas
tacgaham	cas	vhixahgayayun vanicas hinza
tazel	cas	kepa Lukub mexicano zgatemue
temax	cas	taynpicac	cas
tagaal konttelae	cas	tas busil	cas
tagmacin	cas	gokna vic	cas
takom ricac	cas	tabis cabal	cas
tagcazcas	cas	tano sun	cas
Detenaku	cas	koncum	cas
Vxbeton	cas	tapaxua	cas
Vatug colon nixtle	cas	Vaxgopat	cas
takulku	cas	tapob	cas

Ahqimaytun	caç	tabolay	caç
Adomuizcab	caç	tabom	caç
tabcacab	caç	tapulcem ttelal	caç
tiximalindunum	caç	tuçolçam	caç
tabiscabal	caç	tacacjical	caç
Acmomoncab	caç	ootcac	caç
tacijcabal	caç	tajumuycal	caç
tuçolçam	caç	tacchimal	caç
taykbalcun	caç	jaxajintun	caç
tanothich	caç	taskomcal	caç
tamultun	caç	timocz	caç
		taycijlak	caç

67 — Pueblos

Jun Ucaçibae tatecol tacalob tamae tun Ukaba
ta Ubatsan acaean Ukaba ternedizam Upetelmae
tun Uinicob yeUagecel Ukuculcaç DiUic Uçiçilbel
tupatay hayn xaq Ukaba Unocaçilob y kin kanaae
yacaç Uani yaçauob paxbolonaça Ukaba gay nix
Meyuual ya haueee yitçoezhuae Zahaueee baslegon
Nae Unucuin çilob y Lay= mutuzim açau= kinzueri
Daxayato= tamalça xun= Ukabaob yokcadkeeni
Uinicob tuçabie 1527. aç Ukaba capiran donmin
tincortez. Yaoçiob dañodie nimiob tayixçoçiob tun
Domcal caeçutte kotitaiteetelob tacaç tuxaltça a
Daix deeeob yitçe Ucuçuelob caçi Uzitçocbel paxbolon
aça aBauacatzanizi cahixmeabi Umorbel Ubaob
cabbel ahaueee baob= çebaraUunim baaçaueelba
çebaatapain ba açaueelba çeba tacactob aaçaueelba
Ukalnamaç çuKaba yay uueea Uomel Uaiccubelob
ntanamaçob çon KuUelab aicatçeme ahixçmic
Uti Utzin çocbelob ççuKabaem tta Day kil açix Ubi
xel Utçometula Uççun ahau. yaix Uçun Uom

A Kçiabi oknotiçinil Padre fr ai diego de Çeçar tali
tabasco ya ixcabi Vnuyylob caçi caçi Vtçan del tuua
cayum capap vixay atalon ca cacanet Vtçon xcay me
V petel cappenelob La atalon a cac ticotol cacab ya acalon
tamacetuni Vtsappel Vkaba Vkalta licet ay ec recon
tacçi için a cante camon yitsocob tuua Vtçon thu diost
a kay cubi Vpecçil Ditayuual Vyoy elçaa tupom Vinic
akala padre Eti yuual cap Kupan yitsocob sai nix Kal
atalon ca ca canet Laçi çeabi Vtçon paxtina Baçi
thoc Vlotobta Liçix Vyubi Padre fr ai diego de Çeçar
Vtçon Vinicobi = caçi Vtçan bel cappenelob La axay
çaçani caçin Vkal yuual akup mea Vpael a pixon
La tukab ciçinobi y uual akup anea aVubin aca
Nela Vtçan diossi Vkalsain xay cabi çi ec capatçini çi
thocobi padreoni yeix me Enimaya y uual a cacebal
talce Vkaçyon capatan tuya del cir pradrei lo Di
Vtçi tactçan cut Le icetix tVacebal ya atalon = baçi
Campeç Baçan porvnic y a cnuypu caçon cel akala
çeabi Vtçan padri çe xay me cut Vcniob Cixin
cabob ya taca lan tamacetun = tali çix me aebikoti
taçumppel V, Vppiz Kinob Vtaçci y açamcel
padreob taçuculi Vtauio b xay campeçi Çaçanixay
V hin padreob ye eLyeix metali fr ai diego de Çeçar
Kotitamacetun a cacanntu 20. de abrie ñu açabil 1550:
Ae taya uual Vtçaçaçin tel Vkal Vpetel Vinic
caix yitso cintel Vpetel nuc Vinicob = Kinten cab = ce
Lutçolcan = Buluçaçi = çalçin = catçmatç = papcen
çi thoc bel nuc Vinicob Aebi tuua Vkal padre cappe
ne lob La axaçanet acaca non la a ça cme on la ocona t
La hum ppel ço Laçumppel Vkinic atonion ca ta vaner
La macha na caçin Vkal caçapau num yai Ltaçij taçucul
Kain xay na taçul z uual actçome çaba La namay çuual

Vtzin Lintel yatul zumacil ygatul paz zuntul
xacz paz zahinoili ataloncaeme tacala caboleca
tacala Suntun tuldiossi Vxul tu vinci el diospapa
cil dioppeneccil dios espiritu sancto Vgeci vxingan
zitzoc namacz zecel zitzoc yecel Vtzandios tzanci
tubaob = colix zatalic Vpetel agcctez benon fa
cicinge abi tzan tzanci tubaob Vkalpadreob = ca
gix Vzapa az oel Vccanob yeca vicin az aucukut
ygan = yeca vicin ta dunum = yeca tagaotte = yg
ba atapan = tacactto zitzoc ye oec cicinob cagix Vla
ckcoel tupam fraidiego elele sar cagix Vpulcel
caix Vcantezacob tuba Vtzanol Vkatib haa
Paternoster ave maria Credo salve zitzoc arteiu
Los Dono caob _____
fahix akcel Vkabaob Don Pedro Paxtun Vkabali
Ahaudonmateo Vkabali kintencaob don francisco
Vkabali calzin ygcix cagi Vogcel taxplomoil Lob-
clain mucul ga yci viya Vkal vinicobi ge bay ltza
ba Vkaba cicin ge ba atabay Vkaba cicin egagc ba
yxgcl ye bacab tanil cactan zocoken Vkacii nobi
haynixme Vcacanob. tcmaeleecagi lmagca Vcamon
ficicin Vbixel zagameel Vkalob Vpulcob zz akcel
tapacib Vuinci el zitzoc Vgacel tupam tuzut vinic
Vpetel ygeix meta caticiain yeoel tali tupua Kat
Vcati zeoel Vkal Obakat Vcati _____
Axay caga ibi ctama egum tugalub Vinumel cas ticcan
Vinic acalan ctama cctun tunumel fran xil Lorenzo
coroy = zucian donzel = Vnocag clixacz paran V oixo tozael
zatabazco ctamal Vabacppel V = ctamal ycaygayel
V, yeoel naxacz maxg xotzol papa cgama ca xacz
hucuob Vpatmob zitzoc oaob zitzoc ygao porri akacz
nok = buul zg xilm zga il = icz = tinam homisanac

yebel volbacal xag kuxbil bukbil v yocel pariny a
tavazcoy tuba=palma= cayx vlya akcel cag tu tiab dicoy
de aionda macdui yitgocob magimac y yaki cag tubabi
xi hixcanypeig ta cate dicos deaian da acatgani hayniix
vkal cagipatam yatacanpelsi ctacil gami dieco deatan
da nupti ymcisca de belazco yitgoc mtonocica m
ton vencia y xme en vlya bextegi v aci yati celpatam
yilapan gaixme vuual yakcel vatangilapam y uual
huli tomaslopez oy dortali cuatimaca dusabil ge
1552 ao haynix megen vxobijuuil paran tamal va
vacepel v yitgoc z hayppel patam yaa kia tamal va
vacepel v y tomas lopez xag vpa agi vpatrintel
hucub vpa agi a hag nok y xim yao pom buulcaal
oy ctinam hom cab yitgoc yebet vbi kital patanob
ayan tacaoob ctamactim acalam hainxag vkal ya
ki progido hes tuba agauob tacabil cab v geen
gouernar tubabelcag hain xag vtgani tucelobaak
vatan yitgoc yaa akcel v cus casticcon v vini e tugu gurpel
cah yncilan at hunpel pesso yapel desso humpel
tostun lsapel tomin vtocel ycebel tayaxg toticlaah
tamac hun aca aalam gafa lubal xag vbixel padre aca
tganiy =ani padre grai dieco de bexar tucga lub tali
Padre grai miquel de ua. vcina ke gaa ctupam vinic v
Chelen arminiztrar lacorame nt sob

Aa litixeme grai dieco pesquera tul galuboci xme u
ual vtgani v goget cag ctalic tixcget tul galubil xag vgur
tel Lita gouernadoril don Luis ya x ua vppenel vagi ima
Lahiix dibil vkaba. talgani tuguni xme vgabil 1557
ao ctaEnero cagi vtacel ayam potonob yitoca con pegob
v miem aboob ctixgelay vkal gagio vinic vkal yabi
yoconat ayanob ya ata aalam ctamac hun geabi vgic
vbialctacel vadieso b vgelen arminis trak sacamti
ya yitgoc humluub dili l xag takal xag vnimel vnouob
vtacel ctame dico leba. genichan = san agustin // santo

Pesquira. Vtanccib ci bal xag dios ytgoc Ley bixi eo б
za ananobi manotgan Vzic mirne L hoticet La talacai
tun = Sa ynixme v Kal zoco utz zubiob castielanbi
nicob

Au habie miel quinientos nobenta ynueve añu
tazuual vhucelob mazalvinicob vcocob gamcintelob
O Kal pedro zakimmy zatugolga y aij tzoc tmogan
Bimae zaxag y uual vxm breob zaxag aeizuual
Vt fim zena bzpl balob ytgoca cacalgu vbo relob
tacampel 5 ytgoc cadilab rbajtoc vpaeelob na kil
Kakinaeb gencon vxka kaltok — tixeem vza
b meul si eeos maget ytgoc nok vpetel xag zgu
Bom tuba anumeeob zatabij na kil Kakña Bl
taeizubiron paueo Vthan a buecelob a yon a teg
cgecob zatugolgaz ytgoc tang Kal vzucgaama ca
hiu Keta bel comission tuba dondieg o del eecazeo zo
tupeteni Lzucaton vKal bixie tamaltei L vpabani
atepp ege = akaix tuba yunaeib vbixteanvinitob
cotot nalob tigeLga ytgoc apopoLzaaamazab. tigun
tupagi iozaa haynixme cacotizitzbcob numontaes lan
zia tzoobcibij hokta vzue gabau zaixcgecti vpozelob
Onumibaeob ytgoc vbaeLib vKatiob atepp egeob
a catzanigi y beiix tibios hunum izatazuual ñala vtuz
thaneob azizmporonob vcacanob a gteppe geob hainix
Me vtzo xio bzata Kinacnal geix taliv vgoce Batuza
Kol vzuegauam tulab go legelob gaix caigucij tyocob
aca bkotoL tigan Kalob go Kalob ytgoc zixiLtacytgoc
Vfenelob gulob viixcgel tazuual vguardianiL pchaidi
mexia ytgoc v saldit chai Joseph bbzque caix zoziniel
gaa tupamzal vpenelob gaa ayanxag yatul vxiul nu
cobi mag ogol zda tupomnob ecyx vcaze vbel donpaelo
bage vzeaev iligai tubaototel hytgoc tubagiz zpakal
ytgoc vbzKcalau. tubagainixme vKaltazcintigfa Joseph

Vo3 que tzimeab ya ochi çi vaça paçi Vzuelatxm baz
camumon 3it3ocobi ʒa xay numi y çoli tuestancia chan
Macdonado kukix Vʒaxm tuba pance fraide3 m
Xiaʒbage yocotilcas ʒitʒoc telsutelac Vtcal
Vici ʒitʒoc yocono bacal tamiçaneal Vʒ3i vi xic
ototel3ai Vmoge baob a3 popol3a, mma 3aʒcabtian
tunpa caçix Vʒan belob tuba don paulo m Vpakin
mec La3alcas tabatm ba kaliçeic V3iç3 aticlob
ʒotrina ʒitʒoc taka ticob tuba sancto Euangelio, ca
kix niec nca ʒayc Vbel3 bubinuc Vi nicob V3 butʒanobi
caçix aciuabel ubinnuc Vi nicob gun tuba marco
de aguilar Encomendero tubacas tixgelaça çiix
caxix di bauel 3in çitʒocob tuba çun desmauria
desensoz Vkal3a nic Vkatm Vautoil Vliss
ʒl Vbixibal Vinic Vpetel cas ʒata Vʒuel3aexm
kaçnix men Vgeel alcanssar tui a tuiciensia y l Vʒan
dondieco delbcaʒic euu tucaçil calkini aixakei
Licensia tubaob Vkal Vbixibalob ʒatau Vʒuel3aexm
tiamolol Vnopetel bixiccas taci çix guei Licenssia
caiix Vthambel don paulo pax bolon gue madoʒ
Cageaguei Licensia Vbixibal caçta Vueba bati
çata çuual Vuice Vʒano3 Vbixibal Vgaʒiluba l
Padres san franciscob Viracas tixgel Vʒanca ʒun
La ley taci ta espana ogic cleriço talibi xio b pancoʒ
san fran, y ogi cleriço tacam un cas Vi ri xi gelay ʒainiço
Vkalmatʒunpi Vibelcas ʒatau ʒu3aexm Vkalna
malʒ ʒatʒabe3 cel Vabixel Vpetel Viniecocoʒaeç
tuguel Licensia bixiob y caçi Vkabaob çibibiçpet
hun caʒalaç ――――――――――― caçix Vhelee vadre
ʒuan Rodriquez eta Vovicarii Vil tuʒuuaei bʒon ʒuan
Bquierdo delespotu veteni l ʒucatan tuuaepeel ʒki
ni3 V henen tuʒaeil l 1603, ali ʒainixmeer
Vkal Vthani yoconataʒm Vʒueʒa eam Vʒabutul

Gil el duckin hob baal Isa ain pag to Juan
Rodriquez bizquel t sani ca 6 v akita pirabo
cassion il obactionil sanshelisthe san diego ca h
bue habin tu 23 ukinil vabui y uñe
biel mil y seisçientos y catorçe años

En la Villa y Puerto de sanfrancisco
de canpeche de Yucatana veinte y quatro dias
del mes de setiembre de mill y seiscientos y dieca
ante alonsso perez alcalde hordinario en esta
villa por su magestad y juez de comicio nonbrado
para en esta caussa la presento franciscoma[l]
donado con los recaudos que en ella refiere

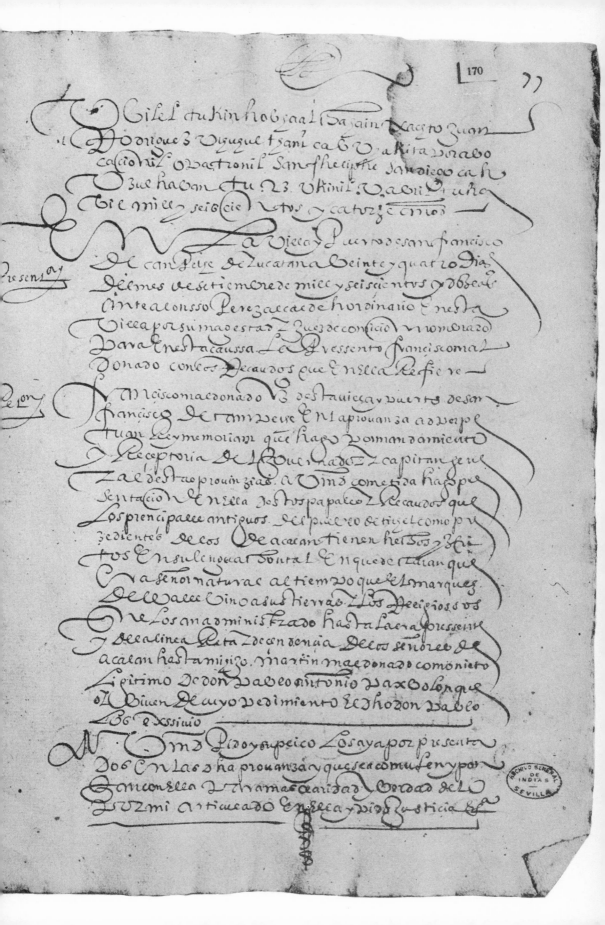

Francisco maldonado vº desta villa y puerto de san
francisco de canpeche en la apicuança ad verpe
tuan ley memoriam que hago por mandamiento
y Receptoria de la vueradez y capitan genel
zal destas prouinzias a uind cometida hago pre
sentacion en ella de los tos papales y recaudos que
los prencipales antiguos del pueço de tixel como pu
zedientes de los de acalan tienen helos y escri
tos en su lengua doutal en que declaran que
tixa señor natural al tiempo que el marquez
del valle vino a sus tierras y los deficioss vs
que los an administrado hasta la era pressente
y de la linea recta y decendencia de los señores de
acalan hasta mi hizo martin maedonado como nieto
ligitimo de don pabeo antonio paxbolonque
oy biuen de cuyo pedimiento el thodon pabeo
B6 e ssiuio

En una pido y supeico los aya por presenta
dos en las dichas prouanzas y ques se comusen y por
que conella vi erama caridad verdad de lo
vsv mi articueado en ella y pido justicia etc

SPANISH VERSION

Trasuntación de la relación que presentó Francisco Maldonado en lengua chontal.

[I]

Yo, Pablo Paxbolon, escribano público en este pueblo de Tichel, aquí traslado lo que está escrito en lengua mexicana por Juan Bautista, escribano, que murió mucho tiempo ha, que empieza de esta manera:

En el pueblo que se llama Santa María de Tichel en la jurisdicción y tierra de la villa de San Francisco de Campeche, provincia de Yucatán, a los diez días del mes de enero de mil quinientos sesenta y siete años, presentes Francisco Felipe y también Luis García, alcaldes, y también presentes Alonso Martín, Pedro Nagua, y Hernando Canan y Antón Quiuite, regidores, representando el gran rey, Su Majestad, y estando yo presente, Juan Bautista, escribano de este dicho pueblo, pareció Don Pablo Paxbolon, gobernador de este dicho pueblo, y dijo que tenía necesidad que tomasen los dichos de los viejos porque quiere saber y oír cómo empezó y cómo vienen sus abuelos y padres, reyes antiguos; lo cual declararon y dijeron los que se nombran Alonso Chagbalam y Luis Tuzin, muy viejos, que empieza como va abajo:

1. En el principio Auxagual, rey, vino de Cozumel, y habiendo cogido los pueblos de aquí, fué a recoger el pueblo de Tanoçica y los grandes principales Avtha llamados y también los Paxoques y también los Chacbalam, cuatro con los Paxmulu, y éstos llevó por compañeros y poblaron y cogieron aquellas tierras.

2. Y luego el segundo rey, llamado Pachimal, que dije arriba, hijo de Auxagual, escrito su nombre arriba.

3. El tercero rey se llamó Chanpel, hijo de Pachimal que dice arriba. Este Chanpel, éste era rey cuando fué a conquistar Tatenam, que es ahora Términos, y los demás fueron juntos a Boca Nueva y otros a Puerto Escondido.

4. Vino el cuarto rey, que se llamó Pexgua e hijo de Chanpel que ya dijimos. Este rey era el que pobló a Tichel. Por tiempo de sesenta u ochenta años estuvieron poblados allí. Empezó a venir guerras por los que poblaban a Chanpoton y Xicalan y Pomeba y los de Tabasquillo, y así dejaron a Tichel despoblado y se fueron a Magtun, que llaman Acalan, y allí estaban el pueblo de los quiaches, Tayel llamado, y también estaban Aziguatespanob[1] en la

[1] Here and elsewhere in the Spanish version the translators retained the Chontal plural ending -ob.

367

junta de los ríos, y desde éstos empezaban su tierra y gente hasta Istapa, de que era rey Paxgua. Y éste cogió el pueblo de los quiaches y los de Mazatecate y los Zulob, y así fueron señores de la tierra de Acalan.

5. El quinto rey se llamó Pachimalays, y también Maquabin, su hermano menor, e hijos de Paxguaob. En tiempo de este rey, a Chagtemal detrás de Bacalar cinco o seis años llegado, metió tributo en ellos.[2] En este tiempo llegaron los Zulob a tomar a Balancan. Ziçimite se llamaba su capitán, y pidióle a Pachimalays, rey, que parta el tributo de los pueblos, y porque no quiso dárselo se hizo con todos los pueblos y tuvieron guerra por tiempo de ochenta días, y a cabo de ellos se volvieron y llegaron [a] Acalan y conquistaron a Chacani. Y entonces empezó a reinar Macabin, hermano menor de Pachimalays que dijimos.

6. El sexto rey se llama Paxbolonacha, hijo de Pachimalays. Este era el rey que pobló Acalan. Y estando allí, vinieron los españoles, capitán, el Marqués del Valle. Este Rey Paxbolonacha tenía tres hijos llamados Pachimalays, que también tuvo un hijo llamado Don Luis Paxua, hijo suyo, y éste se huyó a Chiua; el segundo hijo, llamado Lamaateazel, y éste fué padre de Don Pablo Paxbolon; el tercero hijo se llamó Don Pedro Pastun. Este fué bautizado y no tuvo hijo.

7. Séptimo descendiente, Don Pablo Paxbolonacha, gobernador ahora, hijo de Lamateazel arriba escrito.

Aquí se acabó y feneció lo que se les preguntó y declararon los dos viejos, Alonso Chagbalam y Luis Tutzin. Solos éstos fueron los reyes que declararon, y que éstos guardaron los pueblos. Y así lo decla[ra]ron delante de Hernando Canan, Antón Quiuite[y] Alonso May, testigos, aquí vecinos, y por verdad puse las firmas de alcaldes y la mía como escribano. Francisco Felipe. Luis García. Alonso Martín. Pedro Nagua. Hernando Canan. Antón Quiuite. Pasó ante mí, Juan Bautista, escribano.

Don Pablo Paxbolon, gobernador ahora, se casó con Doña Isabel. Tuvieron por hija a Doña Catalina, que así se llamó, la cual se casó con Francisco Maldonado, español. Francisco Maldonado y Doña Catalina que dije tuvieron por hijo a Martín Maldonado, que vive ahora.

Murió Doña Isabel que dijimos. Se casó Don Pablo Paxbolon, gobernador, con Doña Mencía, hija de Diego de Orduña. Tuvieron una hija que se llama María, que vive hoy día.

[2] This sentence has been punctuated in accordance with what seems to be the meaning of the Spanish phraseology of the manuscript. Comparison with the Chontal Text shows that the translators left out a phrase about going to Chactemal. If we interpolate the word "fueron," the sentence might be punctuated as follows: "En tiempo de este rey [fueron] a Chagtemal; cinco o seis años llegado, metió tributo en ellos." It should be noted, however, that the Text is somewhat obscure at this point, and that this alternative reading may not reproduce the exact meaning of the Chontal. Cf. note 21, p. 385, *infra*.

En veinte y uno del mes de julio de mil seiscientos doce años, yo, Pablo Paxbolon, escribano de este pueblo, presentes los principales, Marcos Tekbalam, alcalde, Juan Chagchan, Francisco Tuzin, regidores, y los demás que se hallaron presentes, Agustín Paxbolon, Alonso Paxbolon, Baltasar Patuzin, les leí que lo oyeron la descendencia y genealogía de Don Pablo Paxbolon, gobernador. Dijeron que estaba cierta y verdadera, que no hay cosa que no lo sea, y por eso puse sus nombres y firmas aquí conmigo, que soy escribano. Marcos Thegbalam. Francisco Tuzin. Juan Chagchan. Agustín Paxbolon. Baltasar Pagtucum. Ante mí, Pablo Paxbolon, escribano.

[II]

En cinco del mes de julio de mil seiscientos doce años, trasladé los nombres y cuenta de los pueblos de los magtunes, que son chontales de Acalan, escritos por los principales, nuestros padres, que murieron antiguos; que empieza el primero el asiento del Rey Paxbolonacha, que así se llamaba, como se sigue:

[1]	El pueblo de Acalan que se llamó Ysancanac, pueblo.	
[2]	Tahobo	pueblo
[3]	Tahcab	pueblo
[4]	Tapib	pueblo
[5]	Xagmucnal	pueblo
[6]	Tanabibcab	pueblo
[7]	Tascabal	pueblo
[8]	Tahahalaez	pueblo
[9]	Tapacabichab	pueblo
[10]	Tixhancubim	pueblo
[11]	Tanaconchute	pueblo
[12]	Tahcehxecche	pueblo
[13]	Taunchelal	pueblo
[14]	Tatoh	pueblo
[15]	Tamabiz	pueblo
[16]	Petenmax	pueblo
[17]	Tachaham, que ahora se llama Chunab y está poblado *meya uinicob*	pueblo
[18]	Tayel	pueblo
[19]	Temax	pueblo
[20]	Tahaalcantelal	pueblo
[21]	Tamalin	pueblo
[22]	Tahomtilal	pueblo
[23]	Tahaazcab	pueblo
[24]	Petenhu	pueblo
[25]	Ubpeten	pueblo
[26]	Batunobonyzte	pueblo

[27]	Taboolho	pueblo
[28]	Tachimaytun	pueblo
[29]	Pambizcab	pueblo
[30]	Tazacab	pueblo
[31]	Tixmalinzum	pueblo
[32]	Tabiscabal	pueblo
[33]	Tazute	pueblo
[34]	Chanhixil	pueblo
[35]	Tahantopoltun	pueblo
[36]	Homolna	pueblo
[37]	Taholcabal	pueblo
[38]	Tahuh	pueblo
[39]	Xacchute	pueblo
[40]	Tahiuiz	pueblo
[41]	Tapontelal	pueblo
[42]	Tapastoh	pueblo
[43]	Tahchauac	pueblo
[44]	Tauhaycab	pueblo
[45]	Talibpetette	pueblo
[46]	Tachicua	pueblo
[47]	Tayaztelal	pueblo
[48]	Tayastab	pueblo
[49]	Taxaha, que tuvo veinte días Cortés, donde se cortó la cabeza al capitán mexicano, Quatemuco	pueblo
[50]	Tanpilal	pueblo
[51]	Tabubuzil	pueblo
[52]	Hohnacic	pueblo
[53]	Tabiscabal	pueblo
[54]	Tanoun	pueblo
[55]	Haulum	pueblo
[56]	Tapaxagua	pueblo
[57]	Yashopate	pueblo
[58]	Tapopo	pueblo
[59]	Tabolay	pueblo
[60]	Tampom	pueblo
[61]	Tapalentelal	pueblo
[62]	Taholam	pueblo
[63]	Tazachilal	pueblo
[64]	Boteac	pueblo
[65]	Tazumuycab	pueblo
[66]	Tamonhab	pueblo
[67]	Tahchicamal	pueblo
[68]	Yahintum	pueblo
[69]	Tahomhab	pueblo

[70]	Temohoche	pueblo
[71]	Tayshilal	pueblo
[72]	Tahichibal	pueblo
[73]	Taholam	pueblo
[74]	Taysbalam	pueblo
[75]	Tanochihe	pueblo
[76]	Tamultum	pueblo

Setenta y seis pueblos

[IIIa]

El principio que empezó, estando en sus pueblos los Tamagtun, que se llama Chontal, y Acalan en mexicano, los indios magtunes, como parece por sus pueblos en que asistían,[3] que la cabecera se llamaba Yxamhanac, y allí estaba el Rey Paxbolonacha, que así se llamaba, que éste era su reino, teniendo sus gobernadores, principales, Mutuzin, rey, Hinzuti, Pazayatomal y Cixun, que así se llamaban.

Vinieron los españoles a esta tierra en el año de mil quinientos veinte y siete. El capitán se llamaba Don Martín Cortés. Que entraron por Tanoçic y pasaron por el pueblo de Taxich y salieron al principio de la tierra de Xacchute y llegaron a proveerse en el pueblo de Taxahhaa. Y estando allí con toda su gente, enviaron a llamar a Paxbolonacha, rey, que ya dijimos, el cual recogió todos sus principales de todos sus pueblos, del pueblo de Taxunum y los principales del pueblo de Chabte y los principales del pueblo de Atapan y los principales del pueblo de Tatzanto, porque no se podía hacer cosa sin dar parte a estos principales. Comunicó lo que se había de tratar del caso, [por] los cuales fué consultado lo que convenía en su gobierno y que envi[a]ban a llamar por el capitán de ellos españoles que estaban en el pueblo de Xachaa; los cuales dijeron no convenía fuese su rey al llamado de los españoles porque no sabían lo que querían. Entonces se levantó y dijo uno de los principales, llamado Chocpaloquem: "Rey y señor, está tú en tu reino y ciudad, que yo quiero ir a ver lo que quieren los españoles." Y así fué con los demás principales, que se llamaban Pazinchiquigua y Paxguaapuc y Paxchagchan, compañeros de Paloquem, en nombre del rey. Y llegados ante el Capitán del Valle, español, y de los españoles no les creyeron, porque debía de haber entre ellos quien les dijese no venía allí el rey de que llamaba. Y así les dijo el capitán: "Venga el rey, que le quiero ver, que no vengo a guerras ni a hacerle mal, que no quiero sino pasar a ver tierra, cuanta hay que ver, que yo le haré mucho bien si él me recibe bien." Y habiéndolo entendido los que venían en nombre del rey, se volvieron y dijeron a Paxbolonacha, su rey, que estaba en el pueblo aguardando; los

---

[3] The Spanish phraseology here is obscure. Cf. English translation and note 62, p. 389, *infra*.

cuales llegados, se recogieron todos los principales y les dijo: "Quiero irme a ver con el capitán y españoles, que les quiero ver y saber qué quieren y a qué han venido." Y así fué Paxbolonacha.

Sabido por los españoles, le salieron a recibir, y el Capitán del Valle con ellos. Y les llevaron mucho presente de miel, gallinas de la tierra, maíz, copal y mucha fruta. Y dijo el capitán: "Rey Paxbolon, aquí he venido a tus tierras, que soy enviado por el señor del mundo, emperador, que está en su trono en Castilla, que me envía a ver la tierra y de qué gente está poblada; que no vengo a guerras, que sólo te pido me despaches para Ulúa, que es México, y la tierra donde se coge la plata y la plumería y el cacao, que eso quiero ir a ver." Y así le respondió que mucho de enhorabuena le daría paso, y que se fuese con él a su ciudad y tierra y que allí tratarían lo que más convenía. Y respondióle el capitán que descansase, que sí, haría. Y antes tuvieron veinte días descansando.

Y estaba allí Quatemuc, rey de Nueva España, que venía con el capitán de México; el cual habló con Paxbolonacha, rey: "Señor rey, estos españoles, vendrá tiempo que nos den mucho trabajo y nos hagan mucho mal y que matarán nuestros pueblos. Yo soy de parecer que los matemos, que yo traigo mucha gente y vosotros sois muchos." Y esto dijo Quatemuco a Paxbolonacha, rey de los indios de Magtunes Chontales. Oído por él esta razón, le respondió: "Veréme en ello. Dejadlo ahora, que trataremos de ello." Y pensando sobre el caso, vió que los españoles no hacían malos tratamientos ni a ningún indio habían muerto ni aporreado, y que no les pedían sino miel, gallinas y maíz y demás frutas que les daban cada día, y considerando que pues no le hacían mal, no podía tener dos rostros con ellos ni enseñarles dos corazones con los españoles. Y Quatemuc le estaba siempre importunando en ello porque los quisiera matar a todos los españoles; y visto e importunado, Paxbolonacha se fué al Capitán del Valle y le dijo, "Señor Capitán del Valle, este principal y capitán de los mexicanos que traes, anda con cuidado con él no te haga alguna traición, porque tres o cuatro veces me ha tratado que os matemos." Oído esto por el Capitán del Valle, prendió a Cuatemuc y le echó en prisiones, y al tercer día que estuvo preso le sacaron y le bautizaron, y no se certifican si se puso por nombre Don Juan o Don Fernando, y acabado de bautizarle, le cortaron la cabeza y fué clavada en una ceiba delante de la casa que había de la idolatría en el pueblo de Yaxzam.

Y luego partió el Capitán del Valle, y con él toda su gente y el Rey Paxbolonacha con toda su gente, y llegaron a la ciudad de Yzamcanac. Y estando allí, empezaron a trazar por qué parte se podía hacer puente para poder pasar el río con todo el ejército, que tendría una legua de travesía con sus bajíos; y así se empezó a henchir los bajíos y a hacer la puente, que se acabó dentro de dos días por la mucha gente que había. Y también limpiaron el camino hasta los quiaches, y se despacharon dos principales que fuesen a llevar el mensaje de la ida de los españoles, que se llamaban Çeluteapach[y]Macuagua. Y el Leluteapeche (*sic*) mataron los quiachob, y el compañero se huyó y volvió a la ciudad de Yzancan donde había salido y con[tó] todo lo que les había pasado, por lo cual los españoles fueron con algún recelo. Y con todo eso mataron cinco o seis de los más valientes a la llegada de los quiaches. Y desde allí fueron los quiaches limpiando camino hasta Tayza. Visto no podían pasar a la isla por el agua, se volvieron y tomaron el camino y salieron a Chanpoton.

Un año pasado que los españoles y el Capitán del Valle estuvieron en Acalan, se fué Paxbolonacha a otro pueblo que se llama Tachacan, adonde murió, y los suyos le metieron en una cano[a] y lo trajeron [a] Acalan donde le enterraron. Tres años había que era muerto el rey y vinieron otros españoles y entraron y pasaron por donde el Capitán del Valle pasó, por el pueblo de Tehix y el pueblo de Çacchute. No se supo si traían capitán. Llamábanse de ellos Francisco Gil y Lorenzo Godoy y Julián Doncel, que eran las cabezas y mayores. Y habiendo llegado a la cabecera, preguntaron "¿Qué es del rey?" Y le respondieron que era muerto. Y preguntaron por sus hijos, los cuales les trajeron delante de ellos; y el mayor de ellos se llamaba Pachimalais, el segundo, Lamateazel, el más pequeño, Paxtun. El mayor de los tres lo metieron en prisión y le cerraron dos días, y le dijeron que les diese tributo, y así se les dió gallinas de la tierra y maíz, miel y copal, frísoles, pepitas y lo demás que había, que de todo fué mucho sin cuenta. Y por la puente pasaron y se fueron.

El Adelantado no pasó por Acalan, que es en Magtun; sólo su mandado llegó por él. Le vinieron a ver a Chanpoton porque allí se detuvo mucho, y allí le trajeron tributo y allí estuvieron con él mucho tiempo, y le pidieron los admitiese en su amparo. Y en este tiempo murió Pachimalays y entró en su lugar su hermano, Lamateazel. Y en su tiempo y gobierno fué la venida de los padres, Fray Luis de Villalpando, Fray Juan de la Puerta [y] Fray Lorenzo de Buenavenida (Bienvenida), los primeros padres de San Francisco. Y en este tiempo se estaban en su gentilidad [e] idolatría, y los españoles y los frailes dichos que vinieron entraron en la tierra y les fueron enseñando el verdadero camino y el verdadero Dios. Iban enseñando a todos, y que nuestros dioses ya habían acabádose y ya habían fenecido y [diciendo]: "En jamás veréis que se tornan[a] adorar y el que los adorare engañado va en su vivir y será castigado el que así lo hiciere, que ya se acabó ese tiempo de tratar con ellos; y mira que nadie engañe a las gentes porque ese tiempo ya pasó." Y esto oyeron todos los principales y el rey y todos sus pueblos lo que dijeron los padres sacerdotes.

Luego murió Lamateazel, su rey, y antes que muriese mandó llamar todos los principales. Y juntos, les dijo: "Ya me muero, y llevo dolor en mi corazón que no [he] alcanzado el ser cristiano y vivir con fe y no como vivimos. En acabándose mi vida os ruego os déis al servicio de otros dioses, porque veo y he oído que han de venir padres sacerdotes a bautizar y predicar y no se ha de acabar ni se ha de ver el fin. Ya viene la verdad y el bien que dicen, y así os encargo que lo busquéis y traigáis los padres predicadores para que os enseñen y encaminen en el verdadero camino." Y con esta palabra murió este Rey Lamateazel.

Entró en su lugar y gobierno Pastun, hermano menor, e hijo de Paxbolonacha. Y oyó la nueva de la predicación y bautismo que hacían los padres y púsose a considerar con todos los principales. Y llamaron todo el pueblo para que vayan a buscar los padres a Campeche, y así vino el Rey Pastun con sus gentes en busca de los padres a Campeche. Y Dios que lo ordenaba así otro día que llegaron a Chinil llegó el Padre Fray Diego de Béjar, que venía de Tabasco. Y allí se encontraron con él y dijéronle: "Padre y señor, aquí venimos a buscarte en nombre de todos mis hijos, y dejo todos mis pueblos y casa, que es Acalan que llaman Chontales, por venir por tí para que nos vengas a enseñar en la palabra de Dios y su fe, porque tengo noticia de que se van bautizando los naturales por vosotros padres, lo cual deseamos nosotros y por eso venimos a buscarte como padre." Y esto le dijo Pastun, gobernador, con sus compañeros.

Y habiéndolo oído el Padre Fray Diego Béjar lo que decían los indios les dijo: "Hijos míos, mucho me huelgo porque deseáis sacar vuestras almas de las manos de los demonios y que deseáis oír y saber la palabra de Dios porque ése es mi oficio y en que nos ejercitamos los padres, mas yo me holgaré poder luego ir con vosotros porque tengo que hacer con mis padres compañeros, y así me parece que os volváis, que presto volveré a Campeche o Chanpoton adonde encontraré los que vengan por mí por vosotros." Y así los consoló el padre y así se volvieron a su pueblo de Acalan de los chontales. Y llegado que fué un mes que señalaron de tiempo de enviar por el padre en canoa, y llegaron a Campeche, de que se holgaron los padres que allí estaban. Y así se vino con ellos Fray Diego de Béjar y llegaron a Matun de Acalan a veinte de abril de mil quinientos cincuenta, y con su llegada hubo gran regocijo en toda la gente.

Y luego llamó a todos los principales, Quintencab, Çelute Holcan, Buluheaçin, Calçin, Catanaz, Papeian y los demás principales y también su gobernador, Pastun, y díjoles el padre: "E hijos, mira que habéis ido en busca nuestra muy lejos, diez o quince días de camino. He venido a buscaros y acompañaros, de que me he holgado de recibir trabajos en el camino y en las canoas. Y mira, lo primero que os digo a vosotros que no se puede servir a dos señores ni a dos padres. A un padre es el que se ha de amar. Eso os vengo a decir, un solo Dios y tres personas, Dios Padre, Dios Hijo, Dios Espíritu Santo, el que crió el cielo y la tierra y todo cuanto hoy hay que se parece," con otras razones de Dios que les dijo.

Quería que viniesen todos a manifestar sus ídolos. Y oído por ellos lo que les dijo el padre, luego empezaron a sacar sus ídolos, y los primeros los ídolos del gobernador que se lleban (sic, llaman?) Huhuelechan y también el Quizin Tazumun y también Tabchete y también Atapan, Tazagto y los demás ídolos, todos los cuales trajeron ante el Padre Fray Diego de Béjar, el cual los quemó. Y luego los empezó a enseñar a rezar el Pater Noster y el Ave María y el Credo y la Salve y los artículos de la fe. Y luego les empezó a dar sus nombres. Don Pedro Pastun se nombró el gobernador. Don Mateo se llamó el sacerdote Quenintencanb. Don Francisco se llamó Halçin. Y así fueron entrando la cristiandad todos, chicos y grandes, que no quedó ninguno. Los ídolos escondidos en sus lugares secretos por los indios, Yhagua, que así se llamaba este ídolo, y otro que se llamaba Tabay y otro llamado Yschel, Cabtanilcab y otros muchos lugares de ídolos, los cuales se buscaron en todos los pueblos. Los que guardaban los ídolos fueron por ellos y los trajeron y quemaron, y echaron presos los que los guardaban y los azotaban delante del pueblo. Y con esto perecieron y acabaron los ídolos en los naturales, de ellos de voluntad, de ellos por miedo del castigo.

Ya dije atrás como desde que pasaron los españoles por Acalan la segunda vez, Francisco Gil, Lorenzo Godoy [y] Julián Doncel, desde entonces se empezó a pagar tributo y llevarlo a Tabasco cada seis meses y cada dos meses. No estaba tasado, sino cuando querían venían por lo que querían, como canoas, remos, miel, copal, gallinas, mantas, frísoles, maíz, pepitas, chile, algodón, calabazas y todo lo que había de comer y beber llevaban de tributo a Tabasco, porque allí empezamos a pagar tributo a Palma en el dicho Tabasco. Y después se encomendó en Diego de Aranda. No sabemos quién puso estos pueblos en la jurisdicción de Campeche. Y cuando murió Diego de Aranda, se casó Francisca de Velasco, su mujer, con Antón García, y el dicho Antón García mandó llevásemos el tributo a Chilapan.

Y en el tiempo vino Tomás López, oidor, de Guatemala en el año de mil quinientos cincuenta y dos años, el cual ordenó y trazó al tiempo que se había de pagar tributo, que es cada seis meses. El cual Tomás López quitó que no diésemos canoas y quitó gallinas, ropa, maíz, miel, copal, frísoles, pepitas, chile, algodón, calabazos, remos y las demás menudencias que dábamos los chontales de Acalan. Y éste dió provisiones a los gobernadores de los pueblos para gober-

nar sus pueblos y el que mandó que se pagase [a] los que llevasen los tributos y
los que cargasen las cargas de los españoles de un pueblo a otro, si era lejos un
peso y dos pesos, y a tostón y a dos tomines según el camino. Y todavía estaban
los pueblos en Magtun Acalan.

Y en este tiempo se fué el padre que dijimos, y volvió el padre otra vez.
Y después vino Fray Miguel de Vera a bautizar de todo punto la gente que
quedaba, y recibían los santos sacramentos. Otra vez volvió Fray Diego de
Pesquera, y les trató como convenía que se bajasen a Tichel, donde habían
estado otra vez, siendo gobernador o rey en esta provincia Don Luis Paxgua,
hijo de Pachimalais, que se dijo arriba. Y al principio del año de mil quinientos
cincuenta y siete vinieron los de Chanpoton y Campeche a desmontar y
limpiar el asiento de Tichel para que se bajasen los indios de Acalan, chontales.
Y porque estaban lejos y no podían los padres venir a menudo [a] administrar
los santos sacramentos, y porque allí era el paso de los padres que venían de
México a esta provincia, de San Francisco y San Agustín y clérigos y Santo
Domingo, y les enseñarían la palabra de Dios cuando pasasen, y también los
españoles, y también porque estarían cerca del gobernador, justicia mayor,
enviado por Su Majestad, el rey, que administra justicia a los maceguales y
naturales; y todas estas causas, movió a los padres a traerlos al asiento de
Tichel; y también porque lo quería el encomendero, Antón García, y por
tiempo de cuatro años les quitó el tributo hasta que se rehiciesen en el nuevo
asiento de Tichel. Y fué en el dicho año de mil quinientos cincuenta y siete a
los diez días de julio. Y a los veinte y dos del dicho mes, día de Santa María
Magdalena, se huyó Don Luis, su gobernador, y se huyó por el Baradero y se
fué al asiento de Chiua donde murió. Y luego el año venidero de mil quinientos
cincuenta y ocho, a veinte y cinco de abril se descubrió este pueblo de Chigua
por Don Pablo y allí supo la muerte, y a todos fué notorio que murió de
enfermedad.

Habíanse pasado el año de cincuenta y ocho y cincuenta y nueve; aun no
habían acabado los indios chontales de dejar su asiento de Acalan, que un
principal llamado Don Tomás Maqua los detenía en el pueblo de Chauhix y
empezaron a tener pleitos y pesadumbres con los que iban de Tichel por de
comer de lo que habían dejado, y allí los cogían y amarraban y azotaban y
les quitaban las canoas. Y también había poblado Tixbavmicha; que idolatraban
sus ídolos, que ya se querían huir todos los indios. Y quiso Dios que viniesen los
españoles en este tiempo a Tichel, que serían treinta soldados. Principales de
ellos eran Castrillo, Juan Vela [y] Tamayo, que no sé cuál de ellos era el
capitán, que a solos los tres respetaban; que los habían llamado los oidores de
Guatemala que fuesen a tomar la provincia de los lacandones y del Popo, y

aquí se quedaron en Tichel porque supieron que se había vuelto el Licenciado Ramírez, que iba por capitán de esta entrada, que había tomado la tierra y gente de los Popos. Y visto por el Padre Pesquera, y que también era servicio de Dios y del rey que fuesen [a] Acalan y que bajasen todos los indios que se habían quedado y alzado, y que podría ser que pasasen bien y pudiesen llegar a los [la]candones; y oído por los españoles, pareció bien.

[IIIb]

Y ellos bajaron al pueblo de Bote y al pueblo de Açilbaob y al pueblo de Tutul y los de Panob y fueron al asiento de Acalan y prendieron a Don Tomás Maqua y a Martín Acha y a Jorge Laon y a Alonso Pacbac y a todo el pueblo bajaron y los que estaban en Tixbaumilha. Y los bajaron a Tichel en el año de mil quinientos sesenta, por lo cual hubo muy grande hambre y ésta fué la causa por qué Francisco Acuz y Diego Pascanan y también Achachu y Gonzalo Pazcanan y Martín Pagtum, que serían sin cuenta, y sus gentes y sus viejos se huyeron. Los cuales sacó Don Pablo Paxbolon y halló en el asiento de Sugte, como más claro consta por la probanza de Don Pablo Paxbolon, gobernador, que en el año que entró a gobernar los fué a buscar. Y se tornaron a huir año de mil quinientos sesenta y ocho, y juntamente los tornó a hallar y con los que se habían huído de antes de ser bautizados, que vivían en el pueblo de Chacam. Y la causa de que se habían huído estos antiguos fué de que los vendrían y los afligían sus amos porque eran esclavos del rey y demás principales. Se llamaban Lamate, Chacantun, Paçimagtun, Atoxpeche, Apastucum, Paxbolon, Chancha, Paloquem y los demás, que serían como seiscientos con sus hijos y mujeres.

Y así como los halló avisó de ello a Don Luis de Céspedes, que era gobernador en esta provincia y estaba en la ciudad de Mérida, en la lengua yucateca se llama Taho, siendo obispo y primero de este obispado Fray Francisco Toral de la Orden de San Francisco, el cual envió a Fray Juan de Santa María de la Orden de la Merced. Este fué a doctrinarlos y bautizarlos los indios descubiertos, y se nombró su pueblo de Sapotitanil por no saber el nombre de aquella tierra, porque algunos principales le nombraban Tachumbay y otros Tachalte y otros la decían Tanaboo y otros Tamucuy, y por esto se le puso el nombre de Xapotitanil; por los cuales pasó este pueblo de Tichel mucho trabajo por la comisión que tenía Don Pablo Paxbolon, nuestro gobernador, del gobernador que asistía en la ciudad de Mérida, con la cual nos hacía que limpiásemos los caminos y rompiésemos los malos saltos del río de Acalan por donde pasase el padre, y le cargásemos en silla por donde no podía pasar, para que viniesen a ser cristianos los infieles que estaban en Xapotitan, según hemos dicho, y para llevar ornamentos de nuestra iglesia, como cáliz, misal, casulla, frontal, aderezo para la misa y también las imágenes. Y nuestros hijos fueron a enseñarles la doctrina cristiana. Y así propio hizo fuésemos otros el año de mil quinientos setenta, que fuimos a Puylha y también a Tabalam a sacar los cimarrones, en que pasamos mucho trabajo en llevar al padre, que se llamaba Gabriel de Rueda, clérigo, y también el Padre Monserrate, que era nuestro vicario en Tichel. Y porque estaban lejos, los trajeron a poblar en Hunlucho y allí vivieron, y allí les llevamos ornamentos y frontal y llevar a menudo el ministro. Y así se poblaron los de Çapotitan y Xoquelha.

En el año de mil quinientos setenta y cuatro, a veinte y cinco de abril, supo Don Pablo Paxbolon como Luis Queh del pueblo de Xocolha había ido entre los indios cimarrones y que sabía su pueblo, y mandóle llamarlo, y también a Juan Chab, a cabeza del dicho pueblo para preguntarles y saber la verdad de lo que habían visto. Y venidos le preguntó Don Pablo: "¿Es verdad que habéis estado con los idólatras?" los cuales respondieron que era verdad que habían visto sus casas y su pueblo, mas que no sabían cómo se llamaba ni qué tanta gente era.

Sabido por Don Pablo, quiso luego ir allá en virtud de las comisiones que tenía de los gobernadores que gobernaban esta provincia para el efecto de sacar los tales cimarrones idólatras. Y llamó sus gentes chontales y escogió hasta ciento de ellos del pueblo de Tichel, y abrimos camino desde Çapotitan hasta Cocolha, llevando nuestras armas de arco y flechas, rodelas y lanzas para lo que fuese menester. Y salimos de Cocolha y llegamos [a] Tachunyupi y allí hicimos noche, y por la mañana partimos todos y a la hora de vísperas llegamos a su pueblo. Y los cogimos descuidados y de las mujeres se huyeron algunos, y los varones tomaron sus arcos y flechas y se vinieron contra nosotros. Y entonces les habló Don Pablo: "No tiréis las flechas ni haya muertes, porque nosotros no venimos a mataros ni tampoco venimos por vosotros, que sólo vengo a veros para deciros a vosotros la palabra de Dios y a lo que me envía el gran Rey, mi señor, que me manda que os ame." De ellos les pareció bien esta razón, de ellos no, y uno de ellos, que se llamaba Pazelic [Pazelu?], fué a desembrazar su flecha para tirar a Don Pablo, y por detrás le asieron el brazo Juan Chab, maestro de Cocolha, que ya dijimos. Y visto por los principales cimarrones idólatras, que se llamaban Paxmulu y otros Paxtun, que era Don Pablo, se fueron a él y le dijeron: "Señor, si vienes a guerra o vienes por nosotros o vienes a matarnos, aquí estamos nosotros. Haz lo que quisieres." Respondióles: "Señores, no vengo a guerra ni vengo a prenderos; sólo vengo a predicaros la palabra de Dios y lo que manda Su Majestad que os diga para que todos nos queramos y tengamos una misma voluntad de un corazón para que amemos a Dios y nos rijamos con la justicia de Su Majestad que es el buen vivir, y esto es a lo que vengo, y abrir camino, que a eso venimos tantos. Y si traemos armas, es para asegurarnos de lo que nos puede suceder, que no sabemos con qué gente encontraremos." Y oídas estas razones por ellos, se asosegaron. Y mientras esto pasó se había ido toda la gente, mujeres, muchachos, que casi no quedaban sino pocos en el pueblo, que no se vieron. Y visto por Don Pablo como no había gente, les preguntó por ella y que los llamasen y recogiesen y asegurasen, y así sosegó sus corazones y así trataron de recoger la gente, la cual se recogió dentro de dos o tres días que no faltó ninguno. Y para asegurarlos, les rogó y llamó que de ellos se fuese a ver el pueblo de Tichel y verían el padre y los españoles.

Y traídos a nuestro pueblo, se les cortó el cabello y los festejaron y los llevaron a ver el padre que nos administraban, de San Francisco, que se llamaba Fray Bartolomé Garzón, en el año de mil quinientos setenta y cinco. Y les empezó a enseñar las cuatro oraciones y los artículos, mandamientos y lo que manda la Santa Madre Iglesia, y habiéndolo aprendido, los bautizó el padre. Y de esta iglesia les llevaron ornamentos e imágenes, que siempre se ha llevado el adorno para el oficio divino y por ello siempre hemos tenido mucho trabajo, y lo propio lo recibieron nuestros padres, como parece a los principios de este escrito, al tiempo que el Capitán del Valle salió a nuestra tierra, y siempre pagando tributo al Rey, nuestro señor, como está escrito en el año de mil quinientos veinte y siete. Es ahora Chiua este pueblo dicho arriba.

Memoria como fueron y entraron [a] hacer cristianos los infieles por nosotros, los indios chontales que vivimos en Tichel.

En el año de mil quinientos ochenta y tres vinieron los que se le escaparon de la muerte, uno de los cuales salió a Chencan, llamado Pedro Chan, el cual, tomando la costa de la mar la vuelta del sur, fué a dar adonde estaba Don Pablo Paxbolon en su estancia, que es junto a Tichel, que allí vive. Y empezó a llorar cuando llegó con sus hijos muy flacos y él flechado en medio de las espaldas, y dijo: "Señor Don Pablo Paxbolon, aquí vengo a decirte que somos las sobras que han quedado y escapado de la muerte, que mataron mis compañeros por los cimarrones de Chunguiyzili, que se llaman Aquebob, que son muchos. Y nosotros somos de Xequelchecan y venimos a Hunguizil y vinieron los Aquelbes (sic) cimarrones a matarnos. De ellos flecharon, de ellos alancearon; mataron nuestros viejos y principales que nos regían y el ahcuxcab Tuyo, que en nuestro nombre se decía Açitiache. Y matamos cinco o seis de ellos. De mis compañeros murieron muchos, y muchos se huyeron, y a mí me flecharon en medio de la espalda. Y de mis compañeros fueron al monte y de ellos se volvieron a Xequelchecan; de ellos y muchachos, mujeres y algunos hombres se fueron por allí sin saber adónde." Y oído por Don Pablo que andaban derramados por el monte aquellas gentes sin saber dónde fuesen y que era de temer no pereciesen de hambre y sed, se fué para Xocola y Sapotitan de su jurisdicción y que había sacado del monte, y los recogió y despachó al monte a partes y lugares que podrían haber aportado, echando cuadrillas de gente por todas partes y encargándoles recogiesen aquellas gentes de Xequelchecan que andaban perdidas y desparramadas por los cimarrones. Los de Xocola los envió a Puila cerca de Chunuitzil donde los habían desbaratado, y fué Dios servido que poco a poco los fueron hallando, que duró el buscarlos cerca de ocho meses o nueve el recogerlos, y pobláronse en Xocola allí junto a los otros. Marcos Balam [y] Gonzalo Çuco, los viejos de Xocola, y Juan Hauiche, que era el más principal de los hallados, visto que todavía se habían juntado como sesenta, habló (sic) con Don Pablo y le dijo como querían poblarse junto al embarcadero de Mamantel porque era lejos de allí y tenían mucho trabajo y allí verían misa. Y así les señaló tierra en medio del camino de Chiua, que llaman Popola, y allí se poblaron Hauiche y sus compañeros.

En el año de mil quinientos ochenta y seis vino el Doctor Palacios a visitar la tierra, y nosotros, los indios de Tichel, le dimos canoas [y] remeros. Le abrimos caminos para que el ministro fuese a visitar estos pueblos, con los cuales siempre tuvimos y hemos tenido mucho trabajo en darles ornamentos para administrarles los santos sacramentos, y todo lo hemos hecho a fin de que sirvan a Dios y al rey, nuestro señor, hasta que fué mandado por la tasa que entre todos sustentásemos el ministro y la iglesia y nuestro gobernador.

Ya tengo dicho en esta relación de la descendencia de los indios magtunes chontales desde que salió a sus tierras el Capitán del Valle, y para que se sepa de nuestro modo de vivir desde el año de mil quinientos veinte y siete hasta el año de mil seiscientos diez, que es éste de ahora, que es menester escribir de sus nombres y hechos para ver lo que somos en nuestros caminos y entradas y en las de los yucatecos, gente de todos pueblos como los que están en Popola, Mazcab, que era Jocola, y los demás pueblos que hay aquí.

[IIIc]

En el año de mil quinientos noventa y nueve años, cuando se empezaron a coger los yucatecos, los que habían quedado de morir por Pedro Zacummay allá en Holha, que es junto a Chencanal, principio del río, y sobre la estancia de Francisco Maldonado, que llaman Usulaban, y las sabanas de Chulnal, que por todas partes andaba y allí mataban a los que iban a cortar cera y por iguanas, que iban de Campeche y de todos los pueblos y también salían a la orilla de la mar a Tixchem y Chemcan y Excacaltok a tomar [a] los que pasaban los cuchillos, machetes y ropa y lo que llevaban, y cuando pasaban por el camino que es junto a la mar. Y así como lo supo Don Pablo de los que iban por el camino y llegaban a Tichel y corrió la voz de los cimarrones de Holhay y en los cuyos de Usulauan, pidió comisión a Don Diego de Velasco, gobernador de esta provincia de Yucatán, para ir al monte a buscarlos y cogerlos. Y así se la dió y para poder llevar los indios que hubiese menester de su provincia. Y así fuimos los de Tichel, y llevó de Popola, Chiua, Mazcab, Tiquintunpa que era Zapotitan, y éstos nos acompañaron, y fuimos y entramos por la estancia y abrimos camino hasta Usulaban. Y allí hallamos una casa por donde andaban los cimarrones y donde hacían fuego. Y quiso Dios en este tiempo que los de Chanpoton, habiendo tenido noticia de ellos, los iban a buscar, y los hallaron en Quinalnal y los desbarataron. Y ausentaron y se vinieron sobre donde estábamos, y así los cogimos los de Tichel, que serían como ochenta en todos. Y los llevamos a Tichel, siendo guardián Fray Diego Mejía de Figueroa, su compañero, Fray Joseph Bosque, y se bautizaron los hijos de ellos y como tres o cuatro de los grandes que no eran bautizados.

Y les preguntó Don Pablo si era buena toda aquèlla tierra que andaban, y respondieron que sí, que era buena para casas, milpas [y] cacaguatales. Y por eso fué enviado Fray Joseph Bosque a que lo viese con algunos indios, y entró por Chiua *paci*[4] por Usulaban y de allí salió por la estancia de Francisco Maldonado. Y vino a decir la bondad de la tierra a Fray Diego Mejía, su guardián, y que podría ir a ella un gran pueblo y hacer muy buenas milperías por haber muy grandes cedros y montañas y que pueden estar allí todos los pueblos de Popola, Tiquintupa, Mazcab, Chiua y Tixchel. Y así se lo dijeron a Don Pablo que allí podía estar todos juntos para poderlos administrar en el santo evangelio. Y tratóselo a los principales todo y a todos les pareció bien; y lo propio se le trató al encomendero, Mateo de Aguilar. Y así entre todos se escribió al defensor para que en nombre de todos los pidiese al gobernador para que juntos todos fuesen al dicho asiento de Usulaban. Y así se dió licencia para que todos juntos fuesen a Usulaban por Don Diego de Velasco, gobernador en la sazón, su fecha en el pueblo de Calquini. Y así como llegó la dicha licencia, Don Pablo Paxbolon, nuestro gobernador, lo dió a entender a todos los pueblos. Y en este tiempo llegó la nueva como los padres de San Francisco se les quitaba la administración de los naturales de esta provincia y se daba a clérigos por orden de Su Majestad, que vino de España la orden. Y eso fué la causa de no tener efecto la ida de los pueblos a Usulaban por

[4] *Paci* is a Chontal word, apparently left untranslated. From the context it would seem to mean "passed."

no tener quien les animase, y así sólo algunos fueron a la llegada de la licencia y así se quedó.

Vino luego Juan Rodríguez, padre clérigo, por vicario de esta provincia, que le envió el Señor Obispo Don Fray Juan Izquierdo de este obispado de Yucatán en seis días del mes de enero del año de mil seiscientos y tres años. Y visto las tierras, dijo que era lejos Usulaban y que los caminos se henchían en tiempos de aguas y él fué el que bendijo la tierra para el pueblo e hizo iglesia y la nombró San Felipe y Santiago a veinte y tres del mes de abril en el año de mil seiscientos y cuatro.

Nos, Francisco de Mena y Alonso de Mesa, intérpretes nombrados por Mateo de Aguilar, alcalde ordinario de esta villa de Campeche y juez comisario del señor gobernador, para el examen de los testigos naturales que Francisco Maldonado presentó en su información, trasuntamos el presente trasunto de los papeles que tiene presentados en su causa en la lengua chontal, los cuales van ciertos y verdaderos, lo cual declaramos debajo de juramento que tenemos hecho. Y lo firmamos en Campeche en veinte y dos días del mes de diciembre de mil seiscientos doce años. Alonso de Mesa. Francisco de Mena.

ENGLISH TRANSLATION

[1]

[1]I, PABLO Paxbolon, public clerk in this pueblo of Tixchel,[2] here translate what is written in the Mexican language[3] by Juan Bautista, clerk, who died a long time ago. It begins in this fashion:

Here in the pueblo called Santa María de Tixchel in the jurisdiction and land of the villa of San Francisco de Campeche, province of Yucatan, on the tenth day of the month of January of the year 1567, in the presence of Francisco Felipe[4] and also Luis García, alcaldes, and also IN THE PRESENCE OF Alonso Martín, Pedro Naua, Hernando Kanan, and Antón Quiuit, regidores, representing the great king, his Majesty, and before me, Juan Bautista, clerk of the said pueblo, Don Pablo Paxbolon, governor of the said pueblo, appeared and stated that it was necessary to take the statements of the old men, because he wished to learn and hear the origin of his ancestors and fathers, the former rulers. Those named Alonso Chacbalam and Luis Tutzin, very old men, made the declaration which begins below.

1. In the beginning Auxaual,[5] KING, came from Cozumel. *He came* to take the pueblos here. He *arrived* to assemble the pueblo of Tanodzic[6] with his great principal men named Huncha, Paxoc, Chacbalam, four counting Paxmulu,[7] and these he brought as companions and they settled and occupied those lands.[8]

[1] In the Chontal Text there is a paragraph preceding the material translated here. It apparently contains Don Pablo Paxbolon's authorization to have made a copy of his papers as requested by his grandson, Martín Maldonado.

[2] This form of the pueblo name, which is consistently employed in the Text, corresponds more closely with that of the deity Ix Chel, who was the goddess of medicine and childbirth and one of the five principal deities of the former Acalan capital, Itzamkanac. The initial *T* is probably a preposition meaning "at the place" (Roys, 1935, pp. 4–5).

[3] Nahuatl was widely spoken in the Chontal area (RY, 1:352). It seems to have been little known among the Yucatecan Maya, although the language of the latter contains a number of words of Mexican origin.

[4] Note that the surnames of Juan Bautista and Francisco Felipe are lacking. In Yucatan we practically never find a name recorded without a Spanish or Maya surname. The famous interpreter, who sometimes signed his name merely as Gaspar Antonio, is an exception.

[5] In spite of Auxaual's recorded origin at Cozumel, the name does not seem to be Yucatecan Maya. It appears on the Alfaro map (Map 2) as the name of a village west of the villa of Tabasco.

[6] The name of modern Tenosique is evidently derived from this Chontal form. The present town is probably at or near its former site.

[7] In the Spanish version these names appear as those of groups, but the Text treats them as individuals.

[8] The Text simply states, "when the lands were taken."

2. THEN *came* the second ruler[9] named Pachimal,[10] WHOM I MENTIONED ABOVE, son of Auxaual whose name is written ABOVE. *He died.*

3. *There came* the third ruler *of the series,*[11] named Chanpel, son of Pachimal, who is mentioned above. This Chanpel was ruler when he went to conquer Tatenam, *which is beyond Bolonlamat,* NOW *called* Términos, and the rest went together to *Dzabibhah*[12] *beside* Boca Nueva, and others *arrived at Holtun,* Puerto Escondido[13] *as they say.*

4. There came the fourth ruler *of the series,* who was named Paxua, son of Chanpel, who has already been mentioned. This was the ruler who settled Tixchel. They lived *at Tixchel* three score or four score years. Wars were begun by the people of Champoton and *Cactam*[14] and Apopomena,[15] *also by Acucyah called* Tabasquillo. Therefore they abandoned Tixchel and went to Tamatun WHICH THEY CALL Acalan; and the pueblo of the Cehache CALLED Tayel was there, and also the people of Çiuatecpan were at the junction of the rivers; and from these [places] began the land and people of whom Paxua was ruler, [and they extended] as far as Iztapa.[16] And he took the pueblo of the Cehache, [or] Mazateca,[17] and [that of] the Dzul.[18] And thus they were lords of the land of Acalan.

[9] The term employed in the Text is *ahau.* In northern Yucatan the word meant ruler and was the title of the *halach uinic* or territorial ruler. As we shall see later, some of the Acalan ruler's principal subordinates also enjoyed the same title.

[10] We are unable to translate the prefix Pa-, which, like Pax- and Pap-, appears to occur only in names of men.

[11] In the Text the number is followed by *-dzac,* which is one of the numerical suffixes so common in Yucatecan Maya. It is defined in the Motul Dictionary as meaning "cuenta de grados y escalones y otras cosas que van unas encima de otras." Farther on we find two brothers grouped together under a single number, and in one case this is done with a father and three sons.

[12] It is very possible that this name should read Dzabibkak.

[13] These are all the names of places leading from Laguna de Términos to the Gulf of Mexico. They were along the main trade route between Mexico and Yucatan and their possession would offer an opportunity to levy tribute on this extensive commerce. The name Bolonlamat, which the Text gives for Términos, is one of the Maya day names (9 Lamat) for which it is difficult to find a satisfactory translation. Holtun, which the Text gives as the name of Puerto Escondido, probably means "the port."

[14] The Spanish version gives the name as Xicalan, and it is of especial interest to find in the Text a Chontal name for this Nahuatl town. This is Cactam, or possibly Çactam.

[15] Apopomena probably means the people of Popomena; the place is called Pomeba in the Spanish version. The close association of this site with Xicalango suggests that the former may have been an older name for a settlement on what is now Laguna del Pom. Modern maps show a settlement called Pom on this lagoon, but we have found no mention of this name in the sixteenth-century documents. The word *pom* means "copal."

[16] A possible alternative translation of the Chontal Text might be: "these [the people of Ciuatecpan] were in the jurisdiction of the people of Iztapa." This is very different from the statement in the Spanish version, but after the conquest of the town by the Acalan, their territory probably extended down the Usumacinta River as far as Iztapa in any case.

[17] The Cehache and the Mazateca, who lived east of Acalan, were the same people and not separate groups, as the Spanish version implies.

[18] Written Dzulob in the Text. This is the plural of Dzul, which means "foreigner" in

5. The fifth rulers *of the series* were named Pachimalahix and also Macuaabin, his younger brother, sons of Paxua. In the time of this ruler (Pachimalahix), five or six years after having arrived at Chactemal,[19] [which lies] beyond Bakhalal,[20] he imposed tribute upon them.[21] At this time the Dzul came to take Balancal.[22] Their captain was named Tzitzimit and he asked Pachimalahix, the ruler, to divide the tribute of the pueblos, and because the latter was unwilling to give it to him, all the pueblos joined together and there was war for four score days. At the end of this time they returned again and arrived at Acalan; they seized *the lands* at Tachakam. Then began the rule of Macuaabin, younger brother of Pachimalahix, whom we have mentioned.

6. The sixth ruler *of the series* was named Paxbolonacha, son of Pachimalahix. He was the ruler who settled *Itzamkanac* Acalan. While they were there the Spaniards came with the Marqués del Valle as their captain. This ruler, Paxbolonacha, *mentioned above,* had three sons. *One* was named Pachimalahix; he had a son named Don Luis Paxua, and the latter fled TO CHIUOHA.[23] The second son was named Lamatazel,[24] and he was the father of Don Pablo PAXBOLON. The third son was NAMED Don Pedro Paxtun. He was baptized and had no child.

7. The seventh in descent[25] was Don Pablo Paxbolonacha, now governor, son of the abovementioned Lamatazel.

Here ended and concluded what the two old men, Alonso Chacbalam and Luis Tutzin, were asked and what they stated. They declared that only these were the rulers and that they watched over the pueblos. And thus they stated in the presence of Hernando Kanan, Antón Quiuit, Alonso May, witnesses, residents HERE. And in attestation I set down the names of the alcaldes [and regidores] and mine as clerk. Francisco Felipe. Luis García.

Yucatecan Maya. It seems probable that they were one of the Nahuatl-speaking groups of Tabasco who had come up the Usumacinta River.

[19] Chetumal.

[20] Bacalar.

[21] The English translation here follows the reading of the Spanish version. We have pointed out (note 2, p. 368, *supra*) that the Spanish translators omitted a phrase about going to Chactemal and that the meaning of the Chontal Text is obscure. The Text reads: "This one was ruler when they [he?] went to Chactemal. It lies beyond Bakhalal. Five [or] six years it was they arrived. During this time entered tribute to them [him?]." This may mean that the going to Chactemal occurred five or six years after the accession of Pachimalahix, or that he stayed there five or six years.

[22] Balancan in the Spanish version.

[23] Here and elsewhere the Spanish version calls the place Chiua.

[24] This part of the Text gives his name as Alamatazel, but elsewhere it is written Lamatazel.

[25] Don Pablo Paxbolon was actually of the eighth generation.

Alonso Martín. Pedro Naua. Hernando Kanan. Antón Quiuit. Done in my presence, Juan Bautista, clerk.

Don Pablo Paxbolon, present governor, married Doña Isabel. They had a daughter named Doña Catalina, who married Francisco Maldonado, Spaniard. Francisco Maldonado and Doña Catalina, whom I mentioned, had a son, Martín Maldonado, who is now living.

Doña Isabel, whom we mentioned, died. Then Don Pablo Paxbolon, governor, married Doña Mencía, daughter of Diego de Orduña.[26] They had a daughter named María, who is now living.

On the twenty-first of the month of July of the year 1612, I, Pablo Paxbolon, clerk of this pueblo, in the presence of the principal men named Marcos Chacbalam, alcalde, Juan Chacchan [and] Francisco Tutzin, regidores, and of the others WHO WERE PRESENT, Agustín Paxbolon, Alonso Patzinbolon, Baltasar Paptucun, read it to them so that they heard the descent and genealogy[27] of Don Pablo Paxbolon, governor. They said it was correct and true, that there is nothing in it that is not. Therefore I set down their names and signatures here with my own as clerk. Marcos Chacbalam. Juan Chacchan. Francisco Tutzin. Agustín Paxbolon. *Alonso Patzinbolon*. Baltasar Paptucun. In my presence, Pablo Paxbolon, clerk.

[II]

On the fifth of the month of July of the year 1612, I copied the names and count of the pueblos of the Mactun, WHO ARE THE CHONTAL of Acalan, written by the principal men, our fathers, who died old men. It begins first with the residence of the ruler, Paxbolonacha, for thus he was named, *written* AS FOLLOWS:

[1] THE PUEBLO OF Acalan, CALLED Itzamkanac[28] pueblo
[2] Tahobo   pueblo
[3] TAHCAB[29]   pueblo

[26] Diego de Orduña lived for many years in Tabasco, where he learned to speak Chontal. In 1573 and again in 1580 he participated in exploring expeditions up the Río de Tachis (San Pedro Mártir) into the Peten. Cf. Appendix D.

[27] The Text reads, "u payolel u uinicilel Don Pablo Paxbolon," which might mean "the jurisdiction [and] the people of Don Pablo Paxbolon."

[28] The lists of towns in the Chontal Text and the Spanish version do not follow exactly the same order. There is also considerable variation in spelling in the two lists. We have given the Chontal forms but have listed the towns in the order that they occur in the Spanish version as a means of facilitating comparison of the variant forms.

[29] As indicated in the translation, Tahcab is found only in the Spanish version and Tacacau only in the Chontal Text. Inasmuch as each list contains seventy-six names, it is possible that Tahcab and Tacacau are variant names of the same place. If not, then there were seventy-seven towns instead of seventy-six.

[4]	Tapib[30]	pueblo
[4a]	*Tacacau*[31]	pueblo
[5]	Çacmucnal[32]	pueblo
[6]	Tanauibcab	pueblo
[7]	Tauchcabal	pueblo
[8]	Tahkakalaez	pueblo
[9]	Tapacauichcab	pueblo
[10]	Tixkancubim[33]	pueblo
[11]	Tanacomchutte	pueblo
[12]	Tahcehxuch	pueblo
[13]	Takunchelal[34]	pueblo
[14]	Tatok[35]	pueblo
[15]	Tamauitz	pueblo
[16]	Petenmax[36]	pueblo
[17]	Tachakam,[37] WHICH IS NOW CALLED CHUNAB[38] AND IS SETTLED BY SERVING PEOPLE (meya uinicob)	pueblo
[18]	Tayel	pueblo
[19]	Temax[39]	pueblo
[20]	Tahaalkantelal[40]	pueblo
[21]	Tahmalin	pueblo
[22]	Tahkomtilal	pueblo
[23]	Tahaazcab	pueblo
[24]	Petenaku	pueblo
[25]	Uxpeten[41]	pueblo
[26]	Uatunhobonnixtte[42]	pueblo
[27]	Takoolku	pueblo
[28]	Tahchimaytun[43]	pueblo

[30] Tapib: "at the pit-oven." This and the following translations of place names are based on the meaning of the syllables in Yucatecan Maya but with frequent allowance for Chontal sound shifts. We believe, however, that they give a correct idea of the general principles underlying Chontal nomenclature of places.

[31] At the cacao trees.

[32] White tomb or burial place.

[33] Tixkançubim would mean "at the yellow acacia."

[34] At the *kunche* trees (*Pileus mexicanus* Standl.).

[35] At the flint or flint knife. *Tok* is also a compound in at least six Maya plant names.

[36] Island of the monkey or wild chile.

[37] At the savanna (*chakan*).

[38] Chunab is a Yucatecan Maya family name.

[39] Where the monkey or wild chile is. There is a well-known Yucatecan town of this name.

[40] Both the *kante* and *kanche* are well-known Yucatecan trees.

[41] Three islands; a possible alternative translation might be "*ramón*, or breadnut tree, island."

[42] Hobonnixtte might be translated as "hollow inclined tree." *Nixche* was the Maya name of *uva del mar*, probably *Coccoloba uvifera* Jacq. in Yucatan.

[43] *Chimay* has been reported as the name of *Acacia milleriana* Standl. and *Pithecolobium albicans* Benth. *Tun* could mean a precious stone, or, in compounds, stone. Chimaytun could mean "stone deer" in Chontal. In Yucatan the Indians still believe in certain supernatural deer called *zip*, which are the guardians of these animals (Redfield and Villa, 1934, pp. 117–18).

[29]	Panuitzcab	pueblo
[30]	Tahçacab[44]	pueblo
[31]	Tixmalindzunum[45]	pueblo
[32]	Tahbidzcabal	pueblo
[33]	Tançut[46]	pueblo
[34]	Chanhilix	pueblo
[35]	Tachantoppoltun	pueblo
[36]	Homolna[47]	pueblo
[37]	Taocabal	pueblo
[38]	Tahuli	pueblo
[39]	Çacchute[48]	pueblo
[40]	Taniuitz[49]	pueblo
[41]	Tappottelal	pueblo
[42]	Tapaxtoh	pueblo
[43]	Tahchacchauac	pueblo
[44]	Takuçaycab	pueblo
[45]	Palibpetette	pueblo
[46]	Tachiciua	pueblo
[47]	Tayaxttelal[50]	pueblo
[48]	Tayaxakcab	pueblo
[49]	Tuxakha,[51] in which Cortés remained for twenty days, where the head of the Mexican CAPTAIN, Cuauhtemoc, was cut off[52]	pueblo
[50]	Taynpilal	pueblo
[51]	Tahbudzil[53]	pueblo
[52]	Hoknadzic	pueblo

[44] At the lime pit.

[45] *Dzunum*, or *dzunun*, means "hummingbird."

[46] At the turn.

[47] Sunken house.

[48] This name might be translated as "white cedar."

[49] At the tip of the hill.

[50] Where the ceiba trees are. It will be noted that several names end in *-ttelal* and still more in *-al*. Those in *-ttelal* appear to indicate localities where a certain kind of tree (*te*) predominates; and we believe that most, if not all, of the others in *-al* indicate a particular type of environment. Lundell has noted that in the south and center of the peninsula the suffix *-al* is added to the folk name of the dominant tree to characterize the association. Such words are formed from Maya plant names in *chechen-al* (Honduras walnut), *naab-al* ("water lily"), and *julub-al* (*Bravaisia tubiflora* Hemsl.). *Zacatal* ("grass") and *zapotal* are derived from Nahuatl forms; *caobal* ("mahogany") and *guarumal* are from West Indian names; and a number of others are taken from the Spanish (Lundell, 1934, pp. 253–355).

[51] Where the waters mingle, which probably means the junction of two streams.

[52] In the Text Cortés is referred to only as the captain. In translating the first part of this passage we have followed the Chontal original, which states that the captain "remained" in Tuxakha for twenty days. The story of Cuauhtemoc's execution is discussed at length in Chapter 5, in which we have cited evidence that Cortés did not remain in Tuxakha for twenty days and that the Aztec chieftain was actually put to death in Itzamkanac.

[53] Where the smoke is.

[53]	Tabidzcabal	pueblo
[54]	Tanohun	pueblo
[55]	Kanlum[54]	pueblo
[56]	Tapaxua	pueblo
[57]	Yaxhopat	pueblo
[58]	Tapop[55]	pueblo
[59]	Tabolay[56]	pueblo
[60]	Tapom[57]	pueblo
[61]	Tapulemttelal	pueblo
[62]	Tuholham	pueblo
[63]	Taçachilal	pueblo
[64]	Boteac	pueblo
[65]	Tadzumuycab	pueblo
[66]	Tamomoncab	pueblo
[67]	Tahchimal[58]	pueblo
[68]	Yaxahintun	pueblo
[69]	Tahkomcab	pueblo
[70]	Temoch	pueblo
[71]	Taychilak	pueblo
[72]	Tachiicabal	pueblo
[73]	Tuholham	pueblo
[74]	Taykbalam[59]	pueblo
[75]	Tanochich[60]	pueblo
[76]	Tamultun[61]	pueblo

Seventy-six pueblos

[IIIa]

In the beginning they were in their towns, the people of Tamactun, who are called Chontal, and Acalan in Mexican, the Mactun Indians, as appears from the towns in which they lived.[62] Their capital was called Itzamkanac. The ruler, Paxbolonacha, for so he was named, was there, for this was his

[54] Yellow earth.
[55] At the rushes.
[56] Where the beast of prey is.
[57] At the copal tree.
[58] At the shield.
[59] Where the black jaguar or puma is.
[60] Where the great bird is.
[61] At the stone mound.
[62] The Spanish version of this passage is obscure and the Text is difficult to translate. The English translation follows closely the word order of the Spanish. A tentative rendering of part of the Text might be: "In the beginning they were settled [?] . . . Tamactun, its name in the language here, Acalan, its name in the Mexican language, all the Mactun people. . . ." At the end there seems to be a reference to the preceding list of towns. Perhaps a free translation of the entire passage might be: "At the beginning [of the Spanish conquest] the Mactun people were settled in the land of Tamactun, which is its name in the language here, and Acalan in the Mexican language, as appears from the list of towns in which they lived."

realm. He had as his governors and principal men: [63] Mututzin Ahau, Kintzucti, Padzayato, and Tamalyaxun, as they were named.

The Spaniards came TO THIS LAND in the year 1527. Their captain was named Don Martín Cortés.[64] They entered by way of Tanodzic[65] and passed by THE PUEBLO OF Tachix[66] and came out at the beginning of the land of Çacchutte, and stopped for a while in the pueblo of Tuxakhaa. While staying there with ALL their followers, they sent to summon Paxbolonacha, the ruler, mentioned above. He assembled all his principal men[67] of all his pueblos, from THE PUEBLO OF Tadzunum, AND THE PRINCIPAL MEN OF THE PUEBLO OF CHABTE, and the principal men of THE PUEBLO OF Atapan, and the principal men of THE PUEBLO OF Taçacto,[68] because no action could be taken without informing these principal men. He informed them of the matter to be dealt with. They consulted concerning what would be the best policy in his realm, in view of the fact that the Capitán *del Valle*[69] OF the Spaniards, who were in the pueblo of Xakhaa, had sent to summon [him]. They said it was not fitting that their ruler should go at the summons of the Spaniards, because they (the Indians) did not know what they (the Spaniards) wanted. Then one of the principal men, named Chocpalocem *Ahau*, arose AND SAID: "RULER AND LORD, remain in your realm and city, FOR I WISH TO GO TO SEE WHAT THE SPANIARDS WANT." And thus he went *before the captain* with other principal men named Patzinchiciua, Paxuanapuk, and Paxhochacchan, companions of Palocem *Ahau*, IN THE NAME OF THE RULER. When they had come before the Capitán del Valle, Spaniard, some of the Spaniards did not believe them because there must have been someone among them who said *to the Spaniards* that the ruler WHOM THEY HAD SUMMONED was not coming there. Therefore the captain said to them: "Let the ruler come, for I wish to see him. I do not come to make war NOR TO DO HIM HARM; I wish only to pass through to see the land [and] whatever there is to see. I will be very good to him if he receives me well." And

[63] In the Text the so-called governors were called *ahau*, and the principal men, *nuc uinic*. In the Spanish version the word *ahau* is usually translated as *rey* (king or ruler).

[64] Cortés passed through Acalan in 1525, not 1527. The chronicler gives him the name of his son, Martín Cortés.

[65] The Spanish reads: "Que entraron por Tanoçic," etc. Although we have translated *por* as "by way of," which is the literal meaning, it would probably be more exact in this case to say "near" or "in the region of." Cortés crossed the Usumacinta at Ciuatecpan, which was apparently located several leagues below Tenosique. Cf. pp. 441-48, *infra*.

[66] Cf. references to the Río de Tachis (San Pedro Mártir) in Appendix D. Note that the words "the pueblo of" are found in the Spanish version only and not in the Text. The passage is apparently intended to record the fact that Cortés passed across or through the region of the San Pedro Mártir.

[67] The Chontal word for principales in this case is *ahau*.

[68] The Text appears to imply that these principal men were the heads of "the four divisions of the town already mentioned" (*chan tzucul cab aca thane*).

[69] Cortés' correct title, conferred upon him at a later date, was Marqués del Valle.

those who had come in the name of the ruler having understood it, they returned and told Paxbolonacha, their ruler, who was in the pueblo of *Itzamkanac* WAITING [for them]. When they arrived all the principal men[70] were assembled, and he said to them: "I want to go to make the acquaintance of the captain and Spaniards, for I wish to see them and learn what they want and for what purpose they have come." And thus Paxbolonacha, *the ruler*, went.

When the Spaniards learned [of his coming], they went out to receive him and the Capitán del Valle with them. They (the Indians) brought a generous gift of honey, turkeys, maize, copal, and a great deal of fruit. The captain said: "Ruler Paxbolon, I have come here to your lands, for I am sent by the lord of the world, the emperor who is on his throne in Castile, who sends me to see the land and the people with whom it is populated. I do not come for wars. I only ask you to facilitate my journey to Ulua, WHICH IS MEXICO,[71] and the land where silver[72] and plumage and cacao are obtained, for that is what I wish to go to see." And so he (Paxbolonacha) replied that he would grant him passage with great pleasure, and that he (Cortés) should accompany him to his city and land, and that there they would discuss what was most fitting. The Capitán *del Valle* told him that he should rest, and he assented. Whereupon they spent twenty days taking their ease.

Cuauhtemoc, ruler OF NEW SPAIN, who had come with the captain from Mexico, was there. He said to ruler Paxbolonacha, *mentioned above*: "*My lord ruler*, there will come a time when these Spaniards will give us much trouble and do us much harm and they will kill our people.[73] I am of the opinion that we should kill them, for I bring a large force and you are many." Cuauhtemoc said this to Paxbolonacha, ruler of the Mactun CHONTAL. When he heard this speech *of Cuauhtemoc* he replied to him: "I will consider it. Leave it for now and we will discuss it later." And, thinking about the matter, he saw that the Spaniards did not commit any abuses nor had they killed or beaten any Indians, and that they asked for nothing except honey, hens (turkeys), maize, and other fruits, which were given to them daily. He considered that since they did him no evil he could not have two faces with them, nor show two hearts toward the Spaniards. Cuauhtemoc, *the ruler from Mexico already mentioned*, was always importuning him about this because he would have liked to kill ALL the Spaniards. In view of this importunity,

[70] The Text apparently states that the ahaus of the entire town assembled.
[71] This statement implies the existence of Nahuatl-speaking people in Ulua. Cf. Roys, 1943, pp. 117–18.
[72] In the Text *takin*, Yucatecan Maya word for gold, is employed.
[73] A tentative translation of the Text suggests that Cuauhtemoc told Paxbolonacha that the Spaniards "will give you much trouble and kill your people."

Paxbolonacha, *the ruler*, went to the Capitán del Valle and said to him: *"My* lord Capitán del Valle, this *ruler Cuauhtemoc,* PRINCIPAL AND CAPTAIN OF THE MEXICANS, whom you bring,[74] watch out for him lest he commit some treason against you, because three or four times he has talked with me about killing you." When the Capitán del Valle heard this, he seized CUAUHTEMOC and put him in chains. On the third day that he was a prisoner they took him out and baptized him and it is not certain whether he was given the name Don Juan or Don Fernando. After baptizing him, they cut off his head, and it was spiked on a ceiba in front of the house of idolatry which was IN THE PUEBLO OF Yaxdzan.[75]

Then the Capitán del Valle and all his force departed, together with ruler Paxbolonacha and all his people, and they reached the city of Itzamkanac. While they were there they began to plan at what point a bridge could be made in order to cross the river WITH ALL THE ARMY, because it was about a league across including the swamps, and so the filling up of the swamps and the making of the bridge was undertaken. It was finished in two days[76] on account of the great number of people there were. They also cleared the road as far as the Cehache, and two principal men[77] were sent, who went to take the news OF THE COMING OF THE SPANIARDS. They were called Çelutapech [and] Macuaaua. The Cehache killed Çelutapech, and *Macuaaua*, his companion, *already mentioned*, fled and returned to the city of Itzamkanac, WHENCE HE HAD SET OUT, AND TOLD THEM ALL THAT HAD HAPPENED TO THEM. For this reason the Spaniards proceeded with some misgiving. Nevertheless, they killed five or six of the most valiant upon reaching the Cehache. From there on the Cehache went clearing a road as far as Taitza. Having seen that they could not cross to the island on account of the water, they returned and took the road and came out at Champoton.[78]

A year after the Spaniards and the Capitán del Valle were in Acalan,[79] Paxbolonacha, *ruler*, went to another pueblo which is called Tachakam, where he died. His people put him in a canoe and brought him to *the city of* ACALAN *Itzamkanac*, where they buried him. The ruler had been dead three years

[74] The Text merely says: "this Cuauhtemoc Ahau, who is with you."
[75] Yaxdzan, which is the name of *Rhoeo discolor* in Yucatecan Maya, does not appear in the list of Acalan towns. It may well have been one of the subdivisions of Tuxakha, where the native author of our Text believed the execution of Cuauhtemoc occurred. See p. 112, *supra*, for a discussion of the place of Cuauhtemoc's death.
[76] The Text says four days.
[77] In Chontal, *nucba uinicob*, meaning the inferior principal men as compared with the ahaus.
[78] The chronicler is mistaken here. Cortés did visit Tayasal, capital of the Itza, situated on an island in the lake, and thence he proceeded to Nito. Avila, who passed through Acalan in 1530, came out at Champoton, but did not go so far inland as Lake Peten.
[79] The Text simply states that it was a year after Cortés and the Spaniards had passed. Acalan is not mentioned.

when other Spaniards came and entered and went through, as the Capitán del Valle had done, BY THE PUEBLO OF Tachiix and the pueblo of Çacchute. It was not known whether they brought a captain. Some of them WERE NAMED Francisco Gil, Lorenzo Godoy, and Julián Doncel, who were the heads and superiors *of the Spaniards.* When they reached the capital, they asked for the ruler, and they (the Indians) replied that he was dead. They (the Spaniards) asked for his sons, who were brought before them. The oldest of the *sons* was named Pachimalahix, the second, Lamatazel, and the smallest, Paxtun. They put the eldest of the THREE *sons, already mentioned,* in jail and locked him up for two days and told him that he should give them tribute. And thus turkeys and maize, honey and copal, beans, squash seeds, and whatever else there was, for there was an incalculable amount, were given to them. And they crossed the bridge, *as the Capitán* [del Valle] *had crossed the river,* AND WENT AWAY.[80]

The Adelantado[81] did not pass through Acalan, which is in Mactun. Only his command arrived IN HIS NAME. They came to Champoton to see him because he stayed there a long time. There they brought him tribute and remained FOR A LONG TIME WITH HIM *at Champoton mentioned above,*[82] and they asked him to admit them to his protection.[83]

Pachimalahix died and at this time HIS BROTHER, Lamatazel, entered in his place.[84] During his time and government the FIRST FRANCISCAN fathers arrived, Fray Luis de Villalpando, Fray Juan de la Puerta, [and] Fray Lorenzo de Bienvenida. At this time they were still in their pagan and idolatrous state, and the Spaniards and the above-mentioned friars who came entered the land and began to teach them the true way and the true God. They went about teaching everyone that our gods were already finished and had already come to an end, [saying]: "You will never see them worshipped again, and he who worships them is deceived in his way of life and he who does so will be pun-

[80] The chronicler's chronology, the statement that the Spaniards followed Cortés' route, and the reference to the imposition of tribute indicate that this section describes the Avila expedition of 1530 rather than the Gil-Godoy episode which occurred six years later. Cf. pp. 126–28, 136–37, *supra.*

[81] Adelantado Don Francisco de Montejo, governor and captain general of Yucatan.

[82] This paragraph probably refers to the years 1531 *et seq.* when Montejo made a second attempt to conquer Yucatan, this time from the west coast. The meeting place of the Chontal and the Adelantado was evidently at Campeche, instead of Champoton, for a document of 1533 states that early in 1532 Montejo sent a Spaniard to Acalan to summon the principal men, and that he brought them to Campeche where Montejo received them and ordered them to bring tribute to that place henceforth (Montejo *v.* Alvarado). It is possible that the paragraph may refer to a later period, when the forces of Montejo's son were stationed for some time at Champoton prior to the final conquest of Yucatan, but the explicit reference to the Adelantado and the sending of his command (*mandado*) to Acalan indicates that the author of the Chontal narrative had in mind the early period when the Adelantado was in charge of operations on the west coast. Cf. pp. 129–37, *supra.*

[83] The Text adds, "and they [the Spaniards] went to Yucatan to seize the land."

[84] The Text says, "entered into the rulership."

ished, for their time is now over. See that no one deceives the people, for that age is now gone by." All the principal men[85] and the ruler and all their pueblos heard what the father priests said.

Then Lamatazel, their ruler, died, and before he died he ordered all the principal men[86] summoned. When they had assembled he said to them: "Now I am dying, and I bear sorrow in my heart that I have not attained to being a Christian and living with faith, instead of as we live. As my life draws to a close, I beg you to give yourselves to the service of another God,[87] because I see and have heard that the father priests will come to baptize and preach, and [the new faith] will not be destroyed, nor will the end [of it] be seen. Now the truth comes, and the good of which they tell, and therefore I charge you to seek it and bring the father preachers to teach you and set your feet on the true road." After this speech this ruler Lamatazel died.

Paxtun, his younger brother and son of Paxbolonacha, entered in his place and power. He heard the news of the preaching and baptism which the fathers were engaged in and took the matter under consideration with all his principal men.[88] They summoned the whole pueblo in order that they might go to seek the fathers in Campeche, and thus ruler Paxtun set out for Campeche with his people in search of the fathers. God ordained it so that the day after they reached Chinil, Father Fray Diego de Béjar, who was coming from Tabasco, arrived. They met him there, and [Paxtun] said to him: "Father and lord,[89] we have come here to seek you in the name of all my children, and I have left all my pueblos and [my] dwelling, which is in Acalan, which they call Chontal,[90] to come for you in order that you may come to teach the word of God and His faith, because I am informed that the natives are being baptized[91] by you fathers. We desire this and therefore we come to seek you AS FATHER." Paxtun, ruler, together with his companions, said this to him.

Having heard what the Indians said, Father Fray Diego de Béjar said to them: "My sons, it gives me great satisfaction that you desire to take your souls out of the hands of the devils and that you wish to hear and know the word of God, because that is my office and the one in which we fathers exert ourselves. Although I should like to be able to go with you at once, I have things to attend to with my father companions. Therefore it seems best to me

---

[85] In Chontal, *nuc uinicob*.

[86] See preceding note.

[87] The Spanish version says, "other gods." The Text reads, *hun tzuc chu*, "one single God." Here we find the Chontal word for God, which corresponds to the Yucatecan Maya *ku*.

[88] In this case the Chontal uses a form of *ahau*.

[89] In Chontal, *ca yum ca pap*.

[90] The Text reads, "Acalan, Tamactun its second name."

[91] In Chontal, *u yochel haa tu pam uinic*: "the water enters to the heads of men." The Yucatecan Maya equivalent of this phrase is very similar.

that you return, for I will come back to Campeche or Champoton soon, where I will meet those whom you may send for me." Thus the father consoled them and they returned to their pueblo of Acalan of the Chontal. At the end of a month, which they appointed as the time for sending for the father in a canoe, they arrived in Campeche, and the fathers who were there were pleased. And so Fray Diego de Béjar accompanied them and they reached Mactun Acalan on April 20 of the year 1550, and upon their arrival there was great rejoicing among all the people.

Immediately he summoned all the principal men,[92] Kintencab, Çelut Hol-can, Buluchatzi, Caltzin, Catanatz, Papcan, and the other principal men, AND ALSO THEIR GOVERNOR, PAXTUN. The father said to them: "*My* sons, consider that you have gone in search of us for a long distance, ten or fifteen days' journey. I have come to find you and accompany you, and I have been glad to undergo hardships on the road and in the canoes. Look, the first thing I have to say to you is that it is impossible to serve two lords or two fathers. Only one Father is to be loved. I come to tell you that [there is] only one God in three persons, God the Father, God the Son, God the Holy Ghost, who created heaven and earth and all there is to be seen today." He told them [this] and other explanations of God.

He wanted everyone to come and display his idols. Having heard what the father told them, they began to bring out their idols,[93] first the idol of the ruler WHICH BEARS [the name of] Cukulchan,[94] and also the devil [of] Tad-zunum, and [those of] Tachabtte, Atapan, and Taçacto,[95] and the other idols. They brought all these before Father Fray Diego de Béjar, who burned them. Then he began to teach them to recite the Paternoster, the Ave Maria, the Credo, and the Salve, and the articles of the faith. And then he began to give them their [Christian] names. The governor was named Don Pedro Paxtun. THE PRIEST Kintencab was named Don Mateo, and Caltzin was named Don Francisco. And thus EVERYONE, YOUNG AND OLD, entered Christianity WITHOUT THERE BEING ANYONE LACKING. The idols hidden in their secret places by the Indians, [such as] Ykchaua (Ekchuuah), for so this idol was called, another called Tabay, another CALLED Ixchel, *another* [called] Cabtanilcabtan, and many other places of idols were sought out in all the pueblos. The custodians of the idols went for them and brought them and burned them. Those who retained them were imprisoned and whipped before the eyes of the people. In

[92] Chontal, *nuc uinicob*.
[93] In the Text the idols are everywhere called *ciçinob*, "devils."
[94] Evidently the same as the Maya Kukulcan.
[95] These are the names of the four quarters of the city of Itzamkanac. The reference here is probably to their patron deities.

this way the idols perished and came to an end AMONG THE NATIVES, some of whom [conformed] willingly, others through fear of punishment.

I have already said above[96] that from the second time the Spaniards passed through Acalan *Tamactun*—[they were] Francisco Gil, Lorenzo Godoy, and Julián Doncel—from then on tribute began to be paid and taken to Tabasco every six months and every two months. It was not levied according to a fixed assessment, but when they (the encomenderos) wished, they came for what they wanted, such as canoes, paddles, honey, copal, hens, mantas, beans, maize, squash seeds, chile, cotton, [and] calabashes. They took as tribute to Tabasco every kind of food and drink there was, because there in the aforesaid Tabasco we began to pay tribute to Palma. Afterwards *the town* was given in encomienda to Diego de Aranda. We do not know who put these pueblos under the jurisdiction of Campeche. When Diego de Aranda died, Francisca de Velasco, HIS WIFE, married Antón García, and THE SAID Antón García ordered us to take the tribute to Chilapa.

At this time, *when the tribute was being taken to Chilapa*, the oidor Tomás López came from Guatemala in the year 1552. He ordained and set the time when tribute was to be paid, which is every six months *and how much tribute every six months*. This Tomás López released us from giving canoes, and also hens, mantas, maize, honey, copal, beans, squash seeds, chile, cotton, calabashes, paddles, and other items which we, the Chontal of Acalan, gave.[97] He issued provisions to the governors[98] of the pueblos giving them authority to govern their pueblos, and he ordered that those who took the tribute [to the encomenderos] and those who carried burdens for the Spaniards from one pueblo to another should be paid, if it was far, one or two pesos, and a tostón or two tomines[99] according to the journey. And the pueblos were still in Mactun Acalan.

During this time the father of whom we spoke, *Fray Diego de Béjar*, went away, and the father returned again. LATER Fray Miguel de Vera came to baptize ALL the people WHO REMAINED [unbaptized] and they received the Holy Sacraments. On another occasion Fray Diego de Pesquera came[100] and

---

[96] The Text reads, "as already written."

[97] This statement is not entirely accurate. The schedule of tribute for Acalan, as fixed by López in 1553, called for the annual payment of 500 mantas, 500 gallinas (one-half to be "gallinas de la tierra," or turkeys, and one-half, "gallinas de Castilla," or poultry of the variety introduced from Spain), and thirty cakes of copal. Moreover, tribute was being paid in Campeche prior to the arrival of López, and it was by his order that payment was made in Tabasco. For a discussion of the early history of the encomienda of Acalan, see pp. 142–55, *supra*.

[98] In Chontal, *ahauob*. This would appear to indicate that the local heads of the various towns had had the title of ahau.

[99] A *tostón* was half a peso; a *tomín*, or *real*, was one-eighth of a peso.

[100] The Spanish reads, "Otra vez volvió Fray Diego de Pesquera," and the Text also seems

talked to them about the expediency of their moving to Tixchel, where they had been once before. This was when Don Luis Paxua, son of Pachimalahix who was mentioned above, was governor OR RULER in this province [of Acalan]. At the beginning of the year 1557 *in January* people from Champoton and Campeche came to clear and clean the site of Tixchel in order that the Indians of Acalan *Tamactun*, THE CHONTAL, might move down there.[101] Because they were far away and the fathers could not come often to administer the Holy Sacraments to them; and because [Tixchel] was on the route of the Franciscan and Augustinian fathers, the secular clergy, and the Dominicans, and also the Spaniards who came TO THIS PROVINCE from Mexico, and they would teach them the word of God when they passed through; and also because they would be near the governor and chief magistrate sent by his Majesty, the king, who administers justice to the common people[102] AND NATIVES: all these reasons moved THE FATHERS to bring them *here* to the site of Tixchel.[103] The encomendero, Antón García, also wished it, and for a period of four years he relieved them from paying tribute until they should reestablish themselves at the new site of Tixchel.[104] It took place in the said year of 1557 on July 10. On the twenty-second of the said month *of July mentioned above*, day of St. Mary Magdalene, Don Luis, THEIR GOVERNOR, ran away and fled through El Baradero[105] AND WENT to the site of Chiuoha where he died.[106] Then the next year, 1558, on April 25, THIS PUEBLO OF Chiuoha was discovered by Don Pablo and there he learned of his death, and it was well known to everyone that he died of an illness.[107]

---

to indicate that he came a second time. We have no other evidence, however, that he had been there before.

[101] That is, down the Río de Acalan (Candelaria) to Tixchel.

[102] Spanish, *maceguales;* Chontal, *chanbel uinicob.*

[103] The Text simply states that for these reasons they were brought to Tixchel.

[104] The Text confirms the statement in the Spanish version that the encomendero remitted the tribute for four years, but it is very doubtful that it states that he wanted to have the pueblo moved. This has some significance in view of the fact that in 1571 García specifically stated that Pesquera moved the pueblo when he was absent in Guatemala. Cf. p. 169, *supra.*

[105] The map of Juan de Dios González of 1766 (British Museum, Add. 17654a) shows two places near Tixchel called Baradero Grande and Baradero Chico. On modern maps we find a site called Baradero on Sabancuy estuary and also a Punta Baradero on the Gulf coast nearby. These names may refer to careening places or portages. The Chontal term is *chinil.*

[106] The Text simply states that Paxua died at the pueblo of Chiuoha.

[107] There is reason to believe that the chronicler is mistaken concerning the year (1558) of Paxbolon's visit to Chiuoha. Don Pablo was then only fifteen years old, and it was not until 1566 that he assumed the governorship of Tixchel. Farther on in the Text we find that in 1574 Paxbolon pacified the Indians of Chiuoha, and it seems probable that the chronicler had this incident in mind. Cf. note 4, p. 171 *supra*, and discussion of the 1574 episode in Chapter 10. Modern maps record a site named Chivoja on the Arroyo Chivoja Grande southeast of Tixchel. We are of the opinion, however, that the pueblo to which Paxua fled and which Paxbolon pacified in 1574 was located farther inland. See Map 3, and cf. discussion of the location of Chiuoha, pp. 226-27, *supra.*

The years 1558 and 1559 had passed and as yet *the people*, THE CHONTAL
INDIANS, had not completely abandoned THEIR SITE OF *Tamactun* Acalan. A
PRINCIPAL NAMED Don Tomás Macua detained them in THE PUEBLO OF Chan-
hix.[108] They began to have disputes and trouble with those who came from
Tixchel for the food supplies they had left behind,[109] and they seized them
there, tied them up and whipped them, and took away their canoes. He
(Macua) had also settled Tixbahumilhaa. They worshipped their idols. By
this time all the Indians [of Tixchel] were about to flee. And God willed that
the Spaniards should come to Tixchel at this time. There were about thirty
soldiers.[110] Their leaders were Castrillo, Juan Vela, and Tamayo, for I do not
know which of them was captain, but they respected only these three.[111] The
oidores of Guatemala had summoned them to go to take the province of the
Lacandon and Popo,[112] and they remained here in Tixchel because they
learned that Licenciado Ramírez, WHO WAS GOING AS captain OF THIS EXPEDI-
TION, had returned, for he had taken the land and people of the Popo. Having
seen this and also that it was to the service of God and the king that they
should go to Acalan and bring down all the Indians who had remained there
and rebelled, and that things might go well and that they might be able to
reach the Lacandon,[113] Father Pesquera *told them so*, and when the Spaniards
heard this it met with their approval.[114]

[IIIb]

And they brought down the pueblo of Bote, the pueblo of Açilbaob, the
pueblo of Tutul, and those of Panob,[115] and they went to the site of Acalan and
seized Don Tomás Macua, Martín Acha, Jorge Laon, and Alonso Pacbac, and

[108] Apparently the pueblo of Chanhilix of the Chontal list (Document II) is intended.

[109] A literal translation of the Spanish would be, "on account of eating what they had left
behind."

[110] The Text states, "fifty (*lahun yuxkal*) soldiers."

[111] For this expedition of Francisco Tamayo Pacheco, Gómez de Castrillo, and Juan Vela,
see pp. 173–74, *supra*.

[112] In Chontal, *poo uinicob:* the Poo men or people. Ramírez' expedition of 1559, referred
to here, was directed against the Indians of Lacandon and Pochutla in southeastern Chiapas.
The Poo Indians may have been those of Pochutla, although it is doubtful whether the names
have a common origin. Pochutla is probably derived from the Nahuatl word *pochotl*, and
would seem to mean "the place of the ceiba trees." The name Popo, which occurs in the Spanish version, is one of the Chontal names found in Tixchel in 1569. Cf. Appendix C.

[113] It appears that the scribe omitted a sentence here in our copy of the Text.

[114] The Text breaks off abruptly here in the middle of this episode, and the next entry is
for the year 1599. Section IIIb of the Spanish version carries on the story without a break and
also records other incidents in the history of the Chontal prior to 1599. Apparently the scribe
who made our copy of the Text carelessly omitted the Chontal equivalent of this section.

[115] These were undoubtedly Chontal settlements, although the names do not appear in the
list of seventy-six Acalan towns. Açilbaob probably means "the people of Çilba." Panob is also
a plural form difficult to explain.

brought down all the people together with those who were in Tixbaumilha. They brought them down to Tixchel in the year 1560. On this account there was a very great famine, and this was the reason why Francisco Acuz and Diego Paxcanan, and also Achachu, Gonzalo Paxcanan, and Martín Paxtun, for there must have been a great number, fled with their people and old men. Don Pablo Paxbolon brought them out after finding them in the site of Sugte (Sucte), as is shown more clearly in the probanza of Don Pablo Paxbolon, governor, who went to look for them in the year he began to govern.[116] They fled again in the year 1568 and again he found them, with those who had fled before being baptized, who lived in the pueblo of Chakam. The reason why these old inhabitants [of Acalan] had fled was lest their masters should come and afflict them, because they were slaves of the ruler and other principal men. They were called Lamat, Chacantun, Paçimactun, Atoxpech, Apaxtucum, Paxbolon, Chancha, [and] Palocem,[117] together with others numbering about six hundred, including their children and women.

As soon as he found them he informed Don Luis Céspedes, who was governor in this province [of Yucatan] and was in the city of Mérida, called Taho[118] in the Yucatecan language. At this time Fray Francisco de Toral of the Order of St. Francis was bishop, the first one in this bishopric. He sent Fray Juan de Santa María of the Mercedarian Order, and the latter went to indoctrinate and baptize the Indians who had been discovered. Their pueblo was named Zapotitlan,[119] because the name of that land was not known. Some of the principal men called it by the name of Tachumbay, and others, Tachalte, and still others called it Tanaboo, and others, Tamacuy. So for this reason it was given the name of Zapotitlan.

On behalf of these people this pueblo of Tixchel underwent great toil because of the commission which Don Pablo Paxbolon, our governor, held from the [provincial] governor who was serving in the city of Mérida. By virtue of this he made us clear the roads and open the difficult rapids of the Río de Acalan where the father would pass, and carry him in a litter where he could not pass, in order that the infidels, who were in Zapotitlan, might become Christians, as we have said; and in order to take ornaments from our church, such as chalice, missal, chasuble, frontal, necessary adornment for the

[116] The Paxbolon-Maldonado Papers, Part I, contain various documents relating to Paxbolon's expedition of 1566, but they do not mention the site of Sucte. There is a place of this name east of Champoton, but obviously it is not the site mentioned here.

[117] These are all pagan names. The spellings have been changed to make them conform to those found in the Chontal Text and in various lists of Chontal personal names found in García v. Bravo.

[118] Tiho in Yucatecan Maya.

[119] This name (Sapotitanil, Xapotitanil, Çapotitan in the Spanish version), unlike other Acalan place names, is Mexican and could mean "place of the Zapote trees."

mass, as well as the images. And our sons went to teach them the Christian doctrine. In the same way he made others of us go in the year 1570, when we went to Puilha, and also to Tahbalam, to bring out the fugitive Indians, in doing which we experienced great hardship in carrying the father, who was called Gabriel de Rueda, secular priest, and also Father Monserrate, who was our vicar in Tixchel. And because [these Indians] were a long distance away, they brought them to settle in Hunlucho and they lived there, and there we brought them vestments and frontal and often carried the minister. And thus the people of Zapotitlan and Xoquelha (Xocola)[120] were settled.[121]

In the year 1574, on April 25, Don Pablo learned that Luis Queh (Ceh) of the pueblo of Xocolha had gone among the wild Indians and that he was acquainted with their pueblo, so he (Paxbolon) ordered him and also Juan Chab[122] to be summoned to the headquarters of the said pueblo[123] in order to question them and learn the truth of what they had seen. When they had come, Don Pablo asked them: "Is it true that you have been with the idolaters?" They replied that it was true that they had seen their houses and their pueblo, but that they did not know what it was called nor how many people there were.

When Don Pablo learned this, he wanted to go there at once by virtue of the commissions he held from the governors who ruled this province [of Yucatan] for the purpose of bringing out such idolatrous wild Indians. He summoned his Chontal people and chose up to a hundred of them from the pueblo of Tixchel, and we opened a road from Zapotitlan as far as Cocolha (Xocola), armed with bows and arrows, shields and spears, in case of need. We set out from Cocolha (Xocola) and reached Tachunyupi, where we spent the night, and in the morning we all departed and at the hour of vespers we reached their pueblo. We came upon them unaware, and some of the women fled and the men took their bows and arrows and came against us. Then Don Pablo said to them: "Do not shoot your arrows or allow any deaths to occur, be-

---

[120] This settlement was evidently the place to which the Indians of Puilha and Tahbalam were moved. Xoquelha is the Hispanicized form of the Chontal word *xocelhaa*, which means "river." The Vienna Dictionary (f. 180v) records *xocola* as a Maya word of the same meaning. In subsequent passages of the Spanish version of this part of the Acalan narrative, for which we have no Chontal equivalent, the Maya form of the name or variants (Cocolha, Jocola) are employed. For this reason and also because most of the people of Puilha and Tahbalam, who resettled at this town, were Yucatecan Maya fugitives, we have accepted Xocola as the preferred form of the town name.

[121] For a discussion of the Zapotitlan episode and the transfer of the Indians to new sites called Zapotitlan and Xocola (later known as Tiquintunpa and Mazcab respectively) nearer Tixchel, see Chapter 9.

[122] Ceh and Chab are Yucatecan Maya names.

[123] *Cabeza del dicho pueblo*. This undoubtedly refers to Tixchel, which was the *cabecera* of this area.

cause we do not come to kill you nor do we come for you. I only come to see you in order to tell you the word of God and the reason why the great king, my lord, sends me, for he orders me to love you." To some of them these words seemed good, to others they did not, and one of them, who was named Pazelu, started to let his arrow fly in order to shoot Don Pablo. And Juan Chab, maestro[124] of Cocolha (Xocola), whom we have already mentioned, seized his arms from behind. When the principal men of the idolatrous wild Indians, who were named Paxmulu and others, Paxtun, saw that it was Don Pablo, they went to him and said: "Lord, whether you come for war or come for us or come to kill us, here we are, do what you like." He replied to them: "Lords, I do not come for war nor do I come to seize you. I come only to preach to you the word of God and what his Majesty orders me to tell you, in order that we may all love one another and have a single desire in our hearts to love God and be ruled with the justice of his Majesty, which is the good way of life. This is my purpose in coming, and to open roads, for this is the reason why we come in such numbers. If we bear arms, it is in order to be secure against whatever might happen to us, for we do not know what people we may encounter." When they heard these explanations, they calmed down. While this was going on all the people, women and children, had gone away, so that only a very few were left in the pueblo or were to be seen, and when Don Pablo saw that there were no people, he asked them where they were, and to summon, assemble, and reassure them. Thus he calmed their hearts and therefore they undertook to reassemble the people, which was done within two or three days so that no one was missing. And in order to reassure them, he asked them and summoned some of them to go to see the pueblo of Tixchel where they would see the father and the Spaniards.

When they had been brought to our pueblo, their hair was cut,[125] and they feasted them and took them to see the Franciscan father who was ministering to us in the year 1575, who was named Fray Bartolomé Garzón. He began to teach them the four prayers and the articles, commandments, and what the Holy Mother Church ordains, and when they had learned it, the father baptized them. Vestments and images were taken to them from this church [of Tixchel] because the adornment for divine office has always been taken [from here] and for this reason we have always undergone great hardship. And our ancestors went through the same experience, as appears at the beginning of this document, at the time when the Capitán del Valle came to our land, as well

[124] Probably means that Juan Chab was *maestro de doctrina* assigned to teach the Indians the elements of Christian doctrine and ceremonial practice.

[125] Long hair was regarded as a sign of paganism.

as paying tribute to the king, our lord, as is written, in the year 1527. This pueblo mentioned above is now Chiua (Chiuoha).[126]

Memorial of how we, the Chontal Indians who live in Tixchel, went on an expedition to Christianize the infidel Indians.

In the year 1583 there came those who escaped death, one of whom, named Pedro Chan, came out at Chencan.[127] Following the sea coast toward the south, he came to where Don Pablo Paxbolon was in his estancia which is near Tixchel, for he lives there. And he began to weep when he arrived with his children, [who were] very weak, and he himself [was] wounded by an arrow in the middle of his back, and he said: "Lord Don Pablo Paxbolon, I come here to tell you that we are those who are left and have escaped death, for my companions were killed by the fugitive Indians of Chunguiyzili (Chunuitzil), who are called Aquebob, who are many in number. We are from Hecelchakan, and we came to Hunguizil (Chunuitzil) and the fugitive Aquelbes (*sic*) came to kill us.[128] Some of them shot with arrows, some of them used spears, and they killed our old men and principal men who ruled us and the ah cuchcab[129] Tuyu, who was called Açitiache in our nomenclature. And we killed five or six of them. Many of my companions died, many fled, and I was shot in the middle of the back. Some of my companions went to the forest, some of them returned to Hecelchakan, and women, children, and some men wandered through that region without knowing where." When Don Pablo heard that those people were wandering about scattered through the forest without knowing where they were going and that it was to be feared that they might perish of hunger and thirst, he went to Xocola and Zapotitlan of his jurisdiction and whose [people] he had brought out of the forest, and he assembled them and sent them into the forest to regions and places where they (the fugitives from Hecelchakan) might have come by chance, sending out parties of men in all directions and charging them to gather in those people of Hecelchakan who were wandering lost and scattered by the fugitive Indians. He sent those of Xocola to Puila, near Chunuitzil, where they had been put to flight, and God was pleased that they should find them little by little. The

[126] For additional data concerning the activities of Paxbolon in 1574 and the founding of a mission at Chiuoha, see pp. 221–25, *supra*.

[127] A site on the Gulf coast south of Champoton.

[128] Aquebob is probably the equivalent of the Maya Ah Kebob and could be translated as people of the Keb name or lineage. Early in the seventeenth century there was a settlement of fugitive Indians from northern Yucatan named Chacuitzil, sometimes spelled Chunuitzil, southeast of Tixchel. This settlement was closely associated with another called Aguatayn, of which a certain Miguel Queb was governor at one time (Paxbolon-Maldonado Papers, Part II). Cf. pp. 263, 275–76, *supra*.

[129] The Yucatecan *ah cuchcab* was a member of the town council and often the head of a subdivision of the town.

search for them and bringing them in lasted about eight or nine months, and they were settled there in Xocola near the others. Marcos Balam [and] Gonzalo Çuco (Tzuc), the old men of Xocola, and Juan Hauiche (Cauich), who was the most important of those found, seeing that about sixty had now been assembled, spoke to Don Pablo and told him that they wanted to settle near the embarcadero of Mamantel,[130] because [their settlement] was far from there and they had suffered great hardship and [that] there they would be able to attend mass. So he assigned them land, which they call Popola, halfway on the road from Chiuoha, and there Cauich and his companions settled.[131]

In the year 1586 Dr. Palacios came to inspect the land,[132] and we, the Indians of Tixchel, gave him canoes [and] paddlers. We opened the roads so that the minister might go to visit these pueblos. In their behalf we always had and have undergone a great deal of trouble in giving them vestments, in order that the Holy Sacraments might be administered to them, and we have done all this for the purpose of serving God and the king, our lord, until it was ordered, in accordance with the assessment [of tribute], that all of us should support the minister, the church, and our governor.

I have already told in this account of the descent of the Mactun Chontal Indians from the time when the Capitán del Valle went to their lands. And in order that our way of life from the year 1527 to the year 1610, which is the present year, may be known, it is necessary to write of their names and deeds in order to show how we go out on our roads and make entradas, even among the Yucatecans, people [who come] from all the pueblos, like those who are in Popola, Mazcab, which was Jocola (Xocola), and the other pueblos which are here.

[IIIc]

[133][It was] in the year 1599 when they began to gather together the Yucatecans[134] who had escaped death at the hand of Pedro Tzakum-May there in Holha, BEGINNING OF THE RIVER, NEAR CHENCANAL AND ABOVE THE ESTANCIA OF FRANCISCO MALDONADO CALLED USULABAN and the savannas of Chunal,[135]

[130] Possibly refers to a site at the end of deep water on the Mamantel.
[131] For discussion of this incident of the fugitives from Hecelchakan, see pp. 229-31, *supra.*
[132] Dr. Diego García de Palacio was visitador of Yucatan in 1583-84.
[133] The Chontal Text begins again at this point.
[134] *Maya uinicob.*
[135] From documents of the year 1615 in the Paxbolon-Maldonado Papers, Part II, we learn that the savannas of Chunal were the place where the pueblo of Sahcabchen was established. A short distance to the east was the Holha River, which flowed into the Gulf at Chencan. Cf. pp. 287-90, *supra.*

for he roamed in all directions. There they (the people of Pedro Tzakum-May at Holha) killed those who went from Campeche and all the pueblos to cut wax and hunt iguanas. And they also went out to the shore of the sea at Tixcem, Chencan, and Uxkakaltok to take the knives, machetes, clothing, and whatever else was being carried by those who passed by WHEN THEY TRAVELED along the road which is near the sea. As soon as Don Pablo learned this from those who WENT BY THE ROAD AND arrived AT TIXCHEL AND THE NEWS ABOUT the fugitive Indians of Holha and in the cuyos[136] of Uzulhaban, he asked Don Diego [Fernández] de Velasco, governor of this province of Yucatan, for a commission to go to the forest to look for them and seize *the fugitive Indians*. And so he gave it to him together with authority to take the Indians that he needed FROM HIS PROVINCE [of Tixchel]. And so we of Tixchel went, and he took some from Popola, Chiuoha, Mazcab, [and] Tiquintupa, WHICH WAS ZAPOTITLAN, and these accompanied us. We went and passed by way of the estancia and opened a road as far as Uzulhaban. There we found a hut frequented by the fugitive Indians *mentioned above* and where they made a fire. AT THIS TIME God willed that the people of Champoton, having had news of them (the fugitive Indians), should go to seek them, and they found them in Kinacnal and dispersed them. And they went away and came *to Uzulhaban* where we were, and so we OF TIXCHEL seized them. In all there were about four score [or] *five score with their women and children*. We took them to Tixchel. At this time Fray Diego Mejía de Figueroa was guardian, and his companion [was] Fray Joseph Bosque. The children were baptized, together with three or four[137] of the adults who had not been baptized.

Don Pablo asked them if all that land through which they wandered was good, and they replied that it was, that it was suitable for houses, milpas, [and] cacao groves. Therefore Fray Joseph Bosque was sent WITH SOME INDIANS to inspect it, and he entered by Chiuoha, passed by way of Uzulhaban, *and we with him*, and from there he came out at the estancia of Francisco Maldonado. And he came back to tell Fray Diego Mejía, HIS GUARDIAN, how good the land was and that a large pueblo could go to it and make very good milperías because there were very large cedars and forested country, and that all the pueblos of Popolha, Ticintunpa, Mahazcab, CHIUOHA, AND TIXCHEL could be accommodated there. Therefore they told Don Pablo that there *religious instruction* [and] the Holy Gospel could be administered to all of them together. The principales[138] were consulted about all of this and all of them

---

[136] Possibly artificial mounds, or *cues*. The Chontal word is *tanhkal*, which we cannot translate.

[137] The Text says two or three.

[138] *Nuc uinicob*.

approved; and the same matter was discussed with Mateo de Aguilar, the en-comendero *for the pueblo of Tixchel*. Therefore, on behalf of all a message was sent to *Juan de Sanabria*, Defender OF THE INDIANS, so that in the name of all he might petition THE GOVERNOR [for] *decree and license* in order that *people of all the towns* might go together to the site of Uzulhaban. Thus permission, dated at the pueblo of Calkini, was given by Don Diego [Fernández] de Velasco, governor at that time, for all to go together to the site of Uzulhaban. And therefore when the said license arrived, Don Pablo Paxbolon, our governor, communicated it to all the pueblos. At this time the news arrived that the administration of the natives of this province was being taken away from the Franciscan fathers, *here at the pueblo of Tixchel*, and given to the secular clergy by virtue of an order of his Majesty which came from Spain.[139] And that was the reason why the removal of the pueblos to Uzulhaban did not take place, because there was no one to encourage them. Therefore only a few went upon the arrival of the license, AND THERE THE MATTER RESTED.[140]

Then Juan Rodríguez, secular priest, came as vicar OF THIS PROVINCE [of Tixchel]. THE LORD bishop, Don Fray Juan Izquierdo, of this bishopric of Yucatan sent him on January 6 of the year 1603.[141] After SEEING THE LANDS, he said that Uzulhaban was a long way and that the roads would fill up in the rainy seasons. And it was *Juan Rodríguez* who blessed the land FOR THE PUEBLO AND BUILT A CHURCH and named it San Felipe and San Diego[142] *of the pueblo of Uzulhaban* on the twenty-third of the month of April of the year 1604.[143]

[139] The missions of Ichmul, Hocaba, Tixkokob, and Tixchel were secularized by virtue of royal decrees dated March 9 and May 1, 1602 (Ayeta, *ca.* 1693; Carrillo y Ancona, 1895, 1:349-50).

[140] The Spanish version omits a sentence which follows here in the Chontal Text. A very tentative translation is: "Their names are to be seen written on the back of the document of my [our?] record [or history]."

[141] Bishop Izquierdo died on November 17, 1602 (Carrillo y Ancona, 1895, 1:354), but he may have appointed Father Rodríguez as vicar of Tixchel prior to that date.

[142] Santiago in the Spanish version.

[143] The Text, which ends at this point, gives the year as 1614, obviously an error on the part of the scribe who made our copy.

APPENDIX B

The Location of Acalan

THE LOCATION of Acalan has been the subject of considerable speculation and argument. Because of the lack of data on the later history of
Acalan in the colonial chronicles, the problem has hitherto been studied in
relation to the expedition of Cortés from Mexico to Honduras in 1524–25, or
to that of Avila from Chiapas to Champoton in 1530. In each case Acalan was
an important place en route. Unfortunately the information concerning the
routes of these early entradas recorded in the traditional sources is not so
precise or accurate as we should wish, and the language of the Spanish originals
is sometimes vague and obscure. It is not surprising, therefore, that students of
the early history of Middle America have held conflicting views on the location of the province.

The divergent opinions on this subject may also be explained in part by
the fact that colonial maps record few of the places mentioned in the accounts
of Cortés' journey. W. H. Prescott calls attention to this in his *Conquest of
Mexico* (1843), and he makes no attempt to give a precise location for
Acalan.[1] It may be noted, however, that the name Acalan appears on a map
of the Gulf of Mexico and the Caribbean made in 1731 by the celebrated
French geographer, Jean Baptiste Bourguignon d'Anville.[2] Here Acalan
marks an area facing the Caribbean coast northeast of Lake Peten and between
Mopan to the south and Tipu to the north. But the location of Acalan on this
map is obviously incorrect, and it illustrates the lack of knowledge concerning
the province in later colonial times.

As far as we know, the first modern map to record a location for Acalan
is the Dudley Costello map of Yucatan, published in 1854 in C. St. J. Fancourt's *History of Yucatan*.[3] Here the legend "Country of the Acalans," appears just below Laguna de Términos and between the Usumacinta and Candelaria Rivers. The map also shows Cortés' line of march to Honduras, but
curiously enough it does not pass through the Acalan area indicated. Instead,
it follows along the Usumacinta to a point above the junction with the Río
San Pedro Mártir, and then turns southeast to Lake Peten.

[1] Prescott, 1843, 2: 371.
[2] Carte des Isles de l'Amerique et de plusieurs Pays de Terre Ferme situés au devant de ces
Isles & autour du Golfe de Mexique . . . Par le Sr d'Anville, Geographe Ordre du Roi, mars
1731. Reproduced in Haring, 1910, and in Cartografía de la América Central (Guatemala, 1929),
no. 19. For an estimate of d'Anville's work, see Encyclopedia Britannica, 1943 ed., 2:90.
[3] This map is reproduced in Cortés, 1908, vol. 2.

In the text of his *History*, Fancourt does not identify any specific area as Acalan, but he clearly implies that the province was located in the interior between the Usumacinta and the Itza territory. It should also be noted that he confuses the province of Acalan with the land of the Chol Acala, where Fray Domingo de Vico, the Dominican missionary and linguist, suffered martyrdom in 1555.[4] In this he was apparently misled by statements in Antonio de León Pinelo's seventeenth-century account of tribes in the interior between Yucatan and Verapaz[5] and by Villagutierre's story of the death of Father Vico and the campaign of Ramírez de Quiñones against the Indians of Lacandon and Pochutla in 1559. There can be no doubt, however, that the Chol Acala, who were neighbors of the Lacandon, were separate and distinct from the Chontal of Acalan.[5a] As we shall see farther on, other writers besides Fancourt have apparently confused these two groups.

Fancourt's ideas concerning the province of Acalan probably explain the direction of Cortés' route as shown on the Costello map. But it is difficult to account for the fact that the same map locates the "Country of the Acalans" so far to the north close to Laguna de Términos. It will become apparent, however, in the course of our discussion that this location is fairly accurate.

A map in Sir Arthur Helps' *Spanish Conquest in America*, originally published in 1855–61, places Acalan between what appears to be the Río San Pedro Mártir and Lake Peten. S. Ruge's *Geschichte des Zeitalters der Entdeckungen*, published in 1881, contains a text map on which the name Acalan appears east of the Usumacinta and south of Laguna de Términos.[6] This location is similar to that on the Costello map of 1854, although Ruge does not cite Fancourt.

In a work entitled *Historia de la dominación española en México*, written about 1849 but not published *in toto* until 1938, M. Orozco y Berra, the distinguished Mexican ethnographer and historian, locates Acalan west of the Usumacinta in the state of Chiapas.[7] This suggests that the author, like Fancourt, confused the Chontal of Acalan and the Chol Acala. As noted above, the Acala were neighbors of the Lacandon, and the major strongholds of the latter were in southeastern Chiapas.

Maler also places Acalan west of the Usumacinta, although farther north

[4] Fancourt, 1854, chs. 3, 4, 12, *passim.* Thompson (1938, p. 586 and map, p. 588) places the Chol Acala southeast of Tenosique.

[5] León Pinelo's report is translated in Stone, 1932, pp. 237–55.

[5a] Ximénez, writing in the eighteenth century, noted that Villagutierre had confused a place called Acalan with the region of the Chol Acala. He suggested that Acalan might be "near Campeche" (Ximénez, 1929–31, bk. 4, ch. 62).

[6] Helps, 1855–61, map in vol. 3; Ruge, 1881, p. 391. Ruge's map is reproduced in Winsor, 1884–89, 2: 384.

[7] Orozco y Berra, 1938, 1: 134–42, *passim.* Part of this work was published in 1906, but most of the edition was apparently destroyed (*ibid.*, 1: ix–x).

than Orozco y Berra's location. In his *Mémoire sur l'état de Chiapa (Mexique)*, published in 1884, he identified the ruins of Palenque as the town of Teutiercas, one of the principal Acalan settlements. Maler's views were accepted by Cyrus Thomas, but Brinton challenged them in a short paper in which he stated that Palenque was nowhere near Cortés' route and that Acalan was located on the southern and eastern shores of Laguna de Términos. In 1910 Maler reiterated his earlier conclusions and identified Canizan, on the left bank of the Usumacinta, as Itzamkanac, the Acalan capital.[8]

In the first volume of his *History of Central America* (1882–87) H. H. Bancroft describes Acalan as "a large province bounded by Laguna de Términos, the broad Usumacinta, and the ranges of Vera Paz, a low-lying country abounding in morasses, miasmatic inlets, and winding rivers tributary to the Términos." This description of the physical geography is accurate, but the territorial limits embrace an area wide enough to include most of the more localized areas which other writers designate as the Acalan lands. On the frontispiece map of the second volume of his *History of Mexico* (1883–88) the name Acalan appears below Laguna de Términos, apparently indicating a more restricted area than the one described above. This location is similar to those on the maps of Costello and Ruge. J. F. Molina Solís (1896) locates the province southwest of Laguna de Términos and states the opinion that Itzamkanac was probably on the Candelaria.[9]

The well-known map of Yucatan and adjacent areas published about 1910 by A. Espinosa is noted for its wealth of ethnographic data and its delineation of cacicazgo boundaries. This map places the cacicazgo of Acalan close to the Gulf coast between the lower course of the Usumacinta (below Jonuta) and the western end of Laguna de Términos.[10]

A study of Cortés' route to Acalan was made in 1910 by M. E. Becerra, a Tabasqueño who has written various works on local ethnography and linguistics. In his paper he attempts to interpret the narratives of Cortés and Bernal Díaz in the light of local geography and the meaning of place names. He concludes that Cortés reached the Usumacinta near Montecristo (Emiliano Zapata), crossed it near Tenosique, and then marched to the San Pedro Mártir, which he identifies as the great estero where the famous bridge was built. The modern hacienda or rancho of Gracias a Dios on the San Pedro Mártir is indicated as the probable site of the bridge. Thus Acalan lay to the east in western Peten, although Becerra does not specify locations for any of the towns.[11]

[8] Maler, 1884, pp. 321–24, and 1910, pp. 165–66; Thomas, 1885; Brinton, 1885.
[9] Bancroft, 1882–87, 1: 546, and 1883–88, vol. 2; Molina Solís, 1896, pp. 217, 436.
[10] Espinosa, *ca.* 1910.   [11] Becerra, 1910a.

In Appendix A of the fifth volume of his translation of Bernal Díaz (1908–16), A. P. Maudslay writes: "I feel fully confident that the province of Acalá was on the Rio San Pedro Mártir, an affluent of the Rio Usumacinta." On the maps showing Cortés' line of march accompanying the same volume the word "Acalá" is spread across the course of the San Pedro Mártir in southeastern Tabasco and the western part of the Peten. The name "Izancanac," followed by an interrogation point, appears along the north bank of the river and east of the site of Progreso, which is located close to the Guatemala-Mexico boundary. The consistent use of the term "Acalá" instead of Acalan in his translation of Bernal Díaz and in his version of Cortés' Fifth Letter suggests that Maudslay also may have confused the province of Acalan and that of the Chol Acala.[12]

S. G. Morley describes the entradas of Cortés and Avila at some length in the first volume of *The Inscriptions of Peten* (1937–38). His discussion is based on a careful study of the colonial chronicles and to some extent on statements in the Spanish translation of the Chontal Text, to which he had access. (It may be noted that other manuscript sources frequently cited in the present volume were not available for his use.) His conclusion as to the location of Itzamkanac, which he places at or near the modern site of Mactun on the north bank of the San Pedro Mártir some 22 km. east of the Guatemala-Mexico boundary, closely approximates Maudslay's tentative location of the Acalan capital. Morley describes the province of Acalan as the area lying between the Candelaria, San Pedro Mártir, and Usumacinta Rivers.[13]

A recent paper (1940) on Cortés' route by P. A. González, who has served as an engineer in the construction of the new Ferrocarril del Sureste from Campeche to Tenosique, clearly shows the influence of Becerra. Indeed, on certain points he reproduces Becerra's conclusions and linguistic arguments. González places Acalan in western Peten, and on the map which illustrates the paper he locates Itzamkanac on the extreme headwaters of the San Pedro branch of the Candelaria, shown as rising only a short distance north of the east-west course of the San Pedro Mártir.[14] Thus the author locates the Acalan capital in the same general region as do Maudslay and Morley, but on a different stream. Although we possess very little accurate knowledge of the

---

[12] Díaz del Castillo, 1908–16, 5: 337 and maps. Bernal Díaz uses the form Acalá, which Maudslay reproduces. But in his translation of the Fifth Letter, Maudslay also uses the form Acalá, although the Spanish text of the Letter has Acalan. This indicates that Maudslay regarded Acalá as the preferred form and suggests, as noted above, that he may have confused the area of the Chol Acalá with Acalan.

[13] Morley, 1937–38, 1: 15–16, 73.

[14] González, 1940.

geography of northwestern Peten, most modern maps do not show the San Pedro branch of the Candelaria as rising so far to the south. According to most maps, González' location of Itzamkanac would be in the region of the Río Escondido, one of the northern tributaries of the San Pedro Mártir.

Dissent from the Becerra-Maudslay-Morley-González school of thought which places the province of Acalan in the interior, is found in the writings of Mrs. D. Z. Stone (1932) and E. W. Andrews (1943). On the basis of her interpretation of certain passages in Cortés' Fifth Letter, as well as other evidence, Mrs. Stone locates Itzamkanac near the mouth of the Candelaria on Panlao estuary, one of the inlets on the southern shore of Laguna de Términos. Andrews locates the province along the Candelaria and states that "Itzamkanac was probably close to the south bank of the river at some point above El Suspiro and below Imposible." In a study of the life of Cuauhtemoc published in 1945 H. Pérez Martínez agrees with Stone and Andrews that Itzamkanac was situated on the lower Candelaria and defines the lands of Acalan as comprising the territory of Términos. It should also be noted that J. E. S. Thompson, writing in 1938, located Acalan "in the vicinity of the Terminos Bay," and called attention to the fact that the Acalan people should not be confused with the Chol Acala.[15]

Thus we find that students have expressed widely divergent opinions on this question during the past ninety years. With the exception of Orozco y Berra and Maler, however, they are agreed on one major point: that Acalan was east of the Usumacinta, a view that is obviously justified by the well-established fact that Cortés reached Acalan en route from the Usumacinta to Lake Peten. The chief problem to be solved is whether Acalan was as far inland as some writers believe, or was closer to the Gulf coast.

Our own study of the problem is based on a wide range of materials, including numerous unpublished sources from the Archivo General de Indias. Unfortunately the new manuscript sources do not provide definitive answers to all disputed points, but they do contain sufficient evidence to resolve the major problem of the general location of the Acalan lands. In the early stages of our investigations, we reached the conclusion that the most important settlements of the cacicazgo, including the capital, Itzamkanac, were situated along the upper course of the Candelaria river system, and above the rapids or falls which impede traffic on this stream. This conclusion is shared by Dr. Robert S. Chamberlain, who is writing a volume on the conquest of Yucatan and collaborated with us in the preliminary phases of the Acalan investigations.

---

15 Stone, 1932, pp. 221–22; Andrews, 1943, p. 21; Pérez Martínez, 1945, pp. 236, 277–80; Thompson, 1938, p. 586.

Certain statements in Cortés' Fifth Letter, describing his journey to Honduras in 1524–25, indicate that there was a route of trade and communication by water from Acalan to Xicalango and other points in Tabasco. (1) We are told that after Cortés reached Iztapa on the Usumacinta River he sent three Spaniards in canoes to the Gulf coast to obtain provisions and transport them "por un gran estero arriba y pasé á la provincia de Acalan," where he would be waiting. (2) In another place Cortés states that "Izancanac . . . está en la ribera de un gran estero que atraviesa hasta el puerto de Términos de Xicalango y Tabasco." (3) In his description of the Acalan area he says: "Esta provincia de Acalan . . . está toda cercada de esteros y todos ellos salen á la bahía ó puerto que llaman de Términos, por donde en canoas tienen gran contratación en Xicalango y Tabasco."[16]

Interpretation of these passages from the Spanish text of the Fifth Letter depends to some extent on the meaning of the word *estero*. It has various meanings, such as estuary, an expanse of water, a swamp or overflow area, and in American usage it may denote a stream or arroyo. P. de Gayangos translates the first passage as "by a great sheet of water communicating with the province of Acalan." In the second he renders the word estero as "gulf, or lagoon," and in the third as "lagoon." MacNutt uses the term "lagoon" in all three cases. In Maudslay's version the word is translated as "river" in the first and second passages, and as "watercourse" in the third. Mrs. Stone quotes MacNutt's translation of the second passage, and she identifies the "lagoon" as Laguna de Términos. As noted above, she also locates Itzamkanac near the mouth of the Candelaria on Panlao estuary.[17]

Although Laguna de Términos undoubtedly formed part of the water route from Acalan to Xicalango, Mrs. Stone's location of Itzamkanac fails to take into account other evidence on this point. Oviedo's narrative of the Avila expedition of 1530 uses the word *río*, "river," to describe the body of water on which the Acalan capital was situated.[18] This alone would not rule out Mrs. Stone's location, since she places the town at the mouth of the Candelaria. Other sources show, however, that Itzamkanac was not located on the coast but some distance upstream. For example, Bienvenida's letter of 1548, from which we quote below, mentions the falls or rapids ("grandes saltos de agua") which had to be passed en route to the pueblo of Acalan. It is apparent therefore that the passages from Cortés' Fifth Letter, if we take them as a

[16] Cortés, 1866, pp. 408, 419, 421.
[17] Cortés, 1868, pp. 21, 38, 42; 1908, 2: 246, 259, 263; 1916, pp. 360, 371, 373; Stone, 1932, pp. 221–22.
[18] Oviedo y Valdés, 1851–55; bk. 32, ch. 5.

whole, refer to a water route consisting of Laguna de Términos and a river system emptying into it.

Additional evidence on this point is found in a probanza concerning the provinces of Acalan and Mazatlan (the land of the Cehache) formulated by Don Francisco de Montejo, Adelantado of Yucatan, in the autumn of 1531. This document is one of a series of five drawn up in 1530–33 to support Montejo's pretensions to jurisdiction over the entire area from western Tabasco to the Ulua River in Honduras.[19]

The probanza was initiated by a petition presented to one of the alcaldes of Salamanca de Campeche on September 10, 1531, in which Montejo stated that he wished to record testimony concerning the results of Avila's recent entrada through the provinces of Acalan and Mazatlan, "which are located seven or eight leagues from the north coast [Gulf coast] and belong to my said government." With this petition he filed an interrogatory of five questions setting forth the essential facts he wished to establish. The fourth and fifth questions are as follows:

iiii. Also, do they [the witnesses to be examined] know that the said provinces of Acalan and Mazatlan are very close to this Northern Sea, [that] the Indians of Acalan trade by sea with the Indians of the coast and in three days come from the pueblos of Acalan to Xicalango, and that from the mouth of the Río de Acalan takes two days and more, and in another day they come from Acalan to the mouth [of the said river]?

v. Also, do they know that the said provinces of Acalan and Mazatlan are in the center of Yucatan and are the most important ones of it and closest to the Northern Sea, and that [coming] from Acalan there is no pueblo closer to the sea than the said Acalan?

Twelve witnesses, all of whom had participated in the Avila expedition, confirmed the general location of the provinces of Acalan and Mazatlan as stated above, and several testified that they knew from personal experience that the Indians of Acalan carried on trade with Xicalango. One also stated that he had been "at the mouth of the river which empties into Términos, [and] which comes from Acalan to the north coast." With regard to the schedule of travel time from Acalan to Xicalango, ten witnesses gave affirmative answers without actually specifying the time involved. Of the two remaining witnesses, one gave the time as three days. The other testified that at one time "Avila wished to send this witness from the said Acalan to Xicalango and the Indians said that they would take him and bring him back in six days."

[19] Sobre las provincias de Acalan y Mazatlan, 1531, *in* Montejo *v.* Alvarado.

The foregoing evidence clearly shows that there were two stages in the water route from Acalan to Xicalango. The first was the journey down the Río de Acalan to its mouth at Laguna de Términos; the second was across the Laguna to Xicalango.

The probanza also indicates that the province of Acalan, or at least its northwestern border, was close to the Gulf coast. It is obvious, of course, that Montejo was anxious to build up as strong a case as possible for his claim to jurisdiction over Acalan and Mazatlan. Consequently we must be cautious about accepting all the evidence at face value. But the probanza, taken as a whole, provides strong proof that the province was not located far in the interior, as some students have believed, but was situated fairly close to the coast.

The schedule of travel time, as stated in the fourth question of the interrogatory, deserves careful analysis, and we shall discuss it later in connection with other data of similar character. It is also a matter of some importance to determine what is meant by the statement at the end of the fifth question, "that [coming] from Acalan there is no pueblo closer to the sea than the said Acalan." Does "the said Acalan" refer to the pueblo of Acalan-Itzamkanac or to the province? It is apparent from Montejo's petition of September 10, 1531, and from the general tenor of the interrogatory that he was thinking in terms of the province as a whole. Moreover, it may be noted that in the entire probanza there is not a single positive reference to the capital of the province as such, either by name or by such a term as *cabecera*. It would appear, therefore, that the passage quoted refers to the province of Acalan, and was intended to stress its proximity to the Gulf coast by indicating lack of settlement in the intervening area.

The statement that the provinces of Acalan and Mazatlan "are in the center of Yucatan" also deserves some comment. What Montejo obviously had in mind was the administrative area, or government, of Yucatan, over which he had been granted jurisdiction as adelantado, governor, and captain general by virtue of the *capitulación*, or contract, of 1526. Because of lack of geographical knowledge, the territorial limits of his government had not been fixed at the time of his appointment. In the course of time, however, Montejo formed definite views concerning the area that should constitute the *adelantamiento* of Yucatan. He believed that the entire region from the Copilco River in Tabasco to the Ulua River in Honduras formed a geographic, economic, and linguistic unit, and he petitioned the Crown to define his jurisdiction in such terms. Consequently, the statement that the provinces of Acalan and Mazatlan "are in the center of Yucatan" evidently means that they occupied a central, strategic position within the larger area which he hoped to weld into a single governmental and administrative unit.

Another link in the chain of evidence relating to the location of Acalan is the letter of Fray Lorenzo de Bienvenida to Prince Philip, dated February 10, 1548. In this letter the famous missionary of Yucatan noted the unhappy state into which Acalan had fallen since the coming of the Spaniards and the urgent need for drastic measures to remedy the situation. Whereas it had once been a prosperous province, it had been reduced to 200 houses in one major settlement, "the pueblo called Acalan," which was undoubtedly the old capital, Itzamkanac. He described the location of the pueblo and the difficulty of travel to it: ". . . y lexos desta tierra yvan por lagunas en canoas á él y tardan los yndios diez dias en yr y con muy gran peligro, que an de esperar tiempos, porque ay grandes saltos de agua. . . ." He recommended that the inhabitants should be moved to a site near Champoton or Campeche, where it would be easier to protect them from injustice and to effect their conversion to Christianity.[20]

The statement that the journey by canoe to the pueblo of Acalan took ten days probably refers to travel time from northern Yucatan. We shall discuss this time schedule later. For our immediate purposes the most important point in Bienvenida's letter is the reference to "grandes saltos de agua," falls or rapids, which had to be passed before reaching the pueblo, for it is one of the basic facts that must be taken into account in locating the Acalan lands and it also indicates that the capital, Acalan-Itzamkanac, was located above these obstacles in the Río de Acalan. Bienvenida's statement is confirmed by a passage in the Spanish version of the Chontal Text which mentions the "difficult rapids of the Río de Acalan" (*malos saltos del Río de Acalan*).

Thus we find that the Acalan lands were located along a river which empties into Laguna de Términos and on which there is a series of rapids and falls. The province was also in fairly close proximity to the Gulf coast.

The most important river systems which empty into Laguna de Términos are the Mamantel, the Candelaria, the Chumpan, and the Usumacinta through one of its lower branches, the Palizada. According to the information at our disposal, only two of these, the Candelaria and the Usumacinta, including its tributary, the San Pedro Mártir, have rapids or falls which impede boat traffic. The rapids and falls on the Candelaria have been described in Chapter 3. In the case of the Usumacinta system, there are rapids on the main stream in the gorge above Tenosique. On the San Pedro Mártir rapids and falls exist between Tiradero and the junction with the Usumacinta (Andrews, 1943, fig.

[20] Cartas de Indias, 1877, pp. 75–76.

27*a*, gives a photograph of the falls at La Reforma), and there is a sharp drop, or salto, in the river just below Mactun in the Peten. Occasional rapids interspersed between overflow areas also occur on the south-to-north course of the river above Tiradero, but these do not constitute serious obstacles to navigation.[21]

The main stream of the Usumacinta is ruled out as a possible choice for the Río de Acalan for various reasons, the most important being the fact that the sources for the Cortés and Avila expeditions clearly indicate that Acalan was located some distance to the east. The San Pedro Mártir deserves consideration because such eminent authorities as Maudslay and Morley locate the principal Acalan settlements on or near this stream. Their views must be tested, however, by reference to the evidence in Montejo's probanza and other data.

As noted above, Maudslay's map of Cortés' route places the Acalan lands along the San Pedro Mártir in southeastern Tabasco and in the western part of the Peten. The area marked "Acala" includes a section of the river extending upstream from about midway on its south-to-north course to the general region of Mactun. Although the rapids and falls between Tiradero and the Usumacinta below this section of the river and the sharp drop near Mactun can doubtless be considered "grandes saltos de agua," which, according to Bienvenida, existed on the Río de Acalan, the entire area is too far inland to satisfy the general requirements of Montejo's probanza concerning the proximity of the province of Acalan to the Gulf coast.

We also encounter difficulties if we attempt to apply the probanza data concerning the water route and the schedule of travel time by canoe from "the pueblos of Acalan" to Xicalango. The probanza shows that the entire journey could be made in three days and was divided into two stages: the first stage comprised the downstream trip to the mouth of the Río de Acalan and was said to take one day; the second was from the mouth of the river to Xicalango and took two days. It is very doubtful that the Indians in canoes could cover the entire distance, exceeding 300 km., from Maudslay's "Acala" to Xicalango in three days. Moreover, since the mouth of the Río de Acalan was at Términos, as the testimony of one of Montejo's witnesses indicates, it would be necessary to assume that the Río de Acalan comprised not only the San Pedro Mártir but also part of the lower Usumacinta and the Palizada. There is no evidence to support such an assumption; in fact, the available data, both specific and inferential, indicate that the Usumacinta and the Río de Acalan formed separate river systems (cf. p. 456, *infra*). It is also evident

[21] Communication from S. G. Morley.

that if the mouth of the Palizada marked the dividing point of the two stages of the journey from Acalan to Xicalango, the time schedules as stated above would have no validity. It would be impossible to travel by canoe in one day from Maudslay's "Acala" to the mouth of the Palizada; nor would the trip from the mouth of the river to Xicalango take twice as long as the downstream stage of the journey.

It would also be difficult to reconcile Maudslay's location of the province with the statement in the fifth question of Montejo's probanza, which indicates lack of settlement between Acalan and the Gulf coast, for there were several towns on the Usumacinta below the junction with the San Pedro Mártir. The only way to solve this difficulty would be to assume that the uninhabited stretch was the region extending overland from the lower course of the San Pedro Mártir across the Chumpan area to the Laguna, for which we have no evidence of settlement at the time of the conquest. We are of the opinion, however, that what Montejo had in mind was lack of settlement on the lower part of the Río de Acalan between the province of Acalan and the coast.

Morley notes that the province of Acalan, according to Cortés, "was completely surrounded by streams, all of which emptied into Laguna de Términos. This was almost literally true, as we have seen, the province lying as it does between the Río Candelaria on the north, the Río San Pedro Mártir on the south, and the Río Usumacinta on the west." [22] This is a rather far-fetched interpretation of the third passage from Cortés' Fifth Letter quoted above on page 411, and we shall have more to say about it farther on (see. p. 460). The northern boundary of the area defined by Morley might possibly be regarded as close enough to the Gulf coast to satisfy the general requirements of Montejo's probanza, but the region as a whole is too far inland. Moreover, Morley clearly regards the San Pedro Mártir as the center of gravity of the Acalan area, for he locates Itzamkanac at or near Mactun on the east-west course of the river in the Peten. [23] In short, it would still be necessary to identify the San Pedro Mártir as the Río de Acalan, and this would involve the same difficulties already noted in our discussion of Maudslay's location.

Thus we find it difficult to reconcile a location for Acalan on the San Pedro Mártir with the data in the Montejo probanza of 1531. Other reasons for rejecting this location may be briefly stated as follows:

1. For administrative purposes the province of Acalan was always regarded as part of the government of Yucatan and subject to the jurisdiction

[22] Morley, 1937–38, 1: 73.
[23] Ibid., 1: 15–16.

of its central governmental agencies. This was true in the time of the Montejos and also subsequent to 1550, when Yucatan was administered by alcaldes mayores or by governors appointed at first by the audiencia to which Yucatan was subject and later by direct nomination by the Crown. If Acalan, and especially its capital, Itzamkanac, had been located on the San Pedro Mártir, it would have been more logical to include the area within the alcaldía mayor of Tabasco. In 1582 the governor of Yucatan appointed Feliciano Bravo corregidor of Campeche, with jurisdiction over the districts of Calkini, Champoton, Tixchel, and the old Acalan area.[24] It is extremely unlikely that Acalan would have been included in such a jurisdictional unit if the province had comprised an area so far away as the San Pedro Mártir.

2. The Indians of Acalan always paid tribute in Campeche, except for two brief periods when the payments were made in Tabasco. (See discussion of the Acalan encomiendas in Chapter 7.) This fact also argues for a location of the province closer to Yucatan proper than the San Pedro Mártir.

3. In 1548 Fray Lorenzo de Bienvenida recommended that the Indians of Acalan should be moved to a site near Campeche or Champoton, where missionary work could be carried on more effectively. This proposal was not carried out at the time, but about a decade later the Acalan were moved to Tixchel on Sabancuy estuary.[25] If their original home was on the San Pedro Mártir, it would have been simpler and more logical to have moved them to a site on the Usumacinta, where other Chontal-speaking towns existed.

4. Finally, we call attention to evidence presented in Appendix D which clearly shows that in 1573–74 citizens of Yucatan and Tabasco regarded the Acalan lands and the Peten area of the San Pedro Mártir (then called the Río de Tachis) as different and separate regions.

From time to time in the succeeding sections of this appendix we shall discuss the San Pedro Mártir location for Acalan in relation to other problems and other evidence. We believe, however, that the arguments already presented constitute a very strong case against the views held by Maudslay and Morley. If we eliminate the San Pedro Mártir as a possible choice for the Río de Acalan, then the only other possibility is the Candelaria. But the case in favor of the Candelaria does not rest solely upon this process of elimination. We shall now present positive evidence to identify this stream as the Río de Acalan.

In Chapter 9 we have described the pacification of the Indians of Zapotitlan

---

[24] Probanzas of Feliciano Bravo, AGI, México, leg. 109. Cf. also Appendix D, p. 498, *infra.*
[25] Cf. pp. 164, 168–71, *supra.*

by Don Pablo Paxbolon, cacique of Acalan-Tixchel, and subsequent events in the Zapotitlan area. After the founding of the mission in March 1569, the governor of Yucatan placed the inhabitants of Zapotitlan under the care and protection of Feliciano Bravo, the chief governmental notary, and on January 15, 1570, they were formally assigned to Bravo in encomienda. The governor's action was based on the allegation that the Indians were settled in "a new land" and were all heathens, ignorant of Christian teaching. These proceedings were challenged by Antón García, the encomendero of Acalan-Tixchel, who claimed the Indians as his tributaries. Evidence recorded in the litigation between García and Bravo and in Document IIIb of the Chontal Text clearly shows that most of the inhabitants of Zapotitlan were Chontal Indians of Acalan who were living in the old Acalan homeland. Some were apostate fugitives who had fled from Tixchel about 1560, and others, who were unconverted, were the survivors and descendants of former slaves of the ruler and principal men of Acalan. They spoke the Chontal language of Acalan-Tixchel; a high percentage of them had Chontal names; and other evidence presented in the lawsuit of García v. Bravo indicates that they had formerly paid tribute to García and to other encomenderos of Acalan.

Travelers from Tixchel to Zapotitlan had to cross Laguna de Términos and then proceed up a river with an extensive series of rapids and falls. From the upper part of this river, above these obstructions, they followed a trail through the forest 5 leagues to Zapotitlan. Although most of the contemporary sources do not record any specific name for this river, a letter of Paxbolon to Governor Céspedes, describing the results of his journey to Zapotitlan in 1568, refers to it as the Río de Acalan.[26] Document IIIb of the Chontal Text also tells about the arduous labor performed by the Indians of Tixchel in opening "the difficult falls of the Río de Acalan" in connection with the missionary activity carried on in Zapotitlan. Moreover, certain statements in Paxbolon's narrative of his first entrada in 1566 clearly imply that "the pueblo of Acalan" (Acalan-Itzamkanac) could be reached in two days' travel by canoe after passing the last of the falls, and there is evidence that on the occasion of Paxbolon's second journey, probably in 1567, some of the fugitives were temporarily resettled at the site of the old capital.[27] Thus it is evident that the pueblo of Zapotitlan was located in the old Acalan lands not far from Itzamkanac and the Río de Acalan. Other data prove beyond any reasonable doubt that this river was the Candelaria.

The general area in which Zapotitlan was located is indicated by two

[26] Paxbolon-Maldonado Papers, Part I, f. 17v.
[27] *Ibid.*, ff. 13–14. Cf. discussion in Chapter 9, pp. 189–91, *supra*.

significant items of evidence. (1) In one of the documents recording Bishop Toral's decision to send Fray Juan de Santa María as missionary to Zapotitlan in 1569, we find this passage: "[The bishop] will send . . . Fray Juan de Santa María . . . who is in charge of the *doctrina* of the Indians of Tixchel, which is on the borders of the said pueblo of Zapotitlan."[28] (2) A witness who gave testimony in a probanza of the merits and services of Feliciano Bravo in 1573–74 stated, in reply to a question about Bravo's visit to Zapotitlan in 1570, that the Indians of this settlement "had been discovered in the province called Acalan [which is] in the direction of the pueblo of Tixchel."[29] The Candelaria area southwest of Tixchel obviously fits the general location of Zapotitlan as described in these quotations better than the more distant region of the San Pedro Mártir.

Additional evidence in favor of identifying the Candelaria as the Río de Acalan is provided by the Alfaro map of 1579 (Map 2). On this map we find a "River called Çapotitan" placed east of the Usumacinta and tributary to Laguna de Términos. Although the Indians of Zapotitlan had been moved to another site prior to 1579, the earlier entradas of Paxbolon, the missionary friars, and Feliciano Bravo and the publicity created by the García *v.* Bravo litigation undoubtedly caused the name Zapotitlan to be associated for many years thereafter with the location of the original settlement and the river which formed part of the route to it. The fact that no settlement is shown on or near the Río de Zapotitlan also indicates that Alfaro knew that the region was no longer occupied.

The position of this river on the map and the manner in which it is drawn leave no doubt that it represents the Candelaria. To the west are two unnamed streams which also empty into Laguna de Términos. The first (counting from west to east) is a branch of the Usumacinta and can be only the Palizada. The second, which parallels the Palizada-Usumacinta, is evidently the Chumpan. Thus the Río de Zapotitlan, in third place from west to east, occupies the position of the Candelaria. Moreover, the course of the Río de Zapotitlan, which extends southward from the Laguna for some distance and then turns sharply to the east, closely approximates that of the Candelaria. Indeed, this sharp, right-angle turn in the Río de Zapotitlan, which was not made neces-

[28] ". . . Tixchel, que es en los confines del dicho pueblo de Zapotitlan." García *v.* Bravo, f. 2161. The word *confines* (translated above as "borders") does not mean, of course, that Tixchel and Zapotitlan were adjacent settlements, or that the territory, or jurisdiction, of one necessarily touched that of the other. It does indicate, however, that the two villages were in the same general region, that they were not separated by great distances, and that there was no important settlement or Indian group between them.

[29] ". . . en la provincia que llaman Acalan hacia el pueblo de Tichel." Probanzas of Feliciano Bravo, AGI, México, leg. 109.

sary by lack of space on the map, more accurately portrays the change of direction in the course of the Candelaria than many modern maps. Although Alfaro apparently had only a vague idea concerning the source of the Río de Zapotitlan, he evidently believed that the headwaters extended into the uncharted region to the east where he filled in the map with hills and sierras said to run from Bacalar to Puerto Caballos. Modern cartography shows that the two major branches of the Candelaria, the Arroyo Caribe and the San Pedro, actually reach some distance inland to southeastern Campeche and to northern Peten. Finally, since the river which formed part of the route to Zapotitlan was characterized by an extensive series of rapids and falls, the Candelaria is the only stream emptying directly into Laguna de Términos that can meet this requirement.[30]

Contemporary accounts of the rapids and falls encountered on the Río de Acalan en route to Zapotitlan bear a close resemblance to later descriptions of similar obstructions on the Candelaria. In the narrative of his first entrada into the interior in April-May 1566, Paxbolon describes the "sierras" (rocky places) and "saltos" (cascades or falls) through which he and his men had to pass, dragging their canoes with ropes "by the sheer force of [our] arms." He says there were seventy of these places, not including others of lesser size which he did not count.[31] Reports of Bravo's journey to Zapotitlan in December 1570 mention twenty "saltos," and tell how it was necessary for all members of the party to get into the water and pull the canoes through by hand.[32] Henry Pawling's description of the Candelaria written in 1859 records the existence of "21 saltos about 2 or three feet in height" below Salto Grande. The latter was a "cascade" 3 *varas* high, and farther upstream at Pacaitun there were "other *altos* . . . formed of hard rock," which had been impossible for boats of any size until he opened a channel at considerable personal expense.[33] A more recent description by Acevedo indicates that the falls formerly

[30] It may be argued that the Río de Zapotitlan does not represent the stream which formed part of the route from Tixchel to the original settlement of Zapotitlan, but the Mamantel, on or near which the Indians were resettled prior to 1579. There are serious objections, however, to such a thesis. (a) The Mamantel occupies fourth place, not third, among the rivers which empty into Laguna de Términos, counting from west to east. (b) If the Río de Zapotitlan were the Mamantel and not the Candelaria, it would be difficult to explain why Alfaro put the Chumpan and Mamantel, two lesser streams, on his map and left out the Candelaria, the most important river system east of the Usumacinta. (c) The Río de Zapotitlan enters the Laguna from the south whereas the Mamantel runs east-to-west throughout its known course. (d) If Alfaro had in mind the stream to which the Zapotitlan people had been moved, he would doubtless have shown the new settlement on the map.

[31] Paxbolon-Maldonado Papers, Part I, f. 14.

[32] García v. Bravo, ff. 2199v–2202v; Probanzas of Feliciano Bravo, AGI, México, leg. 109.

[33] Estadística del Estado de Campeche, Agricultura e industrias anexas, 1859, vol. 5. MS. in the Howard-Tilton Library, Middle American Research Institute, Tulane University, New Orleans.

extended as far as Salto Ahogado (the name means "choked" or "smothered" fall).[34]

Paxbolon evidently counted all the rapids of any size as well as the actual falls, or cascades, whereas Bravo and his associates apparently kept account of only the latter. The number of saltos mentioned in the Bravo documents compares closely, however, with Pawling's count for the Candelaria. It is also clear from Paxbolon's narrative and the reports of Bravo's journey that there was a continuous series of difficult rapids and falls on the Río de Acalan extending over a considerable distance. The obstructions on the Candelaria formed a similar series spread over a distance of some 45 km. from the first rapids above Suspiro to Salto Ahogado.

The group of rapids and falls on the San Pedro Mártir below Tiradero extends for only 12 km., according to Andrews' report.[35] This group is separated from the salto just below Mactun by a distance of 90–100 km. Although occasional rapids exist on the intervening section of the river, they·do not constitute serious hazards to navigation and they are interspersed between extensive overflow areas. In short, the major obstructions on the San Pedro Mártir do not form a continuous series such as existed on the Río de Acalan.

The narratives of Paxbolon's entrada of 1566 and the reports of Bravo's journey in 1570 also provide valuable data concerning travel time from Tixchel. Paxbolon set out from Tixchel on April 25, 1566. He traveled only by day, and we shall assume 12 hours as an average day's journey. Toward the end of the third day (April 27) he reached the first rapids of the Río de Acalan and before nightfall he passed through six of them. If we give him 2 or 3 hours for this last stretch, the total time from Tixchel would be 33–34 hours. Paxbolon spent all of April 28 and 29 in arduous travel through the rapids and falls, and on the morning of April 30 (the sixth day from Tixchel), after getting past nine more of the obstructions, he finally came to the sluggish upper part of the river. The passage through the entire series of rapids and falls must have taken at least 30 hours (2–3 hours on April 27, 24 hours on April 28 and 29, and about 4 hours on April 30). The remainder of April 30 was spent in fishing along the "lagoons" on the upper part of the river. While thus engaged some of the men discovered canoe marks and scattered maize along the shore, and Paxbolon decided to strike inland instead of going on to the site of the pueblo of Acalan (Acalan-Itzamkanac) as he originally intended. On the morning of May 1 he and his men cautiously proceeded overland and about midday reached some milpas, probably the site called Sucte

[34] Acevedo, 1910, pp. 14–18.
[35] Andrews, 1943, p. 54.

in Document IIIb of the Chontal Text, where he later conferred with some of the apostate fugitives.[36]

Bravo set out from Tixchel on the morning of December 8, 1570, after Father Monserrate had said mass. Let us assume that Bravo got started down Sabancuy estuary by 7 A.M. That day he crossed a large lagoon (Laguna de Términos), "and afterward night fell upon us (*y después nos anocheció*) and we went along a placid river" (the lower course of the Río de Acalan below the rapids and falls). Sunset on December 8, 1570 (Julian calendar) and in this latitude (about 18° 30′ N.) occurred about 5:30 P.M.[37] But since the report implies that Bravo started up the placid river at about dusk we shall give him 11.5 hours, instead of the minimum of 10.5 hours to actual sunset, for the trip from Tixchel to the mouth of the river. The next morning (December 9) "at the fourth watch," i.e. before dawn, the boats encountered strong current, and the same day when the moon was up ("con la luna") they began to pass through the rapids and falls. Moonrise on December 9, 1570, was about 4 P.M., but we assume that the reference to the moon means when the travelers first noticed it after dark. Thus it appears that Bravo reached the rapids and falls about 24 hours after entering the river, or some 35.5 hours after leaving Tixchel. The passage through the obstructions in the river took all of the night of December 9–10 and "part of the next day." The last phrase is vague, but 20 hours would seem to be a fair estimate for the entire stretch. From the last of the falls Bravo moved along the "estero," or sluggish upper part of the river, to the place where a trail led off into the interior. Here he apparently spent the night of December 10–11, and the next day (December 11) he marched overland on foot 5 leagues to Zapotitlan.[38]

Thus we find that in 1566 Paxbolon reached the rapids and falls of the Río de Acalan in 33–34 hours of travel from Tixchel. In 1570 Bravo took about 35.5 hours, including 11.5 hours from Tixchel to the mouth of the river and 24 hours from the mouth of the river to the rapids. It should also be noted that Bravo traveled day and night, so that the estimates for his journey represent a consecutive number of hours.

The distance from Tixchel by direct route across Laguna de Términos to the mouth of the Candelaria and thence upstream to the rapids below Suspiro is about 110 km. Both Paxbolon and Bravo could easily have covered this distance in the time indicated above. In Paxbolon's case an average speed of about 3.33 km. per hour would have been required. Bravo's average would have

---

[36] Paxbolon-Maldonado Papers, Part I, ff. 13v–14.

[37] This information was kindly supplied by Dr. Walter S. Adams of Mount Wilson Observatory, Carnegie Institution of Washington.

[38] García v. Bravo, ff. 2199v–2202v; Probanzas of Feliciano Bravo, AGI, México, leg. 109.

been about 3.1 km. per hour. In Father Monserrate's account of Bravo's journey, which provides most of the travel-time data in this case, the first mention
of obstacles in the river probably refers to actual saltos, which would place
the point reached in 35.5 hours from Tixchel a short distance farther upstream
than the first rapids recorded in Paxbolon's account. The extra distance would
not have been great enough, however, to cause much increase in Bravo's
average speed per hour.

For the sake of argument, however, let us assume that the rapids and falls
on the Río de Acalan encountered by Paxbolon and Bravo on their journeys
from Tixchel to Zapotitlan were not on the Candelaria but on the San Pedro
Mártir. This would mean that they crossed Laguna de Términos to the
Palizada and then proceeded up this river and part of the Usumacinta to the
San Pedro Mártir, where the first rapids and falls would have been encountered on the stretch below Tiradero. The distance traveled in such case would
have been very much greater than from Tixchel to the rapids of the Candelaria, and it would have required an entirely excessive rate of speed per hour.

The distance from Tixchel to the mouth of the Palizada by direct route
across Laguna de Términos is about 80 km. From the mouth of the Palizada
to the rapids of the San Pedro Mártir below Tiradero is about 220 km. measured on a large-scale map. The actual distance is undoubtedly greater since
the maps show only the most important bends in the rivers. Thus the entire
journey from Tixchel to the rapids of the San Pedro Mártir would have covered at least 300 km. We do not believe it possible that Paxbolon or Bravo
could have traveled this distance by canoe in the time indicated for their respective entradas (33 to 34 hours for Paxbolon and 35.5 for Bravo).

In Bravo's case, for example, it would have required an average speed of
8.44 km. per hour for the entire distance and for 35.5 consecutive hours.
Moreover, a somewhat greater speed would have been necessary for the upstream stretch from the mouth of the Palizada to the San Pedro Mártir rapids.
For this distance, 220 km. in 24 hours, the average figures out at 9.16 km., or
5.7 miles, per hour. This means that Bravo's paddlers would have had to cover
a mile every 10.5 minutes for 24 consecutive hours. Such a rate of travel by
canoe along the winding courses of the Palizada and Usumacinta Rivers, in
places against strong current, is evidently beyond the realm of possibility.[39]

[39] In the Harvard-Yale boat races at New London, Connecticut, eight-oared racing shells
normally cover a 4-mile upstream straightaway course in 20–22 minutes, or at the rate of 11–12
miles per hour. The oarsmen have had long and rigorous training and they have the advantage
of a light racing craft specially designed for speed. Moreover, they are called upon to exert
maximum energy for only a third of an hour. If they achieve a speed of only 12 miles per
hour (or slightly more if the best record is considered) under these optimum conditions, it is
difficult to believe that Bravo's paddlers could have maintained approximately half this speed
for 24 consecutive hours up the winding courses of the Palizada and Usumacinta Rivers.

As a basis of comparison it may be noted that in 1525 some of Cortés' men took most of one day (10–12 hours) to travel by canoe from Iztapa to Tatahuitalpan, two towns located on the Usumacinta below the mouth of the San Pedro Mártir. Cortés estimated the distance between these settlements as 5 leagues (about 21 km.).[40] This may refer to the shorter overland route. The distance by river may have been somewhat greater. It is evident, however, that the Iztapa-Tatahuitalpan stretch comprised only a small fraction of the distance that Bravo would have had to cover in 24 hours. It also appears that the maximum day's journey upstream on the Usumacinta at the time of Cortés' expedition was 8 leagues (about 33.5 km.).[41] At this rate the distance from the mouth of the Palizada to the rapids of the San Pedro Mártir (at least 220 km.) would have taken between 6 and 7 days (morning to night).

It is also of some interest to compare the time schedules of Paxbolon and Bravo for passing the rapids and falls of the Río de Acalan with a modern report of travel time up the obstructions on the Candelaria. In 1566 Paxbolon, who had to remove many logs and rocks from the channel of the Río de Acalan, took some 30 hours for this stretch. In 1570, after the channel had been cleared, Bravo took an estimated 20 hours to get through. Many of the old obstacles in the Candelaria have been cleared by blasting in recent years. Nevertheless, when Chamberlain went up the river in 1937, his actual travel time for the stretch from Suspiro to Salto Grande (in chicle boats towed by a motor launch) was 12 hours, 10 minutes.[42] It is apparent therefore that the time schedules of Paxbolon and Bravo for a somewhat greater distance (as far as Salto Ahogado) and under less favorable conditions make sense in terms of a passage up the Candelaria.

The foregoing discussion, based on a variety of data, shows that there can be little doubt that the Candelaria is the Río de Acalan of early colonial times. Its proximity to Tixchel, the evidence of the Alfaro map, the basic similarity of early descriptions of the Río de Acalan and later accounts of the Candelaria, and the schedules of travel time for various stages of the journey from Tixchel to Zapotitlan—all these factors constitute arguments which admit no other conclusion.

In 1548 Fray Lorenzo de Bienvenida stated that the journey in canoes to "the pueblo called Acalan," i.e. the capital of the province, took ten days. How does this work out in terms of the Candelaria location for the province? In 1566 Paxbolon reached the upper course of the Candelaria above the falls

[40] Cortés, 1866, p. 407. The Mexican league measures 2.6 miles, or 4.19 km.
[41] Cf. pp. 440–41, *infra*.
[42] Chamberlain to Scholes, April 20, 1937.

on the morning of the sixth day from Tixchel. The following day he advanced overland to the milpas of Sucte. His narrative indicates, however, that he originally intended to go to the site of the former capital, and that he had anticipated reaching it in 2 days' travel upstream above the falls, or apparently by the end of the seventh day from Tixchel.[43] Since Bienvenida's estimate was probably based on a journey from Campeche, the seat of the nearest Franciscan convent, we should add at least 2 more days to Paxbolon's travel time from Tixchel, making a total of at least 9 days. If we take Bravo's 1570 schedule as a basis of estimate, the travel time from Campeche to the Acalan capital would be between 8 and 9 days.[44] It is apparent therefore that Bienvenida's 10-day schedule was not excessive, and that when he stated that the pueblo of Acalan was "far from this land" (northern Yucatan), he was not thinking of some region far in the interior.

It is more important, however, to examine the Candelaria location in terms of Montejo's probanza of 1531. As we have seen, this probanza sets forth three major points: (1) the proximity of the province of Acalan to the Gulf coast; (2) lack of settlement between Acalan and the sea; and (3) a 3-day schedule of travel time from "the pueblos of Acalan" to Xicalango, 1 day downstream to the mouth of the Río de Acalan and 2 days from there to Xicalango. The time schedule is the item which deserves most careful analysis.

In 1570 Bravo covered the 60-km. stretch from Tixchel to the mouth of the Candelaria in 11.5 hours, or at the rate of about 5.2 km. per hour. At a similar speed the journey from the Candelaria to Xicalango (Cerrillos) by direct route across the Laguna (about 95 km.) would take 18.3 hours. The trading canoes in Montejo's time may have been more heavily loaded than those in which Bravo made the trip to Zapotitlan, and they may have followed the coast instead of going straight across the Laguna. Under such circumstances the time would more closely approximate 2 full days of average travel of 12 hours each. In any case it is evident that the journey from the mouth of the Candelaria to Xicalango would have required more than 1 day of average travel and that Montejo's 2-day estimate makes sense.

The vital point in the time schedule is the 1-day estimate for the journey downstream from "the pueblos of Acalan" to the mouth of the river. The phrase "pueblos of Acalan" is vague. It may mean any of the Acalan towns, but we believe that a more reasonable interpretation, taking the probanza as a whole, is that it refers to the border towns nearest the coast. This, in turn,

[43] Paxbolon-Maldonado Papers, Part I, ff. 13–14. Also cf. pp. 187–88, *supra*.

[44] Bravo's total time to the upper part of the river above the falls was some 55.5 hours, or more than 4.5 days of 12 hours each. To these should be added 2 days from the rapids to the Acalan capital and 2 days, Campeche to Tixchel, making between 8 and 9 days in all.

raises the question as to how far downstream the nearest towns were located.

The reports of the Zapotitlan entradas do not record detailed information concerning travel time on the return trip to Tixchel. The most definite evidence we have indicates that in 1568 Paxbolon (traveling by day only) made the journey in 4 days. Most of the first day would have been used up in covering the 5-league overland stretch from Zapotitlan to a point of embarkation on the Candelaria above the rapids and falls, and another day would have been required for travel from the mouth of the river to Tixchel. This leaves 2 days for the downstream stage of the journey. Confirmation of this time schedule is found in a letter of Paxbolon to Governor Céspedes, in which the cacique stated that if the Indians of Zapotitlan were moved to the Río de Acalan, presumably to a site above the rapids and falls, the journey to Tixchel could be made in 3 days.[45] The rapids and falls of the Candelaria would have occupied at least half the downstream stretch to be covered in 2 days. Portages around or over some of the obstructions would have been necessary, thus causing some delay; in other cases it would undoubtedly have been possible to shoot the falls in the boats. It is evident in any case that the downstream passage through the rapids and falls would have required less time than the estimated 20 hours for Bravo going upstream in 1570. Fourteen hours for the rapids and 10 hours for the distance from Suspiro to the mouth of the river might be a fair division of the time; or perhaps it would be better to divide the time equally, giving 12 hours, or a day, for each part of the downstream journey.

It is apparent, however, that for the Candelaria location to meet the probanza requirement of a one-day journey from "the pueblos of Acalan" to the mouth of the river we must assume that some of the towns were located along the rapids and falls, and that the border settlements extended downstream toward Suspiro. According to Andrews, there are "constant mound groups" on the high lands between Suspiro and Salto Grande. Although we know nothing about their age, the existence of such ruins shows that the area was suitable for settlement. In reporting these sites Andrews states: "This region . . . seems to have been fairly heavily populated."[46]

Location of the border towns near Suspiro would satisfy the requirements of the probanza concerning the proximity of the province of Acalan to the Gulf coast. It would also give meaning to the statement in the fifth question of Montejo's interrogatory indicating lack of settlement between Acalan and the sea. As Andrews points out, "the lowest portion of the Candelaria is

[45] Paxbolon-Maldonado Papers, Part I, f. 17v.
[46] Andrews, 1943, p. 45.

swamp, which, except for the coastal fringe, is not suitable for a population of any size."[47] Although we do not know that this area was entirely uninhabited in Montejo's time, it is evident that no towns of any importance, such as existed on the Usumacinta below the mouth of the San Pedro Mártir, would have been located between the rapids of the Candelaria and the sea.

Although it is necessary to postulate the existence of Acalan towns along the rapids and falls of the Candelaria, the major settlements, including the capital, were undoubtedly located on the upper part of the river and its branches. The falls would have served as a protective barrier against raiding attacks from the coast, and in the upper part of the Candelaria drainage the principal towns would have been more strategically located in terms of the overland trade routes across southern Yucatan and the Peten to the Caribbean coast. The major ruins reported by Andrews, whatever their age may be, are all above the falls, and it is rather surprising that he locates Itzamkanac in the zone between Suspiro and Salto Grande, where none of the mound sites are known to be of any size.

The Bienvenida letter of 1548 clearly implies that Acalan-Itzamkanac was situated above the rapids and falls of the Río de Acalan, and this is confirmed by the testimony of soldiers who accompanied Francisco Tamayo Pacheco to Acalan in 1559.[48] We have also called attention to the fact that the narrative of Paxbolon's entrada of 1566 indicates that the site of the Acalan capital was two days' journey upstream above the falls. A strategic location for Itzamkanac would have been near the junction of the Arroyo Caribe and the Río San Pedro, for such a site would command boat traffic on these lesser rivers and on the main stream of the Candelaria. Paxbolon could easily have reached the junction in two days from the last of the falls at Salto Ahogado. The existence of extensive ruins at El Tigre, with "a dozen or more sizable units,"[49] also shows that at some time in the preconquest period the strategic position of the site had attracted a numerous population.

Further evidence in favor of placing Itzamkanac near the junction of the Arroyo Caribe and the Río San Pedro is provided by data regarding the location of Zapotitlan, where the apostate fugitives and former slaves were living when Paxbolon pacified them in 1568. This place, as we have seen, was 5 leagues, or about a day's journey, from the upper part of the Río de Acalan above the falls. North of the Candelaria above Salto Ahogado there is a broad swamp unsuited for settlement, whereas to the south the country is higher and hills are seen in the distance. Consequently we should expect Zapotitlan

[47] *Ibid.*
[48] Cf. Chapter 8, p. 168 and note 7, p. 174, *supra.*
[49] Andrews, 1943, p. 49.

to have been south or southeast of a point on the Candelaria where the trail led off into the forest. Since Bravo in 1570 evidently reached this trail only a few hours after passing the last of the falls at Salto Ahogado, he could not have advanced upstream much farther than La Florida. A 5-league stretch to the southeast measured from a point in this area would reach to the western-most bend of the Río San Pedro on which the town of Mundo Nuevo is now located.

According to Document IIIb of the Chontal Text, the former slaves, who formed part of the population of Zapotitlan, had settled at the site of Chakam when they ran away from their masters, the ruler and principal men of Acalan. We know that Chakam was on navigable water.[50] A location up the San Pedro, or on a creek leading into it, away from the main current of traffic on the Candelaria would have been a logical place of refuge for the slaves and their families. When the apostates fled from Tixchel in 1560, they too would have sought a refuge away from the main stream of the Candelaria. They settled near Chakam, and in the course of time the two groups merged to form the settlement later known as Zapotitlan.

Thus both factual data and inference point to a location for Zapotitlan on or near the Río San Pedro somewhere in the region of Mundo Nuevo. Such a location could have been reached, of course, by following the Candelaria to the junction of the Caribe and San Pedro, and thence up the latter stream, instead of by an overland march from some position on the Candelaria near La Florida. The route across country, however, was much shorter. More-over, in 1566 Paxbolon had first established contact with some of the fugitives after an overland march of half a day to the milpas of Sucte, evidently about halfway between the Candelaria and Zapotitlan, and he apparently followed the same general route in 1568 when he finally reached the settlement. Once the trail had been marked out, it was natural that later visitors to Zapotitlan, such as Bravo and his party, should use it instead of the longer and more circuitous approach by water.

On the occasion of Paxbolon's second entrada into the interior, probably in 1567, some of the apostates were "brought out" and temporarily settled at the site of the old capital.[51] This obviously implies that Acalan-Itzamkanac was downstream from the Zapotitlan area at a place nearer to or actually on the Río de Acalan, or Candelaria. This fact, together with the evidence that the capital could be reached in two days' journey upstream from the last of the falls, clearly points to a location near the junction of the Caribe and the

[50] About 1527 Paxbolonacha died in Chakam, and his body was taken to Itzamkanac in a canoe. Cf. p. 87, *supra.*
[51] See pp. 189–91, *supra.*

San Pedro. Other evidence in favor of such a location will be presented in our discussion of Cortés' journey to Honduras in 1524–25.[52]

The name Zapotitlan, which was applied to the combined settlement of apostate fugitives and former slaves, presents an interesting and perplexing problem.[53] The contemporary sources (1566–71) do not mention Chakam in any way. It is only in Document IIIb of the Chontal Text, written about 1610, that we learn that the slaves had settled there and that Paxbolon found the apostates living with them when he made his third and successful entrada in 1568. This narrative also explains that the name Zapotitlan was adopted because the Indians disagreed concerning the original name of the settlement discovered at that time. "Some of the principal men called it by the name of Tachumbay and others Tachalte, and still others called it Tanaboo, and others Tamacuy. So for this reason it was given the name of Zapotitlan."

The Indians of Zapotitlan were not all concentrated in a single, compact village, some of them living in small groups in the surrounding forests, but there was evidently a nucleus or center of gravity at or near the site of Chakam. Although it is possible that the names mentioned by the principal men may refer to some of the lesser outlying estancias or rancherías, the use of four names and only four in Document IIIb of the Text strongly suggests that they were the names of the four quarters of old Chakam. From other statements in the Text we infer that such a division existed at Itzamkanac, and we should expect to find it in other important Acalan towns.[54]

Why was Zapotitlan chosen as the name for the settlement? On this point we can do nothing more than speculate. We know that some of the Acalan towns had Mexican as well as Chontal names. Itzamkanac, for example, was also known as Acalan, and after Cortés' time this name apparently came into general use among the local Spaniards. For Çacchute and Xakhaa we have Tizatepelt and Teutiercas respectively. It is possible therefore that Zapotitlan was the Mexican name for Chakam. But why the Mexican name should have been adopted instead of Chakam is a question for which we have no answer.

Having cited evidence to show that Acalan was located in the drainage of the Candelaria River, we turn now to a study of the routes of the Cortés and

[52] This means, of course, two days of upstream travel in canoes. On the maps the distance from the last of the falls (Salto Ahogado) to the junction of the Arroyo Caribe and the San Pedro does not seem to be far, but the maps undoubtedly fail to show many bends in the Candelaria which would increase the distance by water.

[53] The name Zapotitlan was applied as early as December 1568, when Paxbolon made his third entrada to the old Acalan area.

[54] See pp. 54–55, *supra*. Documents of 1569 refer to the good lands and cacao groves at Zapotitlan. This would also suggest the site of a former important settlement.

Avila expeditions of 1524–25 and 1530 respectively, in order to see how they conform to this location of the province.

The major purpose of Cortés' expedition of 1524–25 was to reassert authority over the Honduras area, in view of the disloyalty of Cristóbal de Olid who had been sent out to occupy the region in Cortés' name early in 1524. A secondary motive, as revealed by Cortés' own statement quoted below, was to explore and establish jurisdiction over the extensive unpacified country between Mexico and the Caribbean coast. An important question to consider at this point, since it has some bearing on the route of the expedition from the Usumacinta to Acalan, is Cortés' objective on the east coast when he set out from Espíritu Santo in the latter part of 1524.

After Cortés' arrival in Espíritu Santo he summoned Indians from Xicalango and Tabasco (Potonchan) who gave him information concerning the lands through which he would pass en route to the Caribbean. These Indians also made him a map on cloth, "on which," so Gómara says, "they painted all the route from Xicalango to Nito, where the Spaniards were, and even to Nicaragua, which is on the South Sea, and to [the place] where Pedrarias, governor of Tierra Firme, was residing." Herrera states that this map showed the route "to Naco and Nito in Honduras, and to Nicaragua, indicating the government of Pedrarias, with all the rivers and settlements which had to be passed. . . ."[55] At the end of his long overland march to the east coast Cortés actually came out at Nito near the mouth of the Río Dulce. On the basis of the foregoing data it might be assumed that from the time he left Espíritu Santo Cortés' actual objective on the Caribbean coast was Nito and that he consciously sought to follow as direct a route as possible to that place, in accordance with the native map. Analysis of statements in Cortés' letters and other evidence indicates, however, that such assumptions are by no means justified.

Although the passage from Gómara quoted above might be interpreted as indicating that prior to his departure from Espíritu Santo Cortés knew that Spaniards were settled at Nito, he actually had no such information. He had learned that Olid, while in Cuba en route to Honduras, had planned an act of disloyalty, and this report had caused him to dispatch another force under Francisco de las Casas to the Honduras country; but when he set out from Espíritu Santo and for a long time thereafter he did not know the exact whereabouts of Olid and Las Casas, nor did he possess knowledge of the events that had occurred after their arrival on the Caribbean coast. Moreover, he had no information concerning the activities of Gil González de

55 López de Gómara, 1943, 2: 13; Herrera y Tordesillas, 1726–30, dec. 3, bk. 6, ch. 12.

Avila, another Spaniard operating in the Honduras area, who founded San Gil de Buenaventura near the Bay of Amatique, the colonists of which later moved to Nito.[56] It was only after Cortés reached Acalan that he learned that Spaniards were settled at Nito, and on the basis of this information and other data supplied by the Chontal of Acalan he then directed his march to the Río Dulce. He did not know who these Spaniards were, however, until shortly before he reached the east coast.[57]

The most explicit statement we have concerning Cortés' knowledge of events on the east coast when he set out from Espíritu Santo and his actual objective at that time is recorded in the famous Fifth Letter to Charles V, dated September 3, 1526, in which Cortés gave a full report of the Honduras expedition. Referring to his conference with the Indians of Xicalango and Tabasco, Cortés writes:

I learnt from these men much that I wished to know about the country and they also told me that on the sea coast on the other side of the land called Yucatan, towards the bay which is called "La Asuncion," there were certain Spaniards who did them much injury, for besides burning many villages and killing the people so that many places were laid waste and the people had fled to the forests, they had done even greater damage to the traders, and the whole trade of that district, which was very considerable, had been lost.

From personal knowledge they gave me an account of almost all the towns of that district as far as the place where your Majesty's Governor Pedrarias de Avila was residing. They also made me a map of it all on a cloth, from which I gathered that I should be able to march through the greater part of the country, or at least as far as the spot pointed out to me as the abode of the Spaniards. Hearing such good news of the road which had to be followed in order to carry out my plans, and bring the natives of the land to a knowledge of our faith and to the service of your Majesty, and knowing that in such a long march many and divers provinces must be crossed, and that people with strange customs would be met with before one could ascertain whether those Spaniards were followers of the Captains whom I had sent out—namely, Diego or Cristóbal de Olid, or Pedro de Alvarado, or Francisco de las Casas—it seemed to me that in order to carry out the matter satisfactorily it would conduce to the service of your Majesty that I should go there in person, especially as so much unknown country was to be discovered and observed, and much of it might be brought peacefully under your rule, as has since been done.[58]

Thus we find that the Indians of Xicalango and Tabasco gave a report con-

[56] For a discussion of events in the Honduras area in 1524–25, see Bancroft, 1882–87, 1: ch. 17.
[57] Cortés, 1866, pp. 422–41, passim; Díaz del Castillo, 1939, chs. 177, 178.
[58] Cortés, 1916, pp. 348–49.

cerning certain Spaniards who had made depredations on the Caribbean coast, but Cortés was not certain of their identity. Moreover, although the native map may have marked out the location of towns as far as the jurisdiction of Pedrarias, it seems clear that the immediate objective of Cortés, when he set out from Espíritu Santo, was the region of "Asuncion" Bay on the eastern side of Yucatan, where the marauding Spaniards were said to be. This is also indicated by the fact that when Cortés arrived in Iztapa on the Usumacinta he sent orders to his ships waiting off the Tabasco coast to proceed around Yucatan "to the bay of La Asuncion, for there they would meet me or I would send instructions to them as to what they should do next."[59]

The Bay of "La Asuncion" undoubtedly refers to an arm of the sea on the east coast of Yucatan discovered in 1518 by Juan de Grijalva and named by him Ascension Bay. It is doubtful whether the Indians of Tabasco and Xicalango were familiar with the name Ascension Bay, but Cortés, after hearing their reports of marauding Spaniards on the Caribbean coast, apparently concluded that the latter were operating in the region discovered by Grijalva in 1518. That he might have expected some of the Spaniards whom he had sent to Honduras to be in that area is made clear by a statement in his Fourth Letter, in which he says that Olid had been instructed to found a settlement at the Cape of Higueras, and then to send one of his ships "to cruise along the coast of the Ascension Bay, searching for the strait which is believed to be there."[60]

It is obviously a matter of some importance to determine, as far as possible, Cortés' ideas concerning the location of this bay. Bancroft asserts that Cortés applied the name Ascension to the Gulf of Honduras.[61] Although it may be assumed that Cortés did not possess an exact knowledge of places and distances on the Caribbean coast, it should be noted that in the Fourth Letter he also states that Ascension Bay was 60 leagues from the Cape of Higueras.[62] This would place it in the region of Chetumal Bay. On the anonymous Turin map of 1523 we find a "baya de la cention" on the east coast of Yucatan, which evidently refers to Ascension Bay. It is placed too far south to be the present bay of this name, and its location more closely approximates that of Chetumal Bay.[63] It is also significant that in a description of the Caribbean coast written by Oviedo some time prior to 1550 (apparently based on the lost map of Alonso Chaves of 1536) we find mention of three bays on the coast northeast of "the ex-

[59] Ibid., p. 360.
[60] Cortés, 1908, 2: 195.
[61] Bancroft, 1882-87, 1: 543, note 18.
[62] Cortés, 1866, p. 290.
[63] A section of the Turin map is reproduced, with critical commentary, in Harrisse, 1892, pp. 528-33. For additional data on this map, see Lowery, 1912, pp. 25-26.

treme or westernmost part of the Gulf of Higueras," and of these "the nearest to the Gulf of Higueras is called the bay of la Asçension."[64] Moreover, in a passage describing the peninsula of Yucatan, Gómara refers to "Chetemal, which is in the bay of la Ascension."[65] A reference to Ascension Bay in the *Relaciones de Yucatán* of 1579 indicates that at this later date the name was applied to the present Ascension Bay, northernmost of the three arms of the sea on the east coast of Yucatan.[66] But it would appear that in the time of Cortés, Oviedo, and Gómara, it was employed to designate Chetumal Bay farther south. As late as the eighteenth century we also have maps on which Chetumal Bay is named the Bay of Ascension.[67] In view of these facts, it seems evident that what Cortés had in mind was not the Gulf of Honduras, as Bancroft states, but an arm of the sea farther north on the coast of Yucatan proper. Bancroft probably assumed that inasmuch as Cortés came out at Nito on the Gulf of Honduras, this was his actual objective.

The easiest route to Ascension Bay and the east coast of Yucatan would have been by sea. The passage from the Fifth Letter quoted above indicates, however, that after his talks with the Indians of Tabasco and Xicalango Cortés decided that an overland march was feasible and that it would also provide an opportunity to visit the "many and divers provinces" located between western Tabasco and the Caribbean and bring them to obedience to the Spanish crown. As a general guide he had the native map showing the principal settlements of the area through which he would pass. As noted above, Gómara and Herrera state that this map showed the route to Nito and beyond. Bernal Díaz tells us, however, that "all the pueblos we should pass on the way were marked as far as Gueacalá"[68] (great Acalan, or Itzamkanac). We also know that when Cortés reached Acalan, where he learned for the first time of the presence of Spaniards at Nito, he obtained a new map showing in detail the route to the latter place. This suggests that although the first map made by the Indians of Tabasco and Xicalango may have indicated the locations of towns as far as Honduras and beyond, it was meant to serve as an actual guide only as far as Acalan, where the Chontal, because of their trade with the east coast, would be able to give Cortés more explicit information as to the whereabouts of Spaniards on the east coast and the route he should follow.

To sum up, Cortés' objective when he set out from Espíritu Santo was not Nito, but an area on the east coast known as Ascension Bay, which early

[64] Oviedo y Valdés, 1851–55, bk. 21, ch. 8.
[65] López de Gómara, 1931, p. 185.
[66] RY, 2: 199.
[67] Cf. maps by D'Anville, 1731 and 1791, by Bellin, 1754 and 1764, by Kitchin, 1762, and by Hinton, 1755, reproduced in Cartografía de la América Central, 1929.
[68] Díaz del Castillo, 1908–16, 5: 12.

map makers and chroniclers, and probably Cortés himself, identified with Chetumal Bay. It was also his plan to visit and pacify the principal towns en route, as indicated on the map made by the Indians of Xicalango and Tabasco. This map served as a general guide as far as Acalan, where Cortés received more precise information as to the whereabouts of Spaniards on the Caribbean coast. On the basis of this information and a new map obtained in Acalan, he then turned southeast to Tayasal and Nito, instead of going on to the Ascension Bay area. But even if it could be proved that Cortés' objective from the beginning was Nito and the Río Dulce, it would not follow that he necessarily sought to follow a fairly direct route to the southeast after leaving the Tabasco coast, for he was also interested in visiting the principal Indian provinces in the intervening country, one of which was Acalan. In order to do so, he would undoubtedly have been willing to deviate from the direct route if necessary.

The route of Cortés from Espíritu Santo to Tepetitan in southern Tabasco is fairly well established and does not require detailed analysis here. (For a discussion of this part of the journey, see Chapter 5, pp. 93–100, *supra*.) From Tepetitan Cortés advanced to Iztapa on the left bank of the Usumacinta,[69] thence upstream to Ciuatecpan (called Çagoatespan by Cortés and Ziguatepecad by Bernal Díaz), where he crossed the river and marched to Acalan. It is this stage of the journey, Tepetitan to Acalan, concerning which there has been the most argument and debate. Three major points are involved: (a) the location of Iztapa, from which Cortés turned south up the Usumacinta; (b) the location of Ciuatecpan, the point of crossing; and (c) the direction of the route from Ciuatecpan to Acalan.

The march from Tepetitan to Iztapa took three days, during which the main army followed the trail of an advance party across swampy country, where "the horses sank to their girths when riderless and led by hand." Outside the town was a "great lagoon" across which the Spaniards had to swim their horses.[70] Thus the actual settlement was apparently on a neck of land with the river on one side and the lagoon on the other.

[69] Neither Cortés nor Bernal Díaz records a name for the river on which Iztapa and the upstream towns were located, but there can be no doubt that it was the Usumacinta, which is the first major river system that Cortés would have encountered marching east, northeast, or southeast from Tepetitan. Cortés states that the river on which Iztapa was located flowed into the Río de Tabasco, or Grijalva, and Bernal Díaz reports that Ciuatecpan, situated upstream from Iztapa, was on a river which "ended in some lagoons where stood a pueblo named Gueatasta and near to it was another large pueblo called Xicalango." (Cortés, 1866, p. 408; Díaz del Castillo, 1908–16, 5: 18.) These statements obviously refer to the branching lower course of the Usumacinta.

[70] Cortés, 1916, pp. 356–57.

Modern maps do not record any site named Iztapa on the Usumacinta.[71] In his account of the upstream march Cortés mentions the names of seven more towns: Tatahuitalpan, Ozumacintlan (Usumacinta), Ciuatecpan, Petenecte, Coazacoalco, Taltenango, and Teutitan. Of these only the name Usumacinta, a place 2 or 3 leagues below Tenosique, appears on modern maps. Maudslay and Morley identify it as the Usumacinta of the Cortés narrative, but there is ample evidence, as we shall see later, that the colonial settlement was located farther downstream, below the junction of the San Pedro Mártir and Usumacinta Rivers. This lack of dependable modern cartographical data means that in fixing the location of Iztapa and other settlements on the Usumacinta we must depend upon the inadequate data recorded by Cortés and Bernal Díaz, supplemented by any additional information that may be found in other colonial sources.

Unfortunately Cortés does not indicate the direction of his march from Tepetitan to Iztapa. The one sure fact that we have is his statement that the journey took three days. From various statements in the Fifth Letter and in Bernal Díaz' narrative, we find that 6 leagues (approximately 25 km.) was apparently the maximum overland distance covered in one day in swampy country. On this basis the three-day march from Tepetitan to Iztapa probably did not exceed 18 leagues. Consequently the site of Montecristo (modern Emiliano Zapata), which is about 16 leagues by airline in an easterly direction from Tepetitan, probably marks the highest point on the Usumacinta that Cortés could have reached.

Mrs. Stone places Iztapa just above Jonuta, at a point about 8 leagues by airline northeast of Tepetitan, and she locates Ciuatecpan, from which Cortés set out for Acalan, at Montecristo.[72] In fixing the location of these towns so far downstream, Mrs. Stone was apparently influenced by three lines of reasoning, expressed or implied.

In the first place, Mrs. Stone places considerable reliance on the downstream locations of Iztapa and other Usumacinta towns as shown on the Alfaro map of 1579 (Map 2). On this map Iztapa is placed above Jonuta on the right bank of the Río San Pedro y San Pablo. Usumacinta is on the right bank of what appears to be the Palizada, and two more towns, "Petenete" and "Tanoçic," are located farther upstream. Although the map shows some distortion, it actually gives a correct idea of the branching lower course of the Usumacinta system and its connections with the Grijalva River, the Gulf

[71] The modern site of Estapilla below Tenosique is not the same as the sixteenth-century Iztapa. Cortés could not possibly have reached Estapilla in a three-day march from Tepetitan.
[72] Stone, 1932, pp. 217–20, and map.

coast, and Laguna de Términos. Its locations for Jonuta, Iztapa, and Usumacinta, however, are grossly inaccurate.

The modern town of Jonuta is located on the Usumacinta proper, above
the point where the San Pedro y San Pablo branches off. A passage in the
relación of the Villa de Tabasco, written in 1579, the year of the Alfaro
map, indicates that Jonuta was then situated at or near its present site.[73]
Consequently Iztapa must also have been on the main stream above Jonuta.
Usumacinta was higher up the river but below the mouth of the San Pedro
Mártir.[74]

Mrs. Stone apparently places Jonuta at its present site, for her suggested
location of Iztapa on the right bank of the Río San Antonio, which branches
off from the Usumacinta to form Isla del Chinal, puts these towns in the same
relative position as on the Alfaro map. But in order to reconcile these locations with the fact that on the Alfaro map both Jonuta and Iztapa are east of
the Río San Pedro y San Pablo, she is compelled to assume that this river comprises not only the stream actually so named, but also a considerable stretch
of the Usumacinta proper. For example, she says at one point that Montecristo, where she locates Ciuatecpan, is on the San Pedro y San Pablo.[75] Such
a line of reasoning is not justified either by modern cartography or by Alfaro's
map. On the latter the legend, "Río de Usumacinta caudaloso," actually appears on that part of the main stream between the fork where the San Pedro
y San Pablo branches off and another fork higher up where the Palizada turns
off to Laguna de Términos, and it is on this very same stretch that Jonuta was
and still is located. The Alfaro map also shows the connection between the
Usumacinta system and the Grijalva, but curiously enough no such connection
appears on Mrs. Stone's map.

Another line of reasoning employed by Mrs. Stone is her identification of
Petenche, marked on modern maps, as the site of the settlement of Petenecte
mentioned by Cortés, recorded on the Alfaro map as Petenete, and also listed
in other colonial sources. According to Cortés, Petenecte was 6 leagues above
Ciuatecpan, and the modern Petenche is about that distance above Mrs. Stone's
site for Ciuatecpan at Montecristo. Although there is a certain similarity in
the names Petenche and Petenecte, this does not establish the fact that they
were the same. Mrs. Stone may have been misled to some extent by a mis-
reading of the name on the Alfaro map, which she gives as Petencte instead
of Petenete, and also by her mistaking a passage from MacNutt's translation

[73] RY, 1: 346–47.
[74] Cf. Appendix D, p. 499, *infra*.
[75] Stone, 1932, p. 220.

of Cortés' Fifth Letter, in which she has Petenche instead of the spelling (Petenecte) employed by the translator.[76]

Finally, it is obvious that if Itzamkanac was located on Laguna de Términos, as Mrs. Stone believes, Cortés' march along the Usumacinta could not have extended much above Montecristo. Although Mrs. Stone does not argue, as Andrews does, that Ciuatecpan should be located with respect to a known location for Acalan, her conviction that Itzamkanac was on Laguna de Términos may well have had some influence in her general reasoning about the location of the Usumacinta towns. If she had placed Ciuatecpan higher upstream anywhere near the site favored by Maudslay, whom she takes to task more than once, she would have faced almost insuperable difficulties in getting Cortés back to the Laguna. It is our own view that Ciuatecpan was located above the junction of the San Pedro Mártir and Usumacinta Rivers, although not so far as the Tenosique location favored by Maudslay and others. After we have cited the evidence for our own site, we shall give reasons why Mrs. Stone and Andrews are in error in placing the town below the junction.

Maudslay places Tepetitan near the modern town of this name, but on the opposite (right) bank of the Río de Tepetitan. He then states: "If Cortés took an easterly course he would have struck the Rio Usumacinta somewhere near the Laguna de Catasajá, and we may safely locate Ystapa in that position." On his map Cortés' route runs north of Laguna Catazaja, and Iztapa is placed at about the point where the Río Chico or Chiquito, branches off from the Usumacinta to form Isla Monserrate.[77] North of Laguna Catazaja are the swampy Lagunas de San Carlos and a network of rivers and creeks which would have made a march through this region extremely difficult and hazardous, and we doubt that Cortés could have reached the Usumacinta in three days' traveling through such country. It is true, of course, that Cortés refers to swamps encountered between Tepetitan and Iztapa, and he implies that the going was difficult at times. Swamps also exist south of Laguna Catazaja, but descriptions of the country by Charnay and Stephens (see Chapter 5, p. 101, *supra*) suggest that the terrain is fairly favorable and would not present such hazards as the northern route. But our main reason for believing that Cortés passed south of Laguna Catazaja, instead of by the route indicated by Maudslay, is the fact that other evidence, cited below, calls for a location of Iztapa farther upstream on the Usumacinta than Maudslay's site.

Becerra and González discuss Cortés' route on the Usumacinta in rela-

[76] *Ibid.;* Cortés, 1908, 2: 250.
[77] Díaz del Castillo, 1908–16, 5: 336 and map.

tion to local geography and the meaning of place names, with special emphasis on the latter, and they conclude that Iztapa was near Montecristo. They call attention to the existence of lagoons near this town, a point of some importance in view of Cortés' remark that the Spaniards of his advance party had to swim their horses across a "great lagoon" outside the town. The name of one of these lagoons is Saquila. According to the Becerra-González interpretation, this name means "white water" in Maya. A similar meaning is ascribed to the Mexican name Iztapa.[78] We are not especially impressed by the Becerra-González etymologies of the Usumacinta place names, but there appears to be no doubt that Iztapa connotes something white, and Saquila might well have the same meaning.[79]

Although we do not regard the arguments of Becerra and González as conclusive, we agree that a site near Montecristo is indicated as the probable location of Iztapa. Montecristo probably marks the highest point upstream that Cortés could have reached on a three-day march from Tepetitan, but we also believe that a downstream site is ruled out by evidence concerning the relative position of the Usumacinta towns and the distances that separated them.

Various documents of the period 1573–82, including the Alfaro map, list towns on the Usumacinta in the following order looking upstream: Jonuta, Popane, Iztapa, Usumacinta, Petenecte, Tenosique. In two cases, however, the order for Popane and Iztapa is reversed.[80] None of the documents mention Tatahuitalpan, Ciuatecpan, or the three towns named Coazacoalco, Taltenango, and Teutitan, which Cortés places above Petenecte. It is reasonable to assume, however, that Tenosique was one of the three settlements upstream from Petenecte. If Popane was actually above Iztapa, we might identify it as Tatahuitalpan, but most of the available evidence places Popane below Iztapa. The disappearance of four towns between the time of Cortés and 1573, if such was the case, may probably be attributed to the Spanish policy of consolidating Indian settlements into larger units for missionary and administrative purposes. Declining population was undoubtedly another factor in the situation. In 1573 the Usumacinta towns were apparently served by the

[78] Becerra, 1910a, pp. 471–75; González, 1940, pp. 403–04. Becerra, who places Iztapa between Montecristo and the mouth of the Río Chacamax, states that there is also a rancho called Tierra Blanca on the left bank of the Usumacinta a short distance above Montecristo.

[79] In Maya *zacil* means "whiteness," or "something white." For Iztapan, a town mentioned in the Mendoza Codex, Peñafiel gives "sobre la sal, en la salina," from *iztatl*, "sal," and *pan*, "sobre, lugar"; and for Istapa, a place in Chiapas, he gives "lugar blanco," from *iztac*, "blanco," and *pa*, "lugar" (Peñafiel, 1897, pt. 2, pp. 140, 146). Rovirosa (1888, p. 21) defines Istapa (Chiapas) as "sobre la sal," from *iztatl*, "sal," and *pan*, "encima, sobre." A salt marsh would be "white water," but we do not know whether salt marshes exist at Laguna Saquila.

[80] Probanzas of Feliciano Bravo, AGI, México, leg. 109; DHY, 2: 65; RY, 1: 340, 347.

friar at Palenque, the Dominican Fray Pedro Lorenzo, but before the end of the sixteenth century the river settlements were formed into a separate missionary district served by a secular priest stationed at Usumacinta.

According to Cortés, the distance from Iztapa to Tatahuitalpan, the first stop upstream, was 5 leagues.[81] The next town was Usumacinta, visited by some of the Spaniards going upstream in canoes, but the distance from Tatahuitalpan is not recorded. As late as Cogolludo's time Usumacinta was 22 leagues from Petenecte,[82] and the latter, as we have seen, was below Tenosique. Thus Iztapa was at least 27 leagues below Tenosique, to which must be added estimates for the Tatahuitalpan-Usumacinta and Petenecte-Tenosique distances, which we estimate at not more than 8 leagues and 3–4 leagues respectively. (The reasoning on which we arrive at these estimates is set forth farther on in our discussion of the later stages of Cortés' journey up the Usumacinta.) Adding the known distances and the estimates, we get at least 38–39 leagues (about 159–163 km.) for the distance from Tenosique (which we locate at or near its present site) to Iztapa.[83] Although it is difficult to measure distances on the Usumacinta, for even a large-scale map shows only the most important bends and loops in the river, a stretch of 38–39 leagues from Tenosique will not reach to either Mrs. Stone's or Maudslay's location for Iztapa, and will more closely approximate that of Becerra and González near Montecristo.

Finally, a Tabasco tribute document of 1688 records information concerning certain Usumacinta towns, including "Ystapilla en Monte de Cristo." From the context it seems clear that this phrase refers to a downstream site and not to the present site of Estapilla located above the junction of the Usumacinta and San Pedro Mártir between Canizan and modern Usumacinta. In short, this pueblo of "Ystapilla en Monte de Cristo" was almost certainly the sixteenth-century town of Iztapa. This evidence, together with the data

---

[81] Cortés, 1866, p. 407.

[82] Cogolludo, 1867–68, bk. 12, ch. 7.

[83] In 1573, after his return from the first Tachis expedition (see Appendix D), Feliciano Bravo visited the Usumacinta towns from Tenosique to Popane, and on his arrival in Popane, May 8, 1573, signed a document in which he stated that the towns visited occupied a district of 25–30 leagues along the river. If this estimate is correct, then Popane was some distance above Montecristo and Iztapa still farther upstream. It is possible, of course, that prior to 1573 these towns had been moved upstream from their conquest sites, but we have no positive evidence of this. Moreover, Cogolludo's estimate of 22 leagues for the Usumacinta-Petenecte distance, to which must be added estimates for the stretch from Popane to Usumacinta and also for that from Petenecte to Tenosique, constitutes strong evidence that Bravo underestimated to some extent the Tenosique-Popane distance. On the other hand, if Iztapa were located at the site indicated by Maudslay, it would be necessary to assume a margin of error of at least 60 per cent, and more than 80 per cent in the case of Mrs. Stone's location. It hardly seems likely that Bravo's error would have been so great.

already cited, constitutes rather conclusive proof that the town of Iztapa visited by Cortés was at or near modern Montecristo (Emiliano Zapata).[84]

From Iztapa Cortés advanced up the Usumacinta to Tatahuitalpan, said to be 5 leagues distant. Some of the Spaniards made the trip in canoes, and the main army marched overland, crossing a deep river (río hondo) over which a bridge had been built by the Indians of Iztapa. The journey took one day, and Cortés states that the army reached Tatahuitalpan ahead of the canoes, which were delayed by "the swift current and the many bends in the stream." He describes Tatahuitalpan as "a small pueblo which we found burnt and abandoned."[85]

Maudslay locates Tatahuitalpan near Montecristo,[86] an obvious location with respect to his site for Iztapa, for it would have taken Cortés across the base of a triangle, the other sides being formed by the Usumacinta. Airline distance overland is about 6 leagues, and the river route is at least 9–10 leagues. Although we should not raise serious objection to the overland distance from Maudslay's Iztapa to Montecristo, the 9–10-league water route would appear to be a rapid rate of travel for a one-day journey in canoes against strong current. Moreover, Cortés' narrative indicates that although the canoes were delayed by the current and bends in the river, they reached Tatahuitalpan early enough so that he could send some men across the river the same day to search for the natives of the town, who had fled to the opposite bank. In short, there is reason to doubt that the Spaniards in the canoes could have made the journey from Maudslay's Iztapa to Montecristo within the time that can be allowed for the trip.

Becerra and González identify Río Chacamax, which flows into the Usumacinta a short distance above Montecristo, as the deep river bridged by the Indians of Iztapa; and they locate Tatahuitalpan near the Arroyo de Balancan Viejo, shown on González' map as a southern tributary of the Usumacinta, joining the main stream between Pobilcuc and San José.[87] Again they employ linguistic arguments to support their conclusion. According to Becerra, whose definitions are adopted by González, Balancan means "a place abandoned because of fire" in Maya; and the Mexican name Tatahuitalpan, which Becerra derives from Tlatla-uei-tlalpan, is defined as "in the burnt plain."[88] As noted above, Tatahuitalpan was "burnt and abandoned" when

[84] AGI, Contaduría, leg. 920.
[85] Cortés, 1916, pp. 358–60.
[86] Díaz del Castillo, 1908–16, 5: 336.
[87] The Tulane-Carnegie map of the Maya area (based on the work sheets of the 1:1,000,000 maps issued by the American Geographical Society) shows an unnamed lagoon just to the east of Pobilcuc. On González' map this lagoon forms part of the Arroyo de Balancan Viejo.
[88] Becerra, 1910a, p. 505; González, 1940, p. 404.

Cortés arrived. Tlatlaueitlalpan might possibly signify a large place or land that had been burned, but we question the meaning ascribed to Balancan.[89]

It is not clear whether Cortés' 5-league distance from Iztapa to Tatahuital-pan was by water or overland, which would normally be less than the river distance. Cortés says that Tatahuitalpan was 5 leagues "higher up the river" (*el río arriba*),[90] which would normally mean by water. Yet we know that the army was able to make good time, because the trail had been prepared in advance and the deep river bridged, and it could probably have made 5 leagues and still get in ahead of the canoes.

If Iztapa was near Montecristo, a site 5 leagues overland would be near Pobilcuc. The distance by water in this case would not be much greater. A site near San José on the eastern side of the great loop of the Usumacinta above Pobilcuc would lend greater force to Cortés' remark about the "many bends" in the river. Such a location for Tatahuitalpan, however, would not only increase the land distance from Montecristo to 7 or 8 leagues, but would also involve a water route of about 11 leagues, which is too much for a day's journey against current. For these reasons we prefer the suggested location near Pobilcuc. Between this place and Montecristo the river winds somewhat, but not to the extent it does farther upstream, and it seems evident that it was the current more than the bends in the river that delayed the canoes. It may be noted that the Pobilcuc location for Tatahuitalpan is not far from the site suggested by Becerra and González.

Cortés' arduous overland march from Tatahuitalpan to Ciuatecpan, dur-ing which the Spaniards had to cross two broad swamps and bridge a stream, and later got lost in the high forest, has been described in Chapter 5.[91] The most significant item in Cortés' account is the fact that on the last day he directed the march to the northeast and reached Ciuatecpan in the afternoon.

With regard to the travel time as recorded in Cortés' narrative, we can add up three days (two in high forest and the last day to the northeast) in addi-tion to an unstated time for building the bridge and crossing the two swamps. In Bernal Díaz' version of the upstream march we find a similar account of an

[89] Peñafiel defines Tlalpan (from *tlalli*, "tierra," and *pan*, "en, sobre") as "en el suelo, lugar que está en tierra;" Huitlalpan (*huey*, "grande," and *tlalpan*) as "Tlalpan el grande;" and in one case he derives *tlatla* from *tlatlac*, "quemado" (Peñafiel, 1897, pt. 2, pp. 134, 284, 289). Thus Becerra's Tlatla-uei-tlalpan might possibly mean "burnt-great-ground." The last two elements (*uei* and *tlalpan*) no doubt signify a large expanse of ground, but there is less certainty regard-ing the first, since the Molina dictionary gives some 500 words beginning with *tlatla*. Although we are unable to translate Balancan, we can find no grounds for the definition given by Becerra and González. Peñafiel (*op. cit.*, pt. 2, p. 41) suggests that perhaps the name should be Balan-chan, "que significa lagarto."
[90] Cortés, 1916, p. 359; 1866, p. 407.
[91] See pp. 102–03, *supra*.

arduous journey between Iztapa and a place called Tamaztepeque, but the old soldier obviously had in mind the difficulties encountered between Tatahuitalpan and Ciuatecpan. He states that although the Indians said it would take three days, the march actually lasted seven days.[92] A seven-day period fits in well with other facts in the Cortés narrative. The canoes sent upstream arrived at Ciuatecpan ahead of Cortés, after spending some time en route at the town of Usumacinta. At Ciuatecpan they waited two days for Cortés and then went on up the river to Petenecte, not later than the very day when Cortés finally arrived. So counting that day plus two that they waited at Ciuatecpan, and another for the stay at Usumacinta, we reduce the time the canoes were in actual travel from Tatahuitalpan to Ciuatecpan to three days. This suggests that the Indians' estimate of a three-day journey was for the trip by water.

We have already seen that Usumacinta was 22 leagues from Petenecte. According to Cortés the latter place was 6 leagues above Ciuatecpan, so we get 16 leagues for the Usumacinta-Ciuatecpan distance. This is more than we can assume for a one-day journey upstream. Giving it two days, we have one day left for the stretch from Tatahuitalpan to Usumacinta. If the rate of travel was about the same throughout, then the distance to Usumacinta was 8 leagues, or about the maximum daily travel against current. A site 8 leagues upstream from Pobilcuc would place the pueblo of Usumacinta in the region of modern Balancan. This locates the town below the junction of the San Pedro Mártir and Usumacinta Rivers, and fits in with evidence from the Bravo probanzas which also indicates a below-junction location.[93]

In regard to Ciuatecpan, Maudslay states that it "must be somewhere near the modern Tenosique," and his map shows the crossing just above the latter place. His conclusion is based on the fact that Ciuatecpan was higher upstream than Usumacinta, "which is still marked on the maps."[94] In assuming that colonial Usumacinta was located at the modern town, Maudslay completely ignores all the evidence concerning the relative position of the river settlements. The distance from modern Usumacinta to Tenosique is only 3 leagues, whereas we have shown, on the basis of Cogolludo's estimate of the Usumacinta-Petenecte distance, that Ciuatecpan was 16 leagues from Usumacinta. Moreover, if Ciuatecpan was at Tenosique, then according to Cortés' statement we must place Petenecte 6 leagues farther upstream, and colonial Tenosique would be still farther up the river. But this would put both Petenecte and Tenosique in the gorge of the Usumacinta River.

92 Díaz del Castillo, 1939, ch. 175.
93 Cf. Appendix D.
94 Díaz del Castillo, 1908–16, 5: 336–37 and map.

Becerra and González also place Ciuatecpan near modern Tenosique.[95] They base their conclusion in part on linguistic arguments which we do not regard as valid. Becerra derives Çagoatespan, the incorrect form of Ciuatecpan given by Cortés, from Tsauatecpan, which he defines as "palace of the spinners" (evidently from *tzaua*, "to spin," or *tzauani*, "spinner," and from *tecpan*, which means "government house" and has often been translated as "palace"). Seler has long since shown, however, that the correct form of the name was Ciuatecpan, which he translates as "palace of the woman (of the goddess)."[96] Becerra also reconstructs the name of Tenosique and its variants (Tanoçic, etc.) as Tanatziic (*tana*, "house," and *tziic*, "to unravel, to count threads") so as to obtain a meaning in Chontal similar to that ascribed to Ciuatecpan. But the Chontal Text gives the name as Tanodzic, which would appear to be the correct form and does not easily lend itself to such a definition.

Another argument employed by Becerra and González is the statement that Cogolludo places Tenosique between Usumacinta and Petenecte, i.e., in the same relative position occupied by Ciuatecpan in Cortés' time. Actually we find no justification for this in Cogolludo, unless the authors, assuming that colonial and modern Usumacinta are the same, took note of Cogolludo's statement that Petenecte was 22 leagues above Usumacinta, which would place Petenecte above modern Tenosique. They disregard, however, Cogolludo's remark that Tenosique was the last town up the Usumacinta River.[97] González' actual location for colonial Tenosique (and consequently for Ciuatecpan) is at the ranchería of Concepción, a short distance below modern Tenosique, and he places Petenecte at the ranchería of Buenavista upstream from modern Tenosique.[98]

Morley does not express an opinion as to the sites of Iztapa and Tatahuitalpan, but he locates Ciuatecpan "not far below the modern village of Tenosique." This location is based in part on the fact that Ciuatecpan was above Usumacinta, which Morley identifies as the modern settlement of this name, and below Petenecte, which, in turn, was below Tenosique.[99] This means, however, that he has to squeeze Usumacinta, Ciuatecpan, Petenecte, and Tenosique into a 3-league distance, although Cortés separates Ciuatecpan and Petenecte by 6 leagues and Cogolludo states that Usumacinta and Petenecte were 22 leagues apart. It should be noted, however, that Morley also cites other evidence to support his conclusion that Cortés crossed the Usumacinta

[95] Becerra, 1910a, pp. 504–05; González, 1940, p. 409.
[96] See p. 57, *supra*.
[97] Cogolludo, 1867–68, bk. 12, ch. 3.
[98] González, 1940, p. 409.
[99] Morley, 1937–38, 1: 11–13.

a short distance below Tenosique. Before reviewing this data we shall give our own idea as to the location of Ciuatecpan.

On the basis of our general location for the town of Usumacinta near Balancan, Ciuatecpan would be 16 leagues farther up the river in the Canizan-Estapilla area. However, we must also take into account the fact that Ciuatecpan was also 6 leagues below Petenecte, which, in turn, was an unstated distance below Tenosique. Consequently, in order to fix the location of Ciuatecpan in relation to these two upstream settlements we must be reasonably certain of the location of colonial Tenosique and also arrive at some estimate of the distance which separated it from Petenecte.

It is generally agreed that colonial Tenosique was located at or near the modern town of this name, but we submit the following evidence in order to remove any lingering doubt on this point. In all the lists of Usumacinta River towns for the period 1573–82 Tenosique is always farthest upstream. The Alfaro map also locates it in the same relative position. A document in the Bravo papers of 1573 refers to Tenosique as "the last pueblo of Christians," beyond which extended the unpacified area of the interior. During his expedition of 1530 from Chiapas to Champoton, Alonso de Avila reached a place named Tanoche, just below the gorge of a great river which lower down flowed into the Río de Grijalva.[100] Taking into account Avila's march from Chiapas, this river can only be the Usumacinta, and Tenosique, as we know, is just below a gorge on this stream. But do the names Tanoche and Tenosique refer to the same place? Oviedo states that Tanoche was 60 leagues from the Río de Grijalva, which would place the town far upstream on the Usumacinta in the Tenosique area. The Chontal form of Tenosique is Tanodzic. The variant spellings in the colonial papers—Tanoçic, Tenoçic, Tanotzic, Tagnodzic, Tanoci, Tanoçil, etc.—are obviously derived from the Chontal form. Tanoci and Tanoçil are so similar to Avila's Tanoche, and also to Tanochil or Tanochel of the Gil-Godoy episode of 1536, that there can be little doubt that all these names refer to the same place. Moreover, on the Alfaro map the upper part of the Usumacinta above "Tanoçic" is named "Tanochel." Alfaro, of course, places all the Usumacinta towns too far downstream. A correct location of "Tanoçic," or Tenosique, would have been close to the place where the "Río de Tanochel" emerges from the mountains.

Cortés does not record the name Tenosique or any of its variant spellings, but he does mention three towns with Nahuatl names—Coazacoalco, Taltenango, and Teutitan—that were above Petenecte. One of these was undoubtedly Tenosique. From Ciuatecpan Cortés sent word of his arrival to the

[100] Probanzas of Feliciano Bravo, AGI, México, leg. 109; Oviedo y Valdés, 1851–55, bk. 32, ch. 4.

Spaniards who were at Petenecte, and the following afternoon "at the hour of vespers" this group returned to Ciuatecpan. They told Cortés that messengers had been sent to the Indians of the three towns farther upstream, "who would probably come to see me during the next day. And so it turned out, for the next day there came down the river six or eight canoes with people from all these pueblos."[101] Thus we find that within two days Cortés' messengers went to Petenecte and the Spaniards there returned to Ciuatecpan, and that sometime during the third day the Indians came from the towns above Petenecte. Because of the current, which Cortés says was very strong at Ciuatecpan, the 6 leagues upstream to Petenecte would probably have taken from early morning until at least midafternoon of the first day. The journey downstream on the second day would have taken less time, but the Spaniards undoubtedly started before noon. From Cortés' account we also infer that when the Spaniards in Petenecte received Cortés' message, they, in turn, sent word to the three pueblos upstream and obtained a reply before leaving for Ciuatecpan. Unless the three towns were very close at hand, the persons who went up to them probably made the upstream journey the first day, i.e. after midafternoon, and came back down to Petenecte before noon the next morning. This would imply a journey of not more than 3–4 leagues each way, and probably less. Since we do not know whether Tenosique was nearest to Petenecte or the farthest upstream, we can only assume the latter and call the Petenecte-Tenosique distance 3–4 leagues. Adding the 6 leagues from Ciuatecpan to Petenecte, we have an estimated distance of 9–10 leagues from modern Tenosique down to a site for Ciuatecpan.

The modern site of Canizan is approximately 9 leagues from Tenosique. In the preceding discussion we tentatively placed Ciuatecpan in the Canizan-Estapilla area, on the basis of a location for Usumacinta not far from Balancan. But we know that on the last day of his march to Ciuatecpan Cortés followed a direction from southwest to northeast. so he could not possibly have struck the river near Estapilla. A site at Canizan or on the bend of the river above it would, however, permit an approach from the southwest.

Finally, we have two more bits of evidence that deserve mention. Cortés tells that the Indians of Ciuatecpan had fled to a lagoon east of the river. In the Spanish version of the Chontal Text we read that Ciuatecpan was at the "junta de los ríos," a phrase used to translate the Chontal word *tuxakhaa*, which might also be translated as "where the waters mingle." Some modern maps show a stream called the Chicmux[102] flowing into the Usumacinta close

[101] Cortés, 1916, pp. 363–64.
[102] On some maps it is called the Arroyo Mactun; others show the Arroyo Mactun as a branch of the Chicmux.

to Canizan. On one map we have seen this stream parallels the Usumacinta for a short distance, joining the latter at a ranch named Chicmux just above Canizan. The Espinosa and Hübbe–Aznar Pérez maps of Yucatan and Tabasco show a lagoon (Laguna Chixmuc) on this small watercourse. All this would mean little by itself, for there are so many places on the Usumacinta "where the waters mingle," or where there are lagoons, temporary or permanent, near the river. But having worked out a location for Ciuatecpan near Canizan on the basis of other evidence, we believe that the data just mentioned may well have some significance.[103]

We turn now to Morley's major arguments for locating Ciuatecpan close to Tenosique. First, he cites the fact that when Avila reached Tanoche, or Tenosique, in 1530, the Indians guided him to "the road cut through by Cortés four and a half years earlier (the inference being that this road was near by)." Second, he quotes a passage from the Spanish version of the Chontal Text which states that the Spaniards under Cortés "entraron por Tanoçic" and then passed on to the lands of Acalan.[104] This evidence clearly associates the Cortés route with the Tenosique area, but in view of the fact that Tenosique was above Petenecte and the latter, in turn, was also 6 leagues above Ciuatecpan, the place where Cortés crossed the Usumacinta could not have been between the modern villages of Usumacinta and Tenosique as Morley believes. Moreover, the Oviedo data concerning Avila's march and the passage from the Spanish version of the Chontal Text are not inconsistent with our location for Ciuatecpan near Canizan. The Cortés road, to which the Indians guided Avila, obviously was not far from Tenosique (Canizan is only 9 leagues downstream) but not necessarily so close at hand as Morley suggests. Although the Spanish word *por*, used to indicate direction, usually means "through" or "by way of," in this case it probably means "near" or "in the region of."[105] In any case, this evidence clearly implies that Cortés crossed the Usumacinta at some point upstream in the general region of Tenosique, i.e., above the junction of the Usumacinta and San Pedro Mártir Rivers.

As already noted Mrs. Stone favors a location for Ciuatecpan at Montecristo below the junction. She attempts to reconcile Oviedo's account of Avila's march with this location, but her arguments are of dubious validity.[106]

---

[103] It is also interesting to note that the Tulane-Carnegie map shows a ruin on the left bank of the Usumacinta at Canizan.

[104] Morley, 1937–38, 1: 12–13.

[105] It should be noted that the language of the Chontal original is ambiguous, for the phrase *ochiob tanodzic*, which the translators rendered as "entraron por Tanoçic," has no preposition.

[106] Mrs. Stone points out that Oviedo does not state the distance from Tenosique to Cortés'

At the time her paper was written the Chontal Text was not known. Andrews also favors a downstream location for Ciuatecpan, although he does not specify any particular site. His arguments take no account of the Oviedo evidence, nor does he refer to the passage from the Spanish version of the Chontal Text cited by Morley.[107] Pérez Martínez, who accepts the Stone-Andrews thesis of a location below the junction of the Usumacinta and San Pedro Mártir, places the town "near the place where the Río de Palizada branches off from the Usumacinta."[108]

Any discussion of the question whether Ciuatecpan was above or below the junction of the Usumacinta and San Pedro Mártir must also take into account the location of the great "estero" where Cortés built the famous bridge on his march from Ciuatecpan to Acalan in 1525. Avila also crossed this same estero (Oviedo calls it a "laguna") in 1530. Mrs. Stone identifies it as an estuary on Laguna de Términos, a logical location in terms of her sites for Ciuatecpan and Itzamkanac. Andrews does not attempt to locate it, but he does cite reasons to challenge Morley's view that the estero was "a widened or overflow section of the Rio San Pedro Martir."[109]

It is not necessary to examine the validity of Mrs. Stone's and Andrews' arguments, for we now have evidence that the estero was actually on the San Pedro Mártir. The passage from the Spanish version of the Chontal Text mentioned above states that the Spaniards with Cortés "entraron por Tanoçic y pasaron por el pueblo de Taxich [Tachix in the Chontal original]," and then advanced to the lands of Acalan. Likewise, the Spanish version refers to a second expedition, obviously that of Avila, as follows: "vinieron otros es-

---

road, i.e., to Ciuatecpan or nearby. This is quite true, but the Oviedo narrative as a whole clearly implies that the road crossed the Usumacinta in the general region of Tenosique and not at some point as far downstream as Montecristo. Mrs. Stone also states that after arriving at the road Avila marched three days to the great estero where Cortés had built a bridge in 1525. Actually Oviedo gives no time schedule for this stage of Avila's journey. He does state, however, that when Avila returned to Tenosique from the estero, the journey took "almost three days." But this makes a vast difference not only as to the location of the estero in relation to Tenosique, but also as to the site of Ciuatecpan. We see no way of solving the problem in terms of Mrs. Stone's locations for Ciuatecpan and her site for Itzamkanac on Laguna de Términos (Stone, 1932, pp. 231–33; Oviedo y Valdés, 1851–55, bk. 32, chs. 4, 5).

[107] Andrews, 1943, pp. 17–21.

[108] Pérez Martínez, 1945, p. 277. Cf. also pp. 232–33, 277–81, *passim*. The author cites the statement of Díaz del Castillo (ch. 176) that Ciuatecpan was situated on a great river "que iba a dar en unos esteros donde había una población que se dice Gueyatasta, y junto a él estaba otro gran pueblo que se dice Xicalango." Influenced by the Stone-Andrews thesis of a downstream location for Ciuatecpan, he interprets the passage as referring to the lower course of the Usumacinta-Palizada. He also calls attention to a statement in the Chontal Text which refers to the Ciuatecpan people "en la junta de los ríos" (the Chontal for this phrase is *tuxakha*, "where the waters mingle"), and he concludes that this "alludes to the Palizada and Usumacinta." Açtually, the phrase could apply to any river junction or place "where the waters mingle" on the Usumacinta.

[109] Stone, 1932, pp. 220–21, 232–33; Andrews, 1943, pp. 19–20.

pañoles y entraron y pasaron por donde el Capitán del Valle [Cortés] pasó, por el pueblo de Tehix [Tachiix in the Chontal]." It may be noted, however, that in neither case does the Chontal original have words for "pueblo de." The Text merely states that Cortés and the second expedition "passed Tachix." In Appendix D we describe the entradas of Feliciano Bravo from Tenosique to the Peten in 1573 and 1580. In each case he marched overland from Tenosique to a "Río de Tachis," and then advanced upstream in canoes toward the Itza country. This Río de Tachis can be only the San Pedro Mártir. Consequently, the statements in the Chontal Text that Cortés "entered" by way of the Tenosique district and then "passed Tachix" en route to Acalan clearly indicate that he crossed the San Pedro Mártir at some point.

If Ciuatecpan were located at Montecristo or at any other point some distance below the junction of the Usumacinta and San Pedro Mártir, both Cortés and Avila would have had to make a roundabout march to cross, or indeed to have passed anywhere near, the latter stream en route to Mrs. Stone's and Andrews' respective locations for Itzamkanac on Laguna de Términos and the lower Candelaria.

The next stage of Cortés' journey which requires detailed discussion is the march from Ciuatecpan to Itzamkanac, the Acalan capital. Crossing the Usumacinta at Ciuatecpan, Cortés traveled for three days along a narrow trail until he came to an *estero* or *ancón* 500 paces wide (a section of the Río San Pedro Mártir), which blocked his advance. After a fruitless search for a ford, he called upon the Spaniards and Mexican auxiliaries to build a bridge across the stream and although it seemed a hopeless task, the bridge was finally completed, owing in large measure to the commander's leadership and driving energy. On the right bank of the river the army encountered a swamp, where the soldiers had trouble in getting the horses through to solid ground. But once the estero and swamp were crossed, the army was able to advance without difficulty to the lands of Acalan.

The first Acalan town, called Tizatepelt by Cortés, was reached in a two-day journey from the swamp. After a stay of six days at this place, Cortés continued the march to a larger settlement named Teutiercas 5 leagues distant, and from there the army eventually proceeded to Itzamkanac, which was apparently a day's journey or less farther on. The actual travel time from the swamp on the right bank of the San Pedro Mártir to the Acalan capital may be reckoned as about four days. In Acalan Cortés received information concerning the Spaniards at Nito, to which he now directed his march. On leaving Itzamkanac the army crossed a nearby river and advanced through Cehache country en route to Tayasal on Lake Peten.[110]

[110] Cortés, 1866, pp. 413–427.

As we have stated in the first section of this appendix, Becerra places the crossing of the estero, or San Pedro Mártir, near the modern site of Gracias a Dios, southeast of Tenosique. He places the Acalan lands in western Peten, but he does not attempt to locate the capital. González directs Cortés' march even more sharply to the southeast from Tenosique, placing the crossing of the San Pedro Mártir near El Ceibo on the present trail from Tenosique to the Peten. From this point the route turns slightly northeast to the site for Itzamkanac, on the extreme headwaters of the San Pedro branch of the Candelaria, which is shown on González' map as extending a considerable distance southward into the Peten.[111]

On Maudslay's maps the Cortés route crosses the San Pedro Mártir almost directly east of Tenosique and then swings southeast paralleling the river to a tentative location for Itzamkanac east of the Mexico-Guatemala boundary. Morley's route for Cortés is essentially the same. He places the crossing of the San Pedro Mártir between La Revancha and Santa Elena and locates Itzamkanac at or near the modern settlement of Mactun on the north bank of the river in the Peten. Maudslay's location for the Acalan capital is in the same general locality.[112]

Thus all four of these writers agree on a southeasterly route for Cortés from Ciuatecpan to the Acalan lands. It is our own view that Cortés marched northeast from Ciuatecpan, crossed the San Pedro Mártir near Nuevo León, then proceeded to the San Pedro branch of the Candelaria, and finally reached Itzamkanac near the confluence of the San Pedro and Arroyo Caribe. This view is naturally based in part on our belief that the Acalan lands were located in the Candelaria drainage. But in the preceding discussion we have also shown that the province was closer to the Gulf coast than the area in which Becerra, González, Maudslay, and Morley place it, and we have presented various arguments to prove that the Río de Acalan, on which Itzamkanac was located, cannot be identified as the San Pedro Mártir. We now propose to refute the thesis that Cortés followed a southeasterly route from Ciuatecpan to the Peten, where the four writers mentioned above place the province of Acalan and its capital.

1. At Ciuatecpan Cortés conferred with the Indians concerning the route he should take to Acalan. The Ciuatecpan people told him that he should proceed by way of the towns higher up the river, and they had already opened 6 leagues of road before the arrival of the natives from these upstream settlements. The latter insisted, however, that such a route would be very

<hr/>

[111] Becerra, 1910a, p. 413; González, 1940, pp. 411–17, and map.

[112] Díaz del Castillo, 1908–16, 5: maps; Morley, 1937–38, 1: 13–16. On plate 179 of Morley's work Mactun is shown on the south bank of the river, but in vol. 1, ch. 1, note 89, he notes that this is an error.

circuitous ("muy gran rodeo") and that the direct road was by way of a merchant trail leading from the right bank of the Usumacinta opposite Ciuatecpan, "by which they would guide me to Acalan." The Indians finally agreed among themselves that this was the better way.[113] It was evidently the plan of the Ciuatecpan people to get the Spaniards quickly out of town at any cost and to put the onus of transportation across the Usumacinta and provisioning for the journey to Acalan on their upstream neighbors. But when the Indians from Petenecte and the other settlements above Ciuatecpan arrived and talked to Cortés, they promptly put an end to any such scheme. They had geography on their side of the argument, and the Ciuatecpan people finally had to acknowledge it.

In the case of a Peten location for the Acalan capital, a march upstream from the Canizan area (where we locate Ciuatecpan) to the region of Tenosique (one of the upstream towns) and thence across country to the San Pedro Mártir would, of course, have been more roundabout than a route directly to the southeast from Canizan, but it would not have been unduly circuitous. On the other hand, any upstream march, regardless of its distance, would indeed have been circuitous if Acalan was located to the northeast in the Candelaria drainage. In short, the objection to an upriver journey made by the visitors from Petenecte and neighboring towns applies with very much greater force in the case of a Candelaria location for Itzamkanac than it does in the case of a Peten site. If we also take into account the evidence already cited in favor of a Candelaria location, there can be little doubt that the direct road from Ciuatecpan to the Acalan capital was to the northeast and not to the southeast.[114]

2. Morley states that Cortés' march from Ciuatecpan to the great estero was "through continuously hilly country." This statement is evidently based on Cortés' remark that after leaving Ciuatecpan the army traveled for three days along a narrow trail "por unas montañas harto espesas."[115] One meaning of the word "montañas" is elevated or mountainous terrain, and if Cortés used

[113] Cortés, 1866, p. 413, and 1916, p. 365.

[114] The Indians from Petenecte and adjacent towns told Cortés that an upstream march would also take him through "difficult and uninhabited country." This has been interpreted as meaning that the suggested upstream route extended far to the south into the rough, mountainous region above Tenosique. In such case the line of march to a Peten location for Itzamkanac would have been much more circuitous than by way of Tenosique and thence overland to the San Pedro Mártir. But we doubt that the Ciuatecpan people had any idea of sending Cortés so far to the south. Moreover, with Acalan located in the Candelaria drainage, a route by way of Tenosique, east or southeast to the San Pedro Mártir, and thence in a northeasterly direction through the Peten to the headwaters of the Candelaria would have been "very circuitous." It would also have crossed through difficult country, for which we have no evidence of permanent settlements at the time of the conquest.

[115] Morley, 1937–38, 1: 13; Cortés, 1866, p. 413.

it in this sense, a route from Ciuatecpan skirting the wedge of elevated country separating the Usumacinta and the San Pedro Mártir would be called for. The more southeasterly routes from Tenosique to the San Pedro Mártir suggested by Becerra and González would satisfy such a requirement better than the Maudslay-Morley route, which crosses through country where modern maps indicate a maximum elevation of less than 200 m. But the word "montañas" can also mean forested country,[116] and the adjective "espesas" (dense, thick) employed by Cortés strongly suggests such a meaning in this case. Andrews has called attention to this point in his criticism of Morley's route for Cortés from Ciuatecpan to Itzamkanac, and it is also interesting to note that Maudslay translates Cortés' phrase as "through thick forest."[117] Thus a northeasterly route from Canizan to the San Pedro Mártir across low country where the elevation is less than 100 m. would satisfy the requirements of this phase of Cortés' narrative as well as of a southeasterly march across higher terrain. The army would have encountered thick forest in either case.

3. When Cortés was searching for a ford across the estero, or San Pedro Mártir, his guides, evidently from Ciuatecpan, told him that such a search was useless unless he traveled upstream for twenty days "hasta las sierras."[118] The sierras here mentioned (note that Cortés in this case uses the word "sierras" and not "montañas") obviously refer to the elevated country, rising in places to a height of 500 m. or more, extending from near Tenosique southeastward into central Peten. The northwestern, and also the highest, portion of this area forms the wedge or divide, mentioned in the preceding paragraph, which separates the Usumacinta and San Pedro Mártir and forces the latter stream to turn north after crossing the Mexico-Guatemala boundary. Although the guides may have exaggerated the time that would have been required to reach a ford, it is evident that Cortés had struck the San Pedro Mártir a considerable distance downstream from the sierras. The points of crossing at Gracias a Dios and at El Ceibo suggested by Becerra and González respectively are at the foothills of the divide between the two rivers, and the sites indicated by Maudslay and Morley, although farther downstream, are also too close to the sierras to give the statements of the guides much meaning. In short, a site for the crossing of the San Pedro Mártir northeast of Canizan, where we locate Ciuatecpan, would satisfy this part of Cortés'

[116] Chapter 10 of the present volume deals with the history of the "Montañas" missions that were established in 1604 et seq. in the area southeast of Tixchel. These missions were so named because they were located in a bush and forest area, not in mountainous or elevated country.

[117] Andrews, 1943, p. 19; Cortés, 1916, p. 365.

[118] Cortés, 1866, p. 413.

narrative better than those suggested by the proponents of a southeasterly route to Itzamkanac.

4. Mrs. Stone, who places Ciuatecpan at Montecristo, believes that Cortés marched in a northeasterly direction to Itzamkanac, which she locates on Laguna de Términos. Morley raises an objection on the ground that "such a direction would have taken the army a tremendous distance out of the most direct route to the next identifiable point of its itinerary after leaving Itzamkanac and the Province of Acalan, namely Tayasal at the western end of Lake Petén Itzá."[119] This line of argument implies that Itzamkanac should be located in terms of a direct route from Ciuatecpan to Tayasal and other identifiable points of Cortés' itinerary beyond Acalan; that Cortés' objective on leaving Ciuatecpan was not only Itzamkanac but also other points on his later route to Nito and the Caribbean coast. We have already noted, however, that Cortés' objective prior to reaching Acalan was apparently Ascension Bay, which he may have confused with Chetumal Bay, in eastern Yucatan. Consequently, if Cortés, on leaving Ciuatecpan, followed a fairly direct route to an objective beyond Acalan, it would be more reasonable to assume that he marched northeast instead of southeast. It was only after he reached Acalan that he learned of the presence of Spaniards at Nito and directed his march toward the latter place on the basis of a new map provided by the Indians of Acalan. Thus the thesis of a direct route to the southeast is tenable only for the journey beyond Acalan.

Crossing a wide river near Itzamkanac, Cortés passed through certain towns of the Cehache Indians on the way to Tayasal. In Chapter 3 we have shown that the Cehache occupied the lacustrine belt extending from Mocu and Cilvituk south into northern Peten. According to available documentary evidence the southern limits of the province, even at the end of the seventeenth century after the Cehache had been subject to prolonged pressure by fugitive Maya from northern Yucatan, were in the region of Chuntuqui. Consequently, if Itzamkanac was located on the north bank of the San Pedro Mártir at or near Mactun, it would not have been necessary for Cortés to cross the river in order to march through Cehache territory. Moreover, a march from Mactun to Tayasal by way of the southern part of the Cehache country as defined above would have necessitated a lengthy detour to the northeast. In short, the thesis of a direct route to the southeast falls down in the very first case where it has definite validity.

On Maudslay's map the Cehache area, designated as Mazateca, is spread across the San Pedro Mártir southeast of the location for Itzamkanac, and

[119] Morley, 1937–38, 1: 12.

Cortés' route, which crosses the river at the latter place, runs through the southern part of the indicated Cehache territory.[120] Thus Maudslay achieves a direct route through Cehache country to Tayasal, but only by placing the Cehache farther south than is warranted by the documentary evidence.

Morley describes the Cehache province at the end of the seventeenth century as extending from the northern boundary of the Department of Peten to "somewhere around the headwaters of the Río San Pedro Mártir, east of Agua Dulce along the general line from Salchiche to Santa Cruz, roughly 9 or 10 leagues north of the lake."[121] Like Maudslay, he errs in extending the Cehache territory too far to the south. The narrative of Avendaño's journey to Tayasal in 1696, of which Morley gives a summary, mentions no towns or settlements between the Cehache ranchería at Chuntuqui and the first settlement of the Chakan Itza west of Lake Peten. The narrative also indicates a distance of about 29 leagues between these points.[122] In 1525 Cortés marched five days through uninhabited country from Yasuncabil, the last Cehache town, to the lake. The logical route for a march from Mactun to Tayasal through the southern part of the Cehache province as defined by Morley would be north of the San Pedro Mártir and around its headwaters. Cortés' narrative explicitly states, however, that on leaving Itzamkanac the army crossed a "gran estero" (a wide, sluggish river), a point which Morley fails to mention. If Cortés crossed the San Pedro Mártir at Mactun and followed a direct route to Tayasal, he would not have passed through Cehache country as delimited by Morley.

5. Morley's location for Itzamkanac is based in part on his interpretation of certain passages in the Chontal Text and in the Spanish version of the same. He calls attention to the fact that in several places the term Mactun occurs together with the name Acalan in references to the people or to the province of Acalan, and he also states that in one case the capital of the province is referred to as Mactun de Acalan (Tamactun Acalan in the Text). Morley then adds:

The writer regards it as highly probable that while Acalan was the Nahuatl name of the province and, by extension, of its capital or principal settlement as well, the Maya (Chontal) name for the people as likewise for the province and sometimes, by extension, even for its capital was Mactun, though the proper Chontal name of the principal town or capital was Itzamkanac. By referring to plate 179 it will be seen that the name Mactun still attaches to a small settlement

---

[120] Díaz del Castillo, 1908–16, 5: "Map of Guatemala and Adjacent Areas."
[121] Morley, 1937–38, 1: 72.
[122] Means, 1917, pp. 124–29; Morley, 1937–38, 1: 50–51. Means' map (plate VI) places Chuntuqui south of the San Pedro Mártir, but we see no justification whatever for such a location.

on the north bank of the Rio San Pedro Mártir, 22 km. in an air line east-southeast
of the point (Santa Clara) where the river passes out of the Department of Petén,
Guatemala, and into the State of Tabasco, Mexico. This the writer believes must
be very near, if not indeed actually at, the site of Itzamkanac, the capital of the
ancient Province of Acalan.[123]

This line of argument is open to various objections. The duplication of
place names in Yucatan and Tabasco, as well as in other parts of Middle
America, makes it necessary to exercise caution in forming conclusions based
on the appearance of a certain name at any given point on modern maps.
Mactun occurs not only in the case cited above by Morley but also as the
name of an arroyo, or small stream, tributary to the Usumacinta near Canizan.
On the basis of name occurrence it would be just as logical to locate Itzamkanac in the latter area as at the site of the settlement of Mactun on the San
Pedro Mártir. Although the case is not entirely comparable, it may be noted
that Maler's incorrect location for Itzamkanac at Canizan was based on the
similarity of the two names.[124]

The term Mactun appears at least eleven times in the Chontal Text, but
in no case do we find it alone as a name for the Acalan capital. It appears alone
only once (folio 72v, line 4) in the plural form Amactunob, "Mactun people."
In all other cases we find it together with or in association with the name
Acalan, and in almost every passage the reference is to the province or its
people. In only one passage, describing the arrival of the Franciscan missionary, Fray Diego de Béjar, on April 20, 1550, is there any certainty that the
capital is indicated, and in this case the Text reads "Tamactun Acalan" (folio
74r, line 24). In contrast, the Text records the name of the capital four times
as Itzamkanac, once as Acalan Itzamkanac, and once as Itzamkanac Acalan.
These facts indicate that Mactun was probably a qualifying term, and also
that it was normally used with reference to the province or its people rather
than to any particular settlement.

We cannot translate the term Mactun with absolute certainty. *Mac* can
mean that which chokes or obstructs something. *Tun* means some kind of
rock, and it evidently indicates a natural feature of the landscape by which
the country is characterized in the minds of the people. As already noted,
Mactun appears on modern maps as the name of a river and of a river settlement. In the Chontal Text it refers to a province, a people, and possibly a
settlement located on a river, the Río de Acalan. An important feature of the

---

[123] Morley, 1937–38, 1: 15–16. On plate 179 of Morley's work Mactun is shown on the south
bank of the river, but in vol. 1, ch. 1, note 89, he notes that this is an error.

[124] Maler, 1910, p. 165.

APPENDIX B 455

Río de Acalan was the stone ledges which created an extensive series of rapids and falls. Rapids exist on the San Pedro Mártir below the modern settlement of Mactun, as well as below Tiradero. We do not know whether such obstacles exist on the Arroyo Mactun, tributary of the Usumacinta. The foregoing data suggest, however, that Mactun (the name can be either Chontal or Maya) is a term descriptive of a region of rapids or falls.[125]

If our reasoning is correct, then the name Mactun as employed in the Chontal Text indicates that the people of Acalan regarded the rapids and falls of the Río de Acalan as the characteristic feature of their country. In other words, Acalan, which means "land of boats" in Nahuatl, was also a "rapids" province, and its inhabitants, the Amactunob, were "rapids people."[126] It is evident, however, that such a province could have been located on the Candelaria as well as on the San Pedro Mártir.

With regard to any settlement named Mactun on the San Pedro Mártir, we do not know whether it goes back to pre-Spanish times. We find no mention of any such place in the reports of the expeditions of Feliciano Bravo up the Río de Tachis, or San Pedro Mártir, in 1573 and 1580, although on each occasion he undoubtedly passed the site of the modern settlement. It is possible, of course, that a tract of land along or near the rapids on the east-west course of the river in the Peten was always known as Mactun; but it is also more likely that a new and later settlement established close to these rapids would be called Mactun. Moreover, the reports of Bravo's entradas contain no hint that he had entered Acalan territory or that he had passed the site of Itzamkanac on his upstream journeys toward the Itza country. Indeed, witnesses who were asked to testify concerning Bravo's services made a clear distinction between the Acalan country and the Tachis, or San Pedro Mártir, area.[127]

6. We have already taken note of various statements in Cortés' narrative which refer to a water route from Acalan and its capital to the coastal settlements of Xicalango by way of Laguna de Términos.[128] If Itzamkanac was on the San Pedro Mártir, then the water route would have comprised this stream and the Usumacinta. In other words, Itzamkanac would have been located on a branch of the same river on which Cortés marched upstream from Iztapa.

[125] Cf. discussion in Chapter 3, pp. 51-52, *supra*.

[126] This does not mean that the capital of the province and other principal towns were necessarily located on or close to the rapids of the Río de Acalan. In the Yucatan documents towns of the Xiu province are often referred to as "sierra" settlements, although they were actually some distance from the sierra, or range of hills, to which reference is made.

[127] Probanzas of Feliciano Bravo, AGI, México, leg. 109. Also cf. discussion of the Bravo entradas in Appendix D.

[128] Cf. pp. 411-12, *supra*.

At this point we also call special attention to the fact that while Cortés was at Iztapa he sent messengers to his ships waiting off the Gulf coast to obtain food supplies and transport them by water to Acalan, where he would be waiting. This would mean, in the case of a location for Itzamkanac at Mactun, that the supplies were to be transported up the Usumacinta and San Pedro Mártir Rivers, and that Cortés already had at least a general knowledge of such a route. After his arrival in Acalan Cortés would have received more precise information from Paxbolonacha and the Acalan merchants, and he would also have learned then, if not before, that Itzamkanac was located on a branch of the Usumacinta.

We should expect therefore that Cortés would have given some explicit indication of one or more of these facts in the narrative of his journey. But the Fifth Letter contains no statement that clearly and unmistakably defines the water route from Acalan to the Gulf coast as the Usumacinta–San Pedro Mártir system; no explicit evidence that the supplies were to be sent up the same river on which the army was encamped when the messengers were sent to the coast; no statement that Itzamkanac was located on a branch of the great river on which the towns of Iztapa, Tatahuitalpan, Usumacinta, and Ciuatecpan were situated; no statement that the Acalan capital was located on the very river across which Cortés built the famous bridge. The lack of any such data in Cortés' narrative clearly implies that in marching from Ciuatecpan to Itzamkanac the army crossed from one river system to another, i.e., from the Usumacinta–San Pedro Mártir to the Candelaria. That such was the case is proved by Montejo's probanza of 1531, which places Acalan close to the Gulf coast and in which we have testimony that the Río de Acalan (the "gran estero" on which Cortés said Itzamkanac was located) emptied directly into Laguna de Términos. It is evident therefore that the supplies from the ships were to be sent across Laguna de Términos and up the Candelaria, while Cortés and the army followed another route to Acalan. Likewise, the Tabasco merchants who gave Paxbolonacha advance knowledge of the Spaniards undoubtedly came by the Términos-Candelaria route.

7. A final objection to Maudslay's location for Itzamkanac may be made on the basis of the salto, or sharp drop in the San Pedro Mártir, just below Mactun. Neither Cortés nor Bernal Díaz refers to any falls near the Acalan capital. Bernal Díaz traveled by canoe through most of the region surrounding Itzamkanac in search of food for the army, and if he had encountered any such obstructions to navigation he would almost certainly have mentioned them.

González places Itzamkanac on the Candelaria system, but his location for the capital on the extreme headwaters of the San Pedro branch, which he extends farther south into the Peten than do most cartographers of the region, is too far upstream. The records of Paxbolon's entradas into the Zapotitlan area in 1566–68 indicate that Itzamkanac could be reached in a two-day journey above the falls and rapids of the Río de Acalan. It would not be possible to reach González' site for Itzamkanac within two days from Salto Ahogado, in former times the upper limit of the falls on the Candelaria. Andrews reports rapids on the upper part of the San Pedro branch,[129] but these, in turn, are too far from the coast to be identified as the obstacles mentioned in the narrative of Paxbolon's entradas.

The foregoing evidence should be sufficient to refute the idea that Cortés followed a southeasterly route from Ciuatecpan to Itzamkanac. A route to the northeast not only satisfies certain requirements of Cortés' narrative as well as a march to the southeast, but in some cases permits a more reasonable interpretation of the narrative. We shall now describe the line of march we believe the army followed to the Acalan capital and thence across the Cehache country to Tayasal.

As stated above, we place the crossing of the estero, or San Pedro Mártir, in the region of Nuevo León northeast of Canizan. The airline distance from Canizan to Nuevo León is approximately 30 km., a short stretch for a three-day march. But since the army followed a narrow trail through thick forest, the advance was probably slow and arduous; and the actual route, winding through the forest, was necessarily longer than the airline distance. In 1530 Avila took "almost three days" to return from the estero to Tanoche, or Tenosique.

Near Nuevo León a small stream (the Río Nuevo León, also called the "zanja" of Nuevo León) enters the Usumacinta from the east. On some maps this tributary is shown with branching mouths, indicating a low flood area, and on at least one map (Balancan Sheet, Military Intelligence Division, U. S. A., 1935, Map No. 107 E-15-S-III) we find an extensive area of swamp drained by this "zanja." These topographical data fit in with Cortés' account of an estero, said to be 500 paces wide, and a swamp on the right bank of the river, and also with Oviedo's description of a great lagoon 2 leagues wide encountered by Avila in 1530. Avila arrived in the rainy season when the flood waters would have been more extensive, and although Cortés passed through in the dry season, he refers to the "muchas aguas que había," evidently out-of-season rains.[130]

[129] Andrews, 1943, p. 46.
[130] Oviedo y Valdés, 1851–55, bk. 32, chs. 4, 5; Cortés, 1866, pp. 413–14.

Certain statements in Cortés' Fifth Letter and in the narrative of Bernal Díaz have been interpreted as indicating that there was also a water route from Ciuatecpan to Acalan. Cortés tells us that from Ciuatecpan he sent a Spaniard and some Indians "in a canoe by water to the province of Acalan" to announce his coming and to find out whether the supplies had arrived from the ships. Later he sent out another advance party, evidently the one of which Bernal Díaz was a member. In Maudslay's translation of Bernal Díaz' account of the activities of this second party we find this statement: "We did all the journey in canoes by rivers and lagoons. . . ." By reference to the Spanish original we find, however, that this statement ("y todo se andaba en canoas por ríos y esteros") does not refer to Bernal Díaz' journey to Acalan, but obviously goes with his preceding reference to the Acalan settlements and means that communication between these settlements was in canoes by rivers and esteros. In another passage Bernal Díaz also mentions "crossing the swamps with difficulty" en route to Acalan, a remark that would have little meaning if he had made the entire journey by canoe. Moreover, Cortés specifically states that the second advance party was sent "por tierra" with guides from Ciuatecpan who knew the road.[131] Thus the question is how to interpret Cortés' statement that the first party was sent "in a canoe by water to the province of Acalan."

If this statement means that the entire journey was to be made by water, then there would be only two alternatives in the case of a location for Acalan in the Candelaria drainage. One would be down the Usumacinta and the Palizada to Laguna de Términos, thence to the mouth of the Candelaria, and upstream to the Acalan settlements. But this route can probably be ruled out, since it would have taken a long time and Cortés was evidently anxious to learn whether the supplies from the ships had arrived. The second alternative would have been down the Usumacinta to the mouth of the San Pedro Mártir, thence upstream on the latter river to a point where there was some sort of water connection, possibly with portages, to the San Pedro branch of the Candelaria. Some of the older maps actually show a connection, called the Arroyo Pedernal, between these streams across the northwest corner of the Peten. Exact topographical data for this area are not available, but in former times, prior to the blasting of channels through the rapids and falls of the Candelaria, there were probably more extensive swamp and overflow areas on the upper reaches of the river, including the San Pedro branch. Such areas and the swamp, or *zanja*, east of the San Pedro Mártir near Nuevo León may have provided a passage with portages for canoes from one stream to the other.

131 Cortés, 1866, p. 413; Díaz del Castillo, 1908–16, 5: 19–20; 1939, ch. 176.

It is also possible, indeed probable, that Cortés' statement merely means that the first advance party set out by canoe and was expected to proceed by water as far as possible, i.e., to some point on the San Pedro Mártir or to the great swamp east of the river, and then by a short overland march to the Acalan settlements. The main army later reached the first Acalan farms after a march of only a day and a half from the swamp. Advocates of a San Pedro Mártir location for Acalan may argue that the advance party was expected to proceed by way of the Usumacinta and San Pedro Mártir all the way to Itzamkanac, and that Cortés' statements constitute evidence in favor of their location of the province, but there are so many reasons for rejecting a San Pedro Mártir location for Acalan that such an argument does not merit serious consideration. It is evident that canoes could go from Ciuatecpan to within a relatively short distance of the Acalan frontier, and it may be that Cortés thought of the Acalan province as beginning on the farther side of the great swamp. Moreover, as we have indicated above, there may actually have been a water route for canoes, with easy portages, from the San Pedro Mártir to the San Pedro branch of the Candelaria.

From the swamps on the right bank of the San Pedro Mártir, Cortés and his army advanced toward the frontier settlements of Acalan. About noon of the second day they came to some planted fields, and later in the afternoon, after making a detour around a swamp, they arrived at the first town. This settlement, called Tizatepelt in Cortés' Fifth Letter, was apparently the place named Çacchute in the brief narrative of the journey in the Chontal Text.[132] Neither the Mexican nor the Chontal name appears to provide a definite clue to the location of the town.[133] If we assume a distance of 9 or 10 leagues in a northeasterly direction from Nuevo León on the San Pedro Mártir, the settlement would have been situated in the region of the great bend of the San Pedro branch of the Candelaria above the junction with the Esperanza.[134]

The lord of Tizatepelt had his people open a road to a larger settlement 5 leagues farther on. Cortés gives the name of this second town as Teutiercas, evidently the place named Tuxakha in the Chontal Text. The term *tuxakha*, which means "where the waters mingle," is translated in one passage of the Spanish version of the Text as "junta de los ríos." Ixtlilxochitl, who gives the

---

[132] Cortés, 1866, pp. 416–17.

[133] Seler (1904, p. 79) defines Tizatepetlan (the form given by Gómara and Ixtlilxochitl) as "the white earth mountain" or "village of the white earth." We have tentatively translated Cacchute as "white cedar" (cf. p. 388, *supra*).

[134] If Cortés had marched almost due north from the San Pedro Mártir, he would have struck the Candelaria below the rapids. But since neither he nor Bernal Díaz mentions these obstacles, it is evident that the army's route was to the northeast to the upper part of the river above the rapids.

name of the town as Teotilac, indicates that it was on a river.[135] It seems likely therefore that Teutiercas, or Tuxakha, was located on the Arroyo San Pedro somewhere on the lower part of the great bend and possibly at the junction with the Arroyo Esperanza.[136]

From Teutiercas, where Paxbolonacha came to meet Cortés, the army proceeded to Itzamkanac. Cortés does not state the distance for this stage of the march, but it was evidently made in one day or less, and we may assume a maximum distance of from 5 to 6 leagues.[137] Depending on the general direction of the march and also the exact location of Teutiercas, the army could have reached the Candelaria at various points from the junction of the Arroyo Caribe and the San Pedro downstream toward La Florida. But we also have to take into account the fact that Itzamkanac-Acalan was some two days' journey above the rapids and falls, and this would indicate a location near the junction. And we must also assume that it was on the south bank of the Candelaria, since the Cortés narrative gives no evidence that any major stream was crossed between the estero, or San Pedro Mártir, and Itzamkanac.

A site for the capital on the south bank of the Candelaria near the junction of the Arroyo Caribe and the San Pedro also satisfies other requirements of the various accounts of Cortés' stay in Acalan. (1) It is far enough above the rapids and falls to explain why neither Cortés nor Bernal Díaz mention these obstacles in the Río de Acalan. (2) It occupies a position from which Cortés had to cross a river and only one (evidently the Arroyo San Pedro) en route to Cehache country, and it also enables us to plot a march through this area and thence to Tayasal in the time allotted by the Fifth Letter. (3) It is centrally and strategically located in a network of waterways (the Candelaria, its two main branches, connecting creeks, swamps, and overflow areas) that would give meaning to Cortés' remark that Acalan was "surrounded by esteros." González defines the province as the northwestern Peten, with the San Pedro Mártir and the San Pedro branch of the Candelaria as the surrounding waterways. Morley suggests an even larger area bounded by the Candelaria, the San Pedro Mártir, and the Usumacinta.[138] It seems obvious, however, that Cortés was describing the part of Acalan that he actually saw, not a larger area, parts of which he could not have visited if he had taken a

[135] Cortés, 1866, p. 417; Alva Ixtlilxochitl, 1891–92, 1: 412.

[136] Seler (1904, p. 79) derives Teutiercas (recorded as Teuticcac by Gómara) from *teotl-icac* (cf. Ixtlilxochitl's Teotilac) as "the upright standing god," and he calls attention to the fact that at Teutiercas the Chontal worshipped a female deity to whom maidens were sacrificed. The forms recorded by Gómara and Ixtlilxochitl probably reproduce the actual name more accurately than Cortés' Teutiercas, since there is no written *r* in Nahuatl.

[137] Cortés, 1866, p. 419.

[138] González, 1940, p. 415–16; Morley, 1937–38, 1: 73.

southeasterly route from Ciuatecpan on the Usumacinta to the San Pedro Mártir, Mactun, and thence to Tayasal. Moreover, the region of the upper Candelaria and its two major branches would constitute an area surrounded by esteros directly tributary to Laguna de Términos, as Cortés' narrative implies and Montejo's probanza requires. (4) From a site near the junction of the Arroyo Caribe and the San Pedro it would have been possible, as Bernal Díaz relates, for the Spaniards to visit the neighboring settlements in canoes and rapidly accumulate a supply of food for the army.[139] (5) Bernal Díaz also states that some of the towns were on mainland and others on islands.[140] Before the blasting of the rapids of the Candelaria, there was probably more overflow on the upper part of the mainstream and its branches, creating inundated areas surrounding plots of higher ground. Andrews reports that even today the country north of the Candelaria is swamp.[141]

Having obtained information from Paxbolonacha and the Acalan merchants concerning the Spaniards at Nito, Cortés now prepared to march toward the latter area. The Chontal made him a map of the route he should follow, furnished supplies of food, and provided guides to take him to the Cehache country which bordered the province of Acalan on the east.

Itzamkanac lay beside a swamp and just beyond the latter flowed a wide, sluggish river ("gran estero") which it was necessary to cross to march toward the Cehache country. Since the town was apparently on the south bank of the Candelaria near the junction of its two major branches, the estero must have been either the main Candelaria or the San Pedro branch. Cortés also states that between the estero and the first Cehache farms his route lay through level, heavily forested country and was impeded by no river or swamp. Consequently it is difficult to escape the conclusion that he crossed the San Pedro not far above the junction and proceeded in an easterly direction, probably a little south of east, between the Arroyo Caribe and the Arroyo Esperanza to the lacustrine belt beyond Laguna Misteriosa.[142]

If Cortés had crossed the main Candelaria, he would have immediately encountered swampy country north of the river. It would also have been necessary either to cross the Arroyo Caribe or else to make a long detour around the north end of Isla Pac, the great swampy area draining into the upper part of the latter stream. This would have also taken Cortés to the Cehache country, it is true, but he would have been so far from Lake Peten that we find it impossible to reconcile such a route with either his or Bernal Díaz' account of the journey.

---

[139] Díaz del Castillo, 1939, ch. 177.
[140] Ibid., ch. 176.
[141] Andrews, 1943, p. 45.
[142] Cortés, 1866, pp. 419–23; Andrews, 1943, p. 12.

The only other possible route, apparently, would have been to cross the San Pedro above its junction with the Esperanza and proceed to the southeast between these two streams. This might be shorter than the route we have suggested, but it is open to several objections. It would necessitate locating Itzamkanac farther up the San Pedro than seems compatible with the documentary evidence concerning the location of this town. It also seems doubtful that a lake country could have been reached in this direction in less than three days (the time required to reach the first Cehache town in the lake area). Finally, it is open to question whether the Cehache area extended so far southwest that Cortés would have been obliged to travel through it for more than two days in the direction of Lake Peten. As mentioned above, the Cehache settlements, even at the end of the seventeenth century after they had long been crowded toward the south, extended only as far as the neighborhood of Chuntuqui.

Upon leaving Itzamkanac the army spent the first day in crossing the swamp and the river adjoining the town. The second day, after traveling 5 leagues, Cortés met his scouts who reported on the route to the Cehache border. Later two Acalan merchants were seized near a lake and impressed into service as guides. After advancing some distance farther, the expedition stopped for the night in the forest. On the following day a skirmish occurred with an armed Cehache patrol, one of whom was captured, but the others made their escape. That night the Spaniards made a dry camp near some farms, and in the morning (fourth day) they crossed a swamp and reached a fortified town some 3 leagues from where they had slept. This settlement (called Pueblo Cercado by Bernal Díaz) was situated on a rock beside a large lake. Evidently it lay in the lacustrine belt between the heavy rain forest, through which the expedition had passed, and the drier forest of southeastern Campeche. From here the army could have headed only in a southerly direction toward Lake Peten.[143]

Their route now led through a savanna country where they saw many deer; and they passed the sites of two villages which, according to Bernal Díaz, had been burned by a raiding party of foreign invaders.[144] After traveling 7 leagues the expedition came to the town, larger than the first, called Tiac, where Cortés noted that each barrio was separately fortified in addition to a

[143] Cortés, 1866, pp. 423–25; Díaz del Castillo, 1939, ch. 177.

[144] Díaz del Castillo (1939, ch. 177) states that "it seems to me" the Cehache told him that these foreign invaders were Lacandon. It is evident, however, that he was not entirely sure of his memory on this point. We doubt that the Lacandon were ranging farther north than the San Pedro Mártir, although it may have been possible. We are inclined to believe that the invaders were Itza, or groups of the Río de Tachis people, who also were probably Itza, mentioned in the Bravo probanzas.

palisade surrounding the entire settlement. Bernal Díaz adds that it was on an island in a lake, through which they waded to reach the place. Another day's travel brought them to the third and last Cehache town on their route, although the heads of five or six other settlements had also supplied Cortés with provisions. He calls this place Yasuncabil and notes that it was fortified like the others. Bernal Díaz tells us that it was on a large lake and that it took two days to reach it.[145]

If we roughly estimate Cortés' course as extending some 17 leagues east by south from the Río San Pedro to the first Cehache town, and another 14 leagues southeast to Yasuncabil, it would place the latter town in the region of Chuntuqui. (We estimate a day's travel as 7 leagues, partly because the army could have made faster time in this country than in the swamps of Tabasco. Moreover, as we have already noted, Cortés states that he made 7 leagues in one day between Pueblo Cercado and Tiac.) This area, as we have seen, was still occupied by the Cehache at the end of the seventeenth century.

At Yasuncabil supplies were assembled for a five-day journey through uninhabited country.[146] Four leagues were covered the first day, but no other distances are recorded for this stage of the journey. The route crossed the hilly (sierra) country north of Lake Peten. One difficult pass was called Puerto de Alabastro, but the rock for which it was named was probably a very fine limestone. On the fifth day the scouts reached the lake, and that night the army camped on its shore.[147]

The airline distance from Chuntuqui to Lake Peten is approximately 65 km., but the actual travel distance would, of course, have been longer. The narrative of Avendaño's journey in 1696 indicates that the distance traveled from Chuntuqui to the first settlement of the Chakan Itza (5 leagues west of the lake) was about 29 leagues. Maler gives the distance from Chuntuqui to San Andrés on the western end of the lake as 30 leagues, or 127.5 km. Although we are of the opinion that both Avendaño and Maler overestimated the length of their respective routes, we shall use their figures as a basis of calculation for Cortés journey.

Avendaño, who had no local guides and in places had to depend on the *batches*, or blazes on trees, made by Itza travelers, covered his route in six days. Maler followed an old pack trail that runs through Santa Rita and San Miguel and reached San Andrés in four days. Their respective schedules aver-

[145] Cortés, 1866, pp. 425–26; Díaz del Castillo, 1939, ch. 178.
[146] Both Avendaño in the late seventeenth century and Maler 200 years later found the country between Chuntuqui and Lake Peten uninhabited (Means, 1917, pp. 124–29; Maler, 1910, p. 150).
[147] Cortés, 1866, pp. 426-27.

age five days, which was Cortés' travel time from Yasuncabil to Lake Peten. Although Cortés was accompanied by a large force of soldiers and auxiliaries, he also had competent local guides who knew the most direct route to the lake. Moreover, Cortés could take no risk of running short of food on this uninhabited stretch, and consequently he must have traveled as rapidly as possible. Under ordinary circumstances he could easily have covered 29–30 leagues in five days. The only problem is whether the hilly country between the headwaters of the San Pedro Mártir and Lake Peten would have slowed down his rate of travel sufficiently to create serious doubt whether he could have reached the lake in the allotted time. Although Cortés mentions "sierras" and a difficult pass, his account of the journey, to which he devotes about six lines, does not give the impression that the march was especially difficult. Avendaño refers to "rough ascents and descents," but these stretches (including the "Hell of Ytzaes," which apparently caused him little trouble) comprised little more than one-third of the entire distance. Maler does not appear to have considered his own route a difficult one to travel. Consequently, we doubt that the hilly country actually constituted a serious obstacle. Everything considered, we believe that five days were sufficient time for Cortés to march from Yasuncabil in the general latitude of Chuntuqui to Lake Peten.[148]

From Tayasal the expedition followed the trade route already discussed to the rapids of the Sarstoon and, farther on, to Nito near the mouth of the Río Dulce.[149]

In 1530 Alonso de Avila, marching from Chiapa, reached the Usumacinta 3 leagues up the gorge above Tanoche, or Tenosique, and proceeded downstream in canoes to the latter place. The Spaniards rounded up some natives of the town, who guided them to Cortés' road from Ciuatecpan (Canizan) to the great estero, or San Pedro Mártir. The narrative of Alonso de Luján incorporated in Oviedo's *Historia General* describes the estero as "a very large lagoon two leagues in width." Since the rainy season was on, the overflow area was naturally much wider than when Cortés crossed it in late February or early March, 1525. Cortés' bridge was gone, except for a few timbers in the water. Avila and his men set to work to build another bridge, but he was forced to abandon it because the heavy rains hindered the work. So he turned back to Tanoche, a journey of "almost three days," and established his camp in some maize fields near the town. Here the expedition is said to have remained more than four months of the rainy season. At the end of this time the Indians took

148 Means, 1917, pp. 124–29; Maler, 1910, pp. 150–52.
149 See p. 60, *supra*; Morley, 1937–38, 1: 17–19.

canoes to the lagoon, evidently by way of the Usumacinta and the lower San Pedro Mártir, and the Spaniards made the crossing to the opposite shore.[150]

The implication of the Luján-Oviedo narrative is that the expedition had remained in Tanoche until the rains abated some time in the autumn of 1530. We now have evidence that this was not the case, for we have recently found an encomienda grant by Avila dated at Salamanca de Acalan on August 1, 1530.[151] Avila was in Acalan about six weeks. Assuming that the encomienda grant was made during the first or second week of his stay, it would mean that Avila left Tanoche in July, when the rains were at their height. Since the rains had already started by the time Avila first arrived in Tanoche, it is also evident that he did not spend four months in this settlement. We surmise, therefore, that the major purpose of his return to the town after his first journey to the San Pedro Mártir was not to await better weather but to make arrangements for the Indians to take canoes to the lagoon so that the expedition could make the crossing.

On the right bank of the San Pedro Mártir the expedition picked up the Cortés road again, although it was practically closed (*muy cerrado*) and could be followed only with great difficulty. Indeed, it appears that they left the trail and took a route to the west of the San Pedro branch of the Candelaria, for Oviedo mentions no important towns en route. The first Acalan settlements reached by the expedition were some small villages only 3 leagues from the capital.

Oviedo gives the distance from the lagoon, or San Pedro Mártir, to Acalan as 30 leagues. With one exception, Oviedo uses this figure to measure all the stages of Avila's journey from Teapa to Champoton, and it seems likely that it represents an estimate of travel time or a comparative measure of distances rather than distances actually traveled. In this particular case we have a basis of comparison in Cortés' narrative of the expedition of 1525. Cortés took four days to go from the San Pedro Mártir to Itzamkanac, and the travel distance may be estimated as 20–24 leagues, the smaller figure probably being the closer estimate. During the first two days Cortés evidently followed the trail of the advance party, which had brought provisions from the Acalan settlements. On the third and fourth days he proceeded along a road opened in advance by the Indians. Avila, on the other hand, had to cut a path through thick

[150] The Luján-Oviedo account of the Avila expedition is found in Oviedo y Valdés, 1851–55, bk. 32, chs. 4, 5. The discussion of the expedition in the text above is based on this source, except as otherwise indicated in the following notes.

[151] This encomienda grant is found in a lawsuit entitled "Isabel Sánchez, hija de Pedro Galiano, difunto, con Francisco Manrique, vecino de Yucatán, sobre los indios de Yobain y Tixcacal, 1557." AGI, Justicia, leg. 1012, núm. 2, ramo 3.

forest, and, as already noted, he apparently took a route farther west, which may have been somewhat longer. Consequently, a travel time of six days, with an estimated 5 leagues per day, would compare favorably with Cortés' schedule.

Oviedo tells us that during the march from the lagoon to Acalan the expedition suffered from thirst and that the soldiers obtained water from a kind of caña, or bamboolike growth, and also from "cardos" growing on trees (probably a kind of epiphyte). This statement has puzzled students, since Oviedo's narrative implies that the march was made toward the end of the rainy season. It becomes even more puzzling now that we know that the march occurred not later than July, when the rains must have been heavy. It seems obvious that Oviedo garbled Luján's narrative or that Luján had in mind an incident that occurred at some other time and mistakenly introduced it in this part of the narrative.

After a stay of about six weeks in Acalan, Avila set out again early in September 1530, and marched through Cehache country to Champoton. Since his route was to the northeast, he evidently passed through the northern part of the Cehache province, instead of the southern part through which Cortés marched in 1525. Oviedo states that when Avila left the Acalan capital he crossed a swamp two crossbow shots in width, a river, and another swamp on the farther side. He then continued on his journey to a town called Mazatlan, but this was really the name for the entire Cehache area. Oviedo mentions no towns along the way, and the route was said to be so swampy that nowhere were they able to light a fire for a distance of 30 leagues. The latter statement has been regarded as an exaggeration, for it has been supposed that the wet season had ended. The story has more meaning now, since the journey must have occurred in September, when the rains were still in progress. It strongly suggests that the expedition crossed the main Candelaria near where it forks, passed close to the swamps along the north shore of the Arroyo Caribe, and then continued north skirting the edge of the lacustrine belt which extends from Lake Mocu down into Guatemala. West of this area of lakes and swamps is the rolling country covered by rain forest, which one sees along the Ferromex railroad.

The settlement of Mazatlan, which was deserted, was apparently of some size, since it is called a city. It was fortified by a ditch and a palisade of heavy timbers, like the Cehache towns mentioned by Cortés and Bernal Díaz. Excursions were made into the surrounding country, and some Indians were captured; but Oviedo tells us that they died under torture rather than give any information, so the Spaniards learned nothing of any other towns which

might have been in the neighborhood. We doubt the latter statement, however, for a witness in Montejo's probanza of 1531 states that certain lords of
Mazatlan gave Avila tribute.[152] But he evidently regarded the area as poor
and sparsely populated, and he decided to continue his journey.

According to Oviedo, a boy was found who guided the expedition to
Champoton 30 leagues away. Again the Montejo probanza gives a different
story, for here we are told that certain Cehache chieftains accompanied the
force as far as the coast.[153] The Oviedo account states that the expedition
passed through many woodlands and swamps, so it seems likely that they kept
well to the west, following the general direction of the modern road from
Mocu and passing through the region where Sahcabchen was later established.
This would have taken them through a country that would be inundated in
the rainy season.

The location of the Cehache town where the expedition stopped is of
course a matter of speculation. According to Oviedo, it was 30 leagues from
the Acalan capital and 30 leagues from Champoton, but these estimates are a
relative rather than an accurate measure of the distances traveled, and indicate that the town of Mazatlan was about equidistant from Itzamkanac and
Champoton. The northern end of the lacustrine belt, which was inhabited
by Cehache in the sixteenth century is about midway from the fork of the
Candelaria and Champoton. Moreover, Montejo's probanza indicates that the
part of the Cehache country visited by Avila was fairly close to the coast.
The statement that Acalan and Mazatlan were only 7 or 8 leagues from the
coast,[154] which undoubtedly refers to the borders of these provinces, may be a
conscious underestimate, but the general tenor of the probanza shows that
Avila's Mazatlan was not far inland.

As we have noted elsewhere, Andrews has found ruins at Las Ruinas and
Cilvituk which appear to date from the last archaeological period preceding
the Spanish conquest. It is hard to tell whether or not these sites were still
occupied when Avila visited the Cehache area, but it seems fairly certain that
the district was not a part of Acalan or of the cacicazgo of Champoton, and
that we may rather ascribe it to the Cehache.

In concluding this survey of Avila's march, we call attention to the fact
that it would be quite impossible to reconcile Maudslay's location for the
Cehache with the Luján-Oviedo narrative. The part of the area which Maudslay designates as Mazateca is not equidistant nor in any way approximately so
from his locations for Itzamkanac and Champoton. We find no mention of

[152] Montejo v. Alvarado.
[153] Ibid.
[154] This statement occurs in Montejo's preliminary petition initiating the probanza (ibid.).

Oviedo in Maudslay's study of the Cortés route, and he apparently disregarded the Avila phase of the problem of the location of Acalan.

The northern boundary of the Cehache province at the end of the seventeenth century as defined by Morley falls to the south of any midway point between Mactun and Champoton. At the time of the conquest and for some time thereafter there were Cehache settlements to the north of the Peten boundary, and there is evidence that scattered Cehache settlements existed in the northern area even at the end of the seventeenth century. Consequently it would be possible to have a Cehache town equidistant from Mactun and Champoton. But any such location would be too far inland to satisfy the general requirements of the Montejo probanza. Moreover, Morley gives no indication that the Cehache were north of the Peten boundary in earlier times. In his discussion of Cortés' route he states that the province was "east or east-southeast of Mactun," which implies a more southern extension of the area than the limits ascribed to the province at the end of the seventeenth century.[155]

The major points in this lengthy discussion of the location of the province and towns of Acalan may be summarized as follows:

1. The Acalan lands were located in the drainage of an important river system which provided a route of communication and trade to Laguna de Términos and thence to the coastal towns of Xicalango and Tabasco. An important feature of this river was an extensive series of rapids and falls which impeded traffic between the Acalan capital and the coast.

2. Montejo's probanza of 1531 indicates that this river, the Río de Acalan, emptied directly into Laguna de Términos, that the Acalan lands were fairly close to the coast, and that the border towns of Acalan were one day's journey by canoe from the coast.

3. The Candelaria River, which empties directly into Laguna de Términos and is characterized by a long series of rapids and falls, meets the requirements as stated in the preceding paragraphs. On the other hand, we find it difficult, if not impossible, to reconcile these requirements with a location for Acalan on the Río San Pedro Mártir, on which rapids and falls also exist.

4. The reports of journeys made in 1566–70 to the Zapotitlan area, where two groups of Acalan Indians were living after most of the Indians had been moved to Tixchel, clearly indicate that the Río de Acalan was the Candelaria.

5. The Río Zapotitlan marked on the Alfaro map is evidently the same as the Río de Acalan. On the map this river occupies the position of the Candelaria.

155 Morley, 1937–38, 1: 16.

6. The reports of the entradas of Feliciano Bravo up the Río de Tachis, or San Pedro Mártir, in 1573 and 1580, indicate that Acalan was located in another area, which can only be the Candelaria drainage.

7. The Candelaria location fits other evidence such as the administrative status of Acalan as part of the province of Yucatan, and, in 1582, as part of the corregimiento of Campeche, better than a San Pedro Mártir location.

8. The town of Iztapa, where Cortés reached the Usumacinta on his expedition in 1524–25, was located near Montecristo (modern Emiliano Zapata); and Ciuatecpan, where he crossed the river en route to Acalan, was near modern Canizan.

9. From Ciuatecpan Cortés took a northeasterly route to Acalan. The great estero, where he built the famous bridge, was an overflow section of the San Pedro Mártir near modern Nuevo León.

10. From the great estero Cortés crossed over to the San Pedro branch of the Candelaria and eventually reached Itzamkanac on the main stream of the Candelaria.

11. Although some of the Acalan settlements were apparently located along the rapids and falls of the Candelaria, the major towns were situated above these obstacles on the main stream and its branches.

12. We place Itzamkanac, the capital, south of the main Candelaria and west of the Río San Pedro near the junction of these rivers. (The extensive ruins reported by Andrews and Chamberlain at El Tigre indicate that this was a preconquest settlement of importance, but we do not know their age.)

13. Teutiercas, or Tuxakha, was apparently on the Río San Pedro, possibly near its junction with the Esperanza. The town of Chakam, where Paxbolonacha died and where the unconverted Acalan slaves later took refuge, was also on or near the San Pedro; and Tizatepelt, or Çacchute, was near, if not actually on, this same stream.

14. Upon leaving Itzamkanac, Cortés crossed the Río San Pedro near its junction with the Candelaria, marched east by south to the southern part of the Cehache area, southeast through three Cehache towns, the last of them in the region of Chuntuqui, and thence south and southeast to Tayasal.

15. Avila crossed the main Candelaria at Itzamkanac and marched northeast to the northern part of the lacustrine belt occupied by the Cehache, and thence northwest to Champoton. The town called Mazatlan described in the Luján-Oviedo narrative was about equidistant between the fork of the Candelaria and Champoton, possibly in the Mocu-Cilvituk area.

APPENDIX C

Matrícula of Tixchel, 1569

SO LITTLE is known of the social organization of either the Acalan or the Chontal of Tabasco that the *matrícula*, or list, of the tributaries at Tixchel, taken in 1569, is of especial interest. Here are the names of 270 married couples and five widowers. Inasmuch as this list was compiled for purposes of taxation, children and unmarried adults are not included. It begins as follows:[1]

First, being in the house of the said Don Pablo Antonio Paxbolon, governor of the said town, the people of his house were counted, and in it the following tributaries were found:
House. Don Pablo Antonio Paxbolon, married to María Yxnaçe[lu *or* -lut?].
Luis Paxbolon, married to María Yxnahual.
Francisco Paxut, married to Lucía Yxnahuacan.
Alonso Pacoy, to Mencía Yxnoc.
Agustín Ahcat, married to Angelina Yxna[...].
Felipe Champel, married to Inés Yxtunich.
Martín Bol, married to Francisca Yxnapatzim.
Domingo Martín Cab, married to Juana Yxmulu.
Marcos Chanmulu, married to Luisa Ysnahua.[2]

Immediately following we read, "House. Juan Chachan, married to María Yxnaut," and the list continues as above, but there is no indication where the count for this house ends.

This would indicate that Don Pablo's home was a multiple-family house, but it is hard to tell how many others of this type there were at Tixchel. Many

[1] This matrícula (copy in García *v.* Bravo, ff. 2117r–2128v) was made at Tixchel on February 14–16, 1569, as the basis of a new assessment of tribute. The tributary unit in Yucatan at this time was the married couple. Exemption was granted in the case of widows and widowers, the aged and infirm, juveniles (married couples under sixteen years of age), pueblo officials, persons serving as singers (*cantores*) in the village church, and *hidalgos* (persons of noble descent). It was the custom, however, when a reassessment was made, to list all the married couples and heads of families and then subtract those who were exempt. The net total was multiplied by the amount of tribute payable per unit (in the case of Tixchel it was one manta for each eligible tributary unit), thus giving the total tribute assessment for the entire village. Later on, in the 1580's, widows, widowers, and unmarried adults were assessed as half-tributaries. The Tixchel matrícula of 1569 lists 275 married couples or heads of families. Of these, more than 50 were declared exempt. For additional details, see Chapter 8, pp. 182–84, *supra*.

[2] García *v.* Bravo, f. 2117r and *v.* Preferred or reconstructed forms of these names will be found at the end of this appendix. This and the other extracts which follow have been made from a copy by E. B. Adams and compared with photographs of the documents.

of the neighbors of the Acalan had such houses, and those of the Chol Lacandon have already been described. Among the Manche Chol the two largest towns had about 100 houses each, whereas in others the number ranged from ten or twelve to thirty. Here, it was reported, "each house is a family with sons, daughters-in-law, relatives, etc." At Tayasal, the Itza capital, each house contained "an entire collection of relatives (*toda una parentela*), however large it might be."[3] Bienvenida tells us that in northern Yucatan there was "hardly a house which contains only a single citizen (*vecino*). On the contrary, every house has two, three, four, six, and some still more; and among them is one paterfamilias, who is the head of the house."[4]

For the Chontal of Tabasco our information is less definite, but in 1541 Alonso López had moved to another town the people of three houses at Tecoluta containing ten men and from Chichicapa, nine houses in which there were about forty men. Apparently there were also some single-family houses, for five houses at Omitan and five at Culico belonging to widows do not appear to have paid a tribute of cacao. It seems unlikely that multiple-family houses would have been exempted in this manner.[5]

Other evidence, however, points to the existence of a considerable number of homes containing more than one family. Only fifteen houses are reported in Xicalango in 1541. Not only does the description of the place in 1544 give the impression of a town of more than fifteen families, but in 1579, when the population of Tabasco had still further decreased, Xicalango had thirty tributaries. The implication is the same if we compare the statistics for other towns, as we see from the following examples:

Chichicapa: 1541, 3 remaining houses; 1579, 8 tributaries.
Culico: 1541, 15 houses, 5 of them of widows; 1579, 29 tributaries.
Huimango: 1541, 30 houses; 1579, 100 tributaries.
Jalpa: 1541, 20 houses; 1579, 48 tributaries.
Jalupa: 1541, 20 houses; 1579, 60 tributaries.
Maçateupa: 1541, 17 houses; 1579, 31 tributaries.
Nacajuca: 1541, 20 houses; 1579, 60 tributaries.
Soyataco: 1541, 8 houses; 1579, 32 tributaries.

There was some shifting of the population from one town to another during

[3] Remesal, 1932, bk. 11, ch. 19; Villagutierre Soto-Mayor, 1701, bk. 8, ch. 12. Don Pablo was only twenty-six years old at this time and could not have had sons-in-law. Whether or not he had a brother is uncertain. In the absence of any stated relationship it is possible that the eight couples following his name did not belong to his house. We are inclined, however, to believe that they did, possibly as retainers of the cacique.
[4] Cartas de Indias, 1877, p. 78.
[5] Fiscal *v*. López. There can be little doubt that the term *indios* ("Indian men") employed here designates married men.

these thirty-eight years, but we doubt that it was sufficient to invalidate the conclusions drawn from this comparison.[6] Some of the exactions by the Spaniards reported in 1541 would appear to be beyond the capacity of the people on the basis of single-family houses. Two towns, one of five houses and the other of six, each planted 2000 cacao trees for the conquerors in addition to maintaining their own groves.[7]

In Yucatan the Spanish authorities disapproved of several families living in the same house, and separate houses for each family were prescribed by an ordinance of López Medel in 1552, but we do not know how rapidly this regulation was enforced. In Cozumel, where there was little Spanish supervision, the old conditions still prevailed in 1570. A census of this date lists the names of the adult occupants of the houses, and we find from two to seven married couples living in each.[8] After the multiple-family houses fell into disuse in colonial Yucatan, groups of married couples, many of them related to one another, apparently continued to live together on the same ground plot, but each couple with their unmarried children occupied a separate house. This may have been the case at Tixchel, whatever their former manner of living was in Acalan.

At Tixchel, as in Cozumel, the population was counted by houses. At the beginning of the second day of the count it was noted that, "The said Indian alcaldes, regidores, and principal men of the said town, before the captain and in the presence of me, the said notary, continued the said enumeration through the said interpreter as on the first day already passed and declared by their names and houses the following Indian tributaries."[9] At the beginning of the third day this statement was repeated, and at the end of the day it was noted that, "The said Indian governor, alcaldes, [and] regidores of the said town stated that the said enumeration was concluded and that it [the town] does not contain more people, houses, or any other thing bearing on the matter that could be declared."[10] In spite of these notations, however, the only two houses that actually appear in the list are the two which we have mentioned.

Although, with these exceptions, the names are not listed by houses, three-quarters of them fall in what we shall call relationship groups. All the men's names in the list are accompanied by those of their wives, except for four

[6] *Ibid.;* p. 53, *supra;* RY, 1: 332–38. Cf. Roys, 1943, p. 103.
[7] Fiscal *v.* López.
[8] López de Cogolludo, 1867–68, bk. 5, ch. 16; Roys, 1941, doc. 41; Roys, Scholes, and Adams, 1940, p. 14.
[9] García *v.* Bravo, f. 2120v.
[10] *Ibid.,* 2129r.

widowers and one whose wife had deserted him. Immediately following the names of fifty-nine of these men are those of others stated to be related to them by blood or marriage, mostly the latter. Altogether we find fifty-nine brothers-in-law (*cuñados*, including one *concuñado*) of the heads of the groups, sixty-one sons-in-law (*yernos*), nine brothers (*hermanos*), six sons (*hijos*), two stepsons (*entenados*), one uncle (*tío*), and thirteen nephews (*sobrinos*).

Among the 275 married couples and widowers listed, no relationship is indicated for sixty-seven. Of the fifty-nine relationship groups, we find twenty-five of only two couples each, ten of three, thirteen of four, four of five, one of six, four of seven, one of ten, and one of twelve. Although it is not so stated, it would appear that each relationship group was a residence group living either in a multiple-family house or on a single ground plot. To judge by a matrícula compiled at Ppencuyut in northern Yucatan in 1584, it seems possible that some of the unrelated married couples combined to form larger residence groups, but this is a matter of conjecture.[11]

Even taking the Spanish terms of relationship literally, we run into some ambiguity. Only one of the brothers-in-law is called a concuñado ("husband of wife's sister"), but the relationship of the others to the head still remains uncertain. We have defined cuñado as "brother-in-law," but formerly it could also mean an affinal relative in any degree. In our discussion we shall treat the sobrino as a blood relation of the head of the group, but this is an assumption, and he might be a relative of the head's wife.

Dr. Sol Tax, who has kindly studied the data presented here, notes in the case of the large groups that "it is obvious that the relatives referred to must be classificatory in most cases. If the 'cuñados' and 'yernos' were really what they seem, one would have to conclude that the population was increasing tremendously. . . . Therefore one may soundly assume that a man did not normally have the several 'cuñados' and 'yernos' except if farther relatives were called that. I shall assume therefore that the 'groups' consisted of some couples more distantly related. Such terminology is not inconsistent with what Eggan found in the old dictionaries."[12]

The indications of blood relationship occur mostly in the larger groups. In the thirty-five groups consisting only of two or three couples each we find no hijos and only three hermanos and three sobrinos of the heads. The following tabulation offers some idea of the composition of the various groups.

[11] Cuenta y visita del pueblo de Ppencuyut . . . 1584, Archivo General de la Nación, México, Tierras, tomo 2809, exp. 20.

[12] Tax to Redfield, July 6, 1943, and March 14, 1944; Redfield to Roys, July 9, 1943, March 15, 1944; Eggan, 1934, pp. 190–92.

BLOOD RELATIONSHIP INDICATED	NO. OF GROUPS
Hermano only	2
Hermano, sobrino, cuñado	2
Hermano, cuñado	2
Hermano, cuñado, yerno	1
Hermano, yerno	1
Hermano, sobrino, cuñado, yerno	1
Hijo, sobrino, yerno	1
Hijo, entenado, yerno	1
Hijo, yerno	3
Tío, yerno, cuñado	1
Sobrino only	2
Sobrino, cuñado, yerno	1
Total	18

AFFINAL RELATIONSHIP INDICATED	NO. OF GROUPS
Entenado, cuñado, yerno	1
Cuñado only	16
Cuñado, yerno	8
Yerno only	16
Total	41

Since affinal relationship of the men is indicated in 70 per cent of these groups, it seems evident that there was a strong tendency toward matrilocal residence. This brings up the question of inheritance and descent. As we have seen, Don Pablo Paxbolon had come into his chieftainship of the nation through descent in the male line over a period of eight generations, but we have no other specific information regarding inheritance among the Acalan.

Among the Yucatecan Maya, although descent was reckoned in both the paternal and maternal lines, the formal lineage groups, which were exogamous, the inheritance of property, and that of certain political positions were based on patrilineal descent. Inheritance in the male line has also been generally accepted for the Nahua peoples.[13] Although there are indications that the Maya

[13] Roys, 1943, p. 28; Thompson, 1937, pp. 58–61. As we have noted elsewhere, among the Maya of Yucatan the headship of the residence group appears to have been inherited in the patrilineal line; in the Cozumel census the head of the multiple-family house is referred to as the owner (Roys, Scholes, and Adams, 1940, pp. 15, 18). Various Maya phrases designating either the head of the establishment, including family and servants, or the owner of the house indicate that they were the same person. Especially suggestive are such expressions as *u chun na*, defined as "dueño de casa" but really meaning the principal person in the house, and *Juan tah otochi*, "Juan es su dueño y señor" [of the house] (Vienna dictionary, f. 79v; Motul dictionary, 1929, p. 821). Consequently it would appear that inheritance of the headship, like that of the house itself, was patrilineal. Our belief that the same was true of the Nahua is based largely on inferences made from Zurita's account of their political and social organization (Zurita, 1891, *passim*). It will be recalled, however, that in the absence of sons or brothers a woman sometimes inherited the caciqueship. This was not the case in Yucatan.

system differed in some respects from the Acalan, their relations were close, and the culture and religion of both appear to be very similar. Furthermore Mexican influences were very strong; more than 40 per cent of the Acalan had Nahuatl names. This would suggest that, whatever the system might have been at an earlier period of their history, at the time of the Spanish conquest the customs regarding inheritance were like those of the Yucatecan Maya and the Mexicans. These are inferences, however; our only positive evidence is that of the manner in which the chieftainship of the nation was inherited.

The situation presents a problem. Whether or not all the yernos were actually sons-in-law, Tax notes that it is obvious that daughters tended to bring their husbands home. If we include the sobrinos, a considerable minority of the members of the groups are blood relations of the head, but it is difficult to account for the presence of only a single uncle, more alleged brothers than sons, and still more nephews than either brothers or sons. It is also of interest to note that more than half the groups consist of only two or three couples each. Tax has also called our attention to the Chorti, whose language is little more than a dialectal variant of Chontal. Among these people the married couple is permanently attached to the group that pays for the wedding. He notes that under such conditions a rich family tends to become large, and a poor one tends to disappear as a group; and that the large groups listed in the Tixchel matrícula may be considered as "successful" or "rich."[14]

Another question that naturally arises is how far the grouping of relations indicated by the matrícula corresponded to social conditions in Acalan before the population had been moved from their isolated situation in the interior of the peninsula to Tixchel on the coast. Here, during the twelve years prior to 1569, the people were not only subject to Spanish supervision, but they came into closer contact with the Yucatecan Maya. Among the latter in Cozumel both men and women bearing the patronymic of the head were still living in multiple-family houses in 1570, and we infer that a considerable number of them were his sons and daughters. In the case of some of the daughters and their husbands this residence may have been only temporary,

[14] Tax to Redfield, March 14, 1944; Wisdom, 1940, p. 255. Tax, who has not investigated the grounds for our belief that inheritance of property was in the male line, takes patrilineal descent as given and to reconcile this with commonly matrilocal residence suggests "the assumption of a social system by which only one son inherited his father's position as 'head of the house or group' and perhaps the paraphernalia as well. . . . This would account for the paucity of brothers in the same group and also father-sons, if we assumed that all sons but one had to leave the establishment, perhaps being 'set up' in other establishments or else going to live at their wives' establishments. This system is frequently in force in Guatemala, and something like it was present in medieval Europe." He cites the Chorti example and also notes that since the sons, except one, are separated from the group, the remaining married children tend to be women. Noting the problem where no son is listed, he suggests that the head of the group had no sons living to maturity.

since in Yucatan several years of marriage service by the bridegroom has been reported.[15]

Space does not permit publishing the entire matrícula in this study, but a few extracts will give some idea of the manner in which it was compiled.

Domingo Macua, [married] to Mencía Yxzulu.
Marcos Paxcanan, his son-in-law, married to Magdalena Ysnatzin.

Luis Ytzal, married to Ana Yxnaçelut.
Agustín Acha, nephew, married to Isabel Ysna[...].

Sebastián Paxoc, married to María Ysnalamat.
Antonio Max, brother, married to Catalina Ysbolon.

Alonso Quibit, married to María Yxçelu.
Martín Paxoc, brother-in-law, [married] to Catalina Ysinaynucuy.

Luis Çelut, married to Luisa Yxzapa.
Luis Paxmala, brother-in-law, to María Yxnoc.
Agustín Paxmalu, brother-in-law, married to Luisa Yxnabayn.

Jorge Quibit, married to María Yshuan.
Juan Pazoc, son-in-law, married to Luisa Ysnapatzin.
Luis Paxmalu, son-in-law, married to Luisa Çapa.

Juan Ahecha, married to Marta Maybit.
Melchor Pasmala, brother, married to Luisa Chimali.
Luis Achamal, son-in-law, married to Mencía Bol.

Martín Pamalin, married to Inés . . . .
Miguel Pactucum, son-in-law, married to Luisa Yxcochute.
Fabián Paxuyte, nephew, married to Luisa Yxnauyt, right hand crippled.

Alonso Abomay, married to Mencía Yxtzu.
Martín Çelut, son-in-law, married to Isabel Çelut.
Luis Patzin, son-in-law, married to Luisa Ysbolon.
Pedro Pazim, brother-in-law, to . . . .

Martín Paxbolon, married to Francisca Yxnapatzin.
Luis Paco, son, married to Luisa Yxçelut.
Martín Yxquintz, stepson, married to Catalina Yxnahuzuin.
Juan Pactuny, son-in-law, married to Mencía Yxçelut.

[15] Roys, Scholes, and Adams, 1940, pp. 14–15.

Sebastián Pacha, married to María Yspazim.
Fabián Ybit, brother-in-law, married to Francisca Ysnazelut.
Luis Paxmulun, brother-in-law, married to Francisca Ysnoc.
Juan Ybit, son-in-law, married to Mencía Yscoa.

Juan Pacua, married to Inés Natzelut.
Pedro Acha, son, married to Mencía Yxnapatzin.
Luis Paxmulu, nephew, married to María Yxmaqui.
Antón Patzin, son-in-law, married to Juana Yxnapatzin; he is very old and lame.
Agustín Paniz, son-in-law, married to María Yxnacanan.
Agustín . . . , son-in-law, married to . . . .
Luis Ach, nephew, married to Francisca Yxbanex. She is blind in one eye and
    says she sees poorly with the right eye. Also she is bent over.

Alonso Pastun, widower; he has no wife.
Mateo Paxmala, uncle, married to Luisa Yxlamat.
Martín Paxmolo, son-in-law, married to Ana Ysnachavan.
Another Juan Boluch, brother-in-law, married to Lucía Ysnalamat.
Anton Pacha, son-in-law, married to Luisa Yxaba.
Alonso Pamalin, brother-in-law, married to Luisa Yscoanen.
Baltasar Pazelu, brother-in-law, married to Magdalena Ysnalamat.

Francisco Patny, married to Leonor Yxcoy.
Luis Macua, brother-in-law, married to Mencía Ysmalin.
Marcos Canancha, son-in-law, married to Francisca Ysmalamat.
Francisco Ybit, son-in-law, married to María Ysnacha.
Sebastián Panacha, son-in-law, married to Leonor Ysçelu.
Juan Bautista Zelu, step-son, married to María Ysçelu.
Alonso Ybit, son-in-law, married to Francisca Yszelu; singer.

Francisco Pactucum, married to Luisa Yxnalahun.
Marcos Pachaqui, son-in-law, married to Ana Yxnazelu.
Melchor Pacoy, nephew, married to Isabel Canal.
Francisco Nahan, brother-in-law, married to Luisa Yxcomulgada.
Luis Paxmala, nephew, married to Luisa Yxchamal. These are juveniles
    fifteen years old.
Pedro Pazin, son-in-law, married to Luisa Ystaam.
Another Luis Paxmala, the brother of Melchor, married to María Yxnacha.
Agustín Pazai, nephew, married to Luisa Yxmantzin.
Juan Bolay, brother-in-law, married to Luisa Yxnapazin. He is crippled in
    the left foot, the large toe missing.
Domingo Papalahum, son-in-law, married to Ana Yxçipa. He is a singer
    and attached to the church.

Luis Pacohi, married to Isabel Ysmolu.
Luis Maniche, son-in-law, married to Juana Yschimali.

Pedro Lamat, son-in-law, married to Luisa Yxan.
Domingo Paxbolon, brother-in-law, married to Ana Ystuny.
Fabián Chimal, son-in-law, married to María Yxaba.
Jorge Achax, brother-in-law, married to María Ysnamacua.
Francisco Uncha, brother-in-law, married to Ana Ysmulu.
Mateo Zelud, son-in-law, married to Antonia Ysmacua. He has a leg badly
     injured by an old sore; [he is] sickly and covered with boils.
Miguel Paxmolu, son-in-law, married to Ana Yschaque. He is old and sick.
Sebastián Cheue, son-in-law, married to Ursula Ysnaluchcoy.
Juan Buch, brother-in-law, married to Ana Ysnalamat.
Alonso Quivit, married to Ursula Ysnaman, brother-in-law.[16]

It seems obvious that the surnames recorded in the Tixchel matrícula are
neither patronymics nor matronymics, since brothers, sisters, parents, and
children all have different surnames. We surmise, however, that the children
who were born and baptized in Tixchel were given the surnames of their
fathers. A number of these Acalan names are still to be found in a matrícula of
Usulaban compiled in 1688.[17] Occasionally we find in the Tixchel matrícula a
man and wife whose surnames either are the same or differ only in the prefix.
Barring a few exceptional cases, such marriages were forbidden in pre-
Spanish Yucatan, where the surname was a patronymic and indicated mem-
bership in an exogamous lineage group. Not only is it very rare in the matrículas of the seventeenth century, but people say there is a prejudice against such
a practice at the present time. In the Tixchel matrícula, however, the following cases are recorded:

Alonso Acat, married to Luisa Ix-na-acat.
Juan Bautista Çelu, married to María Ix-çelu.
Hernando Pa-çelu, married to Luisa Ix-na-çelut.
Francisco Çelut, married to Catalina Çelut.
Martín Çelut, married to Isabel Çelut.
Fabián Pax-iuit, married to Luisa Ix-na-iuit.
Luis Patzin, married to Antonia Ix-na-patzin.[18]

As might be expected, a number of the heads of relationship groups were
persons of some prominence in the town. Don Juan Pacua, who was one of
the signers of a petition to the Crown for more Franciscan missionaries in

16 García v. Bravo, ff. 2117r–2128v.
17 Matrícula de los pueblos de la provincia de Yucatán . . . , 1688, AGI, Contaduría, leg,
920, exp. 1. A few people with Acalan names were also living at this time in the neighboring
towns of Santo Domingo de Chekubul and San Cristóbal de "Chekubul" (probably Chiuoha).
18 García v. Bravo, ff. 2118r, 2119r, 2121r and v, 2124v, and 2125r. Çelu and Çelut are considered to be variants of the same name.

1567, was no doubt the principal of this name who appears in 1569 as the head of a group of seven couples, but we can not account for the omission of his title in the matrícula.[19] Felipe Acat, who had also signed the 1567 petition, was the head of a group of only two couples, and we do not know his rank. Another principal, Francisco Pactucum, headed a group of ten couples, but the third principal, Luis Paxoc, was a widower. He probably lived with one or more of the couples who follow his name on the list, but no relationship is mentioned. The alcalde, Alonso Quiuit, might be either the head of a group of two couples or another of the same name in the group of twelve couples cited above. It is of interest to note that the two alcaldes called Alonso Quiuit and Fabián Quiuit at the beginning of the matrícula are evidently the same as those who signed the document as Alonso Martín and Fabián González. This is also true of the town clerk, who signed both the first document of the Text and the matrícula as Juan Bautista, but he appears in the body of the latter document as Juan Bautista Çelu, stepson of Francisco Pactuni, who heads a group of seven related couples. No Spanish surnames appear in the actual list of tributaries.

One of the regidores mentioned in the first document of the Text was Hernando Kanan. He appears in the matrícula two years later as the son of the aged Francisco Chacbalam and Juana Ix-na-uitz, who head a group of four couples. Another regidor, Pedro Naua, was a member of a group of three couples headed by his brother-in-law, Alonso Çelut. Alonso Chacbalam, one of the old men who testified as to the truth of the history of Don Pablo's ancestry, heads a group consisting of himself, a son-in-law, and a brother-in-law; but the other aged witness, Luis Tutzin, is not associated with any of his relatives in the matrícula.

There was some juvenile or child marriage among the Acalan of Tixchel, and in such cases the approximate ages are given in the matrícula. Frequently both spouses were young, but in nearly half the instances recorded the age of only one is mentioned, and we infer that the other was considered to be an adult. Of those, where only the age of one is given, one wife was nine years old and had deserted her husband, and two were twelve and sixteen respectively; one husband was twelve or thirteen, and another was fifteen. Where the ages of both spouses are recorded, we learn of one couple, both of whom were twelve; another, fourteen; and two couples, fifteen years of age. In one case the husband was seventeen and the wife, fourteen. Of one pair, both are said to have been juveniles (*muchachos*), and of another it is recorded that they were adolescents (*mozos*).[20]

[19] AGI, México, leg. 367, f. 68r. [20] García v. Bravo, ff. 2117r–2128v.

It is hard to tell what proportion of the older people had been married at an early age and how representative these cases were of conditions in pre-Spanish times. Of the Yucatecan Maya, Landa tells us that formerly the usual age at marriage had been twenty, but in his time they were marrying when they were twelve or fourteen. Pagan baptism, however, seems to have been a puberty rite, and we learn from more than one source that after this ceremony young people were considered to be of marriageable age. Consequently we are inclined to believe that juvenile marriage had not been unusual among the Acalan in pre-Spanish times.[21]

The following list of Acalan names has been compiled largely from the Tixchel list of tributaries and the Chontal Text, but a few have been added from the baptismal records of Zapotitlan. Many names in these manuscripts have been badly garbled by the Spanish scribes, and, wherever possible, the Text is used as a standard for their reconstruction. Some of these reconstructions are obvious, but others must be considered tentative, especially with names of Mexican origin. Indeed, it would require a Nahuatl linguist familiar with the dialects of southern Mexico and Central America to determine the correct forms of these names with any degree of confidence.

The presentation of the names offers something of a problem. The Chontal Text, which we have taken as our standard, is written in the special notation devised by the Franciscan missionaries for writing Yucatecan Maya.[22] In the Tixchel matrícula, the Zapotitlan records, and the Spanish version of the Acalan narrative, however, the names are written, often carelessly, as they sounded to the Spanish scribe and in the orthography of the time. In only a few cases is the glottalized k-sound designated by the letter k, as was customary in northern Yucatan.

Often the two systems coincide, but when they conflict, the name is reconstructed according to the Yucatecan notation, so that it will correspond with the orthography of the Text, and is placed in brackets. The form of the name at the beginning of each entry, if it is not a reconstruction, is to be considered the preferred one, and wherever possible, it is the form employed in the Text. Following the preferred or reconstructed form, variations of the name, as written by the scribe, are recorded so that the reader can form his own opinion of the reconstructions which we have proposed. The numeral in parentheses at the end of each entry refers only to the number of times that the name occurs in the matrícula. This gives an approximate idea of its frequency among the adult population at Tixchel in 1569. Names believed to be

---

[21] Landa, 1941, p. 100 and Tozzer note; Roys, 1943, p. 25.
[22] P. 364, *supra.*

of Nahuatl origin are designated by the letter N. An effort has been made to transcribe most of the men's names in the matrícula, but quite a number of the women's names in this document are either illegible or so garbled that no attempt has been made to reproduce them.

The preferred or reconstructed forms are divided by a single hyphen to indicate a prefix and by a double hyphen to show a compound name. Such divisions, however, are only for the purposes of this study and do not occur in any of the documents, except possibly by accident.

As already noted, the masculine prefixes Pa-, Pac-, and Pax- appear to be variations of Pap-, but we are ignorant of their significance. *Pap* is the word for father in Huaxteca and Chontal. We find the latter both in the Text and in the modern language, but as yet it has not been recorded as occurring in Maya or in the other languages of the Maya stock. In Yucatecan Maya it was formerly *yum* and in Manche Chol, *mi;* but in western Chol, Chorti, the Chiapas group, and several of the highland languages of Guatemala *tat* or some similar word referable to the Nahuatl *tatli* ("father") has been reported. *Papa* has been cited from widely separated parts of Mexico either as a term of respect or meaning "father" or "priest."

Ix- is a feminine prefix in Yucatecan Maya, Chontal, and other languages of the Maya stock. *Na*- means "mother" in various languages of the stock including Maya, Chol, and Chontal. In Chorti it is *tu,* but in others the word is *nan,* which is evidently referable to the Nahuatl *nantli* ("mother"). This prefix, like the masculine, is hard to explain. It does not necessarily indicate that a woman has children, nor does it designate a matronymic as in northern Yucatan. It occurs also among the modern Lacandon. Here the sons of each family are given certain names according to the priority of their birth, and the daughters receive the same names preceded by the prefix Na-. For example, the oldest son is named Kin and the first daughter, Na-kin. In this case the prefix does not seem to indicate a mother, and Tozzer translates it as "house."[23] In Maya and Tzeltal *na* and *otóch* or *otot* both have this meaning, but in Chontal, Chol, and Chorti we have as yet found only the word *otot*.

PERSONAL NAMES OF THE ACALAN

Men's Names

A-BOL. *A*- is considered to be a masculine prefix like Maya *ah*. *Ah bool* is the Maya name of a certain stingless wild bee. (2)

[23] Tozzer, 1907, p. 42. In spite of the negative evidence, it seems possible that *na* was also a Chontal word designating some kind of a building, but doubtful that this meaning is to be associated with the feminine prefix.

[A-CUTZ]. Acuz. Cutz ("wild turkey") is a Maya patronymic. Cf. Roys, 1940, pp. 42–46, for this and other Maya names.

A-CHAMAL. Possibly a variant of Chimal, since Spanish writers sometimes substitute *a* for *i* in Tabasco place names, writing Çagoatan for Ciuatan. *Chamal*, however, is defined as a cigar or a tubular tobacco pipe in Maya. (1)

A-KIN. Aquin, Aquini, †Akin. *Kin* can mean "priest" or "sun" in Chontal. In Maya *ah kin* means "priest"; *kin* is defined as "sun," "day," and the name of a certain insect. (2)

A-KUK. Kuk ("quetzal") is a Maya patronymic. (1)

A-MULU. Cf. Mulu. (N., 1)

A-PAP-PIZON. Reading doubtful. (1)

*A-PAX-TUCUN. Cf. Pap-tucun.

*A-TOX=PECH. Tox, for which no applicable meaning has been found, and Pech ("garapata") are Maya patronymics.

A-TZUK. Possibly A-kuk is intended, since *k* and *tz* have a similar appearance in the manuscript. (1)

[ABIN]. Auin, Avim. Reconstruction based on the name Macua=abin in the Text. Habin is the Maya name of *Piscidia communis* Harms., or dogwood. (2)

ABOMAY. Possibly a compound name, A-bol=may, is intended. (1)

ACAT. Ahcat. Referable to the Mexican day name Acatl ("reed"). (N., 11)

ACAT=PAX-BOLON. Cf. Pax-bolon. (1)

[AÇIPAC]. Atzipac. Cf. Çipac; also Pipil "ā-sipǎket" ("alligator," Lehmann, 1920, 2: 1048). Here the initial *a-* may mean "water." In Aztec it is prefixed to various names of marine fauna and objects associated with water (*atl*). (N., 1)

ACHA. Ach, Hacha. (6)

*ACHACHU. Possibly a compound name Acha=chu.

ACHAX. (1)

AHECHA. Possibly Acha is intended. (1)

*AUXAUAL. Discussed on p. 78, *supra*. (N.?)

[AXMOX]. Asmox. (1)

BOL. Cf. A-bol. Bol is a modern Lacandon name (Tozzer, 1907, p. 42). (1)

BOLAY. Cf. Maya *bolay* ("a beast of prey") and the Acalan place name, Tabolay, p. 389, *supra*. (1)

*BOLON-LAMAT. Apparently 9 Lamat, a day name with its coefficient. Bolon, the coefficient, is here treated as a prefix and separated from Lamat by a single hyphen. Cf. Maya Lamat and Tzeltal Lambat (Seler, 1902–23, 1: 448, 473). A place name, Bolon-lamat, appears in the Text. (1)

[BOLON=PA-ACHA]. Bolonpacha. Cf. Bolon and Pa-acha. (1)

[BULUCH]. Boluch, Buch. Evidently the Chontal word for "eleven." Cf. p. 65, *supra*. (2)

*BULUCH=ATZI. Cf. p. 65, *supra*.

CAB. A common Maya patronymic, but in the matrícula we find a Domingo Martín Cab married to Juana Ix-mulu, whose name is Chontal. (1)

CALTZIN. Apparently a Mexican name, since -*tzin* and -*tzintli* are Nahuatl suffixes. Usually called honorifics ("*reverenciales*"), they are also applied to the possessions

†Found only in the baptismal records of Zapotitlan.
*Appears in the Text as a pagan name and not preceded by a baptismal name.

of the honored person, and the example *caltzintli* ("house") is given. They may indicate merely affection and approval and have been considered diminutives also (Tapia Zenteno, 1885, pp. 15–16; Molina, 1886, pp. 139–40; Galdo Guzmán, 1890, p. 302). The name may be referable to *calli* ("house") or possibly *cacalli* ("crow"). Cf. Aztec *ayotl* ("turtle") and Pipil *ayutzin* (Lehmann, 1920, 2: 1048). (N., 2)

CANTZIN. Cf. Caltzin. (N., 1)

CATAN. (1)

*CATANATZ.

†[CI=PECH?]. Quipeche. Pech is a common Maya patronymic meaning "garapata" in both Chontal and Maya. Here *Ci* is apparently the equivalent of the Maya *ceh* ("deer"). Cf. Acalan Ciach and Maya Cehach, both of which refer to the same tribe or people. Consequently the name of the cacicazgo Ceh Pech in northern Yucatan might be referable to this personal name.

[COAT]. Coate. Apparently referable to the Mexican day name Coatl ("serpent"). Cf. Pa-cua. (N., 1)

ÇELU. Tzelu, Zelu. Although listed here as a separate name, it is evidently the same as Çelut, a contraction of Uçelut and referable to *oçelotl* ("jaguar"). Here, as in *coatl*, the final *tl* does not appear to be an essential part of the word, since the plurals are given as *ooceloh* and *cocoah* (Rincón, 1888, p. 234). (N., 3)

[ÇELU=IUIT]. Çeluit. Cf. Iuit. (N., 1)

ÇELUT. Tzelut, Zelud, Zelut. Referable to the Nahuatl *oçelotl* ("jaguar"), which might be either a day name or that of a military order. Cf. pp. 65–66, *supra*. (N., 12)

*ÇELUT=A=PECH. Cf. Ci=pech.

*ÇELUT=HOLCAN. Holcan, which means "brave warrior," is apparently a title following the name.

†ÇIPAC. Referable to the Mexican day name Çipactli, sometimes defined as "swordfish" and sometimes as "crocodile." (N.)

CHACANAN. *Chac* means "red," and the name might be reconstructed either as Chac-kanan or as a compound name, Acha=kanan. Cf. Kanan. (2)

*CHACANTUN. In Maya *chacan* could mean something apparent or plainly visible, and *tun*, a rock or stone; but such a meaning would seem more applicable to a place than to a personal name.

*CHACBALAM. Chabalam, Chacbalan, Chavalan, Checbalan. In Maya *chac* means "red" and *balam*, "jaguar"; the name is the Chontal word for "puma." (4)

CHACCHAN. Chachan. *Chac* means "red" and *chan*, "serpent"; possibly it is the name of a species. (2)

*CHANCHA. We surmise that this is a contraction of a compound name, Chan=acha.

[CHAN=MUCUY]. Chanmocuy. Chan (Chontal: "four," "serpent," "sky") and Mucuy (Maya: "dove") are both Maya patronymics. (1)

CHAN=MULU. Probably a compound of Chan and Mulu, but if Mulu is referable to a day name, Tzeltal Molu or Maya Muluc, it could be a day name with the coefficient 4. Cf. Mulu. (1)

*CHANPEL. Apparently the Chontal word for four (*chan*) followed by the numerical suffix (*pel*) defined as "times" in the modern language (Blom and La Farge, 1926–27, 2: 468). This suffix is *ppel* in Maya. (4)

CHEUE. (1)

[CHICNAUI]. Chicnabi, Chicnav. Nahuatl, "nine." (N., 2)

CHIMAL. Chimul. Nahuatl *chimalli* ("shield"); also a common patronymic in northern Yucatan. (N., 2)

*HUNCHA. Uncha. (5)

[ICIM]. Yquin. Apparently referable to Maya *icim* ("owl"). (1)

ITZAL. This might be referable either to the Maya *itzam* ("lizard") or to Itza, a patronymic and the name of a people. (1)

[IUIT]. Ybit, Yvit. Apparently referable to Nahuatl *iuitl* ("feather"), and the patronymic of a ruling family in Yucatan. In the Nahual dialect of Pochutla, Oax., *iuit* means "sister," and the word has been referred to the Aztec *icuitl* (Lehmann, 1920, 2: 1077). (N., 6)

[IUIT=ACHA]. Ybitacha. (1)

[IZCINTI?]. Written Yzquintz. It seems possible that the final *z* was an error of the scribe. Yzquinty could well be referable to the Mexican day name Itzcuintli ("dog"). Cf. Ix-na-izcin and the Chontalpa name Izquin (p. 62, *supra*). An early ruler of Tequiziztlan in the Valley of Mexico was named Izcuin (Nuttall, 1926, p. 63). (N.? 1)

KANAN. Canan. *Kanan* is the Maya name of a medicinal shrub or small tree *Hamelia patens* Jacq. It also means "that which is precious or necessary." Seler (1902–23, 1: 464) associates this word with the Tzeltal day name Ghanan. (3)

[KANAN=ACHA]. Canancha. (1)

[KIN=NAL?]. Quinaal. Cf. A-kin, Nal=chan, and Ix-nal=abin. (1)

*KIN=TENCAB. See Tencab.

*KIN=TZUCTI. *Kin* ("priest") is probably prefixed as a title. *Tzucti* (literally, "tuft at the mouth") is the Maya word for "moustache" and apparently has much the same meaning in modern Chontal, where it is defined as "*barba*" (Blom and La Farge, 1926–27, 2: 470, "*tsuctik*").

LAAX. (1)

LAHUN. In Maya and Tzeltal "ten" and probably the same in Chontal. The Chol word "*lujum*" (Stoll) is very similar. (1)

*LAMAT. Cf. Bolon-lamat. (2)

*LAMAT=AZEL. Evidently a compound name, but no name Azel has been found recorded.

MACUA. This name resembles the Nahuatl verb *macoa* ("to help another so that he may help me," Molina, 1880, 2: 50*v*), but *ma* and *coa* appear as syllables of words with various meanings. Cf. Pa-cua. (N.? 4)

*MACUA=ABIN. Cf. Abin.

[MACUA=A-TZUK]. Macuiaatzuk. (1)

*MACUA=AUA. Cf. Ix-aua.

[MACUA=CHAUAN]. Macuachaban. Cf. Ix-chauan. (1)

[MACUIL?]. Macabil. Perhaps referable to the Nahuatl *macuil* ("five"). (N.? 1)

MALNA. Doubtfully referable to the Mexican day name Malinalli ("a kind of grass"). (N.? 1)

[MAMAN?]. Man, Manun. Cf. Ix-maman and Na-maman. (2)

[MAMAN=ACHA?]. Manacha. (1)

MANICHE. We are reminded of the names Manachi, Manicha, and Ix-manichi in the Zapotitlan baptismal records (García *v.* Bravo, ff. 1966r, 1969r). (1)

MAX. *Max* means "monkey" in Chontal, Chol, and Tzeltal and "wild chile" in Maya. *Maax* is the Maya name for a small variety of monkey. (1)

MAY. *May* ("fawn," also a ritual word for "deer") is a common patronymic in northern Yucatan.

MULU. Probably referable to the Nahuatl *molotl* ("sparrow"), but it is also possible that it should be associated with the Maya and Tzeltal day names, Muluc and Molo. Cf. Seler, 1902–23, 1: 473, for a discussion of these day names. (N.? 2)

*MUTUTZIN=AHAU. Evidently referable to the Aztec *mototli*, defined as "a small animal like a squirrel" (Molina, 1880, 2: 60v), and to the Pipil *mutujtzin* ("ardilla," Lehmann, 1920, 2: 1034). Here the suffix *-tzin* appears to be a diminutive. *Ahau* is a title following the name. (N.)

NAHAN. (1)

NAL=CHAN. Nal ("young maize plant") and Chan are both Maya patronymics. Cf. Panal and Ix-chan. (1)

NAUA. Nahua, Nava. Apparently referable to the name of the Nahua people or their language. *Nahual*, however, is a spirit that takes the form of an animal, and *naualli* is defined as "wizard" (Brinton, 1894, p. 5, and p. 78, *supra*). In Maya *naual* is a verb, "to reel with weakness or like a drunken man" (Motul dictionary). Nahuat is a common patronymic in northern Yucatan. (N., 4)

[NAUI-CALI]. Navycali. The Mexican day name Naui Calli ("9 house"), which here includes the numerical coefficient. Cf. Bolon-lamat. (N., 1)

[PA-ACHA]. Pacha. Cf. Acha. (3)

PA-COHI. Coh ("puma") is a Maya patronymic, but Pa-coy may be intended here. (1)

PA-COY. Coyi is a Maya patronymic, but no applicable meaning has been found. (3)

PA-CUA. Cf. Ix-cua. Perhaps referable to the Mexican day name Coatl ("serpent"). Cua apparently corresponds to the Maya "boy name" Ah Cuat and to "*kúa*," the Pipil form of *coatl* recorded by Scherzer at Izcalco (Lehmann, 1920, 2: 1027). (N.? 3)

PA-CUA=NEÇIO. Neçio seems to be Spanish. Possibly it is merely descriptive of the person recorded. (1)

[PA-ÇELU]. *Paçelic (probably an error of the scribe), Pazelu. Cf. Çelu. (N., 1)

[PA-ÇELUT]. Pazelut. Cf. Çelut. (N., 1)

[PA-CHACI]. Pachaqui. (1)

[PA-CHAUAN?]. Pachava. Cf. Ikchaua (p. 57, *supra*) and Ix-chauan. (1)

*PA-CHIMAL. Cf. Chimal. (N. 2)

*PA-CHIMAL=AHIX. Evidently a compound name, but Ahix is not found as a single name.

[PA-CHUCI]. Pachuqui. Possibly the same as Pa-chaci. (1)

[PA-DZAY]. Pazai, Pazay. Dzay ("eye tooth," "tusk") is a Maya patronymic. (2)

*PA-DZAY=ATO. Possibly it should be =a-to. To is a Maya patronymic, but no applicable meaning has been found.

*PA-LOCEM. Paloquem. Near the Lacandon was a large Chol-speaking town named Locen. (1)

PA-NACHA. (1)

[PA-NAUA]. Panaba. Cf. Naua. (N., 1)

[PA-OCO?]. Paco, Poco. Cf. Pax-oco. (N.? 2)

PA-NAL. Cf. Nal=chan and Ix-nal=abin. (1)

†Pa-patzin. Cf. Patzin. (N.)

[Pa-quiuit]. Pacuit. Cf. Quiuit. (N., 1)

Pa-tox. Cf. A-tox=pech. (1)

Pa-uitz. Uitz ("hill" or "mountain") is a common Maya patronymic. (2)

Pac-bac. Found only in the Spanish version of the Text. Cf. Pa-cua.

[Pac-tuni]. Pactuny, Patny. Cf. Ix-tuni and Pax-tun. (3)

*Pap-can. Papcam. Can is a common Maya patronymic. Here *can* is probably referable to the Maya *can* in the sense of "to converse" or "to speak formally," since the Maya *can* meaning "four" or "serpent" and *caan* meaning "sky" become *chan* in Chontal. In the same manner Maya *cab* ("honey") becomes *chab* in Acalan Chontal, but Maya *cab* ("land") still remains *cab* in the language of the Acalan. Maya *cambez* and Chontal *cantez* both mean "to teach," literally "to cause to learn." (2)

[Pap-lahun]. Papalahum. Cf. Lahun. (1)

*Pap-tucun. Pactucum, Patucun. (3)

*Pax-bolon. Bolon means "nine" in Maya and Chol and presumably the same in Chontal. One of the gods at Campeche was named Ah Bolonil or Ah Bolon Ahau (Vienna dictionary, f. *129r*). (12)

*Pax-bolon=acha. Cf. Acha.

Pax-cabam. (1)

Pax-coya. Possibly a variant of Pa-coy. (1)

[Pax-iuit]. Paxvt, Paxvyt, Paxvyte. Cf. Iuit. (3)

[Pax-kanan]. Paxcanan, Pascanan. Cf. Kanan. (2)

[Pax-kin?]. Paxquin. Cf. A-kin. (1)

[Pax-kuk?]. Paxcuc. Cf. A-kuk. (1)

Pax-mala. Pasmala, Paxmalan. (8)

Pax-malin. Pamalin, Paxmalim. Apparently referable to the Mexican day name Malinalli ("grass"). *Malina* is defined as "to twist," as one twists a cord. Cf. Malna. (N., 4)

[Pax-maman]. Paxmana, †Paxmanan. Cf. Ix-maman. (1)

*Pax-mulu. Paxmalu, Paxmolo, Pazmulo, Paxmolu, Paxmulun. Cf. Mulu. (N.? 7)

*Pax-oc. Paxoc. Oc is a Maya day name. See p. 65, *supra*. (4)

[Pax-oc=chacchan]. *Paxhocchacchan. Cf. Chac-chan.

Pax-oco. Paoco. *Oco* is a Nahuatl word meaning "pine." (N., 3)

*Pax-tun. Pastun, Patun. *Tun*, which means "rock" or "stone" in Chontal, is a common patronymic in northern Yucatan, where it has much the same meaning. (3)

*Pax-ua. No meaning has been found for *ua* which seems applicable. The name occurs twice in the Text but only in a compound name in the matrícula.

[Pax-ua=acat]. Paxhuacat, Paxvaca. Cf. Acat. (2)

†Pax-uan. Paxjuan (Matrícula of Concepción de Usulaban, 1688. AGI, Contaduría 920). These two names, which are not in the Text or the Tixchel matrícula, may be variants of Pax-ua.

*Pax-uan=a-puk. Divisions very tentative. No applicable meaning has been found in Maya, and the letter *k* rarely, if ever, appears in names of Mexican origin.

Paba. Possibly Pa-ua is intended, but we are also reminded of the Nahuatl *pauatl* ("fruit"). (1)

*Paçimactun. Perhaps Pa-çima=tun was intended. Zima and Tun are both Maya patronymics.

PATZIN. Pazim, Pazin. The suffix -*tzin* strongly suggests a Nahuatl name. We are reminded of *patli* ("medicine generally, a plaster, unguent, etc."). (N., 10)

PATZIN=BOLON. Cf. Bolon.

*PATZIN=CHICIUA. Evidently a compound name, but no name Chiciua has been found.

[PATZIN=MULU]. Pazinmulu. Cf. Mulu. (1)

POLHAUAN. Reading doubtful. (1)

POPO. A tribe of this name is also mentioned (p. 398, *supra*). (5)

QUIUIT. Quibit, Quivit. Here we have followed the Chontal Text in abandoning the Yucatecan orthography, which would be *ciuit*. The name is apparently referable to the Mexican day name Quiauitl ("rain"). (N., 6)

[QUIUIT=ÇELUT]. Quibitarlut. Cf. Çelut. (N., 1)

[QUIUIT=CHAN]. Quibitcham. Cf. Chan=mulu. (1)

SICABIN. Reading doubtful. (1)

*TAMALYAXUN. *Tamal* might be a Chontal preposition meaning "during" or "among." In Maya *yaxum* (literally "the green bird") seems to be a ritual term for the quetzal (*kuk*). It has also been reported verbally as an unidentified tree (Roys, 1933, pp. 63, 74, 99).

†TENCAB. The Text tells of a Kin ("priest") Tencab (p. 395, *supra*), and a Luis Tencab appears in the Zapotitlan records. *Tem, ten,* and *cab* are Maya words, but we have found no applicable meaning.

TOHXUN. Perhaps referable to the Nahuatl *toxontinemi* ("to be poor and in great need"). *Nemi* means "to live." (N.? 1)

TUTZIN. Tuzin, Tuzi. Perhaps referable either to the Nahuatl *tlotli* ("hawk") or *tototl* ("bird") followed by the familiar suffix -*tzin*. We are reminded of the name of the Chichimec ruler, Tlotzin, and of the Yucatecan patronymics, Tut and Tutul. (N., 6)

[ULUM]. Ulun. *Ulum* means "turkey" in Maya. (1)

[UIAN]. Vian. Perhaps referable to Pax-uan and Ix-uan. (2)

YMBAN. (1)

ZOL. Reading doubtful. The initial letter much resembles *J*. (1)

ZU. Possibly Dzul, a common patronymic in Yucatan, is intended. This was also the name of a people in Tabasco (p. 82, *supra*). (1)

Women's Names

[ACHA]. Abcha. (1)

BOL. Cf. A-bol. (1)

CANAL. Possibly Camal, a common Maya patronymic, is intended. (1)

CANTZIN. The suffix -*tzin* suggests a Mexican origin. (N., 1)

[ÇELU]. Zelu. Cf. Çelu, men's names.‡ (N., 1)

‡Hereinafter designated as m.n.

ÇELUT. Tzelut, Zelut. Cf. Çelut, m.n. (N., 5)

[ÇIPAC]. Çipa. Cf. Çipac, m.n. (N., 1)

CHIMAL. Cf. Chimal, m.n. (N., 2)

[ECAT]. †Ecate. Referable to the Mexican day name Ehecatl ("wind"). In the Zapotitlan records María Ecate appears as the wife of Juan Macua. (N.)

[IX-ACHA]. Yxcha, Yscha. (2)

IX-AN. (1)

[IX-APATA?]. Ysapata. Possibly Ix-zapa is intended. (1)

[IX-AUA]. Yxaba. Cf. Macua-aua. Perhaps referable to the Nahuatl *auatl* ("oak," "cater-pillar," or "spine") or to *aua* ("the resident of a town"). (N., 2)

[IX-BOL]. Yxbol. Cf. A-bol. (1)

IX-BOLON. Yxbolon, Yxbolom, Yxbolum, Ysbolun, Yspolon, Tisbolon. Cf. Pax-bolon. (17)

†IX-CAB. Cf. Cab, m.n.

[IX-COANEN?]. Yscoanen. Probably a garbled compound name. Cf. Ix-cua. (1)

IX-COCH. Perhaps referable to the Nahuatl *cocho* ("parrot"), although *coch* and *koch* are Maya words. (N.? 1)

[IX-COCHAN=CUCO?]. Yscochancuco. Cf. Ix-cuco. (1)

[IX-COCHUT]. Yxcochute. Referable to the Nahuatl *cochotl* ("parrot"). (N., 1)

IX-COMULGADA. Ixcomudo. It is difficult to account for these Spanish forms. (2)

[IX-COY]. Yscoy. Cf. Pa-coy, m.n. (9)

[IX-CUA or IX-COA]. Yscua or Yscoa. Reading doubtful. Cf. Pa-cua, m.n. (1)

IX-CUCO. It is possible that Ix-kuk is intended. Cf. Pax-kuk, m.n. (1)

IX-ÇELU. Ysçelu, Yxzelu. Cf. Çelu, m.n. (N., 6)

IX-ÇELUT. Yszelut. Cf. Çelut, m.n. (N., 5)

[IX-ÇIPAC]. Ysçipa, †Yxçipat. Cf. Çipac, m.n. (N., 2)

[IX-CHACI]. Yschaqui. Cf. Pa-chaci, m.n. (1)

[IX-CHAMALI]. Yschamali. Possibly a variant of Ix-chimali. Cf. A-chamal, m.n. (2)

IX-CHAN. Cf. Chan=mucuy, m.n. (1)

[IX-CHAUAN]. Yschauan, Yschavan. Cf. Pa-chauan, m.n. (4)

IX-CHIMALI. Yschimali. Cf. Chimal, m.n. The reason for the final *i* is uncertain. In Yucatan a final *il* is often added to a patronymic, but people say it still remains the same name. (N., 2)

[IX-ICIM]. Yssiquin. Cf. Icim, m.n. (1)

[IX-KANAN]. Yscanan, Yxcanan. Cf. Kanan, m.n. (3)

[IX-KUMUN?]. Yxcomud, Yxconun. Kumun is a Maya patronymic, but we do not know its meaning. (2)

[IX-KUMUN=COY?]. Yxcomuncoy. (1)

[IX-LAMAT]. Yslamalat. Cf. Lamat, m.n. (1)

[IX-LOCEN]. Ysloquin. Cf. Pa-locen, m.n. (1)

[IX-MACI]. Yxmaqui, Ysmaaqui. (2)

[IX-MALA]. Ysmala. Cf. Pax-mala, m.n. (2)

[IX-MALIN]. Ysmalin. Cf. Pax-malin, m.n. (N? 1)

[IX-MAMAN]. Ysmanan, Ysmama. There may be some association between this name and those of the Mamantel River and the town of Mama in northern Yucatan. The latter is accented differently from most, if not all, other Yucatecan names ending in *a*. (3)

Ix-MANTZIN. The suffix -*tzin* suggests a Nahuatl origin. Possibly Ixnantzin is intended. Cf. Ix-natzin. (N.? 1)

Ix-MULU. Ysmolu. Cf. Mulu, m.n. (N.? 3)

[Ix-NALA?]. Ysnala. Ix-mala may be intended. (1)

Ix-NAL=ABIN. Ysnalavin. Cf. Nal=chan and Abin, m.n. (1)

Ix-NATZIN. Ysnatzin, Ysnazim. The suffix -*tzin* suggests a Mexican origin. Cf. Nahuatl *nantli* ("mother"), also Pipil *nú-nan* ("mi madre," or "mi señora"), and *tu-nantzin* ("the Virgin Mary," literally "our mother" or "our lady," Lehmann, 1920, 2: 1033). (N., 3)

[Ix=NAUA]. Yxnahua, Yxnahual, Ysnahua. Cf. Naua, m.n. (N., 3)

Ix-NAUA=CAN. (N.? 1)

[Ix-NAUAT]. Yxnahuat, Ysnahuat, Ysnahuate. Possibly a variant of Ix-naua. Nauat is a common patronymic among the Maya. (N., 4)

[Ix-PATZIN]. Yspazim. Cf. Patzin, m.n. (N., 1)

Ix-POPO. Yspopo. Cf. Popo, m.n. (4)

[Ix-PUT]. Ysput. *Put* is the Maya word for "papaya," and Pot is a Maya patronymic. (1)

[Ix-SUCHIL]. Yssuchi. Referable to the Mexican day name Xochitl ("flower"). (N., 1)

[Ix-TAAM?]. Ystaam. (1)

Ix-TUCUN. Cf. Pap-tucun. (1)

Ix-TUNI. Ystuny, Ystuy. Cf. Pax-tun and Pac-tuni. (7)

Ix-TUNICH. Less rare at Zapotitlan. *Tunich* means "rock" in Maya, but we have not found the word employed as a name in northern Yucatan. (1)

[Ix-UAN]. Yxvan, Yxven, Yshuan, Yxbanex. Cf. Pax-uan, m.n. (5)

Ix-ZAPA. Ysçapa. Perhaps the same as Ixçipa, a variant of Ix-çipac. Cf. A-chamal, m.n. (N.? 3)

[Ix-ZU?]. A doubtful reconstruction of Yxzua and Ystzu. Cf. Zu, m.n. (2)

Ix-ZULU. Zulu is a Maya patronymic and may be a variant of Çelu. (N.? 1)

[Ix-NA-ACAT]. Yxnacat, Yxnacate, Ysnacat. Cf. Acat, m.n. (N., 12)

[Ix-NA-ACHA]. Yxnacha, Ysnacha. Cf. Acha, m.n. (12)

Ix-NA-CUA. Cf. Pa-cua, m.n. Ix-macua may be intended. (N.? 1)

[Ix-NA-ÇELU]. Yxnazelu, Yxnatzelun. Cf. Çelu, m.n. (N., 2)

[Ix-NA-ÇELU=IUIT]. Ysnaceluit. Cf. Çelut=iuit, m.n. (N., 1)

Ix-NA-ÇELUT. Ysnazelut. Cf. Çelut, m.n. (N., 7)

[Ix-NA-CHAUAN]. Ysnachaguan, Ysnachaua, Ysnachavan. Cf. Chauan, m.n. (3)

Ix-NA-CHIMAL. Cf. Chimal, m.n. (N., 1)

[Ix-NA-ICIM]. Ysnayquim, Yxnaquin, Ysnaquin. Cf. Icim, m.n. (6)

[Ix-NA-IZCIN?]. Ysnazquin. Perhaps referable to the Mexican day name Itzcuintli ("dog"). (N.? 1)

[Ix-NA-IUIT]. Yxnaybit, Yxnavyt, Yxnaut. Cf. Iuit, m.n. (N., 4)

[Ix-NA-KANAN]. Yxnacanan. Cf. Kanan, m.n. (1)

Ix-NA-LAHUN. Cf. Lahun, m.n. (1)

Ix-NA-LAMAT. Yxmalamat, Ysnalamat. Cf. Lamat, m.n. (6)

Ix-NA-LUCH=COY. *Luch* is the Chontal and Maya name of the tree gourd. Cf. Pa-coy. (1)

Ix-NA-MACUA. Yxnamacua. Cf. Macua, m.n. (N.? 4)

[Ix-NA-MAMAN?]. Ysnaman. Cf. Ix-maman. (1)

[Ix-NA-MUCUY]. Ysinaynucuy. Cf. Chan=mucuy, m.n. (1)

[Ix-NA-OC]. Yxnoc, Ysnoc, Ysno, Yxno. Cf. Pax-oc, m.n. (4)

[Ix-na-oco]. Yxnoco. Cf. Pax-oco, m.n. (N., 1)

Ix-na-patzin. Yxnapatzim, Yxnapazin, Ysnapatzin, Ysnapatzma. Cf. Patzin, m.n. (N., 12)

[Ix-na-pez-iuit or Ix-na-piz-iuit]. Yxnapexuyt, Ysnapizuyt. We can find no meaning for *pez* or *piz* that seems applicable to a name. Cf. Iuit, m.n. (N., 2)

Ix-na-tutzin. Ysnatutzin. Cf. Tutzin, m.n. (N., 3)

[Ix-na-uain?]. Ysnabayn. Ix-naua=ain might possibly be intended. *Ain* is the Maya name of the alligator and a very similar word, "*öjin*," is reported by Stoll from the Chontal. (1)

[Ix-na-uitz]. Ysnahuiz. *Uitz*, which means "hill" or "mountain" in Maya, is a common patronymic in northern Yucatan. In Nahuatl *uitz* seems to be associated with a spine or sharp point. (1)

[Na-acha]. Nacha. Cf. Acha, m.n. (1)

Na-çelut. Natzelut. Cf. Çelut, m.n. (N., 3)

[Na-iuit]. Maybit. Cf. Iuit, m.n. (N., 1)

Na-lahun. Cf. Lahun, m.n. (1)

Na-mama. Cf. Ix-maman. (1)

Suchil. Cf. Ix-suchil. (N., 1)

†Yquipac. Possibly Ix-quipac is intended by the scribe. This would be referable to the name Quipaque found in the Chontalpa (p. 62, *supra*).

Zapa. Cf. Ix-zapa. (N., 2)

APPENDIX D

Explorations of Feliciano Bravo in Southeastern Tabasco and the Peten

I N CHAPTER 9 we have described the part played by Feliciano Bravo, *escribano mayor de gobernación* of the province of Yucatan, in the Zapotitlan episode. In 1573 and again in 1580 Bravo was also the leader of exploring expeditions in southeastern Tabasco and the Peten. The story of these expeditions constitutes a new chapter in the long history of Spanish efforts to pacify the Indian tribes which occupied the lands bordering on the provinces of Yucatan, Tabasco, Chiapas, and Verapaz.[1]

Bravo's chief associate in these expeditions was Fray Pedro Lorenzo, a Dominican stationed at Palenque, who had achieved considerable reputation because of his missionary activities and his knowledge of Indian languages. In 1563–64 Fray Pedro pacified some of the hostile Indians of Pochutla in eastern Chiapas and settled them at Ocosingo. Remesal calls him "the apostle of that land."[2] Later he made Palenque the center of his missionary labors and obtained "good results" in converting the Indians of adjacent areas.[3] His linguistic attainments are attested by statements in the Bravo probanzas that he knew four or five Indian languages, including Chontal.[4]

At various times Fray Pedro had sought to get in touch with certain heathen and apostate Indians of the interior, who were a menace to the safety of the frontier pueblos in southeastern Tabasco, especially those located along the Usumacinta. On one occasion he had gone out with a few Indians of Palenque to seek these hostile groups, but without success. Subsequent

[1] Information concerning these explorations is found in the Probanzas of Feliciano Bravo, AGI, México, leg. 109, cited in preceding chapters. The story as told in Appendix D is based on this source, unless otherwise indicated in the notes.

[2] Remesal, 1932, bk. 10, chs. 17, 18. Antonio de León Pinelo (Stone, 1932, pp. 245–46) gives his name as Laurencio.

[3] In 1576 Fray Pedro's work was brought to the attention of the Crown, and on May 15 of that year royal cedulas were sent out to the Audiencia of Guatemala and to the governor of Yucatan instructing them to give him all possible aid. According to these documents, he had settled his converts in a pueblo which had more than 500 inhabitants. (AGI, México, leg. 2999.) This place was undoubtedly Palenque.

[4] After Bravo returned from the expedition of 1573 he took Fray Pedro to the Chontalpa in northern Tabasco, where he preached in Chontal to the Indians of Bravo's encomienda. This was said to have given great pleasure to the Indians, for the clergy who had been assigned to that area had not known the Chontal language. An undated "Memorial de la provincia de Yucatán y Tabasco" (AGI, Indiferente General, leg. 1373) describes Fray Pedro as "a great servant of God, of great learning and good example, . . . who knows four or six languages."

effòrts to locate them had also been unsuccessful because the Indians whom he sent were afraid to penetrate far enough into the bush and forest. So finally Fray Pedro sent letters to Yucatan suggesting that an expedition be organized to find them and effect their conversion to Christianity.

This appeal was received with favor by Don Diego de Santillán, governor of Yucatan, who issued an order February 15, 1573, naming Feliciano Bravo as captain of a force to accompany Fray Pedro on another trip into the interior. In the preamble the governor stated that according to Fray Pedro's report the heathens and apostates were located several days' journey from Palenque,[5] "in the district of Tayça and Tachis." Bravo was instructed to proceed to Tabasco and there organize an expedition to bring about their submission to the king and the faith.

In accordance with Santillán's order, Bravo went to Santa María de la Victoria, capital of Tabasco, where he made the necessary preparations. After presenting his commission to the cabildo, he explained the purpose of the expedition and called upon the encomenderos of Tabasco, or their substitutes, to serve as escort for Fray Pedro Lorenzo, who was to act as interpreter and as preacher of the Gospel. Two Spaniards were also sent to the pueblos of Jonuta, Popane, Iztapa, and Usumacinta on the Usumacinta River to obtain canoes and paddlers, and "to take the canoes by way of the Río de Tachis" to a place where Bravo would meet them by marching overland from Tenosique, the starting point of the expedition.

On April 20, 1573, Bravo and his small force of soldiers arrived in Tenosique, "the last settlement of the Christian pueblos which border the said heathen Indians." Fray Pedro Lorenzo had already arrived from Palenque, and after mass Bravo explained the missionary character of the entrada to the Indians of the various towns who were to accompany him. It is interesting to note that among the latter were some said to have come from the pueblos of "Alacandon," Pochutla, Zinacantan, and Copaltepeque in Chiapas.[6] We suspect, however, that the Lacandon and Pochutla people were Indians moved to Ocosingo by Fray Pedro Lorenzo. It is difficult to believe that any unpacified Indians from Lacandon and Pochutla would have accompanied a missionary expedition.

The next day (April 21) the expedition left Tenosique and started overland to the Río de Tachis. Instead of the usual Indian carriers, more than twenty horses were used to transport the food and supplies. The route was through heavy forest (*montañas*) and some of Bravo's companions later re-

[5] Another document, dated a few weeks later, gave the distance from Palenque as eight days' journey.
[6] The others came from Palenque, Tepetitan, Chilapa, Petenecte, and Tenosique.

lated how the captain went ahead, leading his horse and cutting a path in places with his sword. One of them also stated that the route was through "new country . . . where Christians had never traveled." On the second afternoon (April 22), after traveling 10 leagues from Tenosique, the party reached the place on the Río de Tachis to which the canoes had been brought. This place was named Puerto de la Buena Esperanza.

Here a member of the expedition named Juan de Orduña, "who has experience and full knowledge of the said heathen Indians," made a sworn statement in which he told how these Indians terrorized the frontier pueblos, especially Tenosique, and cited the case of an Indian woman of the latter pueblo who had been carried off and who later escaped from her captors. He also stated:

The said heathens frequent the shores of this river [Tachis], where they have their canoes and near here an isolated Indian hut where they kept their idols, with their settlement a short distance farther in. And it is said now that they have moved to a peñol which is at a lake in that region, and that a short time ago as many as two hundred Indians from the pueblos of Pochutla and Lacandon went to them well armed after their fashion. The said infidels are so harmful, triumphing in doing evil, and without [meeting] resistance, that they went forth and killed [almost] all of them, for only twenty of them escaped. The latter have said, told, and related what has been stated above, and in particular they told it to Juan May, an Indian of Petenecte whom they saw in this company.[7] And for this reason it is a very just thing, of great service to God and his Majesty, that this land should be made safe from the aforesaid infidel huntsmen, because the Christians in their district are so terrified of them that two or three times [when] he has gone up by this river to explore the region, the Indians whom he was taking kept holding back without his being able to move them forward.

On April 23 Bravo and his companions left the Puerto de la Buena Esperanza and proceeded upstream in the canoes. Five days later (April 28) they came to a "bay where the river widened out," later named Bahía de la Ascensión because they celebrated the feast of the Ascension there. At this place they saw "a great deal of smoke and signs of settlement" off to the right. The next day they followed the river looking for a place where they could go inland to these settlements, but their search was unsuccessful and they returned to the Bahía where a camp was established. From here Fray Pedro and a few Spaniards and Indians went to seek a trail to the settlements, but the

[7] We doubt that any of the twenty Indians of Pochutla and Lacandon who escaped the massacre were members of Bravo's expedition. The people who told this story to Juan May of Petenecte were probably Indians from Ocosingo, who had received the news from Pochutla and Lacandon.

forest was so dense that they finally found it impossible to go on, and after two or three days they returned to camp.

On Ascension Day Fray Pedro said mass, and afterwards made a speech in which he proposed that the expedition should turn back to Tenosique. The Indians were tired and restless, and food was running short. Although the heathens had not been found, their location was now known, and Fray Pedro stated that it would be possible to return later and preach to them. Bravo and the other Spaniards agreed, and the same day the expedition set out on the return journey. On May 2 they reached Tenosique.

From Tenosique Bravo went down the Usumacinta, visiting the various pueblos that were located along its shores. In each he paid for supplies that had been furnished for the expedition and inquired into the state of the missions and pueblo affairs.[8] From Popane he turned back to Palenque, and from there went to northern Tabasco where he had encomiendas, and finally returned to Yucatan a few weeks later.

The expedition of 1573 had obviously failed to achieve the results expected. Later in the year Fray Pedro asked Diego de Orduña, one of Bravo's companions, to go back and try to obtain more information concerning the land they had visited. With a few Indians Orduña went out again to the Río de Tachis and advanced upstream for five days. On the fourth day he encountered signs of the "wild Indians," and his companions began to display fear. The next day he had some of them climb a hill in order to look for other signs of the settlement, "and when they returned it was with so much fear and outcry that they did not know how to tell him anything they might have seen, and they were unwilling to go any farther." So he was obliged to return and report to Fray Pedro what had happened. Apparently no further efforts were made to renew the explorations at this time.

We have already noted that Governor Santillán's decree authorizing the expedition of 1573 stated that the heathen and apostate Indians whom Fray Pedro wished to convert were located "in the district of Tayça and Tachis." Reports of Bravo and Fray Pedro, made soon after their return, do not designate by name the region they had explored, but in a document dated at Santa María de la Victoria on July 11, 1573, Bravo referred to the expedition as the "jornada de Tayça." On the same day one of his companions made a sworn statement concerning the entrada in which he stated that "the said Feliciano Bravo entered the land of the heathen Indians which they call Tayça."

[8] Bravo had also been appointed *visitador* in Tabasco, with authority to investigate local administration and correct abuses.

These statements, as well as other evidence to be recorded below, indicate that Bravo and Fray Pedro had entered, or at least approached, the region dominated by the Itza Indians in the central Peten. The Río de Tachis along which they had traveled in canoes for five days was evidently the San Pedro Mártir, which rises in the Peten, flows west across the Guatemala-Mexico boundary, turns north to Tiradero in southeastern Tabasco, and then west to join the Usumacinta above Balancan.

In 1576 reports reached Spain concerning the success of Fray Pedro's missionary activities in the Palenque district, and on May 15 of that year royal orders were sent to the Audiencia of Guatemala and the governor of Yucatan to give him all possible assistance.[9] These instructions did not produce immediate results, but in 1579 Don Guillén de las Casas, governor of Yucatan, authorized a new expedition into the interior. The circumstances which prompted this move are explained in part by an interesting document in Bravo's probanzas.

It appears that for some time Governor Las Casas had been interested in a project for an expedition to the Itza territory and adjacent areas, and that he had sent reports concerning the scheme to Spain. Early in 1579 an Indian of Hocaba, named Pedro Uc, returned to Yucatan from a sojourn among the Itza, and the governor seized the opportunity to obtain additional information about the lands to the south. On April 18 he ordered Feliciano Bravo to receive the Indian's testimony, of which the essential part is given below.

This witness said that he has been in the province of Tahytza, which is of infidel Indians, and at the time Father Fray Lorenzo and Feliciano Bravo went to the discovery of that land, he was in a large settled town which the said Indians have. By rivers and lakes, according to the road they took, and through forests where they wandered, as this declarant and the Indians of the said town were aware and knew, [Lorenzo and Bravo] had arrived as near as a day's journey from the said town.

This said town has a population of about two thousand Indians who dwell in houses of the said place. Each Indian does not have his own house, but many live together in each one of the said houses; and they do not have any stronghold or fortress. And from a great river, by which Fray Pedro and Feliciano Bravo were traveling toward the east, a little estero branches off, and this extends to within three leagues of the said pueblo. By established custom among them the Indians of the [town] do not travel or have any sign of a road toward that river, at least where it can be discovered. When the said Fray Pedro and Feliciano went where they did, the [Indians] believed that they had discovered it and would reach the said place. The said Indians were agreed that they would receive them in peace if they wished to have it, and if they saw and understood that they were not going

[9] Cf. note 3, *supra*.

to do them harm; but if they perceived the contrary, and that they wished to make war upon them, they had decided to wage it with them. This declarant understood this at that time when he was in the said town. He had gone from this province as a boy with other Indians who are now dead.

The aforesaid infidel Indians usually know and have information about what goes on in this land among the Christian Indians, for the Indians of this land go there and have dealings with them. And now they have learned and know very well the character of the said governor, Don Guillén de las Casas, who is governing this land at present, and therefore the [witness] understood from them that they [might be approached][10] with ease and great peace because they are aware that the said governor shows great favor to the Indians and does not wish them to be ill treated.

This declarant is from the province of Hocaba, and a short time ago he came from that land toward the sierras of Mazatlan with other Indians who remained in that region. And this declarant joined some Christian Indians, who were traveling through the forests seeking wax, and came to this land.

The Indians of the said town and those of its environs sacrifice and perform idolatries of their paganism and antiquity, and they have their idols. They sustain themselves by farming, hunting, and fishing.

Part of this testimony may have been elicited by leading questions propounded by Bravo, but the story obviously provided an excuse for sending out an expedition of exploration and reconnaissance without waiting for a reply to the reports which Governor Las Casas had sent to Spain. On November 12, 1579, the governor renewed Bravo's old commission, issued by Santillán in 1573, and instructed him to proceed to Palenque where Fray Pedro Lorenzo was still living and to enlist his support in the organization of a new entrada into the interior. The purpose of the expedition was clearly stated by Fray Pedro in testimony given after his return, in which he described the journey as "an expedition to discover the new land of Tayça, by way of the Río de Tachis, in order to know and learn what there is along the shores and [in the] district of the said river, which borders upon the land of Yucatan and Lacandon."

Preparations for this second expedition were made in the same manner as for that of 1573. Canoes were sent up the Río de Tachis to a designated spot to await the arrival of Bravo and his companions, who were to go overland from Tenosique. About fifty Indians were assembled to accompany the Spaniards, who numbered twelve or thirteen persons. Among the latter were the veteran Diego de Orduña and a certain Francisco Gómez, "experienced in

[10] A few words seem to have been omitted here. They probably refer to the possibility of converting these Indians and inducing them to acknowledge Spanish sovereignty, for when Governor Las Casas renewed Bravo's commission later in the year, he stated that he had been informed that the Indians of the interior desired to become Christians.

measuring altitude and in demarcation of the land." Food and other supplies were collected at Tenosique to be transported overland to the Río de Tachis on horses.

The expedition left Tenosique on Easter Sunday, 1580, and after a day's journey through the forest reached an "embarcadero" on the Río de Tachis where seventeen canoes were waiting. On the following Wednesday the force started upstream in the canoes and after seven days came to a place where it was impossible to proceed any farther because of the "grandes palizadas e impedimentos" which obstructed the course of the river.[11] Here they found signs of habitation, for there were canoes along shore and ."the land was cut over."[12]

Some of the Spaniards desired to advance inland for a day's journey or two in search of the Indian settlements, but the plan had to be abandoned. The Indians who had accompanied the expedition were restless and anxious to return home, and Fray Pedro Lorenzo had fallen ill and was unable to travel on foot. The expedition turned back and reached Tenosique on April 21. The following statement concerning the return trip is taken from testimony given by Diego de Orduña.

They agreed to return and did so, making entradas inland in order to become well acquainted with the country. On one of these [entradas], from a very high peñol which overlooked everything, they descried the location of the capital of Taiça, which is a peñol in a lake at the foot of three sierras which surround it, and so the cacique of Alacandon and Pochutla and others of his nation whom they were taking with them recognized it and pointed it out. . . . The aforesaid cacique is called Çenuncabenal.[13]

The sierras which we saw in this way and which were recognized as the location of the said Taiza were about four leagues away. Two men of the said company taken by the aforesaid captain, who are named Martín de Arriaga and Gaspar Martín, skilled and well-informed with regard to gold and silver mines, saw and considered, [and they so] stated and affirmed under oath, that according to their [mining] experience, the sierras at the aforesaid place which the said Indians held were of great mineral wealth in gold, if any mines existed in the world.

[11] The Spanish reads: ". . . hallaron el dicho río cerrado con grandes palizadas e impedimentos que no se pudieron pasar por él adelante." The meaning of this phrase is not entirely clear. *Palizada* usually means an artificial stockade, or a barrier thrown up for defensive purposes in war. In this case it probably refers to some sort of natural barrier.

[12] The Spanish reads, "la tierra talada." *Talar* means "to fell trees, to desolate, to lay waste a country." The phrase probably describes milpa lands in which the trees had been cut down to be burned before planting maize.

[13] This reference to the "cacique of Alacandon and Pochutla" is, of course, of some interest. Since the Pochutla and Lacandon people on this expedition and that of 1573 were probably Indians of these settlements who had been moved to Ocosingo by Fray Pedro Lorenzo in earlier years, we infer that they continued to have their own cacique and probably a barrio of their own in their new place of residence.

The watersheds in that region ran in a southeasterly direction toward Golfo
Dulce.

In the present state of affairs the entrance to the aforesaid land by way of the
said river is well ascertained, discovered, and known, and this witness considers it
the best there can be, for about thirty years ago this witness, in the company of
Captain Francisco de Montejo with more than thirty Spaniards and two thousand
Indians, made an entrada by way of Yucatan in order to ascertain and discover the
aforesaid Tayça. Although he journeyed many days he was never able to reach it,
or even the present point, and he returned with the loss of more than a thousand
Indians who remained in the forests, dead from thirst, for there was no water along
the route they took nor is there any coming through that region to the said new
land of Tayça, as this witness has seen. And now at one day's journey away from
the said river they will reach the land of the said Tayça, according to what has
been seen and the smoke from fires which was sighted on this occasion and had
also been observed during the side trip [made] during the previous expedition.
Nevertheless, this witness believes that a force and more than twelve harquebusiers
are necessary in order to be safe from the said infidels, who are daring and harmful
according to what this witness has learned from more than twelve years' residence
in this region where he lives.

Thus the expedition of 1580 had apparently taken the Spaniards farther
inland than in 1573, and according to Orduña they had sighted the district in
which the chief Itza stronghold was located. In summing up the results, Fray
Pedro Lorenzo said that "the passage and entrance" to the heathen Indians
was now known, and he had faith that their conversion could be achieved
"with the aid of God, for it is His cause." More than two years passed, however, before plans were made for another entrada.

Upon receipt of the governor's reports concerning the advisability of
pacifying the Indians of the interior, the Crown, on November 1, 1579, instructed Las Casas to take suitable action to achieve this end. Acting on these
instructions, the governor renewed Bravo's old commissions on August 30,
1582. At the same time Bravo was appointed corregidor of the Campeche
district, "so that from there, by way of the province of Tixchel, he might
plan to make the entrada and open the road, both to the provinces of Chiapa
and Tabasco and to the new land which he is ordered to discover." For this
new venture Bravo and Fray Pedro Lorenzo were to receive all necessary aid.
The language of Bravo's appointment shows, however, that it was now the
plan to enter the interior from southwestern Yucatan, instead of following
the Tenosique–Río de Tachis route of the previous expeditions.

Bravo took office as corregidor in October and began to make plans for
the entrada. In order to obtain information concerning the interior of the
peninsula, he summoned for examination certain Indians who knew the coun-

try because they had gone there to hunt and to collect wax. Their testimony contains a few interesting details about sites and Indian settlements they had visited, but it provides very little information of a definite character that would have been useful to Bravo in charting a new route southward from Campeche. In November Bravo returned to Mérida where he petitioned the governor for financial assistance to carry out the entrada. The documentary evidence ends at this point, and we have no record that the expedition was ever made.

The story of Bravo's explorations has been related in some detail because any new information concerning Spanish activities in the unconquered lands between Yucatan and Guatemala is worth recording. Moreover, the data presented above, especially the references to the Río de Tachis, have considerable significance in relation to the Acalan problem.

We have already stated that the Río de Tachis, which Bravo followed in his expeditions of 1573 and 1580, was apparently the San Pedro Mártir. Analysis of the evidence in the Bravo documents clearly indicates this identification.

1. We have already quoted various statements which show that the expeditions of 1573 and 1580 were directed toward "Tayça," the lands of the Itza in the central Peten. The headwaters of the San Pedro Mártir reach to within a short distance of Lake Peten, center of the Itza territory.

2. In 1573 the canoes that were sent to the point of embarkation on the Río de Tachis were furnished by the pueblos of Jonuta, Popane, Iztapa, and Usumacinta, of which the first three are known to have been located on the Usumacinta River below the junction with the San Pedro Mártir. None was sent from Petenecte and Tenosique, located above the junction of the two streams. This suggests that it was Bravo's plan to have the canoes brought up the Usumacinta to the San Pedro Mártir, and thence up the latter stream to a point where he would meet them by traveling overland from Tenosique. (If this reasoning is valid, it constitutes strong evidence that the town of Usumacinta was also situated below the junction of the Usumacinta and San Pedro Mártir. This is a point of some importance in relation to Cortés' route from Iztapa to Ciuatecpan in 1524–25. Cf. discussion on pp. 435–48, *supra*.)

3. The names of the towns which furnished canoes in 1580 are not recorded, but Diego de Orduña stated that the canoes had been brought upstream at the cost of great labor, "because of the great falls and rapids [the river] has." There are falls and rapids on the San Pedro Mártir between Tiradero and the junction with the Usumacinta.[14]

[14] Andrews, 1943, p. 54.

4. The journey overland from Tenosique to the Río de Tachis in 1573 took less than two days. The distance was said to be about 10 leagues, or some 40 km. It is about 30 km. airline by an eastern or slightly southeastern route from Tenosique to the San Pedro Mártir. In 1580 this stage of the journey took one day. The shorter time might be explained by the fact that the route was already known, or by assuming that Bravo followed a more direct route to the river than in 1573. The point of embarkation in each case was probably near the modern site of Santa Elena.

5. In 1573, after five days of travel up the Tachis, the Spaniards reached a place where the river widened out to form what they called a bay (*bahía*). In five days canoes moving up the San Pedro Mártir from a place near Santa Elena on the south-north course of the river east of Tenosique could advance a considerable distance into the Peten. Along the south bank of the river in the Peten are numerous swamp and overflow areas which might possibly be described as bays. According to Pedro Uc's story, the Spaniards reached a point about a day's journey from a western Itza settlement located three leagues beyond an estero that branched off from the stream, "by which Fray Pedro and Feliciano Bravo were traveling toward the east." On the upper course of the San Pedro Mártir in the Peten are many small tributaries which drain lagoons or esteros.[15]

6. In 1580, after traveling upstream for seven days, the Spaniards came to a place where obstacles in the river prevented their advancing any farther. The inference seems to be that they had reached the end of canoe navigation. After turning back they climbed a high peñol from which they sighted the sierras surrounding Lake Peten. In the case of the San Pedro Mártir the end of navigation would probably be reached at Paso Caballos.[16] Assuming that the hill the Spaniards climbed was in the region of Paso Caballos, it would have been possible for them to sight the sierras mentioned. It seems likely, however, that Orduña minimized the distance when he stated that the sierras were about 4 leagues away.

If the Río de Tachis was not the San Pedro Mártir, then the only alternative would be to assume that Bravo reached the confines of Itza territory by traveling up the Usumacinta and its tributary, the Río de la Pasión. It may be

[15] According to Lundell, the northern banks of the San Pedro Mártir "are precipitous. while the southern banks are mostly swampy." He also notes that "in the drainage system of the San Pedro Mártir numerous *arroyos* are found which during the dry season are reduced to a series of unconnected pools." One of these arroyos extends southeastward toward Kantetul, located only a short distance north of Lake Peten (Lundell, 1937, pp. 24–25, and pl. 1).

[16] Lundell (*ibid.*, p. 24) states that the San Pedro Mártir is navigable for small boats as far as El Paso (Paso Caballos). The Hedges map of Guatemala also marks Paso Caballos as the end of canoe navigation on the San Pedro Mártir (communication by S. G. Morley).

argued that the falls and rapids in the Río de Tachis mentioned in 1580 by Diego de Orduña refer to the tumbling torrent of the Usumacinta in the gorge above Tenosique, and that the overland part of the journey in 1573 and again in 1580 was made to by-pass the gorge. If the canoes were sent up the Usumacinta to a point which Bravo reached by traveling overland, it would be necessary, however, to explain why they were brought from pueblos downstream below the junction of the Usumacinta and the San Pedro Mártir, instead of from Petenecte and Tenosique which were nearer at hand. Moreover, it is doubtful whether Bravo could have moved up the Usumacinta and the Pasión to a place bordering on the region dominated by the Itzas within five or seven days. Finally, if Bravo reached the end of canoe navigation in 1580, such a place on the Pasión would have taken him toward the headwaters of that stream and beyond a point close to Itza territory.

Identification of the Río de Tachis as the San Pedro Mártir aids in the interpretation of certain passages of the Acalan narrative. In the Spanish version of Document III we read that when Cortés went to Acalan in 1525 he "entered by way of Tanodzic and passed by the pueblo of Tachix and came out at the beginning of the land of Çacchutte," one of the Acalan settlements. We are also told that a second Spanish expedition, obviously that of Avila, "came and entered and went through, as the Capitán del Valle had done, by the pueblo of Tachix and the pueblo of Çacchutte." Contemporary accounts of the Cortés and Avila expeditions do not mention any settlement named Tachix, or Tachis, along the line of march from the Usumacinta to the beginning of the Acalan lands. Moreover, it should be noted that in both passages the words "pueblo of" are found only in the Spanish version, not in the Chontal original. The Chontal merely records the fact that Cortés, on the way from the Usumacinta to Acalan, passed through or by way of Tachix. The name might refer to a settlement, a region, or, as we know now, a river. If the Río de Tachis was the San Pedro Mártir, then the narrative clearly implies that Cortés crossed this stream on the way to Acalan.

Such an interpretation of the Text complements and confirms other evidence that Ciuatecpan, where Cortés crossed the Usumacinta en route to Acalan, was located about the junction with the San Pedro Mártir. It also proves beyond any reasonable doubt that the great estero, or lagoon, encountered by Cortés and Avila between the Usumacinta and Acalan was an overflow section of the San Pedro Mártir. Moreover, if we reverse the process of reasoning and take into account all the data concerning Cortés' route, including the references to Tachix in the Text, we find that such data constitutes additional proof that the Río de Tachis was the San Pedro Mártir. In short, the early sources concerning the Cortés expedition, the Text, and the evidence in the Bravo papers form a mosaic that fits together in a remarkable manner.

In Appendix B we have noted that Maudslay and Morley locate Itzamkanac, the capital of Acalan, on or near the San Pedro Mártir within the western boundary of the Peten. If their views are correct, it is evident that the Bravo-Lorenzo expeditions of 1573 and 1580 would have crossed former Acalan territory; indeed, in traveling up the Río de Tachis, or San Pedro Mártir, Bravo passed the site of Mactun which Morley identifies as the probable location of Itzamkanac. But there is not the slightest hint in any of the documents relating to these entradas that Bravo had entered the old Acalan area. On the contrary, we find that in both Yucatan and Tabasco the province of Acalan and the Tachis, or San Pedro Mártir, area explored by Bravo and Fray Pedro Lorenzo were regarded as separate and distinct areas.

This fact is recorded in a general probanza of services formulated by Bravo in the autumn of 1573. One of his supporting witnesses was Juan de Montejo, grandson of the conqueror. Montejo gave testimony concerning an earlier entrada by Bravo "to a new settlement of heathen Indians who had been discovered in a province called Acalan toward the pueblo of Tixchel." This statement obviously refers to Bravo's journey from Tixchel to Zapotitlan in December 1570 (see Chapter 9 and Appendix B). The witness then related that Bravo subsequently went to Tabasco where, by order of Governor Santillán, he made another expedition "for the conversion of other heathen Indians who are said to live in another province called Tayça." The latter statement can only refer to the first journey of Bravo and Lorenzo to the Río de Tachis, or San Pedro Mártir, in 1573. Another witness was Francisco de Peñate, a resident of the Chontalpa in Tabasco. After testifying concerning the explorations of 1573, he stated that he had heard that "prior to this [Bravo] went on another journey for the conversion of other Indians who are in the region of Acalan."

Report of Indian Settlements in the Interior of the Yucatan Peninsula in 1604

THE FLIGHT of Indians from the mission towns of northern Yucatan to the swamp and forest areas in the interior of the peninsula created a serious problem to which the provincial authorities gave increasing attention in the latter part of the sixteenth century and throughout the seventeenth. In Chapter 10 we have given some account of this problem, especially in relation to the activities of Don Pablo Paxbolon, cacique and governor of Tixchel, and in Chapter 11 we have described the history of certain forest, or Montañas, missions established in the south-central part of the peninsula.

The history of the Montañas missions dates from 1604, when Paxbolon made a journey to the interior country to obtain information concerning settlements of fugitive and unsubdued Indians. On this entrada the cacique traveled six days from Tixchel to a region called Nacaukumil, where he visited two settlements, or foci of settlement, about 1 league apart. From later documents we learn that this area was some 4–6 leagues east of Popola, the latter being situated on the upper course of the Mamantel River. From the Indians of Nacaukumil Paxbolon received reports of other settlements located toward the east, north and northeast, and southeast. This information was recorded in a *memoria*, or report, later transmitted to Governor Fernández de Velasco by Paxbolon's son-in-law, Francisco Maldonado, and other citizens of Campeche as evidence in support of a petition for formal authorization to undertake the pacification of the interior settlements. In May 1604, the petitioners, having been granted a capitulación, or contract, to carry out their scheme, journeyed to Nacaukumil and thence to another place called Auatayn, where missions were established by Franciscan friars who accompanied the expedition. Subsequently the contract with Maldonado and his associates was suspended, but the Franciscans carried on the work thus begun and founded other missions in the Montañas area.

Paxbolon's report of 1604, of which a translation is given below, has considerable interest, since it illustrates the number, size, and character of the interior settlements already existing at the beginning of the seventeenth century. The large number of apostate fugitives in these settlements is shown by the preponderance of Christian names for the principal men and leaders. In certain cases, such as Ixkik and Tixchalche, we find record of two chieftains, one with a Christian name and the other with a pagan name. Some of these men with pagan names may have been autochthonous residents of the region; others were probably descendants of apostate fugitives who had fled from northern Yucatan in earlier years. It is not surprising to find only pagan names for the leaders of Petox, a Cehache village, since the Cehache had never been converted. In the case of Chunpich, whose chieftains also had pagan names, the situation is not entirely clear, although this may well have been another Cehache settlement, for in Avendaño's time at the end of the seventeenth century Chunpich was in Cehache territory.

Most of the Petox names, especially the long name beginning Caca-, are unfamiliar, although this is not surprising since Petox was a Cehache settlement. These names show, however, that the Cehache had Na- names, as might have been expected, and that the ah kin, or native priest, was an important member of local government. But this was also true among the fugitives.

Unfortunately the report is very vague as to the location of the settlements listed, nor do the meanings of the names, as defined in the notes, help in this connection, except in the case of Nacaukumil. In some cases, however, such as Ichmachich, Ichbalche, Ixtok (Tzuctok), and Chekubul, where missions were later founded, it is possible to work out tentative locations on the basis of other sources. (See Map 4.)

One copy of the report (to be cited as Copy A) is in the Paxbolon-Maldonado Papers, Part II, ff. 9v-11. Another (to be cited as Copy B) is found in AGI, México, leg. 359. In many cases the names are spelled differently in the two copies. In the translation we give what seems to be the better spelling, followed by a reconstruction of the name in parentheses. Variant spellings are given in the notes. In the same way we give in parentheses reconstructions of the personal names, although some of these are doubtful.

[*Translation*]

Report of the settlements[1] of fugitives[2] in the forests, according to what was learned from the Indians who made the declaration to Don Pablo Paxbolon. They are as follows:

[1] Spanish, "pueblos." From other sources it seems clear that most of these settlements were not compact villages but more or less scattered settlements in the general locality of the "pueblo" listed, like the two settlements of Nacaukumil.

[2] "Cimarrones." Although most of the Indians of these settlements were evidently apostate fugitives from northern Yucatan or their descendants, the Cehache and Itza and possibly the Indians of Chunpich (who may have been Cehache) were unconverted heathens who had lived in the interior since preconquest times.

1. In the first place, the first settlement which Don Pablo Paxbolon reached, [called] Nacaucumil-taquiache (Nacaukumil-taquiache).[3] It has about 30 married men and those who command it are called—[names not given].

2. Nequecumil (Nacaukumil)[4] is the second settlement Don Pablo reached. It is governed by Pedro Zeque (Tzek)[5] and has about 50 married Indians.

It is about 1 league from one to the other. They are not in a compact town but are scattered.[6]

3. One day's journey toward the east is the settlement of Yxquique (Ixkik).[7] It was not possible to learn how many people it has. Those who govern it are called Napolcobo (Napol Couoh) and Juan Tuyu.[8]

4. Toward the east and beyond this said settlement there is another settlement called Chunlucho (Chunluch).[9] It is another day's journey farther on. It was impossible to learn the number of people it has. Those who govern it are Juan Cocom and two others.

5. Toward the said east and in the direction of Bacalar is another settlement beyond those mentioned above. No report of its population has been brought. Those who command this settlement [called] Zapebobon[10] are named Luis Cu (Ku) and five others.

6. Continuing toward the said east is the settlement of Tibacab.[11] Those who govern it are Francisco Uco (Uc) and three others.

7. Continuing toward the east is the settlement of Yxtoc (Ixtok).[12] Francisco Canche, Antonio Pech, and six other principal men govern it.

[3] Cacaucumil in Copy A, but other variants indicate that *naca* was the first element. *Ucum*, or *ukum*, can mean "river," and *taquiache* evidently refers to the land of the Cehache. The most applicable meaning for *naca* is hard to determine but it may mean "close to" or "up" the river in question. Since Nacaukumil was a short distance east of Popola, which was situated on the Mamantel, the name shows that this river led toward the Cehache area.

[4] Nequyumil in Copy A.

[5] Pedro Zeque, or Çec, later became governor of the mission town of Nacaukumil (see ch. 11).

[6] The Indians of these rancherías were subsequently congregated into a single settlement of the same name and later known as Chacuitzil. In the Maldonado-Paxbolon probanza of 1612 this mission settlement is also called Ichcun and Yscuncabil (Paxbolon-Maldonado Papers, Part II).

[7] Isquiqui in Copy B.

[8] Tuque (Tuc?) in Copy B.

[9] Chumluchu in Copy A.

[10] In 1615 Francisco Sánchez Cerdán, a prominent citizen of Campeche, told about a journey he had made into the interior country southeast of Campeche in the late 1570's (Paxbolon-Maldonado Papers, Part II, ff. 257v–62v). One of the sites visited at that time was a place called Dzopohobon.

[11] Sánchez Cerdán's report of his entrada of the 1570's (see preceding note) mentions a site called Tubacab located near two permanent lakes or lagoons.

[12] This place was evidently Tzuctok, where a mission was established in 1605 (see ch. 11). In 1605 Francisco Canche was elected governor of Tzuctok and Antonio Pech was named

8. Continuing toward the east is another settlement called Chumpiche (Chunpich).[13] They [Paxbolon's informants at Nacaukumil] declare that it may have 200 houses. The reason for this statement is that they [the inhabitants of Chunpich] are enemies of those who testify. They say that there are many people and that they do not wish to be Christians. [These people] are about four days' journey from the declarants, the other aforesaid settlements being in between. From there [Chunpich] to Bacalar is all populated,[14] so they say. They do not give the names of any settlements or caciques. Those who govern this settlement [of Chunpich] are called Ah Kin Aca (Ake? Acat?)[15] and Namay Queb (Keb) and three others.

9. On the north [from Nacaukumil] is the settlement of Tixchalchel (Tixchalche).[16] Namay Que (Ceh) and Miguel Ucan govern it.

10. Toward the said north is the settlement of Çucmiz.[17] Three principal men govern it.

11. Toward the said north is the settlement of Yxchemachiche (Ichmachich).[18] Three principal men govern it.

12. In the same direction is the settlement of Ichbalche.[19] Eight principal men govern it.

---

alcalde. Moreover, Tzuctok was located near the settlement of Chunpich, which is listed after Ixtok in the report above. Documents of 1668–70 refer to a site named Ichtok east of Chekubul, but this place was not the same as Ixtok, or Tzuctok, since Fray Cristóbal Sánchez reached it en route to Tzuctok in 1670.

[13] Hunpiche in Copy B. *Chun* is a prefix meaning "at the base of something" or "the trunk of a tree"; *pich* is the ear tree, or conacaste, an important timber tree (Roys, 1943, p. 50). In the late 1690's Chunpich was located some 8 leagues from Tzuctok on the route to Batcab and Chuntuqui. It was probably in the region of modern Cumpich north of the Mexico-Guatemala boundary. At this time the Chunpich area was inhabited by Cehache (Means, 1917, p. 117). It is also interesting to note that in 1605 Tzuctok was said to be the "puerta" to the Cehache area.

[14] It was in this area that the mission of Sacalum was later founded. Cf. ch. 11.

[15] Ake is probably indicated here, since we have found Ac for Ake in other documents. Acat has been found only as an Acalan or Nahuatl name.

[16] Tischaloche in Copy A.

[17] Cucomiz in Copy A. *Zuuc* is a general term for grass or zacate; *miz* is *Tillandsia brachycaulos* Schl., an epiphyte. In place names, however, *tzuc* is occasionally a prefix, indicating a locality where the plant or other natural feature which follows is found. Cf. Sucopo (Maya, Tzucop), which means "a grove of anonas (*op*)." Documents of 1615 refer to a site named Çucmiz a short distance west of Sahcabchen in the locality where the pueblo of Holail was founded.

[18] Ychomahuh in Copy A. Other documents record the name as Machich, Chichmachich, Chichimachiche. *Ich* means "in" or "among"; *machiche* is reported as an unidentified timber tree (Standley, 1930, p. 176). We are reminded of Ichmul, a well-known town in northern Yucatan, which means "among the mounds." After the founding of the Montañas missions in 1604–05, Ichmachich was a visita of Ichbalche. In 1615 the people of Ichmachich were resettled at Cheusih together with those of Chacuitzil (formerly Nacaukumil) and Chunhaz (see ch. 11). Modern maps show a place named Machich southeast of Sahcabchen, but this could not have been the site of the mission town of Ichmachich.

[19] Yschebalche in Copy B. Also recorded in other documents as Ysbalche, Esbalche, Ychebaz. *Ich* is here a prefix, as in Ichmachich; and *balche* (*Lonchocarpus longistylus* Pittier), "a tree from which they make wine and become drunk" (Motul dictionary). The mission settle-

13. In the same direction is the settlement of Coobziz.[20] Six principal men govern it. The chief is called Juan May.

14. Toward the said north is the settlement of Yxchan (Ixchan).[21] Ah Kin Pech and two other principal men govern it.

15. Toward the said north is the settlement of Checubul (Chekubul).[22] Miguel No (Noh) and Diego To govern it.

And all these settlements are in the neighborhood and direction as given by the declarants.

16. Toward the southeast [from Nacaukumil] is the settlement of Tazul.[23] These [Indians] scattered because they did not wish to be Christians and they heard that [Spaniards?] were going to them, and so they went to Tayza. The latter attacked them and routed them. Only one Indian died. And since this happened a short time ago, they are not reassembled. They say that they now wish to be Christians. Fifteen captains and principal men govern them.

17. Toward the said southeast are the Quiaches (Cehaches). This settlement is called Petox.[24] Those who govern it are called[25] Ah Kin Cholo (Xol?), Batab Chac, Ah Kin Zel (or Tzel), Nabon Cacaalezuc.[26] There are as many as 20 captains.

18. Toward the said southeast is the famous town of Tayza (Tayasal) and other settlements subject to it, the names of which are not known.

---

ment of Ichbalche was also known as Ichçayab. Although *zayab* usually means a spring, it is also reported as a synonym for the balche (Standley, 1930, p. 297). The Franciscan convent of Ichbalche, founded in 1604–05, was the chief center of missionary activity in the Montañas area until 1615, when the people of Ichbalche and Tzuctok were moved to Sahcabchen (see ch. 11).

[20] Coobçiz in Copy B.

[21] Modern maps show a site named Taschan located between Pixoyal and Lake Mocu. There was also a mission settlement named Texan in the Montañas area, 1609–15.

[22] Hecubul in Copy B. In other seventeenth-century documents the name appears as Chekubul, Chikubul, Chicbul, Chekbul. Modern maps show two sites named Chekubul and Chicbul southeast of Tixchel. The early documents, however, mention only one settlement (cf. references to Chekubul in ch. 13).

[23] Taçul in Copy B. In another document we find the name recorded as Tajul.

[24] *Pet* means "something circular," and in compounds is sometimes applied to tracts of land, like cornfields, gardens, and orchards, even when they are not circular. *Ox* is the breadnut, and it seems likely that a grove of such trees is indicated.

[25] The Spanish text reads, "el q. los rixe se llama," but the names which follow evidently refer to more than one person.

[26] Cacaalliçie in Copy B.

Glossary

[The definitions given here apply to the use of the terms in this volume, and in some cases they are oversimplified. Many terms of Indian origin employed in the preceding chapters, appendices, and explanatory notes and already defined where they occur have been omitted from this list.]

Acalli (Nahuatl): canoe.

adelantado (Span.): a title conferred upon some of the conquerors, which usually implied a considerable measure of independent jurisdiction.

adelantamiento (Span.): the area governed by an *adelantado*.

ahau (Maya): ruler; sometimes the title prefixed to the patronymic of the *halach uinic*.

ahau (Chontal): title of the Acalan ruler and of some of the lesser chieftains; translated in the Spanish version of the Chontal Text as "rey," "principal," and "gobernador."

ah cuchcab (Maya): a member of the town council; the head of a subdivision of a town.

ah kin (Maya): priest.

ah kulel (Maya): a deputy or assistant of the *batab*.

alcalde (Span.): a local magistrate.

alcalde mayor (Span.): a subordinate colonial official in charge of a province or provincial subdivision.

alcalde ordinario (Span.): the elected magistrate of a Spanish or Indian town.

alcaldía mayor (Span.): area governed by an *alcalde mayor*.

alguacil (Span.): a minor peace officer; bailiff.

alguacil mayor (Span.): chief bailiff.

arroba (Span.): a weight of approximately 25 pounds, or a liquid measure of about 4 gallons.

arroyo (Span.): a river or stream, often of seasonal character.

audiencia (Span.): one of the highest judicial courts in the colonies, which also enjoyed a considerable measure of administrative authority; also the area in which an audiencia exercised jurisdiction.

auto (Span.): decree, edict.

ayuda de costa (Span.): pension; grant-in-aid.

ayuntamiento (Span.): a municipal government.

Barrio (Span.): ward, subdivision of a town.

batab (Maya): in pre-Spanish times the civil and military head of a town; during the colonial period the *cacique* and later on the governor of an Indian town.

Cabecera (Span.): the capital, principal town, or administrative center of a province, district, or mission area.

cabildo (Span.): town council or corporation.

cacicazgo (Span.): the dignity or office of a *cacique* and his territory; native province or political subdivision.

cacique (Span.): an Indian chief; in colonial times the holder of a certain hereditary position, and later the governor of an Indian town.

calpulli (Nahuatl): a landholding lineage group; a ward or subdivision of a town.

cantor (Span.): singer, chanter in village church.

capilla (Span.): chapel; altar space.

capitulación (Span.): agreement, contract.

carga (Span.): a measure of cacao or maize.

casa (Span.): house; a line or branch of a family.

cenote (from Maya *dzonot*): a natural cistern or water hole peculiar to the Yucatan Peninsula.

chalchihuitl (Nahuatl): a green precious stone.

chontalli (Nahuatl): foreigner.

cimarrón (Span.): a fugitive Indian.

cimatl (Nahuatl): a medicinal plant believed to be a species of Phaseolus.

cizin (Maya): devil, idol.

comisario (Span.): superior or director of a new mission area.

concuñado (Span.): husband of wife's sister.

corregidor (Span.): a subordinate governmental official with authority over a city or a provincial subdivision.

corregimiento (Span.): area governed by a *corregidor*.

cuñado (Span.): brother-in-law.

cura (Span.): parish priest.

Definidor (Span.): a member of an elected council (*definitorio*) in a Franciscan province to advise the Provincial and assist in the administration of the province between meetings of the provincial chapter. (A *custodia*, or semi-independent subdivision of a Franciscan province, also had a board of *definidores*, as in the case of the Franciscan missions in Yucatan prior to 1561.)

doctrina (Span.): Christian instruction; a town or village of Christian Indians.

ducado (Span.): a monetary unit of 375 *maravedís* in value, equivalent to five-sixths of a gold peso (*peso de oro de minas*).

dzul (Maya): foreigner; also a common Yucatecan Maya patronymic. In the Chontal Text the term is employed to designate a certain foreign nation.

Encomendero (Span.): holder of an *encomienda*.

encomienda (Span.): an allotment of Indians under obligation to give service, tribute, or both, to a Spanish colonist.

entenado (Span.): stepson.

entrada (Span.): an expedition for purposes of exploration or military conquest.

escribano (Span.): notary; clerk of an Indian town.

escribano mayor de gobernación (Span.): chief governmental notary.

estero (Span.): estuary, wide expanse of water, swamp or overflow area, a sluggish river or stream.

expediente (Span.): a file or series of documents.

Fanega (Span.): a dry measure of approximately 1.6 bushels.

fiscal (Span.): crown attorney; prosecuting attorney.

Gallina (Span.): hen. The term *gallina de Castilla* was used to describe the European variety, and *gallina de la tierra* to describe the native turkey.

guardián (Span.): the head of a Franciscan convent and its mission district.

guardianía (Span.): a mission district administered by a *guardián*.

Halach uinic (Maya): a head chief or territorial ruler of an independent Maya state.

hermano (Span.): brother.
hidalgo (Span.): a noble.
hucup (Chontal): canoe.

Juez de comisión (Span.): a judicial officer appointed to conduct an investigation or to deal with some particular case or legal inquiry; a judge-delegate.

Katun (Maya): a time period of 7200 days, or approximately 20 years.

Laguna (Span.): lake; lagoon.
legajo (Span.): a bundle of papers or documents.

Macegual, macehual, mazeual (Nahuatl): a common Indian, not a noble.
maestre de campo (Span.): a certain military officer of high rank.
maestro de doctrina (Span.): a native teacher who instructed other Indians in Christian doctrine.
manta (Span.): a mantle; a length of cloth. In Yucatan the tribute *manta* comprised four *piernas*, or lengths, of cotton cloth measuring 4 *varas* by three-fourths of a *vara* each, making a total of about 10 square yards (English measure).
maravedí (Span.): 0.094 gram of pure silver (Hamilton, 1934, p. 318).
matrícula (Span.): an official count or list, such as a count of tributaries, heads of families, or adult inhabitants of a town.
memoria (Span.): list, report.
mestizo (Span.): a person of mixed Spanish and Indian blood.
mezquita (Span.): mosque; often used in colonial documents to describe native temples or sanctuaries.
milpa (Nahuatl): farm plot; land cultivated according to the customary Maya system of agriculture involving the burning of the bush prior to planting.
milperías (Span.): *milpa* lands.
montaña (Span.): a forested area; also hilly or mountainous terrain.
monte (Span.): bush; forest.

Natural (Span.): native; natural.
nuc uinic, nucalob, nucba uinicob (Chontal): the inferior chieftains or principal men, as contrasted with the ahaus.
nucil, nucil uinicob, nucbe uinicob (Maya): the elders or principal men of a town.

Ocelotl (Nahuatl): jaguar.
oidor (Span.): member of an *audiencia;* in the case of *audiencias* which had separate panels for criminal and civil cases, the *oidores* served in civil cases.

Partido (Span.): a local district or administrative area; the district administered by a curate or beneficed priest.
peso (Span.): a monetary unit, Spanish dollar. The *peso de oro común* (the silver *peso* or piece of eight) had the value of 272 *maravedís*, or 8 *reales* or *tomines* of 34 *maravedís* each; the *peso de oro de minas* had the value of 450 *maravedís*.
peten (Maya): island.
pierna (Span.): a length of cloth measuring 4 *varas* by three-fourths of a *vara;* one-fourth of a tribute *manta*.
pozole (Nahuatl): a drink made of maize dough and water.

principal (Span.): an Indian of recognized noble status; the head of a subdivision of a town.
probanza (Span.): proof; an official record of merits and services.
procurador (Span.): solicitor, attorney, legal agent.
provisor (Span.): a diocesan judge named by the bishop.

Quiçin, quizin (from Maya *cizin*, q.v.).

Ranchería (Span.): a small settlement.
real (Span.): a monetary unit of 34 *maravedís* in value, one-eighth of a silver *peso;* a military camp.
regidor (Span.): a member of the town council.
relación (Span.): an account, relation, or report.
repartimiento (Span.): an allotment; an alternative term for the encomienda; a general term for the system of forced Indian labor for pay; also used in Yucatan to describe the system of forced contracts by which the Indians were obliged to accept advances of money or raw materials in return for which they had to supply stated quantities of beeswax, honey, cochineal, cotton, cotton cloth, etc.
reservado (Span.): person exempt from tribute.
residencia (Span.): an accounting required of the holder of a public office.

Sabana (Span.): savanna.
sacbe (Maya): a paved road.
salto (Span.): cascade, waterfall.
señor (Span.): lord.
señor natural (Span.): a natural lord; a term applied to native rulers and their descendants.
sobrino (Span.): nephew.

Tameme (from Nahuatl *tlamama*): Indian carrier or burden bearer.
tasación (Span.): a tax or tribute assessment.
tecpan (Nahuatl): government house.
tío (Span.): uncle.
tomín (Span.): one-eighth of a silver *peso;* one *real.*
tostón (Span.): half a *peso.*
tun (Chontal): stone or rock.
tun (Maya): a precious green stone; a soft limestone overlying the older rock and shell conglomerate, and in compounds something made of stone; also a time period of 360 days.

Ucum, ukum (Maya): *estero* or river.

Vara (Span.): a linear measure of about 33 inches; a staff of office.
vicario (Span.): a priest to whom certain authority has been delegated by the bishop.
villa (Span.): a town enjoying certain privileges of local government.
visita (Span.): an official visitation, inspection, or judicial inquiry; an ecclesiastical term designating an Indian town with a church but no resident clergy.
visitador (Span.): an official authorized to make a visitation or inspection (*visita*).
viudo (Span.): widower.

Xocelhaa (Chontal): river.
xocola (Maya): river.

Yerno (Span.): son-in-law.

Zanja (Span.): channel, canal.

References

ACEVEDO, J. R.
 1910 El partido de Carmen (Estado de Campeche). Mexico.

ACOSTA, JOSÉ DE
 1880 The natural and moral history of the Indies. . . . Reprinted from the English translated edition of Edward Grimston, 1604. (Works issued by the Hakluyt Society, nos. 50, 51.) London.

ADAMS, E. B.
 1945 Note on the life of Francisco de Cárdenas Valencia. *The Americas*, 2: 21–29. Washington.

AGUILERA MARTÍNEZ, J. G.
 1942 Geografía del Estado de Tabasco. Villahermosa.

ALVA IXTLILXOCHITL, FERNANDO DE
 1891–92 Obras históricas. 2 vols. Mexico.

ANDREWS, E. W.
 1943 The archaeology of southwestern Campeche. *Carnegie Inst. Wash.*, Pub. 546, Contrib. 40. Washington.

ANGHIERA, PIETRO MARTIRE D'
 1912 De orbe novo, the eight decades of Peter Martyr d'Anghiera. Translated from the Latin with notes and introduction by F. A. MacNutt. 2 vols. New York and London.

ANNALS OF THE CAKCHIQUELS
   See Villacorta C., 1934.

ARCHIVO GENERAL DE INDIAS, SEVILLA (cited as AGI)
 [Antón García] contra Feliciano Bravo, escribano, y Juan Vázquez y Juan de Monserrate. 1570–71. Justicia, leg. 250, ff. 1885–2255v. (Cited as García v. Bravo. This expediente forms part of the first legajo of the residencia of Gov. Luis Céspedes de Oviedo.)
 Autos hechos a instancia del defensor de indios, Juan de Sanabria, sobre la reducción de los que había en las montañas de aquella provincia [de Yucatán]. 1609. Patronato, leg. 231, núm. 4, ramo 16. (Copy of materials in the Paxbolon-Maldonado Papers, Part II, ff. 146r–204v, and a few supplementary documents not included in the latter.)
 Autos hechos por Pedro García de Ricalde en virtud de comisión del Sr. Maese de Campo Don Rodrigo Flores de Aldana, gobernador de estas provincias, sobre la reducción de los indios de Sahcabchen y otros pueblos. 1668–70. Escribanía de Cámara, leg. 317B, pza. 8.
 Confirmation of a pension granted to Juan de Ribera y Gárate on half of the encomienda of Pocmuch. 1648–60. México, leg. 243.
 Contra Antonio González por malos tratamientos a los [indios] de Sahcabchen sobre que recibiesen repartimientos de cera, de que resultó ausentarse los indios de aquel partido a las montañas. 1666–70. Escribanía de Cámara, leg. 317C, pza. 4.
 Cuaderno de testimonios de certificaciones dadas por los oficiales de Yucatán y alcaldes mayores de sus partidos de las personas que poseían las encomiendas y su producto. 1688. Contaduría, leg. 920, exp. 2.
 Cuentas de real hacienda dadas por los oficiales reales de Yucatán. 1540–1606. Contaduría, leg. 911A.

ARCHIVO GENERAL DE INDIAS, SEVILLA—*continued*

Documents relating to the missions of Las Montañas. 1604–05. México, leg. 359. (Copy of materials in the Paxbolon-Maldonado Papers, Part II, ff. 1–75*v*.)

Don Francisco de Montejo, gobernador y capitán general de la provincia de Yucatán, con el Adelantado D. Pedro de Alvarado, sobre derecho a una encomienda de indios. 1541. Justicia, leg. 134, núm. 3.

El Adelantado Don Francisco de Montejo, gobernador de las provincias de Yucatán, con Don Pedro de Alvarado, gobernador de Guatemala, sobre el derecho a los términos del Río de Grijalva, que dicho Montejo había conquistado y pacificado a su costa. 1530–33. Justicia, leg. 1005, núm. 3, ramo 1. (Cited as Montejo *v.* Alvarado.)

El fiscal con los oficiales reales de la provincia de Yucatán sobre ciertas adiciones que fueron puestas por el gobernador de ella de varias ayudas de costa que pagaron. 1567. Justicia, leg. 209, núm. 4.

El fiscal contra Alonso López, vecino de la villa de Santa María de la Victoria de Tabasco, sobre haberse titulado visitador y exigido a los indios de la provincia de Tabasco diferentes contribuciones. 1541–45. Justicia, leg. 195. (Cited as Fiscal *v.* López.)

Expediente concerning confirmation of Capt. Nicolás Fernández Maldonado as encomendero of Calkini. 1628–31. México, leg. 242.

Expediente formado a instancia del Capitán Pedro Ochoa de Leguízamo sobre ir a su costa al nuevo descubrimiento del Valle de Suchicane. 1604–05. Patronato, leg. 20, núm. 5, ramo 25.

Información de los malos tratamientos que los españoles hacen a los indios de la provincia de Tabasco. 1605. México, leg. 369.

Información de los méritos y servicios del Capitán Francisco Tamayo Pacheco. 1568. Patronato, leg. 82, núm. 2, ramo 1.

Información de los servicios de Fray Juan de Izquierdo, obispo de Yucatán. 1595. México, leg. 369.

Información de servicios de Alonso Gómez de Santoyo, teniente de gobernador y justicia mayor en la provincia de Tabasco. 1565–66. México, leg. 98.

Isabel Sánchez, hija de Pedro Galiano, difunto, con Francisco Manrique, vecino de Yucatán, sobre los indios de Yobain y Tixcacal. 1557. Justicia, leg. 1012, núm. 3, ramo 3.

Letter of Antonio Laynez to the governor of Yucatan. Aug. 29, 1669. México, leg. 307.

Letter of Bishop Diego Vázquez de Mercado to the king. Mérida, October 12, 1606. México, leg. 369.

Letter of Don Pablo Paxbolon and other native officials of Tixchel to the king. February, 1567. México, leg. 367, ff. 68*r*–69*v*. (Maya text and Spanish translation.)

Letter of Francisco Palomino to the king. Mérida, October 2, 1572. México, leg. 99.

Letter of Fray Cristóbal Sánchez to the provincial. Nacab, August 5, 1670. México, leg. 308.

Matrícula de los pueblos de la provincia de Yucatán con certificaciones de sus vicarios. 1688. Contaduría, leg. 920, exp. 1.

Memorial de la clerecía de la ciudad de Mérida y obispado de Yucatán hecho por su Señoría el Dr. Don Juan Alonso de Ocón, obispo de dicho obispado . . . , Mérida, 8 marzo, 1643. México, leg. 369.

Memorial de la provincia de Yucatán y Tabasco. n. d. Indiferente General, leg. 1373.

Minuta de los encomenderos de la provincia de Yucatán y la renta que cada uno

ARCHIVO GENERAL DE INDIAS, SEVILLA—*continued*

tiene. 1606. México, leg. 1841. (The printed text of this document in Paso y Troncoso, 1939–42, 15: 26–41, contains many errors.)

Nombramiento del obispo de beneficiados a los partidos de Tichel y Tepetitlan. 1606. México, leg. 2606.

Paxbolon-Maldonado Papers, Parts I, II. México, leg. 138. (For a description of these papers, see Appendix A.)

Petitions of Fray Diego de Castro and other documents relating to a request for additional Franciscan missionaries for the province of Yucatan. 1603–05. México, leg. 294.

Probanza de los méritos y servicios de Blas González. . . . 1567–70. Patronato, leg. 68, núm. 1, ramo 2.

Probanza of the merits and services of Don Juan Chan, cacique and governor of Chancenote. 1601–17. México, leg. 140.

Probanza of the merits and services of Iñigo de Sugasti. 1598–1615. México, leg. 242.

Probanza of the merits and services of Dr. Pedro Sánchez de Aguilar. 1599–1617. México, leg. 299.

Probanza of the merits and services of Lorenzo de Godoy. 1562. Guatemala, leg. 111.

Probanza of the merits and services of Nuño de Castro. 1569–75. México, leg. 100.

Probanza of the services of Don Pablo Paxbolon, cacique of Acalan-Tixchel, 1569–76. México, leg. 97.

Probanzas of Feliciano Bravo, *escribano mayor de gobernación* in Yucatan. 1565–78. México, leg. 100.

Probanzas of Feliciano Bravo, *escribano mayor de gobernación* in Yucatan. 1562–82. México, leg. 109.

Ratificaciones de los indios que dijeron en los sumarios secretos de esta Villa de Campeche, su tierra adentro y partido de Sahcabchen y Popola, y matrículas y memorias de los indios de sus pueblos. 1670. Escribanía de Cámara, leg. 315B, pza. 8.

Relación hecha por Luis de Cárdenas sobre la división geográfica de la Nueva España. . . . Sevilla, 30 de agosto, 1527. Patronato, leg. 16, núm. 2, ramo 6.

Residencia de Don Luis Céspedes de Oviedo, governor of Yucatan. 1571. Justicia, leg. 250–53.

Residencia of the officials of the pueblo of Chiuoha. 1667. Escribanía de Cámara, leg. 318B, pza. 9.

Residencia of the officials of the pueblo of Usulaban. 1667. Escribanía de Cámara, leg. 318B, pza. 8.

Royal cedula confirming the authority of Francisco de Montejo as adelantado of Yucatan and granting him jurisdiction as royal governor over the area from the Río Copilco to the Ulua River. Monzón, December 19, 1533. México, leg. 2999, libro D-1.

Royal cedula granting Francisco de Montejo jurisdiction over the region of Puerto Caballos. Monzón, December 19, 1533. México, leg. 2999, libro D-1.

Royal cedula instructing the Audiencia of Guatemala to favor the missionary labors of Fray Pedro Lorenzo. Aranjuez, May 15, 1576. México, leg. 2999, libro D-3.

Royal cedula instructing the governor of Yucatan to take suitable action with regard to the fugitive Indians in the said province. December 31, 1601. México, leg. 2999, libro D-4.

Royal cedula naming Francisco de Montejo as governor of Honduras-Higueras. Madrid, March 1, 1535. Guatemala, leg. 402, libro T-1.

ARCHIVO GENERAL DE INDIAS, SEVILLA—*continued*

Royal cedula to Lic. Alonso López de Cerrato, president of the Audiencia of Guatemala concerning the Indians of the province of Cimatan. Valladolid, July 7, 1560. México, leg. 2999, libro D-1.

Royal cedula to the Audiencia of Guatemala requesting a report on the services of Don Pablo Paxbolon, cacique and governor of Tixchel. Madrid, November 18, 1576. México, leg. 2999, libro D-2.

Royal cedula to the governor of Yucatan transmitting a petition of Gregorio de Funes dealing with idolatry and fugitive Indians in the said province. Barcelona, June 28, 1599. México, leg. 2999, libro D-4.

Royal cedulas to the viceroy of New Spain and to the governor of Yucatan. Tordesillas, July 20, 1592. México, leg. 2999, libro D-3.

Sobre las diligencias que se han hecho para la reducción de los indios de Sahcabchen y otros pueblos. 1668–70. México, leg. 307.

Testimonio de las cartas de los indios de las montañas y administración a los dichos del Rdo. P. Fr. Cristóbal Sánchez, y asimismo administración en el beneficio de Sumacintla. 1671–78. Escribanía de Cámara, leg. 308A, pza. 16.

Título de encomienda de Pocoboco en favor de Antón García. 1546. Indiferente General, leg. 1382B.

Un libro de tasaciones de los naturales de las provincias de Guatemala, Nicaragua, Yucatán y pueblos de Comayagua. 1548–51. Guatemala, leg. 128.

ARCHIVO GENERAL DE LA NACIÓN, MEXICO CITY

Cuenta y visita del pueblo de Ppencuyut. . . . 1584. Tierras, tomo 28, exp. 20.

Probanza concerning the jurisdictional status of Tabasco. 1584. Civil, tomo 932.

ARCHIVO HISTÓRICO NACIONAL, MADRID

Letter of Fray Luis de Villalpando to the King. Mérida, October 15, 1550. Cartas de Indias, caja 2, núm. 54.

AYETA, FRANCISCO DE

ca. 1693 Ultimo recurso de la provincia de San Joseph de Yucatán. [Madrid].

BANCROFT, H. H.

1882 The native races of the Pacific states. 5 vols. (Works, vols. 1–5.) San Francisco.

1882–87 History of Central America. 3 vols. (Works, vols. 6–8.) San Francisco.

1883–88 History of Mexico. 6 vols. (Works, vols. 9–14.) San Francisco.

BANDELIER, A. F.

1880 On the social organization and mode of government of the ancient Mexicans. *Peabody Mus. Harvard Univ.*, 12th ann. rept., 2: 557–699. Cambridge.

BECERRA, M. E.

1909 Nombres geográficos del Estado de Tabasco de la República Mexicana. Mexico.

1910 Estudio lexicológico. *Boletín Soc. Geog. y Estad.*, 5a época, 4: 97–112. Mexico.

1910a Itinerario de Hernán Cortés en Tabasco. *Boletín Soc. Geog. y Estad.*, 5a época, 4: 393–408, 462–79, 502–14. Mexico.

1934 Los Chontales de Tabasco. Estudio etnográfico i lingüístico. *Investigaciones lingüísticas*, 2: 29–36. Mexico.

BELTRÁN DE SANTA ROSA, PEDRO

1859 Arte del idioma Maya reducido a sucintas reglas y semilexicón Yucateco. Mérida. (Originally published in 1746, Mexico.)

BLOM, F., and O. LA FARGE

1926–27 Tribes and temples. A record of the expedition to Middle America conducted by Tulane University of Louisiana in 1925. 2 vols. New Orleans.

BRAINERD, G. W.
1942   Yucatan: pottery. *Carnegie Inst. Wash.*, Year Book 41, pp. 253–57. Washington.

BRINTON, D. G.
1882   The Maya chronicles. *Library of Aboriginal Amer. Literature*, no. 1. Philadelphia.
1884   Nagualism: a study in native American folk-lore and history. Philadelphia.
1885   Did Cortés visit Palenque? *Science*, 5: 248. Cambridge.
1896   The battle and ruins of Cintla. *Amer. Antiquarian*, 18: 259–67. Worcester.

CALDERÓN QUIJANO, JOSÉ ANTONIO
1944   Belice, 1663(?)–1821. Sevilla.

CALKINI, CRÓNICA DE
       [Chronicle and geographical description of the Province of Ah Canul in Maya.] MS. Gates reproduction.

CÁRDENAS VALENCIA, FRANCISCO DE
1937   Relación historial eclesiástica de la provincia de Yucatán en la Nueva España, escrita el año de 1639. (Biblioteca Histórica Mexicana, vol. 3.) Mexico.

CARRILLO Y ANCONA, CRESCENCIO
1895   El obispado de Yucatán. 2 vols. Mérida.

CARTAS DE INDIAS
1877   Publícalas por primera vez el Ministerio de Fomento. Madrid.

CARTOGRAFÍA DE LA AMÉRICA CENTRAL
1929   Guatemala. (Publicaciones de la Comisión de Límites.)

CHAMBERLAIN, R. S.
1936   Francisco de Montejo and the conquest of Yucatan. MS. (Unpublished dissertation for the degree of doctor of philosophy, Harvard University.)
1938   Two unpublished documents of Hernán Cortés and New Spain, 1519 and 1524. *Hispanic Amer. Hist. Rev.*, 18: 514–25. Durham.
1939   Castilian backgrounds of the repartimiento-encomienda. *Carnegie Inst. Wash.*, Pub. 509, Contrib. 25. Washington.
1939a The concept of the *señor natural* as revealed by Castilian law and administrative documents. *Hispanic Amer. Hist. Rev.*, 19: 130–37. Durham.

CHARNAY, C. J. D.
1881   The ruins of Central America. Part 6. *North Amer. Rev.*, 132: 187–94. New York.
1887   The ancient cities of the New World. . . . New York.

CHUMAYEL, BOOK OF CHILAM BALAM OF
       See Roys, 1933.

[CIUDAD REAL, ANTONIO DE]
1873   Relación breve y verdadera de algunas cosas de las muchas que sucedieron al Padre Fray Alonso Ponce en las provincias de la Nueva España. . . . 2 vols. Madrid. (Originally issued in Colección de documentos inéditos para la historia de España, vols. 57 and 58. Madrid, 1872.)
1932   *See* Noyes, 1932.

COLECCIÓN DE DOCUMENTOS INÉDITOS
1864–84 Colección de documentos inéditos relativos al descubrimiento, conquista y colonización de las posesiones españolas en América y Oceanía. 42 vols. Madrid. (Cited as DII.)

CORDRY, D. B., and D. M. CORDRY
  1941   Costumes and weaving of the Zoque Indians of Chiapas, Mexico. *Southwest Mus. Papers*, no. 15. Los Angeles.
CORONEL, JUAN
  1929   Arte en lengua Maya recopilado, y enmendado. . . . *In* Martínez H., 1929. (Originally published in 1620, Mexico.)
CORTES, HERNÁN
  1866   Cartas y relaciones de Hernán Cortés . . . colegidos e ilustradas por Don Pascual de Gayangos. Paris.
  1868   The fifth letter of Hernán Cortés to the Emperor Charles V, containing an account of his expedition to Honduras. Translated . . . by Don Pascual de Gayangos. (Works issued by the Hakluyt Society, no. 40.) London.
  1908   Letters of Cortés; the five letters of relation to the Emperor Charles V. Translated and edited by F. A. MacNutt. 2 vols. New York.
  1916   The fifth letter of Hernando Cortés to the Emperor Charles V. [Translated by A. P. Maudslay.] *In* Díaz del Castillo, 1908–16, 5: 347–447. London.
CUEVAS, M.
  1915   Cartas y otros documentos de Hernán Cortés. Sevilla.
DAMPIER, W.
  1906   Dampier's voyages. . . . 2 vols. New York.
DÍAZ, JUAN
  1858   Itinerario. . . . *In* García Icazbalceta, 1858–66, 1: 281–308. Mexico.
  1939   Itinerario de Juan de Grijalva. *Crónicas de la conquista de México*. Biblioteca del estudiante universitario, 2: 17–39. Mexico.
DÍAZ DEL CASTILLO, BERNAL
  1904–05 Historia verdadera de la conquista de la Nueva España. . . . La publica Genaro García. . . . 2 vols. Mexico.
  1908–16 The true history of the conquest of New Spain. . . . Translated by A. P. Maudslay. 5 vols. (Works issued by the Hakluyt Society, 2d ser., nos. 23–25, 30, 40.) London.
  1939   Historia verdadera de la conquista de la Nueva España. Introducción y notas por Joaquín Ramírez Cabañas. 3 vols. Mexico.
DOCUMENTOS PARA LA HISTORIA DE YUCATÁN
          See Scholes et al., 1936–38.
EGGAN, F.
  1934   The Maya kinship system and cross-cousin marriage. *Amer. Anthropol.*, n.s., 36: 188–202. Menasha.
EMMART, E. W., tr. and ann.
  1940   The Badianus manuscript. . . . Baltimore.
ENCINAS, DIEGO DE
  1596   Provisiones, cedulas, capitulos de ordenanças, instruciones, y cartas, . . . tocantes al buen gouierno de las Indias, y administracion de la justicia en ellas. . . . 4 vols. Madrid.
ESPINOSA, ANTONIO
  ca. 1910 Mapa de la península de Yucatán (México) comprendiendo los estados de Yucatán y Campeche y el territorio de Quintana Roo.
ESTADÍSTICA DEL ESTADO DE CAMPECHE, Agricultura e industrias anexas. 1859. 10 vols. MS. in the Howard-Tilton Library, Middle Amer. Research Inst., Tulane Univ., New Orleans.

FANCOURT, C. ST. J.

1854 History of Yucatan from its discovery to the close of the seventeenth century. London.

FOSTER, G. M.

1943 The geographical, linguistic, and cultural position of the Popoluca of Veracruz. *Amer. Anthropol.*, n.s., 45: 531–46. Menasha.

FUENTES Y GUZMÁN, FRANCISCO ANTONIO DE

1932–33 Recordación florida. . . . 3 vols. Guatemala.

GAGE, T.

1928 Thomas Gage, the English-American. A new survey of the West Indies, 1648. London.

GALDO GUZMÁN, DIEGO DE

1890 Arte Mexicano. Mexico. (Originally published in 1625, Mexico.)

GALINDO, J.

1920 Report of the scientific commission appointed to make a survey of the antiquities of Copan. . . . *In* Morley, 1920, pp. 593–603.

GALINDO Y VILLA, J.

1926–27 Geografía de la República Mexicana. 2 vols. Mexico.

GANN, T. W. F.

1900 Mounds in northern Honduras. *Bur. Amer. Ethnol.*, 19th ann. rept., pt. 2, pp. 655–92. Washington.

1918 The Maya Indians of southern Yucatan and northern British Honduras. *Bur. Amer. Ethnol.*, bull. 64. Washington.

1927 Maya cities, a record of exploration and adventure in Middle America. London.

——, and J. E. S. THOMPSON

1931 The history of the Maya from the earliest times to the present day. New York.

GARCÍA DE PALACIO, DIEGO

1920 A description of the ruins of Copan, by Diego García de Palacio in 1576. *In* Morley, 1920, pp. 541–42.

GARCÍA ICAZBALCETA, J., ED.

1858–66 Colección de documentos para la historia de México. 2 vols. Mexico.

GAYANGOS, PASCUAL DE

1866 *See* Cortés, 1866.

1868 *See* Cortés, 1868.

GIL Y SÁENZ, M.

1872 Compendio histórico, geográfico y estadístico del Estado de Tabasco. Tabasco.

GODOY, DIEGO

1931 Relación hecha por Diego Godoy a Hernando Cortés. . . . *In* Vedia, 1931, 1: 465–70. Madrid.

GONZÁLEZ, JUAN DE DIOS

1766 Plano de la provincia de Yucatán. MS. British Museum, Add. 17654a.

GONZÁLEZ, P. A.

1940 La ruta del Ferrocarril del Sureste y la ruta de Hernán Cortés. *Rev. Mex. de Ingeniería y Arquitectura*, 18: 392–421. Mexico.

HALPERN, A. M.

1942 A theory of Maya tš-sounds. *Carnegie Inst. Wash., Div. Hist. Research, Notes on Middle Amer. Archaeol. and Ethnol.*, no. 13. Cambridge.

HAMILTON, E. J.

1934 American treasure and the price revolution in Spain, 1501–1650. Cambridge.

HARING, C. H.
1910 The buccaneers in the West Indies in the XVII century. New York.
HARRISSE, H.
1892 The discovery of North America. London and Paris.
HELPS, A.
1855–61 The Spanish conquest in America. 3 vols. London.
HERRERA Y TORDESILLAS, ANTONIO DE
1725–26 The general history of the vast continent and islands of America, . . . translated into English by Capt. John Stevens. 6 vols. London. (Translated from the Spanish edition of 1601–15, Madrid.)
1726–30 Historia general de los hechos de los castellanos en las islas i tierra firme del Mar Océano. 9 parts. Madrid.
HOLMES, W. H.
1895–97 Archaeological studies among the ancient cities of Mexico. *Field Columbian Museum*, Anthropol., Ser., vol. 1, no. 1. Chicago.
HÜBBE, J., and A. AZNAR PÉREZ
1878 Mapa de la península de Yucatán . . . revisado y aumentado con datos importantes por C. Hermann Berendt.
JOMARD, E. F.
1854–62 Les monuments de la géographie; ou Recueil d'anciennes cartes Européennes et orientales. Paris.
JUARROS, DOMINGO
1937 Compendio de la historia de la Ciudad de Guatemala. Guatemala.
KIRKPATRICK, F. A.
1942 The landless encomienda. *Hispanic Amer. Hist. Rev.*, 22: 765–74. Durham.
LA FARGE, O.
1930 Choles, Chorties and Puctunes. MS.
LANDA, DIEGO DE
1941 Landa's Relación de las cosas de Yucatán. A translation edited with notes by A. M. Tozzer. *Papers Peabody Mus. Harvard Univ.*, vol. 18. Cambridge.
LEHMANN, W.
1920 Zentral-Amerika. Teil I. 2 vols. Berlin.
LEÓN PINELO, ANTONIO DE
1630 Tratado de confirmaciones reales de encomiendas, oficios i casos en que se requieren para las Indias Occidentales. Madrid.
1639 Report made in the Royal Council of the Indies. *In* Stone, 1932, pp. 236–55.
LÓPEZ DE COGOLLUDO, DIEGO
1867–68 Historia de Yucatán. 3d ed., 2 vols. Mérida. (Originally published in 1688, Madrid.)
LÓPEZ DE GÓMARA, FRANCISCO DE
1931 Hispania victrix. Primera y segunda parte de la historia general de las Indias. *In* Vedia, 1931, 1: 155–455. Madrid.
1943 Historia de la conquista de México. Con una introducción y notas por Joaquín Ramírez Cabañas. 2 vols. Mexico.
LOTHROP, S. K.
1924 Tulum: an archaeological study of the east coast of Yucatan. *Carnegie Inst. Wash.*, Pub. 335. Washington.
LOWERY, W.
1912 A descriptive list of maps of the Spanish possessions within the present limits of the United States. Edited with notes by P. L. Phillips. Washington.

LUNDELL, C. L.

1934 Preliminary sketch of the phytogeography of the Yucatan peninsula. *Carnegie Inst. Wash.*, Pub. 436, Contrib. 12. Washington.

1937 The vegetation of Peten. *Carnegie Inst. Wash.*, Pub. 478. Washington.

MACNUTT, F. A.

See Cortés, 1908.

MALER, T.

1884 Mémoir sur l'état de Chiapa (Mexique). *Revue d'ethnographie*, 3: 295–342. Paris.

1901–03 Researches on the central portion of the Usumacinta valley. *Memoirs Peabody Mus. Harvard Univ.*, vol. 2, nos. 1, 2. Cambridge.

1910 Explorations in the Department of Peten, Guatemala, and adjacent region. *Memoirs Peabody Mus. Harvard Univ.*, vol. 4, no. 3. Cambridge.

MARTÍNEZ HERNÁNDEZ, JUAN, ed.

1929 Diccionario de Motul: Maya-Español. Mérida.

MASON, J. A.

1940 The native languages of Middle America. *In* The Maya and their Neighbors, pp. 52–87.

MAUDSLAY, A. P.

See Díaz del Castillo, 1908–16.

MAYA AND THEIR NEIGHBORS, THE

1940 New York.

MEANS, P. A.

1917 History of the Spanish conquest of Yucatan and of the Itzas. *Papers Peabody Mus. Harvard Univ.*, vol. 7, Cambridge.

MECHAM, M. L.

1934 Church and State in Latin America; a history of politico-ecclesiastical relations. Chapel Hill.

MEMORIAL DE TECPAN-ATITLAN

See Villacorta C., 1934.

MERWIN, R. E., and G. C. VAILLANT

1932 The ruins of Holmul, Guatemala. *Memoirs Peabody Mus. Harvard Univ.*, vol. 3, no. 2. Cambridge.

MOLINA, ALONSO DE

1880 Vocabulario de la lengua mexicana. Leipzig. (Originally published in 1571, Mexico.)

1886 Arte de la lengua Mexicana y Castellana. Mexico. (Originally published in 1571, Mexico.)

MOLINA, CRISTÓBAL

1934 War of the Castes. Indian uprisings in Chiapas. 1867–70. Translated by Ernest Noyes and Dolores Morgadanes. *Middle Amer. Research Ser.*, Pub. 5, pp. 353–401. New Orleans.

MOLINA SOLÍS, J. F.

1896 Historia del descubrimiento y conquista de Yucatán. Mérida.

1904–13 Historia de Yucatán durante la dominación española. 3 vols. Mérida.

MORÁN, FRANCISCO

1935 Arte y diccionario en Lengua Choltí. *Maya Society*, Pub. 9. Baltimore.

MORLEY, S. G.

1920 The inscriptions at Copan. *Carnegie Inst. Wash.*, Pub. 219. Washington.

MORLEY, S. G.—*continued*
1937–38 The inscriptions of Peten. *Carnegie Inst. Wash.*, Pub. 437, 5 vols. Washington.
[1941] The Xiu chronicle. Part I: The history of the Xiu. MS. in Peabody Museum, Harvard University.

MOTUL, DICCIONARIO DE
See Martínez H., 1929.

NOYES, E., ed. and tr.
1932 Fray Alonso Ponce in Yucatan, 1588. *Middle Amer. Research Ser.*, Pub. 4, pp. 297–372. New Orleans.

OROZCO Y BERRA, M.
1880 Historia antigua y de la conquista de México. 4 vols. and atlas. Mexico.
1938 Historia de la dominación española en México. 4 vols. (Biblioteca Histórica Mexicana, vols. 8–11.) Mexico.

OVIEDO Y VALDÉS, GONZALO FERNÁNDEZ DE
1851–55 Historia general y natural de las Indias, islas y tierra-firme del Mar Océano. 4 vols. Madrid.

PACHECO BLANCO, M.
1928 Geografía del Estado de Campeche. Carmen.

PASO Y TRONCOSO, F., comp.
1939–42 Epistolario de Nueva España. 16 vols. Mexico.

PEÑAFIEL, A.
1897 Nomenclatura geográfica de México. Mexico.

PÉREZ MARTÍNEZ, H.
1937 Piraterías en Campeche (Siglos XVI, XVII, y XVIII). Mexico.
[1945] Cuauhtemoc, vida y muerte de una cultura. Mexico.

POPOL VUH
See Villacorta C. and Rodas N., 1927.

PRESCOTT, W. H.
1843 History of the conquest of Mexico. 2 vols. New York.

RECOPILACIÓN DE LEYES DE LOS REINOS DE LAS INDIAS
1841 5th ed. 4 vols. Madrid.

REDFIELD, R.
1938 Race and class in Yucatan. In *Carnegie Inst. Wash.*, Pub. 501, pp. 511–32. Washington.
——, and A. VILLA R.
1934 Chan Kom, a Maya village. *Carnegie Inst. Wash.*, Pub. 448. Washington.

RELACIONES DE YUCATÁN
1898–1900 *In* Colección de documentos inéditos relativos al descubrimiento, conquista y organización de las antiguas posesiones españolas de ultramar. 2d ser., vols. 11 and 13. Madrid. (Cited as RY.)

REMESAL, ANTONIO DE
1932 Historia general de las Indias Occidentales y particular de la gobernación de Chiapa y Guatemala. 2 vols. Guatemala.

RINCÓN, ANTONIO DE
1888 Arte Mexicana. Mexico. (Originally published in 1595, Mexico.)

ROVIROSA, J. N.
1880 Plano del Partido de Macuspana y comarcas limítrofes. N.p.
1888 Nombres geográficas del Estado de Tabasco. Mexico.
1930 El partido de Macuspana, 1875. *In* Santamaría, 1930, pp. 85–208.

Roys, R. L.

1931 The ethnobotany of the Maya. *Middle Amer. Research Ser.*, Pub. 2. New Orleans.

1932 Antonio de Ciudad Real, ethnographer. *Amer. Anthropol.*, n.s., 34: 118–26. Menasha.

1933 The Book of Chilam Balam of Chumayel. *Carnegie Inst. Wash.*, Pub. 438. Washington.

1935 Place names of Yucatan. *Maya Research*, 2: 1–10. New York.

1939 The titles of Ebtun. *Carnegie Inst. Wash.*, Pub. 505. Washington.

1940 Personal names of the Maya of Yucatan. *Carnegie Inst. Wash.*, Pub. 523, Contrib. 31. Washington.

1943 The Indian background of colonial Yucatan. *Carnegie Inst. Wash.*, Pub. 548. Washington.

——, F. V. Scholes, and E. B. Adams

1940 Report and census of the Indians of Cozumel, 1570. *Carnegie Inst. Wash.*, Pub. 523, Contrib. 30. Washington.

Rubio Mañé, J. I.

1942 Archivo de la historia de Yucatán, Campeche y Tabasco. 3 vols. Mexico.

Ruge, S.

1881 Geschichte des Zeitalters der Entdeckungen. Berlin.

Ruppert, K., and J. H. Denison

1943 Archaeological reconnaissance in Campeche, Quintana Roo, and Peten. *Carnegie Inst. Wash.*, Pub. 543. Washington.

Sahagún, Bernardino de

1938 Historia general de las cosas de Nueva España. 5 vols. Mexico.

San Buenaventura, Gabriel de

1888 Arte de la lengua Maya. J. G. Icazbalceta, ed. Mexico. (Originally published in 1684, Mexico.)

Santamaría, F. J.

1930 Bibliografía general de Tabasco. Tomo I. (Monografías bibliográficas mexicanas, no. 16.) Mexico.

Sapper, K.

1897 Das nördliche Mittel-Amerika nebst einem Ausflug nach dem Hochland von Anahuac. Reisen und Studien aus den Jahren 1888–1895. Braunschweig.

Scholes, F. V., and E. B. Adams

1936 Documents relating to the Mirones expedition to the interior of Yucatan. *Maya Research*, 3: 153–76, 251–76. New Orleans.

1938 Don Diego Quijada, alcalde mayor de Yucatán, 1561–65. 2 vols. (Biblioteca Histórica Mexicana, vols. 14, 15.) Mexico.

——, C. R. Menéndez, J. I. Rubio Mañé, and E. B. Adams, eds.

1936–38 Documentos para la historia de Yucatán. 3 vols. Mérida. (Cited as DHY.)

——, and R. L. Roys

1938 Fray Diego de Landa and the problem of idolatry in Yucatan. In *Carnegie Inst. Wash.*, Pub. 501, pp. 585–620. Washington.

Seler, E.

1902–03 Gesammelte Abhandlungen zur Amerikanischen Sprach- und Alterthumskunde. 5 vols. Berlin.

1904 Antiquities of Guatemala. *Bur. Amer. Ethnol.*, Bull. 28, pp. 75–121. Washington.

SHATTUCK, G. C.
>   1938   A medical survey of the Republic of Guatemala, *Carnegie Inst. Wash.*, Pub. 499. Washington.

——, et al.
>   1933   The peninsula of Yucatan: medical, biological, meteorological, and sociological studies. *Carnegie Inst. Wash.*, Pub. 431. Washington.

SIMPSON, L. B.
>   1929   The encomienda in New Spain. *Univ. Calif. Pub. Hist.*, vol. 19. Berkeley.

SOLÓRZANO PEREIRA, JUAN DE
>   1648   Política Indiana. Madrid. (Also later editions.)

SPINDEN, H. J.
>   1913   A study of Maya art. *Memoirs Peabody Mus. Harvard Univ.*, vol. 6. Cambridge.

STANDLEY, P. C.
>   1930   Flora of Yucatan. *Field Mus. Nat. Hist.*, Pub. 279, Bot. Ser., vol. 3, no. 3. Chicago.

STEGGERDA, M.
>   1941   Maya Indians of Yucatan. *Carnegie Inst. Wash.*, Pub. 531. Washington.

STEPHENS, J. L.
>   1841   Incidents of travel in Central America, Chiapas, and Yucatan. 2 vols. New York.

STIRLING, M. W.
>   1940   Great stone faces of the Mexican jungle. *Nat. Geog. Magazine*, 78: 309–34. Washington.

STOLL, O.
>   1884   Zur Ethnographie der Republik Guatemala. Zürich.

STONE, D. Z.
>   1932   Some Spanish *entradas*, 1524–1695. *Middle Amer. Research Ser.*, Pub. 4, pp. 209–96. New Orleans.

TAPIA, ANDRÉS DE
>   1939   Relación de Andrés de Tapia. *Crónicas de la conquista de México.* Biblioteca del estudiante universitario, 2: 41–96. Mexico.

TAPIA ZENTENO, CARLOS DE
>   1885   Arte novísima de lengua Mexicana. Mexico. (Originally published in 1753, Mexico.)

THOMAS, C.
>   1885   Palenque visited by Cortés. *Science*, 5: 171–72. Cambridge.

THOMPSON, J. E. S.
>   1927   A correlation of the Mayan and European Calendars. *Field Mus. Nat. Hist.*, Anthropol. Ser., vol. 17, no. 1. Chicago.

>   1931   Archaeological investigations in the southern Cayo district, British Honduras. *Field Mus. Nat. Hist.*, Anthropol. Ser., vol. 17, no. 3. Chicago.

>   1937   Mexico before Cortez. 2d ed. New York and London.

>   1938   Sixteenth and seventeenth century reports on the Chol Mayas. *Amer. Anthropol.*, n.s., 9: 584–603. Menasha.

>   1939   The moon goddess in Middle America: with notes on related deities. *Carnegie Inst. Wash.*, Pub. 509, Contrib. 29. Washington.

>   1941   Dating of certain inscriptions of non-Maya origin. *Carnegie Inst. Wash.*, Div. Hist. Research, *Theoretical Approaches to Problems*, no. 1. Cambridge.

THOMPSON, J. E. S.—*continued*

1941a A coordination of the history of Chichen Itza with ceramic sequences in central Mexico. *Rev. Mex. de Estudios Anthropológicos*, 5: 97–111. Mexico.

1943 A trial survey of the southern Maya area. *Amer. Antiquity*, 9: 106–34. Menasha.

TIZIMIN, BOOK OF CHILAM BALAM OF

MS. Mexico. Gates reproduction; photostat made for S. G. Morley.

TORQUEMADA, JUAN DE

1723 . . . Los veinte i un libros rituales i monarchia indiana, con el origen y guerras, de los indios occidentales, . . . 3 vols. Madrid.

TORRES LANZAS, P.

1900 Relación descriptiva de los mapas, planos, &, de México y Floridas existentes en el Archivo General de Indias. 2 vols. Sevilla.

TOZZER, A. M.

1907 A comparative study of the Mayas and the Lacandones. New York.

1913 A Spanish manuscript letter on the Lacandones in the Archives of the Indies at Seville. *Proc. 18th Int. Cong. Amer.*, 2: 497–509. London.

1921 A Maya grammar with bibliography and appraisement of the works noted. *Papers Peabody Mus. Harvard Univ.*, vol. 9. Cambridge.

1941 *See* Landa, 1941.

MS. Chol notes. Puctun linguistic material collected at Palenque, Chiapas, in 1902.

VÁZQUEZ DE ESPINOSA, ANTONIO

1942 Compendium and description of the West Indies. Translated by C. U. Clark. *Smithsonian Misc. Coll.*, vol. 102. Washington.

VAILLANT, G. C.

1935 Chronology and stratigraphy in the Maya area. *Maya Research*, 2: 119–43. New York.

1941 The Aztecs of Mexico. New York.

VEDIA, ENRIQUE DE

1931 Historiadores primitivos de Indias. 2 vols. (Biblioteca de autores españoles, vols. 22, 26.) Madrid.

VIENNA DICTIONARY

Bocabulario de mayathan por su abeceario (Spanish-Maya). MS. National Library. Vienna.

VILLA R., ALFONSO

1945 The Maya of east central Quintana Roo. *Carnegie Inst. Wash.*, Pub. 559. Washington.

VILLACORTA C., J. A.

1934 Estudios sobre lingüística guatemalteca. Memorial de Tecpan-Atitlan [Anales de los Cakchiqueles]. *Colección Villacorta*, no. 4, pp. 1–179. Guatemala.

——, and F. RODAS N.

1927 Manuscrito de Chichicastenango (Popol Buj). Estudio sobre las antiguas tradiciones del pueblo quiché. Guatemala.

VILLAGUTIERRE SOTO-MAYOR, JUAN DE

1701 Historia de la conquista de la Provincia de el Itza. . . . Madrid.

WAGNER, H. R.

1942 The discovery of New Spain in 1518 by Juan de Grijalva. Berkeley.

1944 The rise of Fernando Cortés. Los Angeles.

WATERMAN, T. T.
   1917   Bandelier's contribution to the study of ancient Mexican social organization.
          Univ. Calif. Pub. Amer. Archaeol. and Ethnol., 12: 249–82. Berkeley.
WAUCHOPE, R.
   1938   Modern Maya houses: a study of their archaeological significance. *Carnegie
          Inst. Wash.*, Pub. 502. Washington.
   1940   Domestic architecture of the Maya. *In* The Maya and their Neighbors, pp.
          232–41. New York.
WINSOR, J.
   1884–89   Narrative and critical history of America. 8 vols. Boston and New York.
WISDOM, C.
   1940   The Chorti Indians of Guatemala. Chicago.
XIMÉNEZ, FRANCISCO
   1929–31   Historia de la provincia de San Vicente de Chiapa y Guatemala de la Orden
          de Predicadores. 3 vols. Guatemala.
ZAVALA, S.
   1935   La encomienda indiana. Madrid.
   1940   De encomiendas y propiedad territorial en algunas regiones en la América
          Española. Mexico.
   1943   New view points on the Spanish colonization of America. Philadelphia.
   1943a   Orígenes coloniales del peonaje en México. *El Trimestre Económico*, 10:
          711–48.
   1945   Contribución a la historia de las instituciones coloniales en Guatemala. *Colegio
          de México*, Jornadas, no. 36. Mexico.
ZURITA, ALONSO DE
   1891   Breve y sumaria relación de los señores y maneras y diferencias que había de
          ellos en la Nueva España. . . . *In* Nueva col. de doc. para la historia de
          México, 3: 71–227. Mexico.

Index

Chunab, town, 387. *See also* Chakam

Chunal, savannas of, 288, 403

Chunhaz, town, 279, Auatayn moved to, 277, 283; consolidation settlement at, 283–86, 338–39; headquarters of *guardianía* of Chacuitzil-Auatayn, 284–85; location of, 279, 283; mission of San Juan de, 251, 252, 285, 286; moved to Cheusih, 277, 289, 340, 506; shortage of food at, 284; water supply of, 284. *See also* Population

Chunluch, town, 257, 505

Chunpich, lake, 69

Chunpich, town, 50, 257, 278–79; account of, 506; chieftains of, 504; inhabited by Cehache, 257. *See also* Population

Chunpuct, *see* Chunputit

Chunputit, fugitive settlement, 306

Chuntuqui, site, 68, 69, 229, 257; Cehache in region of, 452, 453; Cortés' route referred to, 464; distance to Lake Peten, 463; route to, 506n.

Chunuitzil, site, location of, 230

Chunuitzil, town, 275. *See also* Chacuitzil; Nacaukumil

Church, at Chan Santa Cruz, 341; at Chiuoha, 222; at Cimatan, 33; at Ichbalche, 286; at Itzamkanac, 158; at Sahcabchen, 288; at Tixchel, 179, 195, 202, 209–10, 212, 215, 238, 303; at Tzuctok, 272, 345; at Usulaban, 405; at Zapotitlan, 195, 206–10, 212, 213, 215; cost of building and equipping, 154; near Ichpaatun, 85; records in native languages, 9

Cicinob, defined, 395

Cigar, name meaning, 482

Çilba, *see* Açilbaob, town

Cilvituk, Lake, 71, 72, 128, 257, 278, 307

Cilvituk, site, 67, 68, 70, 72; location of Mazatlan referred to, 469; ruins at, 320, 467

Cimarrones, defined, 186, 224

Cimatan, town, 39, 61, 324; commercial center at, 29, 31–33, 34, 91, 318; description of, 32; encomienda in, 92; Mexican stronghold at, 35; Nahuatl-speaking, 27, 31, 318; pacification of, 32–33, 94, 97, 126, 322

Cimatl, defined, 16, 32

Cipac, name, 37n.

Çipaque, name, 62, 63

Çipaque, Francisco, 37n.

Cithute, town, encomienda of, 143

Ciuatan, town, cacique of, 107; Cortés at, 97–99; named for goddess, 57

Ciuatecpan, town, 25, 27, 438; captured by Acalan, 82; Cortés at, 103, 104, 106, 390, 435, 442, 445, 449, 501; Cortés' route to, 499; location of, 434, 436, 437, 444, 446, 447, 448, 452, 456, 469; name discussed, 57, 63, 443; recaptured by Dzul, 86; relations with Acalan, 384; route to Acalan from, 126, 450, 451, 457, 458

Ciudad Chetumal, 84

Ciudad Real, Antonio de, cited, 19, 41, 42, 60, 237–38, 243, 329, 332; Franciscan provincial, 260, 267, 270

Ciudad Real, town, at Chichen Itza, 130; at Dzilam, 134

Clergy, secular, 178, 205, 235, 237; in Tixchel, 238–40, 300–01, 336; natives of Yucatan, 238–39; report on, 301

Clerk, of Tixchel, 178, 360, 361, 363, 383, 385, 386, 397, 405, 479. *See also* Notary

Climate, 140; of northern Yucatan, 142, 327; of south-central Yucatan, 333; of Tabasco, 124

Cloth, bark, 43; commerce in, 29, 30, 39, 58, 59, 245; exported from Yucatan, 3, 316; from Sacred Cenote, 319; gifts of colored, 224; of Zoque, 38, 39, 319; silk, 38

Clothing, 192, 223; gifts of, 209; travelers robbed of, 404

Coatis, 30

Coatl, name, 33

Coatzacoalco, town in Veracruz, 91, 92, 94

Coatzacoalco, town on Usumacinta, 103

Coatzacoalcos, Veracruz, 31

Coazacoalco, town on Usumacinta, 438, 444. *See also* Coatzacoalco

Coccoloba uvifera, 387

Cochineal, 305; in Zoque area, 39; plantation, 48

Cochistlan, place name, 34

Cochistli, defined, 34

Cocho, defined, 34

Cochuah, people, 321

Cochuah, province, 322; Avila in, 129; chieftains of, 134

Cocola, *see* Xocola, town

Cocom, family, rulers of Mayapan, 34, 57, 58, 76, 77, 319

Cocom, Juan, of Chunluch, 505

Coconut, 170

Cocosqui, defined, 63

Codices, Mexican, 72, 84

Coefficient, of day names, 62, 65

Cogolludo, *see* López de Cogolludo

Cohuanacoch, lord of Tezcoco, 114, 115; in command of auxiliaries, 93

Collars, Indians taken to Tixchel in, 172

Colonies, administration of, 298, 349; island, 346; Nahuatl-speaking, 21; of Mexican merchants, 35

Colonists, 168, 271, 280–81, 287, 291, 340, 342; association with Francisco Maldonado, 250, 336; farms and ranches of, 290; fears of, 352; forbidden to visit interior, 266, 267, 272, 273, 281, 339; of Champoton, 137; of Honduras, 135; of Tabasco, 124, 165; of Yucatan, 132, 239, 246; opposition to friars, 156; pacification of unsubdued areas by, 231, 254, 261–62

Columns, at Cilvituk, 72; at Ichpaatun, 84; sculptured, at Chichen Itza, 80; serpent, 22

Cortés, Hernán—*continued*
from Tepetitan to Acalan, 13, 100–09, 424, 434–52, 455–60, 464–66, 469, 499, 501; from Acalan to Tayasal, 68, 119, 392, 448, 452–53, 461–64, 466; from Tayasal to Nito, 60, 464; mentioned, 406, 407, 408, 415, 429, 430, 468, 469, 501

Cortés, Martín, confused with his father, 390

Costello, Dudley, 406, 407, 408

Costume, Cehache, 344

Cotexmi, *see* Mexicalcingo

Cotton, 184, 305; armor, 126; cloth, 244, 305; in Zoque area, 39; production, 243; trade in, 243–44; tribute of, 59, 149, 152, 396

Cougar, skins, 29

Coughs, chronic, 166

Council men, *see* Regidores

Couoh, Napol, name, 505

Courts, architectural, 71; of justice, 22

Cozcaquauhtli, day name, 63

Cozumel Island, 383; Acalan rulers from 77, 79, 383; census of, 78, 474; conditions on, 323; Cortés at, 90; Grijalva at, 88; houses in, 72; multiple-family houses in, 472; patronymics in, 475; shrine on, 57, 321; situation of, 78; visited by merchants, 3; visited by pilgrims, 33

Crocodile, name meaning, 483

Cross, worship of, 341, 347

Crossbow, Spanish, 120

Crown towns, 143, 152; administration of, 213

Cruz, Juan de la, 281–85, 338, 339

Cuaquilteupa, town, 31, 32, 33

Cuatequil, labor system, 150

Cuauhtemoc, 5, 87, 93, 112–20, 155, 292, 363, 388, 391, 392, 410

Cuba, 89, 90, 94, 430

Cuccacoatel, or Cuccacoatel, name, 63

Cucmiz, town, 257, 506

Cuculteupa, town, 31, 33

Cuilonia, town, 91

Cukulchan, god, 56, 57, 158, 395

Culico, town, change of location, 98; multiple-family houses in, 471

Culture, conflicts, 364; decline of, 322; intrusive, 23, 41, 61, 95; Mazapan, 23; Mexican, 22, 23, 74; Nahua, in Tabasco, 318; of Cehache, 73

Culua, Mexicans called, 86n.

Cumpich, Aguada, 69, 279

Cupul, people, 77, 321

Cupul, province, 130, 134, 322

Cupul, Kukum, name, 77

Curassows, 30

Customs, native, 2, 155, 159, 179–80, 185, 189, 191, 192, 195, 223, 228, 253, 273, 281, 286, 306, 309

Cuyloremiquis, site, 91

Cuyo de las Damas, site, 57

Cuyos, term discussed, 404 n.

Damages, in Maya law, 344

Dampier, W., 31, 33, 94–96

Dances, agricultural, 114

D'Anville, Jean Baptiste Bourguignon, 7, 406

Dávila, Pedrarias, 430, 431

Day names, Mexican, 62, 65

Dean, of Yucatan Cathedral, 210, 224

Decrees, royal, *see* Cedula

Deer, in Tabasco, 30; supernatural, 387; worshipped by Cehache, 67

Defender of the Indians, 217, 235, 405. *See also* Palomino

Definidor, 169

Deities, of forest and field, 341

Delgado, Diego, 280, 342

Delgado, Frutos, 310

Descent, great, 21; Mexican, of Xiu, 22; reckoning of, 66, 474, 475

Devils, 56, 158, 394, 395. *See also* Idols

Dialects, Mexican, 62; of Chontal and Chol, 17; of Mexico and Central America, 480; of Pochutla, 484

Díaz, Juan, 88, 89

Díaz del Castillo, Bernal, 5–6, 91, 93, 94, 99, 155, 166, 316, 349; account of Cehache, 67, 70, 462–63, 466; account of Mexican plot, 113, 117, 119; account of Potonchan, 36, 37; at Ciuatecpan, 86; description of Cimatan, 32; encomienda at Teapa, 98; gives only Mexican names, 63; in Acalan, 50, 51, 52, 59, 87, 104, 106, 107, 160, 456; in Chontalpa, 96, 97; location of Ahualulco, 95; location of Espíritu Santo, 92; map described by, 433; narrative of, 408, 409, 435, 447, 458–61; place names according to, 434; report of Grijalva expedition, 89; towns mentioned by, 25, 27; True History by, 5, 16, 363

Dictionaries, kinship terminology in, 473; lacking for Chontal, 19

Diego the Mulatto, 303

Diocese, of Yucatan, 207, 210; administrator of, 224; secular clergy of, 301

Diseases, 284, 305, 327; in Acalan, 10, 326, 327, 328; in Guatemala, 324; in Tabasco, 166–67, 324; in Tixchel, 247, 304, 405; in Yucatan, 123, 304, 323–24, 325, 326; introduction of, 166–67, 323, 326

Ditch, fortified, 70, 466

Divorce, 334

Dog, name meaning, 489

Dogs, gold figures of, 29

Dogwood, name meaning, 482

Dolores, town, 41, 42, 44, 45

Dominicans, 39, 45, 397, 407, 439

Doncel, Ginés, 145

Doncel, Julián, 393, 396

Dowry, of Paxbolon's daughters, 246, 249

Drainage, 326, 327

Drought, 334; flight to forest during, 309; predictions of, 308–09

Houses—*continued*

288–89; built for Batab Yam, 309, 344; built for Paxbolon, 264, 344; Cehache, 70; cost of building, 154; gardens around, 170; land suitable for, 404; multiple-family, 53, 54, 160, 470–72, 474, 475, 495; of Lacandon, 41, 43; of Locen, 46; of Potonchan, 38; property, 171; sites for, 210, 288; "straw," 238; with rounded ends, 72

Huaxtec region, 319

Huaxteca, language, 481

Hübbe, J., 276, 277, 446

Huimango, town, 31; change of location, 98; houses in, 471

Huimanguillo, town, 95, 97

Huipil, defined, 344

Hummingbird, town named for, 388

Hunabku, *see* Hunabqu

Hunabqu, god, 272

Huncha, name, 79; companion of Auxaual, 383

Huncha, Miguel, native teacher, 192, 209

Hunlucho, site, fugitives settled at, 400

Hunters, oratories of, 89

Hunting, 228, 234; in Lacandon area, 40; in Tachis district, 496

Huntington Library, 16

Ichbalche, town, alcaldes of, 283, 284, 287; alguacil of, whipped, 283; chieftains of, 264, 504; church of, 286; Santa María at, 273; fugitives from, 286; governor of, 283, 284, 287, 289; inhabitants of, 286; location of, 257, 264, 275, 277–78, 504; meeting of officials of Montañas settlements at, 284; mission of, 251, 252, 270, 271–72, 280, 282, 285–86, 287, 289, 337; moved to Sahcabchen, 278, 288–89, 340, 507; petition to Governor Luna y Arellano, 265–67; *visitas* of, 257, 271, 279, 280, 285–86, 289. *See also* Population

Ichcun, town, 275. *See also* Nacaukumil

Ichmachich, town, 257; alcaldes of, 287; chieftains of, 506; governor of, 287; location of, 278, 504; mission at, 338; moved to Cheusih, 277, 289, 340; moved to Chunhaz, 283–85. *See also* Population

Ichmul, town, 506; mission of, 239, 405; *visita* of Ichbalche, 257, 271, 280

Ichpaa, *see* Mayapan

Ichpatun, ruins, 84, 85, 86

Ichtok, site, 506

Icim, defined, 65

Idolaters, 262, 400

Idolatry, 173, 179, 190, 253, 273, 281, 286, 306, 312, 329, 338, 341, 352; house of, 392; measures against, 158, 229, 254, 274, 286; modern, 347

Idols, 191, 224, 286; at Tonala, 94; burning of, 155, 158, 192; destruction of, 286, 330, 395, 396; found near Laguna de Términos, 89; gift of copper, 224; houses of at Ciuatecpan, 102; in Acalan, 56, 57, 119, 157–58, 159, 173,

Idols—*continued*

395, 396, 398; in colonial times, 346; in Tachis district, 496; of clay and stone, 286; of patron deity of *katun*, 309; of Tabasco Chontal, 58; on Isla Carmen, 90; replaced by cross, 347

Iguanas, 30, 404

Ikchaua, god, 57

Images, 195, 202, 204, 207, 210, 262, 401; carved by Paxbolon, 175, 238

Incensarios, 320; at Santa Rita, 84; from Cilvituk, 72; in Candelaria area, 4

Incense, pine resin, 58; tribute of, 59

Incest, cases of in interior settlements, 286

Indies, ecclesiastical affairs in, 239; reports on, 16

Indies, Council of the, 132, 133, 135, 138, 252, 254, 255, 274, 281, 296, 359

Indios cimarrones, see Cimarrones

Industry, at Tixchel, 244, 246, 329, 336

Infections, intestinal, 166, 324, 326

Infieles, 225. *See also* Heathen Indians

Infirmities, exemption from tribute for, 151, 161, 180, 182, 183, 240

Inheritance, among Chontal, Maya, and Nahua, 474, 475; of encomiendas, 147

Initial Series, period of, 354

Inscriptions, not dated at Comalcalco, 20

Insect, Dzul leader named for, 86

Insurrection, at Sacalum, 342; in Bacalar district, 334, 343; in Yucatan and Tabasco, 322; Tzeltal, 40

Interián, Cristóbal de, 262

Interior, Indians of, power and influence of, 305, 306–10, 334, 336, 343–47; raids by, 12, 229–30, 234, 236, 243, 253, 306, 308–12, 334–35, 344–45, 403–04; reduction of, 185–200, 221–36, 237, 248, 250, 251–90, 292, 294–96, 310–12, 333–47. *See also* Apostates; Commerce, with interior; Forest Indians; Fugitive Indians; Heathen Indians; Interior settlements

Interior, missions of, *see* Montañas missions

Interior settlements, at present time, 341; caciques of, 310; Cehache, 228–29, 245, 272, 273, 274, 278–79, 335, 343; of apostate fugitives, 68, 219, 228–29, 232, 245–46, 300, 305–15, 334, 336–47; Paxbolon's report of, 256–58, 503. *See also* Chiuoha; Montañas missions; Puilha; Tahbalam; Zapotitlan

Interpreters, at Tixchel, 472; Gaspar Antonio in Yucatan, 383; governor of Champoton served as, 206; of Avila, 127; of Cortés, 36, 91, 93; of Grijalva expedition, 89; of Maldonado expedition, 262; Paxbolon served as, 223; received testimony of Indians, 294; translated Chontal Text, 294

Intestinal infections, *see* Infections

Inundations, in Tabasco, 98

Iquin, name, 65

Iquinuapa, town, 97

DATE DUE